Praise for *Se*

"Luxenberg gives a three-dimensional an the players involved, drawing on diaries, l

—Journ ...ew York Times

"Luxenberg writes at the outset of his book that the story of *Plessy* is a reminder that 'history is made, not ordained.' In his moving portrait of the many figures who played a role in the case, he confirms that idea as well as another: that even the most hopeless fool's errand can emerge, in time, as an unassailable triumph." —Charles S. Dameron, *The Wall Street Journal*

"[A] richly detailed portrait of America's most turbulent time. . . . [P]rovides a vivid reminder of how intransigent racial inequality has been and of the need to counter it through political as well as legal means."

—David Cole, *The Nation*

"In *Separate*, the context and aftermath of the court's ruling in *Plessy v. Ferguson* are woven into a nuanced history of America's struggles in the 19th century as a civil war was fought, slavery ended and a new, complex racial politics haltingly took form." —*The Economist*

"Informative, engaging, exquisitely written, sensitive to individuals' frailties, flaws, and inconsistencies, by turns inspiring and dispiriting, *Separate* is a splendid work of history." —Glenn C. Altschuler, *Florida Courier*

"Luxenberg's history contains so many surprises, absurdities and ironies that it would be a shame to spoil the final chapters by revealing which justice ended up on which side."

—James Goodman, *The New York Times Book Review*

"In documenting this country's fateful journey from slavery through thwarted Reconstruction to segregation, Luxenberg paints on a broad canvas, elegantly narrating several captivating and scrupulously researched stories that converge in *Plessy v. Ferguson*. . . . [F]ascinating."

—Steve Nathans-Kelly, *New York Journal of Books*

"[Luxenberg] is a fine writer . . . *Separate* reminds us that our history is not simply a narrative of greater and greater freedom."

—Eric Foner, *The Washington Post*

"An ambitious and deeply researched nonfiction account. . . . [Luxenberg] draws on letters, diaries and archival collections to bring the true story to life." —Suzanne Van Atten, *Atlanta Journal-Constitution*

"A surprising, compelling, and brilliant milestone in understanding the history of race relations in America."
—Bob Woodward, author of *Fear: Trump in the White House*

"Riveting and deeply researched, *Separate* tells the story surrounding one of the nation's most devastating acts: drawing a sharp color line between black and white after the Civil War. The *Plessy* case was a knife that cleaved America, and Steve Luxenberg brilliantly reveals that divide with his rich narrative of admirable and flawed characters caught in the battle over racial justice. Every paragraph resonates in today's headlines."
—Walter Isaacson, author of *Steve Jobs* and
professor of history, Tulane University

"Forensically researched, deeply moving, devastatingly relevant."
—Katherine Boo, author of *Behind the Beautiful Forevers*

"This is a compulsively readable work of serious history, the absorbing and timely story of a disastrous U.S. Supreme Court decision, freshly told through the lives of those directly involved. Steve Luxenberg's scholarship is deep and impressive; his writing even more so. This is history as it was lived, giving us a sense not only of the deep racism of the period, but the struggle of decent men and women to overcome it, in society and, most importantly, in themselves."
—Mark Bowden, author of *Black Hawk Down* and *Huế 1968:
A Turning Point of the American War in Vietnam*

"A magisterial assessment of a U.S. Supreme Court's grievous moral collapse . . . a definitive work on the 1896 legal drama that afflicts us to this day."
—David Simon, author and creator of HBO's *The Wire*

"*Plessy v. Ferguson* looms large in American history, and it remains searingly relevant today, but it is ill understood. Steve Luxenberg uses his relentless reporting skills and narrative expertise to reveal the full story. His uniquely valuable book will appeal to fans of Ron Chernow's *Grant* and Doris Kearns Goodwin's *The Bully Pulpit*—and to anyone who wants to understand how America's current racial landscape came to be."

—Garrett Epps, professor of law, University of Baltimore, author of *Democracy Reborn: The Fourteenth Amendment and the Fight for Equal Rights in Post–Civil War America*

"At this critical moment in our nation's struggle for racial justice, Steve Luxenberg's *Separate* provides a compelling picture of an earlier stage in that quest. Unlike *Gideon's Trumpet* or *Simple Justice*, his story does not end with a judicial triumph. But in viewing *Plessy v. Ferguson* through the lives of its protagonists—the plaintiff, his sponsors, his lawyer, the justices who decided the case—he reminds us that the pursuit of justice comes down to individuals, not just institutions. He has written a fascinating, if sobering, volume."

—Peter M. Shane, professor of law, Ohio State University

"The reader's great honor and delight is to follow Luxenberg as he intertwines [the] stories [of the most important people involved in the case] from widely singular strands at the beginning, to their historical moments on stage together in 1896. . . . U.S. history is repeating itself. With this monumental work, Luxenberg shows us precisely how—through the workings of malleable law."

—Y. S. Fing, *Washington Independent Review of Books*

"A rich, complex, and all too human story, replete with ironies and unintended consequences. This is 'big history,' deeply researched and well-told."

—J. Anthony Lukas Award citation

ALSO BY STEVE LUXENBURG

Annie's Ghosts: A Journey into a Family Secret

SEPARATE

THE STORY OF *PLESSY V. FERGUSON*, AND AMERICA'S JOURNEY FROM SLAVERY TO SEGREGATION

Steve Luxenberg

W. W. NORTON & COMPANY
Independent Publishers Since 1923

Printed in the United States of America
First published as a Norton paperback 2020

For information about permission to reproduce selections from this book, write to
Permissions, W. W. Norton & Company, Inc., 500 Fifth Avenue, New York, NY 10110

For information about special discounts for bulk purchases, please contact
W. W. Norton Special Sales at specialsales@wwnorton.com or 800-233-4830

Manufacturing by LSC Communications, Harrisonburg
Book design by Ellen Cipriano
Production manager: Anna Oler

Library of Congress Cataloging-in-Publication Data

Names: Luxenberg, Steve, author.
Title: Separate : the story of Plessy v. Ferguson, and America's
journey from slavery to segregation / Steve Luxenberg.
Description: First edition. | New York : W. W. Norton & Company, 2019. |
Includes bibliographical references and index.
Identifiers: LCCN 2018043111 | ISBN 9780393239379 (hardcover)
Subjects: LCSH: Plessy, Homer Adolph—Trials, litigation, etc. | Segregation
in transportation—Law and legislation—Louisiana—History—19th century. |
African Americans—Civil rights—United States—History—19th century. | Race
discrimination—Law and legislation—United States—History—19th century. |
Harlan, John Marshall, 1833–1911. | Tourgée, Albion W., 1838–1905. |
Brown, Henry Billings, 1836–1913. | Martinet, Louis P., 1849–1917.
Classification: LCC KF223.P56 L88 2019 | DDC 342.7308/73—dc23
LC record available at https://lccn.loc.gov/2018043111

ISBN 978-0-393-35769-1 pbk.

W. W. Norton & Company, Inc., 500 Fifth Avenue, New York, N.Y. 10110
www.wwnorton.com

W. W. Norton & Company Ltd., 15 Carlisle Street, London W1D 3BS

1 2 3 4 5 6 7 8 9 0

To Mary Jo,
forever equal and never separate

To Josh and Jill,
inspirations always

CONTENTS

PART III: ASCENT

PART IV: PRECIPICE

PART V: RESISTANCE

AUTHOR'S NOTE

WHERE SHOULD I SIT?

A simple question, really, the same question that confronts me every time I board the commuter train that shuttles me between my home in Baltimore and my job in Washington for the better part of twenty-six years. If I'm late, and if this is an evening rush-hour train, I'll be lucky to find any seat at all, let alone an aisle seat that will allow me extra room to stretch out my long legs.

Not every passenger accepts this invasion of personal space with politeness or a neighborly smile. For the most part, though, there's an unspoken understanding that we're better off if we get along. There's no way to avoid the press of humanity. No first class for the well-heeled traveler willing to pay for extra comfort, no business class for those accustomed to the expense account. Young or old, black or white, worker or boss, woman or man, it makes no difference. We all share the same status, at least for as long as our ride lasts.

The conductors weave their way through the crowded aisles, checking tickets and occasionally selling one. While doing my initial research for this book, I tried to imagine them on a train at the end of the nineteenth century, complying with the new requirement in many Southern states to direct white and black passengers to separate cars. Those laws gave conductors the authority of a judge and the power of a police officer. They had the responsibility to decide a person's race, although the separate car laws generally offered no specific definitions for black or white—and then the conductors had the legal obligation to enforce their split-second decision. If they didn't, they faced criminal penalties themselves.

Writing about the nineteenth century, a time and place both foreign and familiar to anyone living today, requires choices. For the sake of historical accuracy, and consistent with my goal of telling the story through the eyes of its participants, I have often elected to use the language of their time, as it appeared in their personal letters, documents, diaries, and newspapers. Labels such as "colored" and "mulatto" were mainstays in the nineteenth century, used by white and black alike. Words that we have rightly condemned as slurs were more common in print as well. In quoting them, which I do sparingly, I am seeking to reflect the speaker's meaning, mindset, or intent. If any readers are offended, I ask their understanding. My aim is to learn from our past and, in my experience, authenticity helps serve that cause better than pretense or omission.

Steve Luxenberg
Baltimore, January 2019

PROLOGUE

April 1896

AT HIS SPACIOUS HOME in the quiet town of Mayville, nestled in the farthest corner of western New York State, Albion Tourgée looked at his co-counsel's two-page letter with disbelief. "There is some chance that the case will be argued tomorrow," read the message from Washington. What? *Tomorrow?*

Tourgée glanced again at the date on the letter: April 1, 1896. *Tomorrow?* There was no tomorrow. It was Friday, April 3. Tomorrow was now yesterday. If the oral arguments in the Supreme Court lawsuit known as *Plessy v. Ferguson* had taken place the day before, then Tourgée had missed perhaps the most important oration of his career, one he had spent more than three years preparing to give.

Impossible. Outrageous. Unforgivable.

Cold fury could be felt in every word of his hurriedly composed note to the Supreme Court clerk's office—an icy, personal anger built upon three decades of disappointment with the North of his birth and its failure to erect a citadel of civil rights from the ashes of the Civil War. "I have been ready for the hearing for three months, waiting every day to know when it would probably be reached," he thundered, "but have never heard a word from you." With a characteristic flush of hyperbole, he rushed on. "I represent an association of about 10,000 colored men of Louisiana who raised the money to prosecute these and other cases, and now by some inscrutable mishap they are deprived of the service they had secured."

He was fifty-seven years old, with a glass eye to replace the one blinded in a boyhood gun accident. As perhaps the nation's most famous white advocate for civil rights, he had lived much of his tumultuous life on the outside looking in, and he had a well-deserved reputation for not suffering fools easily. The accent mark in his last name was a Tourgée invention, adopted in his mid-forties, reflecting a personality often characterized by emphasis and embroidery. He was most comfortable on a podium exhorting a crowd, or at his writing table crafting a novel or drafting his newspaper column, rather than socializing in the drawing rooms of New York or Washington. He had gone South after the war, seeking to cement the revolution. When he left after fifteen years of fighting with the established order, some had cheered. One newspaper, bidding him farewell, called him the most hated man in North Carolina. In white supremacist circles, the label might not have been an exaggeration.

His Supreme Court experience could be summed up in half a sentence: two minor cases, twenty-five years ago. He was unfamiliar with the court's practice of notifying only the local counsel about the scheduling of a case. The "inscrutable mishap" turned out to be mostly his co-counsel's fault. He had known for several days that *Plessy* had been assigned a place in the court's queue for oral arguments, but had failed to alert Tourgée right away. Mystifying. Astonishing. Maddening.

Fortunately, as Tourgée soon learned from court clerk James McKenney's courteous reply, the justices hadn't reached as many cases as expected before adjourning for a week's recess. *Plessy* was next in line. The probable date now: Monday, April 13, plenty of time for Tourgée to get there. The location: the Old Senate Chamber, the Supreme Court's home since 1860.

Plessy would not go forward without its architect in chief.

TOURGÉE HAD NURTURED THE *PLESSY* CASE with the care of a horticulturist tending a prized set of orchids. But his involvement was more chance than destiny.

Nearly five years earlier, in the summer of 1891, he had written a particularly acid newspaper column denouncing the new "separate car law" in Louisiana, which mandated "equal but separate accommodations for the white and colored passengers" traveling on trains in the state. His column had acted like a shot of adrenaline for a committee of prominent mixed-race Creoles and several black allies in New Orleans, which was already bent on mounting a legal challenge to the law. At the committee's invitation, Tourgée had assumed command of the case, working with lawyers in New Orleans and later Washington. The committee's leaders couldn't believe their good fortune in having a man of Tourgée's stature on their side. Even better, he had refused to take a fee for his service. For Tourgée, this was more than a case. This was the culmination of a three-decades-long crusade to build a society that paid more than lip service to equal rights.

On Friday, April 10, he boarded the train for Washington, with hours ahead of him to review his arguments. He had done more than anticipate this moment. He had planned for it, imagined it, played out the scene over and over in his mind's eye, calibrating and recalibrating every detail.

His fame drew attention to the case, but it also brought its own baggage. When it came time for his oral argument, the justices would not be looking at a lawyer with a legal claim. They would see a rebel with a cause, a man who had warned in his writings that the country should prepare for a race war if it did not address the wrongs visited every day on people of color.

As an accomplished orator, Tourgée thought he knew how to read an audience. He had studied the nine Supreme Court justices, looking for any advantage, any clue that would help him and his colleagues in constructing a winning argument. He had urged the New Orleans committee to find his ideal candidate for arrest, a man of mixed race who looked white, could pass for white, who could take a seat in a car reserved for whites and throw doubt on the ability of any train conductor to guess the passenger's race by sight. The Louisiana law essentially required the railroad to decide the race of each passenger. What if the conductor couldn't tell?

That scenario would create the most favorable circumstances for his argument. He intended to prove that the separate car law not only violated the Fourteenth Amendment's guarantee of equal protection for everyone within a state's jurisdiction, but that it was unenforceable as well. Tourgée wanted to do more than impress the justices with his logic. He wanted to open their eyes to the inherent contradictions of previous rulings. He wanted to show them the errors in the court's interpretations of the three constitutional amendments enacted after the Civil War to ensure equality. He wanted a triumph.

THE ONLY SURE VOTE, in Tourgée's estimation, was Justice John Marshall Harlan of Kentucky, a slave owner's son and the inheritor of his family's slaves. Despite that background, Harlan's dissents in previous civil rights cases had been noteworthy for their plainspoken language about the dangers of discrimination and inequality. But Harlan was usually alone in his dissents. Was it possible for him to bring others along this time?

Seven of the other eight justices hailed from the North, including several New Englanders who had joined the court since its last major civil rights ruling in 1889. Was it too much to hope that newcomers Henry Billings Brown and his Yale classmate, David Brewer, might form the nucleus of a group more sympathetic to racial equality than their predecessors had been? Both had roots in western Massachusetts, where their families had raised them with an emphasis on tolerance. Both were Republican appointees, and the party still took some pride in its antislavery roots. Both had moved west as young lawyers, Brewer to the Kansas frontier, Brown to Michigan. Their previous writings suggested no resolute position on racial equality. Brown, in particular, had a reputation for an open mind and impartiality.

Tourgée needed more than their votes. He needed them to embrace his arguments. When the justices eventually met in private to discuss the case, he needed someone other than the dependable Harlan to become spokesmen for his cause. Only then would he have any hope of persuading the court's Northerners that this case was different, that separate was not equal, could never be equal—at least not when a Southern legislature was deploying a law to promote the desires and interests of one race at the expense of another.

Taking the case to the Supreme Court was a risk, as Tourgée knew all too well. Defeat could mean an endorsement of separation that would be difficult to undo. "It is of the utmost consequence that we should not have a decision against us," Tourgée had written in October 1893 to Louis A. Martinet, the committee's most active leader and the editor of the New Orleans *Crusader*, a newspaper that had built a following in the city's Creole and black neighborhoods.

Without Martinet, there likely would have been no case, no fundraising, no sustained protest of the legislature's infernal vote to enshrine separation into Louisiana law. Martinet was unflagging. He griped to Tourgée that the committee had thrown all the work on his slight shoulders, but it was the good-natured complaint of an energetic campaigner drawing on a seemingly bottomless reservoir of anger and purpose. As a man of mixed race who could pass for white, and often did, Martinet did not feel the sting of separation as strongly as others in New Orleans. But he had no doubt about its evil effects. "To live always under this feeling of restraint is worse than living behind prison bars," he wrote to Tourgée.

Over the course of the case, the two men had developed a strong personal relationship, exchanging lengthy, often anguished letters about the state of racial inequality in the country. Their similarities stood out more than their differences. Both were men of ego, inclined toward action, yet consumed by misgivings about their mission. Both felt, often, like outcasts. Both were impetuous. Both believed that separation mocked the Constitution's guarantee of equal protection.

Perhaps most of all, both found a good fight hard to resist.

SUPREME COURT CASES often arise out of the ordinary friction of everyday life. Not *Plessy*. It had been a prearranged arrest, the second of two such test cases, both engineered by the New Orleans group that had adopted a name as straightforward as its cause: the Citizens' Committee to Test the Constitutionality of the Separate Car Law, or the *Comité des Citoyens* in French. The railroads had agreed to participate in the ruse, eager to settle the constitutional question before spending a lot of money on extra cars. Which is how Homer Plessy ended up at the New Orleans Press Street depot on June 7, 1892. He was twenty-nine years old, married, and fair-skinned enough to cause confusion. In his neighborhood of Faubourg Tremé, a favorite of the French-speaking free people of color, *les gens de couleur libres*, he blended right in.

It was no accident that the *Plessy* case emerged from the mixed-race culture of New Orleans, a city unlike any other in the United States in 1890. The French-speaking Creoles felt particularly aggrieved by their loss of status after the Civil War. Many had wealth, education, and a strong motivation not to slip farther on the social scale. If the case had come from any other city, it's unlikely that a man who looked white would have been sent to buy a ticket for the whites-only car.

But then, *Plessy* occupies a peculiar place in the American narrative on race. It's safe to say that many people recognize the case as a famous one, and many can place it as the one that sanctioned the "separate but equal" doctrine. But ask about even the basic facts, and the likely reaction is a blank stare. They don't know that the case is one steeped in contradictions, or that it arose from a very public discussion about race, or that there were plenty of advocates working in opposition to the forces of racial injustice.

Just like the people swept up in the case, the story behind *Plessy* is neither plain nor simple. It sprawls and snakes through almost a century of American history, beginning at the dawn of the railroad age in the North, germinating in the soil of slavery and the Civil War, sprouting in the turmoil and tension of Reconstruction, and then bursting forth at the end of the nineteenth century as separation took root in nearly every aspect of American life.

The ruling in *Plessy* drew little attention at the time, but its baneful effects lasted longer than any other civil rights decision in American history. It gave legal cover to an increasingly pernicious series of discriminatory laws in the first half of the twentieth century. Under the banner of keeping the races apart, much of white America stood silent as black Americans suffered beatings, assaults, and murders. Lynching, already a weapon of vengeance and vigilante justice in the years before the *Plessy* decision, became a signature tool for whites bent on domination and repression. This culture of violence flourished, primarily but not exclusively in the South, because some proponents of separation embraced the twisted notion that enforcing laws of racial separation had a higher priority than liberty, justice, fairness, or opportunity.

The *Plessy* case underscores a central fact about the Supreme Court: Its decisions cannot be viewed in isolation. They follow a string of earlier rulings, and they precede a fresh set of issues that can sometimes be foreseen but never guaranteed. Questions about racial equality confronted the country's founders, who embedded their divisions into the Constitution in 1789. We grapple with those questions still, in every new dispute involving voting rights and immigration, affirmative action and school funding, criminal justice and capital punishment.

All Supreme Court stories have their own geography. Remarkable characters populate the landscape of this one: Tourgée of Ohio, Brown of New England, Harlan of Kentucky, Martinet of Louisiana, on separate paths to a shared destination, connected by time, culture, happenstance, and the unresolved struggle between an exhausted North and a bitter South.

Their actions and attitudes, their flaws and foibles—who they were, where they lived, what they said, why they said it, how their views evolved during a tumultuous half century of strife and conflict—serve as powerful reminders that history is made, not ordained.

CAST OF CHARACTERS

Henry Billings Brown, author of the majority opinion in *Plessy v. Ferguson*. Born in Massachusetts, 1836; moved to Michigan, 1859.

John Marshall Harlan, the only dissenter in *Plessy v. Ferguson*. Born in Kentucky, 1833.

Albion W. Tourgée, recruited to argue *Plessy*, also a best-selling author and weekly newspaper columnist for the *Chicago Inter Ocean*. Born in Ohio, 1838; moved to North Carolina, 1865; returned to the North, 1879.

Louis A. Martinet, editor of the New Orleans *Crusader* and guiding force behind the Citizens' Committee to Test the Constitutionality of the Separate Car Law, also known as the *Comité des Citoyens*, reflecting the group's French Creole leadership. Born in Louisiana, 1849.

Caroline (Pitts) Brown, first wife of Henry Billings Brown. Born in Michigan, 1844.

Malvina (Shanklin) Harlan, wife of John Marshall Harlan. Born in Indiana, 1839.

Emma (Kilborn) Tourgée, wife of Albion Tourgée. Born in Ohio, 1840.

Frederick Douglass, abolitionist, orator, author. Among the first passengers of color to be ejected from a railroad car for sitting in seats reserved for whites. Born in Maryland about 1817. Fled from slavery in 1838.

Rodolphe L. Desdunes, member of the Citizens' Committee and a contributing writer to *The Crusader.* Born in Louisiana, 1849.

Daniel Desdunes, chosen by the Citizens' Committee to test the separate car law, arrested by arrangement in February 1892. Son of Rodolphe Desdunes. Born in Louisiana, about 1870.

Homer Plessy, chosen by the Citizens' Committee to test the law, arrested by arrangement in June 1892. Born in Louisiana, 1862.

John H. Ferguson, the state judge whose rulings were appealed by Plessy's team, making him the defendant in *Plessy v. Ferguson.* Born in Massachusetts, 1838; moved to New Orleans, 1866.

James C. Walker, a white New Orleans lawyer hired by the Citizens' Committee to work with Tourgée and act as local counsel. Born in Louisiana, 1837; served in the Confederate Army.

Men hate each other because they fear each other; they fear each other because they don't know each other; they don't know each other because they can't communicate with each other; they can't communicate with each other because they are separated from each other.

Martin Luther King Jr., speaking in September 1957,
at the Highlander Folk School,
Monteagle, Tennessee

PART I

Ambition

EASTERN RAIL ROAD.

THE EASTERN RAIL ROAD IS NOW OPEN BETWEEN

BOSTON & SALEM.

FOR THE PRESENT THE FOLLOWING ARRANGEMENT IS ADOPTED.

From Boston.

Passengers and Baggage will be taken from the Company's Depot, on *Lewis's wharf*, at the following hours, viz:

7 o'clock, A. M.	2½ o'clock, P. M.
9 " A. M.	3¼ " P. M.
12¼ " P. M.	6 " P. M.

From Salem.

Trains will start from the Depot, foot of Washington-street, at the following hours,* viz:

8 o'clock, A. M.	1½ o'clock, P. M.
10 " A. M.	4½ " P. M.
11 " A. M.	7 " P. M.

RATES OF FARE.

Between LEWIS's WHARF and SALEM DEPOTS,	50 Cents.
Between BOSTON and LYNN,	31 Cents.
Between BOSTON and MARBLEHEAD DEPOT,	31 Cents.
Between SALEM and LYNN,	25 Cents.

☞ All the Trains will stop at the *Lynn Depot* and the Trains leaving Boston at 9 A. M. and 3¼ P. M., and Salem at 8 A. M. and 1½ P. M. *will stop at the Marblehead Depot, to take and leave passengers.*

The Coaches of the late Eastern Stage Company will be at the Depot in Salem to take passengers to the Eastward on the arrival of the 7, 9, 12¼ and 3¼ Trains from Boston.

Passengers for Portsmouth and Dover, who take the 7 o'clock Train from Boston, can dine at either place.

Passengers by the 9 o'clock Train will arrive at Newburyport at 1 o'clock, and at Portsmouth at 4, P. M.

Passengers by the 12¼ Train can *dine at Salem, and then proceed to Portsmouth and Portland the same evening in the Mail Stage.*

Passengers by the 3¼ Train will be taken as far as Newburyport.

Passengers by either of the above Trains will be taken to intermediate places, as usual.

ALL BAGGAGE WILL BE AT THE RISK OF ITS OWNERS.

STEPHEN A. CHASE, *Superintendent.*

September 7, 1838.

Calling all passengers: The Eastern's inaugural timetable, September 7, 1838

1

Taking Their Seats

Massachusetts, 1838–1843

SOME CALLED IT, SIMPLY, "the dirt car." Newspapers preferred the "Jim Crow" coach. No matter what name it went by, the abolitionists of Massachusetts wanted the separate car for colored passengers banished from the state's new railways. It belonged, they would say later, in the "receptacle of forgotten barbarisms."

For the abolitionists, the sprawling network of railroads emanating from Boston was nothing short of a godsend. Their organization, the Massachusetts Anti-Slavery Society, was pushing to create and nurture chapters in every one of the state's counties, and to expand their movement's reach into neighboring states. Before steam locomotion, the society's agents had no choice but to spend long, fatiguing days on horses and stagecoaches. Now, they climbed aboard a train whenever they could. With each passing mile, they could feel their movement accelerating.

Among the eight passenger railways operating in the state, only three had chosen the custom of separate cars. But two of those lines served towns north and south of Boston that had emerged as antislavery strongholds. With pairs of white and black abolitionists frequently aboard those trains, confrontations were guaranteed. They could not ride together, the conductors said—not in the whites-only car, not in the dirt car. Resisters could go quietly, or in the rough grip of the crew's strong arms. But go they must.

Jim Crow laws gained velocity in the South at the end of the nineteenth century. But Jim Crow did not originate there. Separation had no role in the South before the Civil War. Slavery required close contact, coercion, and even intimacy to survive and prosper. It was the free and conflicted North that gave birth to separation, in different places and in different forms.

One of those birthplaces was the Massachusetts town of Salem. There, on a late summer's day in 1838, the Eastern Rail Road threw a party to announce itself to the world, accompanied by the kind of pomp and celebration that often heralds a newborn's arrival.

PASSENGERS EVERYWHERE. Passengers in the seats, in the aisles, on the platforms at the ends of each car, a mass of humanity so thick that some riders worried that the Eastern Rail Road's maiden trip on August 27, 1838, would transform triumph into disaster. Would one of the railroad's three newfangled steam locomotives wheeze to an exhausted halt? Would the railroad need stagecoaches—whose owners had predicted that the first train derailment would send frightened passengers streaming back to their carriages—to rescue the top-hatted dignitaries and stockholders, stranded in their finery under ominously cloudy skies somewhere between East Boston and Salem?

The practice tests had gone well. But no trial run could simulate what the locomotives were expected to do on that warm August day: haul three or four overloaded cars on round-trip runs between Salem and Boston. The coaches were designed to accommodate twenty-four travelers each. On this day, though, they would be stuffed with perhaps double that number.

At noon in East Boston, after an hour of hurrahs from several hundred investors, the swollen crowd jammed itself into the three trains for the thirteen-and-a-half-mile ride. The cars were delivering the passengers to a festive dinner for six hundred at the Eastern's new depot in Salem. Newspaper correspondents representing nearly every town along the route were on hand to chronicle the history-making moment. A breakdown would be more than embarrassing. It would be impossible to hide.

Separated by half a mile, the locomotives clattered along at a leisurely pace, allowing the passengers plenty of time to admire the many engineering marvels—overpasses, embankments, stone walls—that work crews had fashioned in the excavated cavities of rock and earth. As the trains crossed the spanking-new Saugus River bridge and rumbled toward the town of Lynn, gasps rose from inside the cars. A full sweep of the sea came into view. The white sails of passing vessels fluttered lazily in the distance, a stark contrast to the noise, heat and acrid smell from the wood-fired steam engines.

The first glitch came at the Lynn station. There, yet another clutch of stockholders waited to join the jolly parade. Their joyful anticipation shifted to confusion as the jam-packed trains thundered past without stopping. Cries, shouts, groans, and hisses filled the air. An empty set of cars came back to retrieve them, but it was too late for some stranded riders. They were so incensed that they decided to boycott the celebration.

No existing form of transportation quite compared to a railroad car's opportunities for throwing together passengers without regard for status or social group. A gentleman could wind up next to a laborer, close enough together to smell breakfast—or worse—on each other's breath. Trains with first-class accommodations offered wealthier patrons a possible respite from the riffraff, but the newspaper advertisements that appeared during the first week of September in 1838, proclaiming "The Eastern Rail Road is now open between Boston and Salem," mentioned no such haven for the well heeled. There was only one fare: fifty cents in each direction, half of what the stagecoaches were charging for the same trip, except that the train would make the journey in less than an hour, while a stagecoach would take the better part of the afternoon.

Fifty cents for all passengers, gentleman or lady, white or colored. One price to fit all. But only, it would turn out, on paper.

THE TAIL END of the opening-day procession trundled into Salem without further hitch, just ahead of an evening downpour. The disembarking passengers joined a Who's Who of the state's business and political elites. Leading figures from the Whig and Democratic parties mingled with the presidents of the state's other rail companies, who had come to salute the latest member of their growing club. Talk of railway expansion to other states brought shouts of "Onward!" from the giddy crowd, which feasted on a bounty of cold meats and other foods from six tables that ran the length of the depot, nearly 130 feet long, by the *Boston Transcript* reporter's measurement.

The Eastern's ruddy-cheeked president, George Peabody, had prepared a grand speech to match the grand occasion. That was typical of the forty-three-year-old Massachusetts native, who was already on his way to amassing the wealth that would eventually earn him the unofficial label, "one of America's richest men." At seventeen, he had left his hometown of South Danvers (later renamed Peabody) to fight in the War of 1812. At nineteen, he and a fellow enlistee founded a wholesale dry goods company in Baltimore. By thirty-two, he was exporting cotton to the British, a beneficiary of the South's slave labor economics. His merchant banking firm, Peabody & Company, was now a powerful financier with investments on both sides of the Atlantic. A sumptuous London home doubled as Peabody's primary residence and a frequent stop for American visitors.

Like the man who wrote it, Peabody's speech to the Salem gathering brimmed with ambition. The railroad was not merely a means of transportation, he told the crowd. It was a force for social change. Steam locomotion would bind together the sprawling United States, which had recently welcomed the new states of Arkansas and Michigan into the Union, swelling the total to twenty-six, a once-unthinkable number. "The extreme states need no longer be farther separated than were the extremities of the 'Old Thirteen' at the confederation," Peabody declared.

The states, in Peabody's sunny view, were the main ingredient in the still-young republic's recipe for success. In other nations, he said, "the provinces not only suffer from the constant tendency" to lavish attention on the capital city, "but the most remote are apt to be neglected and experience little of the fostering care of the government." Not so in the United States, where every state has "its own particular sun, shining with its own brightness, and warming and illuminating its own peculiar sphere."

The men in Peabody's audience—and they were, of course, overwhelmingly men—certainly felt that way. They regarded themselves as citizens of

Massachusetts first, and then, separately, as citizens of the United States. They embraced the Massachusetts Constitution ardently—more ardently, if they called themselves antislavery—than they embraced the U.S. Constitution. The Massachusetts Constitution not only declared that "All men are born free and equal," but it had ended slavery within the state's borders upon its adoption in 1780.

The ever-widening divide between North and South had given even greater meaning to the importance of state citizenship. Natives of Massachusetts, that "inspiration of liberty," could declare themselves as separate from the slaveholding states, where skin color had shoved aside equality as the determining factor in the pursuit of life, liberty, and happiness. Similarly, Southerners could distance themselves from those noxious Northern abolitionists who would prevent the South from "shining with its own brightness," to borrow Peabody's phrase.

But a national railway system, Peabody boldly predicted, would help to "subdue local prejudices." A rail-connected nation, east to west, north to south, would send "a whole people moving onward together in a career of unexampled prosperity, bearing in their front the standard of Equal Rights."

He would have said all that, but he never finished his speech. Peabody "commenced an address of some length," the *Boston Courier* reported, "but from the extreme size of the building, the noise produced by the popping of Champagne corks, etc., he could only make himself heard by a few persons," and he stopped short. A chagrined Peabody turned to *Boston Advertiser* publisher Nathan Hale, and requested that Hale arrange to print the speech in full, so that the people of Massachusetts might read and digest it at their leisure. Hale nodded his assent.

The next day, though, when Mr. Peabody's railroad officially threw open its doors to the paying public, the "standard of Equal Rights" was nowhere in sight. Instead, the Eastern's white and colored passengers moved onward—to separate cars. At first, the practice provoked no outcry, not even from the abolitionist movement, perhaps because people with any shade of color made up a minuscule portion of the Massachusetts population, barely 1 percent in the 1840 census. While a sizable number of the state's 8,669 "free colored persons"—black or mulatto, according to the census designations—lived within hailing distance of the three railroads that ran separate cars, few had the money or regular need for train travel.

If anyone did object, railroad officials would say, firmly: The cars are the same. Separation best serves our passengers, all passengers. Please take your seat.

IN EARLY SEPTEMBER OF 1838, a week after the Eastern Rail Road chugged into operation, an enslaved Marylander slipped away into the night, his bag light, his eyes set on Canada.

Months later, in freedom, he would take the name of Frederick Douglass. But during those initial days of flight, he adopted the last name of Stanley, then Johnson, thin disguises to throw off any slave-hunter looking for the runaway Frederick Bailey. He had no money for bread, let alone shelter. Among the twenty-year-old fugitive's few possessions: the name and address of David Ruggles, secretary of the New York Committee of Vigilance and born free to a Connecticut family in 1810.

Ruggles will help you, the runaway had been counseled, just as he has helped hundreds who preceded you. He may not be a physically imposing young man, but he's a determined one. Go to him. Trust him.

The fugitive ignored the advice. As he would write in his first book, an 1845 account titled simply *The Narrative of the Life of Frederick Douglass,* he cowered in hiding during his first few days in New York City, trusting no one, white or black, "afraid to speak to any one for fear of speaking to the wrong one, and thereby falling into the hands of money-loving kidnappers, whose business it was to lie in wait for the panting fugitive, as the ferocious beasts of the forest lie in wait for their prey." He sought to make himself invisible by melting into the nooks and crannies of New York's wharves, not an easy task for a man of Douglass's powerful build. When the runaway did not show up as arranged, the bespectacled, well-groomed Ruggles went looking for him.

While living under Ruggles's roof on Lispenard Street in lower Manhattan, Douglass got his first good look at the life of a professional resister. Ruggles spent several days in jail for his intervention in a fugitive slave case, and Douglass was impressed by his host's grit and guile in "devising the ways and means" of securing escape routes for the runaways who flowed through the house. "Though watched and hemmed in on almost every side, he seemed to be more than a match for his enemies," Douglass marveled.

The two men would not spend much time together—two weeks at most—but Ruggles would leave a profound impression on the young Douglass. By the time they parted on September 17, Ruggles had turned Douglass away from Canada, pointing him instead toward the Massachusetts whaling town of New Bedford. Douglass's skills as a caulker would be valued there, Ruggles said, and he would have no trouble blending in. New Bedford's black community had swelled in recent years, reaching more than 6 percent of the town's population, and the seaport bubbled with abolitionist activity.

When Douglass arrived in New Bedford, bearing a letter of introduction and five dollars from Ruggles, he was not ready to jump into the fires of the antislavery movement. When the moment came, though, Douglass would prove himself an attentive student.

IT TOOK ONLY six weeks for "Jim Crow" to show up in a newspaper as a label for the colored-only car. The October 12, 1838, item in the *Salem Gazette* told the story of two drunken white sailors, Benjamin King and John Smith, charged with damaging the Eastern Rail Road's track in retaliation for being ejected from the train. Their rowdy and profane behavior on the six o'clock evening run to Salem had so disgusted the other passengers that the crew had halted the locomotive "and compelled Smith, who was the drunkest, to take his seat in the 'refuse' or 'Jim Crow' car, at the end of the train."

The newspaper's matter-of-fact reference to Jim Crow suggested the label was already well in circulation among passengers and railway crews. The *Gazette* offered no explanation for using it. Tellingly, none was needed. By 1838, the astounding success of an entertainer named T. D. Rice, abetted by newspapers on the prowl for a turn of phrase, had turned "Jim Crow" into a commonly understood phrase in New England's lexicon.

Thomas Dartmouth Rice liked to call himself the "Original Jim Crow," although he certainly could not claim to be the first white man to sing in blackface when he bounded on to the stages of New England and elsewhere in the early 1830s. But he could soon claim to be the best known. His buffoonish imitation of slave dialect was only part of Rice's act. He kept his paying audiences coming back by constantly writing new verses for his standard "Jump Jim Crow" tune, often commenting acerbically on the latest political news, sometimes in ways that cut against the grain of the racist stereotype that Jim Crow represented.

Rice's character took on a life all its own. Figurines, touted as the "complete, original Jim Crow," showed up on tables at annual spring fairs in Massachusetts. Boston merchants carried music boxes that played "Jim Crow, Zip Coon and other tunes." A tour of England widened his reputation. On Ireland's racetracks during the 1838 season, a horse named Jim Crow danced his way to several victories. By the time the Eastern Rail Road laid down its tracks, Jim Crow was no longer just the name for a white entertainer dressed in a short-waisted blue coat, threadbare gold pants and mismatched shoes who sang that "Eb'ry time I wheel about I jump Jim Crow." Newspaper editors and letter writers had picked up the phrase, routinely accusing politicians of "jumping Jim Crow" for giving up a principle too easily or for abandoning their party's cause.

It was just a short hop from there to christening the colored-only car as the "Jim Crow." The whites-only car acquired no comparable designation. Whatever George Peabody meant by saying the railroad would bear the banner of "equal rights," it did not extend to nicknames on the Eastern railroad line.

IN JUNE 1841, three years after the birth of the Jim Crow car, David Ruggles arrived in Massachusetts for a series of abolitionist strategy sessions. He did not come to pick a fight over transportation. Only thirty-one years old but with failing eyesight—cataracts would leave him blind by the following year—Ruggles drew his personal line somewhere between fairness and dignity. When he boarded the steamboat *Telegraph* in New Bedford's harbor on

June 19, 1841, bound for Nantucket and a meeting of the abolitionists there, he found fairness and dignity nowhere in evidence.

On that pleasantly sunny Saturday morning, Ruggles learned that there were two fares. For two dollars, passengers could roam the ship, free to go anywhere. For fifty cents less, they could confine themselves to the cheap seats on the forward deck. Ruggles opted for the higher fare. The captain refused to accept it. Words became shouts, and in the ensuing scuffle, the slightly built Ruggles lost his hat and the papers he had brought with him. He never made it to the meeting in Nantucket.

Several weeks later, on the New Bedford & Taunton line to Boston, Ruggles discovered that the railway offered no discount at all for its brand of discrimination. All passengers paid the same two-dollar fare. Ticket in hand, Ruggles made his way to the whites-only car, insisting that he was entitled to sit wherever he chose. The conductor insisted otherwise, summoning reinforcements to eject him. Ruggles put up a fight, and had the bruises and torn clothes to show for it. His baggage went on to Boston. He went to New Bedford to file a formal claim of assault against the railroad company and the men who had manhandled him.

By seeking to bring the railway to account through the legal system, rather than just retreating to lick his considerable wounds, Ruggles had done something extraordinary. This free man of color, battered but unbowed, was fighting back with a weapon unavailable to a slave. Ruggles wanted more than an apology. He was, essentially, challenging the railroad's policy of separation and its authority as a corporation to enforce it.

A few weeks later, at a two-day trial before New Bedford police judge Henry H. Crapo, the railroad president testified that the company's rule benefited everyone because it "separated the drunken, dirty, ragged and colored people from the others." Ruggles told the judge that he saw no benefit in paying two dollars to sit with the drunken, dirty, and ragged. He had paid full price—the same price as white passengers—and that should give him the same privileges. But none of his arguments moved Judge Crapo. He blamed Ruggles for refusing to obey a posted rule. The railroad was entitled, the judge said, to make and enforce whatever rules it deemed necessary. "The cars are the property of the stockholders, and as such are private property," Crapo declared.

Crapo's ruling brought a vehement denunciation from William Lloyd Garrison, the founding editor of the abolitionist newspaper, *The Liberator.* Garrison took to its pages to censure Crapo for "giving his legal sanction to the dastardly assault and battery." In an accompanying article, Ruggles pronounced the trial "the greatest farce I ever witnessed."

Less than two weeks later, with his railroad battle still a fresh wound, Ruggles was the guest of honor at a gala dinner celebrating his contributions to the abolitionist cause. "Action is everything," he exhorted his admirers, a mixed gathering of whites and blacks that defied the calls for separation in public places. "With it, we are successful. Without it, all our enthusiasm is worse than nothing."

ACTION CAME IN MANY FORMS. So did resistance. Two weeks after the gala dinner, the conductor and crew on the Eastern Rail Road found themselves face-to-face with both, in the form of Frederick Douglass and a white abolitionist named John Collins, the general agent of the Massachusetts Anti-Slavery Society.

The Eastern had extended its Salem line across the state border to Portsmouth, New Hampshire, twenty miles north of the Massachusetts line. Grateful passengers included Collins, whose travel time to abolitionist chapters in southern New Hampshire had shrunk dramatically. On September 8, 1841, Collins was heading there for an annual meeting, accompanied by Douglass, the Anti-Slavery Society's newest employee and rising star.

Less than a month before, Douglass had transfixed the abolitionists' midsummer gathering with a spontaneous, eloquent description of his days in slavery. Almost instantly, Douglass went from obscurity to symbol, a flesh-and-blood example of the wonders that abolition could bring. Garrison and his compatriots, shrewd as well as captivated, wasted no time in pressing Douglass into their service for a trial period.

The traveling duo made an odd pair—the excitable Collins, seven or eight years older, born in Vermont, known for his sarcastic pen and long face, and the stern-eyed, broad-shouldered Douglass, not quite twenty-four, unschooled in antislavery politics. Together, they would attract attention in any crowd, but the Eastern conductor had his eye on the only contrast that mattered when he spotted them sitting side by side: Collins was white, Douglass was not.

The conductor ordered them to separate. Douglass stayed put. The conductor laid down the usual ultimatum: the Jim Crow car, or ejection. Collins demanded to know the basis for the conductor's directive. The conductor ripped down a posted placard from the car's entrance and thrust it toward them. Collins treated the placard's words as one more debating point, arguing that the rule violated the Massachusetts Constitution's guarantee of equal rights.

The conductor lost what little patience he had. Collins united with Douglass in refusing to move. The conductor now had two resisters on his hands, one white, one black. Not the usual scenario, but nothing to make the conductor back down. Collins and Douglass proved no match for the half-dozen men who seized Douglass and dragged him out of the car.

Then, a new and complicating series of events: Another abolitionist on the train, George Foster, announced his intention to join Douglass in the Jim Crow car. The conductor stood firm against this unexpected challenge, telling Foster that he "was not black enough to sit there." Foster fumed, but retreated.

The next day at the meeting in New Hampshire, Collins and Douglass ignited the assembled with their account. Soon, the abolitionists had more than another outrage to discuss. Thanks to Ruggles and Douglass, they now had a rallying cry: Ban the separate cars.

THE FALL OF 1841 brought one clash after another on both the Eastern and New Bedford lines. Traveling parties of white and black abolitionists now demanded to sit together, in one car or the other. The tactic of "bearing witness," either by protesting an eviction or by trying to join the evicted traveler in the Jim Crow car, introduced a new level of danger into every encounter. Both sides felt it.

On September 28, Collins met Douglass and two white abolitionists—a female friend of Collins, and James N. Buffum, secretary of the Lynn chapter—at the Lynn station for a trip north to Newburyport, near the Massachusetts–New Hampshire line. The foursome planted themselves in the whites-only car, known as "the long car." Douglass regarded the Eastern long cars as "one of the best railroad carriages" then in operation, with "luxuriant and beautiful" seats. The enraged conductor ordered Douglass out. When Buffum described his intention to go with Douglass, the conductor set down his marker: "I'd as soon haul you out of his car, as I'd haul him from this."

Douglass held fast to his seat. Six men were needed to oust him. "They clutched me, head, neck, and shoulders," Douglass wrote later. "But, in anticipation of the stretching to which I was about to be subjected, I had interwoven myself among the seats. In dragging me out, on this occasion, it must have cost the company twenty-five or thirty dollars, for I tore up seats and all." At the next stop, his white companions were forced to leave the train as well.

Buffum, back at the station, spotted the Eastern superintendent, Stephen Chase, whose name appeared on the placard of rules that the conductor had ripped from the wall. Buffum and Chase belonged to the same Quaker meeting house, and their relationship was already strained. In the pages of *The Liberator*, Chase had been attacked as a hypocrite, a Quaker who believed in the inhumane treatment of his passengers.

Buffum confronted Chase with a Quaker-flavored accusation: "Stephen, I don't think thee does right to utilize a Jim Crow car on thy train."

Chase fired back with his own charge of hypocrisy: "Well, James, I'll tell thee, when thee abolishes the colored pews in the meeting house, then I'll abolish the Jim Crow car."

BY THE FOLLOWING WEEK, the uproar had bloomed into a full-flowered controversy. A hastily organized town meeting in Lynn ended with resolutions denouncing the railroad and Chase, as well as a call for a boycott unless the railroad changed its policy. Chase, claiming he was trying to avoid trouble, came up with a bold idea: He ordered the trains not to stop at the Lynn station. That would prevent Douglass, who was living in the town, from climbing aboard.

The plan backfired. Irate Lynn passengers, their travel arrangements disrupted, turned on the railroad. The editor of the *Lynn Record* dismissed Chase's fear of "mob violence" as a pretense designed to "enlist the sympathies of the people, and to turn their indignation from themselves." Chase quickly rescinded his order.

The abolitionists celebrated the turn of events. "I am convinced that the agitation growing out of these incidents will do much good," Buffum wrote to *The Liberator*, now filled every week with a running chronicle of fresh indignities on Eastern and the New Bedford lines. "Indeed, everywhere I go, I hear men and women talking of these shameful transgressions."

After three years of relative obscurity, the issue of separate railroad cars had vaulted to the top of the abolitionist agenda, reaching parity with the other issues then consuming the movement: petitioning Congress to outlaw slavery in the District of Columbia; protesting the return of fugitives to their Southern masters; ending the state's intermarriage ban.

Dozens of petitions went to the legislature, calling for a law that would forbid separate cars. The most prominent one, signed by Garrison, Collins, and Douglass, minced no words. Legislation was needed so that railroads "may no longer claim the right" of assigning seats "on the sole ground of a difference in color," and to stop railroad employees from "insulting, assaulting and ejecting white passengers" who objected.

That drew several counterpetitions from groups of white passengers, including one arguing that their "comfort and convenience" would be seriously diminished if they had to share "the company of blacks." On an early November evening in 1841, Douglass challenged a rapt audience to see the insidiousness of Northern-style prejudice. "People in general will say they like colored men as well as any other, *but in their proper place*. Who is to decide what is their proper place?" A theme was beginning to run through Douglass's speeches: Inaction and excuses ensured that prejudice would always triumph.

The outcome of the looming legislative battle was not at all certain.

Most legislators stood against slavery, but opposing the South's "peculiar institution" did not translate to a belief that freedom meant the right to mix freely with whites in the North. There were plenty of legislators who viewed anyone of color as inferior, who felt no law could undo what God and nature had created.

EVERY TRAIN TRIP carried the potential for fresh ammunition. While traveling in southern Rhode Island on a late December day in 1841, Douglass and George Foster boarded the Stonington and Providence Railroad, the third line that had adopted separation. Thwarted as usual in their efforts to take seats in a long car, they trudged to the Jim Crow car, where the conductor allowed the two men to ride together for their twenty-four-mile trip to the town of Westerly.

A furious winter storm swirled outside, and "the seats were covered with snow," Foster later wrote. They closed an open door. "After a few miles, four smokers came in. . . . We felt inclined to open the shutters and suffer from the snow and cold, rather than endure the stifling smoke."

Douglass caught a chill that sent him to bed for two days. In his absence, the Rhode Island abolitionists drew up a resolution labeling prejudice on railroads, and elsewhere, as "vulgar, cruel and murderous."

THE SCENE THAT UNFOLDED in the Massachusetts House of Representatives six weeks later, on February 10, 1842, came with no precedent. A special joint committee, chaired by an abolitionist senator from Plymouth, had granted a full hearing to the petitioners seeking a ban on separate cars. Word had gotten out: a man of color would be testifying.

Curious spectators, including legislators, crowded into the cavernous hall. It was not the most comfortable venue for watching an event, momentous or otherwise. The ornate room had the dual distinction of being large enough to accommodate more than four hundred representatives, and too large to keep warm during the winter months when the legislature met. The four fireplaces, one in each corner of the room, did such an inadequate job that the House had adopted a rule. Legislators could stay bundled while seated, but had to doff their hats when standing to speak.

Few in the crowd needed an introduction to the first witness. Wendell Phillips was the son of a former Boston mayor and, at thirty years old, already among the most prominent of New England abolitionists. Like Garrison and Collins, he had chosen to show his support for colored passengers by attempting to ride with them in the separate car. His protest had led the *National Anti-Slavery Standard* to exclaim that separation on railroads would end if only ten other "patricians" would join Phillips in the Jim Crow coaches.

His rousing oratories had mesmerized even the most lukewarm of antislavery supporters. He drew on those skills in delivering an impassioned ninety-minute plea against separation. "There are those who consider this a trifling matter," Phillips told the white men arrayed before him. "To the colored citizen, sir, it is not so." A white passenger could not begin to understand "the inconvenience, the wrong, the disgrace, the insult and suffering of these unconstitutional by-laws of corporations."

Phillips took direct aim at Judge Crapo's ruling against Ruggles: Yes, the railroads might be privately owned, as Crapo had insisted, but they were public in every way that mattered. They ran their trains on public roads. They operated with a public charter. They laid their tracks with public loans from the state treasury. They are, Phillips told the committee, "creatures of your own enactment."

As Phillips sat down, to murmurs of approval, the crowd craned for a good look at the next witness: Charles Lenox Remond, who had come to offer a firsthand account of one colored citizen's travels on the Eastern Rail Road. A year older than Phillips, Remond was no stranger to the abolitionists in the hall. He had just returned from a nineteen-month lecture tour of Britain and Ireland that had brought him acclaim and a place of honor at the Anti-Slavery Society's annual meeting two weeks earlier.

But to most in the crowd, Remond was an unknown. A spectator muttered contemptuously to a correspondent for a New York abolitionist newspaper, "He will have to ask his master what to say." After Remond had finished, the correspondent asked the spectator what he thought now. "Why, I think," said the spectator, "the colored man is the ablest man of the two."

Remond's travels abroad gave him an unusual perspective, and he shrewdly made the most of it. On trains and steamboats in Europe, in hotels and on the street, he said, "in no instance was I insulted, or treated in any way distinct or dissimilar from other passengers or travelers." Yet on his return to Boston, just before Christmas 1841, he was immediately reminded of his inferior status in the land of his birth. Buying a one-price-fits-all ticket to Salem, where his parents lived, he was ushered to a dismal, dirty car for colored passengers. Europe suddenly seemed very far away. "I took my seat peaceably," he told the committee, "unwilling to descend so low as to bandy words with the superintendents or contest my rights with conductors."

A few days later, Remond continued, he ran into the Eastern's superintendent, Stephen Chase. The two men knew each other from growing up in Salem. Chase asked Remond if he was glad to be home after such a lengthy absence, and was taken aback by Remond's tart answer: "I never felt to loathe my American name so much as since my arrival." Remond asked Chase how separation would make him feel—if, for example, passengers with red hair, like Chase, had to ride separately. Chase "could make no reply."

Remond then drove his point home to the committee. He had no control over his skin color, just as Chase had none over the color of his hair. "Complexion," Remond said, "can in no sense be construed into crime, much less be rightfully made the criterion of rights."

The newspaper reports reflected the usual split in public opinion. One Boston correspondent called Remond's delivery "graceful and pointed," and surmised that "equal justice" would prevail. But the correspondent for the *Hampshire Gazette* complained sourly about these "petty" petitions of "trifling importance" taking up the legislature's time. *The Liberator*, with its usual enthusiasm, published verbatim accounts of the testimony.

Several newspapers carried nothing at all.

ANOTHER FAMOUS SON of Boston, Charles Francis Adams, watched the Phillips and Remond testimony with keen interest. In only his second year as a member of the Massachusetts House of Representatives, Adams had decidedly mixed feelings about what to do about separate railroad cars. He deplored the practice, but had grave misgivings about the precedent that would be set if the legislature intervened in the affairs of the corporations. Where would it lead? Where was the line between private and public interests? After listening to Phillips and Remond, Adams wrote in his diary, "I was disappointed at the general character of the argument and my mind was in greater doubt than ever."

Doubt was a place where Adams often dwelled. Other members of Boston's elite families had donned the abolitionist label in recent years, and were wearing it with pride. Not Adams. He was staunchly antislavery, and would later lead a wing of the Whig Party into a national antislavery role. But he rejected immediate abolition as a solution. In 1837, distressed that his close friend and Harvard classmate Edmund Quincy had "come out a warm abolitionist" with a public declaration in *The Liberator*, Adams wrote in his diary: "I wish I could be an entire abolitionist; but it is impossible. My mind will not come down to the point."

Until he had bowed to the Whig Party's entreaties to join its ticket, Adams had spent a good portion of his first thirty-three years looking for an escape from his presumed destiny. The Adams clan was as close to aristocracy as any in the young republic, and Charles felt every ounce of that considerable weight. He revered his grandfather, John Adams, whose resume began with "revolutionary" and peaked at "second president of the United States." He loved and respected his father, the nation's sixth president. He wrote often in his diary of his ambition to leave his own mark in the world. But he claimed to detest the profession that had made his family so influential—not just the practice of it, but everything about it.

Publicly, he hid his distaste. Privately, he filled his diary with withering entries about the business of politics. The Massachusetts legislature was a place of "little consequence," engulfed in a "multitude of harassing local questions," he complained before agreeing to run for a seat. The Whigs, he wrote while serving as a Whig member of the House, were a party "tied together by no principles and led on by political gamblers" who would ensure the party's doom.

He valued independence more than any cause. He was generally an abolitionist ally, but hardly a reliable one. After hearing out yet another abolitionist appeal for help, he scribbled in his diary, "I am willing to advance their principles as far as I can approve them but I will not consent to make myself their slave."

THREE WEEKS AFTER the Phillips-Remond testimony, the special legislative committee on separate railroad cars issued its much-anticipated report. It could not have been more favorable if the abolitionists had drafted the document themselves.

It did not matter, the report said, that some passengers preferred separation. The Massachusetts Constitution had decreed equal rights—at least for its male citizens—and that meant no discrimination by color, descent, or religious sect. The committee recommended a bill making railroads liable for criminal penalties if they discriminated. The proposal brought a howl of protest from one state senator, who warned that "this foolish mixing" would spread to theaters, hotels, and other public places.

The final vote on repealing the intermarriage ban came up first. It passed the Senate by a comfortable margin, but failed in the House by four votes. Adams, who had spoken out in favor of the repeal, wasn't surprised. He had felt the House's mood shifting after the *Boston Advertiser* had come out for keeping the ban. "So hard it is in a community to do away with a deep rooted prejudice," he wrote in his diary. "I must take care and keep myself cool."

The Senate saved him from having to decide on the separate car bill. Opponents, sensing they now had the votes to put the issue on hold, moved for an indefinite postponement. They won, 18 to 13.

Garrison wrote bitterly of the dual defeat: "Humanity and Liberty have yet a mighty work to accomplish in Massachusetts." A month later, he debuted a new tactic in *The Liberator*: A "traveller's directory." Modeled after the train timetables, the directory informed passengers of how they could expect to be treated on each of the state's railways.

On the Boston and Lowell: "*humanity respected.*"

On the Western: "*equality of privileges.*"

On the Eastern: "*an odious distinction on account of color, and a bullying propensity to carry it out.*"

A SECOND YEAR of confrontations did not eliminate Adams's doubts about the railroad bill. As the 1843 session got under way, his attention was elsewhere, primarily on the George Latimer fugitive case. A Virginia slaveholder, claiming ownership of Latimer, had asked Massachusetts to hold Latimer and return him, no questions asked. This was a matter that went directly to the heart of the country's great national divide: Could a Northern state be forced, against the principles of its own constitution, to comply with a slave owner's request? Adams, who was heading the legislative committee investigating the Latimer case, had no misgivings on this issue. He favored enactment of a "personal liberty" law that would prohibit the use of any Massachusetts property or official in a Southerner's hunt for a runaway slave.

The Latimer case had stirred public opinion like none other. It was seen as an affront to state citizenship, and not just by the abolitionists. At the end of January 1843, two men, using a stretcher resting on their shoulders, carried petitions into the State House bearing an astounding sixty-four thousand signatures, more than 10 percent of the state's adult population. Their cargo weighed more than one hundred and fifty pounds.

The abolitionists, who had orchestrated the event, had asked Adams to make the formal presentation to the House. "This is perhaps the most memorable event of my life," Adams wrote that night. "I feel some degree of pride in the fact that I was selected for such a purpose."

HE FELT NOTHING of the sort about the railroad bill. He wished the legislation would disappear. But like a conductor enforcing the separate car rules, he found confrontation hard to avoid. The climactic moment came on February 6, 1843, a cloudy Monday, one week after his Latimer triumph. The House took up the railroad bill for a final debate. After a divisive discussion that pitted Whig against Whig, Democrat against Democrat, Adams reluctantly rose to his feet. He had made up his mind to vote against the bill. But he was eager to avoid saying so publicly, given the "strong undercurrent of prejudice" in the opposition's speeches. Desperate to find an alternate path, he fell back on an unusual ploy: a direct appeal to the railroads themselves.

There was no question in his mind, Adams told his House colleagues, that the legislature "had the right" to pass a bill. But "it would be a kind of entering wedge to a general interference with the charters of all corporations," and he did not think that approach was wise. With a dramatic air, he turned to the legislative reporters, and instructed them to write down his words precisely. Perhaps the offending railroads, he said, "would take the advice of a humble member of the House," and voluntarily rescind their bylaws allowing separate cars. That would "save the necessity of a resort to legislation."

Swiftly, the House seized on the Adams sidestep, postponing any action by an overwhelming margin, 171 to 61. The disappointed abolitionists now held their collective breath. Would the railroads, saved from state interference, take the Adams hint?

The railroads did. By the end of 1843, the Jim Crow cars were gone from the Eastern and the New Bedford lines. Frederick Douglass, in retelling the story of how the abolitionists had forced the railroads to abandon separation, specifically praised Adams. Douglass's account was too kind. Douglass did not know that Adams had written in his diary, on the night after engineering the bill's postponement: "Believing this bill to rest on an erroneous principle of legislation, I opposed it, and was the more inclined to because I thought it dangerous."

IN THEIR CONTINUING campaign against slavery, the abolitionists constantly toured New England in the coming years, speaking about their battles, including the separate car fight. Among the people who showed up to hear a Wendell Phillips lecture in the late 1850s: a young Henry Billings Brown, then in law school, and keen to hear as many famous orators as he could.

The twenty-three-year-old Brown was so taken by Phillips's delivery that he made a special note in his pocket daybook: "Phillips power consists in interspersing his speeches with interesting incidents and telling them in a simple, unaffected and heartfelt way." Inspired, he scribbled down one Phillips line, putting quotation marks around it: "Be true to the dreams of thy youth."

Wedding Day: December 23, 1856, Evansville, Indiana

(Courtesy of Edith de Montebello)

2

Harlan of Kentucky

1853–1857

MALVINA SHANKLIN'S FIRST glimpse of John Harlan, as she would remember it, didn't offer her the clearest picture of the man she would marry three years later. On a late summer day in 1853, she sat in a darkened room at a doctor's office in her hometown of Evansville, Indiana, undergoing treatment for "some slight affliction" of her eyes. Through the nearly closed shutters, she saw a strapping shape, striding down the street, "as if the whole world belonged to him." She took note of "his magnificent figure" and "his broad shoulders well thrown back." She was fourteen years old.

The following February, on a cold winter's afternoon, she was startled to see the same man come prancing into the parlor of her neighbor's house, a rope dangling from his arms and a little boy on his back. She had often daydreamed of this "interesting stranger," even giving him a romantic name: "A Prince of the Blood." Now her daydream had romped right into the room, looking neither princely nor magnificent. He was giving a boisterous "horsey" ride to her neighbor's three-year-old son, who turned out to be John Harlan's nephew. John had not expected an audience for his exuberant performance. He seemed both "very much amused," Mallie thought, and "covered with manly confusion" at being caught "playing the boy."

Hasty introductions followed.

John Marshall Harlan was a Kentuckian, twenty years old, the son of the state's attorney general, less than a year out of law school, and working in his father's private law practice in Frankfort, the state capital. He was visiting Evansville more often these days, now that his older sister, Elizabeth, and her husband had added two boys to the Harlan family tree. John loved his new role of doting uncle.

Malvina Shanklin, known to everyone as Mallie, had come for dinner. She was the only daughter of a prosperous local merchant. She lived a block away with her parents and three brothers, but had spent a portion of 1853 in the faraway city of Philadelphia, boarding at the Misses Gills' School and seeing something of the world beyond provincial Evansville.

Mallie said nothing to John, of course, of her romantic fantasies since the previous summer, or of her fluttery feelings now. After only a few hours in his company, she could feel her infatuation intensifying. "His conversation during that evening greatly interested the young girl," she wrote years later, referring to herself in the third person, "and that night he escorted her home."

Exhilarated, she had rushed to her mother's room, bubbling with the news of "the very pleasant acquaintance she had just made." She already thought of John as more than an acquaintance, of course, and she desperately wanted to see him again. She was taken by his fine blue eyes, his wonderfully clear complexion and his beautiful sandy hair, "which he wore quite long (as was the fashion of the day) . . . parted on the right side, instead of the left, as did all the young men of his family, giving them a most marked individuality."

Whenever she thought about that first night, she remembered her mother's standoffish reaction to her "girlish outburst" about this charming Kentuckian. What did Mallie know of this stranger from another state—a slave state, no less? What did she know of his family in Frankfort, of his beliefs, of his character? Adopting a "very dry, decided and matter-of-fact tone," her mother said firmly, "'You have talked quite enough about a young man whom you have only seen for an hour or two; now you can go up to your room. Good night.'"

MORE THAN A mother's skepticism and a difference in age stood in the way of the young couple's budding relationship. The two families had their roots on disparate sides of the Ohio River, the starkly picturesque waterway that separated North and South. Nearly one thousand miles long, the Ohio in the 1850s served as more than a busy highway for steamboat travelers, freight, and shady gamblers looking for easy prey. It was a dividing line in a divided country.

By a crow's flight, 175 miles lay between John in Frankfort and Mallie in Evansville. But in 1854, John could only envy the crow. He had several options for his visits to Evansville, but none that could be called easy. The Ohio River figured in all of them.

Traveling by horseback meant a week of exhausting rides, with short breaks to rest or change mounts, long nights at unfamiliar stopovers and a final ferry ride to cross the river. Taking a stagecoach offered shelter and a modicum more comfort, if comfort was the right word for a bumpy journey over roads that ranged from rutted to muddy. Then there was the steamboat from Frankfort, a luxurious trip by comparison but also more convoluted—sixty-five miles up the Kentucky River to the confluence with the Ohio, and then a transfer at Louisville (to avoid the treacherous Falls of the Ohio, a twenty-two-foot drop over two miles).

Better yet: John could save a bundle of time and trouble by folding his six-foot, two-inch frame into a plush seat on the latest local novelty, the Frankfort-to-Louisville railway. The train would carry him to Louisville in less than four hours—five hours faster than the stagecoach, fifteen hours ahead of the steamboat—at about the same fare. He would have to put up with the smell of burning wood and steam wafting into the car. But at fifteen miles an hour, the breeze would help to keep the more pungent aromas from spoiling the trip.

Yes, the railroad was a modern miracle, but for the moment, it was a miracle that stopped in Louisville. That left John only one practical option for completing his journey to see Mallie. He could catch a steamer in Louisville for a meandering, 185-mile voyage on the heavily trafficked Ohio. If all went well, it would deposit John at the Evansville wharf as the sun was rising and the town was just waking up.

STEAMERS FOR EVANSVILLE usually left Louisville in late afternoon, making several stops on its overnight journey. The trip itself was an education, especially for a young man whose view of the world to that point had rarely extended beyond the Kentucky side of the river. Anyone traveling those waters felt a hint of danger in the air, the sense that not everyone and everything was as they appeared.

The new Fugitive Slave Act of 1850 required steamboats and ferries to return any runaways caught north of the river. Bounty hunters and U.S. marshals often came aboard with colored men and women in chains. On the Kentucky side, concern about the growing number of runaway slaves had prompted the legislature in 1852 to authorize "special patrol companies" for the two dozen counties flanking the Ohio. These roving bands of "sober, discreet citizens" had the power to arrest, without a warrant, anyone found "lurking about" with the intention of assisting a runaway to freedom. But Kentucky's shoreline ran for hundreds of miles, creating large gaps, and Underground Railroad operatives often received advance word of a determined runaway's likely appearance on the Northern banks. During severe winters when the river froze, the only movement might be the occasional runaway, risking an icy dash to freedom.

On the Ohio, seeing slavery's raw reality required only an open pair of eyes. On the lower deck of steamers heading south to Mississippi and Louisiana, it was common to see slaves, shackled to iron rings and each other, watched over by slave traders as merely another form of cargo, much like the adjacent barrels of flour, casks of cheese, and penned livestock. Paying passengers on the cargo deck slept wherever they could find space. If they were lucky, they huddled next to a cotton bale. If not, within smelling distance of the livestock. The fare was cheap: less than fifty cents from Louisville to Evansville. Enclosed cabins, a level above, cost five times as much.

On the upper deck, swanky saloons and sumptuous tables of food awaited the more prosperous travelers—if they were white. Slave owners could bring a personal servant into the cabin area, but a hostile reception likely awaited any free black passenger making an appearance. The river was rife with stories like the one recounted by a traveler writing for a popular British magazine: A steamer captain on his way from Pittsburgh to Cincinnati had brought "two very respectable negroes" into the dining room, where several white Kentuckians had greeted them with brandished knives.

These "respectable negroes" turned out to be Frederick Douglass and Charles Remond, on a speaking tour of Ohio in the 1840s and already gaining reputations as powerful orators for the abolitionist movement. No strangers to separation on trains and steamboats in the North, the two men saw the knives and began a retreat. They had only entered the dining room by invitation, they said, and not because they were bent on sitting with whites at the dinner table.

Their dignified demeanor won sympathy from other white diners, including none other than Henry Clay, the famous Kentucky Whig politician and longtime friend of the Harlan family. Like John's father, Clay was not an abolitionist. Like John's father, he owned slaves himself, as many as sixty. Clay's stated distaste for slavery, and his crafting of legislation to limit its expansion, had earned him support for his presidential aspirations among many Northern Whigs. But it had also infuriated many of his Southern brethren, who regarded his compromising tendencies with suspicion—or worse, as betrayal.

In the steamer's dining room, Clay now argued for the two black men to stay. Some white passengers sided with Clay. As tensions mounted, Douglass and Remond opted for their own version of compromise. They had no wish to offend anyone, they said. They would eat alone at a side table. As word spread of the outcome, a new invitation went out: Would Douglass and Remond like to deliver a talk the following afternoon, on the very same upper deck?

They would. As the steamer churned its way through the waters separating North and South, a large crowd gathered to hear the two men. "And with such power, with such simple and touching eloquence, did they speak of the wrongs of their race, that the company was frequently moved to tears," a witness recounted. "Mr. Clay himself declared to me that he did not believe that the man existed in the United States who would have spoken more eloquently than Mr. Douglass, and that it was a disgrace to civilization that such a man should only have gained his freedom by flight, or that the race which had produced two such orators should be enslaved."

JOHN HAD NO QUARREL with slavery or with most slave owners. At last count, his family owned fourteen slaves, including five children under the age of fourteen. Most were women, who cooked, cleaned, and served as maids to his mother and three sisters. His father was a lawyer, not a farmer, so the family had no need for an enslaved team of field hands under the thumb of an overseer. But with two houses and three sons—not to mention the likelihood of further expansion, with more marriages and grandchildren on the horizon—the Harlans had plenty of domestic work to be done.

From late fall through the winter, they all crammed into the family's house in town, on one of Frankfort's prettiest streets. But as soon as the blossoms of spring gave way to the suffocating heat of summer, they decamped to Harlan's Hill and the rambling house with its vine-covered wraparound porch, cooler temperatures, and bountiful garden tended largely by "Uncle Lewis."

Only a mile separated the two houses, but the retreat to Harlan's Hill was akin to moving an army, requiring complicated logistics and an assault on difficult terrain. The most direct route, over the imposing slope they called Harlan's Backbone, was so steep that it could only be accomplished on horseback. A wagon carrying goods or the Harlans' slaves had to take the long way around, over roads with gentler switchbacks.

Like most Kentucky slave owners, John's father did not set about to educate or emancipate the men, women and children he held in slavery—with one notable exception. In 1848, he freed thirty-two-year-old Robert Harlan, a light-skinned man of color long treated more like a family member than a slave. That's because he was almost certainly a blood relative, although the court papers setting him free said nothing to settle the mystery surrounding his parentage. He had been part of John's childhood, a fixture in the household, not only sharing the Harlan name but eventually adding his own luster to it. After his emancipation, Robert left for California, where he would make a small fortune in the gold rush before settling in Ohio. Over the subsequent years, his occasional letters to family members, including John, kept them informed of his whereabouts and achievements.

The arguments John heard about slavery—from his father, from his professors, from newspaper editors, from his father's political allies—tended toward the constitutional rather than the concrete. Slavery might be a scourge, they conceded, but it was a legal scourge. His elders defended the status quo, and denounced the abolitionists for their ceaseless "agitation." John saw his father as a compassionate master, genuine in his concern for his slaves' welfare. But neither John nor his father were innocents about slavery's essential cruelty.

John carried a boyhood memory of a Sunday morning walk to church, and his father crossing a Frankfort street to confront a slave driver, whip in hand, herding a line of shackled captives, stark evidence of how slavery tore apart families in the name of property rights. "You are a damned scoundrel," his finger-pointing father roared, shouting to be heard over the clanking chains and ringing church bells. It was the first and only time that John ever heard his father swear, John would claim in recreating the scene for a reporter many years later.

The newspapers offered frequent reminders that slavery was a hard-hearted business, with labor as its raw material. "Slaves! Slaves!" announced a *Louisville Daily Journal* advertisement that appeared in the same month as John's 1853 trip to Evansville. "We will pay the highest cash prices for Negroes at our Negro depot on First Street."

ON JULY 25, 1853, a new advertisement appeared in the *Frankfort Commonwealth*, announcing that "John M. Harlan, Attorney at Law," had arrived on the legal scene. The ad, soon a regular fixture in both local papers, named three prominent Whig politicians as references: a current Kentucky U.S. senator, Kentucky's sitting governor, and John's father, the Honorable James Harlan, attorney general. Not a bad start. But to be expected for a lad who had grown up around nearly every notable Whig in his state, who remembered having his hair tousled by men like Henry Clay.

John's confident stride, which had left such an indelible first impression on Mallie Shanklin, was no accident. He had advantages that most twenty-year-olds could not hope to duplicate. He had an education from two of Kentucky's best-known schools, Centre College in Danville and Transylvania Law School in Lexington, joining a long line that included Kentucky governors, senators, congressmen, and judges. He had graduated to a coveted post in his father's law office, in the shadow of the Kentucky state house, the nexus of law and politics.

John didn't wait long to take his first baby step into politics. The Frankfort city elections were coming up in early 1854. The job of city attorney seemed tailor-made for a Harlan. It was a part-time post, responsible for prosecuting minor criminal cases—breaches of the peace and the like. No one would make the mistake of calling it a high-profile position, but his last name gave him a Harlan-sized edge, especially in a contest with relatively few voters.

When he won, John accepted the job without fanfare. He made no statements to the local newspapers, wrote no letters to the editors, gave no speeches. If he were being honest—and that was certainly his inclination—John would have laughed at Mallie's perception that he walked as if "the whole world belonged to him." At the time of his election as city attorney in January 1854, he still lived largely in his parents' orbit. He relied on them in nearly all the ways that mattered—for employment, connections, companionship, and guidance.

Meeting Mallie a month later took John outside that orbit. He was as captivated by her as she was with him. During his week-long visit to Evansville, he called daily at the Shanklins' house, met her parents, joshed with her three brothers. As the day neared for his return to Frankfort, with their courtship still in its infancy, he proposed. Sure of himself as well as his choice, he wanted to marry right away.

Even by the standards of the age, an immediate wedding would put them on the extreme end of early marriage. Mallie would not turn fifteen for another month; John was still in his first year as a practicing lawyer in his father's firm, too soon to stake a claim to financial independence. In asking Mallie's father for his blessing, John stressed his personal qualities over his earning power. "He said nothing whatever of the worldly or material aspects of the matter," Mallie wrote years later. "After expressing the hope that he could make me happy, he referred my father, for information as to his character, to prominent men with whom my father was acquainted in Henderson, a neighboring town on the Kentucky side of the Ohio River."

Perhaps to allow the reality of marriage to catch up with the passion of youth, both families urged postponement of the engagement as well as the wedding. John and Mallie promised to keep their intentions within the families for now. John returned to Frankfort to solidify his future. Mallie went away to school in Ohio, near Cincinnati.

Hanging over them was the slavery issue, impossible to disguise or fix. Indiana, while a free state, wasn't the most hospitable place for a free black. The state's brand-new constitution, adopted in 1851, included a clause that prohibited any person of color from settling in Indiana. But slavery found no sympathizers in Mallie's clan. "All my kindred were strongly opposed to Slavery," she wrote later, capitalizing the dreaded word. She hoped that one uncle, "an out-and-out Abolitionist," would come around, once he got to know John. But for now, her uncle "would rather have seen me in my grave than have me marry a Southern man and go to live in the South."

Mallie, hopelessly smitten with her "Prince of the Blood," was determined to prevent any derailment of her dreams.

JOHN'S FATHER DID NOT start his life with the kind of privileges that John now enjoyed. James Harlan had earned his way into Kentucky's elite, legal case by legal case, political campaign by political campaign. His credentials marked him as a formidable Whig force: two terms in Congress, then a turn at nearly every Kentucky office except governor. But the law remained his passion, and he planned for his sons to follow in his path. He so admired John Marshall, the former Supreme Court chief justice, that he had named his youngest son after the eminent jurist. Now John had to live up to that legacy.

John's entire childhood had been an apprenticeship of sorts. In his father's company at political meetings, John learned firsthand how words could grip an audience, especially if they came from the mouth of a powerful speaker such as Henry Clay. John and his father had sat within spitting distance of Clay on a rainy November day in 1847, when Clay had delivered his famous Mexican War speech in Lexington to a throng of thousands, including a newly elected congressman on his way to Washington named Abraham Lincoln. John would later say that Clay's sharp criticism of the Mexican War, and of slavery's expansion into the territories, went well over his fourteen-year-old head. But he would forever remember being "charmed by his magnificent, bugle voice." To succeed in law or politics, John concluded, he would need to master this art of mesmerizing a crowd.

But then, John was a born student, inclined to listen and observe. A few months after his fifteenth birthday, John started down a path already trod by other Harlan sons. In the fall of 1848, he arrived at Centre College's small campus in Danville, some forty miles south of Frankfort. Centre's Presbyterian roots suited the Harlans and other Kentucky families with strong ties to that church. John looked around and saw many a familiar face—boys he knew from Frankfort or Lexington, boys from other prominent families. He was younger than many of them, but it didn't take long for him to feel comfortable. He knew he would fit in.

He usually fit in. He was a disciple, not a rebel. He loved to argue, but for him, argument was a skill, not a fight. At Centre, he started a habit of collecting bits and pieces of writing, gravitating toward selections about people who had left a lasting mark in some way. He copied several into a notebook. One was an excerpt from an 1825 essay on the American Revolution, which looked back at the men who had carried the new nation to freedom, whose names now served "as a watchword to the lovers of liberty all over the world." Another was a mournful poem by an Irish writer, expressing a jilted lover's heartbroken wish to have "a place in thy memory, dearest."

He reached the age of eighteen with advantages that grew more abundant with each passing birthday. He even had a political office of his own, a gift from the governor, another friend of his father's. Of all the privileges that came his way, perhaps none was more revealing—and to John's mind, more absurd—than his appointment as adjutant general, head of the Militia of Kentucky. Years later, in recounting the episode, John could not repress his amazement.

It was the spring of 1851. John was seventeen, working as a temporary clerk in the state auditor's office before the next term at law school. Governor John L. Helm entered the room, apparently looking for John's boss. Without warning, the governor headed John's way, as if struck by divine inspiration.

"John," the governor began, "the office of Adjutant General is vacant, and I have a notion of appointing you."

"Governor, you are jesting," John said, hastily reminding the governor of his age.

Helm's unruffled reply made clear that jest was not his aim. "No matter," Helm said. "You can fill the place."

A few days later, on April 16, 1851, John received his commission as Kentucky's fifth—and youngest—adjutant general. It was a part-time job, but it put him on the official list of the state's top officials. His annual salary: $150, half his father's pay as attorney general. The political benefit: invaluable.

YEARS LATER, JOHN WOULD make light of the entire episode. "The position was not one of any special consequence," he wrote, "for the State had no military organization to be controlled and I had nothing to do except keep some old military papers connected with the War of 1812 . . . and perform certain duties connected with two military institutes."

That was modesty talking, from the comfortable distance of time and recollection. True, much of the job was ceremonial, requiring John to attend the commencement exercises at the state's military academies and to appear, in appropriately official attire, at funerals and Fourth of July celebrations. He even gained a title ("General") that he joked about, but never disclaimed. Until his death, letters would arrive at his home addressed to "General Harlan."

But with the prestige came undeniable risks and responsibilities. If the president of the United States was to send out a call to the states for troops, as James Polk had done five years earlier during his Mexican War, all eyes would swivel in John's direction, his competency and youth suddenly on display.

The adjutant general did not control the state's militia. It was a loose network of 143 companies and 82,840 men, as stated in the annual report that John sent to Washington at the end of 1851. But if a crisis came, he would be expected to know their condition and readiness—each company's supply of muskets, rifles, bayonets, and powder horns. The state had a small, separate arsenal. In filling out the state's annual return for 1852, John had left the arsenal line blank, writing in the margin: "No return made to me of the Arms and Accoutrements in the Arsenal." The adjutant general, unable to say what was in the state's stockpile! This was not the sort of ammunition that an aspiring politician wanted to hand over to his political foes.

The ceremonial part of the job went better, but it still reminded John that he was indulged rather than in charge. In June, he acted as a presiding officer for graduation exercises at the Western Military Institute, a modest collection of buildings along the Kentucky River north of Frankfort. As the cadets went marching past in the spring sunlight, John led the review, with several generals "who had won distinction in the Mexican War, standing behind me." He struggled, he later told Mallie, to keep a solemn face.

After all, he was the same age as the graduating cadets.

JOHN DID NOT TAKE his future for granted. Just as the mostly placid waters of the Ohio masked dangerous snags that had wrecked many a riverboat, complacency threatened Kentucky's status quo. One of his favorite law professors, George Robertson, had warned as much in his introductory lecture to Harlan's class in the fall of 1852. "The signs of the time portend an approaching crisis," Robertson predicted gloomily.

He was talking about slavery. If extremists from both sides of the debate kept up their agitation, Robertson warned, they would upset the Constitution's delicate balance, the fulcrum that allowed North and South to stay in the same Union. It was a "radical error," Robertson said, to see the Constitution as a document of loose federation that allowed the states to resist the national laws whenever they chose. The national government could not exist under such anarchy, he said. Northern resistance to the Fugitive Slave Act was but one example.

John found the lecture so compelling that he and two students formed a committee, and requested Robertson's permission to publish it. Robertson replied, with an attempt at modesty, that the speech was intended for their ears alone. But if publication helped "to prevent the unhingement of the Government of our model Union," he wrote, "I shall be more than compensated for my effort."

Robertson was a giant in Kentucky law and politics, a former chief justice of the state's supreme court and a former Whig congressman. A few months before his speech to John's law school class, he had finished his third and final term as speaker of the Kentucky House of Representatives. John had come to regard Robertson with an admiration approaching reverence. Decades later, John would return to Transylvania as a famous alumnus, and deliver a speech hailing Robertson as one of the nation's greatest lawyers. Had Robertson served on the U.S. Supreme Court, Harlan would declare, his reputation would have equaled that of John's namesake, Chief Justice John Marshall.

But John's mentor was also a slaveholder, with no patience for either "emancipationists" or "perpetualists," the labels he used to reject both. In 1849, a crowd had gathered outside Lexington to hear Robertson's thoughts on a new Kentucky constitution. A small abolitionist faction was proposing a gradual emancipation scheme, a matter of considerable interest for a state with thirty-three thousand slave owners and two hundred thousand people in slavery.

Robertson opposed this plan as unworkable and dangerous, as many slave owners did. But he went further, putting his oar sharply into the debate's turbulent waters, scolding his fellow slaveholders for not facing up to slavery's consequences. "I am not one of those who believe that domestic slavery is a blessing, moral or physical, to the white race," he said. "I cannot believe that it makes us richer, more moral, more religious, more peaceful, more secure, or more happy," or that it makes "our children become more industrious, more practical, or more useful." He would be pleased to see slavery "obliterated from the face of the earth." If permitted to "run its natural course," slavery would "find its appropriate grave, in its appointed time."

That "appointed time" might not arrive for several generations, of course, but the "perpetualists" in the crowd didn't cotton to such dangerous talk. They called Robertson an abolitionist sympathizer, a traitor. Robertson protested, but his speeches often seemed to tack from one side of the debate to the other, pleasing few and confusing many. In his farewell oration as speaker of the House in 1852, he tried to make his points again. "I have never believed that the enslavement of the black can be a blessing to the white race," he said. But if slavery was the curse that abolitionists believed, "premature and compulsory emancipation" would be a greater curse, he felt.

Slavery, he warned, "cannot be speedily eradicated without convulsion." That convulsion, however, could be minimized. The best plan, in Robertson's view: Whites should rule and teach blacks, enhancing "the welfare of the inferior and the security of the superior."

THE MOST IMPORTANT influences in John Harlan's life up to this point—his parents, Robertson, and the Whig politicians that his father knew best and respected most—spoke for preservation over passion, conservation rather than change. In the Harlan household, slavery relied on the rule of law, not an overseer's whip. John's father had represented slaveholders in their claims to recover their enslaved "property," but his client list also included two free blacks seized in Ohio and accused of being fugitive slaves. The captured men insisted they were no such thing. Instead, they said, they were victims of a well-known abduction scheme: unsavory slave traders, roaming the Ohio countryside, looking for any black man, free or fugitive, to sell into slavery.

When a friend reported that he was being labeled an "abolitionist" for bringing lawsuits on behalf of these "negroes," the elder Harlan was indignant. Nothing a slave trader could say "will ever prevent me from instituting a suit for freedom if I believe the laws authorize it," he wrote to the friend in August 1851. "The term 'abolitionist' has no terrors for me," but "he who applies it to me lies in his throat." He also wrote, and then crossed out: "I have the same opinion of an abolitionist that I have of a disunionist—Each deserves the gallows."

A free black would not mistake James Harlan for a staunch ally. He supported the view that emancipation, immediate or gradual, was a flawed solution. Because the freed slaves would never fully integrate into American life, he felt, it would be best if they could be resettled in Africa. He pursued the colonization idea—as Clay had, as Abraham Lincoln did—by serving on the Kentucky Colonization Society's board of managers throughout the early 1850s. But in a country that had counted more than three million slaves in the 1850 census, shipping even a thousand souls to Liberia was certainly no answer to the country's irreconcilable differences over whether slavery should continue to exist.

A crisis was approaching, as Robertson had said. The nation's westward expansion ensured it. A choice had to be made—slave or free?—every time a new state was carved from the vast territories west of the Mississippi. There was no status quo in the American slavery debate, as John Harlan would soon find out.

THE HUSH-HUSH CEREMONY in the summer of 1854 took place in the most public of Frankfort's places, the old courthouse. It was strange to hold a clandestine meeting there, stranger still for young John Harlan to look around the room and see many of the county's most venerable Whig politicians, including his father. These were men accustomed to debating political issues before large, noisy crowds. But not on this night. Before the evening was done, John would take a secret oath, pledging himself to a new political movement, the Know Nothings, the heir apparent to Kentucky's disintegrating Whig Party.

John didn't know much about the Know Nothings, except that in a matter of months, they had gained a swift popularity in Kentucky. Born in the North a decade earlier, the Know Nothings could trace their ancestry back to a trio of stealthy societies with a common agenda: preventing immigrants from exerting any influence in American government or politics.

Secrecy was bred in the movement's bones. Claiming a need to protect themselves from the evil intentions of disruptive outsiders, the Know Nothings had thrived on elaborate, mysterious rituals—passwords and secret grips, solemn oaths and initiation rites. New members were directed to answer any prying questions by saying "I know nothing," giving birth to its nickname. Most wore the unflattering label with defiance and pride.

In 1856, when the American Party emerged from the Know Nothing shadows to nominate the movement's first candidate for president, the new party's leaders would discard the secret rituals as a liability, a reason for suspicion. But in 1854, the oath was mandatory and revered. John had just reached twenty-one, the minimum age for membership. Resting his right hand on a Bible and raising his left hand to the heavens, John pledged to vote only for American-born citizens, and never to vote for a Roman Catholic. He swore that he was raised "under Protestant influence." He vowed to support the movement's call for tougher citizenship and voting laws.

Years later, with the benefit of a lifetime of experience, John would remember his secret induction with some embarrassment. "I was very uncomfortable when the oath was administered to me," he wrote. "My conscience, for a time, rebelled against it. . . . I did not relish the idea of proscribing anyone on account of his religion."

If he did not relish it, he still accepted it. John was the disciple, not the rebel. Standing before his father and men he admired, "I had not the boldness to repudiate the organization. So I remained in it, upon the idea that, all things considered, it was best for any organization to control public affairs rather than to have the Democratic party in power. That was the kind of political meat upon which my father fed me as I grew up."

JOHN'S MISGIVINGS ABOUT THE OATH, however heartfelt, did not emerge forcefully until much later. In the fall of 1854, other emotions played on his mind: ambition, pride, impatience, confusion. John's older brother Richard had just died, struck down by illness, the second Harlan brother in five years to go to an early grave. Only John and his brother James were left.

John was eager to participate in politics, but he had suddenly found himself on a Whig road going nowhere. His father's beloved party had finally reached an impasse over slavery. For more than two decades, the party's Northern and Southern wings had found enough common ground to send two Whigs to the White House. Henry Clay himself had nearly won the presidency in 1844. But now the party's elder statesman was dead, and his party was dying, too. The Kansas-Nebraska Act of 1854 had set the country on a new course, ensuring slavery's expansion and undoing the series of compromises that Clay and others had constructed in the name of preserving the Union as it was. If the divide between North and South was a fault line, then the Kansas-Nebraska Act was the earthquake that everyone feared.

In Kentucky and everywhere else, old parties were giving way to untested movements and surprising alliances. The Know Nothings, vowing to do nothing about slavery, appeared like an oasis in the Kentucky heat. John may have lacked the boldness to repudiate the organization's principles. But he had no difficulty in seizing the opportunity that the movement's unexpected popularity offered. He took to the campaign trail with wide-eyed gusto.

RECALLING HIS ORATORICAL debut in the summer of 1855, John dismissed his success as an accident. If so, it was an accident waiting to happen. He had been preparing himself for such a moment for a long time, ever since he had begun copying the words of others into notebooks, ever since he had asked his law professor for permission to publish that opening day oration.

It began on a steamy day in late June. A family friend had invited John to accompany him on a political mission. The friend: Thomas L. Crittenden, son of U.S. senator John J. Crittenden. The mission: ride to a school house in the hamlet of Bridgeport, a few miles outside Frankfort, where Tom would deliver a rousing speech on behalf of the Know Nothing slate of candidates.

They made the jaunt under threatening skies. Tom was thirty-one, a Mexican War veteran, and a new face in Kentucky politics. John, barely twenty-two, was very much the junior partner. Tom would do the talking. John would watch, and listen, and learn.

The rain did not begin in earnest until they had tied off their horses and were safely inside the little school. A curious crowd of a hundred or so awaited them. It wasn't every day that a Crittenden and a Harlan showed up in Bridgeport. Years later, telling the story of that memorable day, John would say that he had no plans to speak, no plans at all. He would not have uttered a word, he claimed, if the rain had not turned into a downpour, trapping everyone inside, and if Tom Crittenden hadn't "run dry" after forty-five minutes.

Even then, John didn't jump in. It wasn't until a farmer, a friend of John's father, cried out, "Let's hear from John Harlan."

No, John protested. I've never given a political speech of any kind.

"That don't matter," came the cry.

John, "as nervous as I've ever been in my life," talked for the better part of an hour, without preparation or notes. Basking in the enthusiastic applause, he relished the moment and what it might mean for his future. "It seemed to me that a new career was then opened up before me," he later wrote, "and I felt that I had <u>some</u> gifts for talking to a miscellaneous crowd."

JOHN WASTED NO TIME in capitalizing on his serendipitous afternoon. Printing up handbills to advertise himself, he repeated his performance at the Frankfort courthouse a few days later, in the very place where he had taken the Know Nothing oath in secret a year before. "I went to bed that night feeling that 'a big thing' had been accomplished."

The modest young man who had "no plans to speak" set about arranging a lengthy speaking tour of the Cumberland Valley, twelve towns in fourteen days, nearly three hundred miles in all. He asked for his father's help. Could he have a reliable horse, a silver watch to keep himself on schedule, some cash for expenses? By early July, John was riding away from Frankfort, "carrying no clothes except such as could be put in a pair of saddle bags."

"Grueling" could not begin to describe his itinerary. Twenty to thirty miles separated most of the towns, which meant on some days, he spent as much time with his horse as he did with the crowds that awaited him. By July 10, he was adding a dozen more stops. His looping zigzag through the hills and valleys of south central Kentucky would end with twenty-six speeches in twenty-three counties, coming home just in time for Election Day on August 6.

The Know Nothing newspapers could not resist him. John arrived in Danville to these words in the local *Tribune*: "He is a young gentleman of fine talents, a most eloquent advocate of the great principles" of the American Party. "Those who desire to hear one of the best speeches they have lately listened to, should turn out to-night to hear him." After his speech, the *Tribune* congratulated him for making new friends among those who admire "eloquence, fairness, modesty and soundness in debate."

He often found himself squaring off with opponents twice his age. Those debates "destroyed whatever bashfulness I had," he later wrote. By the time the summer was over, with his father reelected as part of a Know Nothing sweep of every statewide office, John's view of himself had changed. "I had become conscious of a capacity to say what I desired to say, and to make myself understood by those who heard me."

What did the crowds hear? John had studied the American Party's platforms, and he kept to the Know Nothing script. He denounced foreign influence in state and federal elections, dismissed Roman Catholics as more loyal to the pope than to the United States, and decried the country's citizenship and voting laws as lax and easily abused. He did not call for the intimidation of voters. But the zeal of some Know Nothing members led them to engage in such tactics. Louisville, on Election Day 1855, became the site of "Bloody Monday," a show of force by a Know Nothing mob that started with a promise to "police" the polls and ended with twenty-two dead and a Catholic neighborhood in flames.

The riot was a dark and ominous blot on the party's record, at the very moment that it was winning an impressive electoral victory throughout the state. With the next presidential contest right around the corner, the question hung in the air: If the party's leaders could not control its own supporters, how could they hope to lead the country?

NO LONGER JUST THE DISCIPLE, John entered 1856 with a growing reputation of his own. He had won a third term as city attorney. The new governor had reappointed him as adjutant general. Now the American Party wanted him back on the campaign circuit to stump for the party's presidential candidate, former president Millard Fillmore, an ex-Whig recruited for the run. Fillmore seemed like the perfect American Party choice, a man determined to tamp down agitation over slavery in favor of an unspecified compromise. But slavery was the issue that would not rest. At the American Party convention in early 1856, the meek slavery plank in the platform had led to a split, driving many Northern members to abandon the Know Nothings and join the upstart Republicans, who were fielding their first presidential candidate.

Harlan duplicated his 1855 speaking effort, with a tour that was just as long and no less exhausting. Before leaving, he compiled a scrapbook on the Republican and Democratic nominees. Seeking evidence that Fillmore was a friend of the South, he clipped a reprint of an 1848 Fillmore letter to a Georgian seeking his views on slavery. During his years in Congress, Fillmore told the Georgian, he had often said he "regarded slavery as an evil, but one with which the national government has nothing to do." The Constitution, he insisted, had left slavery to the states, and "if they regarded it as a blessing, they had a constitutional right to enjoy it, and if they regarded it as an evil, they had the power, and knew best how to apply the remedy."

This was the sort of rhetorical balm that John needed to soothe the nerves of his fellow Kentuckians. Again, the Whig press lauded him. The *Louisville Daily Journal* branded him "the young giant of the American Party." After a speech in Evansville, which included a defense of his position on slavery, the *Evansville Daily Journal* quoted him approvingly: "He said he would say nothing in Indiana that he would not say in Kentucky, and that wasn't true of other parties." In the small Kentucky town of Cynthiana, where he spoke for three hours, the newspaper there marveled at his ability to hold "the vast and crowded audience in breathless attention and delight, by a speech of unsurpassed eloquence, ability and power."

But when the voting was done, the worst possible outcome had come to pass. Fillmore had won just a single state, Maryland. The Democrat, James Buchanan, had claimed a resounding victory, winning nineteen states, including a sweep of the South. The most telling result: The Republican, John Fremont, running on an abolitionist platform and not even on the ballot in most of the South, had captured eleven states, all in the North.

The Know Nothing strategy had failed. Sectionalism had triumphed. A year earlier, the way forward had appeared clear. Now, with the future cloudy, John took a needed break from politics. It was finally time, after more than two long years and no second thoughts, for his marriage to Mallie.

THEIR WEDDING DAY showed Mallie's flair for the fashionable. The invitations set the tone—two cards, tied together with white ribbon, one with her name, one with his, announcing an "at home" ceremony on December 23, 1856, at nine o'clock in the evening. Tongues wagged about the union between the daughter of Indiana and the son of Kentucky, but that couldn't be helped.

When the moment arrived, the folding doors just off the parlor flew open, revealing a "tableau" of six bridesmaids and six bridegrooms, family members, and the officiating clergyman, all arrayed around the young couple. It was an "innovation," meant to create a lasting image in people's imaginations. One guest remembered "mounds of macaroons" and "pyramids of wine jelly" among the many delights served at the wedding meal.

After a honeymoon in her parents' house, made several weeks longer by a winter freeze that shut down all travel on the Ohio, the young couple boarded a steamboat for their trip into a new life. He was now twenty-three. She was not quite eighteen. Years later, as Mallie contemplated how her marriage had changed her destiny, her mother's parting words echoed still: "You love this man well enough to marry him. Remember, now, that *his* home is YOUR home; *his* people, YOUR people; *his* interests, YOUR interests—you must have *no other*."

Only upon Mallie's arrival at the Harlan homestead did the full force of her mother's advice begin to register. She was presented with one more gift: her personal slave.

The uneasy graduate: Senior portrait, Yale College, 1856

3

Brown of New England

1856–1857

IN AUGUST 1856, as a summer of pleasant diversions faded into fall's pulse of obligations, Henry Billings Brown could not decide what to do.

This was nothing new. Uncertainty had been Henry's frequent companion for much of his young life. He was just twenty years old, but he sometimes wondered whether brooding was his destiny, whether he was doomed to live in a permanent state of confusion and hesitation. He even had doubts about his doubts. Why couldn't he free himself of indecision's grip? What was his grand plan? Here he was, a freshly stamped graduate of Yale College, Class of '56, with an abundance of opportunities awaiting him. Instead, he fretted that he possessed neither enough ambition nor enough discipline to make his mark in the world.

As he often did, Henry scribbled his latest uncertainties in the palm-sized pocket daybook that he carried everywhere, a habit he had acquired during his junior year at Yale. These leather-bound companions didn't offer much space for his thoughts, no more than a dozen short lines per day, but somehow, that seemed sufficient. Henry disliked self-indulgence nearly as much as he feared that he was prone to wallowing in it. For the most part, his orderly, legible entries stuck to matters close to home—his health, the weather, the appointments he kept, the walks he took, the young women who caught his eye or, better yet, his favor.

He was marooned at his father's house in central Connecticut, a temporary berth while he figured out his next step. "Shall I teach or go to South America next year?" he wrote in his daybook on August 20, a month after he and his Yale classmates had said their goodbyes. On September 12, the bedeviling question remained: "What shall I do next year? Most favour my entering a law office immediately, which I veto."

Anyone looking at Henry's college album photograph for hints of his character might focus on his dark eyebrows, or his gently curved face, or his thickly cut hair, or the set of his mouth above his square chin. But in person, his eyes triumphed. They were blue, attentive without being piercing, watchful as well as observant. No one could have guessed how much trouble they gave him.

He was plagued from an early age by a painful inflammation, cause unclear, remedy unknown, problem recurrent. Henry cursed the affliction, which he blamed on his preternatural love of books, beginning at age three. "Was too fond of books before I could even use them," he wrote in a "Preceding Autobiography" that served as the inaugural entry for his first pocket calendar, in 1855. "Weakened my eyes by overtasking them."

His mother, characteristically, had blamed herself. She had encouraged her precocious son's interest in the printed word. "Books are his source of amusement," she had written in her diary on his second birthday. When the inflammation revealed itself as a regular intruder, she had tried to limit the hours he spent with his beloved books. Motherly pride sometimes blinded her. "I have thoughtlessly indulged him in reading evenings the winter past," was her diary entry on Henry's fifth birthday, during a particularly alarming episode. "I now see my error and lament it exceedingly." She renewed her efforts to police her son's passion. "We find it necessary to divert his mind from his books on account of his eyes failing him," she had written.

It had helped that diversions were readily available in Lee, the western Massachusetts town where Henry was born. Nestled in the Berkshire Hills, Lee hummed with the daily buzz of sawmills, the clang of iron forges, the pulping of paper. Henry was entranced. "I had a natural fondness for machinery," he later wrote, "and was never so happy as when allowed to 'assist' at the sawing of logs and shingles and the grinding of grain in my father's mills."

The distractions seemed to serve their purpose. The inflammation would retreat, sometimes for long periods. Retreat was not cure, however, and a boy of Henry's promise could not meet his destiny without a pair of healthy eyes. In August 1847, when Henry was eleven, his parents took the extraordinary and expensive step of seeking help from a specialist in central New York, more than 130 miles away. This was not just a consultation. To help their son, they uprooted the entire family, said farewell to the Berkshires, and set out for Utica, where they delivered Henry into the hands of Dr. Ebenezer Leach.

They went to Utica with no idea how long they would stay. They only knew that Dr. Leach had acquired a considerable reputation as an oculist, well known for his treatment of eye diseases. Dr. Leach's own eye miseries had caused a temporary loss of his sight when he was forty-one, spurring him to leave behind his jewelry business and devote his full attention to a thorough study of the eye and its disorders. Now fifty, Dr. Leach's eyes still gave him trouble. But when he was feeling fit, he was seeing as many as a hundred patients a day. Many, like the Browns, had traveled from distant points of the compass, looking for relief.

Henry's visits to the oculist still left plenty of time for him to enjoy himself. He wasn't enrolled in school, making Utica feel like an extended holiday. A local dry goods store served as his base of operations. "Amused myself by playing the clerk and errand-boy" at Swarthout & Golden, he would recall, "and flirting with said Golden's wife."

His parents stayed three months, then left Henry on his own for another month's treatment, in the care of others. With no permanent home in western Massachusetts to welcome them back, they relied on family in Connecticut to take them in. Afterward, Henry remembered Utica as a grand adventure. His eyes were feeling fine. Still, he could not escape the feeling that he had not seen the last of the accursed inflammation.

LONG BEFORE YALE, while Henry was still ensconced at his boarding school in Massachusetts, his father had announced his aspirations for his youngest son, declaring, "My boy, I want you to become a lawyer." Henry didn't object. He could conjure no good reason to resist his father's plan.

The idea seemed both appealing and inevitable. "I was naturally obedient," he later wrote. But now that the time had come, he wasn't ready. He told his father, expecting a rebuke, and was relieved that he wasn't angry, that he seemed to understand. Henry thought of his father as quixotic: kind and indulgent, certainly, but quick to mete out punishment. At boarding school, Henry had rarely felt the sting of a teacher's rod. At home, his father seemed to take "a grim satisfaction in atoning for any delinquencies of the schoolmaster," Henry would later write.

In the summer of 1851, after Henry's fifteenth birthday, misfortune had put Henry and his father on an entirely new footing. During a two-month span, death claimed both Henry's little sister and older brother. Etta succumbed first, to a violent attack of croup. She was only four years old. His brother John was not quite twenty-five, the victim of measles and consumption. Another brother had died in infancy, before Henry was born. Growing up, Henry had never felt alone. Now, as his family's only surviving child, he shouldered the benefit and weight of his parents' heightened expectations.

A year later, during his first months at Yale, his mother fell ill. Henry was distraught. He was already struggling to find himself, convinced he had made a mistake by entering the college at the age of sixteen. He wasn't badly prepared for Yale's rigorous freshman curriculum of mathematics, Latin, and Greek. But he was too young, too immature. That was what he told himself after barely managing to survive his first term. He finished his year of "fearful blunders," as he called it, with a firmly mediocre average that put him outside the top third of the class.

Sophomore year would be different, he vowed to himself. Then, right at the outset, an urgent message arrived about his mother. "I was summoned from college to her death bed," Henry would write. When Mary Brown died on October 10, 1853, she was five days shy of her fiftieth birthday. Henry lost his footing once again. "I returned to college and behaved so foolishly as to ruin my college reputation," he confided in his pocket daybook.

He fell behind in his studies, and chafed at the tightly controlled schedule for freshmen and sophomores. "In winter we rose before dawn, attended morning prayers and a recitation by gaslight, then just introduced into the public rooms, but not into the dormitories, and sat down to breakfast around sunrise." He found it "primitive," and could not wait for the freedom of holidays, the sleigh rides of winter, and the sail boats of summer.

But he persevered, determined to prove that he belonged. By the end of junior year, he felt justified in doling out a bit of praise to himself. "I broke away from the miserable crowd I was with, worked hard at my compositions," and shared a first prize in one of Yale's annual writing competitions. "Of a sudden became wonderfully ambitious."

In the fall of 1855, while he was absorbed in his senior year studies and striving to finish as high in the class rankings as he could, his father suddenly remarried. Henry compressed his shock into his daybook's few lines for Friday, November 9: "Learnt that Father was married Wednesday morn. O Dear Dear. What am I coming to? He has gone to Eastern Massachusetts on his bridal tour!!!"

Along with those jumbled feelings came a hefty dose of admiration for the man who had raised him. Billings Brown was a miller and farmer who made up for his lack of formal education with an extensive library of books and a thirst for history and biography that Henry shared. They also shared the family name, Billings, although Henry rarely used it. He opted for a simpler signature, shortening the legacy into a middle initial: Henry B. Brown, straightforward, uncomplicated, blending in.

Henry felt certain about one thing. In the not-too-distant future, he would add a lawyer's title to the end of his name, fulfilling his father's wishes: Henry B. Brown, Esquire. But not just yet. As graduation neared, Henry felt restless, unsettled, much like the country itself, divided over slavery and unable to find a way forward.

SENIOR YEAR AT Yale had ended in a blaze of new doubts. In June, as commencement neared, Henry tallied up his achievements. His final average of 3.01, on a 4.0 scale, put him nineteenth in his graduating class of ninety-five. Not nearly as good as his friend Phineas Calkins's 3.32, or David Brewer's 3.38, or valedictorian Timothy Wilcox's near-record 3.65. But all things considered, "highly respectable," Henry told himself.

He was more pleased with his winning entry for the Townsend Prize, one of five so honored in the prestigious annual competition. His submission was a somewhat bleak essay about threats to liberty, which he had titled, "Public Amusements as Instruments Used by Despotisms to Debase the People." He had worked hard on his composition, which boiled down to an argument that powerful leaders often rely on public pageantry—sporting events, circuses, theater, oratory, even displays of art—to lull the governed, "to corrode every thought of discontent, every breathing for freedom, by substituting a preference for trifling pleasures."

While exultant at his triumph, made sweeter by a twelve-dollar cash award, he had no time to savor it. He was consumed with anxiety about his commencement oration, one of twenty-five chosen. He eyed his oration like a noxious drink made of one part trepidation and one part dread. He ended up disliking his choice of subject, "The Supernatural in Literature." "Half a mind not to speak," he wrote morosely in his daybook.

He felt the pressure of the grand stage. Commencement Day was a four-day extravaganza, with sumptuous alumni dinners, boisterous singing, and excessive drinking, and solemn moments of high-flown rhetoric. The *New-York Daily Times*, now in its fourth year of publication, had staked an early claim to chronicling the spectacle, publishing reports that sometimes ran two columns or more. The final *Times* dispatch for Thursday, July 31, listed all the graduates and their hometowns, along with each of the student speakers and their subjects.

The big day arrived in rain, the appropriate ambiance for Henry's mood. Afterward, he declared his oration "a failure," the result of his "general disgust for labour" after winning the Townsend, "and a knowledge that great things were expected and that many friends would be present." He dreamed of being an accomplished orator, but despaired of ever reaching that goal. Of all his self-described shortcomings, this was the one that bothered Henry most.

"Shall I ever conquer?" he wrote in his daybook. "It is the greatest obstacle to success."

HIS COMMENCEMENT NERVES brought a disquieting end to his four years at Yale. As he read through his friends' scrawled tributes in his college album, doubts thrust their way once again into his thoughts. A. J. Bartholomew had wished him the "success which I am sure your industry will deserve." Phineas Calkins had celebrated Henry's "eloquent, loyal, but ill-starred appeals" during debating competitions. Chauncey DePew had expressed his warm pleasure that their senior year had brought them closer together, which "has enabled me to strengthen some impressions and eradicate others, and to add one more to that golden list of friends."

Henry took up his own pen, and on the page facing his photograph, adopted the persona of an alter ego to add a cheekily contrarian view. "Beloved H.B.," the note began in a gently mocking tone, "our friendship has continued firm and uninterrupted from our cradles upward to the present auspicious moment." After years of knowing each other, the alter ego continued, "H.B." would surely understand why he was "dispensing with the usual complimentary sentiments," in favor "of reminding you of a few of your 'weaknesses' which, I am afraid, will sooner or later prove your ruin. First: your incorrigible laziness. Knowing this habit of yours I am the more surprised at seeing your name coupled once or twice in this book with the words 'Diligence' and 'Industry.' All gross flattery, H.B., and you know it."

His friends might withhold their candor, his alter ego chided. "I, however, have no hesitation in telling you that, unless you rise earlier, sit up later and work harder, you are a doomed individual." Gleefully chastising H.B. for "squandering" too many hours and too much money on whiskey punches and lager beer, the alter ego closed with a brotherly embrace: "I'm sure you can't be offended at my frankness for you well know my every wish is connected with your welfare. Good luck betide you! Yours, heartily and sturdily, Henry Billings Brown."

With that, "H.B." turned to face the world outside Yale's sheltered walls.

AS THE SUMMER FLEW BY, his plans still uncertain, Henry told himself that he was preparing, not procrastinating. "Commenced this day the study of the Spanish language," he wrote on September 20, "in anticipation of spending a winter in Cuba."

Money was one obstacle. Henry wouldn't be traveling anywhere without financial help from his father, or his favorite uncle, Elias, his father's older brother. His father wasn't wealthy, not like Uncle Elias. Billings Brown had managed to carve out a comfortable living from the land, grinding the grain it yielded, cultivating some acres, selling others. Uncle Elias's riches came largely from the sea. His New York City partnership, Everett & Brown, controlled a small armada of a dozen packet ships that sailed the world, delivering goods to foreign ports and bringing European immigrants to America.

Uncle Elias did not call New York City home. He reserved that distinction for Mystic and Stonington, the Connecticut seaport towns where he had established himself as well-to-do and well connected. Over the years, he had served as a local bank director, justice of the peace, town selectman, and representative to the Connecticut legislature. His fleet of ships included several built by one of Mystic's best yards. Henry's frequent visits to Uncle Elias's stately house gave him an early introduction to the advantages that accompanied wealth and stature.

Once, Henry had asked his father how much a man must be worth to be rich. His father's answer was more complicated than Henry had expected. It depended, his father had said, on where the man was living. In the New England countryside, $20,000 in savings was generally thought to be enough for a man to call himself rich. That amount, wisely invested, would provide enough yearly income to cover annual expenses for all but the most extravagant family. His father did not need to say that extravagance enjoyed no status on either side of the family's long line of Puritan ancestors. The conversation made a strong impression on Henry, who remembered it well enough to repeat years later.

Henry found his father's attitude toward money puzzling. Billings Brown could be generous, sending his son to boarding school and then to Yale. But he could be parsimonious, too. Henry gave up trying to anticipate which he would encounter. So, in early October, he was surprised when his father made an astonishing offer: a year of travel in Europe. Henry could not quite believe his good fortune. "I eagerly seized upon this opportunity, then comparatively rare, of seeing something of the older world," he wrote years later.

Weeks of dithering gave way to a whirlwind of arrangements. One of his uncle's packet ships, the *William Rathbone*, would be sailing for Liverpool toward the end of October. When the clipper left New York City's Pier 27, along the East River, Henry planned to be on it.

He set to work, packing up his French- and German-language books, and for the moment, left his doubts and his future behind.

A FEW DAYS after his father's surprise proposal, Henry took his first definitive step toward his year abroad. With his uncle's help, he applied for a passport.

It was October 11, 1856, an unseasonably warm Saturday in New York City. As the temperature marched toward the eighties, Henry accompanied Uncle Elias to the heart of the shipping district, a warren of commercial activity. The city offered the starkest of contrasts to the places Henry knew best—scholarly Yale and tranquil Ellington, the charming Connecticut town where his family had moved in 1849, when Henry was thirteen. "If one could 'put away' all ambition and be content with the simplest of lives," he wrote later, "Ellington was an ideal residence."

New York was neither scholarly nor tranquil. It was a city of half a million, by far the country's largest, more than three times that of runners-up Baltimore and Boston. It was noisy, dusty, bustling, smelly, and audacious. Henry was agog. In describing Ellington, which numbered fewer than thirteen hundred people in the village and surrounding farms, Henry wrote that it had no factories, and therefore no smoke; no commerce, and therefore, no rumbling of carts and heavy wagons. New York City, on the other hand, had so many wagons and so many horses—twenty-five thousand, by one estimate—that it could be described as a giant moving stable. It certainly had the fragrance of one. Mounds of manures could be found everywhere, on streets and in barns, on the soles of many shoes.

Henry and his uncle turned into the Pine Street office of R. L. and S. Godwin, custom house brokers for the shipping industry. There, with Elias as a witness, Henry filled in the passport application's list of ten identifying details, beginning with his height ("five foot, ten and one-half inches") and hair color ("brown"), his eyes ("blue"), and nose ("roman"), and ending with his complexion ("light") and face ("oval"). The broker affixed his notary public's seal, and hurried the document to Washington.

Two days later, the State Department's chief passport clerk assigned passport number 14,845 to Henry B. Brown, and placed it in the mails for New York. Henry would receive it in plenty of time for the *Rathbone's* scheduled sailing to Liverpool.

A PASSPORT WAS A CONVENIENCE, not a legal necessity. But if anything went wrong, the one-page document provided some small hedge against trouble. With it, Henry wasn't a friendless nomad in a foreign land. He was "a Citizen of the United States," carrying a request from his country's secretary of state that he receive "all lawful Aid and Protection" in a time of need. Henry could walk into any legation or consulate, present his passport, and reap whatever benefits it might provide.

That was not true, however, for every native-born American. For years, the State Department had followed a policy of separation in dealing with passport applications. Henry, born in Lee, Massachusetts, on March 2, 1836, could visit a notary in New York City, and within a week or ten days, sail for Europe with a passport among his possessions. But a free person of color born in the same town—of any shade or blend, dark or light, one-half, one-quarter, one-eighth, or less—could not.

Massachusetts might confer state citizenship on its free people of color, but a person of color stood outside the State Department's long-held definition of U.S. citizenship. The department was willing to issue an equivalent "certificate of protection," but not an official passport. As Secretary of State John M. Clayton had explained in 1849, when challenged by two antislavery newspaper editors about the department's policy, "there is no law authorising me to grant a passport to a colored person." All such applications, Clayton said in one letter, "have always been refused by every other Secretary of State." Frederick Douglass's newspaper, the *North Star,* derisively called the secretary's explanation "Clayton's Law of Passports."

It was true, Clayton conceded, that a few people of color had managed to obtain passports. But those were either special exceptions, he informed the editors, or the department had made a mistake, believing the applicants to be white. The application process was an honor system, he pointed out. The passport clerk in Washington was processing several hundred applications a month. He wasn't equipped to investigate each applicant's complexion. The clerk had to rely on the local notaries—who, after all, were casting their eyes directly on the applicants—to provide an accurate description, Clayton said.

White and black abolitionists, in pressing their antislavery views, had seized on the passport system's inequality as one of their many debating points. Every native-born American, the abolitionists argued, was a citizen by birth. Every native-born American was entitled to a U.S. passport. There should be no distinction based on color.

This was not an argument that Clayton, a Whig from Delaware who had served in the U.S. Senate, was prepared to entertain. Clayton was not a slaveholder, but he was a confirmed compromiser, naturally resistant to any change that might cause more trouble. He saw no reason to deviate from the department's policy, especially when it already offered a perfectly good substitute—the "certificate of protection," which was "equally efficient for all ordinary and useful purposes," Clayton said.

His words were telling: *equally efficient.* Equivalent in every way, save one that might truly matter. The word "citizen" appeared nowhere on the "equivalent" certificate.

ON THE EVENING of October 22, 1856, the day before Henry's sailing for Liverpool, New York City's Academy of Music reverberated with the voices of oratory and the hum of several thousand political partisans. The Young Men's General Republican Committee had rented the opera hall for a grand mass rally, paying three hundred dollars and praying that the money would not be ill spent.

It was a lovely fall night, the perfect bookend to an Indian summer afternoon. The presidential election was just thirteen days away. On East Fourteenth Street, a swelling crowd milled outside the academy. The turnout was startling, even by the loose standards of the Republican-leaning newspapers. "ANOTHER GREAT MEETING. THE ACADEMY FULL OF REPUBLICANS" was the headline in the next day's *Tribune*.

Banners from various Republican clubs festooned the stage, including one bearing the popular slogan, "The price of liberty is eternal vigilance." The *Tribune* reporter enthusiastically described the jumble of commotion. "From pit to dome every seat was occupied, [as were] the aisles, behind the circles, and on the stage, all the available space for a standing position. . . . The whole number within the building could not have been less than seven thousand, of whom nearly a thousand were ladies. Large numbers were compelled to return to their homes, because of their inability to get within the auditorium." It was the kind of showing that gave heart to Republican newspaper editors, not that they required much evidence to express their confidence in the fledgling party's chances of winning its maiden national contest.

In a private box sat the Republican presidential candidate himself, forty-three-year-old John C. Fremont. The Southern-born explorer and military officer, a transplant to California, had come to New York City weeks before, and had hoisted his flag there for the campaign's duration. Now he listened as the evening's main speaker drove deep into his subject: slavery, the dangerous threat it posed, and why the country's salvation rested in the hands of the Republican Party and John C. Fremont.

The speaker had more than the usual credentials to make his case, which is why the organizers had chosen him. His name was Charles Robinson, and he was the "former" or the "disputed" or the "exiled" governor of the Kansas territory, depending on which side you asked. A New Englander, Robinson had gone to the Kansas frontier in 1854, joining other northern abolitionists intent on keeping the territory free of slavery. For two years, Kansas had been the front line in the battle over slavery's expansion. Open warfare had led to some calling the territory "Bleeding Kansas." At this moment, slavery's supporters held the upper hand.

The 1856 presidential election, Robinson told the crowd, would determine not only the territory's future, but the country's. If a confirmed compromiser like James Buchanan or Millard Fillmore ended up in the White

House, and Kansas were allowed to become a slave state, it would be too late in four years to stop slavery's invidious spread to other territories, he said.

"What will come before the country during the next four years?" Robinson asked. "What question will come up in Congress? Will not the application of Kansas for admission into the Union be there? Will not the application of Oregon be there? Will not the application of Minnesota be there? And of Utah, perhaps New Mexico, Washington and Nebraska?" Amid shouts of "Yes, yes," Robinson continued his march of logic. "Well, then, here comes the question every time they come up: Shall there be Slavery in those new States, or shall there be Freedom? Must not that be the case? Is there any way we can get rid of that question?"

The Know Nothings avoid all talk about slavery, Robinson cried. They had chosen Fillmore because they thought he could bridge the North-South divide without addressing slavery. Robinson, however, disdained that strategy. The slavery issue would not go away. He told the crowd, "It remains with you to say whether Kansas shall be a Free or a Slave State. If you succeed in electing John C. Fremont to the Presidency, as I am confident you will, then this question is settled!"

With the mention of Fremont's name, lusty cheering resounded through the ornate opera house. As the excited swarm spilled out into Fourteenth Street, a light fog had begun to drape itself over the city's buildings.

THE HEATED ORATORY of the 1856 presidential campaign had caught Henry's interest, but not his passion. He was no stranger to the issues. Several of his favorite Yale professors were immersed in the antislavery cause, and he had grown up among old-line New England Whigs inclined strongly in that direction. But on Thursday morning, October 23, with all three major New York newspapers devoting multiple columns to the previous night's Republican rally, it was a one-paragraph advertisement in Friday's *Herald* that summed up the top item on Henry's agenda: "FIRST PACKET FOR LIVERPOOL. SAILS THIS DAY at noon. . . . Passage in steerage, $18. Second cabin, $20 (including provisions)."

The rest of Thursday had offered none of Wednesday's agreeable weather. A chilly fog loitered through the night, clinging to the morning air as Henry finally boarded the *Rathbone* on Friday, October 24. Nature's sudden shift was a brisk reminder of what the crew knew all too well: A voyage on a packet ship came with discomfort guaranteed and dangers galore. The *Rathbone* had once been struck by lightning on an Atlantic crossing, suffering major damage to its sails and three-masted rigging.

The ship was reliable and well made, a 917-ton workhorse built of handsome oak and chestnut. No one, however, would dare call it luxurious or fleet. The newest, fastest steamships were crossing the Atlantic in ten days flat. With good weather and steady breezes, the *Rathbone* might make it in three weeks. With bad—well, Henry didn't want to think about bad. Major calamities on the water were common enough that newspapers had a standing headline for them: "Marine Disasters." The plural—"disasters"—offered a simple reminder of just how frequent they could be. Thursday's *Times* had offered two such dispatches, a paragraph each: a bark and a schooner, wrecked in separate mishaps off the North Carolina coast.

Henry soon discovered that if misery lay ahead, he wouldn't have much company. He appeared to be the only cabin passenger on the cargo-laden ship. He was dismayed to find his quarters no better than "rude," but he told himself that he was getting the better part of the bargain. His fare was next to nothing and his twenty-three days of seafaring education was free.

What he learned of life on the *Rathbone*, however, appalled him. "Being the only passenger, no attempt was made to conceal or disguise its hardship and brutalities," he wrote later. "The seamen were the most ignorant and degraded foreigners—the very scum of European and American ports. Their treatment seemed to be intended to accord with their rank. They were fed upon the coarsest of food, and were beaten without mercy, even to the shedding of blood, for the slightest dereliction from what the officers conceived to be their duty."

During Henry's three weeks at sea, while he was "brushing up on his imperfect knowledge of French and German" and enduring a "not particularly pleasant" voyage, Henry's countrymen had elected a new president. But when Henry reached Liverpool, his first stop, the winner was still unknown.

The latest news from America was freshly arrived, via the steamship *Arabia*, but it was as stale as ten-day-old bread. Ten days was not just a metaphor. The steamer had left Boston on November 5, the day after the election, carrying newspapers that suggested a Republican upset in the making: Fremont ahead, by two electoral votes, over Buchanan. It was now November 15.

The illusion of a Republican triumph shattered two days later, with the arrival of the next newspaper shipment. Buchanan had captured every remaining state. Fremont's electoral total had not changed. The question that Charles Robinson had posed in his New York speech—"What will become of the country in the next four years?"—had been answered. James Buchanan, the Democrat from Pennsylvania, winner of most of the Southern states, would be the next president of the United States.

AS HENRY SLOWLY made his way south to London, and then to France, he worried about money. He did not want to be forced to cut his trip—or his education—short. In early January, after several days in Paris, his pockets zeroed in on empty. "I am left with two francs," he wrote in his daybook, "and am in momentary expectation of a washing bill larger than that. What am I to do?" He skimped along, longing for help from home. He checked forlornly at the Livingston express office, where American travelers could receive mail and read outdated U.S. newspapers. Finally, on January 20, aid arrived. "O climax of ecstasy! O delightful inconceivable!" he wrote that night. "I went over to Livingston's and at last received my long wished for, long despaired of letter, and I am now the happy possessor of 1000 francs."

It was a substantial sum, about two hundred dollars. Henry resumed his grand tour—France, Switzerland, Germany, the Italian states. While Henry was visiting Italy, Buchanan was taking the oath of office in Washington. In his inaugural oration on March 4, the new president had tried to make the nation's disagreements vanish—merely by saying there was no reason for them to exist.

"All agree," Buchanan said, undoubtedly to the scorn of those who didn't, "that under the Constitution, slavery in the States is beyond the reach of any human power except that of the respective States themselves wherein it exists. May we not, then, hope that the long agitation on this subject is approaching its end, and that the geographical parties to which it has given birth . . . will speedily become extinct? Most happy will it be for the country when the public mind shall be diverted from this question to others of more pressing and practical importance."

Congress, he said, had navigated a route out of the territorial thicket that Robinson had described in his New York speech. The majority in each territory could decide whether to be slave or free. The Supreme Court would be ruling soon on a minor legal question involving when a territory could decide its fate. "It is understood," Buchanan said confidently, that the court case would be "speedily and finally settled."

Two days later, as if waiting for Buchanan to take his oath, the Supreme Court spoke—not with one voice, but with many. This ruling was anything but minor. The justices, each writing separately in a case known as *Dred Scott v. Sandford*, examined the entire edifice of slavery—its history, the central question of what constituted citizenship, and even the constitutionality of Congress's longstanding methods for balancing the rights of free and slave states through legislation such as the Missouri Compromise of 1820.

Chief Justice Roger B. Taney, leading a group of seven justices, declared that Congress had no constitutional power to prohibit slavery in the states or territories. His majority opinion was unambiguous in its language and comprehensive in its scope. The proslavery forces declared that the fight over slavery in the territories was now over. Buchanan, who had advance word of the court's ruling before his swearing in, certainly was counting on it. But Taney's ruling settled almost nothing, while unsettling nearly everyone.

It sent agitation not to its grave, as Buchanan had hoped, but to a new crescendo.

THERE WAS NO HASTE in the Supreme Court's action. The justices had heard oral arguments not just once, but twice. For months, the newspapers had been speculating about the likely outcome, accurately for the most part, and some of the justices had been writing to friends about the court's internal discussions. When the result finally emerged, most of the justices did not stint on length in explaining themselves. The entire decision—Taney's majority ruling, the six separate opinions and concurrences, plus the two dissents—totaled more than one hundred and ten thousand words. It was the equivalent of a good-sized book, the kind that took several sittings to read, and some would say, a lifetime to fully understand.

On March 6, when Taney read the first draft of his decision aloud in the Supreme Court's courtroom on the ground floor of the U.S. Capitol, he had been chief justice for more than thirty years. His biography could be read as a reflection of slavery's unceasing influence on the arc of American life. He was a former slaveholder from Maryland, one of five justices from states where slavery was legal. As a young man, he had inherited his family's slaves, gradually granting freedom to all but two, whom he thought too old to cast out on their own. Yet he was a committed defender of the South and its right to slavery. Now he had reached the stage of declining health, prompting the usual chatter about whether he was up to the job. Justice Benjamin R. Curtis had recently written to his uncle in Boston, "Our aged justice, who will be eighty in a few days, and who grows more feeble in body but retains his alacrity and force of mind wonderfully, is not able to write much." Whatever Taney's infirmities, they did not limit his output in the *Dred Scott* case. Nor did it limit his ambition in using Scott's lawsuit to address the full range of issues surrounding slavery and racial separation.

Dred Scott was a Missouri slave who had been pursuing his freedom for nearly a dozen years, first in state court and then in a federal lawsuit filed in 1853. Scott had argued that he was no longer a slave because his master, an army officer, had taken him to live for two years in the free state of Illinois, where slavery was prohibited, followed by another military posting in the free territory that was now part of the state of Wisconsin. Their return to Missouri in 1842, Scott claimed, made no difference. Once free, he argued, he could not be enslaved again.

Scott lost, slavery won. Taney's opinion declared that a slave owner could take his property anywhere in the United States or its territories, and that Scott, as a slave without citizenship rights, was not entitled to bring the lawsuit at all. On the case's cover, the court's clerk wrote "dismissed for want of jurisdiction."

If Taney and the other justices had wanted, they could have ended the case right there. Having decided Scott had no right to sue, there was no need to say anything else. Initially, that was the majority's inclination. But after the dissenters' view became clear, Taney took over the majority decision and waded into slavery's deepest waters. He declared that Congress had violated the Constitution years before by prohibiting slavery north of the 36° 30′ parallel as part of the Missouri Compromise of 1820. That line was no longer in force, having been superseded by recent legislation. But some, in Congress and elsewhere, harbored the hope that it could be reinstated, that the old balance could be restored. Taney's opinion removed that option.

On the question of citizenship, the seven majority justices agreed that slaves were property, and therefore could not be citizens. But Taney led a group that ventured even further. He took the same position as the State Department had adopted in issuing passports: All Africans and their descendants—free as well as slave, even if native born—were not citizens of the United States. They had none of the rights of U.S. citizens, and were not ever intended to have those rights.

Yes, Taney wrote, the Declaration of Independence had asserted that "all men were equal," and were "endowed by their Creator with certain unalienable rights." Those words "would seem to embrace the whole human family, and if they were used in a similar instrument at this day would be so understood. But it is too clear for dispute that the enslaved African race were not intended to be included, and formed no part of the people who framed and adopted this declaration." They stood separate, apart—"a subordinate and inferior class of beings," in Taney's explicit language—and forever excluded from the benefits that whites enjoyed. Even if "public opinion or feeling" toward the "unfortunate race" had changed since the nation's founding, Taney asserted, the court was duty bound to interpret the Constitution as it "was framed and adopted." By public opinion, the chief justice meant the views of whites in "the civilized nations of Europe or in this country."

Taney carefully picked examples to support his reasoning, while omitting others—the Massachusetts' 1843 interracial marriage law, for one—that suggested separation was a choice rather than the natural order of things. Justice John McLean made precisely that point in his dissent. During the oral arguments, "it was said that a colored citizen would not be an agreeable member of society," McLean wrote. "This is more a matter of taste than of law. Several of the States have admitted persons of color to the right of suffrage, and, in this view, have recognised them as citizens, and this has been done in the slave as well as the free States. On the question of citizenship, it must be admitted that we have not been very fastidious. Under the late treaty with Mexico, we have made citizens of all grades, combinations, and colors."

McLean was a Northerner who had grown up in Ohio. Justice Benjamin Curtis, the other dissenter, was a Massachusetts-born Whig. In his dissent, Curtis directly challenged Taney's interpretation of the Constitution, and echoed the abolitionist argument on citizenship: "My opinion is that, under the Constitution of the United States, every free person born on the soil of a State, who is a citizen of that State by force of its Constitution or laws, is also a citizen of the United States."

Over two days, Taney, McLean, and Curtis read their rival opinions in open court. The dissenters immediately released printed copies of theirs. Taney held back his final version for two months, revising, adding, and responding to points raised by the dissenters. It did not matter. Nothing could calm the surging waters. The Supreme Court, so accustomed to following rather than leading, had thrust itself into the slavery debate.

The majority's proliferation of separate opinions compounded the problem, provoking the sort of easy discord that the majority had wanted to avoid. Republican newspaper editors in the North howled, many pointing out that the court was controlled by five Southern justices, all of whom had owned slaves. In the South, meanwhile, the proslavery newspapers embraced Taney's decision as gospel.

The divide, already deep, had become a chasm.

HENRY CHOSE COMFORT for his return home. The extra fare for a first-class cabin—about seventy-five dollars—was no deterrent. This time, he had plenty of company: ninety-six others were enjoying the *City of Washington*'s plush cabins, plus 189 in steerage, nearly all immigrants who had boarded with Henry at Liverpool. During the voyage, Henry luxuriated in his memories of the past year, knowing that all too soon, he would once again need to confront his future. The passenger manifest listed his occupation as "Gentleman," but for a young man of Henry's ambitions, gentleman was a condition, not a career.

A drenching downpour awaited Henry as the ship disgorged its passengers in New York. It was Monday, November 16, 1857. Much had changed in the year since his voyage on the *Rathbone*. On top of the turmoil over the *Dred Scott* ruling, a banking fiasco was rippling into a wider economic crisis, soon to be known as the Panic of 1857. Henry had left a country on the verge of a momentous political choice. He came back to a nation that had chosen a clear path—Buchanan, rather than the antislavery Republican upstart, Fremont—and yet was hurtling toward the unknown.

Years later, Henry would call his twelve months in Europe "the most valuable of my life from an educational point of view." He would disagree with that towering literary figure, Ralph Waldo Emerson, who had scoffed in a letter to a friend that the American fascination with European travel was akin to "a mild epidemic insanity." Emerson, while no stranger to Europe's delights, had publicly espoused the view that travel was little better than an indulgent distraction. "The soul is no traveler; the wise man stays at home," Emerson had written in his essay "Self-Reliance." "Traveling is a fool's paradise."

Not so for Henry. Traveling, he wrote shortly after his return, "gives a wonderful expansion to one's ideas." His year abroad, he came to feel, "had a strong tendency to correct any false impressions, born of national pride or patriotism, to expand political and religious views, and to teach the lessons so hard to learn at home, that while we have accomplished much in the direction of a higher civilisation, we have still much to learn."

"An orphan in spirit," young Albion called himself

(Chautauqua County Historical Society)

4

Tourgee of Ohio

1858–1860

ON A BRIGHT and beautiful night in late October 1858, Emma Kilborn could not sleep.

Outside her bedroom, fall's familiar nocturnal noises came and went, a reassuring reminder that all was well on her family's fifty-acre farm in the far northeastern corner of Ohio, a few miles from the grand expanse of Lake Erie. Inside the house, though, Emma felt anything but serene. The week's momentous events had left her positively giddy. She was eighteen, and she could not quite believe that Albion Tourgee—clever, feisty, mercurial, ambitious, moody, visionary Albion Tourgee, her talented classmate at Kingsville Academy—wanted to marry her.

Had she sought a diversion from her tumultuous thoughts, she could have wandered outdoors and looked to the stars. For weeks, in various parts of the country, it had become a nightly ritual in some households to stay up late and scan the sky, hoping for a glimpse of the newly discovered comet with its brilliant, breathtakingly long tail. An Italian astronomer had detected the approaching smudge in early June. The bewitching blur, soon to be known as Donati's Comet, had been illuminating the public's imagination ever since. Artists had sped to their canvasses, immortalized the streak in luminous brushstrokes of glowing beams. Abraham Lincoln, on the eve of his third debate with Stephen Douglas in their duel for a U.S. Senate seat, had adopted a hotel porch in Jonesboro, Illinois, as his viewing perch. In northeastern Ohio where Emma lived, the *Ashtabula Weekly Telegraph* had lamented that the "sparkling tail" would not be visible in time to take center stage at the annual township fair. Comet watchers, the *Telegraph* said, would have to wait until late October for the full spectacle.

Late October had arrived, but Emma was too preoccupied with earthly concerns to think about heavenly fireworks. She longed to tell someone—her parents, one of her three sisters, a close friend—her exhilarating news. But she and Albion had agreed to keep their engagement a secret for now. Alone with her feelings, she seized paper and ink. In the night's shadows, she drafted a fevered letter to her "betrothed," as she now thought of him. A river of emotions cascaded from her hand—elation, awe, fright, revelation. "I am wayward, thoughtless, headstrong and you, Beloved, will guide me aright," she wrote. "I will try, Albion, not to love you too much but I almost fear sometimes that I do, that I have an earthly idol."

She was not blind to Albion's flaws. But his razor-sharp wit did not intimidate her. His bursts of brusqueness did not deter her. His piercing gaze, intensified by a childhood accident that had cost him the sight in his right eye, was soft when it fell on her. For a long time after they first met, in the fall of 1856, she had thrown up a wall to protect herself. Once before, she had trusted a young man with her heart, a mistake from what she now called the "dark pages" of her past. As her relationship with Albion bloomed, she had warned him "above all things do not flatter me." He had proven himself to be candid, steadfast, caring. Her wall came tumbling down.

Banter was a favored pastime between them, and Emma gave as much as she got. A few months before their engagement, she had teasingly threatened to "box his ears" when he said he had been laid low by a bout with "the blues." She had scolded him, underlining her words as she often did, demanding to know "what reason you have for ever being afflicted with that dreadful malady. . . . You, that nature has been so partial to, ought to be the last one to have that disease!"

Now, in her new role as fiancée, she chose to be soothing rather than chiding. If he had doubts, she would have none. "I see in the future the realization of your brightest dreams," she wrote, alluding to his ambitions of becoming a renowned lawyer or a celebrated writer. "I see you honored, great beloved, a national homage paid to you. I have no fears of you failing, you will not, you could not, it is an utter impossibility."

Her final thoughts brimmed with conviction: "The future has no clouds for me, all looks so bright."

EIGHT MILES WEST, on his father's thriving farm just north of Kingsville, Albion could not bring himself to share Emma's unclouded optimism. He was twenty years old, brash, stubborn, charismatic when it suited him, belligerent when it didn't, and perpetually at odds with his father. During the past year, he, too, had spent many of his waking hours brooding about the future—his future, Emma's future, *their* future. He felt stuck somewhere between determination and desperation.

Other young men were moving ahead with their lives, but he was still living at home, still attending Kingsville Academy, a fine school, perhaps the best in northeastern Ohio, but not what he needed at this point in his young life. He had made several good friends among the 150 students, and he had met Emma. Not everyone at the school liked him, but many had a wary respect for him as a poet, a promising literary scholar, an accomplished debater. Now he hungered for more, a place to mold himself into the man he wanted to be. This would be his final year at Kingsville. That much was certain.

If his pockets had been full of something more tangible than his dreams, he would have headed east to Harvard, his first choice for the college degree that he coveted but that his father was refusing to support. Instead, he was biding his time, saving what he could from odd jobs, and waiting for a small inheritance that would come his way when he turned twenty-one. Somehow, he would scrape together the money. His ambitions depended on it.

Other than Emma, there was little left in Kingsville to hold him. He told her that he "had no home," and called himself "an orphan in spirit." His mother had died before his fifth birthday. His father had remarried within six months, but Albion had never felt much warmth toward his stepmother,

Rowena. Now, they barely spoke. As for his father—well, their falling out had been years in the making. His father's desire for obedience proved to be a recipe for rebellion. By the fall of 1858, Albion and Valentine Tourgee stood on opposite sides of a wide gulf, separated by mistrust. They inhabited the same house, but lived in different worlds.

Albion's aspirations did not involve a scythe, a plow, a milk stool, or sheep shears. He had never minded what he called the "exhausting slavish work of the hay and harvest field," and he had a deep love for living off the land. The nearby wilderness had offered a refuge from his father and his stepmother, and in his younger days, he had retreated there often to camp, hunt and fish. But now, on the cusp of manhood, he preferred the toil of crafting a poem, the labor of mastering Greek, the sweat of debating a worthy opponent. From those seeds of art and knowledge, he hoped to reap a great novel or a distinguished legal career—something grand, something memorable. Why couldn't his father understand that he needed college to thrive, much as their corn crop needed water and their sheep herd needed grass?

If his father would not help, so be it. As Albion told Emma the following spring, he could see one "grand privilege" in making it on his own. "No one can say," Albion wrote, "that it is to him that I owe my life, my education and my all. My success—if I am successful—will then be attributable only to myself."

AS WINTER CEDED to spring in early 1859, bringing Albion closer to May and his all-important twenty-first birthday, his anxieties took a physical toll. His dark brown hair appeared lank. His blue eyes showed fatigue. Haggard was not too strong a word for how he looked some days, and that was the word Emma chose in urging him to take better care of himself. "I cannot have you suffer," she wrote to him, "and you will be very careful of your health for my sake, will you not?"

He was so slender—a few pounds short of 150, on a frame that came within a few inches of six feet tall—that he could ill afford to lose any of it. He had the sort of slim face that favored a mustache, if only to keep the gaunt look at bay. In the years to come, some version or another—thin, thick, tapered, or twirled—would sit on his upper lip, a Tourgee trademark.

But haggard did not equate to brittle. Albion had a hard-earned resilience that impressed those who knew him. By now, Emma knew him better than most. As they had grown closer over the past year, he had revealed himself in bits and pieces. He had shown Emma some of his poetry, not just verses penned for her, but one that lay bare his enduring grief about his mother's early death. Consumption had claimed Louisa Winegar Tourgee before daylight on a February morning in 1843, after an agonizing eighteen months of illness that had left her gasping for every breath in her final days. Albion was not quite five years old.

Before delirium took hold, she had gathered little Albion in her arms, kissing him one last time, whispering "you must always be a good boy, always love your father, always obey him and try to love God." Albion clung to her, crying, saying "you ain't dying, you will get well." That's how his father later described her final hours, in a tearful letter to Louisa's family. But with the passing years, Albion found to his frustration that he could not remember his mother's features. His poem—a mere sixteen lines, terse by his standards—expressed his continuing sorrow:

In dreams, alone, since that sad hour
I've gazed upon thy face
For Memory has no magic power
Thy lineaments to trace.

DISRUPTION WAS WOVEN into the fabric of his childhood. Moving to Kingsville in 1847, when he was nine years old, meant leaving behind the only home he had ever known, the place that held his indistinct memories of his mother, the place where she "went cold as Winter's air," as his poem lamented. Albion knew the story of his parents' move to Ohio from Massachusetts: How in 1835, as naïve newlyweds, Louisa and Valentine had joined the great migration west, one more New England family in search of cheap land and new opportunity. They had arrived, with their belongings and expectations, fresh from the busy mill town of Lee in western Massachusetts, where Louisa's family, the Winegars, had lived and prospered for generations.

Almost everyone in Lee knew the Winegars. Louisa's grandfather had built Lee's first grist mill. Louisa's father then expanded the business, adding a profitable sawmill that he eventually sold for a pretty penny. One of their competitors was Billings Brown. Had Valentine and Louisa Tourgee stayed in Lee, their son Albion and Henry Billings Brown—just two years older—might have gone to the same school.

Young Valentine, however, despised mill life. He came to think of Lee as "a sink of corruption and ruin." He set his sights on the frontier, specifically Ohio's Western Reserve, a huge swatch of more than six thousand square miles, hugging Lake Erie from the Pennsylvania border almost to Michigan. With their meager resources, Louisa and Valentine settled on a small farm in Ashtabula County, part of the township of Williamsfield, about thirty miles south of Kingsville and Lake Erie.

Adventure quickly turned into adversity. During their first year, as they coped with the harsh winter and a paltry corn crop, Louisa pined for her family in Massachusetts. They hadn't left Lee on the best of terms, but a trip to mend fences was out of the question. Every penny went toward staving off defeat. Valentine promised her a visit as soon as "we are out of debt."

Fortunately, the Tourgees had company in facing those early hardships. Some years before, Valentine's older brother Cyrus had married Louisa's eldest sister, Clarenia Ann, and together, the two couples had struck out for the Western Reserve. They relied on each other whenever tragedy visited, as it did too soon and too often. When Louisa's first two children died in infancy, she leaned on Clarenia Ann. In 1840, a virulent fever caught Cyrus in its fatal grip. The grieving Valentine, only twenty-seven, took on the grim task of settling his brother's estate.

Three years later, as Louisa lay dying, Clarenia Ann had joined Valentine in his round-the-clock vigil. The end was a blessing, she informed the Winegar family. "Last week," she wrote, "her sufferings were beyond description." Valentine did everything he could, and "little Albion feels very bad, almost heart-broken at times."

Louisa's death left searing scars on both her husband and son.

A few months later, Valentine told his in-laws that her gravestone would read, "February 13, 1843, age 33. She taught us how to live and oh! too high the price of knowledge—taught us how to die."

ALBION OFTEN FELT nothing was the same after his mother's death. It was an exaggeration, he might tell himself, but not by much. In a few short years, he acquired a stepmother, a newborn sister, a new house in a new town, a new and larger farm with more work and more responsibilities, and a new and evolving set of expectations that led to tension and conflict with his unyielding and temperamental father.

Remarriage to Rowena Snow had suited Valentine, but it could not mask his lingering grief. His infrequent letters to the Winegars teemed with melancholy and bitterness. New hardships tested the family. Rowena's first child, a daughter, lived only three months. A drought destroyed three-quarters of the year's corn crop. Then, a debilitating attack of rheumatism so enfeebled Valentine that he could not turn over in bed for three weeks, causing the doctor to warn that he might not live. He made an agonizingly slow recovery, spending an entire winter indoors, like a caged bear.

As the family's fortunes improved, so did Valentine's outlook. He and Rowena had a second child, Rosetta, and he delighted in her. The move to a larger and more productive farm in Kingsville, he boasted to the Winegars, had the added benefit of putting eleven-year-old Albion in the company of others with intellectual talents. At five, Albion had shown a love for books that had never waned. It was possible, Valentine wrote, that "we shall all come out some distinguished Literati, as we are near a flourishing academy."

Albion also demonstrated great promise in the art of running a farm. At ten, he was already adept at the hard work of preparing and harvesting the land. He also "came very near getting killed," his father told the Winegars. Albion was overseeing a team of horses as it dragged a nearly-new harrow, its rows of sharp teeth tugging at the earth. Part of the mechanism came loose, and as Albion stopped to rehook it, the horses bolted forward. His bellow brought Valentine in a sprint. "I got there just as he came out the back end," his father wrote. "He was completely harrowed from one end to the other, some 15 teeth at least passing over his body . . . but with the exception of being a little stiff a few days, he never minded it. I think I have never seen a much nearer escape with as little injury."

Otherwise, Valentine rejoiced in his Kingsville kingdom. For fifteen hundred dollars, he was now master of sixty acres, a stable with two horses and a wagon, an abundance of hardy locust trees, and a two-bedroom house with a porch. Prosperity, however, was not enough. Valentine drank too much, and the more he drank, the more rigid he seemed to become.

When young Albion's reading taste expanded to books other than the Bible, his father intervened, weeding out those he felt were immoral, steering his son to those he deemed more in keeping with his Methodist religious values. Albion would long remember having to memorize lines picked by his father from *Paradise Lost,* John Milton's seventeenth-century epic poem of good and evil, God and Satan. But Walter Scott's romance novels, filled with adventure and daring? Off limits. Later, Albion would tell Emma of his plans for his first great novel: a sweeping sixteenth-century tale, in the Scott tradition, set during the Spanish conquest of America. It was "a vast untrodden field for the historic fictionist," he told Emma.

Banning books put Valentine in a decided minority among the tidy villages of the Western Reserve. The New Englanders who first came there in the 1790s, many of them looking to build a more tolerant society than the Puritan one they had left behind, prided themselves on their antiauthoritarian spirit. It was no surprise that the antislavery movement flourished there, that the Underground Railroad had laid down strong connections throughout the Reserve, or that one of the most fervent antislavery voices in Congress hailed from Ashtabula County.

Ohio had its own North-South divide. The state's southern portion, near the Ohio River and Kentucky, had more free blacks, more runaways, more slave hunters, and more tension. The Western Reserve, an abolitionist hotbed, counted sixteen hundred people of color in the late 1850s; fewer than eighty called Ashtabula County home. At the state's political conventions, the Western Reserve delegates often heard a scornful mantra from those worried about the rumblings of secession: Easy for you to embrace the most radical Republicans. Easy for you to resist the federal government's enforcement of the Fugitive Slave Act. You don't have to deal with the consequences. You hardly have contact with the colored race.

In its earliest days, Ohio had enacted "black laws" to limit migration into the new state and control its existing population of free blacks and runaway slaves. An 1804 act to "regulate blacks and mulatto persons" required a "certificate of freedom" and $500 bond to settle in the state. No such certificate or bond was demanded of new white residents. Subsequent laws made the separation even starker. A person of color could not testify against a white, serve on a jury or in the militia, or attend schools with whites. Many of those laws were repealed in a dramatic legislative battle during the late 1840s. But some held on, a reminder that the free state of Ohio was not entirely free for people of color.

The nation's most contentious debate swirled around Albion and his father, a Whig loyalist, but it rarely landed close enough to pull them into its wake.

YOUNG ALBION CHAFED under his father's rule. At thirteen, as 1852 neared, he convinced his father to send him off to live with the Winegars in western Massachusetts, with no fixed date of return. Ever since Louisa's death, the Winegars had been issuing invitations, but Valentine had resisted. "I cannot part with him," he wrote. Each renewed offer made him nervous. Why did they keep asking? Did they think he couldn't care for Albion? Putting aside his reservations, he waved goodbye to Albion at the Ashtabula depot.

While his father fumed in Kingsville, Albion reveled in his newfound freedom in Lee. He felt as if heaven had descended on him. He enrolled in school, amassed new friends, read constantly from the Winegars' extensive library, explored a different religion, watched his grandfather fall sick and die, and opened his mind to a world outside his father's realm.

He also learned the cost of carelessness. While fooling around with a friend and a firearm, something had gone wrong. A piece of a percussion cap went airborne, slicing into the delicate tissue surrounding the cornea of his right eye. In a blink, Albion saw his future altered. He did not relish telling his father what had happened. "Dear Father, I owe you an apology for not writing sooner," his morose letter began in May 1852. After a winter cooped up indoors, a prisoner of his injury and severe weather, Albion was only now starting to feel better. "My eye was hurt very badly . . . it is getting well but it is not out of danger, but blessed be god that it is well as it is. I don't think I shall ever have the sight of it again." His uncle Jacob, however, clung to the few rays of optimism. "Albion is wrong about his eye," Jacob assured Valentine. "I think it out of danger & that he will get the sight as good as the other."

Jacob had good reason, beyond his nephew's well-being, to wish that the injury had never happened. There was enough tension between the two families already, with Albion often in the crossfire. "Well Old Man," Jacob wrote in reply to one of Valentine's complaining letters, "I wish you to remember that your windows have glass in them before you commence throwing stones at mine." He signed off with one final gibe. "I want you to write soon & not keep getting drunk & and laying it to me as you did in your last."

When Albion returned to Kingsville after more than a year in Lee, his sight was no better. He compensated for his disability with aggression, determined not to show weakness. A bad eye? Albion didn't care for the sound of that. A piercing gaze? Much better.

THE FATHER-SON REUNION never quite reached reconciliation. In the spring of 1856, Albion took flight once more, bolting back to Lee. Uncle Jacob had died unexpectedly the previous summer, at age forty-two, leaving a widow but no children. Jacob and Albion had forged a special bond, a counterweight to Albion's fraught relationship with his father. Now his uncle was gone, too, just like his mother.

This time, Albion did not seek Valentine's permission for the trip. He was eighteen now, defiant as well as headstrong, and he had conceived this scheme with his aunts' apparent backing, much to his father's consternation. How dare they encourage Albion to disobey his father? This betrayal was a point of no return, Valentine warned in a clench-fisted letter. He offered Albion one final chance to come to his senses. "I have always told him, as I now tell him, that I will do well by him and assist him to the extent of my abilities," he wrote. "But if he voluntarily and against my will throws himself beyond my authority or control, he must rely on his own resources."

It was a threat cloaked in conciliation. Albion would remember it, resent it, build on it, and keep it deep within, an ember for a fire that he would not allow to burn out. He did not remain in Lee as long this time, only a few months. Back in Kingsville, he was determined to set his own course, with or without his father's endorsement.

He would not allow others to dictate his dreams.

AS THEIR COURTSHIP intensified in early 1859, Emma asked Albion to hold nothing back, and he did his best to comply. The openness and intensity of their relationship was unusual, but in some ways, it mirrored the place where they met. Kingsville Academy was a private school unlike most in the country. It was enrolling female students at a time when schools, whether the newer public ones or the established academies, were almost uniformly divided by gender—and far fewer opportunities existed for girls such as Emma. At Kingsville's annual graduation exercises, an equal number of women and men came to the podium to read, speak, and recite.

Albion and Emma hid their engagement, but not their fondness for each other. When the weather allowed, Albion often walked the eight miles to Emma's house, allowing her family a good look at her suitor. Her three sisters found him charming; her parents found him "disagreeable." Determined to repair the damage, she asked Albion to be less argumentative with her mother and more attentive to her father. After one of Albion's visits, she told him, her mother had asked her father what he thought of Emma's not-so-gentlemanly caller. "Father replied that he hardly knows you, that you were always so taken up with me, that he had hardly had any conversations with you, he thought you rude and rough in your manners."

Rude and rough in your manners. Aware of the resentment these words would bring, she sought to soften the blow. "Do not be angry," she wrote. She had acted as his advocate, she assured him, telling her parents that "you possess great intellect and you would be great and honored and that time would remove all that was disagreeable now." She was sure that he and her father would get along famously if Albion would make the effort. "You will please him," she said, "will you not, Love?"

Albion read her letter with amazement. He thought Emma knew him better than this. She had asked: Are you "displeased because I have spoken so plainly?" Displeased? He was more than displeased. "As to rendering myself agreeable to your parents," he fired back, "I would not sail under false colors, or ever live by false pretenses." Underlining more of his words than usual, some twice, he told her: "I must appear to them as I am." He could not merely seem great and good, he told her. He must be good and great.

Yes, he had flaws, and yes, he could make more of an effort to talk with her parents. But he doubted he could change their minds. "The time was when I could have won their respect and made them acquainted with me very quickly. At present I fear it is different. I think I may say without egotism that I know them. . . . Your Mother especially regards me with something akin to suspicion for having stolen your love without her leave. This to one of my temperament, I need not say, is irksome." Having made his points, he relented a bit. "I feel it is a far more difficult task to please your parents than yourself, your sisters, or even your brothers," he wrote. But "I will try my very best to do so."

He didn't ask for an apology, but Emma offered one anyway. "I am sorry that I have said anything about it, please forgive me, I am always doing something wrong, I might have known that your own way would have been the right one," she wrote. "They will all love you if you will be yourself, they cannot help it, nor do they wish to." Making plain that he was still welcome at her parents' house, she teasingly wrote, "Now my dear Albion, when are you coming to Cherry Grove?"

"Have no hesitations," she told him.

THEIR SECRET COULDN'T KEEP FOREVER. In April 1859, Emma warned Albion that everyone "from one end of the Lake Shore to the other" now knew of their engagement. Emma didn't mind being found out, but she did mind being "universally pitied" by women who could not fathom why she would agree to delay her marriage for several years, until Albion had finished his college studies. Didn't those gossips have anything better to talk about?

She did not have time to dwell on her irritation, however. She was too busy. She had taken another short-term teaching job, her second, no more than a dozen students this time, but they were young and rambunctious, requiring all her attention and most of her energy. The school met in Conneaut, just a few miles from her family's farm, and to make her daily routine easier, she had taken a room in town during the week. She hadn't anticipated how lonely she would feel. She comforted herself by thinking of his next visit and their plans for celebrating a big milestone: Albion's twenty-first birthday, on May 2, 1859.

In keeping with his developing taste for the grand gesture, Albion had resolved to commemorate his landmark day with a poem. Addressed to Emma ("My Love"), his ode was ambitious in scope and sarcasm. He did not finish it for several weeks—a severe toothache sent him reeling for a few days—but when it was done, he had delivered an acerbic commentary on crossing the threshold into adulthood at this perilous moment in the country's political history. His tone was mocking, not joyful; satiric, not sentimental. Yes, he had acquired the freedoms that came to any man turning twenty-one in America, but he wasn't fooling himself—those privileges were an accident of birthplace, gender, and skin color.

I just begin, My Love, to see
How sweet and glorious 'tis to be,
A man, and white—(by courtesy)
In this great nation of the free.

Yes, he could now vote, but the nation did not seem to treasure that freedom as it once did. And yes, he was free to "hold any office I can get," if he wanted the opportunity to "cheat and swindle." He lamented his lack of wealth ("My Birthright's not exceeding great / No princely rank, no princely state"), while slipping in a Northern gibe at Southern prosperity:

I've no estate with rent-roll long
No slaves, to cringe, beneath my thong;
My Manor's scarcely worth a song.

MONEY WAS VERY MUCH on Albion's mind as he composed his birthday poem. His faint hopes of fatherly aid had evaporated, like the morning mist on Lake Erie. In June, when Valentine rejected his latest plea for help, Albion told Emma that he was relieved. Clarity was far better than uncertainty. "I really think that little bit of information which Father imparted to me," he wrote, "has done me more than a little good mentally and physically. . . . Indeed I must say that I feel stronger and happier now that I have only my own strength to rely upon."

For him, money possessed no special allure. It was a means to an end, nothing more. "I scarce know, Emma, whether you will be glad or sorry that your [future] husband has not so strong a love of lucre as many," he wrote. "I do not regard it as an evil and cannot. The fact is I cannot subscribe my aspirations down to the circumference of a dollar. There is no magic about that circle to me. I quite ignore its influence, save as a means of comfort, sustenance & good."

He worried, though, about his suitability to be a husband. Were his dreams too lofty? Too impractical? He might earn a reputation, but could he earn a living? He felt reasonably certain he could make enough money "to satisfy the wants and wishes of any modest conservative man, and more I do not desire." But could he make enough to support a family? "You know I rather dislike, yes hate, detest, the tedium of business," he told her.

Emma had hoped their wedding could take place directly after their graduation from the academy, but Albion had resisted. He wanted to stick to their plan of marrying after he finished college. Yes, the long wait would test them, he told Emma. But it also would deepen their love, make them strong enough to withstand the challenges that life would throw their way. During the long summer hours, while haying in his father's fields, he devised a new strategy: He would go to Lee in early August, ask his aunts Ann and Sophronia to explain the terms of his inheritance, collect the money, and enroll somewhere for the fall term. During his stay in Lee, he would make a start on the historical novel that was rattling around in his head.

If all went well, he would not return to Kingsville any time soon.

THE TRAIN TO ALBION'S FUTURE left the Kingsville depot at noon on a memorably hot Wednesday in early August 1859. Saying goodbye to his father proved harder than he had anticipated. Albion had detected a thawing in Valentine's stiff-necked demeanor as the day of departure neared. "Father and I had quite a talk," he wrote to Emma after his arrival in Lee. "He really felt bad when I came to leave." No promises had been made, no money offered, but Albion permitted some hope to creep back in. If his funds ran short and he had nowhere else to turn, perhaps his father would finally come through.

He felt no such glimmer of warmth toward his stepmother. "You may scold me, Emma, if you wish, (but it will not do any good), when I tell you that I left home without even saying good bye to Rowena," he wrote. In contrast, his affection for his half sister Rosetta, now fourteen, had swelled. "Rosetta mourned almost as if I were dead," he wrote Emma. "I am sure she never realized before how much she loved me. I think however it is well for her, as well as me, that I should go, and leave her."

Much had changed in the three years since his last visit to Lee, he felt. Was it the town? Himself? A bit of both? "I was anticipating very much pleasure in Lee," he wrote to Emma. "I was woefully disappointed in some respects." Many of his friends had moved away, and those who remained did not seem "worthy of my notice and very few if any of them worthy of the friendship of Emma. . . . If that remark be egotistical, then I am most certainly an egotist, for I feel its truth."

His disappointment turned to dismay, then exasperation, as he quizzed his aunt Ann about his inheritance. He was expecting about four hundred dollars, not a "princely" sum but more than enough for a year at Harvard. With the accumulation of interest over the eight years since his grandfather's death, he was counting on another one hundred dollars or so, putting a second year at Harvard within reach.

He listened to his aunt's friendly but frank explanation and couldn't quite believe it. There was no nest egg set aside in his name, no accrued interest. His grandfather had left him one "share" of his estate, but no one had arranged for how that share should be paid once he turned twenty-one. Now his aunt was saying that he might receive the money in installments, twenty-five or fifty dollars at a time. That's all she could afford.

He was angry, but already thinking hard about a new plan. Harvard was out of the question, he told Emma, but what did she think about the University of Rochester? It was far cheaper, perhaps one-third of Harvard's cost, and he had a reasonable hope of entering Rochester as a sophomore, saving an entire school year of expenses. If he could wrest his full inheritance over the next year, he might transfer to Harvard later. Reflecting their shared stake in his future, he asked his "Ministre du Finance," as he playfully called Emma, for her candid opinion of his plan. Asking her to "think of it carefully and seriously," he said teasingly: "I will not agree to abide by your decision in regard to it, but Emma's wishes never shall be unheeded by me."

HOSTAGE TO THE MAILS, Albion retreated to a cozy room in his aunt's house to stew about his predicament and sketch out his novel. On his desk, against his dictionary, he rested a miniature of Emma to keep him company. Two windows gave him a view of the late New England summer. It was, he told Emma, "the nicest little study," the latest of his sanctuaries.

Two weeks crawled by, and the mails brought only a single letter from Emma. Throwing aside convention, Albion wrote to her again. Their notes began to cross, like two shouts echoing down opposite ends of a canyon. While she was answering his first letter, he was surging ahead, not waiting for her input. He had embraced the Rochester idea, and had set aside his novel-writing to concentrate on preparing for his entrance examinations.

Emma, from the distance of Ohio, felt out of step. She answered his letters as soon as they arrived, but she soon saw that the mails could not keep pace with Albion's impatience. She offered support rather than guidance. She had no objection to Rochester, but she frowned about Albion's decision to set aside his novel. "I suppose I must be content, but I do not like it one bit," she wrote.

Nor did she like his description of his latest indulgence: Puffing daily on cigars. She shuddered at the idea that his lips—the same lips that had kissed hers!—would touch something so foul. Surely, she wrote, slyly using Albion's aspirations against him, a man of honor and nobility would not stoop to such low-life behavior? By the time her complaint landed, though, Albion had already resolved to give up the "degrading vice." He framed his decision, as he framed so many others, as a matter of morality and self-discipline, "for if one ministers to appetite in one thing, he is apt to become its slave in all," he told her.

Lee offered other temptations that Albion found hard to resist. Within a few days of his arrival, he confessed to Emma, he had engaged in a brief flirtation with a visiting cousin. He had no interest in her—"She can't talk sensibly. She's a pretty doll"—but he somehow had spent several hours with his head in "the sweet creature's lap saying sweet nothings, feeding her with sugared nonsense." He halted the flirtation when she threw herself into *his* lap. "I said No! None but my Betrothed sits there." Emma, showing no inclination to rebuke her betrothed, dismissed the dalliance with a bantering line: "If she dares attempt [to sit in your lap] again, I'll—I'll— Well, she will find out that I have some grit."

Albion had already profited from Emma's grit. She had been resolute in defending him to her parents and, to her delight, her father's view was changing. On a recent Saturday night, Emma and her father had been alone in the dining room, and their conversation turned to the absent Albion. *Rude and rough in his manners.* Those had been her father's words six months earlier. But no longer. "He said he esteemed you very much and would be proud to own you as a son," she wrote to Albion, still glowing. "He thought that if you did take the profession of law, you should make no common lawyer and undoubtedly would some day stand in the Representative Hall among the first and noblest of our land."

Albion's spirits soared when he read his future father-in-law's words in late August, and then topped them with a few expectations of his own. "I am glad your Father has such high and earnest hopes for me," he replied. "It is my hope and prayer that he nor you may ever suffer disappointment in regard to them. You know, My Love, that it is my hope and expectation, God willing . . . to hold a high place, among the truly noble ones of Earth. I would have true greatness; and for that shall ever strive; and I have no fears, Love, but that you will be a fitting, worthy, yes, more than worthy mate."

IN EARLY SEPTEMBER, his indignation rising and his options fading, Albion summoned the law to his side. Rochester's 1859–1860 school year would start in a few weeks, and he intended to be there, cash in hand. His aunt meant well, and he had come to like her more than ever, but all her explanations and apologies didn't change the facts. He was entitled to his money now, he believed—all of it, not in twenty-five or fifty-dollar increments, not next year, not because he had shown up in Lee to claim it, not because he needed it to pay for college. This was a legal matter, not a family favor. Why should he suffer from someone's negligence? "There will be an uproar in the courts pretty soon," he vowed to Emma, "unless my claim is met immediately."

He had read all the estate papers, both his grandfather's will from 1852 and his uncle Jacob's from 1855, and he had made a startling discovery. Jacob had left him a separate bequest of one hundred dollars, also to be paid on his twenty-first birthday. But again, no money had been set aside. Aunt Ann was pleading patience. Plenty of people owed money to her and the estate—the result of loans that she and her husband had made over the years—but in Lee's current miserable economy, the borrowers were struggling to make their payments.

Albion felt sorry for her, but he could not allow his sympathies to blind him, not even if she had to take out a loan herself at the "almost ruinous" rates that Lee's banks were charging. "She cannot raise money without paying 10 to 20 percent interest," Albion told Emma, "but I can't help it. I must have it & have waited long enough." He did not want to take his aunt to court, but he would, if he had no other option. "I told her last night she might have till Thursday morning to furnish me $150. If she does not do it by that time I shall sue her Thursday."

Bluster? Mostly. Thursday came and went without a lawsuit. For now, he had decided to cobble together enough cash to enroll for his first term and leave Lee without turning his aunt into his adversary. A week later, he went to Rochester as planned. After excelling on his entrance exams—impressing the college president, Martin Anderson, who declared that Albion's knowledge of Greek made him more than fit for sophomore standing—he sent a triumphant note to Emma. He was now a member of the Class of 1862. Send all future letters, he told her, to his quarters at 3 Kent Street in Rochester, where he was sharing a spacious second-floor room with a friend from Kingsville. His dream, to attend college and remake himself, had become a reality.

There was one more reality: His month in Lee had already changed him. He did not need to file a lawsuit to see that the law offered weapons to those who otherwise felt defenseless. In a courtroom, the weak could become stronger. Wrongs could be righted. In his own case, he was sure, he had the facts in his favor. But if the Court of Probate had doubts, he would remove them with his "presence and eloquence," he told Emma.

"I am getting to be quite a lawyer," he wrote.

ALBION THREW HIMSELF into college life with the zeal of a religious convert. Savoring the freedom of days built around intellectual pursuits, he worked hard when a subject engaged him and as little as possible when it didn't. When Emma suddenly declared an interest in learning geometry, he teased her with calculated intolerance. "Why, if I should ever hear you talking about sines and cos, angles and triangles, spheres, spheroids &c, I am sure that I would conceive an unconquerable and everlasting dislike for you. . . . I don't want a triangulated monomaniac for my wife."

Emma accepted his barbs with her usual equanimity. She had a harder time coping with the prospect of a long winter without him. Their separation magnified her worries. When Albion's eyes continued to give him trouble, she imagined the worst. If blindness descended, she promised, they would face it together. "I would be life to your eyes . . . if you should, by God's will, be shut up in darkness and could not look upon the face you loved," she wrote in October 1859, a month after Albion's arrival in Rochester.

In truth, he was feeling better than he had in years. By January 1860, he was crowing to Emma that he had gained a few pounds, boosting his weight to 148. He was sleeping well, and had "none of the haggard which you are accustomed to." But more than that, he was feeling good about the future, *their* future, especially their decision to postpone their marriage. Coming to Rochester offered his best chance "to cultivate, to acquire . . . the steadiness of character" that would "make me a successful man."

Waiting was an ordeal, he wrote, but also an opportunity. He was certain that "this long period of self-denial and self-restraint will do more to give strength and solidity to our characters than almost anything else could."

To weather the inevitable storms, he had to teach himself to control his impetuous nature. His ambitions were great, but ambition alone would not be enough. "I need to learn to endure delay, to wait the appointed hour for action, to wait until my powers are fully developed before I engage in the final, earnest conflict of Life."

The various grades of the coloured people are designated by the French as follows, according to the greater or less predominance of negro blood :—

Sacatra	griffe and negress.
Griffe	negro and mulatto.
Marabon	mulatto and griffe.
Mulatto	white and negro.
Quarteron	white and mulatto.
Metif	white and quarteron.
Meamelouc	white and metif.
Quarteron	white and meamelouc.
Sang-mele	white and quarteron.

A guide to New Orleans: Compiled by a visiting New York journalist, 1853

(Frederick Law Olmsted, from his 1861 book, Journeys and Explorations in the Cotton Kingdom*)*

5

The Free People of Color

New Orleans, 1860

On Sunday morning, January 8, 1860, New Orleans awoke to the annual echoes of booming cannons and rekindled memories. As the horizon welcomed the dawn's early light, militia men from the all-white Orleans and Washington artilleries positioned themselves on the city's four main public squares. On their commander's barked order, they fired into the misty sky, puffs of pungent gunpowder rising to join the fog that was just beginning to burn off. The artilleries repeated their rituals at noon and sunset, the traditional "national salute" marking the famous Battle of New Orleans on January 8, 1815, the last clash of the War of 1812. But after a decade of mounting tension over slavery, the reverberating explosions felt more like a forlorn pause in the seemingly irreconcilable standoff.

If the Fourth of July evoked patriotic thoughts of Nation and Union, the Eighth of January celebration was a distinctly home-grown affair, the city's tribute to itself for forty-five years now. It had become a day to bring out the bunting, stroll on a uniformed soldier's arm, show off a new hat, find a fine viewing spot on one of the new iron-lace balconies, and wave a scented handkerchief at the graying veterans who had fought with General Andrew Jackson's troops on that most memorable day in New Orleans history.

The men from the old Colored Battalions, who hadn't been invited to join the yearly parade until 1851, basked in the limelight they now shared with their white compatriots. Rarely did the ranks of New Orleans's nearly eleven thousand free people of color garner such recognition. Often, their main footprint in public life consisted of a set of initials attached to their names in government and church records, courtesy of an 1808 law that had stamped their separate status with an official designation from birth to death: *f.m.c.*, free man of color, and *f.w.c.*, free woman of color.

Yet of the many threads woven into New Orleans's sinuous history—French colony, Spanish dominion, Caribbean refuge, American territory, and, since 1812, eighteenth U.S. state—the strands featuring the free people of color were among the few that stretched back to the beginning, to the 1720s and 1730s, when Bienville and his pioneer band from France were coaxing a settlement out of a swamp with the involuntary sweat of enslaved men from Africa.

For more than a century, under the governments of three different nations, free people of color had occupied a tenuous middle ground between liberty and captivity. Granted some rights and deprived of many others, they formed the sandwiched layer of a three-tiered society. They could own property, make contracts, obtain licenses, bring lawsuits, and testify in court. But in 1860, they still could not vote. They could not hold public office, or sit on a jury. They could not send their children to the public schools, which had been educating white students for nearly twenty years now, and when they went to the St. Charles Theater or the Gaiety, they had a choice of the Colored Galley (twenty-five cents) or the plusher Quadroon Boxes (seventy-five cents), a favored spot of the elite among *les gens de couleur libres*, as the free people of color were known in the city's French-speaking neighborhoods.

They were free, but fenced in.

AS DESCENDANTS OF WHITE and black and mixed-race parents with roots in Europe, Africa, and the Caribbean, their spectrum of skin colors mocked the stark, standard labels that dominated political discourse elsewhere in America. A New York journalist, after two visits in 1853, was left reeling. How could he explain to his Northern readers that New Orleans was not a white-black society, but French-Spanish-African-English-Celtic, with "nearly all possible mixed varieties of these"? Fascinated, he put together a list with "the various grades of the coloured people"—nine in total—as "designated by the French . . . according to the greater or less prominence of negro blood."

As might be expected of a group that had acquired some wealth and a modicum of influence, *les gens de couleur libres* had ambitions, rising expectations, and a proud history. Many had survived separation by embracing it. French—or, at least, French spiced with a Louisiana patois—remained their first language, even if they knew English. More than a few of the old-timers looked to Paris as much as New York, just as their white grandfathers and fathers had. More than a few could trace their origins to an ancestor who had won freedom generations earlier, during French or Spanish rule. That was true of the Plessys, to name just one of many mixed-race families that dated back to the eighteenth century, and could point to relatives who were Eighth of January veterans.

In September 1814, when Jackson beseeched these French-African-Spanish ancestors to join his army against the British invaders, he had called them "noble-hearted, generous" freemen of color. He was addressing them, he said, with "the sincerity of a soldier and in the language of truth." He began with an apology. "Through a mistaken policy, you have been heretofore deprived of a participation in the glorious struggle for national rights in which our country is engaged," he said. "This shall no longer exist."

Six hundred and nine men had answered his appeal. In exchange for their service, Jackson had promised equal pay, equal rations, and equal bonuses. He did not promise equal respect. Aware that many whites in New Orleans were opposed to putting muskets in colored hands, the general had shrewdly pledged to create two "independent battalions," each under the command of a white "fellow-citizen," so that the colored soldiers would not have to endure "unjust sarcasms." The battalions were divided by birthplace—native-born in the First, émigré in the Second. The *ancien* and the *arriviste*. Over the decades, that distinction had faded. What was left: a desire for full citizenship that still burned brightly in 1860—and was still unrequited.

Now, Jackson was dead, gone fifteen years. U.S. citizenship seemed dead as well, buried by Chief Justice Roger Taney and his unsettling *Dred Scott* decision. The colored veterans' numbers, too, were thinning. Few could fit into the fraying uniforms they had worn in the War of 1812's final, bloody, and largely anticlimactic battle. For most, stooped with age or slowed by illness, their marching days were past. But the youngest—those who had signed up at fifteen or seventeen, pretending to be older—still had enough spring in their steps to walk the three-mile parade route.

No need. The city of New Orleans had grander plans for their aging heroes on this Eighth of January. Shortly before eleven o'clock, a military escort threaded the white and colored veterans through the congested crowds to Lafayette Square, where a string of carriages awaited at the foot of City Hall. The stately building's portico sagged with the weight of hundreds of neck-craning spectators. As the bands blared, the procession pushed off for a three-hour jaunt through the narrow streets of New Orleans's past, present, and uncertain future.

THE NEWSPAPERS MARVELED at the frolicking crowds watching the parade, lured from their houses by the gently warming temperatures. It was the perfect New Orleans antidote to a miserable stretch of cold, blustery weather that had climaxed with a driving rain, leaving some streets swollen with even more mud than usual. The thick crowds were everywhere: on the newly paved granite sections of St. Charles and Camp, in the heart of the American district; along the narrow corridors of Gravier and Common, just a few blocks from the row of thriving slave market dealers and auctioneers; across Canal Street, with its view of the bustling port that sent cotton all over the world; in the nooks and alcoves off Chartres and Royal Streets in the old Vieux Carré, where a visitor was still likely to hear more French than English.

The colored veterans were now a mainstay in the annual procession, but only a few years earlier, in 1851, their first appearance after decades of exclusion had caused quite the stir. The newspapers had nearly exhausted their supply of adjectives in praising their bravery, their gallantry, their love of country. "These faithful men have never before participated in the annual rejoicings," the *Picayune* lamented. "Yet who more then they deserve the thanks of the country and gratitude of succeeding generations? Who rallied with more alacrity in response to the summons of danger? Who endured cheerfully the hardships of the camp, or faced with greater courage the perils of the fight? If, in that hazardous hour, when our homes were menaced with the horrors of war, we did not disdain to call upon the Colored population to assist in repelling the invading horde," how can we now refuse to unite with them in celebrating "the glorious event which they helped make so memorable an epoch in our history?"

Our homes. Our history. In the *Picayune's* narration, the colored veterans weren't defending *their* families or fighting for *their* liberty. Even in tribute, the *Picayune* had drawn a clear and unambiguous dividing line: The free people of color had assisted us in *our* time of need.

The *Picayune* reporter had talked with many whites in the crowd, and "without exception," they had endorsed the colored veterans' inclusion. Inspired, the reporter offered a personal assessment of the free people of color. "As a class," he wrote, "they are peaceable, orderly, and respectable people, and many of them own large amounts of property among us. . . . They have been true hitherto, and we will not do them the injustice to doubt a continuance of their fidelity." But in case rebellion might be on anyone's mind, the accolade ended with a warning: "While they may be certain that insubordination will be promptly punished, deserving actions will always meet with their due rewards in the esteem and gratitude of the community."

If *les gens de couleur libres* had been asked for their views, some might have said that their families had lived in New Orleans longer than the *Picayune's* editors, who were Northern transplants arriving in the 1830s. Some might have said that, during times of crisis, freemen of color had served every government's militia with distinction and loyalty. Some might have said they were promised full citizenship in the treaty that accompanied the American takeover in 1803. Some might have pointed out that fifty years of American rule had eroded some of their freedoms through the enactment of a "Black Code" and other discriminatory laws, proof that "deserving actions" did not always lead to "the gratitude of the community."

Others might have protested the *Picayune's* division between *we* and *them*, perhaps by offering a slice of their proud history to illustrate why the boundary line between white and colored was neither clear nor unambiguous.

MILITARY SERVICE HAD been a principal route to freedom since the territory's earliest days. In 1730, as a reward for fighting the Natchez Indians, the French had liberated some of its soldier-slaves. An incentive was born, one that the French and then the Spanish had used to bolster their militias. That comprised one limb of *les gens de couleur's* genealogical tree.

A second branch consisted of free blacks who had immigrated to the colony from other French possessions. Many had never been slaves. Their children had never been slaves. The largest group had come after 1791, when a slave revolt on the Caribbean island of Saint-Domingue (soon to be renamed Haiti) triggered the chaotic exit of white planters, free people of color, and any slaves their fleeing owners could seize and control. Most went to Cuba, where they started over. But small waves began landing yearly in New Orleans, where they discovered a society with strong similarities to the one they had left.

A third group included women such as Agnes Mathieu, a former slave who bought her freedom with the help of a white French-born soldier and merchant, Mathieu Devaux. A Spanish law, known as *coartación*, gave people in slavery a small but sanctioned opportunity to loosen a master's hold. The system rested on the assumption that every slave had a market value, and if that price was paid, the slaveholder could not refuse. As dictated by the law, two appraisers—one for the owner, the other for Agnes—had determined that she was worth 425 *piastres*, the Spanish near-equivalent of dollars. On December 15, 1778, Mathieu Devaux deposited his payment with the Spanish court, and asked for Agnes's freedom.

During the first decade of Spanish rule, in the 1770s, *coartación* opened the door to freedom for about two hundred people in slavery. Many had the help of their lovers, but not all. While earning enough money for freedom was difficult, it was not impossible. Spanish custom allowed those held in slavery to find extra work on nights or Sunday, and many women did, often in the local markets or by taking on seamstress jobs. Some hoped to save enough to free their children eventually, if not themselves.

Occasionally, even if a slave followed the *coartación* rules to the letter, a defiant owner would put up a fight. That's what happened when a court deputy showed up at Barbara Herterlin Harang's plantation outside New Orleans at the end of 1778, seeking Agnes's release. Harang would not allow "said negro slave her freedom," the deputy reported sheepishly to the court.

Devaux was just as adamant. Agnes's price had been set, and paid. He wanted *coartación* enforced. When a second deputy came back empty-handed, Devaux asked the court not to back down. Finally, the colony's governor, General Bernardo de Galvez, intervened. Devaux was a soldier under Galvez's command, but their military connection didn't appear to be a factor; Galvez had ruled in favor of *coartación* orders in ten other cases. He did so again. Agnes, born into slavery in 1759, now had her freedom papers. She was not quite twenty-one.

Over the next twenty-three years, she and Mathieu Devaux brought seven children for baptism to the St. Louis Cathedral in New Orleans. The Spanish priests recorded the ceremonies in the volume for "Slaves and Free People of Color," using the standard language for a child born to an unmarried couple of different races: *hijo natural de Agnes Mathieu, negra libre, y un padre no conocido.* In English: "child born to Agnes Mathieu, free black woman, and an unknown father." Years later, as he was preparing his will, Devaux named all seven children as his. Some of the baptism records were revised, with "Devaux" scribbled in the margin, adding weight to his legal declaration.

By early 1804, as the Americans were taking over the territory, Agnes Mathieu had carved out her own form of independence. She now owned property in the Vieux Carré. She bought and sold slaves of her own, as nearly half of the free people of color had by the early part of the century. She and Devaux were on the verge of severing their long relationship; within three years, Agnes would marry a free man of color, a marriage that did not last long. But it marked her once again as a woman willing to cross the boundaries that her society had erected.

Her two eldest *mulata* daughters followed her path, creating families with white Frenchmen. Catherina, who went by the nickname Catiche, had met Germain Plessy, a merchant from Bordeaux; they would have eight sons and daughters between 1803 and 1824, some baptized at the St. Louis Cathedral and some at the Catholic church near their country house in St. John the Baptist Parish, about fifty miles west of the city.

The priests at the cathedral were careful to enter the baptisms in their book for free people of color, specifying that the children were *quarteron libre*—free and one-quarter black. But in rural St. John the Baptist Parish, the middle Plessy children went into the white book, with no reference to Catiche's status as a *mulata libre*. Then, for their last two children, their baptism went into the *f.p.c.* books in both parishes. A blurring of the color line was beginning.

For his first two children, Germain was *un padre no conocido*, an unknown father. After that, he openly acknowledged his role. Some years later, completing the circle, he revised the Cathedral's original baptism record for his oldest living son, stating that "Germain Plessy, native of Bordeaux in France" was the boy's father. He signed the alteration with a bold flourish.

The Plessy and Mathieu clans gained a sturdy and visible foothold among *les gens de couleur libres*. Catiche and Germain, like Agnes, accumulated property and slaves. Several of Agnes's grandchildren married other free people of color, often from mixed-race families that had known freedom for two or more generations. When Agnes died in 1818, she left behind an estate for her children and a legacy that loomed larger with each passing decade.

She was the last member in the Plessy line who could say, "I was once a slave."

EXCLUDED BY LAW from any elective office, free people of color couldn't personally press their case for equal rights when the best chance in years materialized in April 1845. A constitutional convention, the first since statehood, had been meeting at the St. Louis Hotel for months, seventy-five elected delegates debating the tiniest details of government and citizenship, with the notable exception on how *les gens de couleur* fit into that picture. Then, on Wednesday morning, April 23, came a surprise from one of the most prominent and flamboyant delegates: Bernard de Marigny of New Orleans, a former president of the State Senate, a slaveholder, and developer of the Faubourg Marigny, a neighborhood dominated by *les gens de couleur.*

Bernard de Marigny was a "Creole," meaning native-born, a label that most whites in Louisiana liked to reserve for themselves. He was fifty-nine years old, well known for speaking his mind and spending too much of his money. He had relatives by marriage who were free people of color, and many buyers of his real estate came from the middle tier. Now, he told the delegates in French, he was offering a proposal that he felt was necessary for the state's "present and future welfare." He asked them to consider a clause allowing the legislature to "confer the rights and privileges of citizenship" on free people of color, if they were native born. It was a small step, only giving the legislature the option, without tying its hands. Take time to think about it, he urged. He would save his arguments for the coming debate.

The proposal died an undignified death a week later, never debated, a casualty of a hostile reception that Marigny said he could not overcome. "I believe it is my duty to withdraw it," he wrote in a statement brimming with disappointment, but "I trust that the members of the Convention . . . will do me the justice to believe my motives were pure."

HOSTILITY WAS NOWHERE in evidence at the same hotel fifteen years later, as veterans and dignitaries gathered for a celebratory dinner on the afternoon of January 8, 1860. Cheering crowds had greeted the parade at every stage of the route, and now, to the jubilant strains of "Hail Columbia," veterans and guests were marching single file into the hotel's opulent domed dining room, primed for hours of hearty fellowship and impassioned toasts.

The host for the dinner: The Association of Louisiana Veterans of 1814–1815, the oldest veteran group, representing the white battalions. The colored veterans, after years without an association, had recently started one. But after their carriage rides in the parade, they had gone their separate ways. No invitation to the sumptuous dinner awaited them.

When Anthony Fernandez, the association's president, offered a toast to

Andrew Jackson's memory, the assembled rose together in solemn tribute, their glasses aloft in the shimmering haze of the room's new gaslights. The toasts rolled on, one homage spurring yet another—"The President!" "The Governor!" "The Mayor!" "The Sons of Louisiana!"—until the usual hurrahs gave way to something more in keeping with the country's ominous mood.

Fernandez took the first step, to sustained applause: "The Union—it shall be preserved in spite of Northern fanaticism and abolitionism."

A military officer added his plea: "Northern and Southern, I hope we shall stand united."

Then, a civilian's defiant vow: "The Sons of Louisiana, if the country was invaded, would fight and give the enemy a thrashing like their fathers did in 1815."

Finally, the toasts and toasters exhausted, Mayor Gerard Stith rose to offer the evening's last words to a special guest: "Old Jordan, the veteran drummer."

The *Daily True Delta* would identify the guest as merely "Old Jordan (colored)." His full name was Jordan B. Noble, a free man of color born into slavery in Georgia. At the age of thirteen, he had drummed his way into history with his sharp, staccato beats as the British attacked on the morning of January 8, 1815. He had served with Jackson's white Seventh U.S. Regiment, not with the First Colored Battalion's band of eleven musicians. Before the morning parade, he had breakfasted with the members of his old regiment—a first for him, he said proudly. Now, he stood before the applauding audience at the St. Louis Hotel, a new medal in hand for his service in three different wars, courtesy of the white association. "I feel greatly honored by my being called to drink a glass," Noble began.

Though now almost sixty, he still considered himself fit enough to beat his drum, he told the crowd. If war should come again, "I would bear arms wherever danger most needed my services as drummer." He would defend Louisiana, against any enemy. "I shall try to gain, if I can, the affections of the rising generation and posterity of my caste in this interest," he said, to shouts of "We know it. We know it."

Cheering erupted as he proclaimed, "No matter what our fate is, we feel in Louisiana free and clear."

WHILE THE WHITE crowd at the St. Louis Hotel hailed Jordan Noble's pledge of loyalty, some *gens de couleur libres* were wondering whether it was time to abandon their beloved native state of Louisiana. They were feeling besieged and unwanted.

Only four years earlier, their status had seemed safe, or at least safer. The Louisiana Supreme Court had put a judicial stamp of approval on the state's three-tiered society, describing whites and free people of color as more alike than different. In a case that did not require such an emphatic ruling, the court had scolded the legislature for regulating the conduct of slaves and free people of color in the same 1855 statute. "In the eye of Louisiana law," the court majority had declared, "there is (with the exception of political rights, of certain social privileges, and of the obligations of jury and militia service), all the difference between a free man of color and a slave, that there is between a white man and a slave."

The ruling did little more than confirm the status quo, and it drew a scornful dissent from two justices, but by describing the contours of the middle tier—the rights it included, and the rights that it didn't—the judges in the majority had issued a warning to those in the legislature who wanted to push free people of color closer to the enslaved class.

Instead of heralding a new sense of security, however, the court ruling was followed by new attacks. A vehement group of state legislators made plain that it would be delighted to see all free people of color leave Louisiana for good. A bill calling for their eviction was introduced at the 1859 legislative session. It failed, but several other laws were enacted that sent the same unmistakable message: We do not want you here.

One law offered "voluntary" slavery, allowing "any free person of African descent, over the age of twenty-one," to select a master and "become a slave for life." Another essentially banned certain jobs, making it illegal for a free person of color to run a coffee house or a billiards hall, or have a license to sell liquor. The third, a ban on newly arriving people of color, caused panic: When it took effect on September 1, 1859, *les gens de couleur libres* streamed into the mayor's office, confused about the law's target and clamoring for protection.

On paper, the third law did not apply to city residents. It called for the arrest of any free people of color arriving by waterway, and their imprisonment until their ships departed with them on board. Because it did not explicitly say that only new émigrés should be detained and expelled, it left open a wide door to misinterpretation. Colored crew members could be taken off their ships and jailed. So could visitors who had no intention of staying beyond a few days. And so could native-born residents who could not prove that they belonged in New Orleans. The clincher: The law offered a ten-dollar reward for the arrest of "such person of color." The incentive guaranteed that some of the city's police officers, not the best paid of public servants, would apply the ambiguous law as broadly as possible.

Some overzealous officers then dusted off an older law, from 1830, that had required free people of color born after 1825 to register with the city or face eviction. Armed with both legal weapons, old and new, police went into the streets. "The first arrests were those of Harriett and Elenora Robinson, colored ladies of Basin Street," the *Daily Crescent* reported on September 2. Unable to produce papers proving their "right to remain," the Robinson sisters sat in jail with a judge's order giving them five days to leave the state.

After several weeks and more arrests, a consensus emerged among city authorities that only the 1859 law should be enforced, and only against arrivals who had never lived in New Orleans. The furor died down, but outside New Orleans, the voices calling for restrictions on free people of color remained loud. The *Opelousas Patriot*, in northern Louisiana, was perhaps the loudest of all. The newspaper was published in St. Landry Parish, home to nearly one thousand free people of color, the second largest community in the state. "We would advise you to flee the society of the white man *voluntarily*, before you are compelled to do so," the *Patriot* wrote. "Take a fair price for your lands, and we will ensure you speedy purchasers. . . . This is the kind of population we want—*all white citizens and their slaves—no free colored citizens in our midst.*"

The middle layer was beginning to feel more compressed than ever. In 1840, nineteen thousand free people of color had lived in New Orleans. But a slow exodus had been going on for years. Some had gone North and West. Some had gone to Mexico, where a small group of New Orleans expatriates had started an experimental settlement for free people of color called the Eureka Colony. A select few, from wealthier families, had gone to France, never to return.

But nearly eleven thousand remained in New Orleans, either because they had nowhere to go or, in most cases, no desire to leave. They were native-born, too, most of them, and long ago, their ancestors had been promised their rights. Louisiana was their home, they proclaimed, just as much as anyone's. They were Creole, and they weren't going anywhere.

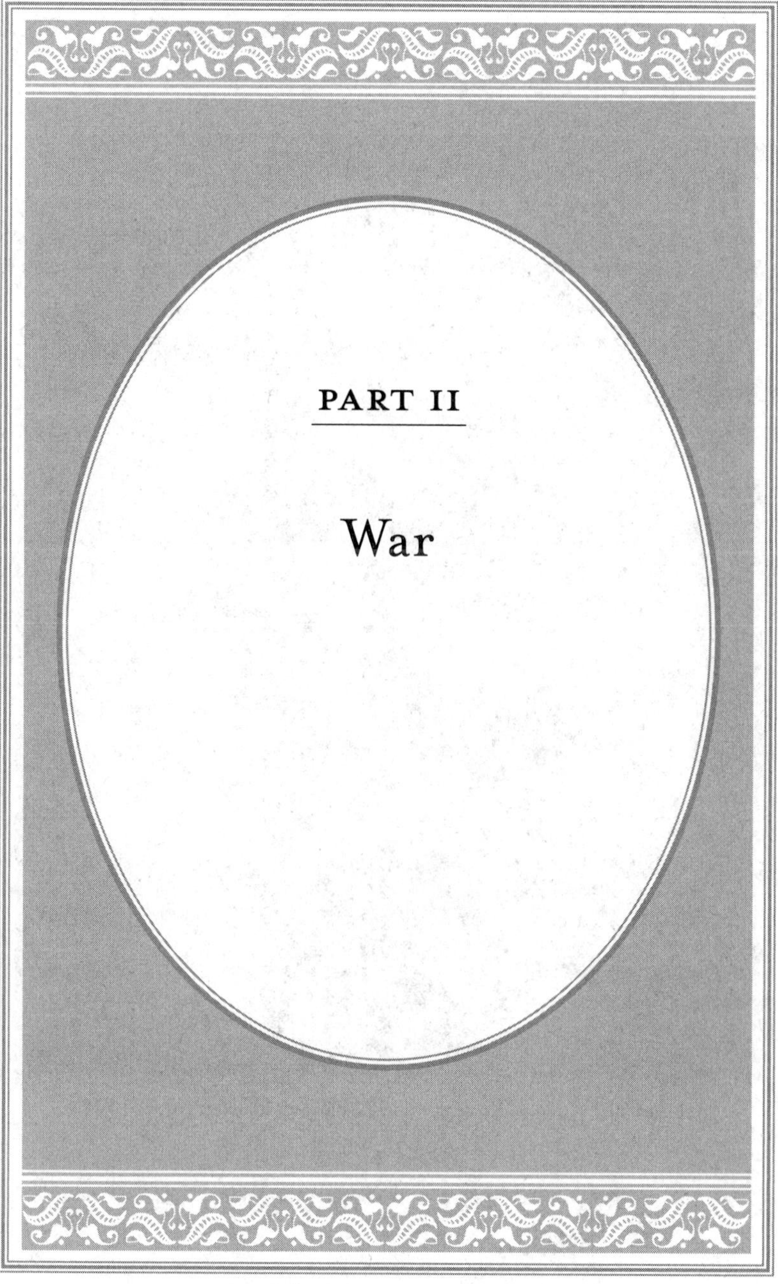

PART II

War

For the Union: Colonel, Tenth Kentucky Volunteer Infantry, November 1861

(Library of Congress)

6

"The Harlan Name"

Kentucky, 1858–1862

THE SCREAMS WOKE the Harlan family in the early hours of a cool October night in 1858. A young girl, an enslaved maid to John Harlan's sister, had stayed up late in the spacious sitting room of the house on Harlan's Hill, preparing for the family's move to town for the winter. The girl had fallen asleep, her sewing basket nearby and a candle on the floor. She awoke to find her clothes ablaze, and family members rushing to her aid. Years later, Mallie's memory remained scorched with the horror: As the "pillar of fire" ran past John, he caught the shrieking girl with his left hand, pulling at the burning fabric with his right. He was too late. A few hours later, the girl died.

Burns blotted the hands of all who had touched her, but John's were the most severe. "The left hand, with which he had gripped the girl with full strength, was seared to the bone and the right arm from the finger tips to the elbow was almost unrecognizable as belonging to a human body," Mallie later wrote. His wounds dressed and bandaged, John joined the mourners on the Harlans' latticed porch for a funeral service. Slaves from neighboring households arrived, and white and black stood together, an African Methodist preacher leading the makeshift congregation in hymn and prayer, connected for those moments in the intimacy of death and grief.

A few days later, Mallie rode her horse to town, accompanied on foot by several slaves. On their return, as the troupe slowly navigated the steep path up Harlan's Hill, a familiar figure came charging toward them on horseback, "at a great and dangerous speed." The family's Irish overseer was sprinting to Frankfort for a doctor's help. John had gone into convulsions.

Her whip flying and her mind racing, Mallie steered her galloping mount toward the house. She arrived to find "panic . . . on the faces of the entire family." During the fretful days and nights that followed, John fought the infection festering in his burns. Soon, the spasms retreated, and soothing salves eased some of his discomfort. But it took months before the young lawyer had full use of the hands. His memory of the intense pain never faded, Mallie said. A cup of hot tea might bring it to the surface.

John's wounds had disrupted a most promising year. Only a few months before, members of his floundering Know Nothing party had gambled on his popularity, pushing him to run for Franklin County judge. John had hurled himself into the race, tromping through farmyards, speaking to any voter who would listen. He squeaked in, one of the few electoral triumphs for the fading party. The judgeship, while limited to hearing civil disputes, gave John a prominence in county politics that no other twenty-five-year-old could claim.

Now, with his hands mending, he watched his father and other former Whigs set about remaking themselves once again. In 1856, the Know Nothings had tried to piece together a national party by skirting the slavery issue, focusing instead on immigration and economic issues. They had failed. By 1859, a party with nothing to say about slavery was about as relevant as a mule at a race of Kentucky thoroughbreds. Slavery was dominating the national conversation as never before. In Washington, the Buchanan administration was working hard to stem the Northern states' growing resistance to the Fugitive Slave Act; Congress was engaged in a daily tug-of-war over abolition and slaveholder rights. The antislavery Republican Party might be "sectional," as its adversaries scornfully said, but it was winning converts throughout the North. The Know Nothings of the American Party were largely talking to themselves.

For the Harlans, losing was a part of politics. Irrelevance, though, simply wasn't acceptable.

DISCARDING THE AMERICAN PARTY label and calling themselves merely "the Opposition," James Harlan and other former Kentucky Whigs emerged from a state convention in February 1859 with a fresh platform that moved slaveholder rights to the very top of their agenda. Almost overnight, they had transformed themselves from silent-on-slavery to proslavery—an amorphous "sectional" party, it was true, but with a platform that had a fighting chance to win in Kentucky. James Harlan readied himself for a hostile reelection campaign as the Opposition nominee for state attorney general, and his son John prepared to help. Then, on a Wednesday in May, an Opposition convention in Lexington forced John to rethink his plans by impetuously considering him for the Eighth Congressional District seat.

The Eighth was, without doubt, the most famous in the state. It was Henry Clay's old stomping ground, known as the "Ashland District," after the name of Clay's famous estate in Lexington. But now it was the domain of John C. Breckinridge, the dashing Democrat elected as Buchanan's vice president at the age of thirty-five, the youngest age possible. Winning the Eighth would be a major victory for the Opposition, as well as a dash of cold water in Breckinridge's face as he prepared for his own presidential run in 1860.

John had come to the convention as a delegate, not a contender. But unexpectedly, one of his enthusiastic admirers had offered Harlan's name to the noisy hall, insisting that the Opposition needed a younger, fresher face. "I started to jump up and say that I was not a candidate," John wrote later. But a fellow delegate restrained him, and John did not resist. After several ballots, he was astonished to find himself in contention. He won by the narrowest of margins.

He was only twenty-five years old, the minimum age required by the Constitution to serve in Congress. If he accepted the nomination, he would have to put his budding legal career on hold. As an upstart, he would have to earn the respect of the party's skeptical elders. These were uncharted waters for John, but also for Mallie, still adjusting to life with a two-year-old daughter and pregnant with their second child. It would be a challenge, far more intense than campaigning for a county judgeship. But when had he turned away from a challenge? That night, at Harlan's Hill, he announced to the family that he had accepted the nomination. His father was "greatly surprised, if not annoyed" at this abrupt turn of events. "Nevertheless," John said later, "he was somewhat moved by this expression of confidence in me by the political party to which we belonged."

John telegraphed his Democratic rival, Captain William E. Simms, proposing a series of debates. They agreed on a grueling schedule, meeting almost daily, crisscrossing all eight counties in the district. An independent candidate would join them, making it a three-way contest. First stop: Paris, at the Bourbon County courthouse, on June 2.

Paris was Simms's home town. The Mexican War veteran's supporters would be out in force. John had less than two weeks to prepare.

ON THE SATURDAY following his nomination, serendipity offered John an early chance to try out his campaign tactics in friendlier confines. He had saddled his horse for a jaunt to Georgetown, the main town in Scott County, twenty miles from Frankfort. The Opposition had a healthy set of allies there, and John would need their energetic help to carry the county in the August 1 election. A day of hand-shaking and a speech would give the Louisville and Frankfort newspapers—which often published lengthy letters from local partisans about a campaign event, under the heading of "correspondence"—something to write about before his debut in Paris.

Having John for the day wasn't enough for his Scott County hosts. They asked him to stay the night, and with his assent, sent a messenger to nearby Paris, inviting Simms for a hastily arranged debate at the Georgetown courthouse. Simms promised to be there. So did S. F. J. Trabue, a renegade Opposition member running without any party's nomination. When the rivals took their places on that Saturday afternoon, they faced a clamorous and curious crowd. It was a fine audience for John to lay a proslavery trap, and dare Simms to find his way out.

John, embracing the Opposition's general strategy, intended to exploit the fault line that had developed between Northern and Southern Democrats since the last presidential election. The Democrats had captured the

White House in 1856 with a platform that said Congress had no constitutional authority to interfere with slavery in the territories. This doctrine of "non-intervention" meant no more Missouri Compromises, no more Kansas-Nebraska Acts, and most of all, no more congressional wrangling over the number of free and slave states. Senator Stephen Douglas had amplified nonintervention into Democratic dogma during his 1858 debates with Abraham Lincoln, his Republican rival for an Illinois Senate seat. It was easy to see the political appeal: Nonintervention had the appearance of neutrality. The territories would choose their own paths on slavery. What could be fairer than that?

But as usual with the slavery issue, a solution born in politics merely proved a breeding ground for new arguments. While most Kentucky slave owners did not have much in common with the large plantation masters of Louisiana and South Carolina—only one-quarter of Kentucky's families held slaves in the 1850s, and half of those owned fewer than five—they guarded their property rights just as zealously. With slave-free Ohio beckoning to runaways, they wanted greater protections for their property, not neutrality. They wanted a workable Fugitive Slave Act, enforced everywhere. The Democratic Party's nonintervention policy felt like a concession at best, a defeat at worst.

As someone who had grown up in a typical Kentucky slave-owning family, John could speak to slaveholders' concerns with credibility. As the Georgetown debate unfolded, John calmly and affably challenged his opponent: Are you *truly* a Democrat, Captain Simms? Will you stand here today, before the good people of Scott County, and *endorse* your national party's position of neutrality on slavery in the territories? If so, what will you tell the Kentucky slaveholder who wants to take his slaves—his *property*—into a territory? Doesn't the Constitution require Congress to protect the property rights of *all* its citizens, Captain Simms? The Opposition proudly stands for slaveholder rights everywhere. The Democrats, it seems, do not. So I ask you now, Captain Simms: If an antislavery Territorial Legislature should pass a law declaring the stealing of slaves to be a lawful way to set them free, would you, if elected to Congress, vote for a bill to punish such an offense and protect slaveholder rights?

Trap sprung.

John was asking Simms to reject his adopted party's position and go his own way, or stick with the Democrats and risk alienating Kentucky voters who did not care a whit about solving the party's North-South split. The crowd waited expectantly. "The Captain was stumped," the *Journal* correspondent crowed. "He wriggled and squirmed and twisted, fretted, and foamed, but if he has answered the question we have never heard it."

Round One, it seemed, to the young, talented, gallant candidate for the Opposition.

ON JUNE 1, 1859, his twenty-sixth birthday, John celebrated and readied himself for Round Two.

He would be on the road for several days, starting the next day in Paris. He packed his clothes with at least one eye on the impression they would leave. A *Louisville Courier* correspondent noticed, offering an elaborate description of this ambitious young man who thought he was ready for high office. "He has red hair and a small side whisker," the correspondent wrote. "He wears straps to his pants, and a standing collar, a scarf cravat with a handsome breast pin, and a snuff-colored cloth coat with a velvet collar." He had the air of someone "high bred and aristocratic." "Aristocrat" wasn't a label that John liked, but given the *Courier*'s low opinion of the Opposition, it was as near a compliment as he could expect.

The ten days since the Georgetown debate had given John time to plot his next move. He had prepared with a lawyer's care, culling evidence from newspaper clippings on the Democrats, party leader Douglas and the Buchanan administration's record in Washington. But this time, Simms was more than ready. When John's dramatic slavery question came his way before the boisterous crowd, Simms's answer was emphatic: If elected to Congress, he would "vote for a law to hang a negro-stealer as high as Haman." No wiggle, no squirm.

Having cast aside Douglas's doctrine, Simms threatened to cast aside Douglas himself. If the Illinois senator were to win the party's presidential nomination, Simms would not support him—not unless Douglas repudiated the policy of nonintervention. John slyly asked: Was Simms still calling himself a Democrat? Why, yes, Simms replied without hesitation, because the Democrats were far and away the best option for preserving slavery as it was. Voting for Harlan and the Opposition, Simms claimed, was as good as voting for the hated "Black Republicans."

John had forced Simms's hand, and now he had to deal with the consequences. The *Courier* editors liked Simms's "high as Haman" retort so much that they declared the election as good as over. "Let us hear no more, then, gentlemen of the Opposition, about Capt. Simms not being sound on the protection question. . . . He stands even with Harlan on the protection of slavery in the Territories, and ahead of him on everything else. Hurrah for Capt. Simms!" But the *Cynthiana News* put its money on John, calling him the best "defender of Southern rights."

On slavery, John and Simms now sounded more alike than different. As they traveled the district during the next month, from Paris to Versailles, from Bald Knob to Peak's Mill, from Cynthiana and Carlisle to Hunter's Mill and Lee's Lick, John shifted his focus slightly. He ratcheted up his attack on the "corrupt" Buchanan administration, asking Simms to defend policies that John characterized as indefensible. After ten days, John felt a surge of confidence. "The general impression was that I had my opponent on the run," he would say later.

That feeling changed on June 13. In the hamlet of Ruddle's Mills, the partisanship turned ugly. Simms used his debate time to denounce an Opposition newspaper essay that had examined his Whig-to-Democrat conversion by mentioning Benedict Arnold and others with a traitorous past. The charge of treason did not sit well with Simms. He called the anonymous author "a slanderer" who "crawls along in his own slime." The essayist, an Opposition leader named Garrett Davis, was in the crowd. He rose to claim authorship, labeling Simms a "liar and a coward." Arrangements for a duel were soon under way.

As the prospective duelists waited in separate rooms at a Cincinnati hotel, friends ferried messages back and forth, hunting a way out. A truce emerged: Davis would retract his essay, and both men would withdraw "all that was said at Ruddle's Mills of an insulting and offensive character." In the end, nothing of substance had happened, but in John's eyes, something fundamental had changed. "The Democratic leaders who, up to that time, were lukewarm and indifferent, were aroused at what they regarded as the attempt by one of my supporters to 'bully' their candidate," John wrote later. Davis's essay, written to wound his opponent, had instead "done me great harm."

John resolved to regain his momentum. In the sweltering heat of July, during one of the warmest summers in Kentucky memory, he spoke as often as twice a day, sometimes three. His voice, barely audible at times, struggled to keep pace. No one could say that he wasn't giving the race his all.

Election Day arrived with John in high spirits. Victory, he felt, was in his grasp.

JOHN STILL BELIEVED he had won, even after the final tally showed otherwise. A mere sixty-seven votes spelled his defeat. Sixty-seven, out of nearly fourteen thousand! He had captured five of the district's eight counties, including Bourbon, his opponent's home county. But he had lost—by suspiciously wide margins—in Scott, Nicholas, and Harrison counties.

Reports of fraud began filtering in, rumors of unfamiliar names on polling books in two counties where Democrats controlled the election boards. The rumors grew into specific allegations: Imports from Ohio, shipped down by train, gone by nightfall. John and supporters examined the records, compiling a list of five hundred questionable names, "persons whom no one knew and no one in the county had ever heard," John said later.

John's friends pressed him to contest the election. They raised $10,000 for the cause. Opposition nominees—including his father—hadn't won any of the state's top offices, but the fledging party had claimed half of Kentucky's ten congressional seats, a stunning achievement. If John could wrest away the Eighth, the Opposition would have a majority of the state's seats in Congress.

John, feeling that the seat rightfully belonged to him, relished the idea of a good fight. But after a hard look, he wavered. Contesting the election would mean a time-consuming, bruising battle, requiring his team to collect several hundred affidavits to present to Congress. He had already spent the summer away from Mallie and the children. Did he want to risk months on a cause with so many uncertainties?

His decision came down to a political calculation. When Congress convened, the Opposition would be a small bloc, no more than eighteen House seats from several Southern states. Who else, then, would take his side against the Democrats? Why, the Republicans, naturally. The Republicans had gained a near majority, ten votes shy. If the Republicans and the Opposition combined to put John in office, then Simms's accusation would have come true: The Opposition would be arm in arm with the party that would destroy the South—or as John put it, arm in arm with "the Abolition Party."

No, he thought, unhappily. Wrong fight, wrong time. The $10,000 went back to the donors. John had not lost his taste for politics. Not at all. But he had debts from the campaign, and now was the time to make a commitment to practicing law and making some money.

His political ambitions would have to wait.

NO ONE HAD TO ASK John in the summer and fall of 1860 where he stood on the great question, "Secession, for or against?" The border state of Kentucky was choosing sides, and John had declared himself a Union-saving man.

Early in the four-way presidential campaign, he had thrown his support behind the brand-new Constitutional Union Party and its promise to support "The Union, Constitution and the Enforcement of the Laws." The party had burst forth as an alternative to the Democrats and the Republicans, offering a haven to the Harlans and other Southern moderates. The Democrats, unable to agree on slavery, had split along sectional lines: Douglas had won the "Democratic" nomination, while Breckinridge was the "Southern Democratic" standard bearer. John could not bring himself to support either one.

John's goals aligned perfectly with the Constitutional Unionists. Like most Kentuckians, he wanted to preserve the status quo, which included slavery and the Fugitive Slave Act so despised by Republicans. But he also wanted to avoid secession, the dangerous word that had gone from a whisper to a shout in some Southern capitals. Less than a year after his congressional defeat, he put the Harlan name back on the ballot, offering himself as the

Eighth District elector for the Constitutional Union's presidential ticket: a South-North combination of John Bell, a prosperous Tennessee slaveholder, and his running mate from Massachusetts, Edward Everett.

Campaigning as an elector meant another sweaty, exhausting summer of travel and debate, promoting the Bell-Everett ticket. "Union Clubs" were sprouting up in every county, and John was a man in demand. On a brilliantly sunny Saturday in late July 1860, thousands flocked to a Union Club gala at the Richmond fairgrounds, about twenty-five miles south of Lexington. From the speakers' platform, John looked out over a red, white, and blue landscape of Union pageantry. Bonnet ribbons, emblazoned with the Bell and Everett names, framed the faces of women strolling through the crowd. A wagon, led by six horses trimmed with flags, carried thirty-four girls, representing all thirty-three states and the District of Columbia, one nation united on a cart. After a picnic dinner, John delivered a ninety-minute exhortation, interrupted frequently by shouts against "disunion."

If John wondered about his popularity, he had only to pick up the friendly *Louisville Daily Journal* after his Richmond oration. A *Journal* correspondent branded him "by far the greatest man of his age in Kentucky, stored with political knowledge to an extent probably unequalled by even any of his elders of greatness. . . . Any Democrat who went away with a determination to vote for Breckinridge either had not brains enough to comprehend the subject or not manliness enough to obey an honest impulse."

Heady words for a twenty-seven-year-old who had failed to win his first congressional race, even coming from a partisan newspaper. Could his political future be any brighter?

IN NOVEMBER, JOHN held his breath to see if Abraham Lincoln and the Republicans would take the presidency without winning a single Southern state. Was it possible?

It was. Kentucky went for the Constitutional Union, much to John's relief and delight. But the more populous North stood unflinchingly behind the lanky Lincoln. Eighteen states ended up in Lincoln's column, giving him 180 of 303 electoral votes and a decisively sectional victory. Breckinridge and his splinter Southern Democrats had captured eleven states, all in the South. Douglas had managed to win only Missouri. So much for the Democratic doctrine of "non-intervention" as a solution to the nation's problems.

Lincoln's triumph fooled no one, certainly no one in nervous Kentucky. So great was the South's antipathy toward the Republicans that Lincoln's name did not appear on the ballot in ten states where secession seemed possible. Lincoln wouldn't take office for three months, giving secessionists plenty of time for a preemptive response. On December 20, 1860, South Carolina took itself out of the Union, the first to go. As other Southern states took up disunion's cry, Kentucky's Democratic governor, a secessionist sympathizer, summoned the state legislature for a special session. He was proposing a convention to determine the "relations" between Kentucky and the U.S. government, an undisguised first step toward separation.

John was one of many Unionists who stood in the way.

MALLIE DIDN'T SEE much of John once the legislature convened. Long days turned into longer evenings, as John and his father met with pro-Union strategists in one tense caucus after another, devising ways to head off Governor Beriah Magoffin's proposed convention. On some nights, Mallie later recalled, John never made it home.

The scene in the state house had no precedent. Mallie, since coming to Frankfort, had spent quite a few hours in the House and Senate galleries. On a winter's day, the Harlan clan might walk over to the legislature for an afternoon outing, the way some families might go for a carriage ride. It was, she remembered years later, a "chief amusement." But this was hardly an amusement now. Politicians from every part of the state—old and young, Unionists and secessionists, makers of Kentucky's past and aspirants to its future—clustered in the stately marble building's corridors. All were bent to the sober business of confronting the unknown.

The dispatches in each day's papers heightened John's sense of peril. By the time Magoffin delivered his opening address on the afternoon of January 17, 1861, secession had claimed three more states, with Georgia on the verge. From New Orleans came even more startling news: A day after their annual march in the Eighth of January festivities, the city's main militias had boarded a steamboat at midnight for a secret mission. Under orders from Louisiana's governor, they had traveled one hundred miles up the Mississippi to Baton Rouge, where they had captured a lightly guarded U.S. arsenal. Simultaneous seizures took place at two other federal forts near the Gulf of Mexico. Swift surrenders brought the surprise raids to an end without bloodshed, but there was no stopping the reverberation: Louisiana had committed the South's first hostile acts against U.S. forces.

In Kentucky, John worried about a slow slide toward secession. Over the next few weeks, he stalked the corridors, corralling lawmakers, asking them to stand firm for the Union. The legislature had rebuffed the governor before, and now did so again. No convention. The majority voted for resolutions aimed at reunifying the Union, perhaps by constitutional amendments that would preserve slavery. Meanwhile, Kentucky would remain neutral.

Magoffin bristled. On April 15, 1861, a few days after Southern forces attacked Fort Sumter in South Carolina, Magoffin received a telegram from Lincoln's secretary of war. The new president wanted Kentucky's help in raising 75,000 troops to put down the rebellion. Magoffin telegraphed his indignant reply: "Your dispatch is received. In answer I say emphatically Kentucky will furnish no troops for the wicked purpose of subduing her sister Southern States."

Hemmed in by the legislature's stance of neutrality, Magoffin refused a similar troop request from the new Confederate secretary of war, but in less colorful language and without a public announcement. But remaining neutral did not mean doing nothing. Magoffin sent agents to buy weapons for Kentucky's defense, explaining to the legislature that he saw no choice because Lincoln had amassed a "standing army of gigantic proportions, gathered exclusively from one section, and mad with sectional hate." Subsequent Magoffin proclamations forbid any outside troops from trespassing on Kentucky soil or transporting arms through the state.

John and Kentucky's Unionists dissented. They would not march in step with their elected governor. They would act for the Union.

TRAITOR. THAT WAS THE WORD that John heard from some quarters during the first summer of war. The venom didn't surprise him. He had established himself as one of secession's staunchest foes. His father was now serving in Lincoln's government, as the U.S. district attorney for Kentucky. John himself had acted as a Union lawyer in state court, arguing that Lincoln had a legal right to impose an embargo on goods being shipped through Kentucky to the South. In Louisville, where he and Mallie were now living with their two small children, John had joined a volunteer company of Unionist "Home Guards," known as the Crittenden Union Zouaves, organized to deter the new rebel militias from making mischief. The Zouaves—a word that came from the French, for light infantry—had elected him as captain.

John had moved to Louisville to establish a new law practice, but he had largely put that aside, choosing to spend most of his afternoons on the city's sidewalks, preaching the Union gospel from atop a wooden box. In August, at the invitation of friends at the *Louisville Daily Journal* who were worried about the paper's celebrated editor caving in to secessionist pressure, John spent several weeks ghostwriting pro-Union editorials, often working past midnight. He would say later that his newspaper nights had helped stiffen the backbone of editor George D. Prentice, until Prentice could show his "natural love of the Union and the Union cause."

John saw his Unionism as logical and consistent. How could he run as a Constitutional Union elector, and then stay silent once calamity had arrived? His support for slavery was unwavering, but so was his commitment to preserving the Union. Then, on a warm August night, that commitment took John in a new and dangerous direction: gun running to Unionists who had established a military camp in the Kentucky woods, in defiance of the Magoffin directive.

Years later, John would write that he was following in his father's clandestine footsteps.

THE GUN-RUNNING OPERATION had presidential backing, of the unofficial sort.

From the war's outset, Kentucky had loomed large in Lincoln's thinking. He was determined to keep the border state—and its river ports—out of the still-expanding Confederacy, but he wasn't sure how to achieve that objective. He worried that direct intervention would smack of coercion and occupation, and he did not want to hand the secessionists that sort of political gift. In early May, a possible solution appeared at the White House in the bearded, burly frame of Lieutenant William Nelson, a U.S. naval officer and native Kentuckian. Meeting secretly with Lincoln, Nelson argued that the Kentucky Unionists needed muskets to lend weight to their stand. Otherwise, he said, the secessionists would never take them seriously.

Lincoln liked the idea, if Nelson could arrange for the Kentucky Unionists to "request" the guns that Lincoln would send. Soon, five thousand federal muskets were on their way to the Ohio side of the Kentucky border. It would be Nelson's stealthy mission to find a way to ferry them across the river, and into the right hands.

A few nights later, in James Harlan's Frankfort law office, eight men furtively plotted to deliver the guns. The men all understood the seriousness of what they were contemplating. John's father was particularly vulnerable: As the U.S. district attorney, he was the federal government's chief legal officer in Kentucky. Now he was entangling himself in a conspiracy that any capable state prosecutor could easily say was illegal, a violation of the Magoffin directive and probably a variety of state laws.

At the end of May, with the first shipment of muskets and ammunition safely in the hands of "true & devoted Union men," John's father and ten others sent a report privately to Lincoln. The plan had worked, they told him. Equipping the Unionist Home Guards had "visibly repressed the violence and hectoring dispositions of the secessionists." These shipments of "Lincoln guns," as the rebels contemptuously labeled them, soon became the talk of Kentucky. Everyone could see that the Union Home Guards had new guns. But mystery shrouded the suppliers and supply routes.

John had inside knowledge of the ongoing operation, but no direct involvement—until an alarming message came his way in mid-August. A rebel band, tipped off to a shipment of Union guns, had converged on the Cynthiana railroad depot, intent on intercepting the cargo. The vigilant conductor, alerted to the raid, had managed to thwart the rebels. He stopped the train short of the station. The thirteen cars backed up, out of danger, and returned to Cincinnati. Urgent messages, delivered by Union loyalists, asked plaintively: What do we do now? How do we get the guns from Cincinnati to Kentucky?

Casting aside the last vestiges of his own neutrality, John arranged with Nelson to ship the guns by riverboat to Louisville, under cover of darkness and "marked to my address." At the wharf, sometime between two and three o'clock in the morning, a team of dray wagons stood ready for the crosstown trek to the Louisville-Lexington railroad depot. The sounds of horseshoes and iron wheels echoed in the near-empty streets as John and a Unionist friend, Judge Joshua Bullitt of the Kentucky Court of Appeals, walked alongside the contraband, their hands on their own guns.

They shepherded their covert cargo onto rail cars, and slipped away into the night.

THE UNION CAUSE now consumed John's every waking moment. Mallie hardly saw him. She was pregnant again, but with no time to look for a house, they had been living since the spring in rooms at Louisville's National Hotel, not exactly ideal for a young family with little children, but comfortable enough. Still, it had none of the charms of Harlan's Hill.

Louisville felt the war's proximity. Across the river, on the Indiana shore, a camp of Union forces grew larger by the day, bolstered by Kentucky volunteers. Meanwhile, John's father and other Union loyalists journeyed to Cincinnati for emergency meetings with the generals in charge of the new Department of the Cumberland, responsible for Kentucky and Tennessee. The day after the meetings ended, September 3, Confederate troops seized the Mississippi River town of Columbus in southwestern Kentucky, the first rebel attack in the state. The rebel commander, General Leonidas Polk, had made up his mind to get "ahead of the enemy," he informed Magoffin in a message written two days earlier.

That was all the invitation the Union army needed. On September 6, General Ulysses S. Grant's forces occupied two Kentucky towns on the Ohio River, near its confluence with the Mississippi. The Kentucky legislature, controlled by large Unionist majorities after elections in early August, voted to expel all Confederate regiments from the state. The Department of the Cumberland moved its headquarters to Louisville, filling the streets with Union troops.

John's thoughts turned toward recruiting his own volunteer regiment. He was twenty-eight, with two children and a pregnant wife. The disastrous Union defeat at Bull Run in Virginia had shown that this war was serious business for both sides, with hundreds dead and several thousand wounded. Was John willing to fight, and possibly die, for the cause? Yes, if the cause was restoring the Union and not ending slavery. But recent events had muddied those waters.

On August 31, acting on his own authority, Union general John Fremont had issued an emancipation proclamation for Missouri. It was a daring act, but Fremont was no ordinary general. As the Republican nominee in 1856, he still enjoyed a certain stature in the party, even though he had lost the election. Abolitionists were jubilant at emancipation's first light, but proslavery Unionists were threatening to bolt. One company of Kentucky volunteers had thrown down their guns on hearing that Fremont had signed freedom papers for several Missouri slaves. Lincoln worried that "the very arms we had furnished Kentucky would be turned against us."

Lincoln felt he could not take that risk. As he soon wrote privately to an Illinois senator and old friend: "I think to lose Kentucky is nearly the same as to lose the whole game. Kentucky gone, we cannot hold Missouri, nor, as I think, Maryland. These all against us, and the job on our hands is too large for us." Lincoln was willing to allow his generals to seize a slaveholder's property, including slaves, for a military purpose. But granting permanent freedom was a political act, he told Fremont—to be accomplished by lawmakers, not military officers. He ordered Fremont to modify his proclamation. The Kentucky Unionists breathed a sigh of relief.

The war came to Louisville on the night of September 17. Large numbers of rebels had attacked the Louisville & Nashville rail line at Lebanon Junction, some thirty-five miles south of the city. They had burned a bridge, cut telegraph wires, and seized train cars heading for Louisville. John rushed to Mallie, telling her that he and the Crittenden Zouaves had been summoned. Their mission: reclaim the railway line, and repel any rebels still there. They would leave via train at daybreak. "That night," Mallie wrote later, "was a most horrible one for me."

Several anxious days later, John returned, exultant. He and his Zouaves had figured out how to float five thousand rounds of ammunition to a Union camp on other side of the Green River, using a makeshift barge. This small taste of military life left him more fired up for the Union than ever, but no less conflicted about the risk for his family. Mallie watched him pace until dawn, wrestling with "his duty to his wife and little ones" versus "his duty to his country." Finally, sitting with Mallie on the bed, he asked her to decide: Should he raise a regiment?

They faced each other, anguished husband and frightened wife. In two months, she would give birth to their third child. "I asked him what he would do if he had neither wife or children," she wrote later. "He said at once, with great earnestness, 'I would go to the help of my country.'" Summoning "all the courage I could muster," she told him: "'You must do as you would do if you had neither wife nor children.'"

A week later, John's decision appeared as a public declaration in the *Louisville Journal*. "To the People of Kentucky," his announcement began. "The time, fellow citizens, has come when even the unpatriotic and the selfish should hasten to take up arms for the common defence of State and country. . . . If our enemies triumph, all our trades, all our professions, all our avocations of whatever character, all our possessions of every description, become valueless. To save ourselves and our families from ruin, not less to save our State and our country from degradation and shame, we must rally now where the National flag invites us. Come, then, let us gird up the whole strength of our bodies and souls for the conflict, and may the God of Battles guide home every blow we strike."

JOHN RECRUITED SOLDIERS for his Tenth Kentucky Volunteer Infantry as if he were wooing voters. In early October, he opened his regimental headquarters at a camp in Marion County, some seventy miles southeast of Louisville. From there, he organized picnics, raised money, hired brass bands, and brought in prominent speakers with impressive Unionist credentials. He offered a lieutenancy to any man who could bring in fifteen to twenty recruits, and placed announcements in newspapers to generate excitement. "Grand Gathering in Old Washington!" was the headline for an October 23 event in that county. "The soldiers will be given a sumptuous dinner by the ladies of Washington. . . . Let the young men of Washington meet Col. Harlan, on Wednesday next, and enroll themselves as members of his regiment."

The day of the Washington County event dawned gloomy, but by one o'clock, the sun was bathing the fairgrounds with a brilliant autumn hue. John and hundreds of his uniformed recruits, their muskets glinting in the afternoon light, marched four abreast into the spacious amphitheater. John ascended the speaker's stand, bedecked with blossoms, and looked out on a crowd of several thousand faces. He was taking up arms, he said, to restore the Union. He would not fight a war against slavery, and he prayed that Lincoln did not make it into one.

He was hoping the war would end quickly, but his recruits were signing up for the standard three years. The pay wasn't much and the incentives were meager—a $100 bounty, a pension for those wounded or killed, and the promise of 160 acres of government land after the war—and yet by mid-November, John had filled eight companies with eighty to one hundred soldiers each, and partial rosters for two more. The Louisville newspapers tracked his progress with nearly as much vigor as they had followed his congressional race, with one major difference: The *Democrat* now joined the *Journal* in embracing him. "He is one of the most talented, energetic and thorough-going men in the State—a glorious champion upon the stump and glorious defender in the field," the *Democrat* declared.

Not bad for a newspaper that had disparaged him during his political campaigning.

WITH JOHN GONE, recruiting full-time, Mallie chose to return for a few months to her parents' home in the free state of Indiana. She was now seven months' pregnant, due in late November. She decided to have the baby in Evansville, surrounded by her family. Boarding the steamboat in Louisville, she discovered a floating microcosm of the war's disruptive consequences. A good number on board were Southerners scrambling to get home; they were hoping to find passage on boats heading further south. "A most exciting trip," Mallie wrote.

The passengers, mostly women, traded stories as the boat made stops on both sides of the Ohio River. Mallie recognized two of them from Louisville. They were on their way to see their husbands, both serving in the Confederate Army near Bowling Green. In mid-voyage, a message arrived: Both men had been killed in battle. The political divisions among the passengers were temporarily set aside in an outpouring of sympathy for the grieving women.

A Harlan cousin was on board. She did not greet Mallie warmly. "[Her] welcome to me," Mallie wrote, "was that she felt 'disgraced' that any one of the Harlan name should be 'enrolled in the Yankee Army.'"

ON THE LAST DAY OF 1861, a rainy Tuesday, John and his Tenth Kentucky Regiment celebrated the New Year with a long march in the mud.

After a month of drilling, John and his eight hundred recruits finally had their orders. They would take their muskets, shoulder their haversacks, and join the Second Brigade, attached to General George H. Thomas's First Division of four thousand troops from Kentucky, Ohio, Indiana, and Minnesota regiments. They would trek some sixty or seventy miles south to the Cumberland River, where rebel forces had taken root. As long as the Confederates held that vital waterway, they had a supply route to support their operations in southern Kentucky and Tennessee. The Union generals hadn't quite been able to agree on a strategy, but in late December, they decided they couldn't wait any longer. The rebels would only grow more entrenched. Now was the time to move.

Before the Tenth could fight the rebels, though, they had to fight the elements. In good weather, on the best of roads, the cumbersome cavalcade and its accessories—tents, food, wagons, horses, mules, tools, and artillery—might make the journey in five days. But the weather was dreadful, the roads worse. Rain was their constant companion. They left in the rain, trudged in the rain, pitched tents in the rain, cooked in the rain, ate in the rain, shivered in the rain, slept in the rain, woke up in the rain. The sun appeared just long enough to tease them. Otherwise, it was rain or the threat of rain, often accompanied by a bone-chilling winter wind.

The unwieldy procession snaked its way south, along an elevated turnpike that gave them a breathtaking view of the Green River, but the soldiers were too busy looking at their feet to appreciate the scenery. Days of rain had softened the road's surface to a pulpy mush, and the heavy wagon traffic had left ruts as deep as six to eight inches. The brigade's progress invited comparisons to a line of lumbering tortoises—except that tortoises wouldn't be sinking further in the muck from all that extra weight on their backs.

On the night of January 8, after a torrential downpour so blinding that they fled the road in search of shelter, John made special arrangements with a farmer for use of his barn. Some of his wet and exhausted troops bedded themselves down "on a pile of tobacco stems, sticks and leaves" for a sound and dry sleep, as one wrote to the *Louisville Journal*. His letter applauded "our gallant Col. Harlan," who had done everything he could to provide comfort "to his weary and drenched soldiers."

In private, John wasn't feeling quite so gallant. The dreary journey had altered his mood. His recent letter to Mallie was missing the enthusiasm of October and November. Instead, he dwelled on the uncertainty of life. The letter struck Mallie as very sad. But she knew better than to rely on one letter to gauge her husband's state of mind. A victory would lift his spirits.

It took nine full days for the Tenth to reach the town of Columbia, just forty miles from their starting point. The pretty village looked "forlorn and desolate," one soldier later wrote, with vacant houses serving as hospitals for two hundred men sick with typhoid fever. The rebels awaited, some twenty miles ahead. After several more days of slow progress, the brigade was finally close enough to establish a temporary headquarters and consider a plan of action.

Just before daybreak on Sunday, January 19, the rebels launched a preemptive attack. Afraid of being pinned against the river, the Confederates had marched nine miles in the middle of the night in hopes of surprising General Thomas's forces at a spot called Logan's Crossroads. John and his regiment weren't there; the previous day, they had been sent a dozen miles north to confront a rebel supply train, which had never shown up.

John's soldiers were having their Sunday breakfast when word arrived of the rebel assault. The men of the Tenth grabbed their weapons, leaving everything else behind. John led them on a lightning march to the front, but the fight was over before they could make it. The Confederate forces, beaten back by the combined efforts of four other regiments, had opted for a hasty retreat to their fortifications on the Cumberland. In the fading winter light, John and his men joined the brigade's pursuit. Crossing the now-bloody farmland, they stepped around the dead soldiers, six times as many Confederate as Union. It was an awful sight, hard to describe, harder still to comprehend.

At the same time, John felt "sore and grievously disappointed" that his men had missed a chance to participate in the Union's triumph, the first of the war. Now he asked his superiors to give his regiment a front-line role in the next day's assault on the rebel fortifications. That night, on a hill overlooking their target, John's men lay in silence on the ground, "without fire, tents, overcoats, or blankets, and with nothing to eat except about one-fourth of a cracker to each man." John, who liked to enjoy an occasional cigar, did not light one that night, afraid the glow would be seen.

At dawn, they crept forward, expecting enemy fire. But most of the rebels were gone. They had escaped across the river in the darkness of the previous night. The abandoned camp yielded both treasure and tragedy:

twelve artillery pieces, horses, wagons, documents, a large cache of weapons, and a miserable assortment of rebel soldiers too sick or too wounded to join the retreat.

John surveyed the scene, taking it all in. In a few short months, so much had changed in his life. He had traded his law books for a musket, his snuff-colored cloth coat for a dark-blue officer's uniform. A full beard and mustache now complemented his side whiskers. He had a newborn son, more than two months old, but had yet to hold him in his arms.

The day before, he had walked across a field, once a fertile farm awaiting the warmth of spring, and he had seen more death in a few hours than he had seen in his twenty-eight years of life. In the coming months, he would be responsible for leading eight hundred men into one battle after another, all in the name of a principle, a belief. On the opposing side were soldiers also fighting for a belief, including men John once counted as friends. A few days later, writing his report on the Tenth's negligible role in the victory, he searched for the right words to describe the intensity of his feelings.

"I do not claim any special honor is due my regiment," he wrote. "But I do claim for the officers and soldiers of this regiment that, under circumstances the most discouraging, they made a march (18 miles in six hours) which indicated their willingness, even eagerness, to endure any fatigue or make any sacrifice" to defeat "those wicked and unnatural men who are seeking without just cause to destroy the Union of our fathers."

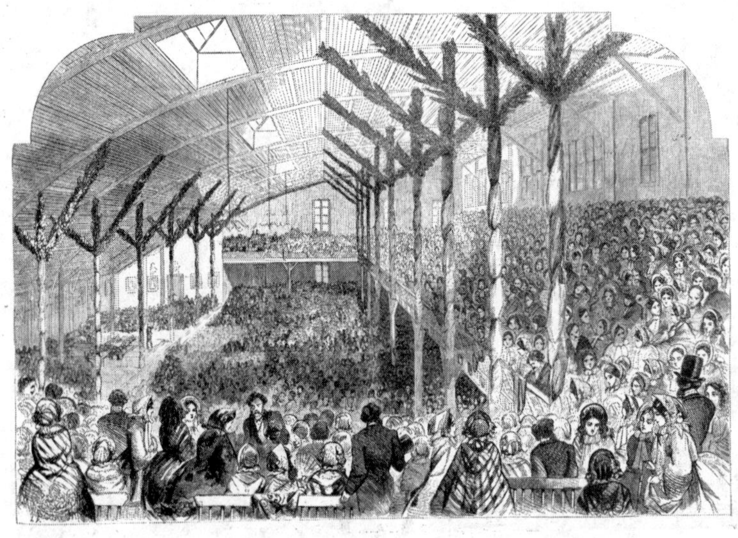

Witness to history: At the Republican National Convention, Chicago, May 1860

(Harper's Weekly, *May 19, 1860)*

7

"A War of Which No Man Can See the End"

Brown in Detroit, 1860–1864

IN THE FIRST FEW HOURS OF 1860, at the start of the year that would lead to war, Henry Billings Brown sat in his dimly lit lodgings at Detroit's Russell House hotel, melancholy and homesick and frightened.

Adjusting the lamp to protect his damaged eyes, Henry reviewed the daily scribbles in his pocket daybook. He was preparing to write his annual year-end summary of highs, lows, and how his life had changed in the previous twelve months. His routine of writing a few sentences a night was ingrained now, as regular as his morning shave. He turned to the daybook's final blank pages. "The last six months of this year have been greatly embittered by the failure of my eyes," he wrote in cramped but legible handwriting. "I have been forced entirely to relinquish reading after sunset and thus am deprived of all opportunity of cultivating literary tastes."

Much had happened during the previous year, both in his personal life and in the country. Yet try as he might, Henry could not keep those events in focus. Everything that had occurred—his switch from Yale Law to Harvard Law, his decision to leave Harvard before earning his degree, his sudden move to Michigan to pursue a legal career, even his hectic social life—seemed peripheral at this moment. They were like distant ships on his port and starboard sides, well within his field of vision, but unimportant compared to the danger straight ahead. He would turn twenty-four in a few months. Was he destined to spend a lifetime of evenings in semidarkness, shielding his eyes, afraid to pick up any of his beloved books? On July 4, after an exhilarating display of fireworks in Boston, he had gushed in his daybook: "Glorious Fourth." The next day, his exuberance had given way to panic: "Eyes feel the worse for the fireworks." Was that his fate? Pleasure followed by pain? The thought was too much to bear.

Since the fireworks, no fewer than a dozen daybook entries had dealt with his eyes. July and August had been dreadful, September not as bad. Miraculously, October had passed with nary an episode. Then, while visiting friends soon after his arrival in Michigan, the scourge returned, with a vengeance. "My eyes beginning to alarm me again, hurt by sitting in a strong light at the Gorhams," he had scrawled on November 28. Two weeks later, he could not read even in daylight. "Eyes broke down again to-day," he mourned. "Began to feel disconsolate and spent most of the afternoon loafing about."

Loafing, Henry knew, wasn't going to help him pass the bar and establish himself as a practicing lawyer. He was supposed to be "reading the law" in preparation, and yet some days, reading was near agony. His infirmity amplified his isolation. He felt torn. He liked Detroit. He even liked his temporary quarters at Russell House—the city's "best hotel," he wrote, as if pinching himself in disbelief. But he longed for New England. His daybook entries offered him a dizzying reminder of Connecticut courtship and camaraderie. Riding with Carrie Champlain. Walking with Louise or Mary Brockway. Taking tea with Louisa Cowles. "Mighty Moses!" he had written on December 19. "How homesick I am."

He had come to Detroit with such high hopes. The river town was booming as a thoroughfare connecting the Great Lakes, a good place to establish himself as a lawyer. But how could he achieve any of his lofty ambitions if he could not rely on his eyes? Closing his daybook on the past year, he inscribed a New Year's wish, not only for 1860, but for the rest of his life: "God grant I may never be blind!"

❖

AS HENRY OFTEN DID in times of turmoil, he fell back on family and friends. Fortunately, he had both in Michigan, all Connecticut transplants. He had traveled west with carpetbags in his hands, a letter of introduction in his pocket, and a hazy plan to find an apprentice-type position in a law office. His first destination would be a familiar and welcoming place: his Uncle Sam Tyler's impressive house, in the flourishing town of Marshall, one hundred miles west of Detroit.

Henry had visited there several times before. After his mother's early death in 1853, Henry had stayed close to her side of the family, particularly her brother Sam, who had migrated to Marshall as a young man, prospering as a farmer and businessman. Henry's grandmother was living with the Tylers, too, yet another Connecticut expatriate. For Henry, Marshall would serve as both comfort and respite, as near as he might come to a home away from home.

Marshall was a small town graced with large aspirations. In Michigan's earliest days as a state, it had been anointed as the capital-in-waiting. The town had even built a modest "governor's house" in anticipation, but political machinations had sent the capital to Lansing. The town's settlers had overcome this setback, largely a tribute to the enterprise of such Marshall luminaries as Charles T. Gorham, a Tyler family friend. When the well-connected Gorham volunteered to shepherd Henry on his visits to Detroit law firms, Henry eagerly accepted.

"Went out with Gorham to seek my fortune," Henry wrote proudly in his daybook.

HENRY WAS FORTUNATE to have acquired such an eminent escort. Gorham, now in his late forties, stood taller than most in Michigan's political circles, especially among Republicans and antislavery advocates. He had a memorably long face, dominated by a high, sloping forehead and a bushy, triangular mustache as robust as his net worth. He had arrived in Marshall during the mid-1830s, when it was a tiny village in a welcoming wilderness. His success as a banker had mirrored Marshall's emergence as the thriving seat of Calhoun County. But it was Gorham's role in the famous Crosswhite fugitive slave case that had altered his political life, thrusting him and his adopted hometown into the heart of the national slavery debate.

At four o'clock in the morning on January 26, 1847, four armed Kentucky slave hunters and a local deputy sheriff broke down the barricaded door of the Crosswhite cottage in Marshall. By dawn on that wintry morning, an opposition throng had surrounded the Crosswhite homestead, freezing the capture in place. By noon, a swelling crowd of one hundred or more was engaged in a spontaneous town meeting with no rules of order.

That slave hunters would be snooping around Marshall was no shock. As a well-known stop on the Underground Railroad, the town had attracted runaway slaves for years. By 1847, the town's eastern edge was home to the "negro settlement," a separate collection of cottages housing about forty free and fugitive people of color, including the Crosswhites, now expanded to a family of seven, headed by Adam and his wife Sarah. The Crosswhite name hinted at Adam's mixed-race heritage, intentionally or not. He was the son of a white master and one of the master's slaves.

Gorham arrived in mid-standoff, with the Crosswhites trapped inside and the Kentuckians stationed at the splintered door, arguing that the 1793 Fugitive Slave law gave them every right to seize the Crosswhites. Along with others, Gorham tried to persuade the slave hunters to abandon their mission. Seeking to show the crowd's unanimity, Gorham put forth a question, asking for a vote: "Resolved, That these Kentucky gentlemen be prevented from taking away the Crosswhite family, by legal, moral, or physical force, and that they leave the State in two hours, or be subject to a prosecution for breach of the peace." A roar of approval left the Kentuckians unmoved. Their leader, Francis Troutman, demanded the names of these interlopers who were blocking their way. "Charles T. Gorham, write it in capital letters," was the banker's reply.

The community's resistance, and its overwhelming numbers, left the Kentuckians with little choice but retreat. By sundown, a lumber wagon was carrying the Crosswhites to a train bound for the Canadian border. The slave hunters were arrested, convicted in an impromptu trial, and ordered to leave town.

The Crosswhite case sent long-lasting ripples through the slavery debate. In Kentucky, it became a synonym for the North's trampling of Southern rights. It helped motivate the Kentucky legislature to enact tougher laws to deter runaways. It helped prompt Henry Clay to push for a stronger Fugitive Slave Act, which passed Congress in 1850. The slave hunters filed a lawsuit for damages against Gorham and another resister in Detroit's federal court, and won.

Meanwhile, in the North, resistance was spreading. Within a few years, the Marshall example was followed by celebrated rescues in Massachusetts, New York, Pennsylvania, and Ohio. In Michigan, Gorham abandoned the Democrats, joining the Republican party after its founding in 1854 and adding his ardent voice to those opposing slavery's expansion.

This was the man who had taken Henry under his wing, who had offered to introduce Henry to Detroit's legal establishment. They left Marshall on the Tuesday afternoon train, arriving in time for what Henry called a "splendid" dinner. By Saturday night, Henry was writing in his daybook, "Engaged to take a seat in Walker & Russell's office," one of Detroit's best.

Henry's family ties had paid dividends, once again.

ON A MISTY AFTERNOON in late February 1860, Henry took a walk to Firemen's Hall, where Michigan's Democrats were holding their state convention. Unlike his mentor Charles Gorham, Henry was still hunting for his place in the swirling political landscape. The Democrats didn't hold much appeal for him—he came from an old-line Whig family, after all—but he thought it might be interesting to hear a speaker or two. He valued that, listening in person.

Where *did* he stand, politically? Somewhere close to the Republicans, he thought. But which Republicans? Not the party's most radical voices, certainly. Their uncompromising rhetoric made him uncomfortable, much as the abolitionists did. During Henry's first month at Harvard, he had hiked into Boston to hear Wendell Phillips once again. Afterward, Henry's dismay had verged on disgust. "Attended a rank antislavery meeting," he wrote. "Absolutely shocked at their blasphemous misanthropic sentiments. Phillips is a dangerous man."

Months later, revisiting his memory of that May evening, Henry found himself separating Phillips's delivery from his ideas. The fiery abolitionist was a gifted storyteller, Henry thought. No question about that. Still unsure of his own oratorical gifts, Henry felt he could learn a trick or two from Phillips without having to adopt the man's radical views.

Henry was drawn to the more temperate voices in the Republican Party. He had plenty of examples close at hand. Four of his professors at Yale, along with the college president and one of his mentors in Ellington, had joined a group of forty-three New Englanders in a sharp letter to President Buchanan, protesting his slavery policy in Kansas. While still at Yale Law, Henry had gone to hear two Republican representatives well known for their strong antislavery views—Joshua Giddings of Ohio and Anson Burlingame of Massachusetts, among others. A "capital stump speech," Henry declared in his daybook after listening to Burlingame's oratory.

Moving to Michigan, he discovered the Republicans in indisputable ascendency. The governor was a Republican, the third in a row. So was Detroit's new mayor, the first Republican to win the city's top office. Just weeks after joining Walker & Russell—a partnership of two Republican lawyers—Henry managed to secure an invitation to a celebratory party at the mayor's house. He might have enjoyed himself more if his eyes weren't failing him again. He brooded later that night: "Find keeping away from books little better than absolute blindness."

When he felt well enough to return to the office, Alfred Russell was waiting with a pleasant surprise. Russell had engineered Henry's appointment as a temporary "commissioner" of Wayne County's circuit court, allowing Henry to take depositions in lawsuits and earn some real money. He would be paid by whichever litigant needed the testimony taken.

"This is the commencement of my professional business," Henry wrote that night.

LUCKILY, HIS EYES cooperated with his new assignment. His first depositions put him on the road for most of April and May, giving him a grand tour of southwestern Michigan's small towns and courthouses. He liked Kalamazoo best ("this really beautiful village," he wrote), but rebelled against its dowdier neighbors ("O! When shall I leave this rotten place!"). In mid-May, after a day of testimony-taking in a place with no charm, impulse seized him.

The Republican National Convention was about to start in Chicago, a few hours away by train. Henry had seen the Michigan Central rail cars steaming by, bedecked in bunting and crammed with delegates. The fare wasn't cheap—two dollars and seventy cents, out of his own pocket—but, well, why not? At four o'clock in the morning on Thursday, May 17, he boarded the train in Niles, arriving early enough to have a decent breakfast before heading to the Wigwam, Chicago's hastily constructed convention hall.

Henry, dazzled by Europe's architectural gems during his year abroad, certainly had never seen anything like the Wigwam. It wasn't historic, it wasn't old, it wasn't attractive, and it wasn't built to last. But Chicago had wanted the convention, and the Wigwam was the city's answer to the Republican party's question: Where will you host it?

Erected in less than two months, the wooden sprawl of a structure was little more than a covered barn for politics. To call the building slapdash would be accurate, but it would miss the point. Spaciousness was its virtue. Five hundred delegates and nearly ten thousand spectators jammed the giant hall for the Thursday session, a remarkable display for a political party only six years old. The hall was loud, chaotic, and, for Henry, unappealing. "Too crowded and got a headache," he grumbled in his daybook. "Took nap in PM."

He spent Friday morning with two friends, enjoying their company more than the convention. Inside the Wigwam, the Republicans marched on. The presumed front-runner, Senator William Seward of New York, fell well short of victory on ballot number one. Second place went to the pride of Illinois, underdog Abraham Lincoln, a surprisingly strong showing in a field populated by a dozen names. On ballot two, Seward lost considerable ground, with Lincoln pulling nearly even. The hometown galleries erupted in noisy approval, while Seward's supporters sagged in disbelief. They could feel the nomination ebbing away.

Henry felt none of this. He was an outsider, a neophyte. He knew nothing about the backroom bartering taking place, how Lincoln's forces were gaining the upper hand. He knew only that if the balloting lingered into Saturday or beyond, history would have to be made without him. He needed to get back to western Michigan, and recoup his two lost days. Fortunately, the convention reached its climatic moment before he had to leave. "Lincoln + Hamlin nominated," he wrote with gusto. "Took cars at 8 PM."

By midnight, he was stepping off the train in Niles. Hours of transcription awaited him. Sunday would be a day of work as well. He had a commission to earn, a deadline to meet. Missing either was unthinkable at this early stage of his shaky legal career.

MOST OTHER SUNDAYS, Henry went to church.

He had no favorite place of worship. Often, he chose the Fort Street Presbyterian Church, where Alfred Russell belonged. Sometimes, though, Henry preferred the First Congregational Unitarian Church, where one Sunday in 1860 he listened to the renowned Ralph Waldo Emerson. He hadn't much cared for Emerson's lecture, declaring it "incomprehensible," but he didn't mind. He went as much for the desire to meet people as he did for the prayers or sermon. Sometimes, in dreary weather or when he felt poorly, he would opt to stay home, but he almost always felt slightly sheepish, like a young boy skipping school. He would make a note in his daybook, his own private confession.

Slowly, Henry was collecting a good list of social and professional contacts, particularly in Detroit's legal community, judges as well as lawyers. Among other notable names, he had forged a friendship with Bela Hubbard, a lawyer who had made a fortune in real estate and lumber. Like Henry, Hubbard was an Easterner who had moved west after college, hired to survey the new state's natural resources. His travels for the government rewarded him with a lifelong love of Michigan's beauty, as well as the profitable understanding that there was money to be made in land and trees. Henry regarded Hubbard, whose Detroit mansion spread over six thousand square feet on vast acreage just north of the city's center, with the wonder and envy of a young lawyer barely able to afford his rent.

Hubbard could open more doors for Henry. But those doors would remain shut if Henry didn't pass the bar. In mid-July, a week before the examination, his anxiety about the exam turned to panic. "Have concluded to go East," he wrote. "I do not feel at home in Detroit." But the exam went well, qualifying him to appear in local courts. Giddy, he rewarded himself, impetuously buying tickets for New England.

He nearly didn't come back. A visit to Providence led to a job offer. Henry was tempted, but local rules required six months of additional study and another bar exam on Rhode Island law. He said no. "Have nearly made up my mind it is my destiny to return to Detroit," he wrote.

Three weeks later, like a soldier summoning courage for a looming battle, Henry reported for duty to a new post, a modest office he had arranged to share with Bela Hubbard. His first forays for clients produced only sporadic success, partly because it's "not in my nature to drum business as most Western lawyers do." By mid-October, he was writing, "Emphatically hard up for cash and creditors pressing." Relief came a week later. His father sent nearly three hundred and fifty dollars, a "long-awaited remittance," enough to pay a few debts and invest in much-needed law books, including a full set of the Michigan Supreme Court's past rulings.

Truth be told, Henry had more reading time than clients. If he was going to succeed in building a local practice, he would need to have a firm grasp of the state's legal precedents. Fortunately, the Michigan Supreme Court's twenty years of published wisdom resided in fewer than a dozen volumes. His eyes weren't rebelling, so he resolved to read through them.

A recently decided case, featuring a dispute between an unhappy steamboat passenger and a stubborn captain, stood out on several counts. Walker & Russell, Henry's former firm, had represented the passenger. The court's ruling was precedent-setting, its first-ever on the legal issues involved. And, the passenger was, as the ruling called him, "a colored man."

Not too many colored men were bringing precedent-setting lawsuits, even in the North. Most didn't have the money. Thirty-year-old William Howard Day didn't have much, but he was willing to make a financial sacrifice "to establish a correct principle," he wrote to an antislavery supporter. He was traveling the same path that David Ruggles had taken in Massachusetts in 1841, asking a court to intervene, to tell the company that it could not create rules based solely on a passenger's color.

The court's unanimous decision in *Day v. Owen* not only made for fascinating reading. It offered a clear glimpse of separation as practiced on Michigan and Ohio steamboats, seventeen years after Ruggles had protested his treatment on the New Bedford and Taunton railroad.

THE FACTS, as laid out in Day's lawsuit, were simple enough.

On October 1, 1855, Day and his wife had boarded the steamer *Arrow* in Detroit. He asked for an indoor cabin for the overnight journey to Toledo. Plenty of cabin space was available, but because Day was a colored man, the steamboat agent said he could only sell them tickets for the cheaper outdoor deck. Now it was Day's turn to object. If they could not have a cabin, they would not ride at all. As Walker & Russell said later, their client "was put to great expense, trouble and delay, and obliged to travel in the night one hundred miles out of his way to reach Toledo." Three weeks later, Day sued the steamboat's captain and owner, John Owen.

Owen was unrepentant in his reply. The *Arrow*, said his lawyer, would not offend its white passengers by sending a colored man into their company. Owen's defense rested on three points. First, the ship was following the routine practice for "common carriers" on the Detroit River. Second, the steamboat's rule was "reasonable," intended to please "the majority" of its customers. Third, it was "well understood" that Day, because of his color, "was excluded from ordinary social and familiar intercourse by the custom of the country."

Routine practice. Company rule. Reasonable. These arguments had been made before, in other courts, in other states, often with success. But "*excluded from ordinary social and familiar intercourse by the custom of the country*"? Not quite. Separation, while a fact of Northern life, was far from universal on common carriers. For example: Did the Michigan judges hear any evidence about the history of passenger trains in Massachusetts, where only three railroad companies had run separate cars and none since 1843? If so, their ruling made no mention of it. Nor did it take note of a recent New York City lawsuit. In that case, the judge had instructed the jury that "colored persons, if sober, well-behaved and free of disease, had the same rights as others" on a common carrier. The jury's verdict: two hundred and fifty dollars in damages for the colored passenger, Elizabeth Jennings.

Also missing from the court's ruling was anything about Day and his background. Day had only two identities in the court's spare narrative: "plaintiff" and "colored man." Yet learning Day's story might have astonished Henry, in part for the many parallels in their lives.

Both had ancestors who had fought in American wars. Both had gone to schools that had emphasized a classical education, giving them comparable foundations in Latin, Greek, mathematics, logic, rhetoric, and literature. Both had college degrees and a fascination with the power of oratory. Both had noteworthy ambitions, but there their goals diverged.

Henry was bent on mastering the law. Day was bent on changing it.

DAY WAS AN ABOLITIONIST in the spirit of his collaborator and sometimes rival, Frederick Douglass, with one important difference: Day had never been a slave.

He had traveled his own unusual path to activism. As a young boy, he sat with his mother at antislavery meetings in New York City, surrounded by talk of fugitive slaves and resistance. At eleven, he so impressed a white visitor to his school that the man asked to become his "guardian." Soon, he was living in Northampton, Massachusetts, with a white abolitionist family whose home served as an Underground Railroad stop for runaways. His "adoptive father," as Day later called him, was a flinty ink manufacturer who encouraged Day's writing but also insisted that his young ward learn the printing trade. Day groused, but the skill repaid him many times over, offsetting expenses during his four years at Oberlin College in Ohio.

Day went to Oberlin for a simple reason: The decade-old school had declared itself open to qualified students of any color, something no other Northern college had done on any regular basis. Whites still predominated, of course. When Day arrived at Oberlin in 1843, he was the only man of color in his entering class of fifty.

Oberlin fueled Day's ambitions. In 1848, only a year after his graduation, he sought and captured a delegate's seat to a National Negro Convention, which was meeting in Cleveland to write a declaration on abolition and equal rights. This gathering of more than a hundred Northern freemen elected Day as secretary, and Douglass as president. Day, Douglass, and three others drafted the convention's final "Address to the Colored People of America."

By the time of the next Negro Convention, five years later in Rochester, New York, Day had added lecturer, political advocate, Underground Railroad operative, and newspaper editor to his list of credentials. After watching Day at the Rochester conclave in 1853, a *New York Daily Tribune* correspondent elevated him to Douglass's level. "There was a young man from Ohio, by the name of Day, a pupil of Oberlin," the correspondent wrote, "whose voice also mingled persuasion with authority, and in music and power was hardly inferior to Douglass."

His successes raised his expectations, only to bring him face-to-face with the harsh realities of life for a free black man in the North. He lost his battle to break the color barrier at the Ohio legislature, which denied him a seat in the press gallery. Then he lost his fledging weekly newspaper, unable to reach a sound financial footing. Disheartened, Day looked to Canada as a cure for his troubles. He was drawn to Chatham, an Ontario haven that runaways had established about forty-five miles east of Detroit.

He and his wife, Lucie, were returning from their initial visit to Chatham when they boarded the *Arrow* that fall afternoon in 1855. Day had endured separation before. Why did he sue this time? Was he fed up after his other defeats? Was this part of a larger mission to confront prejudice whenever it occurred? A reader of the court's ruling would find no answers to those questions. But Day, in asking a wealthy abolitionist for financial help, had hinted at his reason for filing suit.

He was acting, he said, "as much for the colored people generally as for ourselves."

OVER TWO SPRING days in 1858, three of the four judges on the Michigan Supreme Court had heard Day's appeal. Day could not have hoped for a more favorable set of ears. The changing political climate in Michigan had recently created an all-Republican bench. But two months before the arguments in *Day* were heard, Chief Justice Roger Taney and his U.S. Supreme Court majority had unveiled their *Dred Scott* decision. Taney's declarations—that a colored man was not a U.S. citizen and was forever excluded from benefits that whites enjoyed—now loomed like a specter over every legislature and court.

If Michigan's highest court were to rule in Day's favor so soon after *Dred Scott*, its decision would be seen—fairly or not—as Northern defiance by Republican judges. Michigan's legislature had recently declared its disdain for the Fugitive Slave Act, passing a law that banned slave hunters from relying on state jails and requiring jury trials before suspected slaves could be taken south. Would the Michigan Supreme Court now show its displeasure for Taney and *Dred Scott*?

It would not. Without mentioning *Dred Scott*, the judges ruled in favor of both separation and the steamboat owner. It was reasonable, the court ruled, to make the majority happy. It was reasonable to provide cabins "most comfortable and least annoying to passengers generally." The company could not refuse to sell Day a ticket because of his color, the judges said, but it was entitled to make reasonable rules telling passengers where to sit.

For Day, it was hard to feel anything but a new gloom. The newspapers' reaction only made matters worse. In the blunt view of the *Detroit Free Press*, a reliable ally of the Democrats, the Republicans on the Michigan bench had gone a generous step farther than Taney in declaring the superiority of whites. "The Supreme Court of the United States simply passed upon the political status of the negro," the newspaper wrote, while "the Supreme Court of the State of Michigan has passed upon his social status. . . . Both, in our judgment, are eminently right."

BY THE TIME Henry began his study of the court's rulings in the fall of 1860, Day was no longer traveling on Michigan's steamboats. The abolitionist wanted nothing to do with a life in the United States, at least for the moment. He had gone to the British Isles for an extended lecture tour, unsure when he would return, uncertain he wanted to.

Uncertainty described Henry's state of mind as well. Uncertain about his eyes. Uncertain about his ability to make a living at the law. Uncertain about his country's future. There was one certainty, though: The 1860 presidential election would climax on the first Tuesday in November. Political leaders in several Southern states were threatening secession if Lincoln and the Republicans were to win. Were they bluffing? Yet another uncertainty.

For Henry, the thought of having even a tiny role in steering the national ship of state filled him with uncharacteristic excitement. "Election Day!!!" he wrote, adding three more exclamation points than his pen usually produced. He "bolted" to Democrats for a few lesser offices, but otherwise, he went for the Republicans and uncertainty. "Cast my first vote for Abe Lincoln," he wrote after a long night of revelry. "Great Republican triumph."

AS 1861 DAWNED, Henry wrestled with contradictory feelings. A year earlier, he had prayed to God that he might never be blind. Now, writing his annual summary, he thanked "the Lord in his mercy" for a sliver of optimism about his condition. After nine months of being "useless" after sundown, his eyes had recovered enough to read at night, for short stretches, by a coal oil lamp with a porcelain shade—"the only light soft enough for them to endure."

Endurance was an apt word to describe how he felt about the past twelve months. During the year, he had jotted down random, anxious musings about the conundrum of slavery. Those anxieties now permeated his year-end summary. Fond of metaphor, he thought of the mythic story of Diogenes, the philosopher wandering through ancient Greece on a quest to find an honest man, holding a lantern aloft in bright sunlight. "Diogenes searching for a man," Henry wrote. "So we sought for Lincoln." But could any man, even an honest one, bridge the ever-widening divide between North and South? Henry did not see how. South Carolina had already seceded. Other states were beating a similar drum.

"Civil war appears almost inevitable," Henry wrote in the early hours of 1861. "Anything but disunion! God help us!"

HENRY DESPARATELY WANTED the job of deputy U.S. marshal when it came open in the spring of 1861. It was a part-time post, and off the usual career path for an aspiring lawyer, but it promised a reliable stream of income—something that Henry had yet to experience. Deputies received fees for delivering summons and warrants. Equally valuable: The work would bring him into contact with "vessel men of all classes," as he later wrote. The ships on the Detroit River were a big part of the state's economy, and a lawyer well versed in "admiralty law"—the law of the water—had a decent shot at making a good living.

Once again, Henry turned to his friends and family for help. They arranged for Henry's interview with Charles W. Dickey, the new U.S. marshal. Dickey was a Lincoln appointee and a sturdy Republican, but he was also the marshal from Marshall, yet another New Englander who had come to Michigan in the 1830s. He counted two of Marshall's leading citizens, Henry's uncle Sam Tyler and his adviser Charles Gorham, as close friends.

The interview went so well that by the next afternoon, Thursday, April 11, 1861, Henry was moving his few pieces of office furniture into the new federal building. He had no chance to celebrate his new position, though. Sumter was attacked at dawn the next morning.

HEARING THE NEWS of the first Confederate cannonball, Henry's thoughts followed their accustomed pattern, radiating from his vantage point to the rest of the world, and circling back again. That night he wrote: "Tremendous excitement! Affairs come to focus. Attack on Fort Sumpter! War! Called at Miss Reeve's at eve."

The next day, a Sunday bookended by two church visits, his entry was more dramatic but no less pithy. Again, it ended with a reference to the young woman currently drawing his interest. "Fall of Sumpter! Beginning of long war! a war of which no man can see the end. Attended Congregational church in A.M. and Unitarian with Miss Reeve at eve."

Henry's persistent misspelling of Sumter was understandable. Like nearly everyone in Detroit, he didn't have any reason to know much about this tiny military outpost on a spit of land in the sea near Charleston. But the timing of the attack, coming as Henry was taking his oath as a federal officer, made him feel the bombardment's impact in a way that would have been unthinkable a week earlier. He was sworn to uphold the U.S. Constitution, and now the Constitution was under assault.

A few days later, when Lincoln called on each state to provide its quota of volunteers to bring the rebellious South to heel, Henry did not rush to sign up. After a sputtering sixteen months in Detroit, now was not an opportune time for a career detour. He was serving the Union cause in his marshal's job, and that was something, wasn't it? He was also pursuing another part-time government post, as a lawyer in the U.S. District Attorney's office. Word floated back to him that this second appointment would be his, too. Henry exulted like a man at his wedding. "Oh! Lord!" he wrote. "Ain't it good."

Later that week, the Union asked for a public pledge of loyalty from its employees. Henry gave it, with gusto. "Oath of allegiance taken by all Federal officers in front of Post Office this noon," he wrote after the mass ceremony on Saturday, April 20. "Theater girls sang 'Star Spangled Banner.' Whooray!"

A mile away, the new soldiers of Michigan's First Regiment Volunteer Infantry were organizing themselves at the military camp known as Fort Wayne, wondering where they would go. Kentucky? Virginia? Three long weeks later, their orders came through. On May 13, eight hundred men boarded trains for Washington, destined for the Virginia battlefields. If all went well, they were told, they would be home by August, and the South would be back in the Union.

Henry wished them Godspeed.

ALL DID NOT GO WELL. The Union Army's unsettling defeat at Bull Run foreclosed any thought of a quick war. Henry signed up with a local militia, the Holt Guards. Drilling with the company "from time to time" gave him as much of a taste of military life as he desired for now. At year's end, a sense of foreboding colored Henry's otherwise elated summary of 1861.

On the personal side, he gave himself high marks on nearly every front. His government jobs had allowed him to meet some of the "leading men in the state." His health was "superb," and he was making some money, finally. At the age of twenty-five, his only lack of progress had come in his search for a suitable mate. "I haven't found the right one yet," he lamented.

The war, however, brought only apprehension. He foresaw "immense injury" to both sides, no matter the outcome. "As I see its inevitable consequences in the loss of life and property, in the vast issues of paper money and consequent high prices and depreciation of the currency and in the breaking up of the whole social system, it absolutely makes me shudder." He wrote nothing about his own participation in this conflict in which he could see no possible end.

A few weeks later, serendipity forced him off the sidelines and into a public discussion of the war's most divisive issue. Henry had joined the Detroit Young Men's Society, partly to practice his debating skills, and on a frigid Monday night in mid-January, his turn came around. The evening's question: emancipation.

"Was obliged to advocate it," Henry wrote in his daybook. "Oh!"

HENRY STILL DREAMED of becoming a great orator. In late May 1862, he argued his first case before the Michigan Supreme Court. He felt he had done well. The next day, he learned that the judges had ruled against him. "Verily there is little certainty in the law," he griped.

Fortunately, he was too busy to wallow in his loss. In the spring of 1862, Lincoln had appointed Alfred Russell as the new U.S. district attorney. Henry was glad to have his old mentor as his new boss, but Russell was soon traveling a lot, leaving Henry to oversee grand jury sessions and prepare most of the indictments. He was grateful for the experience, but exhausted by the rising number of criminal cases—smuggling, in particular—that the war was generating.

Government business sent Henry into Union-occupied war zones twice, in August 1862 and May 1863. Traveling as a federal official, his hosts came from the officer ranks. He stayed with a colonel, dined with a major, took tea with a major general. Neither visit lasted more than a week, and he spent a good portion of time on trains and steamboats. But each provided him a glimpse of conditions he could only read about in Detroit. He came back from his first trip, to Washington and northern Virginia, with the disconcerting feeling that war had become the country's only profession. "Civil life is getting stale," he wrote. "Shall I go into the army?"

Instead, he threw himself deeper into Republican politics. "Delegate to county convention. President of meeting & Chairman Ward committee!!!" he gushed in his daybook. He could summon no such enthusiasm, however, for Lincoln's handling of the war. "President weak, cabinet divided and paralyzed," he wrote as 1862 ended. "Generals incompetent, armies defeated. We are ripe for some great change. Pray God it may result in our permanent good."

The steamer that took Henry to Memphis a few months later turned into a leisurely trip through Union-held territory. He passed many hours with two "local girls" he met on board, playing game after game of euchre. Arriving near midnight, he opted to sleep on the ship before venturing into the heavily fortified city.

Union forces had captured Memphis a year earlier. The occupation had transformed the city, making it a magnet for both runaways and freed slaves. Strangers needed official passes, proving their identity and loyalty. Henry brought his passes home, tucking them away for safekeeping, souvenirs of the war he was seeing mostly from afar.

BY SPRING 1863, volunteers weren't plentiful enough to replace the Union's fallen, or its many thousands of deserters. Desperate for fresh troops, Lincoln and the Congress reluctantly approved a general draft—much wider than the first one in 1862, which had been limited to militia members. As before, a draft would take place only in districts that had failed to meet their quota. But this time, the draft pool would include all able-bodied male "citizens" between twenty and forty-five. That put Henry—twenty-seven, in good health, his eye inflammation nowhere to be seen—in the line of fire.

If a draft reached Henry's district, he would have three choices if his name was pulled: don a uniform, pay the government three hundred dollars for an exemption, or hire a substitute. Henry wasn't sure what he would do. The army did not appeal to him, but what did that matter?

Luck helped him out. His name wasn't among those summoned. He was grateful, but under no illusions. Another draft was coming, he was sure. "The beginning of the New Year finds me a perfectly healthy man and not exempt from the draft," he wrote in his year-end summary for 1863.

The draft had proved even more unpopular than Lincoln had anticipated. Making military service into a matter of money—those who had it, those who didn't—had undermined Northern support for the war. So had limiting the draft pool to "citizens of the United States." Under Taney's definition of citizenship in *Dred Scott*, that meant only white men were eligible. Riots in New York, featuring angry white draftees who could not afford to buy their way out and who resented that free colored men were not being drafted, caused Congress to amend the law for 1864. Colored men became eligible. The $300 exemption vanished. For any future draftees, the only options would be service or substitute.

Henry had plans for the summer of 1864, and going to war did not figure in any of them. Marriage did. After a steady and romantic courtship—long walks, dances, tea parties, and card games—he had proposed to a "lovely damsel." Her name was Caroline Pitts, the daughter of a local lumber baron. She was twenty years old, considerably younger (by seven years). "I see in her now almost all that I could hope for or desire in a wife," he wrote.

They married on July 13, 1864. Family and friends surrounded them—a Marshall delegation, Carry's brother and three sisters, her father's business associates, judges and lawyers—plus an array of gifts like none Henry had ever seen. They danced until 2 o'clock in the morning. At dawn, as twenty-two thousand Union and Confederate troops prepared for a pivotal confrontation in Mississippi, Henry and Carry left for a month-long honeymoon in Quebec and New England. The war felt far away.

They returned on August 19 to find the war at their doorstep. Lincoln's July 18 order for five hundred thousand more troops had revived talk of a draft. Henry's Second Ward was still twenty-six men short of its quota, by one estimate. Henry was one of three hundred or so on the eligibility list. Not terrible odds, if a draft were to take place. Should he just wait, and hope that the quota was met without a draft? But the newspapers were saying that few were volunteering, that substitutes were becoming more expensive and harder to find. On the morning after Henry's return, the *Free Press* declared that a draft looked unavoidable. "It is idle to act on any other supposition," an editorial warned.

Henry was anything but idle. "Did up some hard thinking about this confounded draft," he wrote. "Busied myself in a calculation of chances." After a long walk with Carry, he decided to act. "Concluded to get a substitute if it be done for $800. Felt uneasy all day."

Having made up his mind, Henry had no time to waste. Other eligible men were taking the same route, putting them all in competition, driving substitute prices ever higher. "Tried to get substitute but failed," he wrote twenty-four hours later. "Getting anxious about it."

The next day was Thursday, August 25. Henry awoke with a firm determination to put the matter to rest. That night, agitated but relieved, he wrote: "Thoroughly disgusted with this substitute business and with the faithlessness of the brokers . . . devoted the whole afternoon, finally getting an excellent sub for $850 . . . John Peterson by name. Enlisted him."

A Certificate of Discharge now safely in hand, confirming that he had hired a substitute, Henry's war was officially over.

War trio: Albion Tourgee, left, and fellow lieutenants of Ohio's 105th Infantry, Tennessee, July 1863

(Chautauqua County Historical Society)

8

"For This I Am Willing to Die"

Tourgee on the March, 1861–1863

On the sunlit Sunday morning of April 21, 1861, Albion Tourgee and some of his University of Rochester classmates trooped to the First Baptist Church for a sermon unlike any they had heard before.

The bombardment and surrender at Sumter, now a week past, was as fresh in their minds as the spring breeze that gently blew in their faces as they walked to the elegant stone sanctuary on North Fitzhugh Street. In the days since Lincoln's public plea for seventy-five thousand volunteers to put down the nascent rebellion, Albion had felt something new in the air. One Rochester newspaper called it "indignation." Another offered "war fervor." Albion, who loved to play the contrarian, could not quarrel with their descriptions. The city felt transformed.

News from Washington and Albany, where the governor and state legislature were drafting rules for enlistment, could not travel fast enough to satisfy the city's appetite. Day and evening, impatient throngs gathered in front of the post office and the city's three dailies, hungry for the latest dispatch. They gobbled up rumor as well as fact. Plenty of both were being served. "One telegram falsifies another so that one hardly knows what to believe," Albion wrote to Emma, now a student at the Gainesville Female Seminary, fifty miles south of Rochester.

Politics had never captivated him. That was Emma's terrain, as he had often teased her. In early 1860, with talk of an irrevocable split over slavery now a staple in the press, he had told her, almost boasting: "I don't look into a newspaper once a month hardly, and when I do, I don't read the Political news." But now, like Rochester itself, he was a young man possessed. "I can't write or think of anything else," he confessed to her on the night of Sumter's surrender.

He had always thought if he craved anything in life, it was solitude and reflection. He dreamed of "a country mansion, among the mountains or by the sea," where he could "live & love & write & study without ever thinking of what the world calls Society." But he did not want society to think him an unmanly coward, so he was already grappling with unfamiliar feelings as he settled into his pew at the First Baptist Church on that April Sunday morning.

In the pulpit stood the university president, as tall and formidable as ever. At six feet three inches, the Reverend Dr. Martin B. Anderson towered over most of his students, including Albion, six inches shorter and thin as a sapling. But Anderson's height was just one small part of his forceful persona. This native of Maine knew his own mind. When he spoke, he expected others would listen. Albion was listening now. He could not quite believe what he was hearing.

Anderson sounded like Lincoln's chief recruitment officer, not like the college professor who had chosen restraint and caution as his personal catechism. What was Anderson saying? Go to war for honor and flag? Avenge the blood that the South had drawn? Those were the words that had appeared in the newspaper after Anderson's rousing speech at a raucous City Hall rally a few days earlier, and those were the sentiments he repeated now.

Albion was bewildered. What had happened to the President Anderson who, seven months earlier, had threatened to arrest him and several friends for daring to start a chapter of the antislavery "Wide Awake" movement? Who had reacted with thunderous outrage at the very idea of associating the university's good name with the Wide Awakes, whose tactics amounted to nothing more radical than marching with lighted torches in a symbolic show of support for abolition? For Albion, it had been mostly a lark. But Anderson had been hopping mad, only easing off when the group agreed not to call itself "the University of Rochester Wide-Awakes."

While moved by Anderson's exhortation to sign up for war, Albion left the church more confused than emboldened. He, too, felt patriotism's pull, but he did not join the stampede to the recruiting stations. His hesitation revolved around Emma, and his duty to her. If he offered himself as a soldier, he might deprive her of a husband. Or perhaps worse, he might return with a crippling injury, a burden rather than a lover. He was not quite twenty-three years old, and she was only twenty, but their youth offered no protection from war's grim realities.

"I am glad you are not my wife," he told her, "for my perplexities would be terribly increased."

AFTER ANDERSON'S SPEECH, Albion wandered the city for hours, observing, thinking hard about what he wanted to do, what the war meant for him. He had been feeling nomadic for months, his life slipping from order to turmoil. In December 1860, he had run out of money—his inheritance was still in limbo, much to his smoldering and unending fury—and he had left the university abruptly at the end of the fall term. He had hidden his departure from Emma, only telling her after taking a teaching job at the Wilson Collegiate Institute, a tiny academy seventy miles north of Rochester, on the lonely shores of Lake Ontario.

The episode was deeply humiliating for him. His carefully laid plans for college and marriage had not included this "experiment in real life." "The fact is," he told Emma after a few weeks at Wilson, "that no one knows why I left the University and came here. I have told my friends, some one thing and some other, all partial truths, and each one thinks he or she knows the reason, but they do not. I am stubborn about it. I do not want to tell. . . . I can't help it."

He was still hoping to earn enough in Wilson to return for the university's third term, beginning April 18. But it looked hopeless. Even if he could scrape together the cash for the rest of the year, he would have nowhere near enough to sustain himself through graduation. In late February, writing to Emma by a "good, warm bright fire" in his lodgings at the academy, he seemed stymied. His primary ambition—"that restless indefinable yearning," he told her—was brash in its simplicity: "I long to write, to speak so that the world shall hear me."

Since coming to Wilson, his weekly letters to Emma had focused almost entirely on himself. Even as seven Southern states bid goodbye to the Union, he took no notice. Only Lincoln's inauguration in early March had brought him to the surface of the world beyond the confines of snow-encased Wilson. "I am seriously afraid that this will be the last inauguration of a president of the U.S.," he wrote Emma on March 3, the night before Lincoln's swearing-in. "I should not indeed be surprised if one month from this should find us in the midst of a long and bloody revolution. . . . I believe that a monarchy of limited powers, will be erected on the ruins of this Republic." For good measure, he underlined "erected on the ruins" and "monarchy" twice.

A month later, with the academy on spring break and no revolution in sight, he headed for Rochester. He wasn't sure where else to go. The university seemed more like home than Ohio. His fraternity brothers, Seneca Coon and Joe Webster and Russ Tuttle, were all there, and he could think about his next step. The academy had invited him back for another year of teaching, but he was clinging to the possibility of working out something with the university so that he could return for the semester.

And then, while he was in Rochester . . . Sumter.

ALBION HAD ALWAYS equated Sunday's familiar sounds—the tolling from belfries, the greetings called out to passing churchgoers—with serenity. But Sumter had shattered that tranquility. "The terrors which have agitated every mind for the last few weeks could not be lulled to rest by the ringing of church bells," he wrote to Emma on the morning after Anderson's call to arms. "Recruiting offices were open, troops were drilling, everybody was in a fever."

Restless, he stayed awake long past midnight, fretting, arguing with himself. In the night sky, a waning moon cast scant illumination. He turned, finally, to Emma, composing a letter to her as if she were in his room, as if she could counsel him on what to do. Before Sumter had made war into a reality, she had told him: "I have no objection my Dear to your going to fight, if it be necessary . . . if it ever is, I'll say go—with great fortitude."

What about now? Had it become necessary to enlist? "I came as near doing it yesterday as I could and not commit the act," he wrote. "I have resisted temptation and hope to do so for some time." He dozed for a while, and when he woke, he finished the letter with a "story" about a "man" who was ill with an extreme case of "war fever."

He narrated this "story" with an aspiring novelist's flair. The "man," after promising to join the militia, asked for twelve hours' grace to think over his decision. Falling into a deep sleep, the man dreamed of entering a "sacred" chamber, where he discovered a maiden-angel, who "welcomed the caresses of his hands and lips." This passionate encounter left the man with agonizing doubts. "He rose from the bed, sank upon his knees beside it, feeling that until his country called still more loudly for his services on the battlefield, he could not go—he had still dearer duties to perform."

Having described his anguished choice in this roundabout way, Albion closed his letter with a blunt question to Emma, his real-life maiden-angel. "Tell me now what you think of the dream," he implored. Posting the letter that Monday afternoon, April 22, he was aware that he could not possibly receive her reply before Thursday.

Even as he sent it, though, he could feel his war fever rising.

FIFTY MILES AWAY, in the sheltered quiet of the Gainesville Female Seminary, Emma awaited Albion's letters with heightened anticipation. Gainesville was but a speck on the map, minuscule compared to Rochester, but the war had left the tiny hamlet in a tizzy. What must the commotion be like in a city of nearly fifty thousand? She longed to hear more. But she would have to be patient. She was at the mercy of the mails, two days from Rochester at best, often three. Gainesville had its charms, but it was not a place where anything moved quickly.

Emma had come to Gainesville in the fall of 1860 to fully immerse herself in her studies of music, mathematics, literature, and history. She was enjoying herself, even putting on a little weight—127½, "most ever," she had gaily informed Albion. Still, she missed him terribly. She felt no embarrassment in saying so in her weekly correspondence, often accompanied by vivid references to their history of stolen kisses and intimate embraces. To her delight, Albion liked to engage in literary lovemaking as much as she did. He rarely closed a letter without one variation or another of the "throbbings" of his "loving heart."

She didn't even mind his flirtations with an ever-expanding stable of female friends, which he made no effort to hide. She knew all about his close friendship with Lizzie Everitt, a Wilson student, and even told him that she approved. She assured herself that her relationship with Albion was an unusually candid one, anchored in trust. She demonstrated that belief by sharing his letters with her two dearest friends in Gainesville—Nellie, another student, and her older sister Angie, a teacher at the seminary.

Early in their courtship, wary of being hurt, she had hidden her innermost feelings. But valuing honesty, she had gradually revealed herself. That meant telling Albion things that she feared might drive him away. She wanted to have children—*his* children—but she did not see pregnancy as a profession or calling. After her mother had broken years of silence by tearfully confiding her profound unhappiness in bearing seven children, mostly at her father's insistence, Emma had poured out the entire sad story into a long, emotional letter to Albion. "Oh, Albion, Albion," Emma had written in that 1859 letter. "Yesterday, she wept as she had not done in years. . . . I have wept with her this morning until my eyes are so weak I can hardly see."

When his reply arrived from Rochester, she read each word with a kind of escalating wonderment. "You wish me to tell you what I think," he wrote, as if he were a judge about to render a difficult verdict. "It is a matter, Emma, in which it is very difficult to decide." He had plunged ahead anyway, his confident tone displaying all the authority of his youth. He understood the problem *exactly*, he said.

Underlining his phrases with abandon, he found fault on both sides of her parents' marriage. "Very few mothers in our land take a sensible view of the wants of their children," he declared, "and their fathers are generally engaged in too much of something else to care much about them." Emma needed no reminder that Albion had family scars of his own—that he was still grieving his mother's long-ago death, that he was barely on speaking terms with his father. How much of the letter reflected these wounds? She did not know, of course. But there was no doubting the intensity of his feelings about married life. "Many men consider their wives only as instruments for legally indulging their gross and sensual passions," he wrote. "This is"—and here he paused to underline every word—"wrong, vile, inhuman."

She read with swelling excitement that he envisioned a marriage unlike her parents. "You are never to wear out your life in caring for my children," he instructed. "I do not believe God designed, and created woman, merely for child bearing." He put a pair of underlines under "child bearing," although Emma hardly needed such emphasis to appreciate his vehemence.

But that was Albion, orating as much as writing.

EMMA FOUND IT CURIOUS that Albion, so ready with his opinions, had not displayed a more forceful interest in the country's political troubles. Antislavery sentiments ran deep in the towns of the Western Reserve, and those sentiments had reached Emma, but scarcely seemed to touch Albion. He had never once commented in his letters on the Oberlin slave rescue trial, yet the celebrated episode had put northeastern Ohio in the national spotlight during 1858 and 1859. The Oberlin case was reminiscent of the Crosswhite standoff in Marshall, Michigan, a decade earlier. Once again, a band of Kentucky slave hunters found themselves locked in a volatile confrontation with a crowd of defiant white and black Northerners. The Buchanan government in Washington decided to make an example of the rescuers, leading to three dozen federal indictments under the 1850 Fugitive Slave Act, the administration's broadest attempt yet to show its respect for slaveholders. Only two of the cases ever went to trial. But the legal battle had played out many months in a Cleveland courtroom, while the rescuers chose to remain in the county jail as a show of unity. Rallies sprang up across the Reserve; thirty-five train cars brought protesters from all over Ohio to the courthouse for a day of parades and speeches. One banner recalled an earlier resistance movement from the country's revolutionary days:

SONS OF LIBERTY:
1775, Down with the Stamp Act!
1859, Down with the Fugitive Slave Act!

Except for Albion's twenty-first birthday poem—with its mocking reference to the "courtesy" of being white, written during the same month as the Oberlin rescue rallies—he seemed content to remain above the political fray. Not even Emma's evolving interest in the antislavery cause drew him in. In January 1860, she had told him about her enthusiasm for "the Helper book," a bestselling antislavery broadside. Hinton Helper, an obscure North Carolinian turned abolitionist darling, had published the book to yawns in 1857. Two years later, Helper took his densely written tome to prominent Republicans in New York. They seized on it—slavery exposed by a Southerner!—and, after forming a committee to raise money, had disseminated the book throughout the North. Emma, at the urging of her uncle, had been reading the book aloud to the family. "You can't imagine what a rank little Republican I am," she told Albion. "I enjoyed reading 'Helper' quite as well as they did listening to me."

Albion's response? To tease her, with unrelenting glee. Calling her a "petticoated Black Republican," he asked: How far did she plan to go? Would she require him to "vote for all Republican candidates and none others . . . before you permit [me] to call you wife?" Would she be praying to give birth to a dozen boys so that she could say, in her old age, that she had "added twelve voters to the strength of the Republican party"? He did not need to say, of course, that they would need to be boys to vote, as girls had no such right in Ohio or any of the other states. And what did she intend to do about the "crying sin of Negro Slavery?" Would she refuse, in protest, to wear any cotton in any form?

Then, he dismissed the entire subject with a haughty declaration. "I verily believe the Union might be dissolved and the whole Creation go to Smash without my knowing anything about it unless some fierce Southern fire-eaters should see fit to honor me with a rope."

THAT WAS THE ALBION she knew, insouciant to a fault, holding himself apart on political matters. This was not the Albion who wrote the pages she held in her hands on Wednesday afternoon, April 24, 1861. The more Emma read, the more foreboding she felt.

This letter, dated Monday, radiated his anxiety in every paragraph. First, his torment over whether to enlist. Then, his strange "story" about the man dreaming of a "sacred chamber" and a "maiden angel," followed by his plaintive plea—"Tell me what you think of my dream, Love." But most of all, his blunt statement about enlisting: "I do not wish to go unless it absolutely necessary."

With dread, she reviewed in her mind the letter she had put in the mail two days earlier, the one Albion might be reading at this very moment. Her words haunted her now. Some of her classmates, she had written, were crying at the prospect of "fathers, brothers, or lovers" going off to fight and perhaps die. Not her. She *expected* her brave lover to go, "if he is allowed to do as he wished." The other girls had thought her "destitute of feeling" because she was so calm about the prospect of Albion becoming a soldier, of putting his life in danger.

She was not calm now. She was frantic. She was horrified. She had to correct any misunderstanding, right away. She had to tell Albion that she had been responding to his previous letter, the one brimming with wide-eyed excitement. "Will my cold heartless letter send you away?" she began, writing in such haste that she put the wrong date at the top, 1860 rather than 1861. "Oh! Albion, I did not mean what I wrote, if I wrote anything I cannot say really whether I did or not." Of course, she would *never* try to stop him from enlisting, but "I would not, would not send you away by my seeming indifference." She begged for clemency. "Can I ever do right, can I ever be worthy of Albion's love?"

Conveying her urgency, she noted the time, "4 p.m.," and said: "I bid this messenger go to you on the wings of the wind, yet something whispers 'too late, too late Emma.'"

IN ROCHESTER, ALBION rose on Tuesday morning, his war fever raging. He had not yet received Emma's letter of Sunday, the one she would soon retract as "cold" and "heartless." Her words were not reverberating in his ears.

In the wee hours of the previous night, he had desperately wanted Emma's advice. Now, he vaulted into action without knowing her thoughts. He hurriedly scrawled a note, his words larger than usual, as if to match the magnitude of the decision itself. "Emma . . . I can stand it no longer. I have had a call to fight, and woe is me if I do not obey it." A few hours later, he returned to his writing desk to add: "Afternoon. It is done, Dearest."

Like a telegraph operator tapping out a fresh dispatch, he rushed through the details. He and Joe Webster had joined a militia group offering itself for cavalry service. If all went as they hoped, "our company will be one hundred strong and when well mounted will be splendid looking fellows."

His concluding thoughts ran toward the cataclysmic, just as they had before Lincoln's inauguration. "There are many, very many chances against my ever meeting you again, but Emma, you will still have the consolation of knowing that I did not shrink to give my life even for my country, when duty called. I may never have children who shall share the liberty for which I expect to struggle. If this should be my fate I know that those who love me will inscribe upon my memory . . . that sweet line of the old poet—'*Dulce et decorum est pro patria mori.*'"

He offered his own translation of Horace's words from ancient Rome, "It is a sweet and noble thing to die for one's fatherland."

ALBION'S LETTER SPED to Gainesville faster than he or Emma thought possible. He had written it Tuesday. It landed Wednesday night, just hours after she had sent off her "4 p.m." note. Now she knew, finally, that her letter had *not* caused him to enlist. She went to bed, trying to sort out her feelings. She did not sleep long.

At five o'clock, the sun just beginning to stir, she threw a shawl over her shoulders and thought about how to begin this most important letter. She had not cried yet, and she would not cry now. Her beloved Albion needed her strength, not her tears. "My Albion," she wrote. "Go, go and Heaven bless my soldier love, and keep him safe from harm and danger." She urged him to think only of his duty to his country, not to her. His struggle was over, and "patriotism was victor." She would much prefer to hear "that my Love fell on the battlefield than that he fled from danger."

As for her, she would pray to God "to make me worthy of a soldier's bride."

COMMITTING TO THE WAR, Albion soon discovered, was easier than accepting a soldier's destiny. His disappointments soon stacked up like the boxes of muskets being shipped by train from the state arsenal. No cavalry companies had been accepted among New York's first thirty-eight regiments, thwarting Albion's first hope. No officer's commission had come his way, leaving him with a lowly sergeant's position. And most distressing of all: no time to grant Emma's fervent wish to marry before his departure for the hastily organized training camp in Elmira, where his Company E of eighty volunteers was to take its place in New York's Twenty-Seventh Regiment.

He was still stewing about the unfairness of it all three weeks later. It was a Sunday, but he had chosen to stay in camp. So many recruits had descended on the town that the churches were overwhelmed. Nine thousand would-be soldiers, the newspapers said, with more on the way. Rather than displace more local worshippers, he and others in Company E had chosen other ways to spend the Sabbath, reading and writing letters, or walking the luxuriant hillsides overlooking Elmira. The spectacular view and idyllic weather, punctuated by the gently flowing waters of the Chemung River below, allowed Albion to forget his maddening situation for a few hours. But he could not keep his ire from creeping into his letters to Emma.

Nothing was going according to plan, he told her—at least, not according to *his* plan. He had the intelligence and background to merit an officer's position, but others were standing in his way. With Company E's leadership ranks filled, he had shifted his focus to obtaining a regimental staff job. When he failed, he took it personally, "for it had been promised me in the most unequivocal terms, by officers very high in the regiment," he wrote. "Through the meanness of the major, I lost it."

He was lucky to be in the regiment at all, he knew. He had kept his blind eye a secret, certain that if anyone knew of his childhood accident, his soldiering days would be over before they had begun. He had made it past the health inspection, only to injure his back in a fall during his early days in camp. The pain and soreness had lingered—he was "half-disabled," he informed Emma. Not that the training was all that arduous anyway. The regiment's commanding officer was a West Point graduate, but most of the Twenty-Seventh's leadership was young and inexperienced. They had no more clue about preparing for war than he did.

Alternating between grand passion and general disgust, he had thought more than once about quitting the regiment, which was now under federal command. He clung to the idea that, until the official mustering-in ceremony, he still had a choice about his two-year enlistment. Even if he quit before the muster—assuming that was even possible—he was determined to have a war experience of some kind, perhaps as a correspondent for a newspaper. "I believe it would be a good thing for me, even in a literary point of view, to go & see & feel the realities of the campaign," he told Emma.

As June marched into July, the regiment learned that it would soon be leaving for a confrontation with the rebels in Northern Virginia. Emma was going in the other direction, home to Ohio, after graduation exercises in Gainesville. Albion had arranged for the *Rochester Union and Advertiser* to be mailed to her family in Conneaut. The newspaper had agreed to publish his correspondence, and he was hoping to send as many as two articles a week, he told her. He suggested she keep a scrapbook of his war letters. He wanted to be able to reread them later.

On June 28, a sunny Thursday, Albion left Elmira for a three-day furlough. He wanted to "say goodbye to civilization." He went to Rochester, then north to Wilson, where his visit with Lizzie Everitt churned up a sea of rumors. The town's gossipers were sure that he had come to make Lizzie a war bride. "We had a good laugh over it, I assure you," he crowed to Emma on his return to camp. A few days later, the regiment's swearing-in finally took place. Seven men refused to take the oath, and were sent home. Albion chose not to join them. He was going to war, after all.

At the very moment the Twenty-Seventh was boarding a train for Washington, the rebellion was casting its long shadow on the University of Rochester's commencement ceremony. Tribute was paid to the students already serving freedom's cause, Albion among them. President Anderson's oration was another passionate call to arms.

"Patriotism is a Christian duty," Anderson declared. The Union must be preserved even though it might require "the sacrifice of a whole generation on the bloody altar of war."

THE TERRIBLE NEWS from Bull Run seeped into Conneaut on Monday night, July 22, 1861, leaving "gloom and sorrow everywhere," in Emma's words. She seized the *Union and Advertiser* as soon as it arrived at her family's farm. She absorbed the descending mountain of headlines, each more disquieting than the last: "A REPULSE!", then "Our Troops Retreating on Washington!" and most alarmingly of all, "TERRIBLE SLAUGHTER!"

Like most Northerners, Emma was staggered by the loss. What had gone wrong? Weren't the Union troops supposed to slice through the Confederate forces and drive on to Richmond, where they would deliver a devastating, perhaps fatal blow to the rebellion? The telegraphs were laboring into the night, but they couldn't bring her the news she most desperately wanted. What about Albion? Was he safe? Wounded? Captured? How could she find out? When?

In despair, she had stumbled outside, into the balmy night air. She wanted to be alone, to stand by the gate where she and Albion had spent so many memorable evenings together. The moonlight, piercing through the trees, lit the way. All seemed so calm, so peaceful. From Lake Erie, a light breeze was blowing. But all she could think about was Albion and the carnage in Northern Virginia.

Over the next few days, as the war correspondents tried to explain how the Union had converted a possible victory into a demoralizing defeat,

Emma scoured the papers for any news of the Twenty-Seventh Regiment, trembling each time she spotted a mention. The published casualty lists were the most maddening of all. They were haphazard, incomplete, and sometimes plain wrong. The Twenty-Seventh's commander, Colonel Henry W. Slocum, dead. Then, the next day, he was "lightly wounded." Emma did not know what to believe. But with each passing day, with each hunt through the many columns without seeing Albion's name among those killed or wounded, she allowed her spirits to soar. He was alive. She was sure of it.

ALBION HAD TROUBLE sitting up in his makeshift bed to write the letter. The hasty retreat from Bull Run had been exhausting enough, miles without pause, without food, without any purpose other than flight. Then, in the chaos, something had gone wrong on a narrow path in the woods. Knocked off his feet and in pain's grip, Albion wasn't sure what had happened. But the company's second lieutenant had seen it—the battery and its gun carriages speeding helter-skelter through the retreating ranks, the heavy wheel shearing off, no time to move out of harm's way, Albion struck in the spine. Years later, Albion would say a wagon had carried him the last twenty miles back to Washington, but only because that's what others told him. He had no memory of it.

Now, after thirty hours of sleep, Albion was trying to figure out how to tell Emma that her husband-to-be had suffered a serious injury—not by being heroic, but during an inglorious retreat, felled by an accident, his own regiment to blame. Scribbling in his notebook at Camp Anderson, the regiment's temporary home in Washington's Franklin Square, he could not stop thinking about the many ifs: If only the regiment hadn't gone into battle already exhausted from an all-night march, "without a moment's rest, a drink of water, or a mouthful of breakfast." If only the civilian teamsters, hired to take care of the wagons and pack animals, hadn't panicked on the retreat. If only his spine hadn't been sore already from his fall at the Elmira training camp. Would his new injury leave permanent damage? He didn't know. For now, on this Tuesday night, July 23, 1861, he just knew he could not walk.

Crafting his letter to Emma, he spared her the details. "Ah! Emma that was a terrible day, a horrible battle, a more terrible retreat and a more horrible night," he wrote. "But I cannot tell you of that now. You must be content to know that I am safe. . . . My feet are so swollen that I cannot put on my shoes, and every bone in my body seems to have been broken." Assuring her that Company E's enlisted men had fought bravely in the "blood and dust and heat," he added wanly, "and I hope I did not disgrace myself."

The letter elated Emma at first—Albion, alive! She even forgave him for his "lack of particulars" about his condition, sure that he would write more when he could. But when a week went by without further word, alarming rumors from town filled the void. Albion's knapsack, "shot to pieces." Albion, crushed "between two cannons." Finally, on August 16, came a frustratingly vague note, written from Kingsville: "Emma, I am at home sick—not dangerously, however, so don't worry about me. Have not a furlough but a discharge. Will write when I can and come down when I am sufficiently recovered. Don't believe any rumors about me. Goodbye, AWT."

Albion at home! A discharge! Recovering at his father's house in Kingsville! Why hadn't he asked for her? She wanted to fly to his side, but the letter's odd tone made her hesitate. She asked her sister Angie to find out more. Angie, furious at Albion for keeping Emma in the dark, wrote to him, her letter full of reproach. He must tell Emma everything, she scolded, "the truth and the whole truth and nothing but the truth."

Even before Angie's reprimand had arrived, though, Albion had already succumbed to Emma's earlier entreaties for more information. "I cannot yet walk," he wrote. And then "the truth," just as Angie was demanding: The doctors had warned that he might never walk again.

ALBION'S TRAIN RIDE from Washington to Ohio had been long, uncomfortable, and mostly spent lying on a mattress. At the Kingsville depot, unable to lift himself, Albion was forced to rely on others to transport him to his father's house. Soon, the whispers were all over town. Did you hear? Albion Tourgee, a cripple.

His most deep-seated fear had come to pass. The army had declared him "wholly unfit for military service," suffering from "paraplegia." He wasn't paralyzed, not entirely. On some days, a prickly sensation gave him some hope that, with time and rest, life would return to his lower body. In late September and early October, miraculously, his legs regained enough feeling to allow short walks, leaning on his friend Joe Warner or using a cane. Ecstatic, he dashed off a note to Emma. His first impulse: "I shall go to war again." He had already written to one of Ohio's senators, asking for authority to recruit a company of his own. "If I keep on getting better as fast" as the past ten days, he told her, "I can go into the field again in two or three weeks."

Then, a stunning, near-total relapse. He blamed himself. He had overdone it. "I am completely discouraged," he moaned to Emma in mid-October. "I cannot live here. I cannot work. I cannot go to war, and what I shall do I don't know."

His blues returned, with a vengeance. He just wanted to be alone. He wanted to brood. He spent much of the fall doing both. He had allowed Emma one visit, and had then told her to stay away. If he could not walk, he did not want to see her. Emma, confused and hurt, had gone ahead with plans to take a governess position in western New York, not far from Gainesville. She would be away at least nine months. Albion still called her "wife" in his letters, but they both sensed that their relationship was adrift. Albion could not help it. He felt lost.

Friends sent well-meaning letters, tinged with pity. He realized, morosely, that he now belonged to that class of people called "lame." He tried to shake his malaise. Embracing his old ambition, he arranged to read the law at an Ashtabula legal office. If he worked hard for a year, he could take the bar, start a career. He moved to town, away from his father and the despised Rowena, taking a room in a boarding house. His disability pension, eight dollars a month, would be just enough to cover the costs.

In April, he made one more decision, the hardest of all: He would not marry Emma—not now, not ever, not unless he could walk. He was heartsick about it, but he felt he had no choice. He had hinted at his feelings in his letters to her, but in mid-May, he let his anger and humiliation burst forth.

"I might as well be dead now, as there is little, if any, hope of my ever recovering sufficiently to take any efficient part in the battle of life," he wrote. "I do not hope ever again to be a man. I am now, and must be, I am told, a cripple." To marry her now would wrong her, he said. "You must not tempt me to do it. It would be a sin of no slight magnitude."

It sounded to Emma as if her beloved had resigned himself to an invalid's life. But she was mistaken. Albion did not tell her that he was about to try a risky treatment. He had visited a Cleveland doctor who said that strychnine, in controlled doses, had helped others with spinal injuries. Desperate, Albion had agreed to take it. In mid-July, Emma received a giddy, astounding one-page note.

"Emma," Albion wrote. "I can walk." And even better news: He would be glad to see her again. But she would have to hurry. He had reenlisted. Yes, *reenlisted.* He was recruiting an infantry company for an Ohio regiment, the 105th, and he finally had the officer's position he had long coveted.

"You can put Lieut. before my name hereafter," he wrote.

ALBION WASN'T AS GOOD AS NEW. Far from it. He had only one good eye, a limp, and spinal pain that would make him a liability on the long marches that this war demanded. But somehow, he persuaded the military examiners that he was fit enough to serve, or at least to act as a recruiter. By late August, after a month of speeches throughout Ashtabula County, he was on his way to Kentucky with Company G and nearly one hundred men he had helped enlist.

The 105th Ohio and its ten companies arrived in Kentucky without adequate training. Their stamina was suspect, especially in the August heat when they were shouldering knapsacks stuffed with summer and winter gear. Albion, cane in hand, had no hope of keeping pace. On a long trek from Lexington to Louisville—the "Hell-March," it came to be called—he fell so far behind that his company went on without him. A buggy picked him up and carried him much of the way.

Nor were most of the soldiers prepared for their first direct encounter with slavery. A good number of the regiment's soldiers had never met a person of color. Now the question of runaway slaves was thrust upon them. On the exhausting march to Louisville, the regiment had acquired a collection of colored men who had appeared along the route, offering to help carry their equipment. When the marchers reached Frankfort and made camp, the Kentucky authorities conducted a kind of raid, rounding up all the colored men as presumed fugitives. A confrontation ensued, with a Union general intervening and ordering the regiment's officers to stand aside.

Union troops were still operating under orders, issued at the outset of the war, to protect Kentucky slaveholders and their property. But Lincoln's strategy, crafted to prevent the border states from bolting to the Confederacy, was a source of continuing friction. As Albion would write years later, in explaining this tension, the 105th was "'an abolition regiment' in a loyal slave state." He told one story with relish: To save an accused runaway, the captain of Company A had falsely claimed him as his personal servant, brought from Ohio. The regiment's commanding general had shouted in frustration: "You are all Abolition nigger-stealers!"

Albion, who in early 1860 had mockingly asked Emma what she planned to do about the "crying sin of Negro Slavery," now confronted the realities of that sin on a regular basis. In October and November, suffering from exhaustion and nursing a reinjury to his back, he spent more than month recuperating at a farm near the Kentucky town of Danville. He savored the few luxuries—wine, apples, sardines, butter, honey—that his hosts had to offer. "I have things so nice," he wrote Emma.

Whatever he saw of slavery during those weeks, he kept to himself, until a Monday in late November. What he saw was something so awful that he could not bring himself to describe it. "Oh! I am sick today—so sick!" he wrote. "Not bodily sick—but so sick at heart! I have seen what would make a cynic heart-sore. My brain throbs—my blood boils! . . . God grant that you may never know its full awfulness, which I could never tell! If it should ever become necessary for you to enter a Slave State I shall wish you to come blindfolded and with shut ears."

Restoring the Union was not enough, he thought now. Slavery had to end. He believed that now, with every fiber of his being. In January 1863, soon after Lincoln's Emancipation Proclamation had declared all slaves in the Confederacy to be free, Albion drafted his own manifesto. His audience: his fraternity brothers at the University of Rochester. He was addressing them both as a soldier and a graduate. The university had chosen to award degrees to those upperclassmen who had heeded the call to service, and that included Albion. He was seeking to drum up new volunteers—not just for the war, but for the struggle that would continue after the battlefield went quiet.

"Dear Brothers of the Upsilon," he began. After establishing his credentials—the humbling defeat at Bull Run, his "long paralyzed limbs," his remarkable recovery—he launched into his central argument about the war's true meaning. Ever since the first shots were fired, he said, the Lincoln administration had repeated the same maxim: "We are fighting but for the Union as it was." This statement was a "sublime hoax," Albion said. Why would the nation want to return to conditions that had brought such terrible bloodshed?

"For one, I don't care a rag for the Union as it was!" he wrote. "I want and fight for the Union better than it was. Before this is accomplished, we must have a fundamental, thorough and complete revolution & renovation. This I expect and hope. For this I am willing to die—for this I expect to die."

"FREEDOM!" ALBION FELT like shouting the word. Shouting it loud and long. Letting it linger in the open air. It was May 6, 1863. He was on a Union steamboat, heading north to Annapolis. For nearly four months—half a winter, half a spring, but more like an eternity—he had been a captive of the damned Confederacy that he had vowed to demolish. But now his captivity was over, ended twenty-four hours earlier, part of a prisoner exchange in Virginia.

The damned Confederacy. That's how he would always think of it. In late January, the damned Confederacy had surprised a 105th supply train, seizing one hundred fifty Union soldiers and thirty wagons. Like slaves to market, Albion and others had been herded to Atlanta first, and then to the notoriously foul Libby Prison in Richmond. He had spent two months in Libby, rotting in the dark and dank. Now he was free—free! Free to walk the deck of the *State of Maine*, free to breathe in the sea air, free to have a smoke to calm his nerves.

"Freedom!" he wrote to Emma while on board. "The word means more to me than it ever did before. It means life, manhood, volition—being—existence and all its pleasures . . ." In contrast: "And prison—bondage! . . . it is chagrin, humiliation—insult . . ." He did not need to make a direct comparison to slavery. The parallels were unmistakable.

Freedom also meant: The freedom to marry. His time in prison had given him plenty of time to think about Emma, about their future. He cast aside his reluctance, once and for all. They met in Columbus, the state capital, far from their home in northeastern Ohio. There was no time for elaborate festivities, only a rushed ceremony on May 14.

He was due back to the 105th, and the fight he had claimed as his own.

HIS BACK INJURY finally caught up with him. The pain was too much, the fatigue too great, the battles with his superiors too frequent. On December 6, 1863, he resigned his commission and returned to Ohio, the war still not won. He was twenty-five years old.

During his year in the South, he had been impressed by many of the colored men he met. In his diary, he often took note of these interactions. Describing a runaway slave who had sought the regiment's protection, he had started with "colored," then had crossed the word out, writing instead "an American citizen of African descent."

Citizen. The very word that Taney and the Supreme Court had denied to people of color.

In June 1863, while still serving with the 105th, Albion had applied to the Bureau of Colored Troops, which was seeking white commanders to lead the newly created colored regiments the War Department had approved in May. Leading colored troops, he wrote in his diary, "is certainly the place for men who would serve the country best and at the same time save valuable lives." The bureau, overwhelmed by more than nine thousand applications, never called him for an interview. Albion was sorely disappointed.

He would have to find another way to make the Union "better than it was."

By color alone: "Vexatious and illegal" mass arrests, New Orleans, January 1863

(Frank Leslie's Illustrated Newspaper, *March 7, 1863)*

9

"Claim Your Rights"

New Orleans and Washington, 1863–1864

FOR MANY IN THE ANIMATED CROWD, the memory would linger for weeks and months, nourishing their hope that *les gens de couleur libres* might finally attain the equal status they had long sought. It was June 29, 1863, a warm summer's evening. The event: a political meeting at New Orleans's Economy Hall. The announced agenda: showing loyalty to the Union during the coming Fourth of July celebration and gaining support for a petition that would extend voting rights to all men born free in Louisiana, regardless of skin color.

In the excited throng stood a smattering of whites, an unfamiliar sight at Economy Hall. Even after Lincoln's troops had reclaimed New Orleans in April 1862, making it a Union-controlled outpost in Confederate Louisiana, everyone understood that certain customs remained unchanged. Separate venues for political meetings was one of them. The white-led Union Association clubs were holding their mass meetings at the Lyceum. The free people of color congregated at Economy Hall, a favored gathering spot for the city's French-speaking free people of color since its founding in the late 1830s.

But the old ways were under assault on this night. The event's organizers—the editors at *L'Union*, the French-language newspaper founded the previous year by and for free people of color—had invited several members of the white Unionist clubs to join the list of orators. Long into the night, the hall echoed with speeches in French and speeches in English, delivered by men of different skin shades and background, bound together by a belief that the way forward from slavery and occupation rested on unity and not division. The boisterous rally wasn't the first time that whites and free people of color had gathered in the same place for a political conversation. But it may have been the first time that they appeared to be acting in concert.

"Appeared to be" was still a necessary caveat. For months, the white and colored groups had been pursuing their agendas separately. The white Union Association's General Committee, after a series of intense meetings, had just put the finishing touches on a three-step plan to gradually return the reins of government to civilian hands. The committee was proposing to hold a constitutional convention to write a new state charter that would ban slavery, followed by a general election once the new constitution was ratified. But to the dismay of people of color, the committee was willing to use the old constitution's voting and eligibility rules. If the plan went forward, if the Union generals gave the go-ahead, the entire process of writing the constitution would be a whites-only affair.

The committee's minutes revealed the undisguised truth: In the absence of free people of color at the meetings, their political rights were never considered. At best, they were an afterthought, expected to be patient while the committee sorted through the many difficult questions surrounding the state's return to the Union fold. At worst . . . well, at worst they were being shunted aside or shunned, once more.

Now, at Economy Hall of all places, the white and colored paths appeared to be reaching a point of intersection. One of the best-known white orators, Anthony Fernandez, thought the meeting was extraordinary, and said so. Invoking a phrase from the Declaration of Independence, Fernandez urged the crowd to act, to seek those rights "that belong to all men." Then the crowd—soldiers and merchants and laborers—pledged themselves to the drafting of yet another petition to the Union generals, the commitment to act as important as the words yet to be written.

Overdue, voices murmured. Long overdue.

IN FARAWAY WASHINGTON, Abraham Lincoln thought the moment was extraordinary, too.

He was not focused, though, on what it meant for free people of color and their long-stifled ambitions. From his vantage point, Union control of New Orleans and the dozen parishes bordering the all-important Mississippi River corridor offered an unparalleled opportunity. Reconciliation and Reconstruction could begin there, on that meandering strip between New Orleans and Baton Rouge, even as the war raged elsewhere. What happened over the coming months—whatever steps were taken by Louisianans themselves to bury slavery and establish a new political order based on a revised state constitution—could serve as a model for other Southern states, and for piecing the fractured country back together.

But figuring out whom to trust in chaotic New Orleans seemed almost as hard as winning the war. As always, the crescent-shaped city was a bewildering place to navigate and understand. Too many schemers, too many factions, too many agendas, too many opportunists. Lincoln had more patience than most, but he could not hope to steer the ship from the distant confines of the White House. He would have to rely on his military governor, Brigadier General George F. Shepley, and his latest commander for all the Gulf forces, Major General Nathaniel P. Banks.

Both had impressive credentials, earned from rival political parties. Banks was a former Republican governor of Massachusetts and speaker of the U.S. House. Shepley was a former U.S. attorney in Maine, a longtime Democrat. Two Northerners, both in their mid-forties, thrown together by happenstance and swept up in the New Orleans maelstrom. Much like the first American military governor after acquisition of the territory in 1803, they had no experience to guide them in ruling this strange new land.

The two generals were supposed to be working in tandem, but no one could accuse them of being a team. Their shared authority was ripe for confusion. With Banks consumed by battlefield pressures throughout the Gulf, Shepley had been left largely on his own to oversee the vestigial government and deal with the local political factions. Now Shepley's job was expanding. He was being asked to shepherd Louisiana from rebellion to restoration, to encourage those who wanted to leave slavery behind without alienating those who wished for slavery's return.

Was Shepley up to the job? Was anyone? Lincoln would soon find out.

AMONG WHITE CREOLES, Anthony Fernandez had done more than most to establish his credentials as a Union loyalist. One newspaper correspondent called him the "noble-hearted old patriot," a tribute to his age (nearing seventy) and his military service (to Andrew Jackson during the famous defense of New Orleans in 1814–1815). Fernandez had owned three slaves at the outset of the rebellion, but within weeks of the federal occupation, he was organizing Unionist rallies. A few days before speaking at Economy Hall, he had acquired a seat on the Union Association General Committee, which was pressing Shepley to approve its reconstruction plan.

Fernandez, an auctioneer who advertised in *L'Union* and knew most of its editors, enjoyed a special stature in New Orleans. He had long served as president of the Association of Veterans of 1814–1815, overseeing the annual Eighth of January parade. At the 1860 festivities, he had brought the overwhelmingly white crowd to its feet with a passionate toast: "The Union—it shall be preserved in spite of Northern fanaticism and abolitionism." Now, more than three years later, Fernandez was facing an altogether different audience at Economy Hall, and he was exhorting them to "defend the Union and claim your rights."

Defend the Union. Claim your rights. Louisiana's colored Union ranks already numbered several thousand men. Was it that simple? Fight for Lincoln's cause, and he will fight for yours? Free people of color could be forgiven for being skeptical. They had heard such talk before. At the outset of the Economy Hall rally, as a symbol of continuity with the past, the organizers had announced ten honorary vice presidents for the night, many of them veterans of 1814–1815. It was a nice gesture, but also a pointed reminder. These men had answered their nation's call in a war against the British. Promises were made to them for their service. Promises not kept.

Overdue, long overdue.

TO THE SURPRISE OF MANY, Lincoln's much-anticipated Emancipation Proclamation had exempted New Orleans and other sections of Louisiana under Union control. Slavery was still legal in twelve excluded parishes. The January 1, 1863, order named them all, ending with "Orleans, including the City of New Orleans." The overly precise language was no accident. Lincoln was emphasizing, once again, that his actions were motivated by military goals, not morality or party platforms. With no military reason for ending slavery in the Union-controlled parishes—or none that Lincoln was willing to claim—his logic dictated that he let them alone.

A "preliminary" draft of the proclamation, released three months early to put pressure on the rebellious states, had said nothing about exceptions. Many Union loyalists were baffled by the final version. Couldn't Lincoln see that dividing Louisiana this way was unworkable, even dangerous? Escaped and newly freed slaves were now streaming daily into the city, desperate for Union protection. Soon, slaveholders began besieging City Hall, clamoring for help in holding onto their enslaved property. It was lunacy, some loyalists felt.

The overwhelmed military authorities decided to control the swelling tide of runaways with mass arrests. In late January, provost guards and police officers swept through the streets, stopping all people of color and carting them to jail if they couldn't produce "freedom" papers or other documents. Anyone without a job would be compelled to work on public projects or pushed into labor contracts with plantation owners, under orders from General Banks, part of a campaign to prevent "vagrancy and crime." Caught in the net were people of color who had never been enslaved, whose parents had never been enslaved, whose grandparents had never been enslaved. It was a frightening echo of the 1859 jailings that had so unsettled the city's free people of color before the war.

The military government seemed unprepared for the fury and fear that these new arrests had caused, and not just among *les gens de couleur.* The local correspondent for the *New York Times*, writing under the pseudonym "Nemo," was a white Union loyalist named John Hamilton. His January 29 dispatch, sent by steamboat and appearing in print on February 11, made plain his contempt for the "arbitrary" seizures. "A few evenings ago," he wrote, "the whole city was thrown into great commotion by the simultaneous arrest of all colored people in the streets, of every age, sex and condition of life, huddling them all into jail. . . . where respectably dressed females and children—some as fair as the fairest Caucasians—were piled ignominiously and promiscuously with the lowest of both sexes, all weeping, imploring, and almost scared to death." It was "something that will not easily be forgotten by those who saw it."

Indignation spread through the Vieux Carré, the Marigny, Tremé, and other neighborhoods where New Orleans's nearly eleven thousand free people of color lived and worked. Did they need a starker reminder of their precarious status between white and slave? Within days, a written protest with more than four hundred and eighty signatures had made its way to Shepley's desk, objecting to the "vexatious and illegal" arrests of people "peaceably pursuing their private business." The list of signers was a cross section of *les gens*: property owners, merchants, slaveholders, tradesmen, officers in the colored Native Guard regiments protecting the city, and veterans of 1814–1815.

The complaint's preamble reminded Shepley that the "illustrious" General Jackson had addressed his colored soldiers as "fellow-citizens." That was more than fifty years ago. Now, those fellow citizens and their descendants were being treated as criminals. Enough, the complaint said. We are not vagrants. We own property. We pay taxes. We helped make New Orleans a prosperous place. We want and deserve respect, not a night in jail while the authorities sort out their ignorance and their mistakes.

The complaint's authors reinforced their anger with specific legal arguments. Carry documents to prove their status? They possessed no such papers. They did not need them. The courts and Louisiana law presumed them "to be free . . . and many of them have been free for several generations."

For free people of color, the irony was inescapable. The Emancipation Proclamation, a document of freedom and joy for so many, was now resulting in harassment and humiliation for them. But like separate railroad cars in Massachusetts for the abolitionists, the mass arrests served as a rallying point for *les gens de couleur.* New Orleans was changing before their eyes. They needed to speak up, to demand a role in the process, to make their case.

As always, there were forces at work that stood in their way.

FRANÇOIS BOISDORE LISTENED in mounting disbelief. He hadn't come to Economy Hall on this Thursday night, November 5, 1863, expecting to hear a speech advising colored people to wait, to be patient. Wait? Be patient? Why should Boisdore and his compatriots be patient? How dare this speaker, this white man named Fisk, this one-time slaveholder from Texas, this relative newcomer to New Orleans, tell them to be "content for the present with achieving their freedom from bondage" and "not to ask for political rights until their freedom was secure"?

Freedom from bondage? Freedom secured? Could Fisk, a Union Association member, be any more insulting? Then, it was suddenly, painfully, absurdly clear. Fisk thought he was talking to a crowd of former slaves. He was so caught up in his conversion from slaveholder to abolitionist, so pleased with himself, that he had made the white man's assumption: colored equated to slave. Colored could not mean freedom at birth, or serving in Andrew Jackson's army, or owning property, or having the liberty to assemble at Economy Hall and demand the right to vote, to have a say in choosing the delegates who would write Louisiana's new constitution.

Boisdore hadn't planned to say anything. But listening to this white man Fisk, Boisdore wanted the floor. Economy Hall was jammed with nearly seven hundred people of every hue, throbbing with noise, the very opposite of patient. "We have waited long enough," Boisdore said. "We have never been slaves." They weren't there to discuss emancipation, he told the buzzing crowd. They were there to move ahead with their now-drafted petition to Shepley, their collective shout for equity. "If the United States has the right to arm us," he cried, "it certainly has the right to allow us the rights of suffrage."

Postpone? No, he said. Now was not the time to retreat. Now was the time to push harder. Do not be deterred. Do not flinch. "If we cannot succeed with the authorities here"—if Shepley would not listen—"we will go to a higher power." As applause rolled through the hall, he vowed: "We will go to President Lincoln, and then we shall know who we are dealing with."

SOME IN THE CROWD had to be wondering: Would the Union Association be daring enough to accept free people of color as partners? A simple question, with no simple answer. The white group was like a system of riverside levees, under constant pressure from the shifting currents. Some members were moving ever closer to outright support for free people of color and their demands. Others could grit their teeth and call themselves Unionists, but no more.

During the summer, several proposals had exposed the group's fissures. Among the most controversial: a revised oath for association members that pledged them to work toward a "*free state* government." This two-word insertion, embracing abolition, drew strong protests from a small faction that still nursed proslavery hopes. Two dissenters resigned, but their departure did nothing to slow the group's conversion. By summer's end, the association's governing council had added the two words to its name: It was now the "Free State General Committee."

All well and good, a significant step widely noted in antislavery circles. But at Economy Hall on that early November evening, not nearly good enough. The teeming throng wanted to hear about rights and equality, not just slavery's end. Why, Boisdore and others were asking, should making Louisiana into a "Free State" put everything else on hold?

A Free State Committee member, speaking after Boisdore, seemed genuinely torn. A. P. Dostie considered himself an ally of free colored people, but he confessed that he thought it best "not to press the question" of rights for free people of color just yet. Still, "if they had well considered the matter and had decided to go on with it," they should "make an honest, persevering effort."

Then, from the crowd, came another impromptu, impatient voice—P. B. S. Pinchback, a former captain in a colored regiment, twenty-six years old, and light skinned enough to be taken for white. Pinchback wasn't a Louisiana native, but after serving in a Louisiana military company, he felt he could speak for his "fellow citizens." They were not asking for any favors or social equality; they were asking for political rights available to *any* male citizen, owed to *any* veteran. If we are eligible to fight, he said, then we are eligible to vote. Treat us as men, Pinchback demanded.

Pinchback's words, a common refrain among colored soldiers, resounded in the hall and beyond. The words appeared in the final petition that would go to Shepley: "We are men, treat us such." Hundreds rushed forward to sign the appeal. In the coming weeks, the numbers would multiply, page upon page, family upon family, generation upon generation.

One surviving 1814–1815 veteran, Michel Debergue, was among the signers who had been waiting a lifetime to claim their rights. Debergue was approaching seventy now, a child of the late eighteenth century, born free in the Spanish era. His father was white and French, his mother was mulatto and born in New Orleans. That made him *quarteron*, the designation that appeared in official records. He and his wife Josephine had several children and grandchildren. The family's newest member was a grandson, born in March amid the upheaval and turmoil of occupation. Their daughter Rosa had married a Plessy, another family from *les gens de couleur libres*, which meant the newborn's New Orleans roots went deep on both sides.

His parents named him Homere Patris Plessy. As a young man, he would come to be known as Homer.

IN WASHINGTON, Lincoln was restless and impatient. He had been waiting months for Louisiana's reconstruction to begin, but the plan had bogged down. Privately, he blamed Shepley for dragging his feet and Banks for not paying closer attention, but blame was beside the point. Lincoln wanted progress, not recrimination. In late July, Shepley had come to Washington seeking guidance. He had spent the better part of a month, making the rounds, talking with cabinet members. Secretary of the Treasury Salmon Chase was the most vocal. He wanted the voter registry opened immediately to people of color. Chase pointed out that the treaty of 1803 had promised citizenship to all inhabitants of Louisiana, with no exceptions. The provision had been "wholly disregarded," Chase said.

For Lincoln, speed was paramount, and the fastest way to achieve his goal—a slave-free Louisiana, created voluntarily by the people themselves—was to propel the process forward without trying to control it. In early August, he wrote a diplomatic letter to Banks, trying to push without being pushy. Abolition came first, he said, but at the same time, "I think it would not be objectionable" for Louisiana "to adopt some practical system by which the two races could gradually live themselves out of their old relation to each other, and both come out better prepared for the new."

Three months later, after learning that no voter registration was yet under way, Lincoln wrote to Banks again, conveying his unhappiness that no progress had been made. "This disappoints me bitterly; yet I do not throw blame on you or on them," Lincoln said. "I do, however, urge both you and them to lose no more time." He feared that inertia was allowing the proslavery faction—the "adverse element"—to gain strength. Give me a "tangible nucleus" that "I can at once recognize and sustain as the true State government," Lincoln urged.

Lincoln addressed the November 5 letter to Banks, but he wanted others to read it and heed it. He made out a delivery list of half a dozen people. As it turned out, Banks was among the last to see it. He was busy outside of New Orleans, commanding troops at the front. Another delay. By the time the general returned to the city in early December and caught up with Lincoln's forceful rebuke, the divergent Washington and New Orleans timelines were beginning to collide and clash.

IN MID-DECEMBER, all twenty of the Union Association's clubs met to choose Louisiana's delegates for a first-ever "Friends of Freedom" convention, a gathering of Unionists in the Southern states to be held in Louisville, Kentucky. Before the all-white assembly could get started, in trooped eighteen free people of color, representing two brand-new Unionist clubs—the Union Radical Association and the Native Central Committee, Left Bank Mississippi.

They wanted to be seated.

The eighteen men presented their credentials, triggering a flurry of parliamentary maneuvering. The chairman, lawyer Thomas J. Durant, skillfully kept the opposition at bay with his rulings. When several unhappy white members threatened to walk out, Fernandez rose to the colored visitors' defense. He said, simply: I know them all. These are gentlemen. Men of education. If we are truly "Friends of Freedom," we have no reason to exclude them.

A headline in the *New Orleans Times* told the unprecedented outcome: "Free Colored Men Admitted to Seats." The official proceedings later gave a full account, listing all eighteen names, including "M. Debergue," Homer Plessy's grandfather.

BANKS FELT HIS TEMPER rising as he read Lincoln's letter. *I do not throw blame on you or the others*, Lincoln had written. As if that were going to fool anyone. Banks's reply was unabashed and unapologetic. Restoring Louisiana's government had been Shepley's job, "exclusively committed to him," he fumed. "My suggestions are respectfully but silently received by the Governor and his associates." Banks blamed the hydra-headed command that Lincoln had created. "Had the organization of a free state in Louisiana been committed to me," he said, "it would have been complete before this day." Give me sixty days and it will done, Banks told Lincoln—"thirty days, if necessary."

Lincoln, meanwhile, had decided not to wait for Banks's reply. He wanted progress, and he wanted it faster than his New Orleans commanders seemed to understand. On December 8, he gave them a specific, concrete way to accelerate the timetable. He issued a "Proclamation of Amnesty and Reconstruction" that made it easier for Union loyalists in any rebel state to establish a government. The proclamation set a "10 percent" threshold for creating a voting registry—that is, 10 percent of votes cast in the state for the 1860 presidential candidates. As soon as 10 percent had taken the oath of allegiance to the Union and had registered to vote, an election could take place to form "a true government of the State."

For free people of color, Lincoln's 10 percent solution felt like a giant step backward. Rather than using "citizen" to define a qualified voter, the president's proclamation was basing voter eligibility on the election laws "existing immediately before the so-called act of secession." Once again, that meant whites only.

Suddenly, it looked as if Boisdore's spontaneous cry—"*We will go to President Lincoln!*"—was the only remaining option. A plan for a direct appeal took shape just after New Year's. A two-man delegation would carry the petition to Washington. Arnold Bertonneau and Jean-Baptiste Roudanez, men of distinction who were well connected with the *L'Union* editors, were chosen to make the long journey.

They would be escorting a document that now exceeded a thousand signatures, including those of Thomas Durant, Anthony Fernandez, twenty other white members of the Union Association, and twenty-eight colored veterans of 1814–1815—among them, Michel Debergue.

BANKS'S ANGRY REPLY reached Lincoln a week before Christmas. The president was privately delighted. He was more than ready to bypass the hapless Shepley, as Banks was suggesting. On Christmas Eve, Lincoln sent a soothing reply, playing to Banks's considerable ego. "I deeply regret to have said or done anything which could give you pain, or uneasiness," Lincoln wrote. "I have all the while intended you to be master . . . it did not occur to me that Gov. Shepley or anyone else would set up a claim to act independently." Banks would be "master of all" from now on. No more confusion. "I wish you to take the case as you find it, and give us a free-state re-organization of Louisiana, in the shortest possible time," he told Banks.

Lincoln knew his general well. If the president wanted a free state government "in the shortest possible time," Banks would give him one. Immediately after receiving Lincoln's reply, Banks went to work on a new decree, superseding Shepley and thwarting the Union Association's convention-first strategy. Louisiana would elect a governor on February 22, Banks ordered, allowing a short six weeks for nominations and campaigning. As prescribed by Lincoln's Amnesty proclamation, voter eligibility would be based on the state's resurrected election law, the one in effect before secession. That meant only white men casting ballots. The winners would take office on March 4;

a constitutional convention would get under way a month later. "This is the wish of the President," Banks declared, although Lincoln's wishes had not covered such specifics.

Fully aware that his decree would cause dissension among the free people of color and their supporters, Banks pointedly said that further debate was not welcome. "When the national existence is at stake, and the liberties of the people in peril," he declared, "faction is treason."

Faction is treason. With an appeal to Banks now pointless, Bertonneau and Roudanez left for Washington in early February. In a final convergence of the Washington and New Orleans timelines, their audience with Lincoln took place on March 4, on the same day that the newly elected governor of Louisiana was giving his inaugural speech before an immense crowd in New Orleans's Jackson Square. Lincoln finally had "his true government of the State," with the free people of color watching from the sidelines, having not participated in the vote.

A MEETING WITH LINCOLN, as Bertonneau and Roudanez soon discovered, was hardly a private affair. It had the air of orderly pandemonium, with people coming in and out, and more people in the hallways. But there was another factor: Bertonneau and Roudanez fit none of the usual categories of White House visitors. The Northerners around Lincoln were curious to meet these light-skinned men of African and French descent, to take their measure, to see how these free people of color from New Orleans presented themselves.

Bertonneau was barely thirty years old and already a wine merchant of some wealth; he had served as a captain in a Union regiment of colored soldiers in Louisiana. Roudanez, nearly fifty, had worked as an engineer on sugar plantations. He and his brother, Louis, were financial backers of *L'Union*. On the petition's first page, Bertonneau and Roudanez had identified themselves as "delegates of the free Colored population of Louisiana." Not the "negro population" or the "black population," and certainly not the growing population of freed slaves.

Lincoln knew of their cause and their arguments—from the persistent Chase, among others—but now he could read and hear their plea for himself.

The petition described the broken promises and endless wait, how the colored veterans of 1814–1815 and their descendants had been "estranged and repulsed, excluded from all rights." Now it had happened again. They had "spilled their blood" for the Union, but when they asked Shepley and Banks "to be placed on the Registers as voters," they heard nothing. In the name of justice, they were now appealing to Lincoln and Congress.

Lincoln's answer was not one they wanted to hear. Their request was a political question, he said, not a military necessity. He was impressed by them and their petition, but he could not help them. They would need to wait for the constitutional convention to take up the issue.

Reporters had no trouble learning what the president had told his private visitors. His rationale, with slight variation, found its way into nearly every newspaper story. The *New York Tribune* was perhaps the pithiest: "Mr. Lincoln substantially told them that he had too much to attend to here to be looking after political morality in Louisiana, and dismissed [them] with the information that if the Convention in their State would give them what they wanted, he would not object to it." The *Chicago Tribune* described Lincoln's reply as "characteristic of the man, and worthy of him. He does not hesitate to avow a lack of personal prejudice against them, but reminds them that the subject matter of their request is not in the range of his present undertaking. This 'big job' must be finished first."

LINCOLN'S FIRM REBUFF left only one more stop for Roudanez and Bertonneau: Congress. They met with Senator Charles Sumner of Massachusetts, the ardent abolitionist. The newspaper accounts said Sumner would present their petition to the Senate on Monday, March 7. But Sumner had his own agenda, and it was broader than speaking up for "the free Colored population of Louisiana." If Bertonneau and Roudanez wanted his help, he told them, they had to revise their petition. They would need to ask for voting rights to be extended to *all* natives of Louisiana, whether born free or born into slavery.

There was no time to consult with anyone in New Orleans about linking their rights to those of freed slaves. On three sheets of ordinary lined paper,

Bertonneau wrote out the requested addendum. Sumner took both documents, and with a strong speech of support, submitted them to the Senate on March 15. The appeal promptly languished in committee.

Postponed, once again.

AT THE WHITE HOUSE, Lincoln mulled over what more, if anything, he wanted to say. As he had told Bertonneau and Roudanez, he had no intention of dictating Louisiana's political choices. But as he had told Banks, he had no objection to extending suffrage in a limited way to some men of color. On March 13, while drafting a congratulatory letter to Louisiana's new governor, Lincoln decided to give the idea a modest presidential nudge.

"I congratulate you on having fixed your name in history as the first free-State Governor of Louisiana," he wrote to Michael Hahn. "Now you are about to have a convention, which, among other things, will probably define the elective franchise. I barely suggest, for your private consideration, whether some of the colored people may not be let in, as, for instance, the very intelligent, and especially those who have fought gallantly in our ranks. They would probably help, in some trying time to come, to keep the jewel of liberty in the family of freedom. But this is only a suggestion, not to the public, but to you alone."

Lincoln's "suggestion" received the constitutional convention's attention when it convened on April 6. But like Hahn, most of the white delegates did not share Lincoln's view. They would only approve a provision allowing the new legislature to *consider* extending suffrage to some men of color—which the legislature then emphatically declined to do.

Overall, though, Banks and Lincoln considered the convention a success—slavery abolished, a free state in its place, the Black Code gone. On August 9, 1864, Lincoln wrote to Banks: "I have just seen the new Constitution . . . and I am anxious that it be ratified by the people."

The free people of color were far less enthusiastic. They would not be among "the people" voting on the constitution. Once again, their ambitions had been waylaid. Once again, they were told to be patient. As 1864 ended, their status felt as precarious as ever.

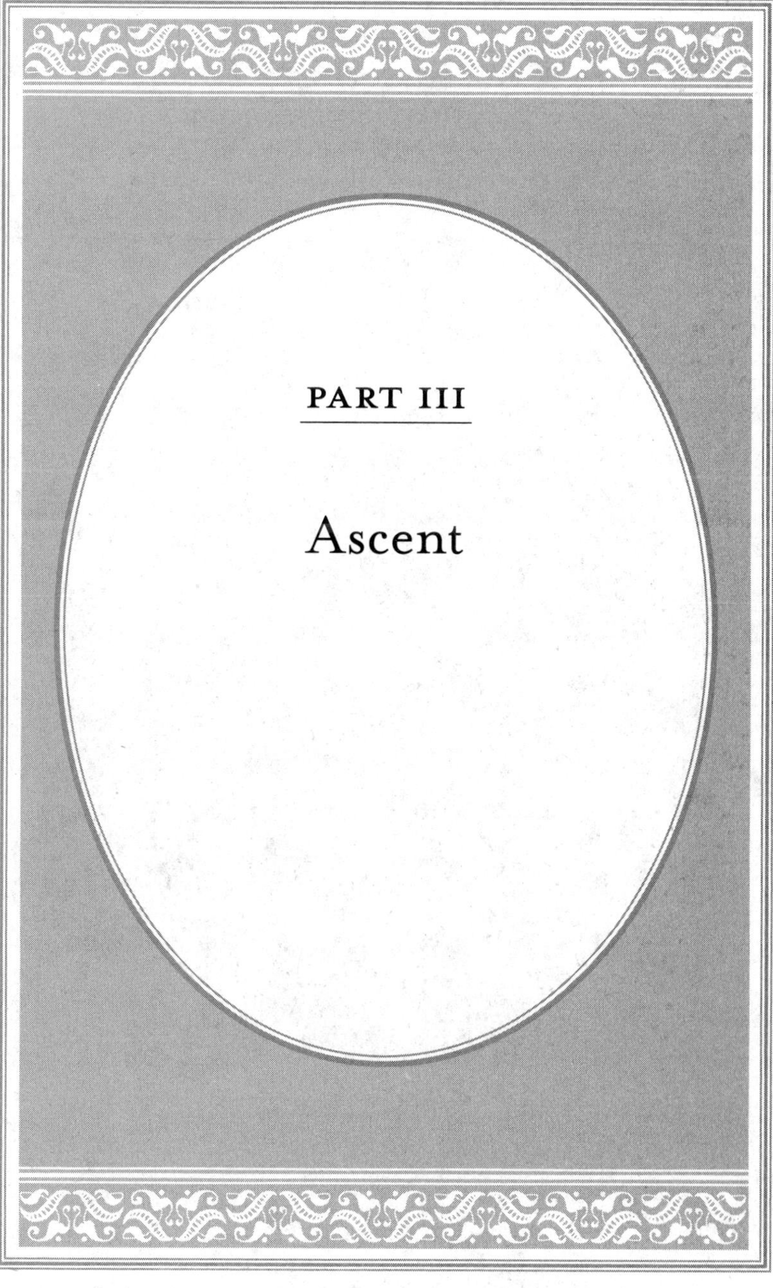

PART III

Ascent

Celebration: Final passage of first federal Civil Rights Act, April 9, 1866

(Harper's Weekly, *April 28, 1866)*

10

Choosing Sides

Harlan in Kentucky, 1865–1871

VICTORY WAS ONLY SIX WEEKS OLD, and John Harlan was finding it almost as unsettling as defeat. He had gone to war to preserve the Union. But not *this* Union. Not a Union where the victors told Kentuckians which laws to make and which to discard. He had not raised a Union regiment in 1861 so that Kentucky's negroes could have immediate freedom in 1865, without fair compensation to their owners. He had not slogged through the muds of Kentucky and Tennessee so that zealots from the North could impose a constitutional amendment that would abolish slavery in one national swoop. He had not asked his men to risk their lives so that negroes could vote, or testify against whites, or exercise any of the "rights" that the ascendant Republican Radicals in Congress were aiming to bestow on colored people everywhere.

Not that John had any affection for slavery. Like his late father, he regarded the "institution" with ambivalence verging on distaste. But Lincoln's Emancipation Proclamation had excused Kentucky, which had remained loyal to the Union throughout the long war, even amid constant rebel attacks. State law still gave slaveholders, including the Harlan family, a legal right to keep their slaves. If slavery were about to die—and in the late spring of 1865, after the triumph at Appomattox and Lincoln's assassination, even the diehards were conceding the likelihood of that outcome—John felt to the depths of his leather boots that it was Kentucky's responsibility to deliver the death blow. *That* was the Union he had sought to save, the one in which Kentuckians ruled themselves.

Principle and duty, he felt, compelled him to make a stand on Kentucky's behalf. As the state's elected attorney general, two years into his first term, he had a ready platform for fashioning legal challenges. As a prominent politician, much in demand as an orator, he had plenty of opportunities to influence public opinion. Perhaps, through a two-pronged offensive, he could bring some order and sanity back to his state.

When it came to finger pointing, as it had during the 1864 presidential campaign, John had not hesitated. He had blamed Lincoln for the wrong turn of events. For the first time in John's life, he had stumped for a Democrat—a Democrat! He had traveled the state, making speech after lengthy speech for Lincoln's opponent and former partner in war, General George C. McClellan. John had even crossed the Ohio River for forays into the free state of Indiana, delivering his well-honed pitch to appreciative crowds in Evansville and New Albany. John's glowing reputation had made him an attractive addition to the McClellan cause. He was an eloquent defender of the Union, a former officer much admired by his troops, and a leading vote-getter in Kentucky's 1863 election, held under military supervision. All that, and only thirty-one years old.

The political gossips had delighted in the incongruity of a Harlan wrapping his arms around the Democrats, a party that John and his father had always denounced with relish. But John saw no other choice. He was as committed as ever to saving the Union, as angry as ever at the Confederate states for breaking it apart. No, John felt, it was Lincoln who had changed. What had started as a noble military campaign to suppress an illegal rebellion had mutated into an unconstitutional crusade to rid the nation of slavery. The 1864 presidential campaign was the ideal forum—the *constitutional* forum—for holding Lincoln to account for usurping powers that rightly belonged to the states.

John threw himself into the campaign fray, just as he had in 1856 and 1860.

WORDS CARRIED EXTRA weight in wartime. John knew that. Another former Union colonel had gotten himself arrested a few months earlier for his anti-Lincoln tirades, accused of fomenting resistance to the president's call for colored recruits. John's speeches, while forthright in their criticisms, stayed on the calmer side of free speech. No name calling, no sly insinuations. He attacked Lincoln's actions but not Lincoln's character. A local correspondent for the *Louisville Daily Journal*, after watching John captivate a packed audience for nearly two hours, marveled at John's "dignity and decorum, candor and moderation."

An air of danger had hung over John's oration on that September afternoon in New Castle, a speck of a Kentucky town some thirty miles northeast of Louisville. While John was taking his shots at Lincoln's presidency inside the courthouse, Union troops were prowling the streets, a show of force intended to discourage rebel guerrillas from any thoughts of a raid.

Having an armed patrol outside a political event offered an ideal backdrop for John's portrayal of a nation divided by Lincoln's "ruinous and destructive policy." Describing himself as a Union stalwart who stood for reunification at any cost, John said Lincoln had forfeited the support of conservative men by pledging "to continue this war until the social institutions of the South are obliterated."

For John, the paramount issue was ending the bloodshed as soon as the rebellion was firmly suppressed. "He would not continue [the war] a day beyond that," wrote the *Louisville Daily Journal* correspondent in his admiring account of John's address. "He would not sacrifice the lives of the white men of this nation, or keep them languishing in Southern prisons, because of the freedom of the negro."

John's support for McClellan did not blossom into allegiance to the Democrats. In Kentucky, he felt, they were making too much room in their party for Confederate sympathizers, who were angling to gain through the ballot box what they had failed to achieve on the battlefield. John was trying to work with them, but he was finding the coalition difficult. He was trying to walk a path of moderation, but by the late spring of 1865, that path was becoming increasingly narrow.

How, he wondered, could he ever hope to influence the country's future if he couldn't find his way through Kentucky's political thicket?

JAMES HARLAN'S SUDDEN DEATH in February 1863 had left John and Mallie with a series of life-altering choices. The first: Should John stay in the Union army—his promotion to brigadier general was pending before Congress—or come home to deal with his father's tangled business affairs?

John knew how he would look if he resigned his officer's commission within a month after Lincoln's Emancipation Proclamation. The secessionists would say he was quitting in protest. True, he had no love for the proclamation. But he did not want anyone to misunderstand his reasons for leaving the battlefield to others. His commanding officers deserved a full explanation, he felt, but his resignation letter also managed to find its way later into the pages of the *Louisville Daily Journal*.

"I deeply regret that I am compelled, at this time, to return to civil life," he wrote on that March day in 1863, from his makeshift command post in Tennessee. "It was my fixed purpose to remain in the Federal army until it had effectually suppressed the existing armed rebellion and restored the authority of the National Government over every part of the nation." But his father's unexpected death had thrust financial problems upon him "which I cannot, with propriety, neglect." That was his sole reason for resigning, not any "want of confidence either in the justice or the ultimate triumph of the Union cause."

John had crafted his words with care, acutely aware of their power to harm the Union cause now and to haunt his political ambitions later. He offered no hint of dissatisfaction with the war—nothing to tarnish his honor, nothing to blemish his record, nothing to comfort the enemy, "for there are no conditions upon which I will consent to a dissolution of the Union."

Leaving the army behind, John felt unmoored. Louisville had been his home briefly before the war, but he had barely lived there since raising his regiment. Mallie and the children had decamped to Evansville, where they had planted themselves with her family. Where should they go now? Frankfort seemed to make the most sense. A summer on Harlan's Hill would give John ready access to his father's papers and the court handling the estate.

Then, in the same week that his resignation letter appeared in the Louisville newspaper, came an unexpected offer that made a move to Frankfort even more appealing. Would John run for attorney general on a Unionist Party ticket? John was enthusiastic, ready—and victorious. He returned to the capital, stepping into several pairs of his father's shoes—taking over his law practice, his political legacy, and his position as titular head of the Harlan household.

AS MALLIE TOLD the story later, John had two thoughts in mind when he decided to keep his late father's slaves in the Harlan family: his mother's comfort and their slaves' well-being. Her memory was kinder than some of the facts—a reflection, perhaps, of her lingering discomfort about those distressing days.

His father's estate was a muddle that required keen attention. John and his brother, James Jr., were both named administrators, but the unenviable task of figuring out what to do fell largely on John's broad shoulders. His father's money was tied up in property—several houses, a tract of land, nine slaves. John was loath to sell off. But what else could he do? His father had left the family in a deep hole. He had guaranteed loans for friends while allowing clients to go years without paying their fees. To make matters worse, his father's ledgers were a mess. John wasn't sure he could compile an accurate list of what his father owed, and what he was due.

If the estate was an intricate puzzle, so were the options. Selling several slaves was the most pragmatic choice; the estate needed a lot of money to pay his father's many debts. According to one appraisal, the family's slaves might be worth three thousand dollars, about half of the available assets. But how would John choose which slaves to keep and which to let go? John had grown up with these enslaved men and women. He had "real affection" for them, in Mallie's words, and "would not bear to think of them falling into other hands through the barter and sale of human beings that was then still in vogue."

Beyond that, John also worried about the devastating effect on his grieving mother—"his idol," Mallie called her. Under Kentucky's inheritance law, Eliza Harlan would receive one-third of the estate, her "dower" interest. The rest would be divided among the children. For years, Eliza Harlan had relied on the family's contingent of slaves, and John "felt it would have been cruel to leave her with the few servants that would ordinarily have fallen to her in the division of the estate." In Mallie's retelling, John avoided the disruption of his mother's household arrangements by making himself "responsible to the estate for the value of the rest of those slaves."

It hadn't been quite that simple. As administrator, John was legally required to put the estate's obligations and debts first. Reuben was sold outright, for $649.60, according to the inventory later filed with the county court. Then, in November 1863, the family's eight other slaves—Robert, Henry, Lewis, Ben, Sarah and her daughter Jenny, Silvia and her daughter Mariah—went on sale at public auction, with John and his mother among the most determined bidders.

They succeeded. They came home with all but Robert, auctioned to a Frankfort man for $230. John bought Lewis, his mother bought the others. They had six months to scrape together the money, nearly thirteen hundred dollars, which they now owed to the estate. Meanwhile, his mother could go on as before, with nearly a full complement of household help. Such were the peculiar twists that arose during the "barter and sale of human beings then still in vogue."

Emancipating some or all the family's slaves had been another available outcome, but the Harlans could not separate themselves from slavery voluntarily. It was stitched into the very fabric of their lives. John's choice: preserve the status quo, for as long as slavery remained legal in the border state of Kentucky.

WITH HIS MOTHER settled with her repurchased slaves, John and Mallie bid goodbye to Harlan's Hill in favor of new quarters in Frankfort. They had four children, all younger than nine, and Mallie wanted help in the kitchen. She had never bought a slave before, but this daughter of Indiana set out to find one now.

Another family, certain that slavery was all but finished in Kentucky, offered to sell them "a very good cook for One Hundred Dollars, a year's hire," Mallie later said. The sellers were leaving the state for good, and wanted to recoup something for their rapidly devaluing property. "Aunt" Fanny was sold to the Harlans.

Mallie, after eight years as a Kentuckian's wife, was no stranger to the master-slave relationship, but she soon found that she could not manage the feisty Fanny. Two strong wills. One stubborn winner. Once or twice, Fanny even took Mallie by the shoulders and escorted her to the door, locking it for good measure.

"You don't know nuthin' 'bout cookin'," Fanny fumed at Mallie, insisting that she had "done it dis way foh Miss Eddie," her previous owner.

"But you are working for *me* now," Mallie had replied, "and you must do it *my* way."

Fanny was unyielding. Mallie was astonished. Her mother-in-law's slaves had never behaved this way. After talking it over with John, they decided to give Fanny her freedom and find another cook.

Her replacement was the aging "Aunt" Charlotte. Her owner was preparing for slavery's demise by looking for buyers or renters anywhere he could find them. Charlotte was sure she would be separated from her husband, George, who was the property of a different family. Charlotte was desperate to remain in Kentucky, near George. Mallie was moved by her tearful appeal. "I determined to close the bargain," she said. She again paid one hundred dollars, securing an enslaved servant and Charlotte's undying devotion, which continued long after slavery's end.

"It was a most fortunate purchase," Mallie later said, fondly.

READING THE NEWSPAPERS in mid-1865 often left John shaking his head. When would Kentucky return to some semblance of normal? It was almost June, and yet the state was still under martial law, still beholden to the federal military command in Louisville, still fearful of unrepentant rebels making guerrilla raids on lightly defended towns, still trapped between slavery and emancipation. It was a tense limbo, with turmoil sprouting here and there, like the goldenrod of a Kentucky summer. The Union general in charge of the Department of Kentucky, a newcomer by the name of John M. Palmer, seemed more interested in provoking havoc than avoiding it. How else to explain his series of orders since his arrival in February?

Palmer was Kentucky born, but Illinois bred, and unknown to most Kentuckians. He had gotten off to a promising start, addressing the legislature on his very first day, appealing for help in bridging the state's bitter divisions. "I did not enter the military service on account of any hatred toward our brethren of the far South," he soothingly told the packed assembly, "or of any peculiar love for the people of the North." He laid out no agenda, saying that impulsive pledges now would only lead to humiliation later. "I feel confident," he said, "that the state and federal authorities will act in perfect harmony" as they carried out their duties.

Perfect harmony never had a chance. A week after Palmer's speech, the Kentucky legislature voted on the proposed national amendment abolishing slavery—and decisively rejected it. Eighteen other states had already voted to ratify. Only one had rejected it. The amendment was going to succeed, but the legislature was determined to make a symbolic stand against outside interference in Kentucky's affairs.

Palmer soon showed that emancipation ranked higher than harmony on his list of priorities. On March 3, an impatient Congress had awarded immediate freedom to all enslaved families of colored Union soldiers, including new recruits. Palmer seized the opportunity. "To colored men not in the army," he announced a week later in General Order No. 10, the congressional act was a chance "to earn freedom for themselves and their posterity" by enlisting. Opposition to his order was immediate. In late March, a judge in Nicholas County declared the congressional action an unconstitutional invasion into the state's affairs. Palmer was undeterred. He welcomed all enlistments. The recruitment numbers soared.

He wasn't prepared, however, for the chaotic exodus that soon descended on Louisville. Hundreds upon hundreds of colored refugees were streaming into the city, asserting their newfound freedom or claiming a husband in the army. In May, angry and accusatory, Louisville's mayor and members of the city's council pressed Palmer for permission to "remove this great evil." They painted the direst of pictures: clusters of colored people, mostly women and children, with no work and no place to live, crowding together, creating conditions ripe for the spread of disease while breaking any number of Kentucky laws.

Palmer, rather than challenging their alarmist claims, capitalized on them. He issued General Order No. 32, granting passage north to any colored person—and family—who could not find work. He directed all ferry and steamboat captains on the Ohio River to honor the Union passes, upon payment of the usual fare. If they refused, they would be arrested and tried by a military tribunal.

Palmer gave pass-seekers a free hand in deciding their destinations. Most chose the short ferry ride from Louisville to the Indiana shore. After years of vigilance in deterring and reclaiming runaways, Kentucky slaveholders could do nothing to stanch the flow. Five thousand crossed by the end of July. As for Palmer's hope of harmony, it had vanished, like the emancipated refugees heading north. Instead, there was ominous talk of prosecuting the hated general for aiding and abetting runaways. A confrontation was looming between federal and state authority. As Kentucky's attorney general, John Harlan stood squarely in the crossfire.

JOHN WAS FLATTERED. A group of "Conservative" Unionists was calling on him to run for Congress again, to seek the nomination for the same Ashland District seat he had failed to win in 1859. While the idea was alluring, John could not see his way clear to another grueling campaign. Not now, with his father's estate still in knots and his own finances in a shaky state.

But why not take advantage of the solicitation to offer his views on Kentucky's political crisis? That way, his answer to the group's leader might end up in a newspaper, and serve as a kind of Harlan manifesto on the dangers facing his state and nation. He sat down to write his lengthy reply on June 1, 1865, his thirty-second birthday.

His primary target: the constitutional amendment abolishing slavery, marching toward ratification. It now stood only five states shy of the three-quarters needed. No matter. He could not support it, he wrote, not even if there were fewer than "a dozen slaves" left in Kentucky. The amendment would be "a direct interference, by a portion of the States, with the local concerns of other States." The amendment opened the door to more federal meddling, he said. No local policy would be safe. Not just in Kentucky, but anywhere, North or South. The "white men of Kentucky," he predicted gloomily, "will regret that any of them ever assented to the surrender to other States, through Congress, of our undoubted right to regulate our own local concerns."

Yes, he had heard the arguments, rooted in political prudence, that ratification was a foregone conclusion. That it was wiser to swallow hard, and move on. But he could not accept this. Why, he asked, should we surrender *our* convictions? Conservative men must do what is right, he said, not what is expedient. "We will then have the proud consciousness that we did all in our power to stay the tide of fanaticism which threatens to sweep away the landmarks erected by our fathers." *The tide of fanaticism.* Strong words from a man who described himself as a moderate Unionist.

John wanted to make himself clear: He had no doubt that slavery's time was ending. But Kentucky must have the power to say how and when. "If left alone, unterrified by armed bands of negro soldiers, the people of Kentucky will, in due time . . . dispose of all questions relating to slavery in their midst, consistently with the interests of the whites and blacks, and soon enough for the comfort, security and happiness of both races," he wrote. Immediate abolition was a mistake, he said. The state needed time to enact legislation that would "protect her white citizens from the ruinous effects of such a violent change in our social system."

John's declaration of principles did not take long to find its way into print. Ten days later, it debuted in the Lexington paper. The headline: "Interesting Letter from Col. John M. Harlan."

AS THE FOURTH of July approached, a new rumor spread: Palmer would free all enslaved people who traveled to Louisville for the annual celebration.

Palmer was dumbfounded. He had no such plans, and no such authority. But rumor prevailed. "The negroes in Kentucky believed I had unlimited power," Palmer would say later. By midday on the Fourth, Palmer's staff told him that thousands were gathered in a grove south of the city, awaiting his declaration of liberation. Palmer resolved to visit the grove, set the record straight, disperse the crowd, and ask them to go home, to wait. The constitutional amendment would free them soon enough.

His plan quickly changed. "When I reached the mass of colored people," he recalled, "I was lifted over their heads and placed upon a platform. . . . When the tumult had partially subsided, I said, 'My countrymen, you are *substantially* free.'"

His nuance was lost in the crescendo of cheers. "They never heard the word 'substantially,'" he later said. Instead, the crowd heard "free" and erupted into song, dance and the sort of praise that Palmer thought "only proper when used in reference to the Supreme Being."

Casting caution aside, Palmer decided he could "drive the last nail" into the coffin of Kentucky slavery. He could do it here, now, on the national birthday, in this nameless grove on the outskirts of Louisville. "My countrymen," he shouted, "you are free, and while I command in this department, the military forces of the United States will defend your right to freedom."

He had been caught up in the moment, but now that moment was over. What next? Turning back was out of the question. Every day brought new reports of colored people in flight, from multiple directions, to multiple destinations. Not just to Louisville, but to Lexington, Frankfort, Bowling Green, Munfordville, Paducah—to any Union outpost where shelter and protection might be found. It was a migration of unprecedented proportions. Most had no place to go, so they ended up in abandoned buildings, barns, sheds—"every nook and hiding-place," as Palmer put it. Most had no money, no prospect of employment. Who would dare hire them?

Exasperated slaveholders called on Palmer to enforce Kentucky law, to send them back. He didn't see how. By his estimate, more than half of Kentucky's two hundred and thirty thousand slaves now qualified as free, thanks to one congressional action or another. How could he and his military force be expected to determine the legal status of every colored traveler?

On July 20, Palmer made his choice. He signed a new edict, Order No. 49, offering passes to *any* colored person who asked for one, not just those who couldn't find work. On the Saturday following his decree, the roads into the Kentucky town of Paris were jammed with refugees of "all ages and sizes, including the lame, the halt, and the blind, in wagons, buggies, on horseback and on foot," the Paris newspaper said. By midweek, the provost marshals there had issued more than thirteen hundred passes.

Few were turned away, in Paris or elsewhere. Palmer was content to have the provost marshals err on the side of freedom, rather than mistakenly send a free man or woman back into slavery. His opponents were content to call him a tyrant and autocrat. Their anger fueled calls for his ouster. Then, from a grand jury led by a Louisville judge, came the first of several indictments of Palmer for aiding runaways.

The showdown had finally arrived. It would be State vs. Federal, the Commonwealth of Kentucky vs. the U.S. Military—and, eventually, Attorney General Harlan's resistance vs. General Palmer's activism.

THE PALMER INDICTMENT could have died a quiet death on December 8, 1865. In the preceding days, three more states had ratified the constitutional amendment, reaching the required three-quarters. As soon as Secretary of State William Seward issued the official verification, the Constitution would have a Thirteenth Amendment, and slavery would be illegal in the United States. In Louisville, Circuit Judge George W. Johnston saw no reason to wait for Seward's signature. Taking "judicial notice" of the amendment's approval, he dismissed the charges against Palmer. The general might be guilty, the judge said, but he could no longer be convicted. The ratification had made Kentucky's slavery laws "a dead letter."

The next day, the state's prosecutor breathed life back into the corpse. He filed notice of a possible appeal, preserving the state's option to argue that Kentucky law had been valid during the many months when Palmer and his troops were issuing their passes, and therefore, Palmer could still be found guilty.

Now it was up to John. As attorney general, he would write the brief.

While he was deciding what to do, the Thirteenth was certified and martial law lifted. Few would blame him for finding a way to duck the issue, and move on.

He chose to stand and fight. In his legal mind, running roughshod over Kentucky's laws was hardly a minor matter. This was a chance to stop the federal incursion into state affairs. If nothing else, John could expect his written brief to receive an attentive reading—one of the three sitting judges was his old law professor and mentor, George Robertson.

John well remembered Robertson's stirring lectures, his description of the Constitution's delicate balance between state and national authority, his warning that slavery "cannot be eradicated without convulsion." Since then, the two of them had evolved into political allies, going back to John's first campaign for the Know Nothings. Robertson had been at the center of Kentucky politics and law for a half century, and in the twilight of his long career, he was now serving his second stint on the Court of Appeals.

John's argument was short, not quite four pages. "All persons from the highest to the lowest, are subject to the laws of the land," he wrote. "Kentucky was never in rebellion and," therefore, "a military commandant has no more right to aid the slaves of our people to escape than the commandant in Ohio had to take, seize or destroy [a citizen's] property in that state." As for Judge Johnston's dismissal of the case, it had been premature. "I insist," John said, "that the court below had no official notice" of the amendment's ratification. But the timing was beside the point, he asserted. What mattered most was that "slavery had not been abolished when the offense was committed."

John won. The court's opinion, delivered by Robertson, lambasted Palmer's order as "a false pretense ingeniously fabricated" to emancipate Kentucky's remaining slaves. Palmer's "unlawful intermeddling" had incited "a spirit of servile insurrection," disrupting the state's system of labor, leaving farmers and others "without their accustomed and necessary help."

Robertson fully embraced John's main arguments. Palmer had no authority to ignore or overturn Kentucky law, Robertson's ruling said, and the Thirteenth Amendment's ratification was irrelevant because Palmer's illegal actions had taken place months earlier. With undisguised sarcasm, the court offered a Kentucky-bred analogy: A horse thief's guilt does not dissolve just because the horse happens to die after the theft.

The ruling had no practical effect. By the time it came out, in October 1866, much had changed. The state legislature, in the wake of the Thirteenth's ratification, had officially dismantled the state's slavery laws. Palmer was gone, back to Illinois, his military career over. No one in Kentucky seemed inclined to haul the ex-general back for a trial.

But for John, prosecuting Palmer had never been his primary objective. Principle and political advantage, not punishment, had been his aims.

BY 1867, JOHN'S FINAL YEAR as attorney general, he had spent a decade jumping from one improvised political party to another. The Know Nothings. The Opposition. Constitutional Unionists. Unionists. Conservative Unionists. It was not a formula for long-term influence.

He was weary of being a political nomad, of joining third parties with little chance of winning, but he still saw no good options. He had given up on the state's Democrats, now thoroughly dominated by ex-rebels. The Republicans, however, offered no comfort. They had followed up the Thirteenth Amendment with the Civil Rights Act of 1866, a far-reaching law that required no ratification by the states, and yet amounted to federal interference in every sector of Kentucky life. To cheers from a full gallery, the Republicans had enacted it over President Andrew Johnson's veto. Colored people had celebrated in the Capitol's hallways after the vote.

The 1866 act was breathtakingly ambitious. All colored people born in the United States were now declared citizens, "in every State and Territory," entitled to the "full and equal benefit of all laws and proceedings." They would have "the same right" as "white citizens" to make contracts, buy and sell property, bring lawsuits, give evidence in court, and benefit from inheritance. Anyone depriving them of these rights was guilty of a crime, and the prescribed penalties were hefty—a thousand-dollar fine or a year in jail, or both. Federal agents were given extensive powers to investigate and prevent violations. They would have plenty to investigate in Kentucky, where in parts of the state, bands of armed white men were undertaking reigns of terror against the newly freed colored population and some white Unionists. These outlaws were calling themselves "Regulators."

There was more. Officers of the new Freedmen's Bureau, established to aid and protect former slaves, were authorized to arrest "every person who shall violate the provisions of this act." Cases ignored or floundering in state courts could be taken or transferred to federal court.

In Kentucky, the act spawned new outbreaks of legal conflict. State law still prohibited "a slave, negro, or Indian" from testifying in cases involving someone white. Such testimony was crucial to prosecuting Regulators who were carrying out violent attacks against blacks. Judges in local courts now had to choose which law to follow: federal or state?

The situation begged for clarity. Nearly all state judges were opting to follow Kentucky law, but not Judge William C. Goodloe, a Republican sitting in Lexington. In Goodloe's courtroom, a white man was convicted of theft on a black man's testimony in January 1867, and then sent to jail. The white man, William Bowlin, appealed his conviction, claiming that the judge was wrong to allow "George Gardner, a negro man" to appear as a witness.

Bowlin's appeal put the case in John's lap. As attorney general, John's duty was to defend the conviction—which, in this case, also might mean defending the state prosecutor's decision to use a colored witness in the first place. John chose to stay silent. He explained his decision in an unusual one-paragraph "Suggestion" to the Court of Appeals.

"The only question in this appeal," John wrote, is "the propriety of the court admitting the testimony of a negro against a white person. Not feeling at liberty, according to my views of that question . . . to uphold the judgment of the court below, the case is respectfully submitted to the [Appeals Court] without argument on behalf of the Commonwealth."

With that extraordinary sidestep, John signaled his disapproval of the Lexington judge's ruling. The Civil Rights Act, in John's view, was another federal assault on Kentucky's prerogatives. Not surprisingly, the Court of Appeals emphatically agreed. Once again, Robertson delivered a forceful opinion that attacked the heart of the Radical Republican agenda.

The Thirteenth Amendment only authorized Congress to enact laws that would ensure slavery's abolition, Robertson ruled. It did not give Congress the power to enact a sweeping Civil Rights Act or intervene in the operation of Kentucky's courts. The Lexington judge was wrong to allow the negro's testimony, Robertson said.

The ruling, overturning Bowlin's conviction, came out in June 1867. It was one of the last of John's cases as attorney general. Two months later, he lost his bid for reelection on his latest third-party ticket, the Conservative Union Democrats. Every state and congressional office went to the regular Democrats by wide and disheartening margins. Thoroughly discouraged, John took a hard look at his political future. With the Conservative Union disbanding, he had to decide: Go with the state's triumphant Democrats, and their white supremacist rhetoric? Or cast his lot with the weaker Republicans, committed to a direction that John had long opposed?

It was not much of a choice, he later said. He could not align himself with men who had worked to break up the Union, or stand with a party that countenanced the "Regulators" and the new "Ku-Klux." From now on, John would call himself a Republican, for better or worse.

ONCE, JOHN HARLAN AND BENJAMIN H. BRISTOW had stood a considerable distance apart, on both the political and legal spectrum. But they had kindled a friendship, despite their differences. Now, in 1869, Harlan and Bristow were contemplating a law partnership that would bring together two of the state's best-known Republicans. It would be a formidable union, but one that had seemed unimaginable only a few years earlier.

As attorney general and Conservative Unionist, John had resisted the 1866 Civil Rights Act. As U.S. district attorney for Kentucky, Bristow had taken the lead in prosecuting these new civil rights cases. By the end of 1867, Bristow was doing exactly what John had opposed as attorney general: He was diverting dozens of criminal cases from state courts, trying them in federal court, asserting that Kentucky's testimony laws left him no choice. The growing list of crimes was horrific—robberies, assaults, murders, lynchings. In one of the most brutal cases, a colored family was set upon in their Lewis County cabin by two ax-wielding white men. Four were killed. One of the victims, sixteen-year-old Richard Foster, managed to give his account of the savage attack before dying. Bristow had the case transferred to federal court.

As long as Kentucky law prevented blacks from giving evidence against whites, Bristow had concluded, there was little or no chance of convicting a Regulator or a Ku-Klux in state court. That's why the Civil Rights Act was so critical, Bristow believed. Without it, he felt, the freedom conferred by the Thirteenth Amendment was almost pointless. As contemptible as slavery had been, masters had an economic incentive to protect their slaves. Who would protect these free people now, if not the federal government?

John was coming around to seeing the world through his new Republican eyes. He had campaigned for General Ulysses S. Grant in the 1868 presidential contest, and found himself on the winning side of a national election for the first time in his life. He had to endure the Democratic catcalls, of course, the constant heckling about his switches over the past decade. Yes, yes, he had voted for McClellan over Lincoln. Yes, he had railed against the Radicals and their constitutional amendments. But no, he was not sorry to call himself a Republican.

In the waning days of 1867, his term as attorney general finished, he and Mallie had decided to move the family back to Louisville. With his father's estate essentially settled, and his bills mounting, Louisville offered more opportunities. The federal court was there. So were the major shipping and railroad companies. As it turned out, the political scene was livelier as well, with many more Republicans than in conservative Frankfort. If John wanted to help build a stronger Republican Party—and his own political fortunes—Louisville was the place to do it.

He and Bristow were now warm friends as well as political allies. In early 1870, they announced their law partnership in the Louisville papers: Harlan, Newman & Bristow, offices at 178 and 180 Jefferson Street. Their past differences posed no obstacle. John had proven himself adept at leaving the past behind, as he often urged others to do in his political speeches.

Bristow's star was rising fast, though, and the partnership didn't last the year. By the fall, Bristow was in Washington, appointed by Grant as the nation's first solicitor general. He would have a major role in establishing the new Department of Justice, recently created by Congress, and arguing the government's positions before the Supreme Court. He and John carried on an animated correspondence as Bristow immersed himself in Washington's political waters.

Bristow's ascension to the top level of national government stimulated John's ambition. Was there also a future for him outside of Kentucky? In November 1870, prompted by a Bristow letter that included firsthand observations about several Supreme Court justices, John gave voice to his internal musings. Speculating about candidates for the court's next vacancy, John told Bristow: "It may be that you will be the man for the vacancy."

Far-fetched? John did not think so, he told Bristow. Grant might want a justice from one of "the late slave-holding states," he wrote. The job held enormous appeal, in John's view. "I know of no more desirable position than that of a Judge of the Supreme Court, especially if the salary should be increased to $10,000—It lifts a man high above the atmosphere on which most public men move, and enables him to become, in every sense, an independent man, with an opportunity to make a record that will be remembered long after he is gone."

Returning to reality, John sounded almost despairing about his native Kentucky and his prospects there. "I have sometimes thought that, if I could, I would leave this rebel state," he confided. But if the Democrats were to capture the presidency in 1872, as some were predicting, where would he go? Not to Washington, certainly. "The probability is that I will plug away here at the law for the balance of my days. . . . It is a hard master, but I love it better than any other except that, if I were a wealthy man, I would enjoy public life."

A year later, public life beckoned once more.

JOHN DID NOT "SEEK" the Republican nomination for governor in 1871, he would insist at the time. Years later, he even professed "great surprise" that the convention had picked him, as if the idea had materialized out of the thin air atop Kentucky's Cumberland Mountains.

Downplaying his ambition might have suited John's temperament, but he had had plenty of notice that the party wanted him. A month before the Republicans convened in Frankfort, the newspapers were saying that the outcome was a foregone conclusion. "It is quite certain that General John M. Harlan, of Louisville, will receive the nomination for Governor without serious opposition," one wrote, "and it is almost as certain he will accept, although he has repeatedly said in reply to the urgent request of his friends that he would not run."

It was true that he felt conflicted. His finances were as precarious as ever, and his children now numbered five. But if the party needed him—and it surely needed somebody, because it was still no match for the Democrats, either in organization or membership—he felt he could not refuse. The nomination, he later said, "seemed a call to duty."

Most newspapers were counting him out from the beginning. A majority of white Kentuckians had supported the Union, but like John in his earlier days, many in that majority regarded the Republicans with suspicion. John's only hope were the thousands of colored men casting their first-ever ballots. The newest constitutional amendment, the Fifteenth, had given them the right to vote. The Fourteenth had guaranteed them citizenship and "equal protection of the laws." Ironically, of course, John had opposed both amendments before his Republican crossover.

In case he had forgotten what he once said about negro equality, negro suffrage, and negro testimony, the Democrats were only too ready to remind him. That would be John's fate in the campaign: He had a lot of explaining to do. His opponent, the incumbent Preston H. Leslie, would make sure of that. Leslie had been governor for only a few months, the beneficiary of a series of political maneuvers that had sent his predecessor to Washington as a senator. Leslie did not have John's gift for oratory, but he still loomed as a formidable opponent. One Democratic newspaper described Leslie's style as "calm, thoughtful and argumentative."

They agreed to an exhausting slate of debates, in towns all over the state, some reachable only by horseback. On June 1, they were in northeastern Kentucky, in lightly populated Lewis County. The campaign was just beginning, and a large crowd was waiting at the courthouse in Vanceburg, along with correspondents for the Louisville and Cincinnati papers. No black voters had dared to join the throng, but a "sprinkling of ladies" could be seen.

Leslie spoke first, and before long, he was quoting from a Harlan speech, delivered in May 1866, describing the treachery of the Radical Republicans. John heard the loud echo of his long-ago claim that the Thirteenth Amendment amounted to "a *complete revolution* in our republican system of government, and, most probably, the *overthrow of Constitutional liberty*." Slyly, Leslie praised John for those long-ago words. "That was the correct view," he told the cheering crowd. "It was the view the Democratic party then took, and it is the view that every fair-minded conservative man must have today."

John knew he could not run away from his past. He could not let the Democrats define him. He had to define himself. "I admit that I have changed some of [my] opinions," he told the crowd, but how could any man do otherwise, given the cataclysm of the last decade? "Let it rather be said of me that I am right rather than consistent," he declared, borrowing from the rhetoric of Henry Clay, who had famously said that he would rather be right than be president. John liked his version so much that he repeated it often during the campaign.

Leslie had his own refrains. He often said that a Harlan victory would be a "negro" victory. "You, General Harlan, will have more negro voters than white voters," he declared at the Vanceburg debate. The consequence? A Harlan administration, Leslie claimed, would force "negro equality" on the state. A Harlan administration would seek to repeal the statute prohibiting marriage between negroes and whites. A Harlan administration would have negro appointees of all sorts—judges, magistrates, tobacco inspectors.

John developed a variety of responses to such scare tactics. "The gentleman may succeed in raising a prejudice against me in the breasts of some poor spirit Kentuckians, but I appeal to your better nature, my fellow citizens," he said. When Leslie complained about the Republican Party's insatiable desire for "negro votes," John would retort that he had seen quite a few "darkies" at Democratic rallies, and that Leslie wasn't turning any of them away.

But as the campaign wore on, John sought to reassure white voters more directly. In late June, he said: "I belong to the white race, and I believe that superior to any other . . . all the equality laws that have been enacted cannot alter that relation." As for schools, they should be equally supported by property taxes on everyone, he said, but it was "right and proper" for them to remain separate.

He accused the Democrats of making false claims about his intentions if elected. "What do they mean by this cry of 'negro equality?'" he said in July. "Do you suppose that any law of the State can regulate social intercourse?" The negro is "your equal before law . . . but he is not your equal socially. . . . Social equality can never exist between the two races in Kentucky."

Just as he felt a need to denounce "social equality," he also separated himself from the Republican Party's Radical wing. But on the three constitutional amendments guaranteeing rights to people of color, he refused to back away. "I have lived long enough, to feel and declare, as I do on this night, that the most perfect despotism that ever existed on this earth was the institution of African slavery," he declared at a July 26 rally. "I rejoice that it is gone."

HE LOST, RESPECTABLY. He polled more than 40 percent of the vote, far and away the most that any Republican had received in Kentucky, fifty thousand more than Grant in 1868. He was still twenty-seven thousand short of victory, but the newspapers—including a few grudging Democratic ones—were impressed. They credited John's sterling oratory and tireless campaigning with putting the Kentucky party on a better footing.

John himself took heart. Though he had failed to win, he had gained something else—a national profile. The *Cincinnati Daily Gazette* suggested that he would make a fine vice-presidential candidate in 1872, while the *New York Tribune* thought a cabinet post might be in his future. The party's leaders soon took notice of this John-come-lately to the Republican fold. A month after John's loss, President Grant was visiting Ohio and Kentucky. The two men—the famous general and the not-as-famous colonel—met in Covington for serious discussions.

Rather than retreating to lick his electoral wounds, John prepared himself for the fight to come with renewed vigor. He was now regarded as the leader of Kentucky's Republican Party. He had found his political home. His conversion was complete, even if his evolution was not.

MICHIGAN REVOLUTIONIZED.

The New Constitution Overwhelmingly Defeated.

Michigan Believes This is a White Man's Government.

THE PEOPLE NO LONGER THE DUPES OF RADICALISM.

The Example of Ohio Followed by the Wolverine State.

Resistance, Northern-style: The *Detroit Free Press*, April 7, 1868, after the defeat of equal suffrage

11

"A Taste for Judicial Life"

Brown in Detroit, 1866–1872

THE MISSING WERE THERE, and not only in spirit.

They were as much a part of Henry Billings Brown's Tenth Yale Reunion as anyone seated at the celebratory dinner on July 25, 1866. They were there in Theron Brown's poem, "Our Class Dead," which the author read aloud in somber voice. They were there in melody, a hundred or so voices singing "in whispering tones of the dead of Fifty-Six." They were there in memory, their names and sacrifices inscribed in the 1856 class report: Bartholomew. Bulkeley. Dunbar. McIntyre. Peck. Walker. Woods. Most had fought for the Union, except Dunbar, a son of Mississippi. Three had died from injuries, the others from disease. Some were Henry's friends. Some he hardly knew. All would have been about his age, just thirty years old, had they lived to see the reunion.

That night, in the warm glow of dining room number two at the New Haven House, Henry could not avoid the war's aura. All around him were men who had served, who had survived, who had come to the reunion, some to share their stories, others to forget them. Henry had no comparable tales to tell or bury. What he had seen of the war was limited to his two brief trips to the South, to Tennessee and Virginia. But he was trying to understand.

Earlier in the year, during a bitter cold snap that had driven much of

Detroit indoors for the better part of a week, Henry had spent his evenings immersed in Edwin Pollard's *Southern History of the War*, written from the Confederate perspective. The just-published book had been attracting attention, and Henry had wanted to see what the fuss was about. For the Young Men's Society, where Reconstruction politics were now a prime topic of discussion, he had written an essay on Jefferson Davis, the Confederacy's benighted former president. Henry had worked hard on it, in the evenings during late February, until his unreliable eyes had rebelled. Carry had to write out the final draft. He managed to read the essay aloud at the society's meeting, but paid the price in several more days of painful inflammation. Would he never be free of this scourge?

Fortunately, his eyes were behaving themselves as he, Carry, and one of Carry's friends prepared for their trip to the East. Henry had arranged to stay away a month, which meant they would be spending quite a few of their pretty pennies on the journey. The final bill would top five hundred dollars, a third of their expenses for the entire year. But traveling was a balm for him, and he was determined to enjoy the extravagance. His good mood had turned sour, though, on their arrival in New Haven. Staying at the Tontine Hotel was a "grand mistake," he groused in his daybook. The "wretched" accommodations were spoiling his fun. Ten years earlier, his rooms at the college had ranked somewhere between austere and spare. But with age came changing expectations. On the steamer from Detroit to Cleveland, the first leg of their trip, he had booked "the best staterooms on the boat."

At the reunion, he luxuriated in the camaraderie of old friends. The legal profession had attracted fully a third of the class, making Henry feel both right at home and apprehensive about his accomplishments. He could boast of five years' experience as an assistant U.S. attorney, and he was building a reputation as an expert on admiralty cases, disputes involving the river or the sea. But some days, he came out of court wondering if he needed to find a new line of work.

Only two months earlier, in his private practice, he had met defeat in a murder trial. His client had been accused of "chopping his sister in pieces with an axe," Henry had written in his daybook. He spent weeks reading about insanity, finding experts, consulting with a doctor at the state asylum in Kalamazoo. After the jury returned a guilty verdict, he judged himself harshly. "Bah! . . . Monstrous poor luck in trying cases. Guess I am not enough of a lawyer after all."

He tried to push aside his anxieties for now. Reunions were a time for celebration, cigars, conviviality, and dinner toasts lasting long into the night. Only fatigue brought a close to his conversations. Dawn had come and gone by the time he fell into his uncomfortable bed.

A WEEK LATER, he and Carry stood on the seashore at Watch Hill, Henry's old summer stomping grounds in southern Rhode Island. He had been eager to come, to introduce her to the ocean and his old friends. Everything was the same—the resort hotels, the waves, the lighthouse, the beauty of it all—and yet Henry felt the irritating creep of disappointment. Something had changed, or perhaps he had. "Watch Hill more than usually stupid and little attraction here now," he wrote. He was finding fault more often these days, recording his barbs in his daybook, sometimes in jest, more often in jaundice. There was the "ogre" of a federal judge, the "execrable dinner," and the "rather insignificant fireworks."

After a scant three days, Henry gladly abandoned Watch Hill for the steamboat ride across Long Island Sound to New York City. They had a grand time strolling the big city's streets. Henry felt revived, ready for his return. On their last leg home, through Canada on the Great Western Railway, he was taken enough with several female passengers to make a special note in his daybook: "Beautiful quadroons in the cars."

Colored passengers, of any hue, were a rarity on the half dozen major rail lines serving Detroit. Michigan had more than a million people now, but only 1 percent—about eleven thousand—were people of color. In Detroit, the state's largest city, the percentage was larger, but still tiny, not quite 3 percent, about two thousand. Yet race—the "negro question," as the newspapers were now fond of saying—was already an outsized political issue in the state, aided by the provocative statements of its popular Republican governor, Henry H. Crapo.

Crapo's improbable rise to political prominence was evidence of the state's longstanding openness to newcomers, especially successful ones. Michigan was still in its youth, fewer than thirty years removed from territorial status. Nearly everyone was from somewhere else, or their parents were. Like Henry, Crapo was a New Englander. Like Henry, he was saddled with health problems. Unlike Henry, he was well into his sixties, the father of ten children, and one of Michigan's wealthier men.

The two men's paths would eventually intersect, to the younger Henry's lasting benefit.

IN SIX SHORT YEARS, Crapo had gone from newcomer to chief executive. He had come to the state from New Bedford, the Massachusetts whaling town. As young man, he had practiced law there, while also doubling as the city's tax collector and treasurer. In the 1830s, he had jumped hard into the buying and selling of Western lands, primarily in Ohio and Michigan. After amassing a substantial fortune, he had moved his large family to Flint in the late 1850s so he could tend to his burgeoning businesses in lumber and salt mining. His investments had caused him to cross paths with Henry's father-in-law, Sam Pitts, also a lumber and salt baron. Not content with his commercial empire, Crapo had branched out into politics.

Crapo was a dedicated Republican, but no firebrand. The party's Radical wing made him uncomfortable. He regarded its leaders as prone to ruthlessness toward the South, and he wanted no part of that. At the same time, Crapo believed strongly in the need for constitutional amendments ending slavery and ensuring political equality. He had met Lincoln twice in the months before his assassination, and had been in Washington for the mournful weeks that had followed, a profoundly moving experience. He returned to Michigan with a determination to stand taller in the fight for equal rights.

Lincoln's unlikely successor had been Andrew Johnson of Tennessee, a

Southern Democrat serving as vice president. Lincoln and Johnson had been thrown together on a "National Unity" ticket in 1864, and now, the Republicans were seeing the consequence of that invented show of conciliation. When Johnson vetoed the 1866 Civil Rights Act, Crapo was crestfallen. Congress was preparing to overturn the veto, but in the meantime, Crapo devised his own unorthodox way of showing his opposition to Johnson's foot-dragging.

On March 31, 1866, Crapo issued an extraordinary proclamation, designating a "Day of Fasting, Humiliation and Prayer." He invoked "the Creator," but left no doubt that his purpose was political, not religious. The "antagonism between the ruling powers" in Washington, he wrote, was impeding Reconstruction. "Millions of freedmen are trembling and weeping for the safety and security of our Government," his proclamation said. "Let us seek, then, the Divine aid . . . to abandon our prejudices, and to reconstruct the Republic upon the broad principles of Right, of Humanity, Justice and Eternal Truth; when all men, irrespective of color or caste, shall be equal in the eyes of the law."

All men, irrespective of color or caste. Equal in the eyes of the law. Potent statements, made even more powerful by a backward glance at Crapo's evolution. Twenty-five years earlier in Massachusetts, as a judge in New Bedford's police court, he had heard the criminal complaint brought by David Ruggles, ejected from a train for refusing to sit in a separate car. Crapo had sided with the railroad, saying it was a private corporation and entitled to make reasonable rules. He acquitted the conductor of the alleged assault that had left Ruggles bruised and battered.

What would Governor Crapo say now about Judge Crapo's ruling? No one was asking, of course. But this much could be said: Governor Crapo was not the same man as the one in that New Bedford courtroom long ago. Not if he believed that "millions of freedmen are trembling and weeping for the safety and security of our government."

Crapo's proclamation provoked a fierce reaction from Democrats and their newspaper allies in Detroit. "Malignant Official Insult to the President and the People," the *Free Press* headline said. The opposition's vehemence startled him, Crapo told his family, but it also made him proud. "You would have thought I had exploded a hundred bomb shells in a crowd of 70,000 people," he wrote to his son. "Its effect shows me I was right . . . let them howl."

THE RIPPLES OF RECONSTRUCTION were washing into Michigan and elsewhere in the North. In Washington, the Radical Republicans were insisting that the rebel states, as a prelude to readmission to the Union, rewrite their constitutions to remove all vestiges of slavery and accept their liberated slaves as part of their population. But what about the Northern states? Michigan's 1850 constitution, for one, restricted voting to "white male" residents. How could Republicans hope to "reform" the South while clinging to such visible prejudice in the North?

Michigan's constitution had a built-in trigger for change, requiring voters to decide every sixteen years whether to undertake a revision. Sixteen years had now elapsed. As the 1866 campaign dawned, Republicans were urging a yes vote for a constitutional convention that would consider equal suffrage and other political rights. Democrats were resisting, but except in Detroit, they were outnumbered in the state.

Henry awoke on Wednesday, November 7, to a smashing Republican sweep. Crapo would have a second two-year term and another Republican majority in the legislature. "Democrats utterly prostrate," Henry noted gleefully in his daybook.

The voters had given a far less emphatic go-ahead for a constitutional convention. Were they worried a revision would go too far? It was hard to know. The Republican-inclined editors at the *Detroit Advertiser and Tribune* put their fingers on the public's pulse, and claimed it was beating strongly in favor of equal suffrage for men of color. "Indeed, so strong is the popular current," the *Tribune* editors wrote, "that the Democratic press, with their traditional hatred of the colored man, have not had the courage to contest the point."

The Democrats had conceded nothing of the sort. The fight over "negro" suffrage would soon reveal divisions in Michigan that were as bitter as those in Kentucky, Louisiana, and the halls of Congress.

THE FAMOUS SENATOR Charles Sumner of Massachusetts was in town. The Radical Republican was there to deliver the opening lecture for the Detroit Young Men's Society's fall-winter series. Henry had marked the date: Thursday, October 10, 1867, 8:00 p.m., admission fifty cents.

As an active member of the society, Henry tried to attend most of its events. But the Sumner oratory held a special appeal—not because of the man's politics, which gave Henry pause, but because Sumner would be calling at his father-in-law's house. Sumner and Sam Pitts were old friends from their student days at Harvard, giving Henry a chance to spend a few minutes with the renowned orator. Henry relished these opportunities. A year earlier, Major General William Tecumseh Sherman, still riding high from his wartime exploits, had stopped in Detroit for a day. Henry had engineered a personal introduction to Sherman, employing "a masterly piece of strategy," he exulted in his daybook.

Sumner's tireless abolitionist efforts had given him prominence long before the war, but his near-murder at his Senate desk had made him a legend. In 1856, an angry South Carolina congressman had roared into the near-empty chamber, and had beaten Sumner unconscious with his walking cane. It had taken three years for Sumner to return to full-time work. If nothing else, the Massachusetts senator was a symbol for never giving up, and never giving in.

Now Sumner was in the thick of a new fight. The latest federal constitutional amendment was slowly making its way to ratification—this would be the Fourteenth, if enough states passed it—mandating "equal protection." Sumner, who had wanted a stronger amendment, thought the equal protection clause would be meaningless without additional legislation spelling out what the phrase meant. He intended to draft a new civil rights bill allowing the nation's colored population to sit, ride, and stay anywhere that whites could.

The senator had infuriated many in the South—and many in his own party—with his uncompromising ways. But few disputed Sumner's oratorical skills, and Henry was eager to hear him in person. They had much in common, these two men of Massachusetts: educations from New England's finest colleges, legal careers, and a love of traveling in Europe. But where Sumner was fiery, Henry was cautious. Where Sumner was unbending, Henry was uncertain. Sumner had eloquence. What did Henry have? Sometimes, he would write out a speech to give at a Republican meeting, and then keep it in his pocket, undelivered.

A miserable late afternoon rain had drenched Detroit, but the Young Men's Hall was nearly full when Henry settled into his seat on the evening of March 10. Sumner had titled his lecture "Are We a Nation?" and for two uninterrupted hours, he wove a tapestry of world history and current politics into a claim that the country had reached a crucial stage in its evolution. "The duel between the Nation and States must forever be brought to an end," he said. States' rights must be "crushed out. . . . We must have a central national authority." Words matter, he proclaimed, and that's why "national" must replace "federal" in the political lexicon. He explained: The courts of the United States are *national*, not federal; the army is *national*, not federal; the debt is *national*, not federal. Exalting *state* governments, he warned, puts the *nation's* future at risk.

From the Democratic paper, the *Free Press*, came a withering review. The senator had given "a thinly disguised partisan speech, with the irrepressible nigger kept just out of sight." But that was to be expected from a "third-rate man" who "has never achieved anything really useful or deserving to survive his memory." From the Republican paper, the *Tribune*, flowed a river of accolades. The senator had "charmed" the audience with his "power and beauty of thought."

That night at home, Henry scribbled his own brief assessment: "He is not a very accurate speaker, but is a man of truly noble presence and magnificent bearing."

LIKE A MOTH circling a light, Henry flitted around Detroit's political scene. He wasn't convinced that he had the temperament for the rough-hewn world of politics, but he would have no chance of finding out if he didn't keep his hand in. He was now a regular at caucus meetings in the Tenth Ward, his home base. A few weeks after Sumner's lecture, he ran for delegate to the county convention, making a decent enough speech, and won. Then in March 1868, much to his surprise, the Tenth elected him as president of its delegation to the state convention.

Henry didn't lie to himself. These were minor victories. But if he wanted to hold public office, he needed to school himself in the not-so-fine art of persuading people to vote for Henry B. Brown. Could he ever become comfortable with such self-promotion? He couldn't see how.

For an evening's diversion, the Young Men's Hall was often Henry's choice. Year after year, the topics and guests remained timely and impressive. He had been in the audience for Frederick Douglass's lecture a month earlier, a performance that the *Tribune* had labeled a "masterly effort" and the *Free Press* had ignored entirely, except to note that Douglass was in town and would be "entertained to-day by a delegation of colored brethren."

A large crowd—men and women of both races, more white than black—had listened keenly as Douglass built a tower of arguments for guaranteed rights. "What we want most is equal suffrage," he said. "Give the negro the ballot and he will carry out the work of reconstruction in the Southern States. Let the plea of inferiority be cast aside."

Were Michigan white voters willing to cast inferiority aside? They would have their chance on April 10, when the revised state constitution would finally have its yea-or-nay moment. After months of wrangling at a constitutional convention, a document had emerged with dozens of changes. The clause granting equal suffrage had survived; the word "white" had vanished from the list of voter qualifications. Remarkably, a move to drop "male" had enjoyed a brief success. But in the end, the men rewriting the constitution could not bring themselves to extend voting rights to women. Female suffrage lost, forty-six to twenty-three.

From reading the newspapers, as Henry did religiously, it was easy to think that "negro suffrage" was the *only* issue that mattered. The *Free Press* warned that the revised constitution would bring negroes swarming into

Michigan. Thousands of former slaves were living in Canadian exile, just across the river from Detroit, the paper said. "Is this the kind of population we want to attract to our state?"

Hogwash, retorted the *Tribune* editors. Other Northern states already had negro suffrage, some for years, and their colored populations were still miniscule. Such arguments were nothing more than a diversionary tactic, the *Tribune* said. Democrats were worried—with good cause, the *Tribune* said—that colored voters would become reliable Republicans.

The rhetorical battle escalated as Election Day neared. The *Free Press* offered "Nineteen Reasons Why the New Constitution Should Be Defeated." The first three took aim at extending suffrage to colored men; the remainder went after a potpourri of other provisions. For its part, the *Tribune* accused the Democrats of planting the seeds of fear, and then watering them with lies and exaggeration. "The great bugbear by which the Democratic party seeks to frighten a portion of their Republican opponents . . . is 'negro equality,'" the *Tribune* wrote. "Concede the ballot to the negro, and he will compel you to invite him to your dinner parties. Make him a voter and you must make him your son-in-law. What nonsense! . . . Equality before the law does not in the slightest degree imply social intimacy."

On Election Day, Henry went to the polls without much enthusiasm. "Voted early but not often," he wrote, his jest reflecting his lack of passion. As the returns trickled in, it became apparent that the *Tribune* and the Republicans had misread public sentiment. The revised constitution failed miserably. It could not muster even 40 percent of the vote.

Equal suffrage wasn't the sole reason for the defeat. The Democrats had done a good job of sowing doubt about a slew of provisions. But it was foolish to think that suffrage wasn't the primary factor. The *Tribune*, searching for an explanation, went deep into the Republican soul. "There are many Republicans, even in Michigan, who are not yet prepared to do justice to all men, and whose fidelity to the doctrine of Equal Rights is [more] theoretical than practical . . . they do not share in the vile and malignant hate of the negro that is common, but nevertheless they have not yet been emancipated from the slavery of prejudice."

The *Free Press* saw nothing to lament. "Michigan Revolutionized," its headline trumpeted, followed by "The New Constitution Overwhelmingly Defeated," and the clincher: "Michigan Believes This Is a White Man's Government."

DEATH ARRIVED in the Brown household on a warm spring Sunday in April 1868, two weeks after the constitution's defeat. Henry and Carry were heading to church when word came that Carry's father was seriously ill. Rushing to the grand house on Jefferson Avenue, they found Samuel Pitts failing. He had been unwell for years, a near invalid at times. By midnight, he had lost his "death struggle," as Henry called it. Sam Pitts was only fifty-eight, and had left behind an unimaginably large estate for his wife, his son, and his four daughters.

Henry had done a bit of legal work for his father-in-law's company. Now, he was pulled into the unavoidable complications that often accompany sudden death. On the evening of the funeral, the family gathered in Henry's parlor. Decisions were made: Tom, Sam Pitts's only son and business partner, would serve as the estate's administrator, with Henry's help. The family business would continue as before, adding new partners. There was no will, so as provided by law, the six heirs would share equally in the wealth built from stocks, lumber, salt reserves, and land holdings in thirteen counties. Fortunately, there was plenty of cash to cover debts. Sam Pitts had left his family in fine shape, financially, for years to come.

It would take months to appraise the many assets and several years, if not longer, before Carry would receive her share. But initial estimates showed the land parcels alone—thousands of acres—were worth nearly three hundred thousand dollars. Henry and Carry would have a solid foundation of income to rely on. Amid the grief, the timing was fortuitous. Only a month before his father-in-law's death, Henry had made a critical career choice. He had resigned from the U.S. district attorney's office after seven years. As of May 1—five days after Sam's death, as it now turned out—he would be on his own, dependent solely on his private practice.

Carry's inheritance, whenever it came, would lessen the risk of the leap he had just taken.

HENRY HAD OTHER WORRIES that money could not mitigate. Carry's health, often precarious, took a bad turn after her father's death. "Carry unable to sit up," he wrote. Henry had been through these cycles before. She would be fine for months, and then have no energy at all. A puzzle that no doctor could solve.

When Carry was on her feet, she and Henry loved to entertain. They finally had their own house, a fine wooden one on a corner of the Pitts property, in sight of the stately main residence where they had been living with Carry's parents and servants. Henry had supervised the construction, recording the slow progress in his daybook, wincing at the cost. Carry's twin sister Fannie and her husband also lived nearby, with their infant son and a second child on the way.

Henry and Carry had no children of their own, and Henry had resigned himself to the likelihood that they never would. "So it seems I am not to become paterfamilias," he had confided to his daybook. He didn't dwell on the reasons, concentrating instead on his disappointment. "Learned something respecting myself which chagrined me exceedingly. Confound it! Why must I be told these things."

Toward the end of May, with Carry feeling better, Henry set his sights on Chicago and the 1868 Republican National Convention. Eight years earlier, on a whim, he had gone to the same city for the conclave that had propelled Lincoln to the presidency. Henry hadn't enjoyed himself, but politics was a part of his life now. He thought he should be there.

He and two Republican friends took the overnight train. One was Charles Kent, a fellow lawyer whose company Henry had come to value. Arriving early in the morning, they set to work on finding a way into Crosby's Opera House. "Luckily," Henry wrote, "got tickets." Alas, General Ulysses S. Grant's nomination had none of the drama of Lincoln's. The speeches took longer than the balloting. Henry, unimpressed, was back on the train by nightfall.

A week later, Henry learned that the Republican Party was considering him for the vacant position of Wayne County circuit judge. Would he let his name go to Governor Crapo for consideration?

"Was completely taken aback," Henry wrote that night. "Asked time to think."

ON THE ONE HAND, what was there to think about? A judgeship on the most important local court in Detroit. Not as prestigious as the federal bench, but still an honor and a welcome break from the strain of being a trial lawyer.

On the other hand . . . there were strings attached. Not conditions, but caveats. Unlike federal judgeships, the circuit court job was an elected post. If chosen, Henry would need to run for a full six-year term. Either that, or act as a caretaker for four months. What were his chances of winning the election, assuming he could secure the nomination at the county convention? Not good. Detroit was still a Democratic stronghold. What if he wanted the nomination, and the convention delegates wanted someone else? That would be embarrassing. What if he won the nomination, only to discover after a few months that he didn't like being a judge? What if . . .

Enough. Henry didn't need to think about all that now. It wasn't even clear that Crapo would pick him. Four days after learning that his name was on the list, he heard that the entire matter would end there. "Prospects for my becoming a Judge look queer," he wrote.

He told himself that being passed over had its virtues. Circuit court judgeships didn't pay much, just fifteen hundred dollars a year, a deterrent for many lawyers. Beyond the money, he had to think about Carry's health problems. She would be leaving in a few days for Saratoga Springs, the famous health resort in New York, accompanied by a retinue of family members. Would it be fair to take on a new job with his young wife ailing? Caveats, more caveats.

News of his appointment came on a Thursday afternoon in late June, in a one-paragraph item in the *Tribune*: "We learn that Gov. Crapo has appointed Henry B. Brown Esq. of this city . . ." The next morning, his official notification was waiting, slipped under his office door.

As was his nature, Henry wondered why he had been appointed. It was possible, given the lousy salary, that no one else had wanted the job. The previous judge had resigned in protest of the low pay. But still . . . *Judge* Brown.

He liked the sound of it.

HENRY WAS NERVOUS. It was July 1, 1868, his first day on the Wayne County bench, and most of the legal community was there. Many were friends—Charles Kent, for one—and soon he would be sitting in judgment of their cases. Henry had prepared a short speech, aiming to sound humble and self-effacing. But embedded in his words were hints of dread—of the responsibility, of the workload, of making a mistake. It did not help that Detroit was in the grip of a blistering heat wave, turning the courtroom into a Saratoga-style steam bath.

"I am painfully conscious, gentlemen," Henry said to the colleagues arrayed before him, "of the interests of liberty, property and reputation that may be imperiled by rash or erroneous decisions. I am aware that there are many gentlemen at the bar more learned than myself, and very many better acquainted with the practice in the State Courts—my own business, as many of you know, having been mostly in the Federal Courts." He took comfort, he said with wry humor, in knowing that the system provided a remedy for his inexperience. Losing parties could always appeal to a higher court, which could correct "the damage I may work."

That night, reliving the moment, he spared himself the agony of excessive detail. "Ye eventful day," he wrote. "Took my seat at 9 a.m. and made my little speech to the Bar. . . . Lord! How I sweat!"

THE FALL DOCKET was a novice judge's nightmare. One hundred and eighty-eight cases, of all shapes, sizes, and specialties. Corporations suing each other. Inheritance disputes. Injury and negligence allegations. Guardianships. Bankruptcies. Some could be dispensed quickly, some required days of testimony and argument, some required written rulings.

Jury trials were the most time-consuming, and Henry had forty-nine on the list. Even if Henry could finish one a day—impossible—he would do nothing else for two solid months. But he had plenty else coming at him: one hundred and twelve scheduled court trials, in which he would sit without a jury and issue a verdict. As the only circuit court judge in the state's largest county, Henry was learning his first valuable lesson. Time was his most stubborn adversary. He had none to waste, and too little available for politics.

He missed his own renomination. On the afternoon of September 14, while the Republican county convention was choosing its candidates for the fall election, Henry was busy on the bench, presiding over a libel suit against the *Tribune*. He adjourned a bit early, but only so he could attend a funeral. Meanwhile, in Dearborn, the convention selected him with a roar of acclamation. If only all his political victories could be this easy.

Running for judge wasn't at all like campaigning for governor. There were no debates, no slate of speeches. Henry managed to set aside a few afternoons for visits to Detroit's ten wards, distributing printed slips with his name through friends and supporters. On Election Day, which dawned clear and crisp, he visited every polling station in the city, an even dozen. After casting his ballot at William Wunsch's house in his home ward, Henry returned to Carry with a severe headache and a glum feeling. "Did not go out again," he wrote. "Beaten without a doubt."

Beaten, yes. But to his amazement, he discovered that he had run ahead of nearly everyone else on the Republican ticket, from president on down. He had more than held his own in Detroit, running ahead by several hundred votes, but he had not fared as well in most of the county's nineteen townships. He sat with the newspapers, studying the results, but no matter how long he looked at them, they all added up to the same dismal conclusion: He had lost by three percentage points.

The Democrats had swept the city offices. "Glorious Results for the Democracy," the *Free Press* rejoiced. But glorious only in Detroit and Wayne

County. The governor, the state legislature, the Congress, the presidency—all in Republican hands. With Andrew Johnson gone, after surviving a bitter impeachment trial, the Republicans could return to the difficult task of looking for common ground on Reconstruction, suffrage, and racial equality.

Freed slaves were a potent political force in the making. Perhaps five hundred thousand colored men had voted in the seven Southern states that had been readmitted to the Union, helping Grant to his closer-than-expected victory. Intimidation by white supremacists kept the turnout from going higher. The former slaves owed their freedom to the Republicans; now the party was hoping to cement their allegiance. Less than a month after the election, the Republicans submitted a new constitutional amendment—"Article XV," the draft said—declaring that no citizen could be denied the vote "on account of race, color, or previous condition of servitude." The Fifteenth was aimed at the North as much as the South. Half of the Northern states still limited suffrage to white men. Michigan, of course, was among them.

In Detroit, after his brief four months on the bench, Henry prepared for his return to private practice. He had arranged to join two of the city's more distinguished lawyers in a new partnership, but he could not help but feel a bit sorry for himself. "As short as my experience was, it gave me a taste for judicial life," he wrote later.

He wanted more than just a taste.

ASPIRING TO A JUDGESHIP, Henry knew, put him on a narrow track with few stops. Other than Wayne County's circuit court, now filled for six years, the only bench worth a shout was the hardest to reach—the federal one. In early 1869, with rumors swirling that U.S. District Judge Ross Wilkins might be ready to retire, Henry dared to let himself think he might have a chance whenever the vacancy came open. He knew one prominent member of the Detroit Bar who was willing to push his candidacy. Would others? He began to ask.

Federal judges in Michigan were paid just enough to stir some competition, thirty-five hundred dollars a year. Even more enticing: These were life-time appointments, eliminating all worry about being cast out by a fickle electorate. The job itself promised stimulating challenges. Detroit was home to the U.S. District Court for the eastern half of Michigan, stretching from the Ohio border to the northern forests of the Upper Peninsula. Much of the Great Lakes—and the legal disputes that surfaced on them—came under the Eastern District's jurisdiction. Henry had more expertise than most in the murky waters of maritime law. That was one point in his favor. He didn't have many others. He certainly couldn't say he had more experience or better political connections than some of his possible rivals.

One was Alfred Russell, the former U.S. district attorney. Only five years in age separated them, but Henry had lived in Russell's shadow for years, first as an apprentice in Russell's law firm, later as Russell's assistant in the prosecutor's office. Russell was a formidable figure—dignified, courtly, and shrewdly ambitious. His Republican roots went back to the party's earliest days, to July 1854, when he and a thousand antislavery activists rallied "under the oaks" in the Michigan town of Jackson, a gathering now famous as the first Republican state convention ever held. Russell had stumped for every Republican presidential nominee, beginning with Fremont in 1856. He knew both of Michigan's Republican senators, not a claim that Henry could make.

Henry had decidedly mixed feelings about his former boss. They were friends, but they weren't confidantes. "Russell is a scamp," Henry wrote in late 1867. "Violates a solemn promise." During their days at the U.S. attorney's office, Henry had grown to resent Russell's extended travels. With Russell away for weeks at a time, Henry was left to handle both the grand jury and trials on his own. It was undeniably good experience, but more work than Henry felt was fair.

Now he was hearing Russell's name for the job that he coveted. "Learn that Russell is a candidate for the District Judgeship, which lays me low," he wrote on March 1, 1869. The next day—his birthday—his mood remained melancholy. "No gray hairs, but growing bald" was his main thought on turning the ripe age of thirty-three.

He was restless. The truth was, he couldn't quite seem to find his niche. "Nothing to distinguish this day from 40 others," he wrote at the beginning of April.

❖

HENRY NEVER HAD any real chance at the district court judgeship, as it turned out. Neither did Russell. On December 20, 1869, a few months after Wilkins's retirement, the *Free Press* delivered the word from Washington: His replacement would be John W. Longyear, a loyal Republican lawyer from Lansing. Henry had no trouble swallowing this outcome. Longyear was fifteen years older, a former two-term congressman, and "the unanimous recommendation" of the Michigan delegation. Henry wasn't in Longyear's league. The question remained: Would he ever be?

Henry greeted 1870 with more gloom than enthusiasm. His father-in-law's estate was still not settled, holding up Carry's inheritance, and their expenses were mounting. He had recently paid nine thousand dollars for a prime lot on Jefferson Avenue—a bargain, he thought, for land on one of Detroit's most exclusive streets—but now he felt strapped. "For the first time in my life, am obliged to borrow—accursed word!" he had written in July, after signing the contract.

Six months had passed since then, and he was still struggling, both with his finances and his frame of mind. "Very blue day," he wrote at the end of January. "Lots of bills, and no money. Heaps of regrets and few prospects."

TWO YEARS. Two long years. But by the spring of 1872, Henry was feeling better about his prospects. He had built his law practice, slowly but steadily, so that now he could write "busy, busy, busy" rather than "no money" in his daybook.

With his business affairs on more solid footing, he was finding more time for politics. At the county and state conventions in May, when he heard his name bandied about for a congressional nomination, he did nothing to put a stop to it. Michigan had gained three seats in the 1870 reapportionment. The First District incumbent was now a resident of the reconfigured Second. If Henry wanted to make a bid for the nomination in the First, this might be the year.

Except for the headaches. The attacks came without warning or cause.

At first they were annoying, but now they were frequent enough—and debilitating enough—to qualify as alarming. "Terrific headache—worst of the season," he wrote after one episode left him too sick to keep a date in federal court. In July, during an intense stretch of meetings with ward leaders to seek their support, he felt another one coming on. The nominating caucus was less than four weeks away. He could not afford any setbacks. To defeat his main rival, the energetic Moses W. Field, Henry would need to have all his wits about him.

Henry still wasn't certain he was ready to do battle. Even after years in caucuses and courtrooms, he still felt awkward on his feet, more likely to leave his audience wanting less rather than more. "Made a short unsatisfactory speech," he moaned. By mid-July, he was wondering if he should withdraw from the race.

Despite his misgivings, he pushed himself to keep going. He even accepted an assignment that required him to give a major speech to an unfamiliar audience. On Thursday night, July 25, he would preach the Republican cause to a rally of colored men, eligible to cast ballots in the first presidential election since ratification of the Fifteenth Amendment. The *Tribune* wanted to publish the text of his speech, which required Henry to write out a full draft. He didn't mind. He felt less nervous with his words on paper. Also, he would be promoting Grant's reelection, which was easier than promoting himself.

The inside of Young Men's Hall could bake an audience in late July, but with temperatures hovering in the seventies, no one would be fainting from the heat. Henry looked out at the black and white faces—the *Free Press* estimated no more than six hundred, while the *Tribune* said "fully one thousand"—and launched into the most stirring speech of his life.

Sounding like a prosecutor making his closing argument to a jury, he portrayed the Democrats as the colored race's unrepentant enemy, past and present. This is the party "that hugged slavery to its bosom . . . that opposed the emancipation of the slaves for fear it might hurt the feelings of the slaveholders . . . that cast its every vote against extending to the colored man the right of suffrage . . . that sought under the name of apprenticeship to hand him back to his old master . . . that [in] Ku-Klux disguise, has broken into his house at dead of night, dragged him from the bosom of his family and shot or hung him in the presence of his wife and children."

He then asked: "Have the authors of these outrages quitted the Democratic party, or has that party, conscious of its guilt, expelled them?" He answered his own question: "Not at all. The Democratic party of today is composed of the same element, led by the same men, animated by the same hostilities to the colored race." Case closed, he might well have added.

He could not end his speech there, however. The presidential election was shaping up as the strangest in years. A group of dissident Republicans, unhappy with Grant, had split away from the party. Calling themselves "Liberal Republicans," they had nominated Horace Greeley, the New York newspaper editor, as their candidate. The Democrats were so happy with the Republican schism that, at their convention, they embraced Greeley as *their* candidate. It was either a clever move, or a desperate one.

Henry warned the colored voters: Don't be fooled. Greeley "may shout till he is hoarse, calling himself a Republican," but if elected, "his will be a Democratic administration, his office holders will be Democrats, his policy will be Democratic." Stay with Grant, Henry urged. Stay with the Republican Party, and "its love for justice, freedom, and equal rights."

In the resolutions drafted after the speeches, the crowd made crystal clear its support for Grant and the Republicans. "We denounce all colored men who vote for Greeley," one resolution said, "as traitors to the principle of equal rights." Later that night, exhilarated, Henry paused to write in his daybook, amazed by the experience, the incongruity of it all, a white man appealing to black voters for support. "Finished my speech and fired it off at a big audience of niggers," he wrote. "On the whole a pretty satisfactory speech—much more than usual."

HE HAD NO TIME to dwell on his performance. He had eleven days left before the First District nominating convention, eleven days of ward meetings all over the city, night after night of asking for votes, of promoting himself, of talking "extempore." He spent the last day with friends, poring over the list of ninety delegates. Remarkably, he kept his usual pessimism at bay. "I can freely say," he wrote, "that I have done nothing and left nothing undone that I regret, and yet I care not a fig for the nomination."

His best effort was not nearly good enough. His troops worked the convention hall, but they were outmaneuvered by Moses Field's army. After the third ballot, stuck in second place, he withdrew. "Mustered 28 votes out of 90—a good compliment but not enough to elect," Henry wrote. "Resumed the practice of law at four o'clock, a wiser but not a sadder man."

ON THE FINAL night of 1872, in the solitude of his study, Henry took a few minutes to jot down his year-ending thoughts. He felt surprisingly optimistic. His father-in-law's estate was near settled. Carry and the heirs would soon receive their shares. As his sister-in-law Isabelle would write years later, Carry's inheritance would make it easier for Henry to pursue his judicial ambitions, should an offer come his way.

Despite "my unfortunate Congressional candidature," he wrote, "the current of life has run smoothly. I have made large additions to my law library, my business becomes steadily more profitable, and think I can safely say that I am not lacking in influence." Veering into his private life, he made a pledge, a pledge he vowed to keep, whatever his future held. "One resolve I make at the close of the year—to devote one mo[nth] of every year hereafter to recreation."

The previous summer, his political ambitions had prevented him from taking any extended holiday. Scolding himself for allowing that to happen, he now added, emphatically: "I mean that nothing shall interfere with that."

On the cusp of adventure: Emma and Albion, spring 1865

(Chautauqua County Historical Society)

12

Tourgee Goes South

North Carolina, 1865–1870

ON A SULTRY SUMMER MORNING, the kind that leaves unprepared Northerners weak in their sweat-soaked knees, a passenger ship from the Goodspeed "Pioneer Line" churned up the Neuse River toward the harbor of New Berne, North Carolina. It was Tuesday, July 25, 1865, and this was the final hour of the steamer's three-day journey from New York City. On board, Albion Tourgee surveyed the unfamiliar landscape and tried to focus on the grand adventure that awaited him. He wasn't having much success. As soon as he reached steady soil, he dashed off a few lines to Emma, waiting nervously in their little cottage in Erie County, Pennsylvania. "Dear Wifey," he scrawled, his handwriting as wobbly as his legs. "Have been most horribly sea sick ever since we left New York and now am sea sick because I am ashore."

He had come alone on this exploratory trip. Emma was content to remain in the North, close to family, but Albion wanted to do something bold, bolder than practicing law in rural Ohio or helping to edit the *Erie Dispatch*, his first dalliance with daily newspapering. He had responded to North Carolina's recruiting call, to the provisional governor's invitation for Northerners to migrate, to bring their capital and their labor, to join the state's loyal Unionists in the noble work of reconstruction. Albion had written to Governor William Woods Holden immediately after Holden's appointment by President Andrew Johnson on May 29, 1865, explaining that he and "an association of young men" were thinking of moving South. What were their prospects if they came to North Carolina?

Holden himself had replied. Remarkable, really. Seductive, certainly. The newly appointed governor had just taken over a state in ruins, with no functioning government and a few handfuls of cash in the treasury. He had a thousand and one tasks to do, and yet he had found time to answer a letter from this unknown twenty-seven-year-old, writing from the obscure hamlet of Belle Valley, Pennsylvania—a nobody with no particular credentials, a lawyer who wasn't practicing law, a Union veteran still suffering from his unglamorous injuries, a voracious reader with only one good eye, a sometimes teacher who didn't want to teach, a sometimes journalist whose duties at the *Erie Dispatch* hadn't left him much time to write.

Albion, already smitten with what he was now calling "his Southern scheme," told Emma after receiving Holden's letter: I'm going to meet the governor. I'm going to find out if North Carolina is our future.

HOLDEN'S LETTER had been warm and encouraging, like a father greeting his son's close friends. The governor's agenda was political, though, not parental. The state's Unionists needed help, at every level of public and commercial life. The mails weren't operating. The telegraph lines weren't reliable. The railroads were erratic, their timetables reduced to the equivalent of suggestions. Abandoned farms awaited replanting, their fields no longer tended by enslaved men and women and children laboring without choice or pay or education.

The U.S. military, uncomfortably balancing its twin roles as helping hand and occupying protectorate, ruled over a population adjusting to this new way of life. No masters. No slaves. In their place, an abundance of animosity, accompanied by alarming episodes of brutality toward white Unionists and liberated slaves. Several cases of murdered freemen were now being heard in military courts. The U.S. commander for North Carolina told Holden that "acts of unlawful violence toward the freedmen are becoming more frequent," and that local authorities often were doing nothing to investigate or stop them. The military's intervention was, he said, "the only adequate remedy for the existing evil."

Rebels and their sympathizers were clamoring to resume their roles in public life, but President Johnson's May 29 amnesty proclamation had excluded fourteen different classes, essentially anyone from the Confederacy's upper ranks—political leaders, legislators, judges, and military officers above colonel. Pardons were available to those who vowed to repudiate their rebel actions and uphold the Constitution, but they weren't automatic. Holden was reviewing the applications, but the final decision rested with the president himself. The process was slow, subjective, and prone to influence. Then there was the most difficult question of all: How could anyone test the sincerity of those pledging their allegiance to a government they had done their best to overthrow?

Still, for all the conflict and chaos, Holden felt he had something of value to offer enterprising emigrants from the North. Good land was cheap, he had informed Albion. Northerners with money would find "many and very advantageous" opportunities for investment, and Northerners with ambition would find a dearth of capable rivals. They would "only have to compete with the uncertain and unskillful negro," the governor told him.

In his first official proclamation, Holden had delivered a stark message to liberated slaves about their place in postwar North Carolina. Declaring his sympathy for them as "the weaker race," the governor said he would help them—if they labored diligently to help themselves. "I will see to it, as far as I can, that you have your liberty; that you are protected in your property and persons; and that you are paid your wages. But, on the other hand, I will set my face against those of you who are idle and dissipated, and prompt punishment will be inflicted for any breach of the peace or violation of the law." Like a school master lecturing his students, he admonished them on how to behave. Learn to read, he urged. Treat marriage sacredly. Above all, work hard. "If you are idle," he warned, "you will become vicious and worthless; if vicious and worthless you will have no friends, and will at last perish."

In contrast, Holden's letter to Albion had been a kindly arm around the shoulder, one white to another. "Should any of the young gentlemen or yourself come to North Carolina, I would be most happy to welcome you," the governor wrote, "and to show to you the fraternal feeling which the loyal people of this state entertain for their northern brothers." North Carolina had a healthy share of Unionists like Holden, a longtime Raleigh newspaper editor who had supported secession when it looked inevitable in 1861, but who had spent much of the war calling for peace and a return to the Union fold.

North Carolina offered a climate that Albion's doctor thought might be better for his precarious health, but that wasn't its main attraction. Among the Southern states, it seemed like the place to pursue his dream of making the Union "better than it was." The rebels didn't frighten him. He knew their prejudices and resentments. He had been their prisoner. He was looking to make new allies in North Carolina, but he was fully prepared to face old enemies.

In mid-July of 1865, he left Emma in Belle Valley and boarded the train, armed with a tentative plan, a plethora of questions, a suitcase, and a borrowed revolver.

SOMEWHERE BETWEEN ERIE and New York City, Albion's eagerness gave way to doubt. He was chatting with two fellow passengers, both ministers, men he knew slightly. As they talked late into the night, Albion found himself thinking about his ambition and God's plan. What if they did not align? What if his desires conflicted with the Almighty's design?

Arriving at New York's St. Nicholas Hotel in the late afternoon of July 20, Albion retreated to his room after an early dinner. Confessing his tortured soul to Emma, he wrote: "I know I wish to do good, but do I wish to do good anywhere God may put me?" The day's temperatures had barely cooled, and he found himself sweating as he let his feelings flow. "Suppose for instance I should find insuperable obstacles in the way of my Southern scheme or should see the will of God . . . pointing out my path as a teacher, or some such profession which I have already declared that I would not follow. What would I say?"

This was Albion's ultimate, unavoidable dilemma. His wishes or God's will? He wanted to say, without hesitation or qualm, that he would go with

God. But he knew that he could not. He had prayed to the Almighty, asking for leeway to pursue his aspirations. "I do not know," he told Emma, if "my prayer is of itself blasphemous."

Blasphemous or not, Albion had no intention of turning back now. In the hotel's lobby, a pair of North Carolinians, brand-new owners of a land agency, had established a base of operations. With Holden's backing, they were promoting the state's opportunities. "They offer for sale or lease large quantities of land, gold, iron, and lead mines, and water power, and offer liberal inducements to emigration," a *New York Times* reporter wrote enthusiastically on July 22. "This is the first step of the kind taken by any State."

Albion and a friend were thinking of taking over a nursery in North Carolina, calculating that in a state decimated by war, a seller of plants and seeds could hardly go wrong. He still intended to practice law, but he would need time to establish himself as a lawyer. During his two days at the St. Nicholas, he talked with "some heavy capitalists" about the nursery venture. He heard discouraging words. His confidence began to wilt. But after a night's sleep, he resolved to plow on.

"I have faith that God will open a way," he wrote to Emma before leaving New York, and "nothing shall discourage me if I can help it."

LANDING AT THE PORT of New Berne put Albion at the doorstep of North Carolina's revival. The evidence was everywhere. The streets hummed with the sounds of buyers, barterers, and agents. The decks of schooners, loaded with goods, stood ready to sail. In the warehouses, cotton bales and casks of turpentine awaited shipment to Northern markets. Watching over it all were the federal troops, colored as well as white, a reminder of the unfinished business between North and South.

New Berne stood in spirited contrast to the deprivation elsewhere in the state. Skeptics had scoffed when the Goodspeed company had decided, a month after the surrender at Appomattox, to open a New York–New Berne route. A failure in the making, the doubters had said. They were wrong. There was so much demand that a competing line had joined the armada. The week of Albion's voyage, two steamers and several schooners left for

New York "rammed and jammed" with goods and passengers, the *New Berne Times* marveled.

Albion had no time to linger in the port's lively streets. He was eager to reach Raleigh, to take advantage of Holden's generous offer of a personal welcome. Within hours of arriving in the capital, however, Albion discovered he was hardly alone in his quest. Raleigh was swarming with supplicants. Loyalists seeking jobs. Confederates seeking pardons. Rebel landowners protesting confiscation of their property. Northerners whose ambitions ran from profit-making to political access. Holden could hardly see them all, even if he weren't preoccupied with his most pressing task: filling official posts with men swearing fealty to the Union. Mayors. Magistrates. Sheriffs. Town commissioners. Justices of the peace. Three thousand five hundred appointments in less than two months.

On the very day that Albion hoped to see the governor, Wednesday, July 26, the *Raleigh Daily Progress* published an unwelcome bit of news. "We regret to announce that Gov. Holden was confined to his bed yesterday, and too unwell to see anyone on business." Even North Carolina's former governor, hoping to see Holden about expediting his pardon request, was turned away.

Albion had plenty else to do. He spent his day walking the streets, making appointments, asking questions, absorbing answers. He could hardly contain his euphoria. "I have obtained more information than I expected to acquire in a month," he wrote to Emma after twenty-four hours in Raleigh. He saw no reason to journey further south, or even visit other parts of North Carolina. "Everyone that has anything to sell, or [wants] a pardon or an office or anything else . . . is at Raleigh trying to get it now," he told her. "I see men hourly from every part of the state, and in fact from all over the South."

Emma, aware that he had been bent on seeing Holden, would be eager to know how their meeting had gone. Albion did not disappoint her. "I have had two very satisfactory interviews with Gov. Holden," he wrote. But he made no mention of what they had discussed—or how he had secured not one, but two interviews with a busy, sick man who was confined to his bed, seeing no one. Details, details. What mattered most was conveying to Emma that all was well, all was hopeful. He would be home soon, he told her. The scorching weather was a strong incentive to leave. "I dare not remain at the south long as the season is unusually dry and hot," he wrote.

Then, imagining Emma reading this, he added: "Do not fret about me."

EMMA WAS FRETTING, mostly because Albion did not come home as promised. At the end of his first letter from Raleigh, he had added a brief postscript: He had been asked to defend a Union Army lieutenant from Ohio at a court martial, and might be "detained several days." His estimate was wrong. Several days turned into a week, then two. Albion had something to prove, other than his client's innocence, and if that took some extra time, well, he knew Emma would understand. She had to.

It wasn't entirely his fault, Albion told himself. Everything had happened so quickly. On July 27, his second day in the capital, he was merely a visitor sporting a droopy mustache and a Northern accent, wandering the city, finding his bearings. The next morning, he was standing in a military courtroom, hearing himself introduced as Albion W. Tourgee, a "Captain of the 105th Ohio Volunteers." Captain was not his rank at retirement, but Albion made no objection to this sudden promotion. The official record would show that "Captain Tourgee" was now serving as counsel for the accused.

At first blush, the case seemed neither complicated nor winnable. The military prosecutor had hard evidence showing that Lieutenant John Clingman had filed a false monthly payroll report, allegedly with the intention of diverting government wages owed to a dozen colored laborers. But the prosecutor hadn't counted on facing a young lawyer determined to show the world—or at least this seven-member tribunal in Raleigh—that he would not shrink from a tough fight.

What others saw as a losing cause, Albion saw as a misunderstanding masquerading as a crime. Yes, Albion admitted, Clingman had filed a false report. But the lieutenant was no thief, Albion insisted. He was a man caught in postwar confusion and bureaucracy. Inept, perhaps, but nothing more.

Albion felt that he understood the wounding nature of injustice. In July 1863, he had endured his own court martial after nicking a fellow soldier with his sword. The military accused him of "conduct prejudicial to good order." Albion called it a playful moment gone awry. The case had ended with his acquittal and a reprimand, but the proceedings had left a scar.

Now, Albion set out to win his client's exoneration, just as his army lawyer had once won his. He conducted a whirlwind investigation, found new witnesses, drew different conclusions. On the trial's climatic day, Albion appeared with a twenty-nine-page closing argument, challenging every prosecution point. Reading it aloud, Albion implored the panel to think hard about the logic of the charges. Would a decorated officer, owed six months' salary and soon to return home to his family, risk his reputation and pension for "the paltry sum" of a couple hundred dollars? Money that had never made its way into his pocket? The evidence, he argued, was ambiguous at best.

There was no ambiguity in the tribunal's verdict. Guilty, on all three charges. For Albion, a sound defeat. For Clingman, a dishonorable discharge and a year in a New Hampshire prison. Six months later, a prominent group of Ohio politicians and military officers managed to accomplish what Albion had not. They won Clingman's freedom. They collected letters of support, portraying him as a trusted officer whose superior record had been "sullied by a single crime." In January 1866, President Johnson granted clemency.

Clingman's war was finally over. Albion's was about to begin anew.

OTHERS SAW ALBION as brash. Impertinent. A mite arrogant.

Albion couldn't worry about that. Reticence would not put the nation on the path to equal rights. So yes, he was brash enough to think those in power needed to hear his ideas. Brash enough to walk, with his slight limp, into the Bureau of Refugees, Freedmen and Abandoned Lands in Raleigh, and ask to see Colonel Eliphalet Whittlesey, the assistant commissioner for North Carolina. Brash enough to believe that Whittlesey would give serious attention to Albion's plan for molding former slaves into citizens by making them landowners.

His brashness was rewarded. Whittlesey asked for a draft of his plan. Working late into the night after a long day at Clingman's trial, Albion produced a ten-point proposal to "improve the condition of the Freedmen of the South." Like a salesman wooing a new customer, he chose enthusiasm over accuracy in describing his enterprise. Earlier, he told Holden of an "association of young men" interested in moving to North Carolina. That "association" was a trio at most—Albion and two friends. His plan for the Freedmen's Bureau created a vastly different impression.

Without using precise numbers, he depicted the group as "a large number of the young men of the Army of the Cumberland, composed principally of practical Farmers and Mechanics of all kinds." Separately, these men had "but little capital," he said. Together, their enterprise could become a model for the entire South. They intended to buy land at reasonable rates, hire freedmen to cultivate it, and then sell small tracts—ten to twenty acres—to the "most industrious and capable" employees. The freedmen's wages would go toward their payments, and the association would act as seller, bank, manager, and landlord. The association also planned to establish schools for the freedmen's children, "under the control of the managers of the Farms."

Whittlesey was impressed. He swiftly sent Albion's proposal to Washington with a note of ringing support. "Any scheme which will ensure to Freedmen homes & farms of their own is worthy of encouragement," he told the bureau's director.

Albion also had asked Whittlesey for a job, and Whittlesey was keen to give him one. "From personal interviews with him and the testimony of those who know him well, I am convinced that he would be a valuable assistant in my work," Whittlesey wrote to his superior. Whom had Whittlesey consulted about this newcomer? How would they "know him well"? Whittlesey did not elaborate. But this much was certain: Albion had charmed a high-ranking federal official, someone positioned to be helpful once he and Emma moved to North Carolina.

Unfortunately for Albion, the timing wasn't in his favor. The bureau's director, Major General Oliver O. Howard, had left Washington for a lengthy summer respite at his home in Maine. His aides were sending him only the most pressing correspondence. Albion's plan—along with Whittlesey's offer to hire the man who wrote it—languished.

It did not matter. A job with the Freedmen's Bureau wasn't crucial to

Albion's Southern scheme. He had seen enough of North Carolina to conclude that the state was fertile ground for cultivating a more equal Union, better than it was. By the end of 1865, he and Emma had rooted themselves on a large farm outside Greensboro, along with Emma's parents and her sister Millie. His two business partners would soon join them.

Albion had chosen his path. He hoped God approved.

ALBION AND EMMA had come south with a smattering of possessions, among them a recent photograph. They had gone to the well-respected Dolph Brothers studio in Erie, where the photographer had posed the young couple standing side by side, arms touching, staring at nothing—not at each other, not at the camera. Albion exuded an air of eager anticipation. His eyes were bright, his face fuller than his wartime photos, his mustache curling toward his chin, his body leaning forward. Emma looked weary, the corners of her mouth sloping southward, not a grimace exactly, but close. The photographer had managed the impossible: Albion and Emma stood together and they stood alone, much like their posture toward North Carolina.

They had opted for Greensboro rather than Raleigh, lured by the city's reputation for greater tolerance. The city was home to an established community of Quakers, who were busy setting up schools for colored students with the support of their Philadelphia-based compatriots and the Freedmen's Bureau. Albion and Emma did not belong to the Society of Friends, as the Quakers preferred to be known, but they applauded the society's education movement, which Albion saw as essential to any long-lasting success in eliminating the stigma of slavery. He and Emma quickly went to work on founding their own school.

The nursery was a partnership with two of Albion's Northern friends, including his old college roommate, Seneca Coon, who had changed the spelling of his last name to Kuhn since coming south. Albion and Seneca had scraped together two thousand dollars each to start the business. They had signed a fifteen-year lease for seven hundred and fifty acres, paying a yearly rent of one thousand dollars—reasonable, if the nursey made money. As spring arrived, their weekly ads in the *Greensboro Patriot* announced that the new enterprise of Tourgee & Kuhn had tens of thousands of apple, peach, pear, and plum trees for sale, as well as shrubs, bulbs, and seeds of all varieties.

They couldn't afford to begin the freedmen's land scheme that Albion had described to Whittlesey, not without aid and approval. But Tourgee & Kuhn did offer employment at a respectable wage to several dozen laborers of color. Elsewhere, there were reports of colored workers being treated as little better than the slaves they once were. Whittlesey had described this brutal treatment in a letter to his superiors in Washington: "Some refuse to employ negroes except at low wages. Others claim the right to whip and 'buck' them at will, as in former times. And a few openly declare that they will either have them as slaves again, or exterminate the whole race."

THE NORTH CAROLINA of spring 1866 was not the North Carolina that Albion had visited the previous summer. Holden no longer sat in the governor's chair. His provisional term had ended in December with the election of a successor and state legislature, preceded by an all-white convention that had done little more than endorse the Thirteenth Amendment abolishing slavery. Whatever the minimum threshold for readmission to the Union, the convention seemed determined to reach it and stop there. It wasn't good enough. When the new Congress met at the end of 1865, it refused to seat any representatives from any of the former rebel states.

Several months later, Albion watched the North Carolina legislature's first postwar session with escalating disappointment. Rather than enumerating a set of rights for its colored citizens, the legislature had enacted an act "concerning negroes, persons of color or of mixed blood" that leaned heavily on prewar prejudices. Vote? No. Carry a gun? No. Testify in a court case that involved whites? Not without the consent of the white parties, and only if proven "competent." Buy and sell property worth ten dollars or more? Only if a literate white witnessed the transaction. Marry? Yes, but only another "person of color."

Underscoring this color line, the legislature gave each county the discretion to create dual systems for taking care of the state's destitute—a warden for the "white poor" and another for the "colored poor." Equal responsibilities, separately handled.

To ensure white superiority in numbers as well as in law, the legislature had erected a racial wall at the state's borders, the same wall that had stood tall in prewar days. Before secession, no "free negro" could migrate legally to North Carolina. Now, any "person of color" who took up residence in the state would be guilty of a misdemeanor. The penalty if convicted? Five hundred dollars. Those unable to pay would be "hired out" until the fine was met. Servitude, it was clear, was not dead after all.

It was hard to imagine a more dismal beginning—except, perhaps, by looking at the more severe Black Codes approved in Mississippi and South Carolina.

IN APRIL 1866, a few weeks after the legislature's adjournment, Albion sat with pen in hand, drafting an essay about his first six months in North Carolina. The nation was in crisis, he wrote, and "intelligent voters of the North" needed "a true understanding of the real status of affairs at the South."

He paused, searching for the right word. Above the phrase "true understanding," he added another: "true conception." That was it. Northerners needed a "true conception" of Southern ways. Albion thought it was his duty—indeed, the duty of "every loyal man at the South, native or alien"—to provide one. He felt equal to the task.

In his mind, the people of the South fell into "three distinct classes." The smallest had resisted secession and remained loyal to the Union, privately if not publicly. The largest had embraced the Confederacy, but more with trepidation than enthusiasm. The third was the dangerous one, populated by unrepentant rebels pining for slavery. For skeptical Northerners inclined to think this third group did not exist in significant numbers, Albion offered an artful "sample" conversation with a man he identified only as "L":

"Are you a Yankee?" L asked.

"Yes, sir," said Albion. "So reported."

"And served in the Army during the war?" L said.

"Yes, sir."

"Well, by God, I'm a rebel, an out and out secessionist, always have been, and always shall be. I hate a Yankee worse than Satan hates holy water. I fought them as long as I could and did them all the damage I could, and I always will. If I could have my way, I'd smash the whole Yankee government."

"But," said Albion, "did you not swear allegiance to the same Yankee government before you got your pardon?"

"Oh," replied L, "Of course! We all had to do that to save our property, you know. But you don't think we care a straw for that, do you? Not by a heap. A man isn't bound to keep an oath which he is forced to take."

Men like "L" weren't relics, in Albion's view. They weren't fiction. They were a present and very real threat—to freedmen, to Reconstruction, to North Carolina's readmission to the Union. By the summer of 1866, the state's Unionists were warning publicly of the state's dangerous drift. They wanted, as one resolution put it, to "restore the State to a condition to be received into the Union, and deliver it entirely and forever from the misrule of traitors."

ALBION CHOSE ONE of those Unionist gatherings, at Cobles Schoolhouse on the outskirts of Greensboro, for his political debut. It was a brief speech, on a steamy August evening, to a crowded assembly from three neighboring counties. Soon, the *Greensboro Patriot* had taken note of this Northerner speaking up for the rights of negroes at "radical meetings." The *Patriot* wanted this interloper to know that "true Southern men"—defined by the newspaper as "men born and reared in the South"—had nothing but contempt for "the presence of strangers amongst them, whose only aim is to excite contention and promote discord."

The *Patriot* report did not bother to mention Albion by name. Still, he seized the opportunity, firing off a lengthy and indignant response to the *Patriot*'s "unprovoked assault." The newspaper, he wrote, was wrong about nearly everything it had said. Wrong to characterize all Southerners as holding the same opinion. Wrong about these "strangers" and their motives. Wrong about the country and its future. "[T]he South as such must die," Albion wrote. "If the men, institutions or traditions of the South stand in the way of this inevitable destiny it will be worse for them, for they will be ground to powder. . . . You may talk of 'Southern pride' and 'Southern rights,' 'Southern principle' and 'Southern will,' but you will find that Human rights, 'eternal justice,' and 'the will of the people' will override all."

A few days later, he was off to Philadelphia, chosen by his Unionist brethren to represent North Carolina at a national convention of Southern loyalists. The *Patriot* editors were outraged by his presumption. "What right has he, a mere disunion Yankee adventurer, to speak of affairs in North Carolina, or any other Southern State?" the newspaper asked.

Albion's defiant answer to such charges: The same right as any citizen, a right he intended to "exercise as long as I have an existence."

EMMA COULDN'T WALK without excruciating pain. The doctor was calling it neuralgia, and her nerves certainly felt as if they were on fire. Ordered to bed, her foot propped up on a pillow, she managed to write Albion. She could not possibly join him in Philadelphia, as they had hoped. "I don't think a month will see me able to walk many steps without assistance," she said. "I have written this lying down and it has tired me all out."

In distant Philadelphia, working feverishly on convention business during that first week of September 1866, Albion had Emma's health on his mind. She was ailing when he left. Had he made a mistake in coming? "I have been haunted all the way up here, with the thought that you would be worse and then I could never forgive myself for leaving you," he had written as soon as he reached Union League headquarters, where he had taken a room. Was she better? "I have heard nothing from you and am getting very anxious indeed," he wrote.

He was too busy to worry more, too caught up in the thrill of the convention. His days began at dawn and ended after midnight. Late in the evenings, though, he would sneak away to one of the Union League's "gorgeously appointed" sitting rooms, and write to Emma. From his nook, he could hear the noise from tens of thousands in the streets below, a nightly show of Northern support. "I never saw such a crowd before," he wrote on Thursday.

He had another long night ahead of him. The next day, September 7, would be the convention's finale, and Albion was planning his first major speech. He had secured a seat on an important committee, representing the "unreconstructed states," as the non–border states were called. He was helping to draft a report that, he hoped, would cause a much-needed ruckus. The committee of seven men was going to call for negro suffrage—not through state legislation, but through an act of Congress, or a constitutional amendment. That was the only way to douse the "spirit of disunion" still burning brightly in the South, the committee's report said. If black citizens could not vote, the rebel element would gradually "gain by the ballot what it failed to achieve by the sword."

The convention had already adopted a full set of resolutions, and none had mentioned suffrage. The border state delegates from Kentucky, Maryland, Missouri, and Tennessee—all safely in the Union—were bent on avoiding the divisive issue. Many had already left for home by Friday morning, when Albion stood to give a passionate defense of the committee's report. But a large crowd remained, including Frederick Douglass and attentive correspondents from the New York and Philadelphia newspapers.

Albion used a startling series of numbers to seize the convention's attention. In the past three months, he said, "nearly twelve hundred Union men" have been driven from North Carolina by former rebels. Between "seven and eight hundred" Union loyalists had signed a petition, seeking protection. On the train to Philadelphia, he heard from an unimpeachable source—a Quaker, he said somberly—that "the bodies of fifteen negroes" had been found in a South Carolina pond, "murdered by disloyal men." The only way to stop this campaign of violence, he declared, was to extend the vote to all former slaves throughout the South, and to deny it to all rebels. If not, he said, they should prepare for "rebels in office, rebels on the bench, rebels in jury boxes, and Union men in dungeons."

The newspaper correspondents rushed his impassioned words to print. As their accounts filtered down to North Carolina, Albion became a marked man in his adopted state. No more anonymity for "Captain Tourgee." Even the new elected governor, Jonathan Worth, took notice. He wrote to a Quaker friend, asking: Who is this Tourgee? How dare he make such outlandish claims? Worth fired off a private letter to the *Greensboro Patriot*, suggesting the newspaper might want to investigate "this Tourgee" and his lies at the "Philadelphia Radical Convention." Then, he dashed off letters to several friends, fuming about "this vile wretch Tourgee." He was concerned, he told one, "lest the Quakers make this Tourgee their leader."

And to another, he wrote: "I believe all the pretended facts he states [are] intended to make the North hate the South."

EMMA HAD LOST track of Albion. Her first few letters to Philadelphia had come back, "Not Found" stamped on the envelopes. Having never seen those letters, Albion had no idea how sick she had been. Now it was late September, and he still hadn't returned. He had written to her after the convention, his words shimmering with satisfaction. The Republicans wanted to send him on a speaking tour in the North. He would promote Reconstruction during the fall congressional elections from a transplant's perspective. Soon, he was on the move, a different city every few days, unaware that Emma was frantically trying to find him.

She needed to warn him. After his Philadelphia speech, two ominous letters had shown up in their mailbox, suggesting not so politely that the Tourgees should leave town. "Your stay in North Carolina had better be short if you expect to breathe the vital air," said one. Scared by the turn of events and annoyed by Albion's continued absence, Albion's two business partners were talking of dissolving the floundering partnership. Emma couldn't believe it. Everything was falling apart. She talked with her father, and they dispatched a young man to Pennsylvania, carrying the threatening letters and Albion's revolver. His mission: Find Albion. Tell him to come home. Now.

After ten days of traversing Pennsylvania, leaving notes for Albion in various places, their emissary wrote to Emma. He hadn't found Albion, but he was pretty sure that Albion had collected one of his messages. "I suppose he is back in Greensboro by now," he wrote.

No such luck. Emma was panicked. Where was her husband? She felt alone, abandoned. On Sunday, October 7, she wrote Albion a letter unlike any she had written before. "Your entire ignorance of the storm brewing here, which has increased from a cloud no bigger than a man's hand to a perfect hurricane of indignation and falsehood, seems strange enough," she told him. "You are needed here my dear Husband more than I can begin to write to you."

A month of fear and frustration came pouring out. "The firm has dropped your name from their card," Emma told him, "and they make it known abroad that such an obnoxious individual such as yourself is no longer connected with them in business." To make matters worse, the partners were refusing to pay the colored workers, as well as giving her a cold shoulder. "I am politely informed when I send down for potatoes that I have no right to them and anything else likewise."

She wanted to rush to the safety of the North, but "duty forbids that I should leave our folks in such an unsettled state." The colored workers were relying on her. "The boys," as she called them, "look upon me as the only protector of their rights while you are away. They have had but half rations for some time and not a cent of money and some of them are getting barefoot and with the cold weather coming on, they need their winter clothing. . . . I have distributed over ten dollars among them and fed them time and again when they had no rations."

She did not understand why Albion was still in the North. "I know you are working hard to do right for us and your country," she wrote in closing, "but dear Husband, what will it all be if you wear yourself out doing it. You need health and nerves when you return and I fear you will have exhausted both."

Emma's patience was certainly exhausted. By the time her letter caught up with him, Albion had been away more than six weeks. He left immediately for Greensboro, contrite but also combative. Politics and public life were now embedded in his destiny. He told Emma: We're staying. I will not retreat. We can make North Carolina better than it was.

His success as a traveling spokesman for the Republican Party was not matched at home in Greensboro. They were awash in debt. His business partnership broke apart at the end of the year. After buying out his partners, he was forced to close the nursery. Later, Emma would remember the winter months of 1867 as the nadir of their early years in North Carolina, living in a "little log cabin, cold, hungry and alone."

ALBION'S PRINTED HANDBILL, distributed to Guilford County voters in late October 1867, couldn't have been more explicit. The coming state constitutional convention was a referendum on the very nature of government. What did voters want? Aristocracy or democracy? Freedom or serfdom? Albion knew what he wanted. "Let then our battle cry be 'Manhood. Equal Rights. Free Schools. Free Juries. Free Offices. Free Press. Free Speech. Free Men!'"

He was running for delegate to the convention, which would rewrite North Carolina's constitution, a required step for returning to the Union. Earlier in the year, in a series of Reconstruction acts, Congress had made clear its terms for readmission: The military would oversee elections for new constitutions and governments in every rebel state. Qualified black men would be allowed to vote, while white men from the Confederacy's higher ranks would be excluded. What Albion had called "a necessity" in his Philadelphia speech—the ideas that had brought him condemnation from North Carolina's Conservatives—was essentially now the law of the South, thanks to the Radical Republicans in Congress.

Albion had made himself into a regular fixture at local political rallies, often called upon to deliver a speech, which he did with relish. The constitutional convention offered a chance to embed his revolutionary ideas directly into the state's permanent charter. His campaign pitch was tailored to cut across racial lines, to demonstrate that poor whites and freed slaves shared common interests and concerns.

He won by a scant margin, forty-three votes, much to the chagrin of his expanding list of enemies. And much to Emma's relief, the seat came with a per diem. At least she would have a source of income while Albion was away in Raleigh for the historic session.

He was predicting it would be "a long one."

WHEN THE CONVENTION convened on January 14, 1868, Albion was the youngest of the one hundred twenty delegates, and one of eighteen transplanted Northerners. Republicans held a commanding majority, with one hundred and seven delegates, including fifteen men of color. The leadership awarded Albion a prime seat, "third in front of the president, on the right hand side," he told Emma. He pronounced himself "well satisfied" with the opening session.

The old white guard, running under the "Conservative" banner, had won but a baker's dozen worth of seats. Their bitterness matched their weakness. They could erect parliamentary roadblocks, but their best weapon was to wage war through the press. Several papers in the Conservative camp mocked the proceedings. The *Wilmington Morning Star* adopted "The Gorilla Convention" as its standing daily headline for "the great Unconstitutional Convention." The *North Carolinian* in Raleigh chose the more straightforward "Nigger Convention."

On the convention floor, in the caucus rooms, Albion demonstrated a rhetorical nimbleness beyond his twenty-nine years, devising parliamentary maneuvers, offering amendments to replace a troubling phrase, making impromptu speeches. One Friday in late February, after a strident Conservative oration promoting white superiority, Albion rose to reply. He said he had once been under the spell of such "unmanly prejudice." In his early days as a Union soldier, he had "recoiled at the idea the uniform I wore should ever cover a black breast." His war experience had cleansed him of that bigotry. "I confess it now with shame," he said.

He could mark one moment in his awakening, he told them. It was the notorious Confederate massacre of colored troops at Fort Pillow in Tennessee. Calling the scene "a picture photographed forever on my mind," he told the riveting story of a "young officer" walking through the carnage, bending over one colored soldier's body, unbuttoning the man's blood-stained vest, searching for a memento to send the slain man's family. Albion didn't say that he was "the young officer," although he certainly left that impression.

Nor did he say that at the time of the slaughter, in April 1864, he was back in Ohio, his war career over.

Visibly emotional, he vowed never to forget that terrible day or its unpunished perpetrator. He would work unceasingly for equal rights. "There is no color before the law," he told the chamber, for "black and white are citizens alike of our glorious nationality . . . with the glories purchased in mingled blood."

Mingled blood. A provocatively chosen phrase, bound to infuriate his white adversaries, bent as they were on supremacy and separation. The next day's *North Carolinian* offered a glimpse of their fury. "The Tourgee brayed," the paper said. "In listening to his tribute to their valor and patriotism during the war, the uninformed hearer would have thought the nigger alone 'crushed the rebellion.'" The newspaper's motto was printed daily under its masthead: "A Daily Democratic, White Man's Newspaper."

Over ten intense weeks, the delegates visited nearly every question of how a government should be run. From his perch on a half-dozen committees, and as the lead drafter of the judiciary section, Albion immersed himself in issues large and small, with mixed success. A majority endorsed equal suffrage, and beat back Conservative attempts to mandate separate white and black militias. But it shied away from endorsing a broader range of civil rights.

At times, Albion could do little more than oppose or moderate a pernicious proposal. When a move to create separate schools gained momentum, he offered a compromise that would allow dual systems, but only if the state provided equal funding and facilities, "entirely adequate for all." His amendment failed, but not before he had put forth the principle that separation could not take place without equality.

When the vote on education came, the delegates chose not to support—or prohibit—separate schools, deciding it would leave that question to the legislature, along with several other contentious issues. Feeling a need to counter the Conservative drumbeat about their work, the delegates approved a clarifying message for the voters who would be asked to ratify their final product. "The charge is, that [the convention] favors *social* equality of the races. It is untrue." Those matters "must be left to the taste and choice of each individual."

EVEN BEFORE the constitutional convention had ended, Albion had laid the groundwork for his future. He had worked his way into the Republican Party's outer circle, landing a spot on the state executive committee. He had set his sights on Congress, specifically the Fifth District seat that included Greensboro. Several party members said they would back his candidacy, and he was soliciting petitions of support in the counties that made up the district.

The party's leaders had other plans. They wanted him to run for superior court judge. He wasn't happy. "I cannot help but think there has been a breach of good faith somewhere," he told a friend on the committee. He stubbornly left his name in contention for the congressional nomination, but could do no better than six of the thirty-two votes.

It was clear that the party wanted him in North Carolina, not Washington. During the constitutional convention, he had been appointed to a prestigious new post. He would serve on a three-member commission to rewrite North Carolina's entire civil code. It wasn't Congress, but he was pleased. Here was a chance to leave his permanent stamp on the state's legal system. First the Constitution, now this. Even better: The job paid $200 a month, and came with a three-year term. "*Se bon dieu*," he wrote to Emma. She knew his version of the French phrase: God is good.

A few months later, the judgeship was his, too, part of a Republican sweep of every significant office in the state, including governor. The new constitution was also approved, by a wide margin. The Conservative press screeched, calling it a "bogus" constitution approved in a "fraudulent" election, the handiwork of the "Radical Congress" and its military "enforcers."

Albion was more than a marked man now. He was a synonym, "*Tourgee*," hauled out by Conservatives when a bogeyman was needed. Albion took a puckish pride in such accounts, snipping them from the newspapers, saving them for his scrapbook. As he wrote to one Ohio friend, "To be a radical here is to set myself up as a target for every possible vilification."

And to be a radical judge? That made him an even larger target. He made known that he would use his powers, as overseer of the grand jury, to root out and prosecute the perpetrators of assaults, murders, and lynchings in the eight counties of his judicial circuit, bringing him into a direct confrontation with the white supremacists from the Ku-Klux.

As before, he vowed not to back down. As he would tell a Northern audience a few years later, North Carolina was now his state, too. "In other words, I am a 'carpet bagger,'" he said, defiantly using the disparaging label that Southerners had adopted for Northern transplants. "There is my business; there is my interest; there is my home. There I live, there I shall die, God willing, a carpet bagger!"

God willing.

Murder in the streets: The New Orleans Massacre, July 1866

(Harper's Weekly, *August 25, 1866*)

13

Equal but Separate

New Orleans and the North, 1867–1871

THE MULE-DRAWN STREETCAR, number 132, bore no star. That meant only whites could board. As the coach trundled up Canal Street, passengers were queuing up, reveling in a dazzling New Orleans afternoon. It was Sunday, April 28, 1867. The swarms in the streets and tropical temperatures prompted the *Daily Picayune* to gush the following day: "Gay parties were going in every direction. . . . There is no population anywhere that goes out of doors to enjoy the lovely weather more than the people of New Orleans."

In short, a perfect afternoon for taking a stand and getting arrested.

The driver reined the hulking streetcar to a stop, wheels shuddering on the iron track. William Nichols stood ready, fare in hand, intent on occupying a seat among the contemptuous white passengers. Intent on defying the driver's order to leave. Intent on telling the driver, I have as good a right to be here as any white man. Intent on saying, no, sir, I'm not waiting for a star car this time. People of color have been waiting for years, and what has all this waiting gotten us? Among other injustices, it's given us streetcars with black stars, too few of them, and half the time, especially on a crowded Sunday like today, the impatient white passengers taking them over. They can ride our cars, but we can't ride theirs? Yes, we know, there are many more white riders than colored. But that's not our fault. This indignity must end. As the

New Orleans Tribune wrote in February 1865, in one of its earliest protests, "our exclusion from the 'white cars' is a brand put upon us, and a relic of slavery that ought not to be tolerated."

Les gens de couleur libres, the French-speaking free people of color, saw the star cars as a particular insult. An impressive number of *les gens* had money, education, status. Why, they huffed, should they be consigned to a separate car? Wasn't their freedom equal to a white man's freedom? It was humiliating, just as it was humiliating that they still did not have a permanent right to vote or hold office. Lincoln had publicly declared, in his last speech before falling to an assassin's bullet on April 14, 1865, that he favored suffrage for Louisiana's "very intelligent" men of color and the colored soldiers "who serve our cause." And still they waited.

William Nichols wasn't waiting any longer. Determined to test the City Railroad Company's separation rule, he climbed the steps, two white allies at his side. The driver said the car was going nowhere until the colored man left. Nichols stayed put. The driver summoned Edward Cox, the "starter," responsible for helping to put mule teams in motion.

The confrontation envisioned by Nichols had arrived. By the time he put his foot on the edge of Car 132, he had already decided to treat "no" as merely the beginning of the discussion.

THE PREVIOUS SUNDAY, the *Tribune* had issued its latest call to action—actually, two calls, one in English and one in French. The newspaper had been campaigning against the star cars for two years now. It had positioned itself as the city's leading spokesman for people of color, but because its founders came from *les gens*, it sometimes struggled to find the right voice. Bridging the divide between the city's French-speaking Creoles and the newly liberated slaves was both difficult and necessary.

The *Tribune* was a six-day-a-week pulpit. Four pages, two in each language, often with separate editorials. The issue of Sunday, April 21, 1867, had delivered a double-barreled dose on equal rights. The English version, headlined "The Colored People and Their Friends," was a model of moderation. It lamented the glacial pace of change, an ongoing theme of *Tri-*

bune editorials. For three years, ever since Union forces had occupied New Orleans, white supporters had been counseling patience. The people of color had been patient, the *Tribune* said. The time had come for more whites in power to "shake off the old prejudice." Those who do so will be "the first to be lauded and remembered."

The French version was more insistent. It put forth a list of "*Nos Demandes*"—"Our Requests." Voting rights first. Public office open to all qualified candidates. Schools available to all children, regardless of color or race. Then, the coup de grâce, the concluding *demande*, one of singular interest to *les gens de couleur*. "Finally, we ask the eligibility of all, to all public places—the steamers, railways, hotels, cafés, theatres, entertainment of all kinds, public baths, shops." One system for all. No discrimination. End of discussion.

The mixed-race class, which spanned the color spectrum from nearly black to nearly white, had families with enough money to attend the opera, dine at finer restaurants, and travel. The former slaves had few. This division made for convoluted politics and even more convoluted relationships. If pressed to choose, many of *les gens de couleur* would say they felt closer to white than black, but more French than anything else. Mostly, they felt trapped. Why did they have to choose at all? They were Creole, meaning native born, and that should be good enough. The newly liberated slaves, their numbers in New Orleans swollen by the flight from plantations to the city, had legitimate reasons to wonder: Could *les gens de couleur* be trusted as allies?

Aware of this tension, the *Tribune* editors preached common ground from its earliest months of publication. "These two populations, equally rejected and deprived of their rights, cannot be well estranged from each other," the *Tribune* editors wrote in late 1864. "The emancipated will find in the old freemen, friends ready to guide them, to spread upon them the light of knowledge, and teach them their duties as well as their rights. But, at the same time, the freemen will find in the recently liberated slaves a mass to uphold them; and with this mass behind them they will command the respect always bestowed to number and strength."

Number and strength. After a half century of putting distance between themselves and those held in slavery, the Creoles of color could not afford to separate themselves any longer. They needed a unified front to achieve their long-sought goals.

THE STANDOFF BETWEEN Nichols and Cox evolved as so many standoffs had before. A company rule invoked. Nichols ejected. A police officer summoned. Cox demanding that the rule-defying, disobedient negro be carted off to jail. Uncertain that a crime had been committed, but certain that the confrontation was over, the officer said he would only make an arrest if the railway swore out an official complaint. Cox had said, yes, officer. Take him away.

The battleground shifted from street to courtroom. Two white lawyers announced themselves as Nichols's defenders, a hint that his arrest had been anticipated. Newspaper coverage divided along color and party lines. The *Picayune*, a firm supporter of the star cars, dismissed the episode as a regrettable stunt, blaming "ambitious mulattoes" for stirring up racial trouble. The *Tribune*, in contrast, saw a case "of vast importance," an opportunity to settle unresolved questions about the Civil Rights Act of 1866. In the *Tribune*'s enthusiastic view, the Civil Rights Act was a beacon of justice and the City Railway Company was in for a licking.

On Tuesday morning, April 30, Recorder Louis Gastinel found his courtroom overwhelmed with spectators. One observer stood out—a military officer from the staff of General Philip H. Sheridan, commander of the just-created Fifth Military District, which included the Union forces occupying New Orleans. The Ohio-bred Sheridan was, for now, the most powerful man in Louisiana. Under the Reconstruction Act, passed by Congress the previous month, Sheridan had the authority to remove any officeholder seen as a hindrance to bringing the state out of slavery and into civilian rule. Flexing his new muscles immediately, Sheridan had replaced the city's Democratic mayor with a Republican, Edward Heath. On the day of Nichols's arrest, Heath had presided over City Hall for exactly one month.

For this minor crime, Gastinel was both judge and jury. After hearing from witnesses, he declared himself in a quandary. The police officer was saying he had arrived to find no disturbance of the peace. The company's lawyer, instead of backing up employee Cox, agreed with the police officer. This isn't a criminal matter, the lawyer told Gastinel. It's a test of the star car system, and the Recorder's Court was not the appropriate venue for debating the company's policy of separation, he said.

The outcome seemed orchestrated, much like an evening at one of the city's masked balls. The streetcar company did not want a provocation or an unfavorable legal ruling. Following the company lawyer's lead, Gastinel said his sole concern was the charge against Nichols. His verdict: no breach of the peace, no crime. Case dismissed.

Nichols had won a hollow victory. He was free to go, but his test would not blossom, as the *Tribune* had hoped, into a legal case of "vast importance." Trying to keep the issue alive, he and his lawyers made one last move. Nichols swore out his own affidavit against Cox, alleging assault and false imprisonment. That prompted the sympathetic editors of one of the city's Republican newspapers to write: "Until the final settlement of the matter, the colored people of our city will claim the right, under the Civil Rights [Act], to ride in any of the street cars, whether they bear the single star or otherwise."

The City Railroad Company braced itself for more challenges from colored riders.

THE "CAR QUESTION" vaulted back into the streets three days later, on May 4, a gusty Saturday that sent stinging dust clouds into the faces of waiting riders. Car number 148 lumbered along its Rampart Street route, skirting the Marigny, the neighborhood long dominated by families of *les gens de couleur libres*. As a "dusky son of Africa," the New Orleans *Times* reported the next day, Joseph Guillaume had no business boarding the whites-only car.

Guillaume thought otherwise. He thought Car 148 was exactly the place to be. No star. No hesitation. Just before noon, Guillaume hailed the driver. When the driver refused to stop, Guillaume leapt aboard the slow-moving car, and grabbed the reins. The mule did not stop.

This was new territory. The Railway Company's instructions to its crews—avoid altercations—hadn't anticipated a driver battling with a colored rider for control of a car. When the dust had settled, two police officers had Guillaume in their grasp. A few hours later, in Recorder's Court, Judge J. A. Letten sorted through the confusion. Like Gastinel, he had a hard time finding a crime. He sent the young Guillaume home with some advice. Bide your time, the judge said. Let the courts rule on Nichols's affidavit against Cox. It might be resolved in a few days. In the meantime, no need for further clashes.

Too late. That night, along various stretches of Rampart, groups of colored men prepared for a long evening of protest. Rumors were as rampant as verified reports. A City Railway security officer told police that colored men "in open riot" were attacking the cars. A city police sergeant saw a throng of fifteen to twenty, wielding clubs. He informed his superiors that he was "under the impression that mischief will be done."

The protests spilled over to the Opera House, where a popular set of French plays was playing to enthralled audiences. The Opera House's storied history made it a symbolic target. The venue had long attracted the crème of New Orleans society, white and black. After an evening there in 1852, the wife of a Hungarian dignitary wrote in her diary, "Coloured people have separate seats in the upper gallery. Some were pointed out to me as very wealthy; but no money can admit them to the pit, or to the boxes."

Several colored men were preparing to storm their way into the theater, the alarmed chief cashier told a police lieutenant. By nine o'clock, the police captains in the Second and Third districts had dispatched extra forces for the evening performance, but they were ill-equipped to handle a moving mélange of protesters. Dashing off urgent telegrams to the chief of police, the captains essentially asked: What should we do?

They all remembered the appalling bloodshed of the previous July. A smattering of Radical Republicans, unhappy with the Louisiana legislature's adoption of a new Black Code, had organized a freestyle constitutional convention to establish a new state government. Only a few dozen delegates had turned up at the Mechanics' Institute hall, along with several hundred colored supporters, but they were met by armed ex-rebels. The federal troops arrived too late. It was a massacre, in the words of General Sheridan. The city police force, seen as a haven for ex-Confederates, was either ineffective or in cahoots, depending on whom you asked. The death toll: thirty-four men of color, three white Republicans. Forty-eight were severely wounded.

The city's new leadership did not want a reprise. Coincidentally, a shake-up was under way at the police department, intended to curb the rebel influence. Just two days earlier, Sheridan had ordered that former Union soldiers be added, enough to make up half the ranks. Heath had dismissed thirty-nine policemen as unfit. The depleted force was overwhelmed.

When the urgent telegrams arrived on the night of May 4, police chief Thomas Adams chose to deliver his answer in person. He visited the precincts, issuing his orders for the next day, another Sunday: Keep the peace, as best we can.

BY EARLY AFTERNOON, hundreds of people of color lined both sides of Rampart near Congo Square, poised for resistance. Like a boisterous crowd perched along a Mardi Gras route, they waited for the parade of streetcars to appear. The scene was chaotic, but a loose strategy had emerged—"an understanding, a concert of action," according to the *Times* account. "Negroes" would board the whites-only cars, ride a short distance and then step off, their point made. But also, a new twist: They would converge on the star cars as well, shouting at the colored passengers to get off, to abandon those symbols of discrimination and join in liberating the white cars.

The *Times* thought the teeming crowd showed "a decided tendency to bring on a riot," but the *Picayune* was impressed that protesters were taking over cars "without using any violence." The somber weather may have put a damper on the crowd's more fiery elements. Rain clouds clung to the sky, finally opening their spigots in late afternoon.

After hours of watching, Mayor Heath felt the mood shifting toward unruly. He could summon Sheridan's troops for help, but first, he wanted to try a face-to-face appeal for calm. Heath was something of an enigma. Born in Maine but a New Orleans resident since 1842, he was a prosperous merchant who stood somewhere between the moderate and radical Republicans, depending on the moment. The *Tribune* had been pushing him to appoint men of color to the police force, but Heath had shown no inclination to take that unprecedented step. Still, he hoped to make his voice heard at Congo Square.

Go home, he urged the milling mass. Let us discuss the star cars with the City Railway. Riotous behavior will accomplish nothing. Remember the massacre of the previous summer, he told them, and "refrain from doing anything that might cause a rupture of that kind again." One protester interrupted. He was willing, he claimed, to "spill the last drop" of his blood. Heath, laying his hand on the man's shoulder, told him that he wasn't looking for that sort of advice. Then, his voice firm, he promised the arrest of anyone, black or white, who disturbed the peace.

Most of the crowd melted away. The next day, Heath kept his word. He held a whirlwind of meetings with railway officials, Sheridan, and the police chief. The company wanted reinforcements from Sheridan to stop the disruptions, but the general said no. He would not order his troops to protect drivers or cars. That night, the police chief issued a new directive. "Have no interference with negroes riding in cars," the chief's telegram read. "No passenger has a right to eject any other passenger, no matter what his color. If he does so, he is liable to arrest for assault or breach of the peace."

Without military or police protection, how was the company to enforce its policy of separation? It had more than one hundred and fifty cars to guard. More than two hundred employees. More than thirty-two miles of track.

The next day, the company told its drivers: Let everyone ride.

THE QUESTION WAS impossible to ignore: If colored passengers could sit with whites on streetcars, what about the other places on the *Tribune's* list of *Nos Demandes*—"the steamers, railways, hotels, cafés, theatres, entertainment of all kinds, public baths, shops"? Were they next? Mayor Heath certainly seemed aware of that possibility. A week after the streetcar company's white flag of surrender, he asked the city attorney for a legal opinion on whether merchants and managers could refuse to serve "any portion or portions of citizens."

The city attorney, Henry D. Ogden, was a Democrat, an ex-Confederate officer, and a known defender of discrimination. He would soon make Sheridan's list of officials to remove from office. What was Heath hoping to accomplish by seeking Ogden's opinion? Was this a shrewd step to focus attention on a rebel sympathizer still in office? Or a calculated attempt by the mayor to maintain separation beyond the streetcars?

Ogden needed less than a day to deliver his adamant conclusion: Merchants and managers had a legal right to refuse anyone they wish. "I entertain no doubt," he wrote on May 15. Their licenses did not turn them into public places, Ogden advised. As private individuals operating private businesses, they could make any reasonable rule they "deem proper." It was the same rationale that judges in Massachusetts and Michigan had used, before the war, in turning aside legal challenges from colored passengers.

Ogden's opinion did not carry anything near the weight of a judge's ruling, but the *Tribune* could not contain its scorn. Under the headline "The Black Laws to be Perpetuated," the editors wrote: "The Mayor had no use to ask for the opinion of pro-slavery men; he only had to read the civil rights bill to find our clear title to equal rights at the merchant's counter."

The *Picayune* editors, meanwhile, kept searching for ways to preserve separation on streetcars, and everywhere else. A May 16 editorial laid out their latest idea, one they liked so much that it became the centerpiece of subsequent commentaries. Freely acknowledging that "white people frequently overfilled the star cars, so that colored people could not get seats," the paper urged whites to restrain themselves. If whites would stay off the star cars, the editorial said, separation could work. Black riders would have "all the rights which the white people have, and all the accommodations which are given to them, and neither can intrude unwelcome company on the other." Everything—availability, access, comfort—would be the same.

Equal, but separate.

TWELVE HUNDRED MILES to the north, in the city of Philadelphia, George H. Earle and his client of color, Mary Miles, had reason to feel optimistic about their ongoing legal fight against separate cars on the West

Chester and Philadelphia Railway. It was a mirror image of the battle in New Orleans, proof that the North had yet to free itself of separation's stubborn grip.

Miles, a young teacher, was working at a school for the orphaned children of colored Union soldiers. Boarding the train one day in Philadelphia, she had refused a conductor's order to sit in a section cordoned off from the white passengers. Such arrangements were nothing new on the railway or the city's horse-drawn streetcars; neither was resistance. Months earlier, in mid-1866, a twenty-six-year-old colored leader named Octavius Catto had coordinated a public protest of the city's streetcar companies and their longstanding policy of exclusion from the inside sheltered seats. In rain or snow or sun, riders of color—including women and children—were confined to the cramped outside front platform, if allowed to ride at all. Catto and his allies had taken their campaign to the state legislature, with the support of the Union League of Philadelphia and the state's Radical Republican duo in Congress, representatives Thaddeus Stevens and William Kelley.

For Miles, her moment of rebellion had earned her a conductor's demand for compliance, a stalemate, and a forcible ejection. She was left stranded, miles from her destination. Described by her lawyers as a "well bred, intelligent and respectable colored woman," she wanted damages for her trouble. At trial, the judge had delivered an important finding in her favor: The West Chester Railway, he had instructed the jury, had no legal authority to make a rule of exclusion based on her color.

She won the jury's vote, along with five dollars in damages. The railroad then appealed the verdict to the five-member Pennsylvania Supreme Court. The company was relying on an 1861 ruling, also from a Philadelphia court, which found that carriers had a right to exclude. George Earle and his law partner thought the 1861 precedent was obsolete, a remnant of prewar days. The appeal gave them a chance to write a powerful brief, citing two more recent cases. They called separation a "public mark of degradation."

Just days before the oral argument, on April 1, 1867, came a well-timed gift from the state capitol in Harrisburg. After two years of lobbying from white and black groups, along with the election in 1866 of a bevy of Radical Republicans, the once-resistant legislature approved a sweeping new law, making it illegal to exclude anyone from any railroad car because of color or race. The law wouldn't take effect right away, but it was hard to see how the appeals court could take a firm stand against Miles, now that the legislature had spoken.

But as Earle awaited the appeals court's 1867 fall term, he wasn't celebrating just yet. As a longtime observer of Pennsylvania's racial divide, and heir to his family's legacy of activism, he had learned not to make any assumptions about what Northern courts might do.

NOW IN HIS MID-FORTIES, Earle came from fine abolitionist stock. Two decades as a practicing lawyer had taught him that the law could be a curse as well as a blessing. Before the war, while defending people of color fleeing slavery, he had seen how the Fugitive Slave Act had become an instrument of oppression, requiring the North to act as the South's enforcement arm. Now Northern prejudice was drawing more of Earle's attention. In January 1865, sixty-nine white Philadelphians announced a public effort to pressure the city railways into allowing "respectable" colored passengers to sit in the cars. Earle was enlisted as a legal adviser.

Philadelphia had embraced street railways with wide-eyed zeal in the late 1850s. Nineteen new companies sought charters in just two years. They laid tracks at a frenzied pace, leading observers to say that "passenger railway insanity" was gripping investors. By the early 1860s, streetcars of eighteen or twenty-four seats were carrying fifty thousand customers a day, most of them white. Answering the inescapable question—are colored passengers allowed to sit?—the railways had chosen exclusion from the outset. In a city with more black residents than any other in the North—nearly twenty-three thousand, greater than New York or Boston, but still a sliver of the white population—friction was inevitable.

The new committee's first move: Send delegations to meet with the nineteen railway presidents—white men conferring with white men—and ask them to drop the exclusion rule. The result was an unprecedented referendum, a "car vote," proposed by one of the railway presidents. Over a two-day period, conductors handed paper slips to all white passengers, asking them to mark either For or Against "colored persons riding on all the cars." Overwhelmingly, the white passengers said no. Sorry, the railways said. Our passengers don't want any change.

Earle felt the courts had become the best option for attack. In May 1865, he and his law partner, brother-in-law Richard White, won a significant verdict on behalf of an ejected colored passenger in the case known as *Derry v. Lowry*. The lawsuit echoed so many others, but with a Civil War twist. A conductor on the Lombard and South line had confronted Mrs. Derry, a "very respectable colored woman, almost white," as she sat in a near-empty car. It was late, about eleven o'clock. She was on her way home from her church, where she was helping to nurse wounded colored soldiers. As the judge later wrote, the conductor "told her that she must get out; that no d----d niggers were allowed to ride on that line." Stopping the streetcar, he enlisted "two friends standing on a street corner" and "ejected her from the car with great violence, tearing her clothes."

The trial judge, aware that the 1861 ruling had applauded separation as a means of keeping racial peace, told the jury that the war had changed everything. It has "cleared our vision and corrected our judgment," he said. If colored men could wear the Union soldier's uniform, they "should not be denied the rights common to humanity." Verdict for Mrs. Derry. Fifty dollars for her distress.

Attaching the *Derry* judge's written findings to their brief in the *Miles* case, Earle and White rooted their argument in both law and morality. The company had justified separation, they said, by claiming that "a large majority of the people of this city are opposed to mingling with colored people." Even if the claim were true, the brief said, it was unthinkable to base a rule on such blatant bigotry. Where would it stop? Would the courts endorse the separation of Catholics, despised in some parts of the country? Of Union soldiers, hated in much of the South? Of immigrants, scorned nearly everywhere?

Earle and White put the question plainly. "Is this Court prepared to say that common carriers are to sit in judgment on a man's complexion, race, religion or politics . . . to be slaves to popular prejudice," no matter what that prejudice might be?

"A doctrine so monstrous," they wrote, "can require no refutation at our hands."

IF POLITICAL AFFILIATIONS were any guide, the Pennsylvania Supreme Court tilted slightly in Miles's direction. The five judges included two Democrats and three Republicans. They could have issued a narrow ruling, citing the legislature's new law as a complicating factor. But Daniel Agnew, a Republican, chose instead to write a majority opinion that amounted to a treatise on the wisdom and legality of separation. It was extraordinary in its fervor.

Agnew declared a "right to separate," perhaps a first for the court. In Agnew's view, there was no shortage of good reasons. Preventing violence was one. "If a negro take his seat beside a white man or his wife or daughter, the law cannot repress the anger, or conquer the aversion which some will feel. . . . It is much wiser to avert the consequences of this repulsion of race by separation, than to punish afterward the breach of the peace it may have caused." A railroad rule is reasonable to "preserve order and decorum," he wrote, "and prevent contacts and collisions arising from natural and well-known customary repugnancies, which are likely to breed disturbances by promiscuous sitting."

Summoning God to his side, Agnew said "the Creator" had ordained separation by making two such dissimilar races. But, he said reassuringly, "to assert separateness is not to declare inferiority in either. . . . It is simply to say that following the order of Divine Providence, human authority ought not to compel these widely separated races to intermix." Separation was the status quo in Pennsylvania society, he said. "Blacks live apart, visit and entertain among themselves, occupy separate places of worship and amusement, and fill no civil or political stations." Why, he suggested, should trains be the exception?

The railroad had asked the trial judge to tell the jury that Miles was offered a "comfortable, safe and convenient seat, not inferior in any respect to the one she was directed to leave." Equal but separate. The trial judge had refused. Agnew said the trial judge was wrong. Three of his colleagues agreed. One dissented, without explanation.

Miles's only consolation was Agnew's final paragraph. The justice said his ruling was based on the law at the time of her ejection. He could not say how the court might react to a challenge based on the new law.

Newspapers of every region took note of the ruling, often mentioning Agnew's political pedigree. The Democratic ones were gleeful, and not just in the South. "Judge Agnew is a Republican, was elected by the Republican party, but he is also a lawyer of high character, and great moral rectitude as a man," said the *Ohio Statesman* in Columbus. "He does not believe in the mixture of races, nor in forcing a negro into the society of the white race. . . . His opinion in this case covers the whole ground, and all who read it must be satisfied with its marked ability."

Republican papers were more cautious, but few chose to quarrel. "This is Republican doctrine enunciated by a Republican judge and sustained by a Republican colleague," said the *Harrisburg Telegraph*. "We are satisfied with the decision."

Other Republicans were far from satisfied. The Radicals in Congress wanted stronger civil rights laws, and were determined to enact them. So were some Republicans in Louisiana. In early 1868, the constitutional convention ordered by Sheridan gave them the opening they needed.

INSIDE MECHANICS' HALL on January 2, 1868, the delegates to the Louisiana constitutional convention rang in the New Year with a raucous debate over "the right to travel and to be entertained." It was a clear and pleasant Thursday, the convention's twenty-ninth day. But the mood in the hall, near the site of the 1866 massacre, was anything but agreeable. As the *Picayune* headline said the next day, the nearly ninety delegates in attendance were engulfed in "The Vexed Subject of Social Equality."

The delegate roster included equal numbers of colored and white delegates, elected in September 1867 under the watchful eyes of the Union command. Colored voters had outnumbered whites. The result was the most lopsided in the state's history, with all but two delegates calling themselves Republicans. But there was nothing uniform about the assembled group, which had as many layers as the muddy sediment in the Mississippi. White and black Radical Republicans from New Orleans. Conservative white Unionists from upstate parishes. Northern newcomers who had come during the war, some as soldiers, others as opportunists. French-speaking *gens de couleur*, including signers of the 1864 voting rights petition.

Most white newspapers had belittled the convention as an illegitimate gathering, created by the occupying military. The *Picayune* said "it should be called the Unconstitutional Convention." The *Times* preferred bigoted mockery, naming it the "Bones and Banjo Convention." Several papers outside New Orleans settled on the "nigger convention," and in a show of equal offensiveness, applied the same insult to any white delegate willing to vote for equal rights in education, suffrage, courts, or public accommodations.

On the last day of 1867, the convention had accomplished two essential tasks, adopting articles that banned slavery and conferred citizenship on "all persons" born or naturalized in the United States, "without regard to race, color, or previous condition." Without those, Louisiana had no chance of readmission to the Union. But as the delegates debated the specifics that came along with that citizenship, their divisions became glaringly apparent.

P. B. S. Pinchback, a debonair New Orleans delegate of growing notoriety, triggered the uproar. Four years earlier, the light-skinned Union captain had made an impassioned speech at an Economy Hall political rally, saying if we're eligible to fight, we're eligible to vote. Treat us as men, he had demanded. Now thirty, he was Georgia-born, Mississippi-reared, Ohio-schooled, and eager to engage in political battle.

He wanted the constitution, as the state's fundamental expression of rights, to serve as a battering ram against the color line. But it must be done, he urged, without relying on racial politics. This is not a "colored convention" or a "Radical Republican Party Convention," he admonished. The delegates needed to frame a constitution that applied fairly to all, while ensuring that people of color obtained their long-denied rights.

Achieving that goal, Pinchback felt, required explicit language. Broad statements like "the right to travel and be entertained" could be ignored or twisted. He offered an amendment, adding but eleven words: "The right of all persons to travel *on the common carriers* and to be entertained *at all places of a public character* in this State, shall not be infringed." It passed by a wide margin, sixty-seven to eight.

That wasn't good enough for George Wickliffe, a white Radical Republican. For years, he said, companies had claimed the right to make "reasonable" rules for how they treat their patrons. Those rules were the problem, he said. He proposed an amendment, limiting that power: "No company or municipal, parish or chartered corporation shall make any rules or regulations creating any distinction between persons on account of race, color or previous condition."

With those few words, Wickliffe was willing to impose on companies what Charles Francis Adams had resisted twenty-five years earlier in the Massachusetts legislature. Had such a constitutional provision existed in Pennsylvania, Mary Miles might have won her lawsuit against the West Chester Railway. Had one existed in Michigan, William Howard Day might not have lost his case against the steamboat company in 1858.

Several of the conservative delegates in Louisiana were determined, however, to stop the "social" fabric from fraying any further.

FOR TWO DAYS, the delegates dueled over the Wickliffe amendment. John L. Ludeling, from the upstate parish of Ouachita, spoke in apocalyptic tones. The Wickliffe amendment, he said, was a "lawless license to trespass upon private or social rights, such as the rights of men to control their own property." Such a provision, he said, "could have no effect in law, and would only create a war of races."

From William H. Cooley, a white judge representing Pointe Coupee parish, came a divide-and-conquer strategy. The Wickliffe amendment, Cooley said, primarily benefited *les gens de couleur* and their ambitions to achieve the same social status as whites. It was "of no earthly use to the freedmen." Cooley thought the constitution should stay silent on theaters and other public places of entertainment. Mandating "social equality," he felt, was absurd.

One of the New Orleans delegates was Arnold Bertonneau, half of the duo that carried the 1864 voting rights petition to Washington. He had been told to wait then. He was hearing the same now. He rose in rebuttal. I don't want to force white people to drink *with* me, he said. I simply want to have the privilege of drinking in the same saloon, without fear of ejection.

Late on Friday afternoon, January 3, a hefty majority coalesced around an alternative amendment, defining all businesses operating with a government license as public places, and therefore open to anyone of any color. The weary delegates approved it, fifty-eight to sixteen. Ludeling and Cooley voted no—as did Wickliffe, disappointed that his version had failed.

The constitution would not include any restrictions on a company's right to make rules. But it would have this new clause, Article 13, guaranteeing the right to travel and be entertained at all public places holding a government license to operate.

Would it be enough to ensure equal treatment?

THE MAJORITY LAYERED the final draft with safeguards against discriminations of other kinds—in schools, holding office, the militia—and also enacted an article that denied voting rights to a broad swath of ex-rebels. Anger was festering among whites, but they did not have the votes to prevent ratification. Three months later, at the election of April 1868, Radical Republicans and colored voters combined for a winning margin of twelve thousand. The rest of the balloting was a Republican sweep. A man of color was now lieutenant governor. Men of color had been elected to half of the seventy House seats. By July, after ratifying the Fourteenth Amendment, Louisiana had more than met Congress's requirements, and was back in the Union.

After a bitterly contested tally, Pinchback was awarded one of the thirty-six seats in the State Senate, joining six other men of color. He intended to do more than sit in it. In early 1869, he pushed through a bill to "Enforce the Thirteenth Article." The act specified that companies could exclude customers for "vulgar" conduct or refusing to pay, but never for color or race alone. Businesses that violated the act could have their licenses revoked, and victims of discrimination could sue for damages. "We are told, do not legislate on this subject," that now was not the right time, Pinchback said. "If left to time, the time will never come."

The *Tribune*, wobbling financially but back in print after a hiatus of eight months, urged people of color to use the protections in the Pinchback law to full advantage. To make separation vanish, the paper said, the color line needed to be crossed, again and again.

Separation did not vanish. Many places of a "public character" pretended the law didn't exist or refused to comply. Enforcement was feeble. Lawsuits were few, and *les gens de couleur* were bringing the majority. C. S. Sauvinet, the light-skinned civil sheriff of Orleans parish, sued a New Orleans saloon for refusing to serve him in March 1871. He emerged with a thousand-dollar damage award, later upheld by the Louisiana Supreme Court. But even with Sauvinet's lawsuit pending, the Metairie Race Course was debuting a new venture into separation.

The track's spring meet was an annual rite of merriment, drawing thousands daily, a pageant for the fashionable and the ordinary. When the gate swung open on April 3, the happy hordes were greeted with a spanking-new, colored-only viewing stand.

It would take more than a new constitution and new law to vanquish the spirit of separation.

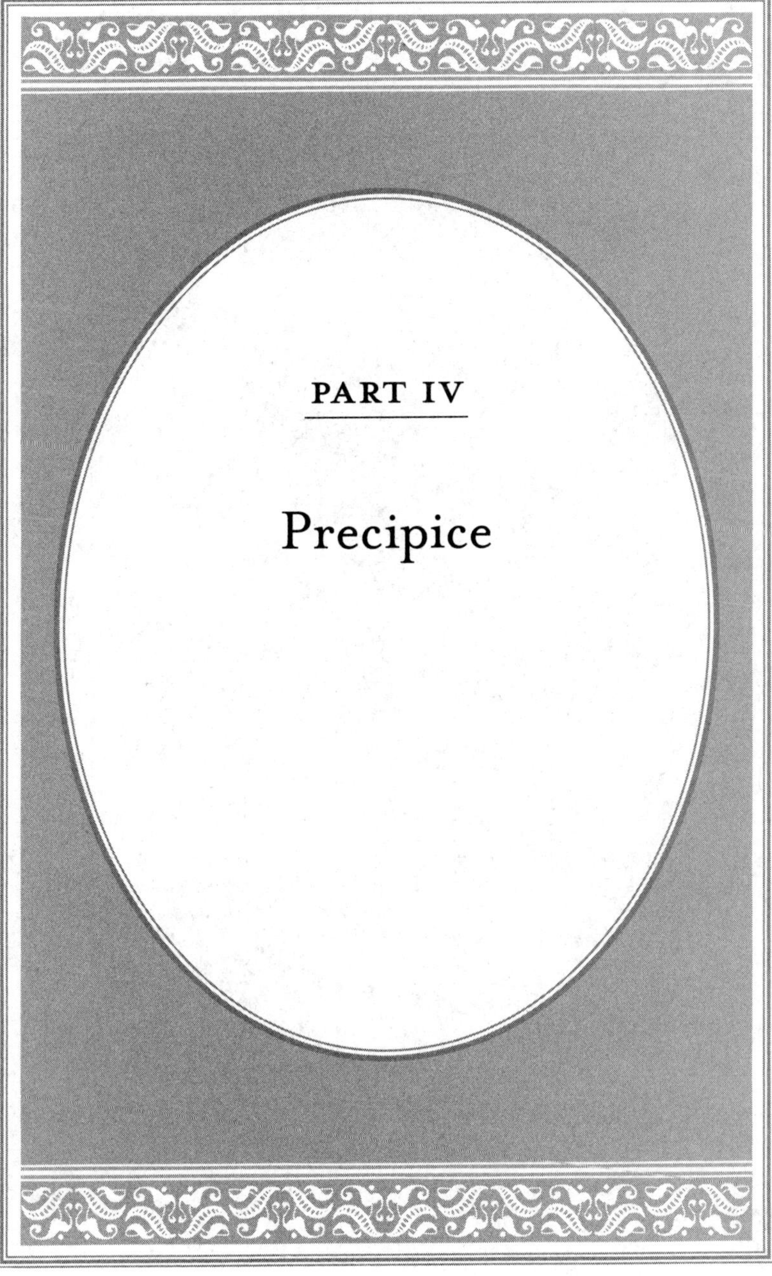

PART IV

Precipice

A rising star: Party leader, candidate for Kentucky governor, convention power broker

(Courtesy of Anderson Americana)

14

"Is Not Harlan the Man?"

Kentucky and Washington, 1875–1878

JOHN MARSHALL HARLAN knew he couldn't win. He knew his second run for governor in 1875 would end with the same result as his first in 1871. In defeat.

There was no shame in losing, if the cause was served and the campaign was serious. But still, there were consequences. For him, for Mallie, for their six children and two servants, and perhaps most painfully, for the family pocketbook. This time, John wasn't being coy or modest when he protested to friends that he didn't want the nomination. He had a major lawsuit coming to trial in mid-June. If he gave it up, he would sacrifice a one-thousand-dollar fee. He was almost forty-two years old and a man of some fame and accomplishment, but wealth was not among his many achievements. He needed the money.

It made no difference. On May 13, when the faithful gathered at Louisville's Masonic Temple, it was Harlan, Harlan, Harlan for governor. He was in the hall when acclamation came. "I was disinclined to accept the nomination," he wrote years later, "but under the circumstances, it would have been ungracious of me to do so."

More than ungracious. Unthinkable. As the unofficial head of Kentucky's Republican Party, described by one Democratic paper as possessing "the brains of his entire party in this State," John could not bring himself to say no. How could he recruit others, how could he ask them to defend the party's principles, if he stayed away from the fray? How could he look his friends in the eye, especially those praising his "sense of duty" and his willingness to put his party first?

He made up his mind: He would juggle both responsibilities. He was no longer young, not quite as spry, not quite as svelte, but in the weeks before the August 2 balloting, he would saddle up his horse again, ride from county to county, from valley to mountaintop, giving two or sometimes three speeches a day. He would exhaust himself, he would endure the mocking editorials, and he would almost certainly lose. He resolved to go down fighting.

In late May and early June, he wrote dozens of appeals to Republicans in the state and beyond its borders. His message was blunt: Winning would require every ounce of effort from every Republican in every one of Kentucky's 116 counties. He scolded, wheedled, demanded, cajoled. Whatever it took to stir his troops and raise enough money to make it a contest.

The scold: "We ought to make a vigorous fight, or none at all," he told his man in Marion County. The wheedle: "We have 65,000 white Republicans and 30,000 colored Republicans. It seems to me that we are entitled to aid from our friends in the North," he pleaded to George M. Pullman, the Chicago railroad car tycoon. The demand: "The gentlemen who got me into this canvass must stand by me. If they do so, and have a thorough organization in each county, I will poll a larger vote than I did in 1871," he huffed to a Henry County supporter. The cajole: "I am sure that every generous man will say that it is not right to put me in this fight, and then withhold the aid which is essential to any successful canvass," he beseeched a Bourbon County backer.

A *successful canvass*. Now that was the tallest of tall orders. John had lost by thirty-seven thousand votes the first time around, polling barely 41 percent. He believed the party could improve on those numbers, but only if it built a much larger base of colored voters. He was certain that many hadn't voted in 1871, when they were new to the ballot box. But how many? Enough to tilt the long odds in his favor? Probably not.

He knew this much: Whatever the reasons for their absence—

intimidation, ignorance, indifference—he would lose, and lose big, if he wooed only white voters.

Could he attract one without alienating the other? Did he want to?

ANOTHER TOWN, another courthouse, another curious crowd. Narrating the tale years later, John would remember a friend stopping him as he entered. Be alert, the friend warned. A mischief maker is plotting to ask some ugly questions.

The moment materialized as John, well into his oration, paused for a few sips of water. "General Harlan," said a man, rising from his seat. "It is rumored among the people here that you sat by the side of a negro at a dinner table in Maine a few years ago. How is that?"

A negro at a dinner table in Maine. John knew the crowd, mostly Democrats, shared the man's presumptions and prejudice. Yet he sensed a discomfort in the room. No one had applauded the man's question or murmured in smug approval. These were Kentuckians, he thought, known for good manners and fair play. In answering, he would appeal to those instincts, not to their fears. He would not deny or dodge or disguise his views. There was a risk, but he decided to shoulder it.

"I am taken aback," he said genially, "by the great issue now unexpectedly thrown at me." It seems the contest for Kentucky's highest office now depends on "whether I ate dinner at the same table with a man of the negro race." Well, he said, the crowd should know "the facts." He had gone to Maine to aid his party, to stump for General Grant's reelection in 1872. He was asked to come by James Blaine, speaker of the U.S. House of Representatives, who was assembling a grand collection of Republican orators on Grant's behalf. As a Kentuckian, John said, he was proud to be representing their great state on this vital mission in the North.

Invited to dinner at Blaine's home, John arrived to find himself seated next to Frederick Douglass, the "negro" the man had mentioned. Douglass needed no introduction to a political audience in 1875. He was, perhaps, the best-known black man in America. John asked the audience to stand in his

Kentucky shoes. "Would you, Kentuckians, have expected me to rise from my seat and lecture Mr. Blaine at his own table? Would you have expected me to rise from the table and leave the house? I ate my dinner in entire comfort, eating neither more or less because of Douglass's presence near me."

Having earned a few appreciative laughs, John could have stopped there. He had done his duty as a Kentucky gentleman, acting courteously while maintaining his distance. But that was not the story John wanted to tell. "Why, fellow-citizens," he went on, "I not only ate by the side of Douglass at Blaine's house, but during the campaign sat at the same table with him in public hotels and spoke from the same platform with him."

As this image of equal status was sinking in, John doubled the stakes. "And here let me say that there is no man of any party in Kentucky who can make an abler address before a public audience than can Frederick Douglass. . . . I not only do not apologize for what I did, but frankly say that I would rather eat dinner any day by the side of Douglass than to eat with the fellow across the way who sought to entrap me with a question that has nothing to do with this contest."

In John's memory, the applause was long and loud.

EMBRACING REPUBLICAN PRINCIPLES placed John on the periphery of his home state, gazing into a cavernous racial divide. He was a Kentuckian marching to the beat of a different drummer. Too often, though, that beat was emanating from Washington, not from Frankfort or Paducah or Munfordville. During his first run for governor in 1871, John had set himself apart from Charles Sumner and the party's radical Northern wing. He had said "social equality can never exist between the two races in Kentucky," and he had meant it. But four years had passed. His adopted party's views on civil rights had continued to evolve. John knew he could not stand still, not if he intended to remain a Republican with an eye on the national stage. His only choice was to adjust and amend.

Every year seemed to bring some new challenge. In 1875, it was yet another civil rights act, enacted a year after Sumner's death but carrying his stamp on every section. For the first time, Congress had thrust itself into the question of how railroads, steamboats, innkeepers, and theaters were treating their patrons. In a few paragraphs, the legislation brushed aside the longstanding claim that private businesses had a right to sort out their customers as they saw fit, if their rules were reasonable. "All persons," the new law said, "shall be entitled to the full and equal enjoyment of the accommodations, advantages, facilities and privileges," regardless of race or color or previous condition of servitude. A five-hundred-dollar fine, paid directly to the victim of discrimination, awaited anyone convicted of a violation.

That wasn't all. The act also intervened directly into the operation of state courts, requiring them to accept jurors of any color and race. Anticipating resistance, the bill's drafters had embedded an eye-opening fine of five thousand dollars for any official found guilty of excluding people of color. This, too, was extraordinary. Congress had unquestioned jurisdiction over the nation's federal and territorial judiciaries. But state courts? Did Congress now have the power, under the new Thirteenth and Fourteenth amendments, to tell Kentucky and the other thirty-six states how to run their judicial systems? Or, for that matter, to tell private companies and individuals how to operate their businesses?

The Supreme Court would have the final say on those legal questions. Congress had set the stage for such a ruling, stating in the act's fifth and final section that all convictions were "reviewable" by the high court, as if begging the justices to weigh in, to say yes, to ensure equality, to form a more perfect union, Congress can now delve deeper into local affairs. If that was the Radical Republican hope, it was a thin one. The justices had already signaled, in earlier cases, that they intended to interpret the new amendments narrowly, that they would aim to preserve the "balance between State and Federal power," as they had said in one recent ruling.

The John Harlan of 1865 and 1866, confronted with the Thirteenth Amendment abolishing slavery and then the first civil rights act, had argued strongly against such federal incursions, labelling them "a radical change in the fundamental law of the land." What would he say now, in 1875, while running for governor?

He could not duck the question. James McCreary, his Democratic rival, had been harping on it, demanding to know if John supported this "revolutionary" legislation, disparaging the Civil Rights Act of 1875 as one more example of failed Reconstruction policy. "Look at Louisiana, Mississippi, South Carolina and others of the Southern States, and see their deplorable conditions," McCreary thundered in early June. "Mixed schools, negro officers, and the rampant rule of ignorance, venality, and brutality."

It was hard to blame the act, only a few months old, for these "deplorable" conditions. But if John wanted to call himself a Republican, well, McCreary was glad to call him to account for every Republican idea. Especially the Radical ones hatched in Washington.

JOHN'S FEELINGS ABOUT the Civil Rights Act of 1875 were complicated. As a student of the U.S. Constitution, he still had qualms about the national government intruding into local affairs. But after years of violence toward Kentucky's colored citizens, he recognized the dilemma at hand. In 1871, after a series of Ku-Klux outrages in the county that included Frankfort, John had told a friend that federal intervention was the only way to "root out the evil." In early 1873, the new U.S. Justice Department had hired him to assist in prosecuting civil rights cases against the Ku-Klux and others. It was a temporary appointment, but it had left a permanent impression. Patience would not cure prejudice. Equality required enforcement.

As John wrestled with what to say about the new law, he looked closely at how federal judges were reacting. Several had already taken opposing views of the act's constitutionality, offering a potpourri of legal positions. John was particularly drawn to the words of Halmer H. Emmons, the chief judge for the four-state circuit that included Kentucky, Ohio, Michigan, and Indiana. Emmons was a Republican appointee from Michigan, a well-regarded jurist, sixty years old, one of only nine circuit judges in the country, six years of service on the federal bench. When the act became law on March 1, 1875, Emmons happened to be sitting in the Memphis federal court for a month, part of his circuit-riding duties.

The existing grand jury had asked Emmons for his guidance on enforcing the law, including the act's threat to punish any U.S. district attorney who "willfully" refused to bring a prosecution, and the judge had taken an extraordinary step. On March 22, he prohibited the grand jury from issuing *any* criminal indictments under the act. His action captured headlines, North and South. "An Important Decision by Judge Emmons," the *Free Press* informed its readers in Detroit, where Emmons lived. "Congress Cannot Pass Laws to Regulate Theaters and Hotels."

It was a dramatic moment, and Emmons knew it. Here was this Northerner, this visitor to Memphis, this near-stranger. The ink was hardly dry on this new national act, and he was declaring the law's criminal provisions to be unconstitutional. His view didn't bind other federal judges, even in his own circuit, but his stature gave his conclusion extra weight.

"In ordinary circumstances," he had told the grand jury, he would have given them their instructions and said nothing more. But the circumstances were anything but ordinary, he said. Racial violence was rampant in the South. Colleagues had urged him to put his ruling into a wider context—"in a simple and untechnical form." Adopting their advice, he had drafted a 3,000-word explanation, which he read aloud in the courtroom.

He sympathized, he told the jurors, with the impulse behind these repeated congressional forays into civil rights. The Southern states and their justice systems had failed to stop or punish the men responsible for "those mean and cowardly murders which are so frequently disgracing our civilization before the world." Without mentioning the Ku-Klux or any white supremacist group by name, the judge spoke with undisguised contempt about "elegantly dressed, socially well-connected, and shameless murderers" who had "not only confessed but boasted of their crimes, and who had either not been indicted at all, or, when tried, had been acquitted by juries."

And yet: Unlike the federal Enforcement Act of 1870, Emmons said, this new law was not aimed at the murderers who had burst into "the humble homes of those peaceful toilers who quietly and inoffensively labor to support their wives and little ones." Instead, he lamented, this "almost grotesque exercise of national authority" had been deployed for less serious purposes. Adding a critic's hat to his judicial garb, he said he had but "small sympathy with the right of the negro to see the immodest and vulgar display in the ballet dance, which in modern times so universally disgraces the best theatrical productions."

Emmons urged victims of discrimination to bring civil lawsuits to federal court. That would allow a test of the new law. Emmons, though, had made up his mind. Based on his reading of the amendments, Congress had no basis to "interfere with the private and internal regulations of theater managers, hotel keepers, or common carriers within a state," he said. "Those are matters which the state government alone controls."

John latched on to Emmons's words, like a man clinging to a rope over a dangerous precipice. Emmons is "a distinguished Republican jurist," John said in his campaign speeches, and "I concur" in his conclusion. Public accommodations "are matters of local concern, to be determined and regulated by local authority."

In other words, by Kentucky authorities, not those in distant Washington.

JOHN COULD HAVE shied away from saying anything more, but that was not his inclination. "I desire to speak upon that subject," he told a noisy audience in Elizabethtown on an oppressively hot day in early July 1875, "so that no one can have any doubt as to my position."

Equality before the law was right and just, he said. But recent history had shown how difficult it was to achieve. After emancipation, he reminded them, the Kentucky legislature had refused to allow colored witnesses to testify in cases involving whites. Finally, in 1872, after years of "cruel delay," the legislature had reversed itself. This was progress, but it hadn't happened by luck or accident. "Popular prejudice on that subject had given way to the demands of civilization," John said, "and we are now all agreed that what was finally done by the Kentucky legislature ought to have been done many years before."

We are now all agreed. Hardly. Many white Kentuckians, if asked, would still say that a negro man's testimony was about as valuable as a spittoon of tobacco juice. John himself, during his time as attorney general, had done his part to prevent such testimony. But his thinking had changed. In the face of continuing injustice, he felt, fairness demanded that the state's colored citizens have equal access to the courts. Otherwise, they would have no shield against the "outrages against their life, liberty and property," John told his campaign audiences.

By endorsing the act's overall purpose, even with caveats, John was leaving himself open to scorn. Kentucky politics in the 1870s offered little room for ambiguity, especially around the heated subject of race. McCreary was fond of attacking the act by saying that it gave "greater rights" to colored citizens than to whites. That a white man, traveling alone on a train, could not enter the ladies' car, while a black man could now go "anywhere he wanted." This was an "absurd" interpretation, John said. "The clear and manifest purpose of the act was to secure equal, not superior, privileges to the colored race."

John repudiated McCreary's inflammatory statements, calling them a breeding ground for more acts of violence by "bands of lawless men" against colored citizens. "There is no necessity for this continual war upon that race," he said in Elizabethtown. "This country is broad enough for us all to live in." But equality did not require the two races to like each other, John assured the crowd. Whites and blacks can "move along in this free land of ours, each cherishing, if you please, the prejudices of race without at all interfering with the just rights of the other."

It was an artful argument, tailored to a Kentucky audience. *Cherish your prejudices, but keep them to yourself.* Then, addressing himself to those whites who did not want to let bygones be bygones, John threw down a gauntlet, one that he would carry forward, beyond the campaign. "Anyone who proposes to deny [people of color] such rights is no friend of the law, is an enemy to our free institutions, and no friend of peace," he said.

John had no trouble winning admiration for his rhetorical gifts. His gubernatorial scorecard, though, remained unblemished by victory. By an almost identical margin, thirty-six thousand votes, Kentuckians chose McCreary, the Confederate veteran, over Harlan, the Union colonel. Once again, the Democrats emerged with every top office in the state, making John even more determined to burnish his national profile.

EXCITEMENT RIPPLED THROUGH Louisville's Liederkranz Hall on May 18, 1876, a feverish hum filling the second-floor Opera House. John could look out at the swarm of delegates—more than four hundred Kentucky Republicans, including a "goodly mixture of the colored element," as one Louisville newspaper felt compelled to note—and think with satisfaction about the months of work that had led to this moment, all the exploratory letters to party leaders around the state and elsewhere. All the organizing of "Bristow for President" clubs in Philadelphia, Chicago, Boston, Cincinnati, and Detroit. All the hours promoting Benjamin H. Bristow, John's good friend and former law partner, to sympathetic journalists. All the newspaper accounts, clipped and saved, on Bristow and his half-dozen rivals for the nation's highest office.

It was a relief to be running a campaign for someone else, even the reticent Bristow, who believed that the best way to prove his fitness for the presidency was not to seek it. An honorable stance, but as John well knew, hardly a realistic one. The mountain they were ascending was steep enough without having to carry their candidate on their backs.

John and his disciples now had less than a month before the Republican National Convention met in Cincinnati. Less than a month to chip away at James Blaine's substantial lead. As matters stood, no candidate seemed anywhere close to the three hundred and eighty delegates or so needed to win. If Blaine fell short after the first few ballots—as many believed the Maine Republican would—the party would have to turn to a second choice. Why not Bristow?

By now, John's pitch was well honed. Bristow had the right combination of sterling record and Republican integrity. As U.S. district attorney in Kentucky, he had prosecuted Ku-Klux murders. Now, as secretary of the treasury, he had distinguished himself with a long-running investigation into government corruption. He was the only candidate, other than Blaine, who could claim a truly national reputation, and he was also the only Southerner—a big plus, John felt, for a party that desperately needed to bolster its cross-sectional appeal after its disastrous showing in the 1874 election.

After a decade of controlling Congress, the Republicans had lost the House. In one fell swoop, the Democrats had gained more than ninety seats. Ninety seats! A brutal referendum on Reconstruction. That's what most newspapers were saying. If the party had a prayer of keeping the White House, it had to nominate a candidate who could bridge the North-South divide. Bristow was that man, John believed. "My candid conviction is that he is the strongest man today that the Republicans can run," he told a Kentucky friend.

Everyone remembered 1860, when Lincoln had emerged from deep in the pack after the front-running Seward had stumbled. Could history repeat itself?

That was the swelling hope for John and the rest of the Bristow camp.

BRISTOW'S PATH to second choice was neither easy nor clear. Running as a reformer did not endear him to some members of his party. Allegations of corruption had dogged the Grant administration for years, and Bristow's investigations had added potent fuel to that smoldering fire. His agents had exposed a broad conspiracy, involving government officials, to siphon off federal tax revenues owed on whiskey production. With every prosecution of the so-called "Whiskey Rings," though, Bristow found himself in less favor among Grant loyalists. In a deadlocked convention, Bristow would not be their second choice.

The proceedings at Liederkranz Hall were orchestrated to showcase Bristow's strength at home. Speech after speech brought bellows of approval from the crowd. John had taken on the crucial job of leading the platform committee. Bristow would be tied to this "declaration of principles," so the words had to be right. John shepherded through an eleven-point plan that any Radical Republican could cheer. Number Ten: Schools for all children, at public expense and under public control. Number Eleven: "Equal rights before the law of all citizens without regard to race or color, and full and equal protection in the exercise of those rights."

Typically, the Opera House and its thirty-six-foot-high ceiling played host to the lofty music of grand balls. Today's sounds were different. As one newspaper wrote, John's speech for Bristow brought forth waves of "great applause, hand-shaking and hat-throwing." Here was a candidate, John said, who was calm, courageous, and steadfastly true to Republican ideals. "As Kentucky gave Abraham Lincoln to his country and to mankind . . . she now presents Benjamin H. Bristow." The Opera House reverberated in agreement. All twenty-four delegates, including two of color, pledged themselves to Bristow. Unanimity.

Now it was on to Cincinnati. John would find out for himself just where Bristow stood among the party faithful.

HOLDING COURT at Cincinnati's world-famous hotel, the domed-top Burnet House, John was a jovial host with an undisguised agenda. Not that he didn't enjoy joking and jousting with journalists, especially Republican ones. John had friends at a variety of newspapers, not just in Kentucky, but in Ohio and Indiana and beyond. He needed more than their fellowship now. He needed them to listen.

The city resembled a street carnival, teeming with the sounds and smells of politics. Thousands of strolling visitors. Impromptu speeches from balconies. Musicians and their brass bands rambling from block to block. Inside the hotels, the candidates' surrogates were touting their wares, explaining how Indiana senator Morton could beat Blaine, where New York senator Conkling's strength was hiding, why Ohio governor Hayes was the brightest of the dark horses.

John was one more circus barker, hawking his candidate. He was running into skepticism. If the air went out of Blaine's balloon, the prevailing wisdom was that Bristow would deflate as well, unable to line up the necessary alliances. A correspondent for the *Chicago Inter Ocean*, after attending a dinner of Bristow and Hayes supporters, wrote that the event was "really a wake over Bristow's dead hopes."

John had three days to prove otherwise.

AMID THE BARTERING and brokering and bantering about delegate counts, it was easy to lose sight of the issues that had defined the Republican

Party since the war. Near the end of Wednesday's opening session, a surprise speaker brought those questions back to the fore. Addressing his first presidential convention, Frederick Douglass sharply reminded the delegates that equal rights was still a goal to be attained, not an achievement to be celebrated. He said: "You say you have emancipated us. You have; and I thank you for it. You say you have enfranchised us. You have; and I thank you for it. But what is your emancipation?—and what is your enfranchisement? What does it all amount to, if the black man, after having been made free by the letter of your law, is unable to exercise that freedom, and, after having been freed from the slaveholder's lash, he is to be subjected to the slaveholder's shot-gun?"

Douglass spoke for no candidate. His status as a District of Columbia delegate was in limbo, mired in a credentialing fight. He was both outsider and insider. He could be seen in the hotel lobbies, tall, bearded, a striking figure in frock coat and derby hat, conferring with colored delegates, chatting with white ones, his head bent, serious. He was serious now as he addressed the full convention. "You turned us loose to the sky, to the storm, to the whirlwind, and, worst of all, you turned us loose to the wrath of our infuriated masters," he admonished the delegates. "The question now is: Do you mean to make good to us the promises in your constitution?"

Your law. Your constitution. Words carefully chosen, reflecting the sting of separation.

MOUNTING THE MAKESHIFT platform to nominate Bristow late on Thursday afternoon, the convention's second day, John had one more card to play. He had arranged for three New Englanders, all from different states, to second the nomination. John wanted to demonstrate, front and center, that the Southerner had plenty of Northern support.

Bristow the reformer made only a brief appearance in John's speech, overshadowed by Bristow the defender of equal rights. John reeled off Bristow's bona fides—Union colonel, vocal supporter of the three Reconstruction amendments, prosecutor of Ku-Klux murderers—before quoting Bristow, two powerful quotes, leaving no doubt where this Southerner stood, and no doubt that John stood there with him.

On education: "I would tax the rich man's property to educate his poor neighbor's child. I would tax the white man's property to educate the black man's child, and vice versa. In a word, I would tax *all* the property of the state to educate *all* the children of the state." On Kentucky once denying blacks the right to testify: "This denial is a monstrous and a grievous wrong to both races. It is a practical denial of freedom to the colored race. Yes, it is even worse than that: it is a license, if not an invitation, to base miscreants and cowardly Ku-Klux to gratify their brutal passions and satiate their murderous propensities on this unoffending and defenseless race."

Unflinching words, unlike any in the other nominating speeches. The applause came, but as one observer wrote, perhaps more ardently from the galleries than the delegates themselves.

JOHN WATCHED the first four ballots with growing gloom. Bristow's delegate numbers had hardly moved: 113, 114, 121, 126. He had achieved little more than a firm grip on a weak second place. John's only consolation was Blaine's equal lack of progress. When Michigan broke ranks on the fifth ballot, awarding all twenty-two of its votes to Hayes, John was crestfallen. Had the stampede to second choice begun? John thought so. "As soon as it was done," John later wrote Bristow, "I felt that our case was hopeless."

Hayes had been stalled in sixth place before the Michigan move, with barely half of Bristow's delegate total. Now, pandemonium reigned in the massive hall. "The effect was electrical," was one reporter's description. "Two thirds of the convention and the audience were on their feet in an instant, shouting and yelling, waving hats, handkerchiefs. . . . Everyone felt that the Rubicon was passed, that the next President was already named."

Not quite. There was no mass movement to the Ohio governor. The Rubicon remained uncrossed, reviving John's wilting hopes. If Indiana could be persuaded to abandon Morton and come over to Bristow's column . . . well, that could change everything. John awaited the next ballot, tense, awash in a sea of conflicting sentiments. As Bristow's friend, he felt obliged to stick with him to the end. But as leader of the Kentucky delegation, he felt pressure to make their votes count for something if Bristow could not win.

Just after four o'clock in the waning afternoon, the secretary called for the seventh ballot. When Indiana's turn came, the delegation's chairman revealed that he was withdrawing Morton's nomination. The hall thrummed with expectation. The second choice was finally at hand. "Indiana casts twenty-five votes," and now he had to shout, "for Rutherford B. Hayes . . ." The rest of the sentence disappeared in an explosion of foot-stamping and hand-clapping.

Ten ear-splitting minutes later, John hoisted himself to his feet. Ten thousand pairs of eyes followed his deliberate walk to the platform. The reporters readied themselves to take down the words that telegraph operators would soon transmit to the country. John had planned those words with care. What was said in defeat, he well knew, could be as meaningful as what was said in triumph.

"The Republicans of the State of Kentucky feel deeply grateful," John said, to "those gallant men of Massachusetts and Vermont and other states of New England." When others had insinuated that Bristow could not be trusted to be president "because he was born and reared in the South," the New Englanders had "refused to believe it." They had told him: Bristow was true. Bristow was trustworthy.

It was hard to hear much amid the din, but a *New York Times* reporter found the moment so memorable that he wrote "never did a man facing such an audience say so much in so few words." John did not prolong the suspense. "I have come upon this stand" to withdraw Bristow's name, he said, and cast "the entire vote of the state of Kentucky for Rutherford B. Hayes!"

RUTHERFORD B. HAYES was making a list. It was January 17, 1877, and the president-elect was at his desk in Columbus, Ohio, jotting the names of possible cabinet officers. Evarts for secretary of state. Rice or Forbes or maybe Sherman for treasury. General Harlan—"of Kentucky," he noted—for attorney general. A suitable job for the man who had delivered twenty-four crucial votes at the convention.

But nothing for Blaine or Bristow. Hayes wrote in his diary: "I am inclined to say that I must not take either of the leading competitors for the

Presidential nomination, nor any members of the present Cabinet." He preferred to start fresh, if he ever took office.

If he ever took office. Remarkably enough, the election remained unsettled. Disputed results in three Southern states, accompanied by dueling accusations of fraud and ballot manipulation, had sent the country spinning into a constitutional quandary. The Republicans were claiming a one-vote victory, 185 electoral votes for Hayes, the absolute minimum—achieved, they contended, despite Democratic efforts to intimidate colored voters in the South. The Democrats said nonsense, the Hayes triumph was a concocted fiction, conjured out of foul air by Republican-controlled election boards in Louisiana, South Carolina, and Florida, which had invalidated enough Democratic ballots to steal twenty electoral votes from Samuel J. Tilden—winner of the popular vote by 250,000, as the Democrats were eager to point out.

No one knew how to resolve the mess. No mechanism existed for investigating the contested results. As the crisis wore on, the finger pointing turned nasty. Newspapers were quoting dark talk of "well-armed men" threatening to march on Washington if the Republican president of the Senate tabulated the electoral votes, as the Constitution required him to do, and dared to declare Hayes the victor.

The stalemate led to an unprecedented, untested idea: creating a commission of fifteen—five Republicans, five Democrats, and five Supreme Court justices—with the exclusive power to decide the election. Was it constitutional? Hayes thought not. But he was staying away from the fracas, leaving the negotiations to others. "I will abide the result," he wrote to a friend. "No one ought to go to war, or even to law, about it."

Hayes prepared for either outcome, making notes for an inaugural speech, fiddling with his cabinet preferences. John remained in the running for one of the seven coveted posts. Hayes was keen to demonstrate that sectionalism would not govern his administration. If given a chance to deliver an inaugural address, he would say that it was time to bring the Reconstruction era to a close, and to remove all federal troops from the South. "We do not want a united North nor a united South. We want a united country," he scribbled. Make sectionalism disappear, and "that will tend to wipe out the color line."

Hayes had no illusions about Southern Democrats. He was sure that most of them thought it was "a monstrous wrong" to allow colored people to vote. But he was still set on erecting a bridge rather than wielding the bludgeon of military power. "I would like to get support from good men of the South, late rebels," he mused in his diary. "How to do it is the question. . . . I could appoint a Southern Democrat in the Cabinet. But who would take it among the influential and good men of those States?"

PRESIDENT RUTHERFORD B. HAYES assembled his cabinet shortly after 10:00 a.m. on March 21, 1877, a gray Wednesday morning, with one primary item on the agenda—discussing "the Southern question," as some newspapers were politely calling what amounted to political insurrection. Hayes had emerged with his brokered presidency, but in both Louisiana and South Carolina, there were now rival state governments, each claiming to be legitimate. It was like having double vision. Two governors. Two state legislatures. Two political parties refusing to blink. There was pressure on Hayes, from within his party, to order federal military forces to back up the Republican claimants in New Orleans. Hayes was thinking of deploying a five-member commission of inquiry instead.

The cabinet had only one Southerner to advise him, and it wasn't John Harlan of Kentucky. Opposition from a powerful Republican senator had derailed John's appointment. The president had another job in mind for John, a temporary one: He would dispatch him to New Orleans as part of the commission of inquiry. Hayes wanted his emissaries to gather facts, take testimony—to prod but not push. "It is not the duty of the President of the United States to use the military power of the Nation to decide contested elections in the States," Hayes wrote in his diary after two days of cabinet meetings. "The wish is to restore harmony and good feeling between sections and races. This can only be done by peaceful methods. We wish to adjust the difficulties in Louisiana and South Carolina so as to make one government out of two in each state. But if this fails . . . we must then adopt the non-intervention policy, except so far as may be necessary to keep the peace." If that meant conceding parts of the South to the Democrats, so be it.

Reconstruction was limping to an end. John would be there to witness and perhaps influence some of its final days. Mallie made plans to go with him to New Orleans, but decided at the last minute that she "could not, with any peace of mind, be absent so long from my children." John took their eighteen-year-old son, Richard, instead. The lad was eager to go along. It would be an education, to use one of Mallie's favorite words, for the two of them.

An education it was. "Of all the states that I have ever visited, this beats all," John wrote to Bristow from New Orleans. "Its politics are an utter confusion, and it will puzzle anyone to get at the exact matter."

HAYES WANTED A SOUTHERNER for the Supreme Court. That was the heart of the matter. Handed a court vacancy at the beginning of his term, Hayes had been weighing his options for months. The last justice from the South had been appointed in 1853, during Democrat Franklin Pierce's administration. Ten vacancies since then, and all had gone to Northerners. Hayes was determined to break with that past. He had kept his pledges to name a Southerner to his cabinet and pull back federal troops. Now he wanted to go one step further.

The president had several possible nominees on his list, John and Bristow among them. But he was also looking farther south. He expected loud opposition from the party's Radical wing. He was prepared to ride out the howls.

John was paying close attention to the rumors, of course. His ambitions were at war with his loyalties. By his reckoning, if a judgeship was destined for a Kentuckian, then his friend Bristow stood first in line. But if Bristow wasn't in the running or wasn't interested . . . well, John had long thought of the Supreme Court as the ideal job. "I know of no more desirable position," he had written to Bristow back in 1870, wondering if Grant might appoint Bristow to the bench. Did John dare dream of it now, for himself?

In May, after his return from New Orleans, John had an encouraging if sobering letter from Wayne MacVeagh, a fellow member of the Louisiana commission. MacVeagh, a Hayes confidante, had spent three intense weeks with John in the madhouse of Louisiana politics. MacVeagh had liked what he had seen of the forty-four-year-old Kentuckian. "Your career ought to be judicial," MacVeagh wrote now. "It is your ambition. . . . I see not only great usefulness but great happiness in it for you." But forget about the current Supreme Court vacancy, he advised. The job would not go to anyone from John's circuit, which already had a justice on the bench. Instead, MacVeagh suggested, "Why not make up your mind to take the Circuit Judgeship when it is vacant?" Whenever the moment came, MacVeagh promised to speak up on John's behalf.

John had a chance to press his own case. In mid-July, he was in Washington to arrange a presidential visit to an industrial exposition in Louisville. A private meeting with Hayes turned into a kind of job interview. Hayes asked John: "Would a first-class foreign mission tempt your ambition?" The president had England in mind, the most prestigious post of all.

John, while flattered, resisted the idea. "I think not, Mr. President," he said. "My ambition has not led me in that direction. I do not see how a man of my limited fortune and large family could afford to live abroad." John preferred something "in the line of my profession."

In other words, what about a judgeship?

JOHN'S AMBITIONS DOVETAILED with MacVeagh's growing unease about Hayes's intentions. The president seemed set on plucking a nominee from the deepest South. MacVeagh felt it would create a ruckus within the party that Hayes did not need. On August 21, MacVeagh sent Hayes a lengthy note, urging him to find "a thoroughly sound Republican" from "the more Northern States of the South." MacVeagh had someone in mind. "I believe General Harlan of Kentucky meets all the requirements, and that you could not possibly do a wiser or better thing for the country as well as for your Administration, than to offer him the existing position."

Weeks later, Hayes wrote to another friend, William Henry Smith, of the Western Associated Press in Chicago: "Confidentially and on the whole is not Harlan the man? Of the right age—able—of whole character—industrious—fine manner, temper and appearance. Who beats him?"

Smith's reply was guarded. Yes, Harlan might be the one, "a much better man in every way than Bristow, if a Southern man is to be taken." But, Smith warned, it "will offend a good many people of both parties" who favor a Midwestern nominee.

MacVeagh and Smith weren't the only ones whispering in Hayes's ear. Bristow's most passionate advocates had been promoting their man's interests, and they were fuming. Why wasn't Hayes turning to Bristow? Was John elbowing Bristow aside? If so, how dare he?

A rift was developing between the two old friends, rooted in misunderstanding and their competing ambitions. On the same day that MacVeagh was writing to Hayes, John was putting his own thoughts on paper, in diary form. His words verged on bitterness. John had fought hard and true for Bristow over several years. What had Bristow done in return? Nothing that John could see. When Hayes was considering John for attorney general, Bristow had stayed silent. He seemed to treat John as a rival. "Thus has an exhibition of selfishness snapped the cords of a friendship," John wrote in sadness and anger.

The tension surfaced publicly when word circulated that Hayes had made his selection. "Happy Harlan" was the *Cincinnati Enquirer*'s main headline on October 12. Directly underneath: "Bristow on the Ragged Edge of Disappointment and Disgust." The story hinted, vaguely, at dire political consequences for Hayes should Harlan "walk off with the prize that Bristow has so coveted."

Four days later, Hayes sent John's name to the Senate.

THERE WAS NO escaping the ruckus. Too many Republicans were upset with Hayes's Southern policy, and John's nomination offered an easy target for expressing that anger. They had no trouble compiling a litany of John's sins. Defending slavery, both before and during the war? Voting for McClellan over Lincoln in 1864? Opposing the Thirteenth and Fourteenth amendments? Yes, yes, and yes. It was admirable that Harlan had changed his stripes, but was this man the best that Hayes could do?

John had no way to know if his nomination was in serious trouble, but when one of Kentucky's senators advised him of the "stories being circulated" about him, he decided to defend himself. At home in Louisville, he drafted a seventeen-page reply. "My dear Senator," he wrote on October 31. "You know very well that I do not claim to have been a Republican" since the party's founding. But that did not make his conversion any less sincere, he said. He now believed he was wrong to have supported McClellan, and wrong to have opposed the amendments. Asking only to be judged for what he had actually done and said throughout his life, John authorized the senator to use his reply "as you deem fit and proper."

The senator, James Beck, was a Democrat who had worked against John's bids for governor. But loyal to Kentucky, Beck was now working hard for John's nomination. Late in November, after a nervous few weeks, Beck wrote a hurried note to John, predicting "you can't be beaten." A last-minute maneuver to block the vote failed to gain any traction.

On December 10, in the Old Senate Chamber that served as the Supreme Court's home, John took his oath as the nation's forty-fourth justice. Mallie beamed in her seat, the president's wife at her side. They had come to the Capitol in Lucy Hayes's carriage, the start of a friendship that Mallie would say made moving to Washington much easier than she had feared.

As for John, he was feeling his way. He was now the youngest justice, by almost two decades. By tradition, as the most junior member, his turn to speak would come last at the court's discussions and votes. It seemed wise to take advantage of that, to watch and learn. During his first week, he asked Chief Justice Morrison Waite not to assign him to write the ruling in a difficult case.

Given "the importance of the questions involved," he wrote in a note to Waite, "the opinion should come from one of the older members of the court."

JOHN FOUND DOZENS of pending cases on the court's current docket, the briefs already filed, the oral arguments heard weeks before, if arguments had been held at all. There was no rule preventing John from voting if he hadn't heard the oral argument, but for the most part, he let those go. He didn't need to worry about breaking any four-four ties. During his first two months, only six of more than sixty cases drew a dissent of any kind, and in no instance was the court divided by more than six to three.

Constitutional questions could be esoteric as well as important, and the court dealt with both extremes. But the Reconstruction amendments had given rise to an entirely new area of legal dispute. One such lawsuit was resting on the docket when John took his seat. *Benson v. Decuir* was a Louisiana case involving steamboats, separation, and a set of facts that seemed ready-made for applying point Number Eleven of the Kentucky party platform that John had helped draft seven months earlier: "Equal rights before the law of all citizens without regard to race or color, and full and equal protection in the exercise of those rights."

In July 1872, Josephine Decuir had boarded the *Governor Allen*, a Mississippi River steamboat operating between New Orleans and Vicksburg in the neighboring state of Mississippi. Decuir wasn't going that far. For her overnight 120-mile journey to the Louisiana town of Hermitage, where she and her late husband had owned a plantation, she asked for a room in the upper cabin area reserved for whites. The ship refused, offering Decuir a place in the lower "bureau" set aside for colored passengers.

This did not sit well with Decuir. She was in her mid-forties, a proud member of *les gens de couleur.* She did not accept her assigned place in this stark division, black and white, upper and lower. "The plaintiff in the case is a lady of color, genteel in her manners, modest in her deportment, neat in her appearance, and quite fair for one of mixed blood," the judge in New Orleans would say in his ruling. "She was never a slave, nor is she the descendant of a slave."

Decuir passed the July night, upright, on a deck chair near the upper cabin. On landing at Hermitage, she paid the lower-cabin rate of two dollars. Nine days later, she sued Benson in a New Orleans court, asking seventy-five thousand dollars in damages. Unlike William Day in 1858, Decuir had state law on her side. Louisiana's new constitution, enacted as part of the state's effort to rejoin the Union, declared that "all persons shall have equal rights and privileges upon any conveyance of a public nature." To back up that provision, P. B. S. Pinchback's 1869 public accommodations law had spelled out the consequences of a violation, including the victim's right to sue for damages.

Two Louisiana courts had found in Decuir's favor, awarding her one thousand dollars. The steamboat captain, John Benson, had taken his protest to the Supreme Court. His primary objection: The state was violating the federal constitution by regulating a business involved in interstate commerce. His business would be hurt, Benson said, if his ship couldn't offer separate accommodations. He portrayed the cabin spaces as equal in quality and comfort. Decuir's lawyer countered with testimony from passengers describing the colored quarters as dreary, dark places—"a kind of prison."

The Supreme Court justices, led by Waite, sided with Benson. The U.S. Constitution's interstate commerce clause trumped Louisiana law, the chief justice wrote for the unanimous court. Commerce must be "free and untrammeled" along the ten states bordering the Mississippi, Waite ruled. The majority ruling was brief—seven paragraphs, fifteen hundred words—but it made clear that the court saw no need to disturb the custom of separation. "If the public good requires such legislation," Waite wrote, "it must come from Congress, and not from the states."

Congress had passed such legislation since Decuir's ill-fated trip in 1872, but Waite chose not to make any mention of the 1875 Civil Rights Act, already so hotly debated by Halmer Emmons and other federal judges. Why not? Was the chief justice leaving that for another day? Or had he already made up his mind about the 1875 act and its requirement that "all persons" were entitled to "full and equal enjoyment" of public accommodations?

As for John, he did not participate. He had gone to Louisville for the Christmas holidays, and wasn't in the courtroom when the decision was announced. Whenever the issue of equal accommodation came up again—as it inevitably would, with three challenges to the 1875 Civil Rights Act making their long journeys through the lower courts—John would not have the option of staying away from the fray.

Sumner's posthumous victory: The Civil Rights Act of 1875

(Harper's Weekly, *April 24, 1875)*

15

"Uncongenial Strifes"

Brown and Tourgee, 1875–1879

THE HEADACHES WOULDN'T GO AWAY.

No matter what Henry Billings Brown did, or how often he consulted a doctor, they kept coming back. Some days, he would stagger through his schedule, grateful to reach his bed at night. But if they came on suddenly and blindingly, as they were doing now in the early months of 1875, he would have to sleep all day, postponing his cases in federal court. It was embarrassing. Everyone has a headache now and then. How could he possibly describe his agony to anyone else? The pulsing pain? The fear—the dread—that he would never be free of it?

Otherwise, taking stock of his life and career, he had much to savor. Carry's inheritance had cleared the last legal hurdles, giving them a measure of wealth and security. He was putting the finishing touches on a legal volume to be published as "Brown's Admiralty Reports," reflecting his knowledge of disputes arising primarily from the Great Lakes and their voluminous ship traffic. At thirty-nine, he had achieved a level of esteem—and even some sway—that other men might envy. Yet how could he enjoy it? For years, he had been coping with his infernal eye inflammations. Was he now doomed to endure debilitating, draining headaches, too? Some months, his daybook read like a medical log. "Hard headache" appeared as frequently as "lovely weather" or "walk with Carry." He felt cursed.

The headaches seemed to take an extended vacation whenever he wasn't working. They were nowhere in evidence during the summer months of 1873, when he was squiring Carry around Europe, their first overseas adventure together. They had invited Carry's younger sister, Isabelle, and together with a trusted servant, they had taken the grand tour—England, Scotland, France, Belgium, Germany, Italy. He reveled in escorting Carry and Isabelle to the Louvre and Notre Dame, places he had visited in '57 and '58 during his glorious year abroad.

This trip, though, felt different. He wasn't a twenty-year-old on a belt-tightened budget. In Paris, he bought dozens and dozens of books, 159 in all—"marvelously cheap," he wrote. In Brussels, he went "head over ears" for art, spending two thousand dollars in an afternoon. It was a major undertaking to ship everything to the States, but it would be a balm for his soul to have bits of his beloved Europe in their home on Detroit's Jefferson Avenue.

Later that fall, he had traveled to Washington for his first argument ever at the Supreme Court. It was a minor insurance dispute, but it had given him the opportunity to meet six of the nine justices and gain admission to the Supreme Court bar. He left feeling as if he had accomplished something grand. "Swell court, big dignity," he had written in his daybook. Several months later, a telegram brought the news that the court had ruled in his client's favor. Victory! His elation was fleeting, though, swept away by a new wave of headaches. He wrote in despair: "Oh! will never they cease except with death?"

Desperation edged into his days. Henry loved the law, but not the pressure that came with the practice of it. By early 1875, he felt his health "giving way under the uncongenial strifes of the Bar." He would gladly swap the stress of litigation, "where one's main ambition is to *win*," for a judgeship, "where one's sole ambition is to do justice," he wrote. But there were no vacancies, and none on the horizon. Judge Longyear, in the federal district court, was fifty-four. Judge Emmons, in the U.S. circuit court, was older, but only sixty-one. These were lifetime appointments. Henry was facing a long and uncertain wait.

Then, near midnight on a clear Wednesday night in March 1875, a heart attack changed everything. "Judge Longyear dead! Oh God! How horrible!"

was Henry's astonished scribble in his daybook. "Already plenty of talk of his successor. Offers of friendship and aid freely made."

Offers freely made—and gratefully, ardently, eagerly accepted.

RESOLVING TO USE every bit of his small store of accumulated influence, Henry devised a hasty strategy. Armed with letters of support, he would undertake a quick trip to Washington and plead his case in person. A bit dramatic, but he felt as if his life—and his health—depended on the outcome.

He booked a Tuesday night train. Before leaving, he stopped to see his friend Charles Kent, a possible rival. Was Kent interested in the judgeship? No, Kent said. Would Kent support Henry's candidacy? Yes, Kent said, with pleasure.

The urgency of Henry's visit made a strong impression on Kent. Henry wanted this job, no question. Fortunately, Kent thought, Henry had an advantage over most other suitors. Quite simply, Carry's nest egg made it possible for him to seek the judgeship without financial concerns. "The salary of a district judge," Kent wrote later, recalling their talk, was but $3,500 a year, "too small to attract competent lawyers" wholly dependent on their earnings for income.

Henry's train ride turned into a nerve-wracking crawl. Snow trapped him in Rochester for much of Wednesday. An ice-damaged bridge in Pennsylvania cost him "twelve precious hours," he moaned in his daybook. He finally reached the capital around nine o'clock on Thursday night, praying that he was not too late, that the nomination had not slipped away in the winter weather. He arrived to learn that President Grant had sent his name to the Senate that morning. The next day, from the Senate gallery, he watched his speedy confirmation.

The next few days were equally dizzying. At the White House, he met with the president. He visited with Treasury Secretary Benjamin Bristow. He had a private moment with Chief Justice Morrison Waite. In a few weeks, he had gone from recurring misery to near euphoria. The curse was lifting. Unlike his long-ago appointment to the local bench, he would not have to run for election. He would be giving up about two-thirds of his annual income, but it was a sacrifice he was more than willing to make for this lifetime appointment.

"The difference in the nervous strain," he wrote later, "gave me an incalculable relief."

ALL RISE FOR U. S. District Judge Henry B. Brown. Not just in the Memphis federal courtroom, where Henry was on temporary assignment for the first two months of 1876, but seemingly everywhere he went in the Tennessee city. At his hotel, where he and Carry greeted an unending stream of callers. At receptions, where they were "the favored recipients of the most refined hospitality." At the courthouse, where he was treated with unfailing kindness. Years later, he would write of his Southern sojourn: "Although it was then less than eleven years since the termination of the Civil War, and the passions that it had aroused were by no means extinct," we "were received with a cordiality which not only disarmed all criticism, but captivated us by its apparent genuineness."

He did not have much of a standard for comparison. This visit to Memphis was his longest stay ever in a state south of the Ohio River, as well as his longest stay in a city with a sizable population of former slaves. When Judge Emmons had asked him if he would go to Memphis, Henry hadn't hesitated. He knew that the circuit-riding duties were wearing on Emmons after six years, and Henry was eager to learn something about "the laws and lawyers of neighboring jurisdictions," as he put it.

He did not know what to expect in Memphis, but he did not expect to be charmed. One social event stood out, among all the others. He had learned, on his arrival, of a legendary Southerner in residence there: Jefferson Davis, former president of the Confederacy. Just as he had with General Sherman in 1866 and Senator Sumner in 1867, Henry resolved to meet this man of notoriety. This time, though, he needed to take care in arranging it. Sherman and Sumner were merely famous. Davis was infamous. "Occupying the position I did, I felt that I could not call on him without exposing myself to unfriendly criticism at home," he wrote.

Aware that Davis did not make "first calls" to strangers, Henry asked Memphis lawyer William Humes for help. Humes was a former Confederate general with a law practice that brought him regularly into the federal courts. Humes "solved the problem by making his house a sort of neutral ground and inviting us all to dine with him," Henry later wrote. "Of course we were only too glad to accept, and I am bound to say I never spent a more delightful evening."

Having never served as a Union soldier, Henry had not faced Davis's rebel army or seen the carnage the war had wrought. His knowledge of Davis was limited to what he had read and heard. In 1866, he had written an essay on Davis for Detroit's Young Men's Society; now, a decade later, he was meeting his subject in person. The dinner gave Henry a fresh and favorable impression. Davis was "a most courteous and agreeable gentleman of the best Southern type, without a suggestion of arrogance or hauteur. It was difficult for me to realise that ten years before he had been a prisoner of State . . . awaiting a trial for high treason."

Davis's wife and daughter also intrigued him. Mrs. Davis was a "handsome woman of refined and elegant manners, with a suggestion of imperiousness." Davis's daughter, Winnie, was "a beautiful young girl of fifteen" who bravely entertained the dinner's guests with a recited monologue, "an accomplishment much in vogue in the South."

Enveloped in the warmth of a winter's fire and the conviviality of wine and food, Henry found it hard to reconcile Davis's demeanor with Davis's deeds. He later wrote: "I then appreciated for the first time that an honourable, conscientious man, removed as far as possible from the criminal classes, may be guilty of treason," a most villainous crime "when committed by an officer of the army or navy in time of war, but in civil life and in time of a general peace, often involving little more than a radical difference of political opinion."

Little more than a radical difference of political opinion. In reflecting on his evening with this erstwhile enemy, Henry took refuge in the idea that Davis had not acted alone, and should not be judged alone. As "his action led to a great revolution in which half the States took sides against the government," Henry concluded, "it would have been a grave mistake to apply the legal canons of interpretation and put him upon trial like an ordinary malefactor."

The battlefields where so many had died, where so many had been maimed, seemed far away that Memphis night, in time if not in distance.

MUDDY STREETS and miserably wet weather could not deter hundreds of theatergoers from showing up in their finery at the Memphis Theater. It was the last weekend of January 1876, two weeks after Henry's arrival, and one of the country's best-known minstrel troupes was in town for three days of sold-out performances. Both Memphis newspapers had heralded the group's impending visit, extolling "Callender's Georgia Minstrels" for their entertaining sketches of slave days, captured through song, dance, banjo picking, and comic repartee. The company's ads promised that the "Great Southern Slave Troupe" would be giving an "UNEQUALED! REFINED! UNIQUE!" performance.

The two dozen performers had no need for blackface. They were "genuine negroes and mulattoes," enthused the *Memphis Daily Appeal*, "whom nature had accorded that peculiar and characteristic talent which other minstrels"—that is, whites—"can at best endeavor to exert." They were fresh from another wildly successful tour of the North. In Chicago, they had utterly charmed the *Tribune*'s reviewer, who had praised their style of humor as "wholly free from the coarseness that makes many minstrel entertainments unpleasant to mixed audiences."

The "mixed audience" at the Memphis Theater meant separate audiences. The venue's proprietor, Thomas W. Davey, had made a point of that. On the evening after the Civil Rights Act became law in March 1875, a few patrons of color had found a way into the dress circle seats, customarily the province of whites only. The next night, fearing a revolt of his white customers and damage to his bottom line, Davey had declared his firm resistance to the act. He would insist on separation, he said, even if it meant his arrest. The *Appeal* applauded his stand, saying Davey had earned "the solid and enduring friendship of every white man in Memphis"—that is, every white man "not tainted with the virus of miscegenation."

Davey wasn't a Southerner. He was British born, an émigré who arrived in America at the age of eighteen. After a decade as a comic actor in second-tier shows, he had gravitated to the business side, evolving into a colorful, gregarious impresario with a larger-than-life personality. He was now running theaters in both Memphis and Detroit, where he owned a home not far from Henry and where he spent most of his time.

No one, Davey vowed, was going to tell him how to operate his business, least of all a bunch of lawmakers in Washington. "I will either run the theater as I have heretofore, or I will close it," he told the *Appeal*. "So long as I pay my rent and license, and put such plays upon the stage as are acceptable to refined and cultivated audiences, I care nothing for oppressive and insulting laws like the civil rights bill. And I will contest them as long as I have a dollar."

DAVEY'S DOLLARS STAYED safely in his pocket. A few weeks after his declaration of defiance, Judge Emmons issued his instantly famous instructions while presiding in the Memphis federal court, telling the grand jury not to bring any criminal charges under the act, calling it an unconstitutional intrusion into local affairs. Unless another federal judge said otherwise, Davey and others in the Western District of Tennessee were free to separate their customers without fear of being charged with a crime.

Henry would not be the federal judge to say otherwise. Not only was he the circuit's most junior member, but he regarded Emmons as "one of the greatest minds" in the legal world. "No one could look into his keen black eyes, overhung by beetling brows, and observe his alertness and decisiveness of manner without being satisfied that he was in the presence of no ordinary man," Henry wrote years later.

Henry had to look no farther than the Detroit newspapers, though, to see that Emmons's view of the Civil Rights Act was far from universally held. Opinions on the law's constitutionality varied from North to South, circuit to circuit, district to district. Tom Davey could keep colored ticket-holders out of the dress circle in Memphis without fear of prosecution, but a proprietor named Tom Maguire was charged with a crime for enforcing the same policy in San Francisco. It was legal anarchy, with little geographic rhyme or reason.

There was widespread agreement on one point, though. The Supreme Court needed to weigh in, and the sooner the better.

AFTER TEN YEARS in North Carolina, Albion Tourgee considered himself something of an authority on the South—Southern customs, Southern politics, Southern economics, Southern fears, Southern hopes, Southern bitterness, Southern violence, and especially Southern hostility toward Northerners meddling in Southern affairs. Albion felt compelled to share his wisdom with others, particularly those in the North who presumed to understand the South.

In May 1875, an earnest Northerner sought Albion's advice about moving to North Carolina, perhaps to do some farming. Albion celebrated his thirty-seventh birthday by drafting a sixteen-page reply of somber guidance, laced with a generous helping of sarcasm. He did not know the writer, Mr. Edward J. Taylor, Esq., but it was clear to Albion that Mr. Taylor had all sorts of ideas about the South, most of them wrong. Wielding his pen like a pin about to prick a balloon, Albion set out to deflate this pompous Northerner with a little pomposity of his own.

Calling himself "a carpet-bagger of the very worst sort," Albion wrote: "You are, of course, aware that nothing is to be believed or relied upon which is written or said by one who had the misfortune to have been born at the North and has become a resident of the South since the affairs at Appomattox." On the unlikely chance that Mr. Taylor was missing his point, Albion jabbed the pin a bit harder. "Indeed—if you will allow me to say so—I must confess that I have rarely seen a Northern man who had been in the state twenty-four hours who did not understand its conditions better than I, and I have frequently [met] those who have never crossed its borders, who were in the same condition."

Answering Mr. Taylor's specific questions was "almost useless," Albion wrote. But he could offer "some brief rules which I have sometimes given to Northern men" who are looking to move to the South. Rule 3: "If you want to make money at once, don't come." Northern farmers had the mistaken belief that Southern planters needed Northern know-how, that Southerners had no idea how to farm without enslaved labor, Albion said. That was as ridiculous as it was arrogant. Growing tobacco and cotton was nothing like farming in New York or Michigan, he warned, and the Northerner was "a thousand times more apt to become insolvent than to startle the nation by his success."

Even his closing bit of encouragement was tempered by one last attempt to set Mr. Taylor straight. "I like living here," Albion said, "and think well-to-do Northern financiers may find health, comfort and profit here—if they will come with reasonable ideas, and not expect to comprehend everything by intuition."

He signed it, "Yours respectfully, A. W. Tourgee."

IT SEEMED LIKE a lifetime ago now, but Albion had once been in Edward J. Taylor's nervous shoes. In the spring of 1865, living in Pennsylvania, Albion had sent an inquiring letter of his own, to the provisional governor no less, seeking "guidance for an association of young men" interested in planting new roots in North Carolina. The governor, who was recruiting Northern labor and capital, had made the alluring promise to show Albion "the fraternal feeling which the loyal people of this state entertain for their Northern brethren."

What a laugh, to think now about how naïve and innocent he had been then. He and Emma had settled in Greensboro with grand plans and grander hopes. He was going to complete the revolution for equal rights that the war had started. He was going to help the newly enfranchised people of color buy land and educate themselves. He was going to build a career for himself as a lawyer and politician. He was going make enough money to bring Emma the comforts that she deserved, and together, they were going find a community for themselves—and, since 1870, for their darling daughter Lodie—that would support and sustain them.

Albion had made headway on some of his goals. He had established himself as a potent force in North Carolina's Republican Party. He had helped rewrite the state's constitution and its civil code. He had won an election to superior court judge, and had spearheaded investigations into Ku-Klux violence. He had burnished his reputation as a wickedly clever writer and orator. But it had turned out to be so much more difficult than he had imagined. He could endure the assaults on his character, and the taunts from opposition newspapers, and even the threats from white supremacists. But in his darker moments, he could not bear the thought that he had hurled Emma into this political and racial maelstrom.

He knew he made matters worse by being cross with her at times. He had made a New Year's resolution, a year earlier, to change. He felt he had improved. "I don't believe I do talk as harsh and get angry about business matters so often as I used to," he wrote to her. "I know I have become terribly selfish and worldly but after all, it is a selfishness of which you are at the bottom of, in the main." He explained what he meant. "I want to see you have everything that you can desire—to see you clothed like a queen. . . . I want to enjoy all the world's good things through you."

Sometimes, though, he felt as if they had lost as much as they gained.

BY SPRING OF 1875, Albion's career had taken a detour into uncertainty. He was no longer a judge. His six-year term had expired in 1874, and with the Democrats gaining strength in his district, winning the job a second time had looked like a lost cause. He had gladly stepped aside. His perpetual battles with the Ku-Klux had taken a serious toll on Emma's equanimity.

After Lodie's birth, Emma had fled to Pennsylvania, to Erie and her sister. She had come back, but more than once, she had been tempted to scoop up Lodie and escape for good. Albion knew she was staying for him, so he could pursue his ambitions, his dreams of higher office. Leaving now, returning to the North, would mean starting over. It would mean admitting defeat. Having invested a decade in the South, he wasn't keen to do either.

He had his eye on a congressional seat—"that Canaan of my aspirations," he had described it, in a May 1874 letter to Martin Anderson, still the president of Rochester University, once a mentor and professor, now a trusted friend. In Albion's view, the Republicans in Congress needed to hear a voice like his, a Radical voice with a Southern perspective. Albion was not a cheerleader for Reconstruction. He approved of the principle, but not of the policy. From his standpoint, it was a series of ill-conceived measures designed by ill-informed Northern legislators who, like his inquiring correspondent Mr. Taylor, did not understand the South. Charles Sumner's civil rights bill was a perfect example of the kind of legislation that provoked Albion's ire. "It is just pure folly," he fumed privately to his college professor.

Albion's primary objection: Sumner had included public schools among the list of public accommodations requiring the "full and equal enjoyment" of both races. "If we get this fool's notion imposed on us, good bye schools in the South," Albion told his professor. "They are not overfond of education here at the best. Our poor white people have to be fed a heap of soft corn to get them to take much stock in it, and the old slave owners etc., do not see any great need in general education."

Congress would drop schools from Sumner's bill eventually, largely because of a Southern outcry. But at the moment that Albion was writing his letter, Sumner's original version was the one being debated. The senator had died two months earlier, and his death had breathed new life into his pending bill.

Many Republicans were still mourning Sumner's death. Lengthy newspaper accounts of his life and final days reflected their veneration of him as a hero worthy of all acclaim. The vicious caning he had endured on the Senate floor in 1856, and his lengthy recovery, remained imprinted on the national memory. But he was also a polarizing figure, despised in much of the South, much like Albion, much like anyone who fought for equal rights and slavery's abolition. As the senator lay dying, with his closest friends gathered around his sick bed, Sumner implored them to "take care of my civil rights bill," and "don't let it fail."

That made no difference to Albion. His critique of the bill, and its author, was as merciless as it was withering. Sumner was "a visionary quack," whose cure of unified schools would set back the South's "thorough and complete rehabilitation" by "ten or twenty years," Albion wrote to his former professor.

Congress should do less, not more, in Albion's view. "The most important thing in the world," he went on, "is to let the South forget the negro for a bit; let him acquire property, stability, and self-respect; let as many as possible be educated; in short, let the race itself get used to freedom, self-dependence and proper self-assertion, and then let this bill come little by little if necessary. Of course, if it becomes law, it will be constantly avoided. No man can frame a statute which some other cannot avoid."

Before Albion could urge anything to Congress, he needed to get himself elected. Securing a nomination would be no easy task, despite his prominence in the party. He had fallen just shy at the Fifth District convention in 1874, a marathon session that required seventy ballots to produce a nominee. The eventual winner had turned into a clear loser in the general election, just one more defeat in a dismal Republican showing around the country.

Still, a part of him—the combative, haughty, never-say-die part—wondered if he could have produced a different outcome. "I believe I can carry the Dist.," he wrote to his mentor in Rochester, "but I honestly think I am the only one who does believe it."

BY ANY STANDARD, Northern or Southern, Albion and Emma had built an unconventional life for themselves in Greensboro. They faced ostracism for their involvement in a school for colored children. They had people of color to their home as guests. They adopted a young girl of mixed race, Addie Patillo. Albion had met her, and captivated by her intelligence and promise, he had arranged for Addie and her sister to come live with him and Emma. They hired Addie's mother to do some cooking and other chores for them, and they later paid for Addie's schooling, sending her north to Vermont and Ohio, and then to the new Hampton Institute in Virginia, an academy of higher education for colored students.

Writing had joined lawyering and political agitation as Albion's primary occupations. No one could say that he wasn't prolific. Essays, speeches, lectures, poems, legal briefs, novels set in the South (one published under a pseudonym, a second in progress). Words were Albion's most potent weapons, and in the spring and summer of 1875, he was wielding them with abandon. The Republican losses in Congress had emboldened the Democrats throughout the South, making Albion feel that it was more imperative than ever for him to make known his provocative views. In North Carolina, the Democrats had engineered a new constitutional convention, to be held in the fall, with the intention of repealing or rewriting many of the reforms he and his allies had embedded in the 1868 constitution. Albion was determined to thwart this retrograde assault. He had put his name forward as a candidate to the convention, and had again won one of Guilford County's two seats.

As he had since his earliest years in the state, he still reserved much of his indignation for North Carolina's "white aristocracy" and their determined efforts to replace slavery with a system that would preserve their power. White superiority was a settled, immutable doctrine for many white North Carolinians. When Congress was giving final approval to the Civil Rights Act in early 1875, the *Raleigh News* urged whites to wake from their slumber and resist this new threat to "the superior right of the white race to lead in laws and legislation and society."

Unlike some North Carolina Republicans, Albion rejected the concept of white superiority, fiercely and publicly. It violated everything he had fought for, everything he hoped to accomplish. "It matters not how honest a man may be in that view" or "how much he may honestly pride himself upon Caucasian complexion, or his *unmixed* Anglo-Saxon-Norman-Celtic lineage," he wrote to a North Carolina newspaper in May 1875. "The very assumption of exclusiveness, or superior right to rule or govern in our land, is repellant to my instincts."

At the same time, he was now a full-fledged critic of Reconstruction. He had long harbored reservations about the Radical Republicans' cornerstone policy, and had said so, in speeches and letters. But after the party's devastating defeat in the 1874 congressional contest, he decided to make his case more forcefully. Reconstruction had cost them control of the House, he believed, and would cost them the White House and the Senate in 1876 if the party didn't make a strong effort to jettison it. He assembled his thoughts into a series of essays and letters to newspapers, asserting that Reconstruction was now a "proven" failure.

Albion stressed that he heartily endorsed Reconstruction's overall aims.

Instead, he was quarreling with the method. The Radical Republicans had gone too far, too fast. Allowing the rebellious states to return to the Union fold, once they had abolished slavery and adopted new constitutions, was a "cruel and ruinous error," he wrote. Giving people of color the *right* to vote wasn't enough. They needed education, employment, protection. When white supremacists rose in defiance, Albion said, the Republicans in the South were not strong enough to stop them.

What would he have done instead? He would have kept the South as a territory under federal control. For how long? For years, a generation, more if necessary—"until the freedmen could become familiar with the duties of citizenship, until schools could be established, and the blight of generations of slavery partially removed." If Congress had adopted this slower path, the Ku-Klux and White Leagues would never have flourished, he argued.

He laid a share of the blame, as usual, on Northern ignorance about the South. Albion had once said in a speech, trying to explain someone's serious political misjudgment: "It is the tendency of our nature to look at what we desire, and believe that it exists." Many Northern legislators viewed Reconstruction as a magnanimous policy. They could not understand why the South did not agree. The Northerners had seen what they wanted to see, Albion thought.

Haste had made their hubris worse. Slavery had existed for two hundred and fifty years. How could these foolish Northerners expect to cure its consequences in a few years? "I doubt if this generation will see the end of those questions which a majority of the nation fondly believe to have been settled by the war," Albion warned. "I seriously fear that the struggle is not only unconcluded, but also that it has not yet reached the climax of intensity."

A RADICAL BRANDING Reconstruction a "failure"—and saying so in multiple forums—was a guaranteed attention-grabber in North Carolina. Albion's views were intricate and nuanced, but the Democratic newspapers didn't worry about that. They sorted through his words, and found much to celebrate or mock. "Judge Tourgee," that notorious carpetbagger, has seen the errors of his ways! Tourgee, that "scoundrel," admits his colored friends could benefit from a little education before getting the vote! Tourgee, a thorn in our side for a decade, has come to the same conclusions that the "leading people of the South held ten years ago"!

A few editors, though, focused on his solution—keeping the South in territorial purgatory for a generation or more—and bristled. This was the same old Tourgee, except worse. This Tourgee would prefer "the North, as conqueror, to rule the South, as a province," for years to come. "That is the statesmanship of one of the leading Republican politicians of this State," wrote the astonished editor of the *Alamance Gleaner.* "No reconciliation, no peace, no quiet, no freedom, no self-government for this generation, for the South."

Albion rarely passed up the chance to duel with his many foes. His retorts often relied on mocking humor, and the pretense that nothing delighted him more than being attacked. "One of the amusements of my life, for the past eight years, has been to keep a scrapbook of the good (?) things printed about me in the Democratic journals," he wrote to the editors of the *Wilmington Post* in May 1875.

Emma did her best to follow Albion's defiant lead, but it wasn't easy. Behind the war of words, she felt, lurked the threat of something more sinister. In September 1875, while Albion was away in Raleigh for the constitutional convention, Emma opened his latest letter to read that his disagreements with the convention's president, an "independent" Republican named Edward Ransom, had escalated into a volatile feud. That very night, Albion informed her, he had heard that his adversary would be waiting in the corridor for him after supper, "having declared his intention to shoot me on sight."

Was it a real danger? Or a bit of embroidery, for drama's sake, as Albion was sometimes wont to do? How could Emma know? Albion was making light of the whole episode. "You will have no fear," he told Emma coolly, "as I am now fully armed and he is a miserable coward."

No fear? Emma had an abundance of fears. But she was trying to keep them in check. "I don't feel very much alarmed at Ransom's threat," she said in her reply. Naturally, she would feel better if there had been no threat at all, "but I feel God has protected you through too many dangers seen and unseen to allow you to fall now by the hand of a cowardly assassin."

She enclosed a second note, from Lodie. Their little girl wasn't yet five years old, so the note was in Emma's hand. "I told Mamma when she read me in her letter about the bad Ransom who wanted to shoot my Papa that we would send you down our revolver," the note said. "I ask God every night when I say my prayers to take good care of my dear Papa and bring you home safe to Mamma and Lodie, 'cause we love you so much."

ALBION CAME HOME safe from the constitutional convention, but discouraged. As leader of the Republican caucus, he had been at the center of a near tug-of-war. The thirty-one days of wrangling had ended with some significant defeats, although fewer than Albion had feared. A ban on intermarriage had passed. So had a mandate for separate public schools.

Albion had argued that the school amendment was unnecessary, a duplication of a law already on the books. His objection was brushed aside. Switching tactics, he put his shoulder behind a Republican delegate's attempt to attach a clause requiring that "colored children shall have equal advantages with whites" in their school districts. That, too, had failed.

The final vote on schools was overwhelming. One hundred and thirteen for separation, including nearly all the delegates of color. Three opposed. Albion joined the one hundred and thirteen. His reason? While he "did not like the language" of the amendment, one Republican newspaper reported, he chose "to put at rest the other side" by voting for it. It was a rare case of Albion making a concession, trying to create some political capital that might prove valuable for a future fight.

Even before the convention's end, he and the Republicans were hatching a plan for the 1876 elections. The idea: Send Albion to Raleigh for the year, where he would take charge of organizing the party's efforts. Albion had agreed to go, but only if he could secure a federal job that would keep him from tumbling into a financial abyss. In late October, several letters went to President Grant, soliciting his direct help in finding a federal job for Albion, hiding nothing. "We ask, in order to secure the services of Judge Tourgee in the fierce canvass of next year, that he be appointed Pension Agent at Raleigh," said one, signed by ten Republicans from various counties.

Albion collected a thick sheaf of testimonials from Republicans throughout the state. Their man was well qualified, his endorsers assured Grant. "He has always been an active, zealous, and successful advocate of Republican principles," the head of the Republican State Executive Committee wrote. "I know of no one who deserves more at the hand of the party."

A month went by. No news. Impatient and worried, Albion headed for Washington to lobby his own cause. He arrived to find the capital in a tizzy. The vice president had died while Albion was en route, and funeral preparations were taking precedence over everything else. Bemoaning his fate, Albion scribbled a hurried one-page note to Emma. It would be days, he said, before he could see anyone.

"I am afraid the whole thing will fall through," he wrote.

ON A COLD NIGHT in December 1875, eight days before Christmas, Emma sat before the dying fire, oblivious to the creeping chill. She felt her world collapsing around her. Albion was still in Washington, trying to arrange that pension agent job. She had let him go, keeping her terrible news to herself. But then, as his absence went from days to weeks, she found the burden of secrecy too much to carry, just like the baby she feared was growing inside her.

She had to tell him. But how? When? She took herself to bed, and lay there for hours, composing a letter in her head, trembling, tossing. She rose early, still distraught, to find all her tenderly nurtured indoor plants either dead or dying. In the fog of her despair, she had not felt the plunging temperature, and she had done nothing to shelter them from the early cold snap. "I was just completely broken hearted," she wrote.

She muddled through the day, praying once again to see some sign of her period, now weeks late. To her relief, it arrived that very night, an early Christmas present. Her spirits soared, and she had no trouble at all writing to Albion. She revealed everything—her awful night, her frozen plants, her shameful joy at discovering she wasn't having a baby after all. She explained why she had kept her suspicions to herself.

At first, she told him, she had clung to the hope that time would prove her wrong. But a few days later, she felt a tingling sensation in her breasts. Hope turned to anguish. "I was going to have a baby I did not want and did not know when I got, and that I had not intended to have," she wrote. "I think I was in the deepest distress I have known since I was in the same condition in the little log cabin, cold, hungry, and alone eight years ago." Then came her reprieve, and just like that, "The horrors of the last week have been dispelled as by a fairy wand."

Signing the letter, "God keep you Darling," she went to bed, feeling lighter than she had in weeks.

ALBION WAS PREPARING for a fight on his pension agent nomination. Grant had finally sent his name to the Senate on January 6. A week later, Albion heard some alarming news: Augustus S. Merrimon, one of the state's two Democratic senators, was scheming to raise objections to "his character." It was hard to believe that Merrimon, an undisguised partisan with a Confederate history, could make much headway with a Republican majority in the Senate. But Albion wasn't taking any chances. He retreated to his desk, drafting and redrafting a lengthy statement, searching for the right level of dignified outrage to fend off the accusations he assumed Merrimon would make.

Some of these charges had been following Albion around for years, like a homeless dog who won't take "Go away!" for an answer. He answered them now. No, he said, he had never been an inmate in an Ohio penitentiary. But come to think of it, he had been a prisoner of war in Virginia, sharing "the bounteous hospitalities" of his Confederate captors. Yes, he would admit to being a carpetbagger, despised by the "unscrupulous and blatant portion of the Democracy to which Mr. Merrimon belongs." Yes, he had borrowed thirty-five hundred dollars from a businessman with legislative interests. But it was a legal, interest-bearing loan to buy the Greensboro property where he now lives, not a bribe to help with legislation in a body where he did not serve.

The Merrimon threat failed to materialize. The committee quickly approved Albion's nomination, and the full Senate soon followed suit. Albion could finally give Emma some good news: We can breathe easier, my darling wife. We won this round.

SURVEYING THE LANDSCAPE for the 1876 elections, Albion saw trouble everywhere in the state. In midsummer, he took it upon himself to write a letter that he suspected—no, he knew—would cause a ruckus. He was going to urge a man of mixed race, James O'Hara, to withdraw as a Republican candidate for presidential elector.

The state had ten electors, and the party was fielding a full slate. O'Hara had won his nomination at the Second District convention. He had every right to run. But Albion wanted O'Hara to sacrifice his ambitions for the good of his party. "You may perhaps be surprised at the tenor of this letter from me," Albion began cautiously, "since you are well aware how little I am accustomed to heed the clamor of our weak-kneed Republicans upon the question of color. I have just returned from a trip to the west and I am seriously afraid that your candidacy" will cut into the Republican vote. "I am of the opinion, in all sincerity, that you will neither benefit yourself nor your race by continuing your candidacy, and that you will seriously injure your friends and your party by doing so."

Albion's letter generated more than surprise. It produced fury. O'Hara wasn't a newcomer. He wasn't an upstart. He was a Northern-born lawyer who had come South after the war, like Albion. His father was an Irish merchant, and his mother was from the West Indies. O'Hara had even won a previous election, capturing a delegate seat at the 1875 constitutional convention. There, he had served alongside Albion. Now Albion was asking him to bow to the fear of white prejudice? To put equal rights on hold? How dare he! How dare the party!

O'Hara's "torrent of abuse," as Albion called it, earned him a pointed reply. "I consulted no one," Albion coldly told O'Hara. "I wrote upon my own responsibility, without the knowledge and suggestion of any man on earth." Albion, as usual, was not inclined to back off. "I am at a loss to understand," he wrote, "how a colored man will claim any especial credit for his conduct should it result in the defeat of his party. . . . It is all very fine to complain of unfair treatment, 'masters' and 'servants' etc., but it is the result which tests ideas. When the colored man was made a citizen, he was not made angelic (as your letter proves) nor was he exempted from the ills of humanity."

Renewing his request for withdrawal, Albion ratcheted up the pressure. "Of course, it is none of my business what you do. You have a right to make or break, rule or ruin, to the extent of your power." But, he warned, "you must take the consequences and bear the responsibility."

O'Hara was unmoved. Two months later, with Election Day drawing near, the Republican State Executive Committee made a sudden decision to replace him with a white candidate. The Republican newspapers gave no reasons for the swap.

The switch did not help. Nothing helped. The Democrats swept to victory in the state. Albion's year had gone mostly for naught. He had written the party's platform, raised money for its candidates, and stumped from east to west, speaking nearly every day over the final six weeks. Exhaustion was his only reward.

Next time, he would chase his own ambitions. He would seek, once more, the Canaan of his aspirations. He would try again for Congress.

PLEASE DON'T RUN, Emma had said to Albion.

She couldn't dissuade him. More to the point, she couldn't stand by him. Not this time. She was scared—a few months earlier, a political grudge-holder had attacked him with a cane, drawing blood, at the Raleigh train depot—and she was tired. Tired of the partisan warfare. Tired of the bitterness. Tired of North Carolina. On a Saturday afternoon in late August 1878, when Albion was declaring his candidacy for Congress from the steps of the Guilford County Courthouse in Greensboro, she and Lodie were long gone, five hundred miles away, back in Erie, Pennsylvania, in the shelter of her sister Angie and the North.

Albion soldiered on. But here he was, pitching himself into one of the toughest fights of his life, and instead of feeling buoyant, he felt bereft. "I do not know why it is," he wrote to Emma within hours of her departure, "but I have the awful feeling that I shall not see you again." They had not made that decision. Their separation was . . . what? Temporary? Provisional? He did not know. He only knew that he needed her. Instead, he had driven her away.

His letters, dashed off between campaign stops, alternated between solicitude and self-pity. For Emma's thirty-eighth birthday, he sent fond wishes wrapped in remorse. "Oh, my darling, why did I ever bring you here to experience such sorrow," he wrote. "How happy we should always have been, if we had remained in Erie. I do think it was the greatest mistake of my mistaken life. . . . I would not have you come back into this old sad life again, for anything in the world."

He tried mightily not to carp at her, but resentment sometimes crept into his words. Assessing his election chances, he grumbled that her flight to the North might be a deciding factor. "I shall lose 500 votes by that," he wrote, "and I have no reasonable prospect of overcoming the difficulty."

The Democratic newspapers were too busy recycling stories from Albion's past to take note of Emma's whereabouts. The fabricated tale about his stint in the Ohio Penitentiary made an appearance. So did a few of Albion's more memorable embellishments. His Southern Loyalist Convention speech from 1866 was dredged up. Albion had claimed, in describing the rise of Southern violence since the war, that fifteen murdered negroes had been pulled out of a South Carolina mill pond. Years later, he revealed that he had merely repeated what a Quaker friend had told him. He trusted the friend, and believed the story. "Whether it was true or not, I do not know or care," he wrote, "I told it as 'twas told to me."

The contest itself, however, did not revolve around these old episodes. Instead, it reflected the South's new reality. With the end of Reconstruction, Albion had chosen to run primarily on economic issues, not racial ones. He cast himself as a "hard-money" man, opposed to the newfangled idea of issuing currency backed only by the federal government's "full faith and credit."

He was keeping his tongue in check, he told Emma, and might finish the campaign without making "a single Democrat angry." That didn't placate his enemies, of course. The *Raleigh Observer* reminded its Democratic followers that this was the same Tourgee who "rode roughshod over us" during Reconstruction—and "now the wretch is down on his all-fours begging us humbly for office as a mangy cur would for a bone."

As October wore on, Albion felt certain he was gaining ground. Was he seeing what he wanted to see? With two days left, he allowed himself to think that victory was in sight. He would triumph by two hundred, he told Emma.

The final results crushed more than his dreams. They crushed his soul. "I think every county has gone against me," he wrote to Emma after hours of staring at the bleak totals. "I can see nothing before me but the most pinching and hopeless poverty. I am utterly cut down." He stopped there, unable to write more. When he picked up his pen a few hours later, his despair had deepened. "I just wish to die. That is all. I can see nothing to look forward to—nothing to hope for. I have ended a life of bright promise in utter ruin. . . . Pity me darling and forgive me."

AFTER A DESOLATE November and December, Albion met the New Year, 1879, with a cold-eyed look at his life. He told Emma, still in Erie, that his political aspirations were probably dead—in North Carolina for sure, perhaps everywhere. "This is very bitter, but I cannot complain," he wrote.

The past few months had been hard. He would not deny it. But from the ashes of his ambitions came new ones. He would compile the digest of North Carolina legal cases that he had been working on. He would finish the novel that he had started with a burst of enthusiasm in 1877, the one called *A Fool's Errand, By One of the Fools*, drawn from his Reconstruction experiences. He would sell their Greensboro property, and reunite with Emma and Lodie.

As spring returned to Greensboro, he was ready to say goodbye to the South—well, not exactly ready, but resigned. "There is nothing for me here and yet I hate to leave," he wrote on April 13, a brisk but lovely Sunday. "I have strung so many sweet hopes on bright dreams here that I seem almost to have knit my heart into the land."

Where should they go? The West? Erie held no appeal for him, he told her. "Let me have your preference, darling, and I will be content," he wrote. "I shall see you again soon, and I trust . . . without any shadow of doubt to obscure our future."

Hoping for better times: Emma and Lodie, before leaving North Carolina for good

(Chautauqua County Historical Society)

16

Fool's Errand

North and South, 1880–1883

FOUR THOUSAND. TEN THOUSAND. Twenty thousand copies. In the first few months of 1880, bookstores could not keep up with the accelerating demand for the season's surprise sensation. As soon as the publisher could print, ship, and deliver the orders for *A Fool's Errand*, they were gone. Snapped up by readers panting to read "a thrilling novel of life in the South, written by a bona fide Northern settler of prominence," as one of the publisher's newspaper advertisements had promised.

It was a phenomenon, that's for sure. The book seemed to have come—literarily, at least—from nowhere. The author's identity? Unknown. On the cover, where the writer's name would ordinarily be found, it said simply, "By One of the Fools." Anonymity added to the mystique. "No book on the shop counters sells better," the *New York Tribune* reported within weeks of publication, "and the fame of it has been carried on the wings of newspapers into every state if not every county in the land."

Albion Tourgee could not quite believe that his family's blood, sweat, and travails in North Carolina had produced a runaway best seller. Based on the paltry sales produced by his first novel of the South, he had allowed himself no more than modest expectations when he had offered *A Fool's Errand* to his publisher in September 1879. He had hoped the book, written over eight months in alternating throes of depression and determination, might generate enough income to provide some breathing room for the family's faltering finances, and some cash for their next adventure: a move to Denver.

Exhausted by the South's racial strife and fed up with the North's reluctance to press ahead on equal rights, Albion had fastened on the Far West as a place to live. Perhaps the frontier, without the burdens of the past and the bitterness of the present, might be a more hospitable place to build a just and equitable society. As if he needed any more proof of the divisions he was leaving behind, the North Carolina newspapers had serenaded his departure with opposing sendoffs. To the *Greensboro North State*, Albion was "Another Reconstruction Hero Gone," a brilliant advocate for "political freedom" who had endured fourteen years of vitriol with "the patience of a martyr." The *Charlotte Observer*, in contrast, bid farewell to "a vindictive, malicious man," who at "every opportunity ridiculed and reviled the best people of North Carolina and of the South. . . . From the day that he set foot upon the soil of the State to the day he quit it, Judge Tourgee's constant and untiring endeavor was to make himself as odious as possible."

A year earlier, in the wake of their separation, Albion had told Emma that taking her South was the "biggest mistake of my mistaken life." Now his fictionalized tale of that "mistake" had turned into the biggest boon of his volatile career. The *New York Tribune* devoted four full columns to its review, nearly two-thirds of a broadsheet page. The reviewer praised the narrative's "luminous exposition of historical facts." A half dozen other Northern papers had proclaimed that *A Fool's Errand* had done for Reconstruction what Harriet Beecher Stowe's *Uncle Tom's Cabin* had done for slavery: made it real and alive and palpable.

Speculation about the anonymous author's identity had blossomed into a literary parlor game. Albion had cropped up as a guess on a few lists, only to be dismissed as nowhere near good enough to have written such a splendid work. Once it was revealed in early 1881 that the "Fool" was indeed Albion W. Tourgee, Ohio native and now North Carolina exile, the newspapers had seized the story. As always, Albion made for colorful copy: one-eyed, outspoken, injured soldier, powerful orator, battle-hardened judge, defiant foe of the Ku-Klux.

His publishers, Fords, Howard & Hurlburt, had milked the mystery.

They had urged Albion to come East, to add a chapter or two for "a new and fuller" edition. He had done as they had asked, leaving Emma and Lodie to fend for themselves in still unfamiliar Denver. Emma wrote that she was "dreadfully lonely" at first, but she had plenty to do. They were staying at a boarding house while she searched for more permanent lodgings, to buy or rent, but in either case, a house they could call their own.

After years of skimping, their sudden good fortune had made her slightly giddy. She asked Albion to go shopping in New York for a "new black silk dress." She wanted to look as "elegant" as the other Denver ladies, she teased. And how about music and dancing lessons for Lodie? They could afford that, couldn't they?

Thirty thousand. Forty thousand. Fifty thousand copies by June 1880, and climbing fast. For the first time in their lives, the Tourgees could say yes, we can afford that.

ENTHUSIASM WANED, NATURALLY, as *A Fool's Errand* traveled South. The *Louisville Courier-Journal* judged it to be "bigoted and malignant, betraying a small mind painfully warped, a blind prejudice, a bitter hatred to the South and a reckless disregard for truth or honesty." The *Raleigh Observer*, accepting the comparison to Stowe's famous work, lamented that *A Fool's Errand* was "destined, we fear, to do as much harm in the world as *Uncle Tom's Cabin*." The *Memphis Daily Ledger* saw it as a "Radical campaign volume," intended as a slur against the South in advance of the 1880 presidential contest.

Commercially, there had been every reason to believe that *A Fool's Errand* would prove its title to be correct. Not that Albion hadn't poured his heart and soul into the narrative. He had done that, and more. He had borrowed bits and pieces of their lives—not just from his life, but from Emma's, Lodie's, their families, friends, and enemies—and woven them into a story that was part romance, part derring-do, part polemic. The main character, a Northern carpetbagger and former Union officer with the unusual name of Comfort Servosse, was a toned-down version of a Northern carpetbagger and former Union officer with the unusual name of Albion Tourgee.

Servosse was the "Fool" of the title, but he also had an alter ego—an unidentified narrator who interrupted the story occasionally to offer historical context and score political points. Through this omniscient bystander, Albion renewed the arguments he had made years before in branding Reconstruction a failure. Referring collectively and sarcastically to Reconstruction's creators as "the Wise Men," the narrator said these Northerners "knew less than nothing" about the South, but they "prescribed remedies anyway." They "never dreamed that investigation, study and time were necessary to restore a nation which had just outlived the fever-fire of civil war."

The novel seemed to make its debut at exactly the right moment. Northerners were hungry to understand what had gone wrong in the South and what might be done about it. President Hayes, the unpopular architect of the post-Reconstruction era, had pledged early in his presidency not to seek a second term. His abdication guaranteed a mad scramble at the party's convention in Chicago, set for early June. According to the newspapers, *A Fool's Errand* had attracted a strong following among leading Republicans, including some of the dozen or so being mentioned as possible presidential candidates. One was the Ohio congressman and former Union general, James A. Garfield, who told a Washington correspondent that the book's influence "will be of great assistance" in the party's campaign to keep the White House.

The journalist agreed. "No better campaign document could be disseminated by the Republican party," he wrote.

ALBION'S PUBLISHERS WANTED a sequel. Of course they did. Only a few years earlier, the company had been in serious financial trouble. Now the partners were "coining money," in Albion's words. If lightning could strike once, why not again?

Albion was resisting. He and Emma and Lodie were just getting settled in Denver, their new home, their new life. He had taken over as editor of the *Denver Times*, a decent-paying arrangement that suited them until he could establish a law practice in Colorado. But back East, his friends at Fords, Howard & Hurlburt weren't taking his "no" for an answer. On a spring day in 1880, Albion and Emma opened their door to find Edward Ford himself. He had come all the way from New York to make his pitch. Albion, he said, you have the public's attention. Sales are astonishing. Now is the time to capitalize.

Sorry, Albion said. He had no book to offer. The publisher had brought out his two earlier novels at the same time as *A Fool's Errand*, both under Albion's now famous name. The first was a story of the South, the second of the North. Why not promote those?

Ford was resolute. So was Albion. Just because he had written one moneymaker, he told Ford, "it did not follow that he could do so again." For several days, Ford kept at him. Finally, Emma said, Albion handed over "eight or ten chapters" of a novel he had laid aside to finish *A Fool's Errand.* Ford sat, read, and smiled. "He was delighted," Emma later wrote.

The following morning, Ford left Denver with the pledge that he had journeyed eighteen hundred miles to obtain. Returning to New York, he spread the word to journalists: Albion Tourgee, author of *A Fool's Errand,* is hard at work on a new book, which will tell the haunting story of the colored race in the South since the Civil War. He's calling it *Bricks Without Straw.* Soon, tantalizing items were popping up in Chicago, New Orleans, Washington, and New York newspapers, announcing that Judge Tourgee had "retired" from the *Denver Times* to "devote himself wholly to literary labors," in the words of the *Chicago Tribune.*

Within a few weeks, though, Albion was telegraphing Ford, reneging on his promise. He had written "page after page," and it wasn't working. Telegrams buzzed back and forth. Ford summoned him to New York. Albion reluctantly agreed to go, assuring Emma that he would be back in a week, "that he was not going to write any book, anyhow, oh no." He would stop in Chicago on the way. The Republicans were holding their convention, and he wanted to be there. His old political instincts were stirring.

AMID THE FRENZIED thousands in Chicago's Exposition Hall, Albion witnessed history in its messy making. On the afternoon of June 8, after thirty-six ballots and two exhausting days, James Garfield burst forth as the convention's compromise choice. His backers had been promoting this precise scenario, but few had dared to believe it would happen. Certainly not Garfield.

Whatever his faint hopes, Garfield had come to Chicago as a delegate, not a candidate. He had authorized no one to trumpet his candidacy, and no one had. Instead, he had delivered one of the nominating speeches, a restrained rallying cry for his fellow Ohioan, Secretary of the Treasury John Sherman. By claiming the role of Ohio's favorite son, Sherman had left Garfield on the sidelines, where he felt comfortable enough, at least for now.

Garfield lived with the ambivalence of his ambitions. He had long ago resolved, as he wrote in his diary, that "I would never permit myself to let the Presidential fever get any lodgement in my brain." In the weeks leading up to the convention, Garfield had told his supporters privately that he would do nothing to thwart Sherman's chances, nothing that might put a blot on Garfield's honor. Ballot after ballot, he stood steadfast by Sherman, while the convention deadlocked. Neither Grant, seeking an unprecedented third term after four years out of office, nor his main rival—the dogged James Blaine, trying yet again to capture his party's trophy—could muster enough momentum to steer the weary convention to a majority.

It was 1876 all over again, but even more intractable. Six, twelve, eighteen, twenty-four, thirty ballots came and went, with no evident end in sight. On the thirty-fourth round, the first wave of votes flowed Garfield's way from sixteen rebellious Wisconsin delegates. Garfield immediately objected. "No man had a right" to put any name before the convention "without the consent of the person being voted for," Garfield protested. To no avail. The convention president told Garfield, essentially, to sit down and be quiet.

Garfield's supporters surged into action. Two ballots later, the Wisconsin trickle turned into a deluge. As chants of "Hurrah for Garfield" swelled to a roar, the dazed nominee remained rooted to his seat. The military band struck up a rousing rendition of "Rally 'Round the Flag," the Civil War standard. Thousands of pro-Garfield voices sang the chorus's first line: "The Union forever! Hurrah, boys, hurrah!" After fifteen boisterous minutes, a speaker called for a vote of acclamation. A nearby cannon thundered. The massive hall's windows rattled from the reverberations.

Albion had no role in the proceedings, official or otherwise. He was there, largely, to bask in the aura of *A Fool's Errand* and to make plain his desire to speak in the coming canvass. He was now known as the "famous author," a label vastly preferred to "failed congressional candidate." During the vice-presidential nominations, one speaker drew cheers when he said, "You have all read *The Fool's Errand*." Well, the speaker said, the man I am nominating was the inspiration for one of the novel's characters, and the author is "my friend, Judge Tourgee."

Albion left Chicago with more than his ego stroked. Grant had been his preferred candidate—Albion felt loyal to the former president for appointing him as a pension agent in 1876—but he saw Garfield as a fine second choice. Perhaps better than fine, perhaps even fortuitous. By the luck of Ohio, when Albion was eleven years old, he had spent a summer with relatives in the northwestern part of the state. Boarding with those relatives was a kindly and energetic seventeen-year-old student named James Garfield. Despite their age difference, the two boys became brotherly pals.

Now Albion's boyhood friend was a step away from the presidency. Albion arranged a meeting with Garfield, eager to revive their friendship. He promised to give Garfield as much help as he could manage.

ALBION'S FAME MADE him a coveted name for the Garfield campaign. But he had a book he had again promised—reluctantly—to write. His publishers wanted the manuscript by early September. They intended to bring out *Bricks Without Straw* in the campaign's final weeks.

Still, he didn't have to pass up every speaking opportunity, did he? He had points he wanted to make, and his publisher was right: He had the public's ear. On June 12, four days after Garfield's nomination, he ascended the platform at New York's Cooper Union for what the *New York Times* called the "first grand ratification meeting of the campaign."

Unfazed by the uncomfortably warm night, spectators filled the hall's seats and stood in the aisles, applauding with gusto at the mere mention of Garfield's name. Cheers went up when the celebrated author of *A Fool's Errand* was introduced, but a few jeers could be heard when he professed that his "heart and hopes" had been with Grant. "I am sorry to hear those hisses," Albion said, "but as I have faced the Ku Klux down South, I can face these hisses."

Down South, of course, was what he had come to talk about. Looking out at the ocean of faces, he had to let them know that he was the genuine article, the Northerner who had gone South, who had seen things they could only imagine. To establish that identity, he talked about "my State," as if he were still living in North Carolina, and he chose an opening gambit no Northern politician would dare attempt: He told a "darkey" story, complete with dialect, like a performer in one of those touring minstrel shows, eliciting laughter with a knowing tale.

Having set himself apart, Albion stayed in character. A previous speaker, he told the crowd, had talked about the coming election as if it would be the swan song of "the solid South," an oft-used shorthand for the Democrats' electoral grip on that wide swath of states. "Don't congratulate yourselves too soon," he counseled. "The hair that is brown tonight will be gray before you cease to meet a solid South."

He had been warning of such Northern naïveté for years, but rarely with members of the national press capturing his words. He left them with a bold message. He had a "cure for the solid South," he said—a cure he had offered at the end of *A Fool's Errand*, a cure he had watched the Republicans embrace for the first time in their Chicago platform, partly at his urging: direct federal aid to local public schools.

Education, he said, was the most effective counterweight to white dominion and black inequality. The national government should subsidize free and open schools, he said, "not for the sake of the people, but for its own sake; not because they were slaves, but because they are free; not because it will do them good, but because it will save us. . . . That was the cure, and the only cure, for a solid South."

A month later, in a formal letter accepting the Republican nomination, Garfield placed federal aid to education at the forefront of his political agenda. "Next in importance to freedom and justice," he wrote, "is popular education, without which neither freedom nor justice can be permanently maintained. . . . Whatever help the Nation can justly afford should be generously given to aid the States in supporting common schools."

ALBION HAD GARFIELD'S EAR, just as he had once hoped to have Grant's. Either suited him. In August, when Garfield asked him to bring his oratorical gifts to the campaign, Albion promised he would, as soon as he finished *Bricks Without Straw*. He had an additional motivation now to write the novel. Telling the fictional story of a black preacher and teacher-in-training named Eliab Hill—portrayed as a man of courage, intelligence, and morality who is sorely tried by the circumstances of Reconstruction—was Albion's way of drawing attention to the plight of freed slaves, the South's resistance to helping them, and the North's timidity in pushing for laws and policies that would ensure equality. At the same time, the novel offered yet another forum for promoting federal aid to education, Albion's "cure" for "the solid South."

After less than a year in Denver, the Tourgees' Western experiment had come to a quiet end. Summoned by Albion, Emma took ten-year-old Lodie to her sister in Erie, and hastened to New York. While Albion seemed to thrive on the nomadic life, she longed for more than a suite of temporary addresses. "I had broken up my pretty Western home and hurried half across the continent at his bidding," she later wrote. But her presence seemed to speed his writing. She found an apartment that gave him a place to work, overlooking a quiet garden. She served as his courier, ferrying pages to the publisher at the end of each day.

By early September, the manuscript was done. Albion immediately traded his secluded quarters for the stump. After hearing Albion speak, an Ohio supporter wrote enthusiastically to Garfield: Tourgee is a "good 'popular' talker . . . make no mistake." The word went out: Get Mr. Tourgee as many appearances as possible. We'll pay his expenses. Also, tell him to stop at Garfield's home in Ohio. Garfield wants to confer.

Six weeks. Twelve states. Dozens of events. Wherever he went, Albion spoke up for federal aid to public schools as well as for Garfield. "Education means death to Ku-Kluxism, death to intolerance," he told an immense crowd in Chicago. Education would make the South "as free, as prosperous, as intelligent as we are at the North."

IN THE WANING weeks of December 1880, Albion and President-Elect James Garfield engaged in a deepening dialogue. Albion was flattered and somewhat startled by Garfield's eagerness to solicit his opinion. But not daunted. Or tongue-tied. No, anything but that.

Garfield had asked: How would the election results affect the South? The president-elect did not need to explain what he meant. The "solid South" had lived up to its nickname. Garfield had won the presidency without capturing a single state below Mason's and Dixon's line. Not since Lincoln had the outcome so starkly shown the country's North-South divide.

Now Garfield wanted to know how the South would react. Albion did not sugarcoat his answer. The election results would not change the South at all. "While the South is depressed and made almost desperate by the defeat, it is not shattered or broken," he wrote. Even if leading Southerners abandon the Democratic Party because it "cannot offer a reasonable hope of victory," they will remain "the 'solid South'—just as solid and just as dangerous as ever."

What should Garfield do? Beware the Hayes fallacy, Albion told him. Hayes had hoped that withdrawing all forms of federal interference would be enough to stimulate the South's evolution into a more just society. That was a grave mistake, Albion said. "I do not think it is possible for you to adopt a mere negation," he wrote, and "call it a policy." He saw two ways to influence the Southern mind. First: Appoint only Republicans of integrity—including men of color—to federal offices in the South. Second, and this was the "master key": Create a national education fund to send money to towns or schools, bypassing the state governments, with the goal of wiping out illiteracy and protecting people of color from white exploitation.

Bypass the state governments. It was a revolutionary idea, but it was an expansion of federal authority that Garfield had yet to embrace. In his letter accepting the nomination, Garfield had specifically called for sending education aid to *state* governments. Albion vigorously disagreed with this method. The money had to go *directly* to the schools, he believed, or it would never get there. The state governments in the "solid South" would do their best to subvert the goal, he said.

Pressing his case, Albion sent Garfield a proof of his forthcoming essay for the influential *North American Review*, which laid out his arguments with full force. The essay addressed, head on, whether it was legal to bypass the state governments. Direct federal aid could be considered constitutional, he wrote, because education was fundamental to "national existence," as essential as national defense. "A nation has not only the inherent right to exist," his essay asserted, "but also to secure its future and perpetuate its life."

Albion had been promoting his education ideas for a decade, without much success. But now he believed their time had come. Why? His book sales, for starters. "The fact that a quarter of a million copies of my books have been bought and read in the short space of fifteen months," he told Garfield, "shows that somebody had been thinking about the subject besides me."

WAVERING BETWEEN SKEPTICAL and intrigued, Garfield asked his trusted friend Burke Hinsdale to look at Albion's letters and published works. Hinsdale was president of Ohio's Hiram College, and their friendship spanned more than twenty-five years, back to the early 1850s, when Garfield was teaching at Hiram and Hinsdale was one of his best students. In two letters to Garfield, before and after Christmas 1880, Hinsdale delivered his verdict.

A Fool's Errand "is a book of great power," he wrote. He was less enamored with the novel's "scornful" criticism of Reconstruction, saying he could not see "what could have been done to have averted the last twelve years." As for Albion's federal aid scheme, he worried about its legality. "I think I see great difficulties. . . . A good deal of discussion must precede the doing of anything on an extensive scale." Garfield might want to use his inaugural speech to draw attention to the problem of illiteracy, Hinsdale said. But beyond that, he advised caution.

Following Hinsdale's lead, Garfield shied away from endorsing Albion's specific plan. His inaugural address, however, devoted considerable attention to racial issues. Praising the "emancipated race" for its "remarkable progress" since the end of slavery, he declared that the country had "special obligations" to end the scourge of illiteracy, so that all citizens and their children could participate fully in voting and other aspects of national life. The new president's words were forceful, but notably vague on how this would be accomplished. He made clear, however, that the States should be involved in any such effort. He would not bypass them.

It was not what Albion had wanted to hear, but still, a step forward. He declared himself "heartily pleased." With Garfield willing to listen, there would be time to make progress. On the night of the inauguration, Albion wrote his friend an ebullient note, calling his speech "the dawn of a new and brighter era." The next day, deciding he wanted to be part of this era, he petitioned Garfield for a judicial post, perhaps on the U.S. Court of Claims, saying it seemed like the kind of workload that would "permit me to continue my literary labors and studies."

Adding "office seeker" to his agenda put Albion's relationship with Garfield into uncertain territory. For months, they had been discussing ideas, policies, the nation's welfare. Now, he became a frequent visitor to Washington, lobbying for himself as well as his other interests. No job offer came his way, but in early April, he persuaded Garfield to appoint a Raleigh friend to a postmaster's job. "The Judge was greatly moved," Garfield wrote in his diary. North Carolina's senators, however, did not take kindly to the carpetbagging Tourgee's sudden reemergence. Their irritation showed up in a *Washington Post* item, which described Albion's White House visits as "meddling" and another "fool's errand."

In early June, Albion returned to the lecture circuit, pushing hard for his education plan. During a provocative speech at the Union League Club in New York, he said the North had reaped immense profits from slave labor, turning all that cotton into textiles. By his calculation, the North owed millions in compensation to former slaves. Plow those ill-gotten gains, he urged, "back into the South in spelling books and readers." Coverage of the speech appeared in newspapers beyond New York.

Then, on July 2, an assassin's bullets tore everything to shreds. The news came to Albion at his new summer home in western New York, a fifty-acre haven overlooking Chautauqua Lake, a gift to themselves, courtesy of *A Fool's Errand*'s success. In playful tribute, Albion had named the estate "Thorheim," a concocted stand-in for "Fool's House." As Garfield clung precariously to life in Washington, Albion went feverishly to work on a Fourth of July poem, an anguished ode to his bloodied friend, calling for Americans to pray together for "the balm of healing rest." The poem went on:

Oh East! from whence his life he drew!
Oh West! of which his life is part!
Oh North! that hath no type more true!
Oh South! that better friend ne'er knew!

ON THAT JULY MORNING, as assassin Charles Guiteau lurked at a Washington train depot waiting to ambush Garfield, Henry and Carry Brown were settling into their first-class cabin on the steamship *Main*, barely an hour into another long voyage across the Atlantic.

Traveling to Europe still topped Henry's list of life's great pleasures. He knew more about London, Paris, and Rome than he did of Charleston, Atlanta, or New Orleans. He had seen enough of the Western European countries to be smitten, but not enough to see beyond their art work and museums, their architectural gems and lively cafes, their reverence for kings, queens, and courtiers. To take account of their competition for empire, their history of conquest, their pursuit of economic power, he would have needed to visit their colonial outposts in Africa, the Caribbean, Latin America. There, he might have seen enough to round out his education and correct "false impressions," a phrase he would later use to describe the virtue of travel.

This was his fourth trip abroad, his second as a federal judge, and he was envisioning many more. He was working hard, handling more cases than ever, but he had found that he could "easily dispose" of his judicial workload in nine months, leaving his summers free for the extended holidays he relished. "There are doubtless higher offices," he later wrote, "but I know of none in the gift of the government which contributes so much to making life worth living as a district judgeship."

As he had hoped, leaving behind the stress of his law practice had restored his "natural vitality." His headaches had disappeared. His eye inflammations still flared up now and then, but at forty-five, he felt better than ever. He was looking forward to a relaxing ten weeks on his favorite continent, far away from the humdrum of his daily routine.

Guiteau's shots rang out just before ten o'clock. Within the hour, the telegraph offices were tapping out the dire news of Garfield's wounds. The *Main* churned on, its passengers oblivious, a ship in a vacuum, a ship in a bottle. When it reached Southampton a week later, the president was still alive, but Henry's hopes of a tranquil tour had gone up in the smoke of Guiteau's gun.

He and Carry kept to their itinerary. Reports of the president's unstable condition awaited them at each stop. Garfield was convalescing on the New Jersey shore, away from Washington's heat, humidity, and fears of malaria. When they returned to Southampton for their voyage home, weary but well pleased with their tour, the latest bulletins offered more hope than gloom. "The president passed an unusually good night," the doctors said.

When Garfield died on September 19, Henry and Carry were on the steamer *Oder* in the middle of the Atlantic, unaware of the momentous news. Another ship in a bottle. Who could have imagined it? They had left in the bright sun of a July morning, filled with anticipation and excitement, and they returned in the darkness of a late September evening to find a nation in mourning and a new president in the White House.

A journey to remember, certainly, but not the journey that Henry had envisioned when he had planned their summer of relaxation.

SEVEN MONTHS LATER, after a night of musical delight at the First Congregational Church in Washington, pastor Jeremiah Rankin stepped forward to tell a story of rank prejudice less than twenty-four hours old. Behind him were arrayed the visiting Fisk Jubilee Singers, whose stirring voices had brought the large crowd to its feet in thunderous applause. Next to him stood Frederick Douglass, one of his parishioners. Together the two men—one white, one black, both fuming—offered a glimpse at the state of public accommodations in the nation's capital, seven years after the 1875 Civil Rights Act's attempt to ensure equal treatment.

The previous night, a Wednesday in mid-February 1882, the touring troupe of eight had arrived at the Baltimore and Potomac train depot in Washington to learn that their lodging arrangements had fallen through. The hotel claimed a mix-up, but the confusion only seemed to arise once the proprietor realized the color of his guests. At least, that was Rankin's suspicion.

Fortunately, it wasn't a cold evening. The temperature hovered in the low forties as Rankin and others went on an extended hunt for accommodations, visiting a dozen of the city's hotels. Most were full—or said they were—but three had space. They also had a policy: whites only. One hotelkeeper's rejection was especially pointed. He said he would not rent his rooms to anyone of color, not even a celebrated troupe of vocalists, not for five hundred dollars each.

It was after midnight when Rankin trudged back to the now-closed depot. Two colored-only boarding houses would take them in, he told the waiting troupe. They would move to the St. James Hotel in the morning, when enough rooms would be available. They were grateful. They had been on the road for weeks now, and would be giving four concerts in the next five days.

This wasn't the first time that the Jubilee Singers had run into such trouble. There were those well-publicized episodes with hotels in Springfield, Illinois, and across the Canadian border in Ontario, both in the past year. But to encounter such unconcealed prejudice within sight of the Capitol, where Congress had conceived and enacted the Civil Rights Act, well, that was a symbolic juxtaposition that some newspapers could not let pass. "Where is civil rights and negro equality now?" asked the *Decatur Herald* in Illinois, while the *New York Times* pointedly observed that "something of the old pro-slavery spirit of caste yet lingers in Washington."

Two days later, the Jubilee Singers were ushered into the Blue Parlor at the White House. Listening to their powerful voices sing "Steal Away to Jesus," President Chester A. Arthur wept. He told Rankin afterward, "I have never in my life been so much moved." The *Chicago Tribune* brought the two episodes together in a single headline: "The Jubilee Singers. Cordially Received at the White House, Though Denied Admission to the Hotels."

THAT VERY CONTRADICTION—welcomed in some places, rejected in others—had come to define the Civil Rights Act. The Supreme Court's inaction had left the law in a protracted limbo. By the fall of 1882, when John Harlan sat down to read through the public accommodation cases that had finally made the Supreme Court's calendar, more than seven years had elapsed since Judge Emmons had challenged the act's legality. Six years since judges in California, Missouri, Kansas, and elsewhere had sent test cases to Washington, asking for the court's swift guidance. Three years since the Justice Department had filed its first brief.

The cases had languished for so long that it had become common for newspapers, especially in the South, to disparage the act as a relic, widely ignored, rarely enforced. That wasn't true everywhere—in 1879, a federal grand jury in New York had indicted the doorkeeper of the Grand Opera Hall—but generally, U.S. district attorneys weren't bringing charges. Most ran their tiny offices on meager budgets. To properly prepare the cases was time-consuming and expensive, they said. It didn't make sense to enforce the law vigorously until the Supreme Court had spoken, and had settled the law's constitutionality one way or the other.

Not that many expected the justices to say the act was constitutional. They had made plain, in earlier cases, their intention to stick to a narrow interpretation of the Thirteenth and Fourteenth amendments. For those who felt that the Radical Republicans had gone too far, too fast in pushing the country toward equality in civil rights, the Supreme Court stood as a braking influence. Hadn't Chief Justice Morrison Waite, writing for the court in the 1876 *Cruikshank* case, decimated a federal indictment against an armed band of white Democrats, accused in a brutal attack on Republican freedmen in rural Louisiana? Waite had ruled that the Fourteenth Amendment did not extend to the actions of individuals, that it was intended only to prevent the states from interfering with the equal protection now due to its people, regardless of their race. The *Cruikshank* indictment was brought under an 1870 law, not under the Civil Rights Act. To endorse the act's constitutionality, the justices would have to ignore Waite's ruling or carve out a new legal theory.

Truth be told, many colored travelers and theatergoers had given up on the government. If prosecutors weren't willing to enforce the law, well, the act allowed them to file civil lawsuits on their own. When the Robinson family sued the Memphis and Charleston railroad, prompting a court hearing in early 1880, the *Memphis Daily Appeal* thought it strange to see such an action "at this late date, when the civil rights bill was almost forgotten, and had become a useless and played-out political page upon the statute book."

Eighteen months later, the *Appeal* had gone from puzzled to alarmed. "There seems to be an epidemic of 'civil rights' on [the] railway, prevailing among the negroes of Middle Tennessee," the *Appeal* said. Colored riders were boarding trains, demanding to sit in coaches reserved for white ladies and their escorts—and for no good reason, in the newspaper's opinion. A new Tennessee law allowed separate cars for negroes if the coaches were "similar to those" for whites, the *Appeal* said, "thus knocking the stuffing out of the designs for a case in the courts."

As the number of passenger-conductor conflicts mounted, the Nashville federal court felt the pressure, like a dam threatened by a rising volume of water. Trying to prevent a flood of new cases, the circuit and district judges called for a moratorium. "Our Colored Friends Advised to Hold On for a While," was the *Nashville Daily American* headline in October 1881.

For white passengers, free of worrying about which car they might ride in, patience was easy to come by. Colored passengers, on the other hand, had to cope with a maddening, shifting kaleidoscope of practices that differed from Southern state to Southern state, from railroad to railroad. As long as the Civil Rights Act cases remained in limbo, equality would have to stand in line behind whim, confusion, and the predisposition toward prejudice.

Hold on.

THE OMINOUS TELEGRAM came on a Sunday night as John Harlan was preparing for a busy week ahead. In two days' time, on Tuesday, November 7, 1882, a new round of briefs was due in the collection of civil rights cases on the court's docket, a significant milestone that promised to move the long-delayed proceedings along. But John's mind was not on his work, thanks to the telegram. His daughter, Edith, was seriously ill in Chicago. She was losing her battle with some sort of fever. Typhoid? Malarial? The doctors weren't sure. Dashing off a hasty note to Chief Justice Waite, John left Washington for a long train ride to sorrow, joining Mallie at her bedside vigil.

Edith died the following Sunday. She was barely twenty-five years old, married the year before, the mother of a three-month-old girl also named Edith. John and Mallie returned to Washington, accompanied by their daughter's casket and a wellspring of grief that would linger in unexpected ways. Their Massachusetts Avenue home, with its vivid memories of Edith, seemed "so changed to us that we felt we must give it up," Mallie later wrote.

They agreed to look for a new place to live, hoping they could find one to suit their strained pocketbook. With three sons completing their educations, and John's alcoholic brother in Louisville constantly pleading for financial help, the family did not have the luxury of behaving as if money did not matter. The pinch was strong enough that John would soon add a law school teaching job—one class, three nights a week—to his busy schedule.

Edith's funeral drew hundreds of mourners to the Presbyterian Church on New York Avenue—lawyers, of course, but also members of Congress and several cabinet officers. All the justices were there. Two by two, Chief Justice Waite at the forefront, they led the funeral procession, a moving display of unanimity for their stricken colleague.

DISSENT, NOT UNANIMITY, was John's increasing inclination in the civil rights cases. As he resumed his review after Edith's death, he kept wondering: What did Congress intend when it drafted the Civil Rights Act? He decided to find out. He took the extraordinary step of arranging a private conversation with Senator George Edmunds of Vermont. Edmunds would know as much as anyone on Capitol Hill about the legislative history. He had worked with Sumner and others on various civil rights bills, and after Sumner's death, Edmunds had helped shepherd the 1875 act to final passage.

For John, a meeting with Edmunds was not exactly an amiable chat with an old friend. Edmunds, as chairman of the Senate Judiciary Committee, had shared the doubts about John's nomination in 1877. In the end, Edmunds had not tried to block the appointment, but he remained a skeptic about John's Republicanism.

Both men understood the "delicacy," as Edmunds put it, of a justice and a senator holding such a meeting. Afterward, Edmunds sent John a letter brimming with neutrality. Enclosing documents on the civil rights bills, he told John that the Senate had fully explored the "scope of the Fourteenth Amendment" in its deliberations. "I refrain from making any summary on the tendency and effect of the debates for reasons that your sense of delicacy will appreciate," the senator said.

The longer John reflected on what Congress had been aiming to achieve in crafting the Thirteenth and Fourteenth amendments, the more certain he felt that his judicial colleagues were heading in the wrong direction. Winter gave way to spring, and still the court did not release a ruling. Then, in late March 1883, the justices added a new case to those under consideration, this one from Tennessee. Unlike the other four, which all involved government prosecutions of theater owners and innkeepers, *Robinson & Wife v. Memphis and Charleston Railroad* was a lawsuit for damages brought by a colored train passenger. At trial, a Memphis jury had trouble reaching a verdict. The judge, asked by the jurors for guidance in interpreting the act, had given them a nudge toward the railroad's view.

Ordinarily, a ruling could be expected within several months of a case appearing on the court's calendar. Not this time. When their summer recess came, the justices went their separate ways without a resolution. John was partly at fault. He had decided to break from his eight colleagues, who had agreed to declare the act unconstitutional, but he was struggling to find the right words.

As the lone dissenter, as the only justice born in the South, he knew he could count on his minority opinion being dissected, challenged, even attacked. He already had a habit of working late into the evening, but now his "absorbing labor, his interest and anxiety" was interfering with his sleep as well. Years later, Mallie would still remember John rising in the darkness to "jot down some thought or paragraph which he feared might elude him in the morning." He wanted his dissent to be crystal clear, to hold up under scrutiny, to change minds if possible.

When the justices reconvened in October for the fall 1883 term, the majority had its ruling ready.

John did not.

ON MONDAY, OCTOBER 15, 1883, Justice Joseph Bradley read his opinion aloud. It took more than an hour, but he finished in time for the evening papers to report that the Civil Rights Act, barely breathing in some places, was now "void" everywhere. The *Baltimore Sun*'s correspondent, in his dispatch, said the decision could not come a surprise to anyone familiar with the Constitution. "The bill was a legislative extravaganza, which never should have been put on the statute books, and the Supreme Court, in wiping it off today, has done no less than the oath of office of its members demanded," he wrote. "It has affirmed the doctrine that Congress has no right to regulate the social habits and the social customs of the people of the States."

Congress has no right. That wasn't John's view at all, and he certainly didn't think he was violating his oath of office by saying so. He thought it was a fiction—a shrewd distortion—to describe the act as regulating "social customs." From his perspective, the law merely guaranteed the legal right to accommodations of a public nature.

When Bradley was done, and with the press corps at rapt attention, John announced in his booming voice that he was dissenting. In an ordinary case, he said, he might hesitate to "set up his individual opinion in opposition to that of his eight colleagues." But these circumstances were anything but ordinary. He had read the majority's opinion, but he "had not had time" to finish his written objections. He would file his dissent as soon as he could.

Within a few days, the mail had brought letters from friends, strangers, judges, lawyers, Kentuckians, Republican stalwarts, including people of color, praising his courage and asking for copies of his dissent whenever it was ready. "You, sir, have won a place in the hearts of my race," wrote Walter S. Thomas, on stationery of the Ohio Republican Central Committee, "that shall never be usurped by another." A Kentucky friend and current U.S. attorney, George M. Thomas, declared himself in full agreement with John, writing: "Of course you will prepare the opinion with great care as it will be one of the 'landmarks' and will stand the test of time."

John had yet to explain his reasons for dissenting, and already he was being treated as a hero. Some newspapers were calling him a leading candidate for the 1884 Republican presidential nomination. It was just foolish talk. Still, when the foolishness persisted, John thought it best to say publicly that he had no such aspiration, that his only ambition was to prove himself worthy of the office he already held.

But this much was true: John had managed to magnify the pressure he already felt. As Walter Thomas told him, "The colored men of the nation look to you as their only hope in this, our hour of need, and from every house and cabin in the land, anxious hearts are waiting to read the text of your decision. God! grant that it may come very soon."

Now John had to write a dissent worthy of these premature accolades.

"An act of surrender": Frederick Douglass's critique of the Supreme Court's ruling in the *Civil Rights Cases*, 1883

(National Archives, Frank Legg collection, 1879)

17

The Color Line Sharpens

1883–1888

PROGRESS CAME SLOWLY. Some days—and nights—it didn't seem to come at all.

John Harlan would retreat to his writing table, and emerge with a frown. As Mallie watched her husband wrestle with his dissent in the early fall of 1883, she thought she understood why. "In point of years," she wrote later, "he was much the youngest man on the Bench, and standing alone as he did . . . he felt that, on a question of such far-reaching importance, he must speak not only forcibly but wisely." But his thoughts refused to flow easily. "He seemed to be in a quagmire of logic, precedent, and law," she said.

Seeking to inspire him, Mallie came up with an inspiration of her own. It required her to reveal a lie of sorts, a secret she had been keeping for months. Her deception had started with good intentions, but as she "never hid anything" from John, she felt more than a tinge of guilt. Her fib revolved around a wooden inkstand, of all things.

This was not just any inkstand. This was an antique with a yarn. The vintage gem, with its two glass wells and grooved channel for pens, had once belonged to Chief Justice Roger Taney. After Taney's death in 1864, the antique had gone to the marshal's office at the Supreme Court. That's where John had spotted it. Taney had drawn his ink for the *Dred Scott* decision from this very stand. That's what the marshal claimed. Seeing that John was taken with the heirloom and its story, the marshal had said: Please, take it. Years later, Mallie could still recall John's excitement when he brought his "great treasure" home.

Not long afterward, though, John promised his prize to someone else. He was chatting with a senator's wife during a Washington party, and they had chanced upon the topic of unexpected discoveries. John mentioned his recent find. The woman, exclaiming that she was a Taney relative, said: "I would so love to have that little inkstand." John, ever the Kentucky gentleman, offered to send it.

When he told Mallie of the encounter, she was seized by a less-than-chivalrous impulse. "I won't let him part with it," she vowed to herself. John was the better guardian, she reasoned. He understood the inkstand's dubious place in the nation's history. The next day, when John said he could not find it, Mallie feigned ignorance as to its whereabouts.

Now, setting her plan in motion, she slipped away to the inkstand's hiding place. When John headed to his writing room for another morning's battle, she told him: "I have put a bit of inspiration on your study table. I believe it is just what you need." When he returned, confused and wide-eyed, she confessed all. "He laughed over my naughty act," she wrote later, "and freely forgave it."

She loved the "poetic justice" of her idea. John, in championing "the black man's claim to equal civil rights," would now be dipping his pen in the same wells Taney had used to write his oft-repeated line—that at the nation's birth, "a black man had no rights which a white man was bound to respect." Whether it was the inkstand or her imagination, Mallie believed her gambit to be a turning point.

"The memory of the historic part that Taney's inkstand had played in the Dred Scott decision . . . seemed that morning to act like magic in clarifying my husband's thoughts," she later recalled. "His pen fairly flew on that day."

WHATEVER THE SOURCE of John's inspiration, his ink now flowed in abundance. When he filed his final version on November 17, it totaled nearly fourteen thousand words, twice the length of Bradley's ruling. John's opening line—a polite but direct attack on the majority's reading of the Constitution—set the tone. "The opinion in these cases proceeds, it seems to me, upon grounds entirely too narrow and artificial," he wrote. The majority had "sacrificed" the "substance and spirit" of the Thirteenth and Fourteenth amendments through "a subtle and ingenious verbal criticism." Essentially, he was saying, the majority had twisted words to thwart Congress's goals on equal rights.

John wanted his dissent to do more than disagree, though. He wanted to show, by logic and law, why his eight colleagues were wrong. His talk with Edmunds had given him a basis to write about Congress's intentions. He could not answer every point in Bradley's ruling. But he could challenge the central ones. At the top of his list: their divergent views of the Thirteenth and Fourteenth amendments.

The majority had sought, following its rulings in earlier cases, to severely limit the scope of the amendments. The Thirteenth "simply abolished slavery," Bradley had written, while the Fourteenth prohibited the states from interfering with the rights of its citizens. Neither amendment, he said, gave Congress the authority to regulate the actions of individuals and corporations. In passing the 1875 Civil Rights Act, Congress was taking "the place of the State legislatures." That was "repugnant" to the Tenth Amendment, which reserved all rights to the States that weren't expressly given to the federal government and Congress.

There was no quarrel among the justices, for the most part, about the need to protect States' rights. Not only was that principle embedded in the Constitution, as Bradley's ruling pointed out, it was embedded in their upbringings. North or South, it was common to hear people proudly declare themselves to be citizens of their state first, and citizens of the United States second.

In scrutinizing the amendments, Bradley was particularly firm in dismissing the Thirteenth's relevance. It had no place in the current discussion, he insisted, and none in settling future disputes involving discrimination. Yes, the amendment gave Congress the power to prohibit "all badges and incidents of slavery." But discrimination did not qualify as such a badge. "It would be running the slavery argument into the ground," Bradley wrote, "to make it apply to every act of discrimination which a person may see fit to make as to the guests he will entertain, or as to the people he will take into his coach or cab or car, or admit to his concert or theatre."

Nonsense, John said in rebuttal. The Thirteenth did not just "simply" outlaw slavery. As the majority ruling had conceded, it had also *created* something, and that something was monumental: freedom for this new group of citizens. Freedom was not an empty vessel, he said. It did not just mean "exemption from actual slavery." It came with inherent rights—rights that the white race had enjoyed since the nation's birth, John pointed out. Congress, in passing the amendments and subsequent laws to enforce them, was seeking to "secure and protect" these fundamental rights—"nothing more" than that, he said, but also nothing less.

Unlike the majority, which had dismissed any possibility that discrimination could be tantamount to a badge of servitude, John strongly embraced the concept. Wherever the color line persisted, he believed, it was an extension of conditions rooted in slavery and superiority. Masters once had absolute power over their slaves' lives. There was no freedom of movement. Continuing to restrict the right of travel, or where people of color could sleep, or limiting their access to a theater, was a remnant of that bondage. The Thirteenth gave Congress the power to "eradicate" those vestiges, he wrote. That's what Congress had done by passing the Civil Rights Act.

As for Bradley's contention that the Fourteenth Amendment did not apply to individuals or corporations—an echo of Waite's ruling in *Cruikshank* eight years earlier—John emphatically disagreed. "In every material sense," he wrote, "railroad corporations, keepers of inns, and managers of places of public amusement are agents or instrumentalities of the State." Railroads run on public highways. Innkeepers have a legal duty to serve all travelers. Places of amusement operate with a public license. All come under the Fourteenth Amendment, John asserted, making an argument that put him at odds with precedent and popular preference.

Taking aim at one of Bradley's most memorable lines, John chastised the majority ruling for saying that a former slave, at some stage in "his elevation," must cease to be "the special favorite of the laws." How, John wondered, could the colored race have "special" status when it had never enjoyed—and still did not enjoy—the same freedoms and protections as whites?

John wanted today's court to show the same reverence for freedom that Taney had once shown for the claims of slaveholders. "I insist that the national legislature may, without transcending the limits of the Constitution, do for human liberty and the fundamental rights of American citizenship, what it did, with the sanction of this court, for the protection of slavery and the rights of the masters of fugitive slaves," he wrote.

In confronting the majority, John was confronting his own past. Fifteen years earlier, while serving as Kentucky's attorney general, he had registered his strong objections to the new amendments. A few years later, after joining the Republicans, he repudiated that stance. Now, his evolving views had reached a new level. Any remaining doubts about the depths of his "Republicanism" could be laid, finally, to rest.

JOHN CARED MORE about his dissent in the *Civil Rights Cases*, as the ruling came to be known, than any he had written so far. This was not one to be filed and forgotten. Some newspapers published it in full; some carried excerpts. In the weeks that followed, he collected the clippings, like an author accumulating reviews.

As expected, the Southern newspapers were largely a lost cause. Several of the New York papers, while more gracious, were critical as well. The *Tribune* impatiently dismissed John's argument that the conductors and hotelkeepers were "agents" of the state, saying "This is surely straining the Constitution until it cracks." The editors at the *Times* praised Bradley's opinion as "easily understood and convincing," while faulting John's reasoning as labored and a search for meanings in the amendments that did not exist. The *Chicago Inter Ocean* gave him a much better reception, calling his dissent a "profound discussion" of discrimination. "There is no escape from his logic," the *Inter Ocean* wrote.

He found more comfort in the personal letters that came his way. He heard from Wayne MacVeagh, the Pennsylvanian who had urged Hayes to nominate John in 1877. "I have just finishing reading your strong and well-reasoned dissent," MacVeagh wrote, "and I am sure you are right." Hayes sent a kind note of his own, saying the majority might be correct on the law, but that John's dissent was "important" and "in every way noble." Six weeks later, Hayes had edged closer to John's side. "The truth is that you have the general judgment of the public with you," he wrote in a second note. "The people who made the amendment meant by it all you claim."

Frederick Douglass was far more effusive. He had been quoted extensively about the dissent, expressing his admiration, but he wanted to tell John directly how he felt. "It seems to me absolutely unanswerable and unassailable . . . for there is not a single weak point in it," Douglass wrote. "It should be scattered like the leaves of autumn over the whole country, and if I had means, I would cause it to be published in every newspaper and magazine in the land."

Echoing the eloquence that John had heard eleven years before, when they had canvassed together for Grant in Maine, Douglass said: "I am glad, sir, in this day of compromise and concession, when it is so much easier to drift with the current, to sacrifice conviction for the sake of peace, you have been able to adhere to your convictions. . . . I wish to assure you that if you are alone on the Bench, you are not alone in the country."

Then there was the heartfelt letter from William Howard Day, of Harrisburg, Pennsylvania. Twenty-five years earlier, before the Civil War, a Detroit River steamboat captain had refused a sleeping cabin to Day and his wife because of their color. They had sued, and they had lost. Day did not mention his case now, but he enclosed an interview he had given to a local newspaper, voicing his pain about Bradley's ruling. He was writing, he told John, to thank him on behalf of "thousands of the Colored Citizens and for myself."

For John, who was hoping to win converts as well as compliments, a conversation with a former Supreme Court colleague, William Strong, proved so gratifying that he penned an immediate note to Mallie, and sent it home. "Dear Mallie, I met Judge Strong this morning & after a brief talk he said: 'I have read your dissenting opinion through twice with great care. It is a very able opinion—the best you have ever written. It does you infinite credit. At first I was inclined to agree with the court but since reading your opinion, I am in great doubt. It may be that you are right. The opinion of the court, as you said, is too narrow—sticks to the letter, while you aim to bring out the spirit of the Constitution.'"

Too narrow. Spirit of the Constitution. Exactly. But John wasn't going to change the minds of his current colleagues on that score. He would have to wait for new blood to come to the bench, and see if he could find common cause there. He had just turned fifty. With any luck, he would be on the bench for a while to come.

AMONG THE CLIPPINGS in John's collection was a Douglass essay for the *American Reformer*, a year-old publication in New York. Titled "Civil Rights and Justice Harlan," it laid a foundation for going forward, while also rebuking the court and others—including Republicans—for turning their backs on the nation's colored citizens.

In his early days of the antislavery struggle, Douglass wrote, abolitionists were few in number, and often dismissed as extremists. To keep up his spirits, he would console himself with the thought that "one man with God was a majority." That comforting notion had returned to him as he read Harlan's "heroic" dissent. The majority's ruling was superficial and abstract, "an eggshell." Harlan's dissent was broad and relevant to daily life in America, "a cannon ball."

Douglass had hoped for more from the court than this "act of surrender." All nine justices were Republican appointees. Eight of these "nine pillars of the highest court in the land" were born in the North. And yet the only dissenter was the Kentuckian? "The marvel is that, born in a slave State, as he was, and accustomed to seeing the colored man degraded, oppressed and enslaved, and the white man exalted," that John Harlan, alone, "should so clearly comprehend the lessons of the late war and the principles of reconstruction," Douglass wrote.

Already, the majority's ruling was emboldening their Southern enemies, Douglass warned. If the newspaper editorials were any guide, a grim future awaited. "Well may the newspapers all over the South laud and magnify this decision," he wrote. "Well may they gloat in triumph over the negro citizen and declare they have now got him just where they want him. They can put him in a smoking car or a baggage car, take him as freight or as a passenger, take him or leave him at a railroad station, exclude him from inns, drive him from all places of amusement and instruction, without the least fear that the National Government will interfere."

DOUGLASS HAD GROWN into the role of elder statesman without growing weary of the fight. He was in his mid-sixties now, his distinctive head of white hair framed by a salt-and-pepper beard that he kept on the trim side of unruly, and he was impatient. Where did the Republicans stand now on civil rights? Douglass was increasingly unsure. While he still thought of the Republican Party as the colored race's best political hope, he wasn't waiting to find out.

Waiting wasn't a plan. Waiting was what too many whites, even sympathetic ones, had suggested for too long. The *New York Evening Post* had said it again in a recent editorial that made Douglass cringe: Be modest in your expectations, the *Post* had advised. Only twenty years have elapsed since you were in bondage. White officeholders fear your aspirations.

Only twenty years. How much longer were they supposed to wait? "We have been given numerous platforms" by the Republicans since the end of the war, Douglass had reminded a National Convention of Colored Men during its recent stormy meeting in Louisville, "but still we are in the same condition." To make progress beyond tokens of equality, he said, they could not rely on a political party's timeline. They could not rely on others to speak for them. They had learned to talk, and now they must make their voices heard. Otherwise, the color line would only grow sharper, firmer.

The Louisville convention had been largely his idea. A national conclave had struck him as the "best means of bettering our condition as a class," he had told a newspaper correspondent. He had formed a committee, which had called for a gathering in Washington. It would be the first such meeting of colored men in nearly five years, and if all went as planned, the largest ever. Civil rights, education, and labor conditions would be debated, for starters.

But other men of color did not agree with his proposal. From various corners of the country came contrary views: What was Douglass's agenda? Was he trying to speak for the entire colored race? Wouldn't holding such a convention at this moment cause a rift with our friends, the Republicans? Shouldn't such a meeting take place away from Washington, closer to the people and their everyday problems? Washington was easy enough for Douglass. He lived there, worked there as Recorder of Deeds for the District of Columbia, a presidential appointment. But the nation's capital was hardly a central location, now was it?

Bombarded with questions about his intentions, Douglass tried to brush them aside. He was surprised, he said, by the antagonism to the idea. Conventions, he said, "are the safety valves of the republic. . . . There is no use for dynamite where men can assemble in conventions." As for those who felt excluded from his committee, he invited them to take charge. "Let them come and do it better," he said.

Whatever Douglass's agenda, it didn't include a pointless donnybrook over the convention's location. Within a few weeks, he relented, and Louisville emerged as the compromise choice. In late September 1883, a few weeks before Bradley's ruling, he journeyed South to find that nearly three hundred delegates from twenty-seven states and the District of Columbia had answered his committee's summons. They were just as feisty as advertised, a mixing bowl of North and South, young and old, free since birth and freed since emancipation.

Their fractiousness served as a noisy reminder that, as with the Republican Party, it was a mistake to think that people of color were all of one mind, one voice, or one purpose.

THEY MET IN the ornate confines of Louisville's Liederkranz Hall, the same place where John Harlan and the Kentucky Republicans had gathered in 1876 to make Benjamin Bristow their nominee for president. After the opening session on Monday, September 24, the *Louisville Courier-Journal* sized up the delegates and pronounced them to be "a fine body of men—men of spirit and energy who would attract attention anywhere." As if caught by surprise, the *Courier-Journal* assured its readers that "an unusually large number of them were men of intelligence, learning, industry, and familiarity with parliamentary laws."

This fine body of men had a mostly Southern hue. Every former slave state, except Florida, had a delegation. All the border states were represented, while the Far Western and New England states were absent, save for Massachusetts. The list of delegates included an ample supply of local-level politicians, federal officials, and editors of the "colored press," a label that now encompassed a proliferating number of publications. The *New York Times* correspondent observed that "black" delegates were few, with most being "olive-colored or almost white." That was certainly true of the sizable Louisiana contingent, which reflected the usual New Orleans spectrum of skin color and social background.

The convention had elected a slate of vice presidents, one for each state. The Louisiana pick was Louis A. Martinet, the thirty-four-year-old editor of a fledgling Republican weekly, the *Louisiana Standard*. His party work had landed him a federal appointment as a deputy customs surveyor in New Orleans. At the convention, Martinet's excitable contributions drew attention from several newspaper correspondents. They called him "a French colored man," as if that description alone explained his exuberant personality.

The Martinet family's story was the familiar Louisiana tale of mixed race and delayed marriage. His father was a French-speaking European. His mother had been enslaved, until his father bought her freedom in 1848, shortly after the birth of their first son. Louis came next, one of eight in the large family that would become a prominent one in St. Martin, a rural parish west of Baton Rouge. At twenty-seven, after studying at Straight University, a college for colored students established in the aftermath of the Civil War, the young Martinet had won himself a seat in the Louisiana legislature. He lasted one term.

Law was his training, but politics and education were his passions. Whether he was jousting with his fellow officers at the Republican Party's Third District congressional committee, or serving on the New Orleans school board before separation took hold in the 1880s, he could often be found in the middle of a vigorous debate. In Louisville, when the Convention of Colored Men took up a recommendation that Congress allocate seven million dollars for Southern schools, Martinet waded into the fray with a fervor that "raised the uproar to its highest pitch," according to one reporter's description. Just as Albion Tourgee had strong feelings about keeping national education aid out of the hands of state governments, Martinet did not want federal money helping districts that were toeing the color line.

The convention's many divisions were on display from the opening gavel. Mild opposition immediately arose to electing Douglass as the presiding officer, but after an afternoon of clamorous wrangling, it was clear that the elder statesman's supporters far outnumbered his detractors. He took the chair, hardly ruffled. The next morning, arriving for a keynote speech, he found an immense audience waiting. One reporter, scanning the crowd, saw many of the city's "leading lawyers, merchants, doctors and military men of the white race."

They had come to see the "most celebrated colored man in the world," the reporter wrote.

DOUGLASS MOUNTED the platform with his handwritten text, revised just the day before. He often spoke without notes, but this Tuesday morning was not one of those times. As he warmed to his task, though, he inserted new ideas and phrases, sprinkling in sarcasm and amplification, particularly as he pressed his points about the perniciousness of prejudice.

Though the colored race "is no longer bought and sold," he said, bigotry hampers every step of our progress, shutting us out of "all respectable and profitable" callings. Trade unions reject us. Mechanics refuse apprenticeships. Schools deny admission. Polling places turn us away. Stores shut their doors. Railroads shunt us to inferior cars. Not everywhere, of course. But the exceptions only serve to illuminate the color line's insidiousness. For our people, he said, liberty is so far only a name, "our citizenship is but a sham, and our suffrage thus far only a cruel mockery." If the colored man tries to better himself, he is ridiculed, resented, and resisted. “If we come as cart-drivers and servants, we are received,” Douglass said. But “when we come as scholars or statesmen, the color line is raised.”

The color line was not the creation of colored people, he pointed out. Whites had imposed it. How, then, could whites be surprised to see the members of that proscribed race banding together in protest? Who else would do so? “The man outraged is the man to make the outcry,” he said. “Men will not care much for a people who do not care for themselves.”

Caring for themselves, speaking out for themselves, had taken on a new urgency, Douglass said. Outrages against people of color—solely *because* of their color—were proliferating in the South. White mobs were hauling away people to “lynch courts,” accusing them of a crime, meting out “impetuous justice,” overthrowing the legal system in favor of murder and torture. Douglass sketched out a typical scene in graphic detail, sparing nothing, certainly not the sensibilities of his white spectators: A captive, startled, alone, frightened, “dragged with a rope about his neck in midnight-darkness to the nearest tree, and told in the coarsest terms of profanity to prepare for death.” And the final outrage in this “hell-black” horror: silence by the authorities who could stop it, silence from the local press.

Douglass would not be silent. People of color could not be silent. They could not settle into a “servile and cowardly submission” to injustice. They must “keep their grievances before the people and make every organized protest against the wrongs inflicted on them,” he said. “While we recognize the color line as a hurtful force, a mountain barrier to our progress, wounding our bleeding feet with its flinty rocks at every step, we do not despair. We are a hopeful people.”

A hopeful people, perhaps, but far from a harmonious one. There were regional and political differences among the delegates that no speech, not even a Douglass speech, could paper over. Some wanted to adopt Douglass’s nearly two-hour oration as a statement of the convention; others did not. Over the next three days, they seemed to agree, mostly, that they could not agree. The resolutions that managed to pass were mildly worded. One on civil rights violations in the South made no mention of violence or lynch courts. General statements endorsing the Republican Party could not muster majorities, with some delegates arguing that "politics" had no place in the proceedings.

For the most part, the white press was unimpressed. The kinder correspondents said little had been accomplished. The unkind ones characterized the gathering as "a roaring farce," marked by "buncombe" and "a ceaseless stream of valueless talk." Douglass, who had hoped to start a new movement, instead found himself fending off criticism from a variety of directions. Returning to Washington, he could not keep his frustration from showing. "I hope to continue to deserve your thanks and support," he wrote to a well-wisher in early October. "I am not ashamed of my words and work at the Louisville Convention."

Two weeks later, when Bradley's ruling dealt its death blow to the Civil Rights Act, Douglass had yet more evidence that, in defiance of the familiar adage, good things did not always come to those who wait.

IN NEW ORLEANS, reaction to Bradley's ruling was as varied as the city's multihued population. The *Picayune*, which still saw itself as the primary voice for English-speaking whites, said it wanted to "congratulate our readers upon the progress made in overturning that objectionable and abhorrent legislation known as the civil rights acts." Not just objectionable, the newspaper said, but unwarranted. The state of Louisiana—not Congress—was the proper authority to punish any illegal acts that interfered with someone's civil rights.

Now that the Supreme Court had removed the offending law, the *Picayune* said, it would be a mistake for the state to reimpose one of its own. Discrimination was not a criminal matter, the *Picayune* said. "When a citizen is excluded from a hotel, railway carriage or place of amusement by another individual or a corporation . . . this is no attack on civil rights or privilege of citizenship. It is simply a private grievance . . . between two individuals, to be redressed in the courts of such State."

Such lawsuits had become harder to win in Louisiana since the Supreme Court had struck down P. B. S. Pinchback's 1869 public-accommodation law, which gave victims of discrimination the right to sue for damages. But the *Picayune* thought there was no need for colored people to worry. Economic imperatives would protect them. "In the race for commercial and industrial supremacy," the newspaper wrote, no State is likely to "fall seriously short of its duty of protecting its citizens in the enjoyment of all legal rights and privileges."

Less than two blocks from the *Picayune* building, on the other side of Canal Street at 123 Chartres Street in the Vieux Carré, Louis Martinet and his *Louisiana Standard* found nothing to like in Bradley's ruling. Yes, it was true that in practical terms, the law had long been "a dead letter," the newspaper said. But even in a moribund state, the act had stood as a vital statement of national principle, an acknowledgment that a vulnerable group needed shielding "against a people, prejudiced and more powerful than we are." For the Supreme Court to cripple the Fourteenth Amendment, leaving its humblest citizens to the whims of unfriendly state governments, was "a farce, if not a disgrace."

It was a delicate time for Martinet's weekly newspaper. Only a dozen issues into a wobbly existence, the *Standard* was still establishing its identity, trying to build a readership among all people of color, whether French or English speaking. The masthead left no ambiguity about its political leanings: "Official Organ of the Republican Party." But now, echoing Douglass's misgivings, the *Standard* fired several editorial shots in the party's general direction.

With one notable exception, the *Standard* said, this court of "supposed unbiased Republican judges . . . has solemnly decreed that the government—the government to which we owe allegiance—has no power to protect its citizens." It was a bitter denouement for the Civil Rights Act, expected or not. "Morally, this is the heaviest blow that has been struck at us—and the blow comes from those who we have been taught to believe were our friends," the *Standard* wrote. How "can the negro remain faithful to a party, no matter what its services have been in the past, which slaps him in the face?"

LIKE AN OASIS in a parched landscape, the Interstate Commerce Commission opened for business in the spring of 1887, offering an unforeseen stopping place for anyone with a grievance against the powerful corporations that controlled the nation's railways. Two months later, at his own expense, William H. Councill journeyed from Alabama to testify in person about his bloody and all-too-believable encounter with the color line on the Western and Atlantic's "night train" from Chattanooga to Atlanta. On a muggy July morning, Councill became the first colored passenger to appear before the five ICC commissioners and ask directly for their help.

The Councill case was transporting them into uncharted territory. Whatever the commissioners did on the case known as Docket No. 21—even if they dismissed his complaint as beyond the commission's jurisdiction—it would encompass a series of "firsts." The commission's first passenger request for damages. The first opportunity to decide whether the ICC's authority extended to civil rights as well as to policing the railroads' business practices. The commission's first exploration of the policy of separation.

The five commissioners—all appointees of Grover Cleveland, the first Democrat to be elected president in twenty-eight years, since before the Civil War—had a legislative road map from Congress, but few precedents to guide them in establishing the federal government's first autonomous regulatory agency. Their task was David versus Goliath: five commissioners regulating some twelve hundred railroad lines, owned by some five hundred companies, operating on more than one hundred thirty-three thousand miles of track. Every month brought new companies into the industry, and every year saw the laying of five to ten thousand miles of new rails.

To protect the commission's independence, Congress had prohibited the commissioners from holding any other job while serving. Their mission was to prevent the nation's railways from engaging in favoritism or collusion, to make sure shipping rates were "reasonable and just," and promote fair competition. They were to conduct hearings, issue findings, and write reports.

The commission had an array of untested powers. The ICC law authorized them to compel testimony, but were the commissioners the equivalent of judges? Did the ICC chairman—the well-respected Thomas Cooley, elevated to the top post by his four colleagues, with a nudge from Cleveland—have any greater power than the others in deciding how they should operate? "As your commission has not yet to our knowledge published any rules of procedure, please notify us whether we can try the case on depositions and witnesses, one or both," wrote Councill's lawyer as he prepared for his client's July hearing.

The ICC was inventing itself, much as the Supreme Court had done in 1789. Cooley, a former chief judge of the Michigan Supreme Court, was acutely aware of the risks of doing it wrong. At this late stage of his distinguished career, Cooley had no interest in presiding over anything of questionable legality or relevance. He was sixty-three years old. His health wasn't what it used to be. He had left his wife, Mary, and the comforts of Ann Arbor to take this important post. He intended to make a success of it.

He was flinty, intimidating, and so hardworking that he thought a long walk constituted a vacation. He also valued independence more than party loyalty. Fed up with the Republican Party in 1884, he had backed Cleveland, the Democrat. When Cleveland won, Cooley's name was bandied about for various appointments, including the Supreme Court. No vacancy had come along, but Cleveland had persuaded him that the new ICC needed a man of his stature. Also, the new law said no party could have more than three of the five seats. Cooley's maverick political history allowed Cleveland to count him as a Republican, and that's how he was described when his appointment was announced, much to the dismay of loyal Republicans.

As a young lawyer, Cooley had served as the Michigan Supreme Court's official reporter. He had brought discipline to a once-haphazard system of compiling, editing, and publishing the judges' rulings. The ICC's credibility, he believed, would be enhanced enormously by handling its decisions much the same way. There should be an "ICC Reports," he said, just as there was a "Supreme Court Reports," a formal record of all completed cases.

Cooley, in his daily letters to his wife in Michigan, had been sharing his impressions of his fellow commissioners—three Northerners and a Southerner from Alabama—but he rarely said much about the cases themselves. Freight and rate disputes didn't make for interesting reading. On the morning of the Councill hearing, however, Cooley had something to say that he knew would catch her attention. "We are to hear the colored man's case today," he told her. "It is a case on which there will be a good deal of feeling."

UNTANGLING THE FACTS in the Councill case did not prove as difficult as some legal clashes. For the most part, the two sides agreed on what happened during William Councill's April 7, 1887, trip, even as they disagreed on the railroad's role in it and on whether the Western & Atlantic's separate cars were truly of equal quality and condition.

Councill made an impressive witness, the commissioners felt, articulate in telling his story. He was a minister, lawyer, and principal of the State Colored Normal School in Huntsville, Alabama. He often traveled to neighboring states, visiting other schools, but usually on trains other than those operated by the Western & Atlantic.

Boarding the train in Chattanooga, Councill said he was confronted with two cars that looked nothing alike. One was a nicely appointed "ladies' car," or so the railroad called it. But plenty of gentlemen were sitting in it, unaccompanied by a lady. The other was the colored car—dirty, partitioned, poorly lit, with a thick tobacco haze in the air, courtesy of the smokers occupying one-half of the car. Nothing suggested it was a first-class accommodation, and Councill was holding a first-class ticket. He passed it by.

He sat in the better car, only to be told that he must move. He refused, unconvinced that the order had come from the conductor. An infuriated white passenger, taking matters into his own hands, fetched the brakeman's lantern and smashed it against Councill's head, glass shattering, shards flying, blood spurting. No one, including the train crew, interceded.

Councill's attacker, at his deposition, had proudly described his method of teaching the colored man to obey orders. "I knocked him out of his seat," testified Charles Whitsett, once a railroad employee himself. "He fell to the floor, and as he raised up, he came toward me, and I let him have it again with the lantern. I hit him several times before I conquered him and then rushed him right out of the car into the darkey's car. He was willing to go by the time I got through with him."

As Whitsett and others were carting Councill to the colored car, they met conductor George Ferguson. He was upset. He was responsible for protecting his passengers. Whitsett told him: "George, we are taking him in the negro's car where he belongs, we cannot put up with his insolence any longer."

Insolence was not Councill's explanation for his behavior. He was used to separation on Southern trains, he told the commissioners. That wasn't his complaint. He had sat in the colored-only cars of the Memphis & Charleston, as well as the East Tennessee & Georgia, but those were full coaches, similar conveniences, no partition, no smoking. Not always as nice as the car for whites, but close. That's what he had expected to find on the Western & Atlantic.

The railroad didn't see it Councill's way, of course. The cars were similar in comfort, said the railroad's lawyer, and met the Western & Atlantic's legal obligation to provide equal accommodations to passengers paying equal fares. The partition in the colored car was a matter of economics, not discrimination, the lawyer said. The railroad didn't have enough colored passengers for a full car, so the railroad had divided it, half colored, half smoker.

As for the assault, the railroad said that its crew could not be held responsible for Whitsett's vigilante actions. Besides, Councill was as much to blame as anyone, the railroad argued. If he had gone to the proper car, as directed and as he knew the rules required, nothing would have happened. Instead, the railroad said, he sat in the whites-only car, defying the color line, trying to stir up trouble in a "bid for notoriety."

The commissioners listened to it all, hours of lengthy depositions read aloud by the opposing lawyers, followed by testimony from Councill, Ferguson, and the brakeman. The more they heard, the more they kept coming back to the same points of contention. What were the conditions of the two cars? Was one better than the other? On other lines that run separate cars—is the colored car usually partitioned with a swinging door, with smokers assigned to the front half? "This rule you talk about," Cooley said to Ferguson as the conductor explained how separation was handled, is that the general policy "down there, upon other roads, as well as your own?"

Whitsett's attack on Councill, as troubling as the commissioners may have found it, did not draw their scrutiny. The commissioners had decided that the ICC law gave them no options on that front, except to highlight the violence in their ruling. They could not punish Whitsett for it, or award damages to Councill, or penalize any railroad employee for failing to prevent it. Anyone accused of assault had a constitutional right to a jury trial, and the ICC had no power to hold one. If Councill wanted to pursue such charges, he would have to bring them in state court. The ICC's sole authority was to find that the railroad had treated Councill with "undue prejudice," and issue a "cease and desist" order.

On December 3, 1887, that's exactly what the commission did. The ruling released that day was a clear victory for Councill and the principle of equal accommodations. But as written by Commissioner William Morrison, a Democrat from Illinois, it turned out to be an even more emphatic triumph for separation and the color line.

IN PLAIN LANGUAGE, Morrison's ruling declared that "fair dealing and common honesty" required railroads to provide first-class cars to all first-class ticketholders. Equality was not "a half car, half lighted . . . dismal, less clean, and less comfortable" than the white car. That must stop, the ruling said.

But how was this principle to be enforced? By leaving that question open-ended and issuing no specific regulations, Morrison seemed to be relying on the railroads to be self-policing. That hadn't worked in the past. Was there any reason to think it would work now?

On separation, though, Morrison's ruling was explicit. Councill had not challenged the policy, so there was no need for the commission to address it at length. Morrison did so anyway. "Public sentiment, wherever the colored population is large, sanctions and requires this separation of races," he wrote. "We cannot, therefore, say that there is any undue prejudice or unjust preferences in recognizing and acting upon this general sentiment, provided it is done on fair and equal terms. This separation may be carried out on railroad trains without disadvantage to either race and with increased comfort to both."

On fair and equal terms. With increased comfort to both. The commissioners had added their voices to the chorus: Separate is legal, if equal.

TWO MONTHS LATER, in February 1888, the commission took its second run at a colored passenger's complaint of "undue prejudice." William Heard's first-class ticket, from Cincinnati to Charleston, required a journey over several railways through several states. He had enjoyed a fine ride on his first two legs, he said, with "no distinctions" between white and colored passengers. The trouble began in Atlanta, when he switched to the Georgia Railroad for the portion to Augusta.

He and his two traveling companions were barred from the white car, with its upholstered seats, clean carpet, and fresh ice water. They had to sit, instead, in the "dusty and dirty" colored portion of the smoking car, with its wooden seats, bare floors, and unpleasant stench. The conductor, invoking the company's separation rule, said he would lose his job if he allowed Heard's group to sit in the white car.

The Georgia Railroad adopted a more defiant stance than the Western & Atlantic. Answering Heard's charge that he was forced to ride in the "Jim Crow Car," the railroad's lawyer had replied with sarcasm. He had never heard the railroad's colored-only car called by that name, the lawyer said. But if the commission had proof of the "Jim Crow" label, then it might want to use its "large powers" to give "appropriate relief" to Heard for having to hear the offending term. The lawyer did not offer a suggestion for what that relief might be.

The railroad argued that the ICC had no jurisdiction in the case because the Atlanta-Augusta route did not cross state lines, and therefore, did not affect "interstate" commerce. The commission disagreed. Heard's ticket had given him passage all the way from Ohio to South Carolina, crossing multiple borders. By participating in interstate ticket sales, the commission ruled, the Georgia Railroad had brought itself under ICC regulation.

While the facts were different than in Councill's case, the outcome was the same. Heard's complaint was upheld, the Georgia Railroad was told to cease and desist. Commissioner Augustus Schoonmaker, of New York, wrote the decision this time. Showing that he wasn't satisfied with Morrison's vague language on equal accommodation, Schoonmaker offered a forceful revision. "Equality of civil and political rights, and the equal protection of the laws," he wrote, invoking language from the Fourteenth Amendment, "are subjects not open for discussion."

Heard's lawyers, both men of color, had specifically asked the commission to rule that separation was "unlawful," asserting that the policy qualified as "undue prejudice" under the ICC law. Schoonmaker had taken their argument seriously, questioning them closely about it during the hearing. In his ruling, he praised an existing alternative to separation. There were railroads in Virginia, South Carolina, and North Carolina that did not divide their passengers by color, he said, opting instead for first-class and second-class cars with different fares. "A method like this does not appear to be in violation of the law," he hinted.

In the end, though, the commissioners chose not to disturb the precedent set down in the Councill case. Instead, Schoonmaker emphasized that separation, to be equal, required constant vigilance. The railroads must show that "equality in separate cars is real and not delusive."

Real and not delusive. The commission had laid down its law, stronger this time: Separate, yes, but only if truly equal.

TOURGEE ON THE NEGRO QUESTION.

BELVIDERE, Ill., Jan. 23.—*Special Telegram.* —The Hon. A. W. Tourgee, the "Bystander" of THE INTER OCEAN, lectured to a large audience in Union Hall here to-night. He devoted his entire attention to the negro problem from the time of the African's first appearance in this country up to the present. He stated that the solution of the colored question was the most important one with which the American people would have to deal, and that it was no more settled now than it was before the war of the re-

In demand: Tourgee on the lecture circuit, January 1889

(Chicago Inter Ocean, *January 24, 1889/Library of Congress)*

18

"The Negro Question"

Mayville, Washington, and New Orleans, 1889–1890

THE LETTERS ARRIVED from all over the country, as many as fifty a week by the fall of 1889, many addressed simply to "Albion Tourgee, the Bystander." That was the persona he had adopted the previous year for his new Saturday column in the *Chicago Inter Ocean*, a national newspaper with ambitions as expansive as its name. For months now, ever since the Bystander had devoted himself largely to the subject of race, his volume of letters had been climbing. "I have never seen such an outburst," he had proudly told the *Inter Ocean* editor, the estimable William Penn Nixon, in July.

When the Bystander returned from a three-week Lake Michigan vacation at the end of August—his first holiday in years, he confided to his readers—a mountain of mail welcomed him home. The collection included the usual diatribes from irate correspondents, eager to tell him that he was wrong about almost everything. These screeds would be useful fodder for future columns. The Bystander liked nothing better than picking a good fight with his querulous opponents. Fortunately, he also had his supporters, "earnest-hearted lovers of liberty and right," he called them.

But no letter in the pile was "more highly prized," the Bystander informed his readers, than one from a "colored Mississippian." Unable to write in his own hand, the man had asked his daughter's help. His message? He was subscribing to the *Inter Ocean's* weekly edition so his children could read the Bystander's column to him, so he could hear what the Bystander has to say in "vindication" of his race's rights and the "encouragement of its hopes."

That gem was followed a few months later by an equally affecting note from the secretary of the Wisconsin Civil Rights League. His name was William Green, and he was writing to convey the league's "heartfelt thanks for the brave and noble stand which you have ever taken in defence of the Negro Race." By revealing "the real status of our people," Green said, the Bystander was doing something extraordinary. He was converting skeptics, "convincing those who have hitherto been unconvinced" that a crisis was at hand. Colored people everywhere "are looking to you as their noblest, grandest and most powerful champion," Green wrote.

While the column's name suggested a detached, observational perspective, the Bystander was anything but. He tried out different voices the way some men tried on a new suit—with relish and a keen eye for the right fit. He could warble about the sorry history of the "campaign song," or rage at the white-ruled South for its "miasma of intolerance." He could scold the North, along with the Republican Party, for abandoning the colored race. He could brag about himself, estimating that "probably ten million" had read his books. He could lament his graying hair and weakening vision, saying though he was only a year past fifty, he now had to "rely somewhat more than his wont on other eyes and other hands."

Writing in the third person seemed to liberate him. He could embellish for effect, or reprimand like a parent, or mount his high horse. But remain detached? Never. That was not a natural posture for Albion W. Tourgee, the radical who had gone to North Carolina to complete a revolution, the man who had vowed during the Civil War to create a Union "better than it was."

THE BYSTANDER'S MAIL wasn't the only evidence of his growing reach. Within a few weeks during the summer of 1889, editors at several national publications had contacted him, soliciting his thoughts on the "Negro Question," the au courant phrase in Republican circles and literary discussions. *Frank Leslie's Illustrated Newspaper* wanted an essay of fifteen hundred to twenty-five hundred words on "what the colored man is doing for himself," while the *New York Tribune* would grant him twice as many for "an analysis of the colored race . . . and how their position will be affected by their progress in wealth, education and refinement."

Quite a turnabout. Only a year earlier, he had tried to sell just that sort of essay for possible syndication, and had received a tepid response. "In regard to the article on the Negro Question," the man at *McClure's* had said in March 1888, "I will offer it to the newspapers and push it to the best of my ability. . . . That is the best I can do with an article of this kind, and it is impossible for me to say what market there would be for the matter."

There had been no market, it turned out. But that was before the Bystander's debut, before he had made race into a centerpiece of his column, before Benjamin Harrison and the Republicans had won it all in the 1888 election. Now editors were hovering at the Bystander's door. The Bystander found their interest immensely satisfying, as well as immensely valuable in his ongoing efforts to solidify his seemingly tentative status at the *Inter Ocean*, which was paying him fifty dollars a week.

He told Nixon of the many offers flowing his way, but truth be told, he found it a bit humiliating to resort to such self-promotion. Couldn't Nixon see for himself that the column was a success of the first order? That the Bystander had catapulted the *Inter Ocean* ahead of its competitors on the race question, bringing acclaim as well as a passel of new subscribers? Yet just a month earlier, Nixon had informed him, in the middle of a letter about something else, that the *Inter Ocean* would be dropping the Bystander! Just like that. No warning.

Oh, Nixon had been diplomatic enough, if you liked your bad news served off-handedly, with a side of insincerity. "While the *Inter Ocean* is doing splendidly," Nixon had said after a page of throat clearing, "I find it necessary to reduce expenses. . . . and that leads me to say that after this month we will have to try to get along without the Bystander. I do not like to lose you as a contributor and hope to be able to take you on in some other way after I have gotten the ship trimmed and lightened."

That was the sort of babble the Bystander was fond of tearing apart. He did no such thing, of course. Instead, he sought a stay of execution, appealing to Nixon's competitiveness and pride. "You may wonder that I keep banging at . . . negro matters," he wrote. "If you have noticed how [often] the Bystander has been quoted of late you will not wonder." This was the best of bargains for the *Inter Ocean*, he argued. "You get the credit and I take the 'cussing!'"

As he had for some years now, Albion signed his letter to Nixon with an accent mark in his last name: Tourgée. It was part affectation, part futile attempt to produce his preferred pronunciation. *Tour-zhay.* Like an apparition, the tiny slash appeared only sporadically in print. His books featured it, but most newspapers either didn't know or didn't care—or, perhaps, didn't have the accent in their typography cabinets. The *Inter Ocean* certainly knew his preference, but at the end of his Bystander column, his name remained Tourgee, sans slash.

By late August, Nixon had amiably reversed his decision to eliminate the Bystander, saying "the more I think about it the less do I desire to give you up as a contributor." Albion responded with a magnanimous pat on the editor's back, while attempting to thwart Nixon's suggestion that they should meet to discuss how to "change the Bystander somewhat." Albion saw no need for adjustment. "I will continue the Bystander as you desire," he wrote, but "judging from the big box of letters and the table full of notices which awaited my return, it would be very poor policy to discontinue or change its character materially."

Harmony restored, the Bystander gave Nixon a glimpse of his latest thinking about the "race question" and its reemergence as a major issue. "Even dilettante New England is getting stirred up and the South is ablaze with excitement on it," he wrote. "The subject will never grow cold again until it has reached some sort of a settlement." What sort of settlement? The Bystander wasn't sure. But he could make one prediction with confidence: "It will furnish food for controversy and be a controlling issue for years."

THE BYSTANDER DIDN'T mention to Nixon that he desperately needed the money.

Jettisoning fifty dollars a week wasn't going to do much to lighten the

Inter Ocean ship, but for the foundering Tourgée household, the income was significant ballast. He and Emma were living, essentially, from column to column, essay to essay, lecture to lecture, book to book. If he didn't write and talk, they couldn't pay their many bills. *A Fool's Errand* and *Bricks Without Straw* had brought him fame and a small fortune in the early 1880s. But he had squandered much of that cash, ploughing it into a new magazine, *Our Continent,* a literary journal with a dash of politics, headquartered in Philadelphia. Albion's creation. Albion's dream. Albion's obsession. But not just his. Emma's too. Her time. Her burden. Her anxiety.

It was a handsome publication, a daring venture, and a commercial disaster. The debts and lawsuits were still trailing them. Years later, Emma would remember the strain and declare: "My poor husband! How his life was embittered, ruined, by his trying to do what he had no capacity to do. His mind was too large to take in business details, and without that ability no one can succeed in such ventures as the *Continent,* which took all his fortune, his ambition, his hopes—everything but his wife."

Albion's renown guaranteed that his ruin went on public display, like a man being shamed in the town square. The *Boston Globe* reduced his financial devastation to a quip: "Had he stayed in the South, he might be a millionaire now instead of an unfortunate, penniless novelist." In South Carolina, the *Watchman and Southron* took special delight in learning of his tumble. "Tourgee is disappointed and poor and sick," the *Watchman* crowed at the end of 1884, "and the next best thing for him to do is die and get out of the way."

By the spring of 1885, he and Emma had retreated to Mayville, to their beloved "Thorheim" overlooking Chautauqua Lake, essentially to start over. His fortune was mostly gone, but he still had his fame. He could make something of that. In early 1886, he conjured up the idea of a six-week lecture tour, one that he and a hired business manager would arrange themselves, without the help of a speakers' bureau. At fifty cents a seat, perhaps one dollar in some places, he was hoping to clear one hundred dollars or more a night, after expenses.

He would stay on the circuit as long as possible, until "we whip this debt."

❖

EMMA WARNED ALBION not to do it. A self-financed tour was too risky, she said, and they couldn't afford another of his money-losing mistakes. Stubborn as usual, he had gone ahead, only to discover that Emma was right, as usual. "Good houses" proved scarce. At Detroit's Opera House, a cavernous place, he drew a few dozen, leaving an embarrassed *Free Press* reporter to write, "A person in a very small audience cannot help feeling a certain sense of shame that his city doesn't show to better advantage."

The nadir came near St. Louis, a night of less than twenty dollars, not enough to "half-pay expenses." Depression set in. Albion found it hard to give every audience "their money's worth," as he had promised himself after the fiasco in Detroit. Writing to Emma from his St. Louis hotel room, he looked up to find his business manager, glum, reporting another weak advance sale. "I don't know how I am to live through another night of shame and horror," he told her. "I have simply outlived my time—the world has forgotten my thought and, almost, my existence."

Their financial woes were unrelenting. He would send her fifty or seventy-five dollars from the road, and as soon as the check arrived, she would head to the bank to pay the overdue interest on one of their debts. At the end of February, after more disappointing crowds in Kansas and a new lecture topic, he declared himself at wit's end. "If not for the notes and present straits, I would quit," he told Emma. "I am a man that was. It is of yesterday and not of today that they think when they see my name."

His "blues," his companion since college days, resurfaced with a vengeance. So did self-pity, another of his bugaboos. On March 1, from Kansas City, he wrote to Emma's sister Millie, who was living with them at Thorheim. He felt more desperate than usual, he said, and could not bear writing to Emma. "I have gone all to pieces," he wrote. Could Millie, or someone, join him for the tour's final weeks? "I must have someone to guard me from myself or I shall be really insane pretty soon," he wrote. "So do not be surprised at a telegram demanding instant attention."

That telegram was never sent. Instead, six days later, Albion composed an entirely different one, to Emma. As if heaven sent, a Buffalo industrialist had emerged, willing to open his wallet for a Tourgée book on the power of monopolies such as Standard Oil, which was a threat to the industrialist's business interests. The contract came with a $2,500 advance. "This strange chance, which seems too good to be true, is just what you have always desired, staying at home with plenty of work and good pay," he wrote the next day to Emma. "Of course I will have to go away to look up the business and learn what I can of its detail; but almost all the summer I will be there . . . I do not see why we should not be perfectly happy."

IT DIDN'T WORK OUT quite as happily as he had envisioned. He and his Buffalo benefactor clashed, leaving hard feelings on both sides. Meanwhile, he and Emma had made progress in paying down their debts, but they were still far from free of them. Trying to protect themselves from new legal trouble, assets now went under Emma's name. To keep themselves afloat, they needed more income. As 1888 dawned, he broached the idea of a weekly column to the *Inter Ocean*, to be called "A Bystander's Notes."

He was a well-known quantity to *Inter Ocean* editors, but a well-kept secret from the newspaper's readers. For three years, he had been writing for the Chicago paper under various pseudonyms, all hugely popular during their limited runs. His "Man of Destiny" attacks on President-Elect Grover Cleveland, published under the pen name "Siva," had mushroomed into a national sensation, prompting a fierce guessing game over Siva's identity. Just as Albion's publisher had done with *A Fool's Errand*, the *Inter Ocean* had capitalized on the mystery, printing letter after letter of conjecture. The editors stoked the speculation, offering a few teasing clues, some misleading, while assuring their readers that Siva is "one of the most courageous and most dashing partisans of the time."

Guesses came from near and far, demonstrating the breadth of the *Inter Ocean*'s subscription list. Through it all, the *Inter Ocean* kept mum. Siva's secret remained Siva's secret, as Albion had requested. He believed that putting his real name on newspaper work would be a mistake. "My name has become a trademark that is worth $10,000 on any book I may write," he explained to a Buffalo editor in offering an article under a pseudonym. "I cannot afford to lessen its value by frequent newspaper or magazine articles."

It was a sensibility that, ultimately, didn't make sense. "Siva" had brought heaps of attention to the *Inter Ocean*, but no lasting benefits for Albion Tourgée. For the Bystander column, he reversed course, opting to sign it, even adding his place of residence: "Mayville, N.Y."

A sound business decision, for once. The Bystander helped to revive his sagging career. He was now, arguably, the best-known white advocate for civil rights in the country. He was certainly one of the best read.

THE DISCREET VISITOR registered at the Deer Park Hotel as "H. B. Brown," not that the presidential reporters were fooled by the omission of his title and hometown. Everyone knew why Judge Henry B. Brown of Detroit had shown up at the mountaintop resort in far western Maryland, and it wasn't for a walk in the ferny woods. Henry had arrived unannounced on July 25, 1889, with a more urban pastime in mind: pursuit of a Supreme Court seat. If all went well, he would meet with President Benjamin Harrison at his vacation cottage, and they would talk about his qualifications for the four-month-old vacancy.

Harrison and his wife had decamped from Washington to spend the better part of July and August in the fresh air of the Alleghenies. The president's aides had insisted that Deer Park was a respite and not a "summer capital," and they had put out the word: "Office seekers" would be turned away if they showed up, broad-brimmed sun hats in hand. So how to explain Judge Brown's visit? The official line was hazy, like the morning mist on the mountains. The judge "was on his way to the Virginia springs, it was stated, and stopped over merely to pay his respects," the *Chicago Tribune* correspondent wrote.

Pay his respects? In the middle of summer, on a circuitous train route from Detroit? No, this was no stopover. This was an audition. A few days earlier, on July 23, Harrison had written privately to a friend in Indiana, a prominent Republican lawyer, asking his opinion of three men for the

Supreme Court vacancy: Henry Hitchcock of St. Louis, president of the American Bar Association; David Brewer, a federal judge in Kansas; and Henry Brown of Detroit. "Write me what you know about them," the president said, "and extend the list if you choose."

Among that trio, Henry was leading in newspaper speculation. But as Henry well knew from twenty-five years in and out of public life, the press's tea-leaf reading wasn't going to matter one whit in helping him to secure the appointment. The *Tribune* correspondent, writing from Deer Park, agreed. "Some of the politicians and newspapers have got ahead of Gen. Harrison in making the appointment, but he takes the matter placidly and doesn't allow a little thing of that kind to interfere with him in the careful search he is making." Still, the *Tribune* reporter observed, Brown's call on the president "means something."

Something, but what? Henry did not know, but he had allowed himself to hope. As he had fourteen years ago in seeking the federal judgeship, he had done his political homework, writing letters, visiting friends, lining up support in Michigan and Washington. He could tell the president, honestly, that his health was good. His eyes gave him the usual occasional trouble, but his headaches were mostly a problem of the past. At fifty-three, he saw no impediment to giving the court two decades of hard work.

Shortly after breakfast, Henry left the Deer Park Hotel for the walk to the president's rustic quarters. The correspondent for the *Pittsburgh Commercial Gazette* was there, watching. He had never met the judge, and now, recording his first impressions, he called Henry a man of "distinguished bearing," marked by "a smooth-shaven face, massive square jaw, overhanging brows, and keen black eyes."

When Henry emerged an hour later, he was congenial but pensive. "He walked slowly," the correspondent wrote, "although the rain was coming down in a way unpleasant to anyone but a preoccupied man."

HENRY LEFT the following morning, his respects paid, his prospects unclear. The correspondents all seemed to be talking to the same sources, citing the same favorable points. Brown, they wrote, had the strong backing of Michigan's senior senator, Republican Francis B. Stockbridge. A "goodly portion of the Michigan bar" had endorsed him, and he "was said" to have the support of "three or four" Supreme Court justices, who were "anxious to have him."

Other aspirants had their champions, naturally. Michigan's junior senator, Republican James McMillan, was pushing a different candidate—none other than Alfred Russell, Henry's once and forever rival. Losing out to Russell would be crushing for Henry. On the other hand, the federal judge from Kansas, David Brewer, was an old friend and a Yale classmate. If Brewer ended up as the nominee, at least that would bring honor to the class of '56.

The president's aides said the choice would be announced before summer's end, but by late September, the president still had not decided. There was no rush. The Senate wasn't back in session until early December. But the press was wondering: What was the holdup? The *Tribune* correspondent wrote that Michigan's senators had put Harrison in a box by backing different candidates, making the president choose and, possibly, offending supporters on the losing side. There was irony at work here. Henry's supporters had been making the argument that it was "Michigan's turn" for a Supreme Court seat. Twenty-five justices had been appointed since Michigan's statehood, none from the Wolverine State. Now it looked as if the senators' inability to present a united front might leave Michigan out in the cold once again.

Stockbridge, frustrated, told the *Free Press* that he was "unable to tell what impression Mr. Brown's candidacy is making on the mind of the president." Russell's supporters claimed that his star was rising. It was clear, mostly, that confusion reigned. On November 26, after meeting with Harrison, Stockbridge's spirits lifted. The president told Stockbridge that he had narrowed his list to two—Brown and a U.S. circuit judge from Iowa.

Neither was chosen. On December 4, the coveted seat went to Brewer, the nearly forgotten man from Harrison's original list. What had swayed the president? According to the *Detroit News*, one factor was a private letter from Brewer to a supporter, "stating that he did not wish to be a candidate if his old school friend, Brown, had a chance of appointment." Impressed by

Brewer's generous spirit, "and already favorably disposed" toward him, the president had "decided to appoint him." How did this private letter find its way to the president? The news accounts did not say.

Stockbridge and McMillan were disappointed but not disconsolate. Harrison had praised both Michigan candidates. The senators hoped, they told the *Detroit News* correspondent, "to get Brown or Russell into the next vacancy." But who could say when that might be? By then, there might be a Democrat in White House again.

Henry had every reason to think his moment had passed.

ON JANUARY 1, 1890, public celebrations brought a festive air to the first day of the Nineties for many Americans. At Thorheim, however, New Year's was much like most days: A long afternoon and evening of work for Albion and Emma Tourgée. It was Wednesday—"Bystander Day," as Emma had taken to calling it—which meant finishing the column so that she could copy it and send it to Chicago in time for Saturday's paper. Missing Wednesday's mail meant paying the extra cost of a special delivery stamp, ten cents rather than two, a small expense, but one that seemed extravagant to Emma in their perennially pinched circumstances.

For his first column of 1890, the Bystander was taking aim at the evils wrought by "Southernism." That was his name for a philosophy that he defined as "the inherited, incarnate, unconquerable belief that 'the South,' 'the Southern people,' 'Southern life,' 'Southern society'—all Southern conditions and environments—are distinctive, anomalous, unique," making the South into a civilization unto itself.

Southernism, he told his readers, lay at the root of the white South's war on the colored race. Southernism explains "that Southern determination to 'keep the nigger down,' which has so long been announced as the ultimatum of 'Southern civilization.'" Southernism declares that "Southern prosperity" demands controlled labor. Southernism tolerates "the killing of negroes about election time," which "has become so common a thing for a score of years that nobody pays any special attention to it." Southernism is only now being recognized by people of the North as "important an element of our past as slavery," and "a much more dangerous element in our future than the difference of race." White Southerners, he said, are "prouder of this 'Southernism' than of anything else."

Among his many targets, the South remained the special favorite of the Bystander. Even in his columns about something else, the South lurked nearby, ready to leap out as an aside or comparison or rhetorical device. Occasionally, the Bystander would remind his readers that his knowledge of the South was firsthand—that he had fought in the Civil War South, spent time as a Southern prisoner of war, lived in the Reconstruction South for fifteen years, and had served as a judge on a Southern court. His novels of Southern life had sold hundreds of thousands of copies, and he still read Southern newspapers, scouring them for examples of "Southernism."

The Bystander didn't expect much from the Southern newspapers, but he was sorely disappointed by many Northern ones. He accused them of a general indifference, of caring more about attacks on Irish patriots in Ireland than on "colored patriots" in the South. Such killings would continue, he suggested, as long as the North shrugged and accepted these brutalities as part of the "Southern way of life." He would not accept them, which was why he had decided to ring in the New Year with a clarion call about "Southernism."

He worked on the column until late on Thursday morning, missing the Wednesday mail. It ran nearly three thousand words, longer than usual. To the accompaniment of a steady rain, Emma typed the final copy, and set off for the post office to buy a special delivery stamp.

TWO MONTHS LATER, on a cold Monday in early March 1890, John Harlan made his way through Washington's icy streets, heading for the Capitol and a morning of dissent about the South's latest addition to its way of life—state laws mandating separate railroad cars. At the Supreme Court's chambers, the justices prepared for a busier-than-usual day. Rulings in fifty cases would be announced. Among them was the first challenge to a two-year-old Mississippi law requiring "all railroads carrying passengers" in the state to provide "equal but separate accommodation for the white and colored races." For significance, the case ranked in the upper echelon. The Mississippi law had broken fresh ground. Not only did it impose separation, overriding the railroads' longstanding contention that *they* should set the rules for seating passengers, but it made failure to comply into a crime for railroads and their employees.

The act seemed to trigger several new constitutional questions. Among them: Did it run afoul of the Fourteenth Amendment, which said "No state shall make or enforce any law which shall abridge the privileges or immunities of citizens of the United States"? And: If used to prosecute a railroad with a line that began in one state and ended in another, did the law violate the interstate commerce clause?

Upholding the Mississippi law would most likely embolden other Southern states to follow the same path. It would shove separation into an entirely different category—not just a custom, but a legislative declaration that separate was the standard, separate was the norm. Even the Tennessee law, passed in the early 1880s, had not *mandated* separation. It had merely required that all separate first-class cars be equal.

Unlike previous "equal and separate" cases, no dramatic confrontation between passenger and conductor had triggered this legal battle. Instead, on August 1, 1888, a grand jury in Tunica County had indicted the Louisville, New Orleans & Texas Railway Company. The railroad had "willfully neglected and refused to provide equal and separate accommodations," the indictment said. The jury's verdict: guilty. Punishment: a $250 fine.

In appealing to the Supreme Court of Mississippi, the railroad essentially argued that it was trapped in an impossible situation. Its trains ran daily between Memphis and New Orleans, crossing Mississippi. To comply with the new law, the railroad either needed to put on extra cars at the border, or configure the entire train from the outset according to Mississippi's specifications. For true separation, the railroad said, it would need duplicates of everything—two passenger cars, two parlor cars, two buffet cars, two sleeping cars.

Either option, the railroad's lawyer said, interfered with interstate commerce and created an unfair burden on the railroad. Either option, he asserted, breached the principles that the U.S. Supreme Court had laid down in its unanimous *Decuir* ruling of 1878. In that case, the justices had said interstate commerce must be "free and untrammeled" in the states along the Mississippi River. A Louisiana law mandating equal accommodations, the court ruled, could not be enforced on a steamboat traveling beyond the state's borders.

The Mississippi case seemed to be a mirror image of *Decuir*: another state law, another imposition on interstate commerce, but promoting separation rather than enforcing equality. The railroad had good reason to believe that its argument was a winner, if not at the Mississippi high court than certainly at the Supreme Court.

The railroad was wrong.

JUSTICE DAVID BREWER of Kansas, a Republican, a New England native and the court's newest member with just two months' experience, had written a majority ruling in the Mississippi case that had left John Harlan perplexed. Brewer and six justices had agreed that the law did "no violation" to the interstate commerce clause.

Brewer's opinion rested on the narrowest of foundations. He had drawn a tight circle around the case, offering a lengthy list of what it was not. It was not a "question of personal insult." It was not an alleged violation of "personal rights." Most importantly, it was not for the U.S. Supreme Court to question the Supreme Court of Mississippi's interpretation. The Mississippi justices had said the law "applied solely to commerce within the state, and that construction, being the construction [of] its highest court, must be accepted as conclusive here," Brewer wrote.

Must be accepted as conclusive? The railroad's lawyer had specifically asked the Supreme Court *not* to trust the state court's conclusion. The railroad's lawyer had accused the Mississippi justices of revising the legislature's words, of substituting more tailored language to "save the Mississippi act from condemnation." Nowhere did the law limit itself to "commerce within the state," the railroad's lawyer said. That was the Mississippi court's rewrite.

Don't be fooled by this "judicial manipulation," the railroad had pleaded in its brief to the Supreme Court.

Brewer gave no weight to the railroad's arguments. He barely mentioned them.

John could not fathom how Brewer and the majority had reached their conclusions. Not only did the ruling's reasoning seem tortured but, in John's view, it defied *Decuir* while claiming—remarkably—to be mindful of the precedent. John's brief dissent could be reduced to the old adage: Good for the goose, good for the gander. If Louisiana's law had interfered with interstate commerce, then Mississippi's law did, too. "I am unable to perceive," he wrote, how *Decuir* could be read any other way.

Unlike the *Civil Rights Cases*, John had not agonized for months on what he wanted to say. He kept his dissent short, not even a thousand words. In the *Civil Rights Cases*, he had painted on a large canvass. Here, he sketched in miniature. There were "other grounds," he said, on which the Mississippi law could be seen as "repugnant" to the Constitution—a clear reference to the Fourteenth Amendment. He could have explained that repugnance. He did not.

It might have been a mistake, if John wanted to draw the public's attention. In contrast to the *Civil Rights Cases*, his dissent provoked no commentary. Newspapers did not reprint it or quote from it. A dispatch that went out from Washington, widely used around the country, treated the dissent as an afterthought: "Justice Brewer read the opinion of the court, from which Justices Harlan and Bradley briefly dissented." That was it. Not a word on their reasons for dissenting, or that Bradley had written the majority ruling in the *Civil Rights Cases*. Many papers, reflecting a weariness with the "Negro Question," treated the news like an old, familiar shoe. "Once More the Color Line," said the *Dodge City Times* in Kansas.

In New Orleans, the *Times-Democrat* cheered the majority ruling. The "negro apologists" like "Tourgee and the *Inter Ocean*" may yell about the Supreme Court's decision, but "it is comforting to know that fifty millions, more or less . . . will rejoice," the newspaper wrote. "Fifty millions" was a bald reference to the estimated number of whites in the country.

Now that the Supreme Court had spoken, the newspaper predicted, other states in the South would soon follow Mississippi's notable example and enact their own separation laws.

THE PRESIDENT'S INVITATION, addressed to the "Hon. Albion W. Tourgée," was waiting at the hotel desk when he and Emma arrived in Washington at the end of that same week in March 1890. Albion had written to Harrison before leaving Mayville, and now the president's private secretary was replying in the most encouraging way, saying the president "will be pleased if you will come at about quarter past one o'clock Saturday, and take lunch with him."

The Bystander, on the strength of his growing fame, had no shortages of doors opening to him on this hastily arranged trip. Speaker of the House Thomas Reed had asked him to come by. So had several senators. House committees would hear his testimony on two proposals he had been nurturing in his column for months. Both had bloomed into bills, drafted by the Bystander at the behest of two eager congressmen. Now the time had come to harvest his crop. He would tell the House Committee on Education about his plan to wipe out illiteracy in the South through direct federal aid to public schools. Then he would try to persuade the House Committee on Elections that congressional contests belonged under federal rather than state supervision.

He had one more item on his already full agenda: He was there to lobby against the Blair Bill, a competing education aid plan that the Bystander had derided in print as "a weak, inefficient, dangerous and unjust method of seeking to effect a very desirable end." Under New Hampshire senator Henry W. Blair's proposal, the money would go to state governments through a formula that seemed to favor white students. It also allowed for the money to be spent for other purposes, such as constructing new schools or higher education. After several previous failures, the bill had passed the House and was coming up for another vote in the Senate.

Albion had long opposed what he called the "State rights" approach to education aid. As he had told Garfield a decade earlier, he wanted to bypass state governments in the South, which were in Democratic hands. These governments could not be trusted, he said. They would divert the money, or find other ways to cheat the colored students. Send the money directly to public grammar schools, the Bystander had advised in his column. To eradicate illiteracy, we must apply "the remedy . . . to the seat of the disease," and nowhere else.

A hearty number of colored leaders and editors were dismayed by the Bystander's adamant stance. They had their own misgivings about the Blair Bill, but most were willing to take "half a loaf" over going hungry. The Bystander was unmoved. In a private letter to J. C. Price of North Carolina, recently chosen as president of a new Afro-American League, Albion's tone swung from blunt to hectoring to haughty. "I cannot see how men of your intelligence and character" can support the Blair Bill, he wrote. "A Northern man is excusable for being a fool upon these matters," he said, "but a Negro of intelligence who knows the facts is responsible to his race, to civilization and to God for mistakes so grievous and so plain."

Emma, reading the draft of Albion's letter, had tried to rein him in—to no avail. Her husband was in a lather. The Bystander told Price, "Pardon my plainness. It has fallen to my lot to speak the truth very plainly to those whom others flatter."

Albion had not lived in the South for more than a decade, yet he still felt certain he understood its conditions. Price wasn't so sure. Yes, he told the Bystander, the "Old South" and its bitter prejudices remained strong. But there was a "New Old South" that Price found heartening. He thought it would be a "calamity" to reject the Blair Bill because a few thousand dollars might go missing. "I cannot see all the evil results of the Blair Bill to which you refer," Price wrote in his friendly reply.

The Bystander had heard such arguments before. His broadsides against the Blair Bill had brought him letters of "vituperation of an amusing sort" from all over. But convinced that his plan was superior, he had published *his* entire bill in a December column, preceded by a detailed explanation of why it was superior. "If the Nation is not willing to do justice to the colored man," he wrote, "let it at least refrain from doing further injustice."

IN THE HOURS between meetings and testimony, Albion had little time to rest. To help pay for their three-week trip to the capital, he had arranged two lectures, and he still had to produce the week's Bystander column. He also had applied for a reinstatement of his long-dormant Civil War pension, gathering affidavits to justify his disability claim, and he had arranged to appear before the pension examining board while in Washington. On top of all that, when Howard University officials learned that he was in town, they began pressing him to speak at a national conference on educating colored youth, set for March 24.

Emma was worried that he would crumble from overwork, and her fears proved justified. Five days into their stay, Albion was "much exhausted and very nervous," she wrote in her diary. His ailing condition even made the newspaper. "Judge and Mrs. Tourgee are in the city," the *Evening Star* reported. "Judge Tourgee is in poor health."

But he rallied. He did not want to miss the Senate vote on the Blair Bill. On Thursday, March 20, he and Emma sat in the gallery, smiling, as the bill went down to a surprise defeat. Pleased but wobbly, Albion returned to their rooms. He spent the rest of the day in bed.

Their last week in Washington was no less a whirlwind. He met with Speaker Reed for a third time, discussing the long odds of moving his two bills forward. He spoke at the colored youth conference, where he fired off a good line about his years of civil rights work, saying he "could not be classed as an educator of colored young men, although he might be said to be an educator of white old men."

An *Evening Star* reporter was there, and wrote afterward that the "well-known author" seemed a bit frail. "He is still lame and leans heavily on a cane."

BY LATE MARCH, Albion and Emma were back in Mayville, where they found an unusual invitation in the mail. The organizers of the "first Mohonk Conference on the Negro Question" wanted Judge Tourgée to join their discussion at Albert Smiley's famous lakeside lodge in upstate New York. Mr. Smiley, a Quaker, had held previous meetings on "the Indian Question." This conference's focus would be "the uplifting of the Negro through his Christianization and education," and it would convene the first week in June. The prestigious list of confirmed attendees included former president Hayes; former Supreme Court justice Strong; the former director of the long-extinct Freedmen's Bureau, and other prominent names from both the North and South. Would he and Mrs. Tourgée please come? All expenses would be paid.

There was one rather large obstacle, as Albion soon learned: No people of color were invited. The organizers seemed to feel that their absence would allow a freer discussion. Before arriving at the conference, the Reverend Lyman Abbott explained why it wasn't necessary to hear their voices. "A patient is not invited to the consultation of the doctors on his case," Abbott had written in the *Christian Union*, the newspaper he was serving as editor.

Several editors of the colored press reacted with scorn to Abbott's metaphor. It was bad enough to keep harping on the "Negro Question," as if people of color were a problem to be solved. But casting whites as medical experts, studying the colored race as if it were a disease? While a patient may not attend "the consultation," wrote William H. Anderson in the *Detroit Plaindealer*, he is "always questioned" about his symptoms, "and his answers control the diagnosis." The editor of the *New York Age*, T. Thomas Fortune, was even more incredulous. The nation had "20,000 Afro-American teachers," twenty bishops and one hundred editors, he wrote. Surely someone with their firsthand knowledge could help the "white doctors" cloistered "a thousand miles distant at Lake Mohonk." Even Fortune's use of "Afro-American" was a challenge to the established order, a rejection of labels ("colored" and "negro") that relied on color to describe and set apart an entire class of people.

A few other invitees were boycotting. Albion thought about joining them, but curious, decided to go. Anderson gave him some advice, showing his disdain for the event with a mocking bit of wordplay on the venue's name. "Don't be silent at Podunk if views contrary to justice are likely to prevail," he said. Anderson hardly needed to worry. To make sure no one could miss his reason for coming, Albion had titled his main speech: "The Negro's View of the Race Problem."

The conference participants had chosen Hayes as their chairman. As president, he had ended Reconstruction, prompting a split in his party that he could never repair. Now, nearly a decade later, he listened intently as Albion, rotund and mustached, delivered a friendly but firm reprimand in a speech lasting more than an hour.

Much of what this august gathering believed about the negro "condition" was rooted in ignorance, Albion told them. "The man who wear the shoe knows better than anybody else just where it pinches," he said. "We wise white people may know more about remedies . . . but the Negro owns the bunion, and his testimony is worth more than that of all the rest of mankind" in understanding where it hurts.

Later that night, writing in his diary, Hayes recorded his review. "He is an orator—pungent, dramatic, original and daring. He rebuked the churches, the North, the South, and stood for the negro." Elsewhere in the lodge, Emma was writing in her diary as well. This time, she had no reservations about her husband's tone. "Albion spoke this morning and it was the sensation of the Conference," she wrote. "He covered himself with honor."

HONOR WAS NOT among the words that Louis Martinet had in mind a month later as Louisiana's lawmakers rushed to enact a "Separate Car Act" in the closing hours of their session. Just as the *Times-Democrat* had forecast after the Supreme Court ruling that upheld Mississippi's law, a bill had materialized when the legislature opened for business in May 1890. Described benignly as "an act to promote the comfort of passengers on railways," House Bill No. 42 had passed the House over the protests of several members, who decried the idea of enshrining "Jim Crow cars" into state law. The bill then sat motionless for a month until, finally, it sprang from a Senate committee in early July, gathering speed amid a throng of white cheerleaders.

Long before that, Martinet had been working on multiple fronts to derail it. His main weapon: the *New Orleans Crusader*, a weekly founded the year before under Martinet's leadership. But Martinet wasn't content to write editorials denouncing the "iniquitous piece of legislation." On May 24, he and sixteen other members of the American Citizens' Equal Rights Association journeyed to Baton Rouge to appeal directly to lawmakers. The ACERA group was a mix of familiar names—Pinchback, Trévigne, Auguste—as well as new ones from the younger generation, including Martinet and forty-year-old Rodolphe Desdunes, a customs clerk and cigar merchant who was making a name for himself as a *Crusader* contributor.

Like *les gens de couleur libres* of 1814 and 1864, they came armed with a petition. Characterizing the bill as "unconstitutional, un-American, unjust, dangerous and against sound public policy," they sought allies among white legislators while urging colored lawmakers to stand fast. "Citizenship is national and has no color," their petition declared.

Senator Henry Demas of New Orleans amplified their arguments when he rose to speak against the bill on July 8. As a white legislator, he was proud of Louisiana's progress since the end of the war. Sharply drawing a line between the two races, he said, "destroys that harmony which should exist at all times between them," and puts "an undeserved stigma on the Negro."

Demas reminded his colleagues that Louisiana's color line was blurry—that "owing to the intermingling of the races," it is sometimes difficult "to determine—from a standpoint of color—the white from the Negro." Reflecting his own bias, he said that forcing the cultured colored class to share an inferior car with the "worst class of the Negro element . . . would be an unmerited rebuke upon the colored men of finer sensibilities."

The Senate fell three votes short of passing the bill. It looked like victory, but the political winds and white newspapers were blowing hard for a reconsideration. If a "New Old South" existed, it had not taken up residence in the offices of the *Times-Democrat*. Southern whites are insisting, the newspaper wrote, "that the two races shall live separate and distinct from each other in all things, with separate schools, separate hotels, and separate cars." They want this not out of "hostility to the negroes," but "to prevent any such dangerous doctrine as social equality, even in its mildest form. . . . We cannot afford to surrender anything in this case."

The bill had become a pawn in a Senate feud over other legislation, and there was no stopping its revival. Despite several spirited speeches against reconsideration, it passed by a wide margin. Martinet sent a hasty telegram to the governor, the only man left who could prevent the Separate Car Act from becoming law.

New Orleans, July 10, 1890.

Gov. F. T. Nicholls, Baton Rouge:

Governor, thousands good and true men petition you to veto separate car bill.

L. A. Martinet

Martinet's appeal failed. The governor signed the bill that same night. Martinet reprinted his telegram in that week's *Crusader*, along with an audacious promise. "We'll make a case, a test case, and bring it before the Federal Courts," he wrote in an editorial. "No such case has been fairly made or presented."

They would be raising money to finance their cause, starting now.

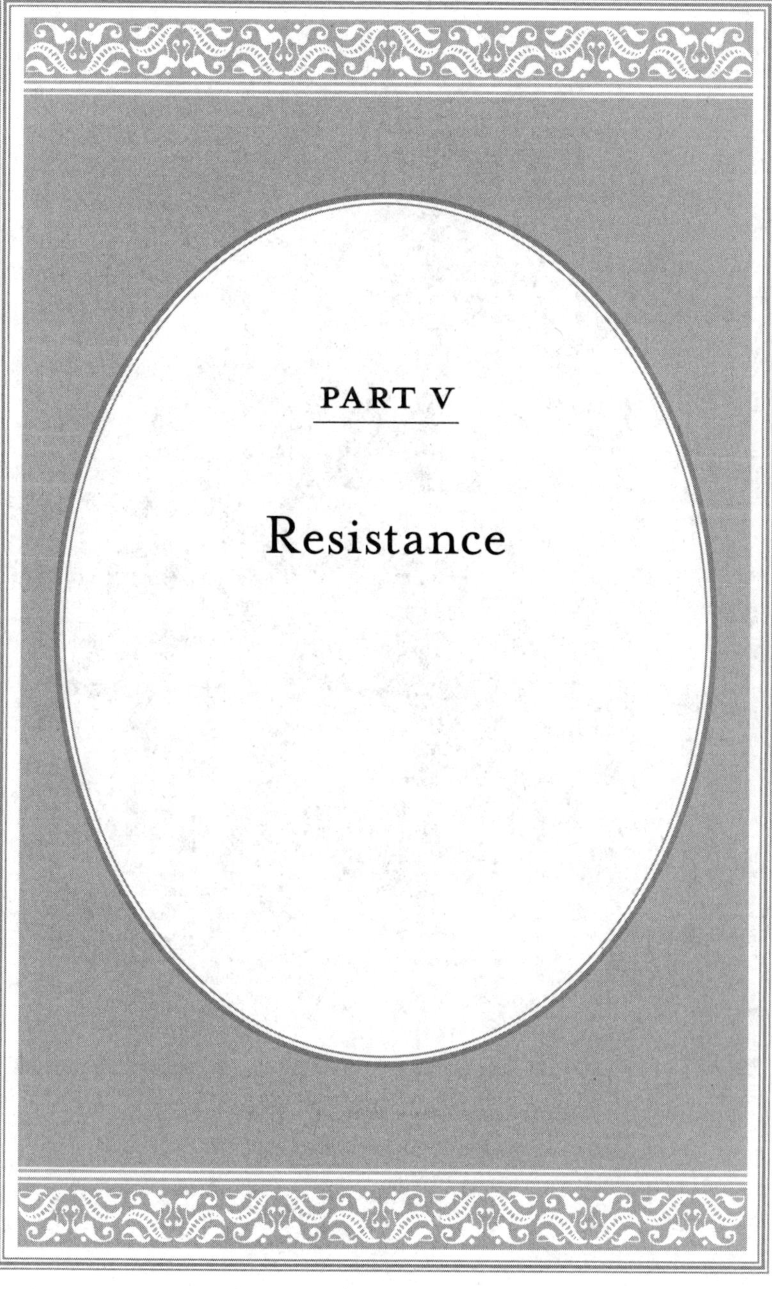

PART V

Resistance

Making waves: Tourgée in his library, circa 1890

(Chautauqua County Historical Society)

19

"In Behalf of 7,999,999 of My Race"

New Orleans, Mayville, Detroit,
and Washington, 1890–1891

How, exactly, does an intelligent, infuriated group of men transform its indignation into a lawsuit? Louis Martinet had hinted at a strategy, an argument, in his *Crusader* editorial vowing a legal challenge to the Separate Car Act. His group would claim, he said, that the new law invaded "the right to a person to travel through the states unmolested." Was there such a right, under federal or state law? Had such a right ever been asserted before?

Martinet was a lawyer, but he had no particular expertise in constitutional matters. He had served in various federal posts, none in the courts, and then had secured for himself the position of civil law notary, an influential cog in the New Orleans legal system. Unlike notaries in most states, the Louisiana version didn't just witness and sign documents. They ran the show, acting as impartial arbiters for creating contracts of all kinds—property transfers, loans, wills, acts of incorporation, marriage covenants. They resolved disputes, drafted the paperwork, and maintained the records, like a branch office of the courthouse. Martinet's notarial practice shared space with the *Crusader* in his cramped Vieux Carré office at 117 Exchange Alley.

Notarial work had little to do with civil rights, but it gave Martinet connections in the city's legal circles. Meanwhile, other members of his civil rights organization, ACERA, were taking steps of their own. One was young Eli Freeman, another Straight University attendee, class of 1884, and now a man of ambition in the Kansas town of Manhattan. Not quite thirty years old, the Louisiana native was holding down two education jobs, serving as principal of Manhattan's colored schools while teaching in the younger grades. A Kansas newspaper had called him "one of the most intelligent and thoughtful colored men of the state."

Freeman was back in New Orleans for the summer, visiting family, and had gotten swept up in the outcry over the Separate Car Act. Freeman thought: Why not ask the famous Bystander for help? On August 4, 1890, three weeks after Martinet's editorial, Freeman scrawled out a letter to "Mr. Albion W. Tourgee, Mayville, N.Y." "Dear Sir," he began. "You are perhaps aware of the class legislation that has recently been enacted by the law-makers of this state. It provides separate first-class coaches on all roads for persons of color."

Preliminaries done, Freeman marched to his point. "We feel very indignant at the presence of such a law and propose to test its constitutionality in the federal courts. But before we proceed, Mr. Tourgee, we would seek your advice. Only a few lines will suffice. And now in behalf of the 7,999,999 of my race whose interest and whose rights you have ever championed, I thank you. . . . An early reply would greatly oblige."

In Mayville, the Bystander was only too happy to offer his suggestions. The law was a great insult to the colored people, he replied. Of course it should be challenged. Good people everywhere had a stake in defeating this odious act. Spread ACERA's fundraising efforts to other states, he urged. Take up a "dime collection" for the legal costs of testing the act's constitutionality. He was confident that a well-planned, well-argued case would succeed if it should end up at the Supreme Court.

Freeman's teaching duties in Kansas limited his involvement in creating the test case. By late August, he was back in Manhattan for the opening of school. He would help organize a meeting there, rally support, take up that dime collection. Anything to help ACERA in its fight. But others, in New Orleans, would have to be the ones to carry it forward.

AT THORHEIM, THE BYSTANDER had a lot on his mind, and not a lot of time to think about Louisiana's Separate Car Act. In the final weeks of August 1890, during a spate of showers that drenched Mayville for five days running, a new deluge of legal threats washed up at the big house on the shores of Chautauqua Lake.

The Bystander's fame had come with unexpected consequences. When Tourgée was clearly down and almost out, his creditors had little choice other than patience. Now that he was enjoying a modicum of success, several had renewed their old claims. It didn't help, ironically, that federal pension examiners had approved his disability application, prompting a flood of newspaper stories about the famous writer being awarding thirty dollars a month plus $2,519.20 in retroactive benefits, from the end of his Civil War service in 1863. "A handsome sum," several accounts had labeled it, accompanied by a few barbed headlines like the one in the *Pittsburgh Press*: "The Celebrated Novelist Can Spend His Declining Years in Ease."

Ease? With thirty dollars a month? The newspapers had no idea what his "declining years" were like. He was fifty-two years old, in poor health, yoked to his writing desk for hours on end, except in summer and early fall, when he sometimes granted himself late-afternoon breaks for a few hours of fishing on Chautauqua Lake. He was months behind on his latest novel, and the publisher was making noises about breach of contract. A minor threat, but one that he sought to snuff out with a stiffly worded letter. The Bystander was not going to be bullied. The editors at Robert Bonner's Sons would get their manuscript, if they would leave him to it.

More worrisome were the creditors trying to collect on long-ago debts. One, seeking repayment of $2,500, had aimed his legal efforts at Emma, accusing her of hiding the couple's assets under her name. The Tourgées' lawyer was trying his best to fend off the attack, but the subpoenas and writs kept trickling in, like a leaky faucet that wouldn't be fixed. Determined to protect Emma, Tourgée himself had spent hours drafting a motion, laying out the reasons why the court had no business putting Emma through such an ordeal.

While the two sides were battling over her in court, she stayed away. On September 1, that strategy took an unexpected turn. A county judge, unhappy with her absence, found her in contempt of court. He ordered her to appear, threatening her with thirty-five days in jail and a thirty-five-dollar fine. A second judge upheld the order. Emma's lawyer was appealing, but she found the process nerve-wracking. When she saw the press clippings about the case, she became frantic. Some newspapers had her behind bars already, like some sort of common criminal. "Mrs. Tourgee Goes to Prison," headlined the *Evening Star* in Washington. Even the *Inter Ocean*, the Bystander's newspaper, got it wrong, saying "Mrs. A.W. Tourgee in Jail."

It was embarrassing enough to have their financial woes on public display again, but these headlines were more than Emma could bear. She wanted to sue. Their lawyer, Adelbert Moot, was sympathetic, but he thought a series of expensive lawsuits in multiple states wasn't the answer. He favored swallowing hard and doing nothing. "From experience," he wrote, "I know how keenly we feel such newspaper thrusts, but I also know from experience how little they affect us in the estimation of our friends, or the public, in the end, and how quick they are forgotten."

Emma swallowed hard. She was trying hard to hold herself together, but some days, Thorheim itself felt like a prison. Her diary entries had a monotonous rhythm—copied a chapter of Albion's new book, copied the Bystander column, copied a letter. Copied, copied, copied. There was no escaping the work—or their "troubles," as she called them—for long. "Wind blew so Albion could not go fishing," she wrote in her diary on a Friday in late September, "and it upset him so he could do nothing. So the day was lost."

In their straits, they could not afford many lost days.

FOR TOURGÉE, WRITING the Bystander offered another kind of refuge. Once a week, he could retreat to the column, where he had the freedom to express himself about nearly any subject he deemed worthy of scrutiny. The week after the "lost" day, he returned to his favorite topic—the South—and the unsettling discussions in some Republican quarters about how the party could break the Democrats' domination of Southern politics.

Supposedly "wise and learned" men were saying, the Bystander wrote in his column for September 27, 1890, that the party needed to "cut itself loose" from the negro to become "respectable" in the eyes of Southern whites. Emphasize economic issues, the Wise Men were saying, and "drop the negro, ignore his cause and forget his claims." Give the party a Southern face to go along with its Northern one.

The Bystander vigorously shook his head. It wouldn't work. He knew these Southern whites—at least the ones aligned with the Democrats. They would never forget what the Republicans had wrought. "The negro, *as a citizen*, is a creation of the Republican party," the Bystander wrote. Even if the party were to cast out every negro in the South, take away the negro's right to vote, and require every party stalwart to present proof of "unmixed Caucasian ancestry," he warned, it would still be reviled as "the black Republican party."

Imagine, he said, trying to explain this "cutting loose" idea to the party's colored members. It would be bewildering, beyond comprehension. To illuminate his point, he offered a hypothetical conversation between a "Wise Man" and a "colored voter." The Wise Man suggests the colored voter might "go Democratic" on some issues, such as tariffs and free trade. The colored voter can't believe what he's hearing. He says, wait, we're both Republicans. We agree that I am mistreated in the South. That I'm denied the same access as whites to the ballot box. That I'm forced to ride in a "Jim Crow" car. Yet you think I should worry about "free trade?" What do I care about free trade unless I have free speech, equal opportunity, and a free ballot?

The Republican Party, the Bystander wrote, had linked its destiny to "human freedom, the right of citizenship, equal opportunity." Those principles had defined the party since its founding in 1854. "Every act for which it can claim credit, every success it has achieved, every bright page in its history, is a direct result" of these beliefs, the Bystander proclaimed. Abandon them now, and the party would crumble in self-betrayal.

The party could not divide itself, and conquer.

THE FIRST WAVE of speculation surged forth within hours, before the funeral arrangements could be announced, before Justice Samuel Miller's casket could be carried to the Supreme Court for a final, solemn tribute. The news of the justice's late-night death, and early rumors about his successor, clacked out over the telegraph wires simultaneously on Tuesday, October 14, 1890, a Washington pas de deux, mourning and machination in graceless tandem.

For Michigan's senators, the unexpected vacancy revived the previous year's dashed hopes. Harrison had all but promised that Henry Brown or Alfred Russell would be the first in line for the next opening. At the time, a retirement was the most likely scenario. Three justices, including Miller, were in their seventies and eligible for a full pension. But none had showed any inclination to bow out. Then, three days before the term's opening session, Miller had collapsed.

The early word on a replacement: Harrison had ruled out anyone from "south of the Ohio River," as the *Detroit Free Press* correspondent put it. "Although of Southern blood," the correspondent wrote of the Virginia-born Harrison, the president "does not take kindly to the people of the South, and the feeling he bears for them is heartily reciprocated."

For Henry Brown, at home in Detroit, the *Free Press* account had one other eye-catching sentence: "The death of Justice Miller may prove to be Judge Brown's opportunity to win the gown which he came so near receiving recently." No mention of Alfred Russell. Did the *Free Press* have some inside knowledge? Were the old rivals no longer in competition?

Over the next month, as the newspapers bandied about a dozen names, the president "was said" to favor the attorney general, his former law partner, and was only holding back because of rumblings of Senate discontent. Another favorite "was thought" to be Wisconsin senator John Spooner, about to lose his Senate seat. As for Brown, he "was believed" to be the president's preference if the other choices didn't work out.

On November 21, a *Free Press* headline declared that the president had made up his mind. "Mr. Alfred Russell Said to Have Been Selected." What?

The missing man, suddenly the victor? The *Free Press* correspondent thought so, but like a gambler relying on the questionable word of racetrack touts, he was hedging his bets. "The intelligence has reached here to-night by way of New York, which, if true, would indicate that Michigan is at last to be honored with a place on the United States Supreme bench," he wrote. "The lucky man is to be Alfred Russell of Detroit, and the gentleman who furnishes the news says he is giving a straight tip."

If true. This "intelligence" from New York, whatever its accuracy, seemed to be a calculated plant from the Russell camp. A "straight tip" would have come straight from the White House, or from one of Michigan's senators, Stockbridge or McMillan. The White House said nothing to give credence to the *Free Press* story. Michigan's senators stayed silent, too.

It looked as if there might be hope left for Brown after all.

ON A CHILLY SATURDAY at the end of November, Senator Francis Stockbridge went to the White House to put his full weight behind Brown. Congress was reconvening in two days, making the president's decision imminent. Stockbridge couldn't read Harrison's mind, but he had read the papers. If Harrison was bent on nominating his law partner, there was nothing Stockbridge could do. But if the president wanted a skilled jurist with a reputation for fairness, Brown was his man. Brown's book on admiralty law had cemented his preeminence in that field, expertise that the court lacked. His party loyalty was unquestioned, and he had the support of his circuit judge—a Tennessean and a Democrat—who had spoken personally with Harrison on Brown's behalf.

Afterward, Stockbridge told reporters that he found the president "well disposed toward Judge Brown." But then, Harrison had said much the same a year earlier before naming Brewer. One thing seemed clear, though: Despite the "intelligence" from New York, Russell's candidacy seemed to be going nowhere.

Senator John Spooner of Wisconsin was the wild card this time. He was a Harrison ally, and in need of a new job. If the president chose to rescue Spooner with a nomination, disappointment would be Brown's destiny once again. Fortunately for Brown, Spooner's ambitions were more political than judicial. When Harrison offered him the seat in mid-December, the senator took a week to think it over, and then quietly said no.

Brown was in his chambers on December 23, drafting an opinion, when he learned of his nomination. He was elated, and amazed. He immediately headed home to tell Carry. A *Washington Post* correspondent found him there a few hours later, in the center of a congratulatory clamor, surrounded by "a party of young ladies who were tugging at his coat," playfully measuring him for the judicial robe that he hoped to be wearing soon.

After preparing himself for defeat, Brown's spirits were soaring. But as he chatted with the *Post* reporter, he did not want to sound too eager. "This upsets my winter plans a little," Brown told the *Post* reporter. "I had thought so little of this turn of affairs that my wife and I had planned a long visit to Cuba."

The reporter was impressed with the Browns' "palatial home," which he judged to be "the handsomest" in Detroit. The stately mansion on Jefferson Avenue was built over several years in the mid-1880s, financed by Carry's inheritance. Brown loved its comforts, its memories. Leaving it behind would be hard, he confessed. "I will take a residence in Washington," he assured the reporter, "and presume that in a social way our life will be no less pleasant."

The nominee caught himself. He had gone too far. He had *presumed*. He did not yet have the job. He took a step back, a small step. "I am sure that I shall like Washington, but perhaps it is not in good taste to say much of this until I am confirmed by the Senate."

UNLIKE HARLAN, who had to defend himself as a Republican latecomer, Brown provoked no opposition. On December 29, six days after the nomination and the brief Christmas recess, the committee sped Brown's name to the floor. Unanimous approval followed hours later. No public hearing, no testimony, no debate. It could not have gone any faster.

In Detroit, the Browns prepared for their move with keen anticipation and more than a little sadness. They were "much attached to Detroit," he wrote years later, and "if the duties of the new office were not so congenial to my taste as those of a district judge, it was a position of far more dignity, was better paid and was infinitely more gratifying to one's ambition."

Ambition. Carry had it, too. That's what her sister Isabelle emphasized in recounting the story of Henry's rise. "She was quite ambitious as he, and wished him to 'go on the bench,'" Isabelle wrote. Carry's inheritance income had allowed Henry "to give up his fine practice, and begin his ascent." He was always grateful for this good fortune, Isabelle said, explaining "that without the help that came to him through my father, he might never have realized their ambition, a place on the Supreme Bench."

Ascent, dignity, money, stature. All the goals that Brown had laid out for himself as a young lawyer in Detroit. All the ambitions he had once worried he would never achieve.

ON NEW YEAR'S EVE, with barely a day's organization, three hundred guests toasted Michigan's first Supreme Court justice at the Detroit Club. Thumbing their noses at winter, the Club's managers had tracked down tropical plants and miniature palms. The guests had their names announced, and shook the hand of the beaming Brown. Alfred Russell was among them.

The train ride to Washington was no less grand. Courtesy of Michigan's former governor, lumber tycoon Russell Alger, Brown and his entourage had traveled in luxury, aboard Alger's private railroad car, the "Michigan." It was a Pullman Palace Car Company coach, outfitted to Alger's specifications. The car's name was everywhere. They dined on "Michigan" china, stirred their coffee with "Michigan" spoons, slept on "Michigan" linens.

Carry had made the trip, with her two sisters and their husbands. A niece and a nephew came, too, along with several friends. Others joined them in Washington. One member of the group stood out. That was Richard Bush—"Old Bush," he called himself—a bailiff from Detroit's federal court. He had been in Brown's office when the telegram arrived with news of his appointment. "Richard," the judge had said, grinning and grasping the colored man's hand, "I will not take my seat on the bench unless you promise to be present at the ceremony." As the bailiff later told the *Free Press*, he was speechless, his eyes filling with tears. He stammered, "What . . . Old Bush?" Brown had replied, "Yes sir, you must be there."

On the morning of January 6, 1891, Bush arrived at the Supreme Court chamber, so crowded with Michigan well-wishers that most could not get in. But arrangements had been made. The court's marshal escorted Bush to his reserved seat, next to Mrs. Brown. "Old Bush" watched with pride as Brown—in another justice's borrowed robe, so large and loose fitting that his ears seemed to disappear in its folds—took his oath as the nation's fifty-second justice.

NEARLY A YEAR had passed since the *Crusader*'s vow of a "test case," but by the summer of 1891, Martinet and his allies were no closer to bringing their promised lawsuit. They had no legal strategy. No lawyer. No consensus on how to proceed. The ACERA group, mired in dissension and ennui, was essentially defunct. If nowhere was a destination, they had arrived.

Martinet hadn't given up, though. He and Rodolphe Desdunes were keeping the idea of a "test case" alive in the pages of the *Crusader*. For his July 4, 1891, column, Desdunes had issued his own declaration of independence, urging a new movement to defeat the tyranny of separation. "Among the many schemes devised by Southern statesmen to divide the races," he wrote, "none is so audacious and insulting as the one which provides separate cars for black and white people on the railways running through the State. It is like a slap in the face of every member of the black race, whether he has the full measure or only one-eighth of that blood."

The full measure or only one-eighth. In less than half a sentence, Desdunes had deftly surfaced one of the *Crusader's* most uncomfortable questions. Did the newspaper speak for anyone other than *les gens de couleur*? A look at the editorial masthead was all it took to see that the power behind the throne rested in the hands of men with French names: Joubert, Jacques, Labat, Martinet. None of the principal editors and writers had "the full measure" of African blood. Their race was mixed, their skin color lighter, their heritage proud, their anger generations in the making. They had been born free, before the Civil War, and while their rights had been circumscribed by custom and law, they had never felt slavery's brutal weight. For decades, many of *les gens* had done their best to distance themselves from "the Negroes."

Now, under the mandate of Louisiana's Separate Car Act, any "colored" passenger would have to ride separately. What defined "colored"? The law did not say. But if one drop of blood was all it took, well, so be it. Desdunes was calling on the entire "black race" to stand together, fight together. If they accepted this "badge of Negro inferiority," he wrote, they could expect separation's spread into other sectors of society. They must resist. "It is our fault," he scolded, if we do not "exhaust every legal remedy which the law holds out against such evils."

ACERA had made a start, raising some money and seeking advice. The famed Albion W. Tourgée had been among those who had offered suggestions, he wrote, but the effort had floundered for "a want of proper and effective direction." Desdunes urged the formation of a new group, led by men with "nerve," men willing to carry justice's banner, just as their predecessors had done in 1815 and 1864. They might fight and lose, but fight they must. "We are not afraid of the end," he declared. "Our cause is a just one."

A month later, frustrated by a naysayer's gloomy letter in the *Crusader*, the columnist responded with an even more vigorous call to arms. The naysayer had described the Jim Crow fight as "forlorn." The courts had already spoken, the naysayer said. Desdunes's rallying cries would not succeed because people knew better than to rally to a hopeless cause.

The naysayer's pessimism only added fuel to Desdunes's passionate ire. Defenders of liberty have "always had a hard road to travel," he reminded his readers. Think of Patrick Henry, John Adams, Garrison, Sumner. All had faced naysayers. None had given up. It was certainly possible that the courts might not be friendly to a test case, Desdunes said. But courts were not temples governed by scripture. They were run by men, and men can change their minds.

There was "nothing forlorn" about their cause, Desdunes wrote. This was a "*guerre à mort*." A war to the death.

AS AN AVID CONSUMER of the colored press, Albion Tourgée was coming to think of the *Crusader* as a new beacon of bravery in a landscape dominated by timidity. In a column about the latest wave of lynching and violent attacks in the South—"fifteen killed and two whipped in one week, in four or five states"—the Bystander had stridently trumpeted his disappointment in much of what he was reading. "There are more than one hundred newspapers in the country owned and edited by colored men," he wrote in his column for August 15, 1891, and yet "not one of them has ever had the courage and the enterprise to learn and publish the names of those scores of victims" slaughtered in a Mississippi massacre a few years before.

The Bystander's blanket denunciation did not sit well with some of those colored editors. Several sent letters to Mayville, objecting to his rebuke. The editor of the *Richmond Planet*, while applauding the Bystander's "stirring articles" on behalf of colored people, wanted him to know that the *Planet* had published many a piece on lynching. Louis Martinet took a different tack. He suggested the Bystander might be more charitable if he better understood the dangers that an outspoken colored editor faced.

Martinet had put his finger on a natural tension between Tourgée and his admirers. Yes, the Bystander had spent fifteen hard, sometimes harrowing years in the South. Yes, he was a champion of the colored race, revered by many. But he could not stand in their shoes. He was now living in the North, he was white, and he could write what he liked in the *Inter Ocean*, without fear of a midnight visitor or some other threat to life and limb.

Characteristically, the Bystander was making no apologies. In his private replies to several editors, as well as publicly in his column, Tourgée readily acknowledged their critical comments—and then hurled himself into a brasher, broader indictment. "The Bystander meant no reproach to anyone," he wrote in his September 12 column, and "certainly not to one who has shown the courage of the editor of the *Crusader*." But, he said, "What is the use of watchmen if they do not sound an alarm? And how shall a race reach a higher level of manhood if its leaders are silent when their rights are trampled upon?"

The Bystander leavened his harsh views with a layer of humility. In his younger days, he wrote, he did not join with the abolitionists, and "none of their glory reflects on him." But he was not backing off from his overall critique. "I believe I fully realize the difficulty of the task before the colored race—more fully than many of the race themselves," he declared in his private reply to the *Richmond Planet* editor.

He respected the intrepid *Planet* editor, he wrote, and had intended no insult to him personally. "At the same time," Tourgée told him, "I meant every word I wrote on the subject—I always do, for that matter—and I fully believe the time has come for the race to stand up and be counted in its own behalf. It was given freedom; it must conquer liberty. Not necessarily with the sword—though a good many will have to die for their rights before they are fully won—but the main thing is to convince the world that they are in earnest and are ready to die if need be."

Looking at the present crop of colored leaders, Tourgée harbored severe doubts about their capabilities and motivations. "The truth is," he told the *Planet* editor, "a good many" of your race "think too much of being considered 'good niggers,' rather than true men." Where were the radicals? The risk takers? The colored race, he wrote in his Bystander column two weeks later, was "advertising very urgently for heroes—men who think more of their race than of themselves—and the most important question . . . is whether the race will be able to supply this demand."

Tourgée favored fresh leadership. Younger members of the post-emancipation generation had a better understanding of the current crisis, he said, and could bring to light "the essential injustice and inequality of conditions" in the South. "Remember," he told the *Planet* editor, "the Northern people are tired of killings. They have become an old story." To counter this indifference, the Bystander had been plucking stories of prejudice and cruelty from Southern newspapers, and making them a regular feature in his column. He wanted others to do the same. He wanted a cascade, a crescendo, a chorus of strong voices.

Silence was the servant of oppression.

THE *CRUSADER* EDITORS had succeeded in spurring action. On September 1, a group had gathered in the newspaper's offices to discuss "legal resistance" to the Jim Crow car law. From that meeting had emerged the "Citizens' Committee to Test the Constitutionality of the Separate Car Law"—or, as the eighteen members called themselves in their appeals to the French-speaking community, the *Comité des Citoyens*. French names dominated the committee's letterhead, and the crossover with the newspaper's leadership was plain for all to see: Martinet, Esteves, Joubert, Labat, Luscy, Desdunes.

Four days later, the committee's manifesto appeared in the *Crusader*. Invoking decades of broken promises, the appeal promised "an earnest effort to vindicate the cause of equal rights and American manhood." While some were saying that a test case would be a fool's errand, that the courts had declared themselves, Martinet and company were determined to prove otherwise. Echoing Desdunes's column, their appeal declared: "We ask the people not to be discouraged by such reports; they have been invented and put in circulation by the enemy to stop the wheels of progress. Our friends hold very different views, and we are justified in asserting that the chances of success are at least on par with the dangers of defeat."

One of those friends was Albion W. Tourgée. He, too, had come to think of the courts as the best route to progress. Legislatures were color-controlled, and the controlling color was white. But the law could be color-blind—in theory, at least—and perhaps the courts could undo these malicious insults to liberty known as the Jim Crow car laws. That's why, the Bystander argued in his column, "there will never be any other question for the colored man" until his rights are "enforced and protected by the courts." That's why Tourgée was eager, when asked for a second time, to give his advice to Martinet and his committee.

And they were just as eager to hear it. By early October 1891, the Bystander was offering to join the legal team, without taking a fee, and Martinet was offering to put him at the head of it. "The revival of interest in the Jim Crow car matter is owing to you more than to anyone else," Martinet wrote on October 5. "We know we have a friend in you and we know your ability is beyond question. We know you will give more time and attention to the preparation of the case than any other, and you shall have control from beginning to end."

MARTINET COULD HARDLY believe his good fortune. The Bystander himself, Albion Tourgée, in charge of their legal strategy! Bursting with ideas, Tourgée had already sent Martinet a variety of scenarios and questions. But as Martinet read over Tourgée's list, he came to a sobering realization: Their new legal strategist from the North needed some tutoring on the racial history and customs of New Orleans, a place he had never visited.

Tourgée had asked, for example, about the possibility of recruiting a woman, fair-skinned enough to pass for white, and sending her to the whites-only car. Martinet, while willing to consider the idea, didn't think it would work. Most likely, he said, the conductors would not bother her. "Walking up and down our principal thoroughfare, Canal Street," he told Tourgée, "if you were not informed, you would be sure to pick out the white for colored, and the colored for white." People "of tolerably fair complexion, even if unmistakably colored, enjoy here a large degree of immunity from the accursed prejudice. In this respect, New Orleans differs greatly" from other parts of Louisiana and neighboring Mississippi, he wrote.

Martinet agreed with Tourgée that they needed to engineer an arrest rather than bring a lawsuit. A civil suit involving a state law might never make it to the justices in Washington. But a criminal conviction would allow them to file a writ of habeas corpus, arguing unlawful detention. That was the "speediest" route to having their appeal heard in the federal courts.

Designing the test case required meticulous planning and vigilance. Whether they chose a light-skinned woman, or a man with "the full measure of African blood," their cause would be lost at the outset without the right sort of arrest. A "breach of peace" charge was useless, Tourgée told Martinet. They were challenging the constitutionality of the Separate Car

Act, so they needed their passenger to be charged under Section II of the law, which made it a crime for any rider to insist on "going into a coach or compartment to which by race he does not belong."

The situation demanded a passenger with tact, Martinet said, someone who could resist firmly but calmly, without angering the crew. There was no point in a struggle. They wanted an arrest, not an injury. "I would try it myself," the *Crusader* editor told Tourgée, "but I am one of those whom a fair complexion favors. I go everywhere, in all public places, though well-known all over the city, and never is anything said to me. On the cars it would be the same thing."

COULD THEY ENSURE the "right" arrest? It would be difficult, but they did not have to resolve all these questions now. Nor did they need to risk everything on one attempt. They could send out several passengers, on multiple railways. Their strategy would evolve, once they had their legal team in place. For now, momentum was the important thing.

Martinet waited several days to mail his letter. He wanted to be able to tell Tourgée that the Citizens' Committee had met and approved his role as lead counsel. In the meantime, the *Inter Ocean* had arrived, with the Bystander's October 3 column praising the New Orleans fight and the people leading it. Martinet was beyond grateful for the Bystander's public endorsement. "Your mention of the *Crusader* helps us a great deal," he wrote. "People from far and near send for the paper . . . it strengthens the backbone of our friends, and confounds our enemies."

Martinet also had read, with appreciation and astonishment, the words of praise the Bystander had written about him. He did not feel entirely comfortable with being placed on such a pedestal. "I thank you sincerely for the kind things you say of me," Martinet told Tourgée, "but do not call me a hero. I am a plain, ordinary man. I prefer that. In that way, I'll not disappoint you."

Intent on deepening their budding relationship, Martinet felt it was important to make a confession. He had once strayed from the Republican Party, he told Tourgée, attaching himself for a time to the Democrats.

He had fallen for the sales pitch, believing that "a division of the Negro vote" might provide the colored race "a measure of protection" and make the South a more "habitable" place. It had worked for a while, Martinet wrote. The Democrats, firmly entrenched in the state's elected offices, did appoint a few men of color to various jobs. But then, a sharp reversal. A reactionary faction, proclaiming "white supremacy all along the line," began waging "a constant warfare" against the party's more liberal members.

This poisonous atmosphere had led to a horrifying new round of white-on-black outrages, Martinet said. "I had seen many mean and cruel things on the part of the Southern whites, yet I had not seen the worse side of their nature—their inborn and ingrained hypocrisy and treachery." With his eyes now opened, he had resigned from the Democrats with a public letter, returned to the Republican fold, and founded the *Crusader*.

"All this, my dear Sir, will perhaps burden you," Martinet told Tourgée, "but I thought best that you should know them."

IN WASHINGTON, the court's newest justice did more than participate in the capital's social whirl. Henry Brown dove into it. He was particularly impressed by the diplomatic corps, "which contains representatives of the most refined society of all the leading countries of the world." When the invitations came to the season's dinner parties and receptions, Brown sent back his RSVPs with relish. Often, Carry joined him, but not always. Her fragile health sometimes forced her to bed for days at a time. Brown feared her condition would leave her an invalid. His friends noted his devotion to her, but also a despair that bordered on grief.

Within a few months of their arrival, Brown had begun scouring the city, looking for land. He envisioned another magnificent home, larger than the one on Detroit. He found a prime parcel on Sixteenth Street, a dozen blocks north of the White House. He and Carry paid twenty-five thousand dollars for it, more than twice his annual salary of ten thousand. The red-brick house, with its gabled roof, grand staircase, ornate parlors and eighteen rooms, would cost forty thousand to build and two years to complete. Even with six servants—the Browns eventually took on a cook, two maids, a laundress, butler, and footman—there was more than enough room for Carry's visiting family and the social events they were keen to host.

At the court, Brown had found the workload heavy but manageable. The bench had six Republicans and three Democrats now, but as far as Brown could tell, politics stayed on the sidelines when they gathered in conference to discuss cases. Chief Justice Melville Fuller, like his predecessors, parceled out the majority opinions as he saw fit. Expertise seemed to dictate the chief justice's choices. If Fuller played favorites, Brown did not see it. Admiralty law and patent cases usually went to Brown and two others. Constitutional cases could go to anyone, while disputes involving land and property were often split among four justices, including Harlan.

Brown was observing, cataloguing, taking the measure of the men who were now his frequent companions. His evaluations were generous. Bradley of New Jersey was, by common consent, "regarded as the most learned and acute lawyer." Harlan, the affable Kentuckian, impressed him as "a strong Federalist, with a leaning toward the popular side of cases and a frequent dissenter from the more conservative opinions of his brethren." Lucius Lamar—the court's other Southerner, a Mississippi Democrat appointed by Grover Cleveland—was "a man of brilliant talents and one of the most genial and delightful companions I ever knew."

Brown was working as hard as ever, but the court's eight-month schedule had left intact one of his most cherished routines: traveling during the summer. Europe beckoned once again. He and Carry had arranged another lengthy tour, returning in late September, two weeks ahead of the court's fall term. Before their departure, he headed to Yale for his thirty-fifth reunion, perhaps his most gratifying yet. The Class of '56 now boasted not one, but two Supreme Court justices. On a sunlit morning, Brown and David Brewer accepted honorary degrees during a pageant-filled commencement that the *New York Times* called a "Big Day in Yale's History."

The night before, the Class of '56 had celebrated itself in the usual Yale fashion—with satire and song. Brown, presiding at a mock trial, was asked to decide the case of "Father Time vs. The Fifty Sixers," an "Action of Trespass and Larceny of Scythes." The justice ruled in Father Time's favor. There were no dissenters.

Then, to the tune of "Rally 'Round the Flag, Boys," these men in their mid-fifties crooned their way through class poet Theron Brown's latest reunion ditty, which included a tribute line to the Supreme Court duo: "On the highest Bench, boys—don't they do us proud!"

THE BYSTANDER, busy with the phenomenal success of his new National Citizens' Rights Association, was leaving the early planning of the test case to the New Orleans committee, based on his earlier guidelines. His letters to Martinet brimmed, instead, with details of the NCRA's remarkable start. During the fall of 1891, the Bystander had been publishing a subscription blank at the end of some columns, promising a "certificate of membership" to anyone who sent a two-cent stamp and pledged themselves to the NCRA's aims. More than ten thousand people—white and black—had sent applications. "A million names on the roll," he exhorted, "are worth more to the cause of liberty than a million dollars. Send them in!"

He and Emma were unprepared for the torrent of envelopes that followed, upwards of a thousand a week, inundating the little Mayville post office. Emma was now spending a portion of every day on "the Association," sorting the applications, mailing out certificates, updating the membership list, sending out new blanks to NCRA volunteers in other states. The workload was staggering. By early December, they had hired a local woman to help.

Tourgée had little time to share in the monumental task he had created. Not only did he need to keep writing, but he was about to leave for an extended trip out West with their daughter Lodie. Now twenty-one, she was in the early stages of trying to establish herself as a commercial artist. She had a commission to do some illustration work for a coming exposition in California, and Tourgée had arranged to give several lectures while he was out there with her.

He and Martinet would stay in touch by letter, but the bulk of the work would fall on Martinet's shoulders.

MARTINET WAS ELATED. It was the last Monday of 1891, three days after Christmas, and he had finally succeeded in making an important ally out of a possible adversary. He had met that morning with lawyers for the Louisville & Nashville Railroad, and they were willing to be a silent partner in the test case. The railroad's assistance looked like the answer to ensuring an arrest of the "right" kind.

For more than a month now, Martinet had been working on this part of the puzzle, talking with officials at several railroads. Some of them had made plain that they wouldn't mind seeing separate car laws disappear. That wasn't the case on some Southern lines. The Georgia Railroad had argued strenuously for separation in hearings at the Interstate Commerce Commission, both as a matter of prejudice and profit. Fortunately for Martinet, the men who ran the Louisville & Nashville felt differently. "They are willing that we shall make the case on their road," Martinet wrote to Tourgée after the December 28 meeting.

Why were some of Louisiana's railroad directors willing to help? Whatever their personal feelings about separation or colored people, Martinet learned, they were businessmen. Putting on extra cars to handle the relatively few number of colored riders did not make economic sense. "The roads are not in favor of the separate car law, I find, owing to the expense entailed," Martinet told Tourgée, "but they fear to array themselves against it." What did they fear? The wrath of public opinion, they told Martinet. They meant, of course, the wrath of *white* public opinion.

The L&N's solution? Stay in the shadows. It would not bring the charge or make the arrest. It would act only as stage manager. "We will have to have somebody on the train—a white man—to object to the presence" of our passenger in the whites-only car, Martinet told Tourgée. "The conductor will be instructed not to use force or molest, and our white [witness] will swear out the affidavit. This will give us our *habeas corpus* case, I hope."

Martinet was pleased, as well as relieved. He had been feeling the burdens of his ambitions to bring down the Jim Crow law. The other members of the Citizens' Committee seemed content to leave much of the work to him—too content, he had lamented to Tourgée, and too much work. Hiring a local lawyer to serve as Tourgée's co-counsel had been particularly draining. They had chased candidates who turned out to be too expensive, or too tied to the white establishment, or too afraid of being denounced for helping the colored race. Martinet would have liked a colored lawyer on the team, but he had given up on that idea. "Those here are of limited attainments," he told Tourgée, and "practice almost exclusively in the police courts. . . . Therefore we will have none, unless it be myself, and I am not willing to get into the case."

Martinet had considered the idea briefly, but only briefly. Not only was he far too busy, but he had done a good deal of the fundraising, and he didn't want anyone accusing him of bringing the case to earn a fee. To avoid any claim of personal gain, he would have to work for free, and that was impossible. The committee now had two thousand dollars in hand; better to spend it on someone with no such conflict.

They had settled on James C. Walker. He was a noted criminal lawyer in New Orleans, but not a constitutional one. A Louisiana native, fifty-four years old, he had served three years in the Confederate army, and returned to make a name for himself in the New Orleans courts. Martinet considered him "a good, upright, conscientious man," he told Tourgée.

Walker would come on board just after New Year's. The committee needed to find a volunteer for the arrest, and choose a date. It wouldn't be long now.

Their strategy was finally coming together.

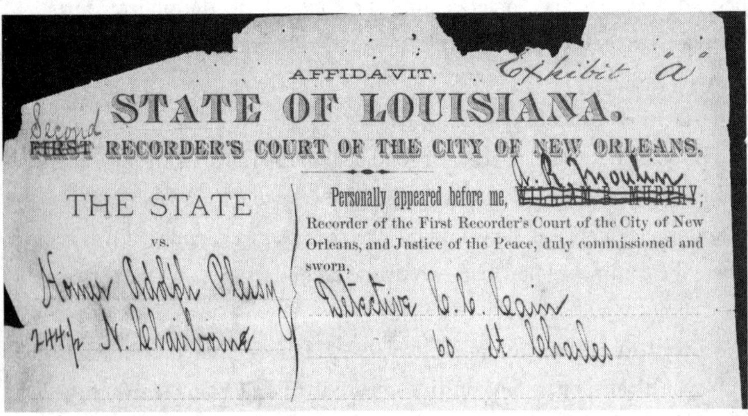

Exhibit "A"

AFFIDAVIT.

STATE OF LOUISIANA.

~~FIRST~~ Second RECORDER'S COURT OF THE CITY OF NEW ORLEANS.

THE STATE

vs.

Homer Adolph Plessy
244½ N. Claiborne

Personally appeared before me, ~~[illegible]~~ A. R. Moulin, Recorder of the First Recorder's Court of the City of New Orleans, and Justice of the Peace, duly commissioned and sworn,

Detective C. C. Cain
60 St. Charles

Reaching his destination: Homer Plessy's arrest, June 7, 1892

(Historical Archives of the Louisiana Supreme Court/University of New Orleans)

20

Arrest

Mayville and New Orleans, 1892–1893

THE BYSTANDER DIDN'T have enough strength to leave the house, much less answer lawyer James Walker's piercing queries about the test case with anything approaching clarity. Walker's three-page letter, introducing himself and raising a host of legal concerns, had arrived during the first week of January 1892, in the middle of a memorable winter storm, six consecutive days of heavy snowfall, with drifts of up to six feet and bone-chilling temperatures, as if the weather gods had confused western New York with Alaska or Antarctica.

Tourgée had been ailing now for nearly a month. A severe bout of grippe had caught hold of him in Denver while he was traveling out West with Lodie, in the early weeks of a trip that was supposed to last through January or later. It wouldn't let go. His telegram to Emma on December 22 had been alarmingly blunt: sick, coming home. Lodie would go on to California and keep her appointments. Tourgée wasn't about to let the grippe knock her off course, too.

He had to cancel several lectures he had arranged for California, but what could he do? He was weak, washed out from the fever, unable to eat. On top of his persistent back woes and glass eye, he felt close to useless, fifty-four years old creeping toward seventy. As a frightened Emma awaited his return, she wrote in her diary on December 25, "Never in my life do I remember so depressing a Christmas Day. To be absent from Lodie was enough to wring my heart, but to be in distress about Albion also was too much."

She welcomed him home the next day, relieved to find him in better shape than she had feared. But another week went by before he felt well enough to tackle Walker's questions. By then, Walker had written a second time, sketching out a tentative plan for traversing the tricky territory between the planned arrest and a date with the U.S. Supreme Court. Getting the case to Washington would not be easy. They could make all the right choices—and there were many choices to make—and still not succeed. Walker had flagged some "practical" obstacles, eager to learn what his co-counsel in distant Mayville might be thinking.

Topping Walker's list of worries: A Supreme Court majority had already blessed Mississippi's separate car law, saying there was no constitutional conflict with Congress's exclusive power to regulate interstate commerce. How did this affect their chances? "I beg to be favored with your views" on this, Walker said.

If they had to forgo the interstate commerce claim, Walker said, they would have to rely primarily on the Thirteenth and Fourteenth amendments. Would the Supreme Court be willing to revisit those arguments, already addressed in the *Civil Rights Cases*? Then, gingerly, Walker raised the last of his "perplexing questions," as he called them. This one went to the heart of the ambitions of the Citizens' Committee in bringing the test case, to the core of Tourgée's purpose in offering his services: Was the law truly "a discrimination as to class, color or condition?" Quoting a recent editorial's claim that "the privileges are equal" in the separate cars, which was the New Orleans newspaper's way of suggesting there was no prejudice in such arrangements, Walker pointedly asked: "What of this idea?"

There were many in the South arguing that "equal but separate" was legal. But those people did not include Martinet, Tourgée, or the members of the Citizens' Committee. Was it possible that the committee had hired a lawyer who did not understand the humiliating, malicious, discriminatory intent of such laws? Or was Walker merely playing the role of a good lawyer, scrutinizing the pluses and minuses of their arguments? Tourgée didn't know. He had no reason to distrust Walker. The New Orleans lawyer had not expressed any reservations about joining the legal team. To the contrary. In his introductory letter, Walker had said that he was "more than impressed" with Tourgée's dedication to the cause, and that he regarded the committee members as "respectable and educated colored men."

But was that enough? If Walker and Tourgée were to work together, they would need to be standing more firmly on common ground.

CATALOGUING PROBLEMS AND SHORTCOMINGS, as Walker had diligently done, was one way of approaching an appeal. Necessary, of course, and sensible. But they were playing for larger stakes than Walker's letters had outlined. The "real fight," Tourgée wrote when he finally drafted his reply, will come on "broader grounds."

Feeling compelled to educate his new partner, Tourgée launched into a lengthy explanation of what he and the committee were hoping to accomplish. They would be raising fundamental questions, including several the Supreme Court had never addressed. Among them: Does the state have the power to "compel" a railroad to sort passengers by race? To put conductors in charge of deciding a person's color? To make it a crime—*a crime*—for a passenger to reject a conductor's classification? To exempt a railroad and its employees from damages for their actions? To take away a passenger's constitutional right to sue for wrongful conduct or injury?

There was a risk, hardly small, that their challenge might make matters worse—that separation could become even more entrenched. But it was a risk they felt compelled to take. The committee could not fight injustice from the shadows. "I take it," Tourgée wrote, "that what our clients most desire is a square out adjudication by the Supreme Court" of the many important issues at stake. "If these questions are to be answered in the affirmative by the highest tribunal, they want to know it; if in the negative, they want to know it."

Tourgée was all too aware that the court's previous rulings made their mission daunting, if not impossible. As Walker had pointed out, the Mississippi separate car law had passed muster in 1890. But as with any legal dispute, no two cases were identical. In Mississippi, the railroad had been convicted for refusing to run separate cars. Here, a passenger would be the one accused of "the crime." Surely that was worth testing. Tourgée's task, with Walker's help, was to fashion their arguments so that the justices could see this case in its own light, distinct from its predecessors.

Walker's last letter had laid out the plan for the day of arrest. Their passenger, not yet identified, would board the Louisville & Nashville in New Orleans, with a ticket for Alabama. That would make him an interstate traveler, preserving that argument on appeal. As already worked out with the railroad, the committee would supply a "white onlooker" to make the accusation. Walker was drafting the onlooker's affidavit. It was vital, Tourgée told him, for the affidavit to mention only the Separate Car Act. They needed a conviction under that law, and no other, Tourgée explained, so that "the court above" could not "dodge the real issue."

Success might well depend on these initial steps, Tourgée said. They had to raise their arguments fully and sharply. They didn't want to end up in Washington without the weapons they needed to destroy the law. To that end, Tourgée wanted Walker to have an early look at the "broader" issues. He set them out, one by one, twelve in all. "It is better to have too many points," Tourgée said, half apologetically, half stubbornly, "than not enough."

Most of the points revolved around the Thirteenth and Fourteenth amendments, but some reflected Tourgée's determination to break new ground. "Race is a scientific and legal question of great difficulty," he wrote for Point Eleven, and no state can authorize "the agent of a corporation" to decide which citizens are white and which are colored. This idea—What is race?—was one that the Bystander had explored in his columns and books. Now he wanted to test it into a legal context.

As he was finishing his letter, already eleven pages, a final thought sprang to mind. "Is there a statutory definition of 'colored race' or persons of color in your state?" he asked Walker. "If so, what is it?" These questions seemed particularly relevant in Louisiana, a place that had long ago embedded gradations of race into its everyday language—griffe, mulatto, quadroon, octoroon, Creole of color. As Martinet had schooled him, it was easy enough in New Orleans to mistake white for colored, and vice versa. Without some standard, Tourgée was saying, how could any conductor, especially one from outside the state, sort his passengers?

Another possible point, well worth researching, well worth tossing into the mix.

ON JANUARY 19, 1892, New Orleans's Odd Fellows Hall was crammed with five hundred Republican delegates and an atmosphere of new optimism. On and off the floor at the state convention, Martinet and Desdunes were making their presence felt, advocating for candidates of color and exhorting party members to take a firm stand against the Jim Crow car law. For fifteen years, since the bitter end of Reconstruction, the reins of political power in Louisiana had rested firmly in Democratic hands. But now, fractures in both parties had injected uncertainty into the political mainstream. In this election year, there would be two Democratic tickets for governor and the other offices. The Republicans were split, too, but the rebellious faction was only a sliver. If the Republicans could rally around their strongest slate, the party stood a chance of capturing an office or two. That was the hope on the floor at Odd Fellows Hall.

The *Times-Democrat*, for one, did not regard the possibility as farfetched. In the last election, an editorial pointed out, registered colored voters had outnumbered whites by more than one thousand. Anyone looking at those numbers will see "real cause for danger," the newspaper said. The Democrats could win only if "the negro vote" remained divided. "All who do not appreciate the gravity of the situation should watch the course of the Republican convention," the *Times-Democrat* cautioned, "and convince themselves that the old enemies of the State and white civilization are confident of a return to power." *The old enemies of the State and white civilization*. In nine words, the *Times-Democrat* had turned Republicanism into an act of treason.

A rambunctious mood permeated the Odd Fellows Hall. The platform committee had set the tone, presenting a report that showed no signs of "cutting loose from the negro," as some national Republicans had been urging. Of the ten or so resolutions, half reflected the influence of Martinet,

Rodolphe Desdunes, and their allies. One endorsed the Citizens' Committee for its "noble work" against "that infamy of infamies," the Separate Car Act. Another demanded the repeal of "all caste or class legislation, and particularly of the separate car law, which is here declared a blot on the statute books and a breeder of discord and turmoil among its citizens." A third denounced lynching as "unjustifiable homicide" and scorned "white supremacy" as "rank political heresy." Two others paid tribute to none other than Albion W. Tourgée, "the sage of Mayville," recuperating from a "sickness brought on, probably, by excess of work done in behalf of human rights."

If the delegates found it odd to be making a fuss over a man they knew only by reputation, if they knew him at all, none made enough noise to matter. Instead, they passed a resolution wishing a speedy recovery to "the brave and uncompromising champion of equal rights" and assuring him of "our unspeakable gratitude for the services, the sacrifices and the sympathies he has devoted to the neglected cause of the downtrodden and lowly of this land."

No candidate on the ticket was described with such unambiguous, glowing reverence.

AS MARTINET LATER told Tourgée, he had not gone to the convention seeking any nomination for himself. But when the proposed slate arrived on the floor with only one person of color for the eight offices, several delegates leapt to their feet in vehement protest. As the debate grew boisterous, Desdunes rose twice to make passionate speeches. He wanted more colored men chosen for the party's delegation to the national convention, and he wanted to nominate a better candidate for attorney general: James C. Walker. The white lawyer's nomination would do nothing to alter the slate's racial composition, and Walker couldn't possibly win, but it was a grand show of support for the man soon to be speaking for the Citizens' Committee in court.

Banding together, half a dozen delegates put forth Martinet's name for the office of state superintendent of public education. Unlike Walker, Martinet had no trouble sweeping aside his competition. Two weeks later, he modestly accepted Tourgée's effusive congratulations. More gratifying, Martinet said, was the generous spirit displayed toward the *Crusader* contingent. "The manipulators had hold of the machinery of the convention," he proudly told Tourgée, "but the sentiment and the large majority of members were with us."

Martinet confessed that he wasn't sure he would stay on the ticket. Too many of the party's leaders were beholden to Louisiana's lucrative state lottery, he said. They were "corruptionists" who would "sell out" the party's principles in an instant. He didn't want to be in league with a crowd that cared more about gambling revenue than equal rights. If they impeded his candidacy, if they "refused to yield something to decency and honesty," he would bow out. He was far too busy to fritter away his time on a doomed campaign, especially with the test case about to launch.

"In a few days the case will be in court," Martinet told Tourgée. "Mr. Walker has sent you a copy of the affidavit he wants to have made, and is anxiously awaiting your reply."

A FEW MINUTES before eight o'clock on February 24, 1892, a mild Wednesday morning in New Orleans, a young musician named Daniel Desdunes boarded the Louisville & Nashville Railroad. His stated destination: Mobile, Alabama. His first destination: the car reserved for white passengers. His hoped-for destination: police custody.

Daniel's father was Rodolphe Desdunes, the *Crusader* columnist, who had been championing a challenge to the Jim Crow cars since the law had gone on the books. Now his oldest son, just shy of voting age, was volunteering for arrest. If Tourgée intended to pursue a legal argument about the difficulty of determining a passenger's race, then Daniel fit his requirements nicely. He was light-skinned and soft-spoken, allowing him to blend in, rather than stand out, while sitting in a car set aside for "whites." A conductor might very well pass him by. But not on this Wednesday morning. On this trip, the crew on this train had a script to follow.

As the L&N departed the Canal Street depot, the brakeman approached Daniel at his seat, and asked him to move. Daniel politely refused. The crew member insisted, summoning the conductor. Daniel was adamant. He was an "interstate passenger," he said. He wouldn't go unless forced. The conductor took his cue. He halted the train, two miles in its journey, so Daniel could be arrested. Conveniently aboard was a police captain. He beckoned to two waiting detectives. The three men escorted Daniel off the train and into the Second Recorder's Court. The captain swore out his affidavit, crafted to make sure that Daniel was charged under the Separate Car Act. The treasurer of the Citizens' Committee, Paul Bonseigneur, was waiting to pay the five-hundred-dollar bond to ensure Daniel's release.

None of the daily newspapers had cottoned on to the choreographed nature of the unfolding drama. Left to their own interpretations, the editors played up the "standoff," with Desdunes cast in the role of unapologetic scofflaw, causing discomfort for white passengers. In the *New Orleans States*, Desdunes "Wouldn't Budge When Told He Was Out of His Element—Then the Police Laid Hands on Him." The police "lost no time," the *States* said, in apprehending "this disturber of the peace, and soon he was hurled out of the train." No hurling had taken place, and no explanation was offered for why two detectives happened to be close at hand.

The *Times-Democrat* declared that the "great interracial conflict between negroes and railroads in this State . . . is at last before the courts." Each side had chosen a duelist, the paper said, with "D. F. Desdunes championing the blacks, and Capt. Ed Flood the pale faces." Desdunes was "a bright young mulatto . . . destined to become famous among his people," while Flood was the calm restorer of order. Acting on a flick of Flood's "crooked finger," two detectives had swiftly removed the offending Desdunes, and the "train then puffed victoriously on its way."

Walker was not quoted. He saw no advantage in talking to the city's white newspapers about the case. He recommended that "our clients be instructed to avoid sensational discussions in the matter." Tourgée seconded his motion. "Our clients should make no clamor," he replied.

They were bracing for a long and convoluted fight. No need to stir up their adversaries.

WAITING IMPATIENTLY for the district attorney to file his charges against Daniel Desdunes, Walker was hard at work, ironing out the final strategy with his co-counsel in Mayville. They still didn't entirely agree. Tourgée had anticipated the possibility of friction, and had tried to smooth the way. "A man who has been substantially out of practice for half a dozen years," he had told Walker, "has no right to an opinion on such points besides one who has been in the traces right along."

Inevitably, though, Tourgée had expressed his opinions, and while he had done so deferentially, he could imagine that his partner "in the traces" was fuming. Here was Tourgée, having never practiced law in New Orleans, freely making suggestions to Walker, the local expert, about shepherding the case through the Louisiana courts. One point of contention: Walker saw a defect in the law's form, a possible mistake made by the legislature in drafting the act. He wanted to add that issue to their attack. Tourgée blanched. Hadn't they gone over this? The Citizens' Committee wanted to force a *broad* ruling. Winning on a technicality would be a "virtual defeat," he protested to Walker in early March.

Walker's reply carried an unmistakable hint of irritation. "Only one motive actuates me, and that is to conduct our case skillfully towards successful termination," Walker wrote. "To this end, I am schooled to accept every suggestion, modify every plan, and sacrifice every conviction." *Sacrifice every conviction? Successful termination?* There was a sourness in Walker's words. That wasn't a good sign. Tourgée decided to say so, plainly.

In disagreeing from time to time, Tourgée wrote, he wasn't intending to "override" Walker's judgment. He did not "distrust" Walker in any way, and he "should be very angry" to learn that Walker distrusted him. He urged Walker: Read my letters with a "presumption of common sense, sincerity, and intended courtesy." If that could be done, "I think we shall enjoy our association and come out of it better friends, at least knowing each other better."

MOLLIFIED OR NOT, Walker made no effort to prolong the discussion. By the time Tourgée's air-clearing letter had arrived, the district attorney had filed his formal charges. The document had left out one important fact: Desdunes's destination. Walker immediately alerted Tourgée. "Our adversaries have not been so generous as to allege that the L&N RR was carrying Desdunes as a passenger for Mobile," Walker wrote, revealing his dry sense of humor. To keep the interstate commerce argument in play, they would need to highlight that fact in their written plea at Daniel's arraignment, scheduled for Monday, March 21.

Tourgée had seen Walker's final draft of the plea, and had sent it back with a buoyantly concise evaluation: "I like it." For the point on racial classification, Walker had added one more objection: that no one had a right to determine someone else's race "without testimony." If the court agreed, then it would be impossible to ask conductors to make an instantaneous decision while walking through a railroad car. It would make the law unenforceable.

They were launching a two-stage attack. First, they were relying on Judge Robert Marr to reject their constitutional arguments, clearing the way for a trial on the charges. Then, they were counting on a conviction. Losing twice was an integral part of the plan. Once convicted, Daniel would refuse to pay the twenty-five-dollar fine, and the judge would order him to jail for twenty days.

Having the young musician locked up was unfortunate, but necessary. That would allow Walker to march over to the U.S. Circuit Court, and file a writ of *habeas corpus*. He would assert that Daniel was in jail under an illegitimate law, with no appeal because the crime was too minor to qualify for one. Having no remedy in the state courts, Walker would argue, Desdunes had no choice but to seek federal intervention.

When Tourgée saw the wording of the district attorney's official charge, he dashed off a one-page note to Walker. Let's add a point to our plea, he wrote. Let's deny that Desdunes "is 'of the colored race' by asserting that he has not more than one-eighth of colored blood (which I suppose to be the fact)." The district attorney was certain to object to this contention, Tourgée said. So much the better. Tourgée was eager to make that idea a part of the record—"if for nothing else, to let the court sharpen its wits" on the question.

Too late. By the time Tourgée's suggestion reached New Orleans, Walker had filed the plea. They would have another chance to make Tourgée's point in their brief to the Supreme Court, if they got that far. For the moment, they could do nothing more. As soon as Marr rejected their plea for the case to be dismissed, Walker told Tourgée, "I propose to go to trial as early as I can, to submit gracefully to the verdict . . . and then to turn our client over to the Sheriff, to be put in prison."

JUDGE MARR WAS MISSING. He had left his house on the morning of April 19, Election Day, to vote. He had not returned. A last sighting put him on the banks of the swirling Mississippi, walking in the early evening, setting off speculation that he had slipped into the water, probably accidentally, perhaps voluntarily. He was a frail seventy-three, and his friends reported that he seemed troubled in recent days.

A month later, with the mystery of Marr's whereabouts no closer to being solved, it was becoming apparent that Criminal Court, Section A, could not remain without a judge for much longer. Much of Marr's docket was fossilizing. Trapped, along with many other cases, was *State v. Desdunes*. Walker and Tourgée were frustrated, but what could they do? Until Marr was declared dead, no vacancy existed to name a permanent replacement. A death watch, in reverse. It was ghastly.

On May 25, a decision by the Louisiana Supreme Court further roiled their carefully constructed plans. The court ruled, in a case pushed by the Pullman Palace Car Company of Chicago, that the Separate Car Act could not be enforced against the company's interstate travelers. The previous September, Pullman conductor W. C. Abbott had been indicted for refusing to eject "a negro" from the lone sleeping car attached to a Texas & Pacific Railway train. Abbott insisted that he had done nothing wrong. As he read the act, it specifically limited itself to travel "within the state of Louisiana." Confronted with a colored passenger holding a ticket from Louisiana to

Texas, Abbott said, he had no choice but to allow him to take his berth. The Louisiana Supreme Court was now saying Abbott was right.

The Pullman ruling's effect on the *Desdunes* case was as straightforward as a railroad timetable. As an interstate passenger, holding a ticket to Alabama, Daniel couldn't possibly be convicted now. It was a great victory. Or was it? The law, while wounded, still stood. It could still be applied to passengers traveling solely "within the state." And what about long-distance trains taking on Louisiana-only passengers? Would the state make them add a car? No one could say for sure. Instead of a "square out adjudication," Martinet and the Citizens' Committee had confusion.

This much seemed clear, though: Separation had survived, and the committee's test case was now obsolete. Tourgée needed to know immediately, Martinet decided. Just after 2:00 p.m. on May 26, 1892, an urgent telegram went out to Mayville: "In Pullman Company case from Shreveport, state Supreme Court yesterday unanimously decided separate car law as applying to interstate passenger unconstitutional."

Five days passed. On June 1, having heard nothing from the Bystander, a restless Martinet sent a second dispatch, more insistent than the first. "Case must drop. Walker wants new case wholly within state limits. Committee wants to hear from you. Wire at our expense."

AT THORHEIM, TOURGÉE was even busier than usual. In a few days, he would be leaving again for the Midwest, an extended trip revolving around the Republican National Convention in Minneapolis, opening on June 7. He had speeches to give at preconvention rallies in Chicago and St. Paul. He was backing his friend Tom Reed, the Maine congressman and former House speaker. Reed had no chance of being nominated. But the Bystander, as "a lover of liberty," would promote Reed as a white politician who would bring "better and grander things" to the country's eight million colored citizens.

In his role as president of the National Citizens' Rights Association, Tourgée was planning a splashy showing at the convention. Thanks to the *Inter Ocean*'s printing press, he would have on hand twenty-five thousand copies of his NCRA pamphlet, "Is Liberty Worth Preserving?" He and his volunteers would distribute as many as possible, free of charge. For months now, the NCRA had been selling the essay for twenty-five cents, raising more than five hundred dollars, aided by promotions in the Bystander's column. The revenue had become the organization's primary source of income, necessary to keep up with the NCRA's ballooning postage costs. Its rolls now exceeded one hundred thousand, Tourgée was proud to say.

Martinet's second, impatient telegram landed as Tourgée was preparing to leave for the Midwest. Replying hastily with a telegram of his own, Tourgée issued his instructions: "Have not seen full opinion. Agree with Walker and approve anything he may advise."

Tourgée trusted his co-counsel. They had a perfectly good strategy. They could quickly modify their plea. All they needed was a new defendant. Less than a week later, they had one.

HOMER PLESSY STEPPED to the ticket window at the Press Street depot on June 7, 1892, a warm Tuesday afternoon in New Orleans, a perfect day for a picnic. As arranged, Plessy bought a first-class fare on the East Louisiana Railroad's 4:15 p.m. train, the No. 8, heading sixty miles north to Covington and the resort towns on the north shore of Lake Pontchartrain. Plessy had no intention of going that far. If all went well, he would see a Recorder's Court judge while the picnickers were enjoying the weather and the lake.

Plessy shared many of the qualities that had made Daniel Desdunes an ideal candidate for arrest. He was light-skinned, a neat dresser, polite. He had never been arrested before. At twenty-nine, he had nearly a decade's head start on Daniel in carving out a life for himself. He was married, working as a shoemaker and renting a house in Faubourg Tremé. His family tree featured every color of the New Orleans spectrum, but no enslaved member since his great-grandmother had gained her freedom in 1779. He could trace both sides of his family's origins back to the century of French and Spanish rule. If *les gens de couleur libres* could be considered a club, his ancestors were founding members.

He had heard the family stories of his maternal grandfather, Michel

Debergue, who had answered Andrew Jackson's call for freemen of color to join his army in 1814. Then, fifty years later, Michel had joined a thousand other men of color in signing a petition to Lincoln, demanding equal rights. The year was 1864, and Michel's new grandson, christened Homere Patris Plessy, was not quite a year old.

Twenty-three years later, Homer Plessy's interest in education and politics led him to serve on two different committees of colored men. There, he had become friends with several Creole stalwarts: Rodolphe Desdunes, L. J. Joubert, Eugene Luscy, and Pierre Chevalier, all of whom went on to form the Citizens' Committee. Those relationships had helped bring him to the Press Street depot on the afternoon of June 7.

A trip wholly within the state's borders required arrangements with a new cast of characters. The Louisville & Nashville wasn't an option. All its trains were interstate. The East Louisiana Railway was a fine substitute, if everything could be carried out just as before. This time, the committee had hired a private detective, Chris C. Cain, to act as the arresting officer.

Plessy knew he was placing himself in some jeopardy. While Desdunes's arrest had gone off without a hitch, the Citizens' Committee could not predict what might happen once the trip was under way. The other passengers would not know what was afoot, and any reader of the *Crusader* could recount a story about white travelers all too eager to aid a conductor in enforcing the rules against colored resisters. But Plessy did not flinch. He boarded the train, crowded with holidaymakers, and made his way to the whites-only car. The conductor approached. The *Times-Democrat* reported a crisp dialogue.

"Are you a colored man?" the conductor asked Plessy.

"Yes," Plessy replied.

Simple enough. Except in the *Crusader's* account, the conductor's question was framed in the reverse: "Are you a white man?" Plessy's reply: "No."

White? Colored? Plessy might have said: Neither. Both. Or he might have asked Tourgée's question: What is the definition of colored? None of those replies, however, were in the script.

In all the newspaper accounts, Plessy refused to budge. Cain came forward, and everything went as planned. After the arrest, five members of the committee, led by Martinet, descended on the Fifth Precinct police station. They wanted to make sure that Plessy did not spend the night in jail. Having accomplished that mission, Martinet turned his attention to telling *Crusader* readers why a second test case was necessary. "The infamous act," he wrote, "is much damaged" by the Louisiana Supreme Court's ruling in the Pullman case. Now the committee intended to finish the job, so that all colored passengers, local as well as interstate, could travel "unmolested and without danger of legal affront and indignity."

The white newspapers had other ideas. In their view, the committee's continuing campaign against separation was pointless. The U.S. Supreme Court had already approved the Mississippi act, the *Times-Democrat* reminded its readers. The *Picayune*, weary of the issue, treated Plessy's arrest as routine. "Another Jim Crow Car Case," said the headline over a three-paragraph item. "Arrest of a Negro Traveler Who Persisted in Riding With the White People."

The newspapers weren't publishing photographs routinely, but they were offering facial sketches of people in the news, a popular innovation. None appeared of this presumptuous "Negro Traveler" who dared to ride with whites.

DANIEL DESDUNES'S JOURNEY, envisioned as a lengthy trip from police custody to the U.S. Supreme Court with many stops along the way, ended prematurely on the morning of July 9, 1892, in the busy confines of Criminal Court Section A, before a newly appointed judge with bushy eyebrows and an even bushier moustache.

This was Judge John H. Ferguson's first week on the bench, replacing the missing Judge Marr. Ferguson was well briefed, and ready. The Separate Car Act could not be enforced against interstate passengers, he said. The district attorney, agreeing that Desdunes fit the definition of interstate traveler, announced that he was abandoning the case. *State v. Desdunes* was over.

Only a partial victory, to be sure. But in these disheartening times, with new outrages happening weekly to people of color in the South, it was a victory that Martinet and the *Crusader* could hail and celebrate. Readers opened that week's edition to a startling headline: "Jim Crow Is Dead." Not just dying. *Dead.* "The Jim Crow Car is ditched, and will remain in the ditch," Martinet's editorial said. "Reactionists may foam at the mouth, and Bourbon organs may squirm, but Jim Crow is dead as a door nail."

The "Bourbon organs"—newspapers like the *Times-Democrat* and others—would scorn that categorical declaration as wishful thinking. As Martinet well knew, they would be right. Jim Crow was wounded, but far from dead. To truly kill it would require a string of victories. Acknowledging as much, Martinet wrote in the *Crusader* that the Citizens' Committee "will no doubt" expand its efforts into neighboring states, "to drive the Jim Crow car out of the South entirely."

For now, though, the *Crusader* was savoring this triumph, incomplete though it was. Martinet and the committee had proven the naysayers wrong. "Negro leaders—national leaders" had rebuffed the committee's early requests for aid or encouragement, the *Crusader* said. That had included Frederick Douglass, "the greatest of all Negroes." Douglass had presumed they would lose, the *Crusader* said, and had withheld his support. But the committee had persevered, showing Douglass to be "unpardonably ignorant . . . of the constitutional rights of his race."

In contrast, the *Crusader* heaped praise on Daniel Desdunes for "the manly assertion of his right." Now, the *Crusader* said, the equally courageous Homer Plessy had taken his place. Sometime soon, the district attorney would file his new charges, and Walker would be ready, revised plea in hand.

They were back to their original strategy. They needed to lose, so that Plessy's test case could go forward, so that they could bury Jim Crow deep in that ditch.

MARTINET SPENT MUCH of the summer of 1892 brooding. Over the past year, even as he was leading the charge against the Separate Car Act, he had entertained thoughts of fleeing New Orleans, abandoning the cause to others. That's what he confided to Tourgée, while trying to finish a letter that he had started on the Fourth of July and had yet to mail. By late August, the letter had come to resemble a personal diary, with six different entries over six weeks, twenty-eight pages, a running commentary on Louisiana politics, the Jim Crow car fight, and Martinet's unsettled state of mind. "I ought to rewrite this and shorten it by one-half or two-thirds," he confessed to Tourgée, when he finally sent it. "But really, I can't."

Martinet found it particularly distressing—and, yes, infuriating—that several leading men of color had shown no interest in the committee's calls for help. "The fight we are making is an uphill one under the best circumstances, and yet those for whom we fight make it still harder," he told Tourgée.

Frederick Douglass's dismissive response had stung the most. Martinet had been a delegate at the 1883 Convention of Colored Men in Louisville. He had heard Douglass's stirring words about fighting the color line, how no one should settle for a "servile and cowardly submission" to injustice. He had listened as Douglass had exhorted the delegates to "make every organized protest against the wrongs inflicted on them." Throughout his long career, the brilliant orator's message had been strongly consistent: We must act now, we cannot wait, whites will *always* tell us that the time is not right.

Perhaps Martinet had expected too much from the man who had pioneered resistance to the Jim Crow car, at the dawn of railway travel in the early 1840s. But reading Douglass's reply to the Citizens' Committee, he felt the rush of bitter disappointment. As he explained to Tourgée, Douglass had "childishly reprimanded" the committee for addressing him as "the Hon. Fred Douglass" on the envelope. "His name was Frederick Douglass, he said, and he expressed his disapproval of the project," refusing to give any aid. Why? "He saw no good in the undertaking," Martinet explained.

No good? Martinet made no effort to contain his scorn. "No good," he fumed, "in protesting against encroachments on your rights!" Martinet's anger led him to question the sincerity of Douglass's reply. "Was that a dodge to protect his pocket?" he said. "Of course, we were not after his money. We wanted his endorsement and moral support."

THE UPHILL FIGHT was wearing on Martinet. Like Tourgée, whose Bystander columns had been needling the national party for its waning interest in the cause of equal rights, Martinet had lost his patience with Republican politicians who purported to be friends of "the negro," but stood silent while conditions in the South worsened and violence escalated. But what choice did he or others have? "Unfortunately for us in the South," he told Tourgée in a late July section of the letter bursting with fury and sorrow, "there is no other party we can affiliate with."

Martinet felt isolated, alienated, and surrounded by political men he did not trust. In Louisiana's April elections, as he expected, he and the rest of the Republican ticket had gone down to a depressing defeat. Uncomfortable with the "manipulators" on the party's campaign committee, he had stayed away from any canvassing. "I took no part in the campaign beyond the advocacy of the ticket in the *Crusader*," he told Tourgée.

Since then, his distress had only deepened. As much as he loved New Orleans, he had grown disgusted with its "prejudiced, rotten atmosphere." Their crusade for equal rights was a blessing, but it wasn't enough to offset his gloom. "I am tired of living here," he revealed to Tourgée. "I wish to be in a place where one can be free. Besides, I see no future here for my family. I am fighting in the common cause, it is true, but it is too great a sacrifice, not to me, but to my wife and child. I have no right to deprive them of the joys and comforts of life."

Despite his jubilant editorial in the *Crusader*, Martinet was harboring doubts about the *Plessy* case. He did not foresee "the same favorable result" as they had achieved in *Desdunes*. He wanted to believe that they had already made significant progress, that the Jim Crow car could not survive all the legal battering, that it might just fade into oblivion, more trouble than the railroads could handle. But history and experience—his own, his state's—suggested otherwise.

He didn't want to give up, but he was finding optimism hard to come by. "What have I to gain in fighting this battle? Like you, I have asked myself this question a thousand times," he told Tourgée. "I want no political influence, no prestige, no office. Why do I do this?"

He answered his own question. "Like you, I believe I do it because I am built this way."

ON NOVEMBER 18, 1892, with Plessy in the courtroom and Tourgée in Mayville, Walker waited cheerfully for the defeat he knew was coming. Once Judge Ferguson ruled against their plea, once he declared the Separate Car Act to be a legitimate exercise of legislative authority, they could finally spring ahead. The white newspapers would misunderstand the moment. They would cast Ferguson's ruling as the end, rather than the beginning.

The *Times-Democrat's* sigh of relief came the next day. "We are glad to see that Judge Ferguson has decided the separate car act [is] constitutional," the *Times-Democrat* wrote, "and thus put a quietus to the efforts of some negro agitators to disobey it and sweep it aside." Now that Judge Ferguson's ruling has "completely disposed of the African claim . . . it is to be hoped that what he says will have some effect on the silly negroes who are trying to fight this law."

Quietus? African claim? This was too much for Rodolphe Desdunes. The *Times-Democrat* "has a perfect right to be happy" with Judge Ferguson's ruling, he wrote in the *Crusader.* "But when it says that the decision will put a quietus to the efforts of most Negro agitators, it is entirely in the dark." Those "silly Negroes"—Desdunes kept repeating the phrase, scornfully—were "agitating for liberty, for justice, for life, for property, by peaceful and constitutional methods." The courts aren't the exclusive domain of whites, he said, and these "silly Negroes" aren't "foreigners or parvenus." They and their ancestors "have built up this country from its incipiency, and have defended its soil at the cost of their blood and their treasures."

There is no "quietus," he declared, and "the colored people are not alone in this agitation." Ferguson's ruling was "only the beginning," he promised.

WALKER AND TOURGÉE had wanted Ferguson to overrule their fifteen-point plea, and they got their wish. But Ferguson did more than that. He issued a full written decision, briefly addressing the constitutional questions.

He also held off on setting a trial date. No trial meant no conviction, no sentence, no habeas corpus opportunity. A delay.

As Walker saw it, though, this pause was a gift. Ferguson's written ruling had opened an alternative avenue to the U.S. Supreme Court. Walker could now seek a "writ of prohibition" from the Louisiana Supreme Court, asking for the case to be stopped in its tracks so the constitutional issues could be argued at the higher court. That's the path the Pullman Palace Car Company had followed. Of course, the Pullman company had won. Walker was expecting to lose. But no matter. Loss in hand, Walker and Tourgée could go directly to the U.S. Supreme Court on a "writ of error"—the errors they would find in this new ruling, as well as the errors in Ferguson's. This route had one clear advantage over habeas corpus. Plessy would not have to spend a minute in jail. The Citizens' Committee liked the sound of that.

Four days after Ferguson's ruling, Walker filed a quickly prepared writ with the Louisiana Supreme Court. The mails could not move fast enough to give Tourgée a chance to review the documents that Walker needed to prepare in the coming weeks. But from their long and evolving correspondence, Walker knew the points Tourgée wanted to include. On each document, he put Tourgée's name first, and then his. Their partnership was complete.

He filed the writ on November 22, a Tuesday. Within a few hours, the chief judge asked for Ferguson's response. It was due Friday. *Friday!* Three days.

After months of glacial movement, their challenge was picking up speed.

A FOOT-DRAGGING JUDGE could do plenty to impede a test case. But Ferguson did nothing of the sort. He was willing to play his part in advancing the matter, in having it debated and settled. He promptly answered the writ of prohibition. Walker referred to him, in letters to Tourgée, as "my friend."

Walker and Ferguson had known each other a long time from their years in the legal trenches. By background at least, they had little in common other than the practice of law. Walker was a New Orleans native and former Confederate. Ferguson was a Massachusetts native, a Unionist who went South after the Civil War. Walker called himself a Republican, while Ferguson owed his judgeship to aligning himself with the Democrats.

In contrast to the *Times-Democrat*'s contempt for the "silly negroes" and their Jim Crow fight, Ferguson made plain his respect for the arguments Tourgée and Walker had mounted. Their plea "displayed great research, learning, and ability," he wrote. He was rejecting it only after "mature deliberation and careful consideration."

Ferguson's ruling showed no hint of any reservations about dividing the races. Separate was legal, he said. Many courts had said so. His only question: Were the cars equal? If not, no one had said so. "There is no pretense" that Plessy was denied equal accommodations, he wrote. "He was simply deprived of the liberty of doing as he pleased."

The outcome was the same at the Louisiana Supreme Court. On December 19, with no dissent, the five judges gave their unanimous approval to separation on trains that did not travel across state lines. The Separate Car Act treats the races with "perfect fairness and equality," they said. Whites are banned from colored cars, and vice versa. Whites can be arrested, and vice versa. In fact, the judges said, the law was so even-handed that they were at a loss to understand the complaints they were hearing "from a portion of the people." They did not accept Tourgée and Walker's assertion that the law was aimed at people of color.

The judges ignored many of Tourgée and Walker's other points, but they also signaled their interest in seeing the test case go forward. They had no doubt about what the justices in Washington would say. Previous majority rulings—including the Mississippi case—had shown no inclination to interpret the Fourteenth Amendment as broadly as Tourgée and Walker wanted.

Besides, the Louisiana judges warned, overturning the Separate Car Act as a violation of the Fourteenth Amendment would have a revolutionary effect. It would nullify dozens of state laws based on the principle of separation. No separate schools. No bans on intermarriage. But the Louisiana judges made one notable concession. As Ferguson had pointed out, the legislature could not forbid passengers from suing for damages. That was unconstitutional. A conductor's decision had to be subject, as Ferguson had put it, to "judicial investigation."

A small victory, but one that Martinet and the *Crusader* quickly added to the list of the Citizens' Committee's achievements.

THE CHRISTMAS HOLIDAYS had arrived, but James Walker wasn't able to leave work behind entirely. He had a deadline to meet. He was polishing the petition for rehearing that he would file on December 26 at the Louisiana Supreme Court. Nearly a year earlier, Tourgée had told him that "it was better to have too many points than not enough." They had made plenty of points already, and they had no hope that the judges would reverse themselves, but this was a final chance to shape the record that would be sent to Washington.

Their initial plea had omitted any mention of Plessy's color, a kind of silent protest of racial classification. Then, in their first filings to the Louisiana Supreme Court, they had described Plessy as a man of mixed descent, "in the proportion of seven-eighths Caucasian and one-eighth African blood." Those who knew Plessy's genealogy would say that the proportion was closer to one-fourth, but for the sake of their argument, the fractions weren't as significant as Plessy's appearance. His "mixture of colored blood was not discernible," Tourgée and Walker wrote. That entitled Plessy to all the rights and privileges of "the white race."

Now, they were making a slightly different claim, a more radical one. Color is not "merely a question of fact," they said in their petition for a rehearing, "but a question of law," to be enacted by the legislature and interpreted by the courts. Other states had legal definitions of "negro" or "colored race." Louisiana did not. Without one, they argued, Plessy could not be classified as colored. His "lawful status," they said flatly, "is that of a white man."

The judges were unmoved. Petition for rehearing denied.

The crossover moment to federal court had arrived. On January 5, 1893, Walker filed their writ of error. The case had a new title to go along with its change of venue, reflecting Plessy's transformation from defendant to plaintiff. Instead of *State v. Plessy*, it was now *Plessy v. Ferguson*.

Another evolution had taken place as well. On the train in June, Plessy had been asked, according to the *Times-Democrat*, "Are you a colored man?"

He had said, "Yes." Or he was asked, according to the *Crusader*, "Are you a white man?" He had said no, a colored man. Those were the only answers he could give, if he wanted to be ejected from the white car and arrested. But now, his lawyers were contending that his "lawful status" was that of "a white man," *not* a colored man.

It wasn't a contradiction. It was New Orleans. Plessy's race? Either. Both. Depends on who's asking, and where, and why.

16343

OCTOBER TERM, 1892.

Albion W. Tourgee S. F. Phillips F. D. McKenney 15248. M. J. Cunningham Alex. Porter Morse	Homer Adolph Plessy. v J. H. Ferguson, Judge of Section "A" Criminal District Court for the Parish of Orleans.	In Error to the Supreme Court of Louisiana.
1893. Jan. 31.	Record received and filed.	

Received and recorded: The *Plessy* docket at the Supreme Court, 1893

(National Archives)

21

"You Are Fighting a Great Battle"

Washington, Mayville, and New Orleans, 1893 1895

JUSTICE HENRY BROWN had a favor to repay, and with the newspapers saying that President Harrison would act swiftly to fill the Supreme Court's latest vacancy, not much time to repay it. On the morning of February 1, 1893, the fifty-six-year-old justice stopped by the White House to deliver a brief but warm message: Take a good look at Howell Jackson, U.S. circuit judge from Tennessee. I served with him. I can vouch for him. "An ideal judge," Brown would later say.

A few years earlier, when Brown's name had appeared on the president's short list for a vacant seat, Jackson had arranged a special trip to Washington to urge Brown's nomination. Jackson was a Democrat and a Southerner, but he had put aside party ties and regional loyalty to speak up for Brown. "I was naturally surprised," Brown later wrote, because "my appointment involved a promotion over his head." Jackson's generosity had lodged deep in Brown's bones. He vowed to himself that he would do the same, if the opportunity ever came.

A Jackson nomination was not going to bring Republicans to their feet in unified approval. Several Southern members were vocal in their opposition. A Tennessee representative said Harrison would be betraying the party by nominating Jackson. Others, while conceding Jackson's legal qualifications, said the president could do better. There were several fine Southern Republicans on the federal bench. Why not one of them?

In any other year, at any other moment of his presidency, Harrison would not have given more than an obligatory glance at someone with Jackson's biography. But this was no ordinary moment. Harrison was a month away from forced retirement. Grover Cleveland, rising from his own ashes to regain the White House, would replace him in less than six weeks. Harrison was not inclined to leave the vacancy to his rival. But he recognized that his weakened political clout left him with limited options. He had already appointed three Republicans to the court, including Brown. None had been hard-edged in their politics; they were lawyers more than politicians.

If the president were to gravitate toward a Southern Democrat, especially a former senator with a Confederate history, it would help to have a Republican judge like Brown attesting to Jackson's abilities. The *Chicago Tribune* was describing Jackson as "popular" in both parties, known for his "moderation" while serving in the U.S. Senate alongside Harrison in the early 1880s. The *Inter Ocean* had chimed in, "He is not a Bourbon Democrat, and is a much broader man in his political views perhaps than anyone whom Cleveland might now select."

Brown didn't know Jackson the politician. But he admired and liked Jackson the judge. Whenever court business had brought Jackson to Detroit, he had stayed with the Browns. "I found him the most delightful of guests," Brown wrote years later. "He had a fund of droll anecdotes," which he "told in his peculiar Southern accent."

Their backgrounds reflected the North-South divide. Jackson had opposed secession initially, but when war broke out, he had accepted a legal position with the Confederate government, handling sequestered property in western Tennessee. That had lasted a year, until the Union seizure of Memphis in the fall of 1862. Nine months later, when Brown made his brief visit to the occupied city, Jackson and his family were gone. They had fled to Georgia, where they spent the rest of the war.

Brown was one of ten or so official visitors to the White House on the busy Wednesday morning of February 1. Years later, Brown would recall the brief chat with pride. "I was instrumental in inducing President Harrison to appoint Mr. Justice Jackson," he wrote. "This was the culmination of a friendship which continued without interruption until his death."

Whatever the extent of Brown's influence, Harrison did not wait for opposition to build. The next day, he made his choice, and Jackson's nomination moved ahead without significant resistance. Less than three weeks later, on February 18, the Democrat from Tennessee was sworn in.

Debt repaid.

BROWN WAS DELIGHTED to have his friend on the bench. The Bystander was not. His first column after the nomination, even before Jackson's confirmation, was contemptuous of both Harrison and his selection. Here was a politician, the Bystander wrote, whose "words of patriotic promise" had "thrilled the hearts" of so many during the 1888 campaign. Four years later, he railed, that same man had become a "cold, calculating economist," eager to "eliminate the 'negro question' from politics."

The Bystander said he was saddened and frustrated by the Republican president's evolution. Lynching had proliferated in the Southern states during Harrison's term, but had the president taken any action to stem the horrific acts? No, said the Bystander. Instead, Harrison had stood by helplessly, essentially saying "the President regrets that he has no power" to intervene in the Southern States and their local problems.

Now, as if determined to bolster his infamy, Harrison had appointed this "State-rights Democrat" to the Supreme Court. A Democrat! Such a betrayal would have been unthinkable in the era of Sumner and Stevens, the Bystander said. But today's crop of Republicans were unworthy heirs to those legislative lions. "The Senate chamber, so long the battlefield of liberty, no longer echoes with patriotic eloquence," the Bystander wrote, "but is noted only as a cozy place for crafty dickering and as affording unparalleled opportunity for the enhancement of already overgrown fortunes—a 'Millionaires' Club.'" His pen red-hot with the fire of an unfinished revolution, the Bystander raced on. "Justice and humanity are forgotten themes of political disquisition; only pelf and profit are worthy of consideration now," he fumed.

The Bystander's loyal readers would have no trouble understanding that "pelf" meant plunder, not just money. Nor would they be surprised by the Bystander's growing disillusionment with the Republican Party.

WITH THE *PLESSY* case pending, the Bystander had more than a columnist's interest in the court's composition. If Harrison had pushed through a Republican nominee, that might have been a boost for the Jim Crow car cause. But Harrison's pick had left the court unchanged. Jackson was replacing Justice Lucius Lamar of Mississippi. Another Southern Democrat was not a likely vote against separation. With Cleveland soon to be in the White House, Tourgée and Martinet could only hope that no other vacancies would occur before their case was called.

There was no chance of a *Plessy* hearing before the end of the court's current term in May, but Tourgée and Martinet were hoping for a date sometime in the fall. They were already making the necessary preparations. Two days before Jackson's nomination, the Supreme Court had received the full printed record from Louisiana. The clerk's office had docketed the case as number 15248 in the court's cumulative record. At Tourgée's suggestion, the Citizens' Committee had approved the hiring of an eminent Washington lawyer to serve as its local eyes and ears at the court. His name was Samuel F. Phillips, and he would help to write and file their all-important briefs when the time came.

Picking Phillips seemed like a shrewd move. Phillips could say, without exaggeration, that he knew his way around the Supreme Court as well as any lawyer in Washington. For nearly thirteen years, from late 1872 to the spring of 1885, Phillips had served as U.S. solicitor general, the second appointee to that prominent job. He had argued scores of cases on the government's behalf, including the 1883 *Civil Rights Cases.* He had been on the losing side, but then again, Tourgée and Walker wouldn't want to work with the winner. Phillips was a year shy of seventy, but showed no signs of slowing up. The justices respected him for his knowledge, temperament, and professionalism. In this uphill fight, any advantage would be welcome.

Tourgée had seen Phillips in action. Years ago, during Tourgée's days as a North Carolina judge, Phillips had been a lawyer in Raleigh. He had appeared in Tourgée's courtroom. As reform-minded Republicans, they had fought on the same side, pushing for the expansion of equal rights and against the rise of the Ku-Klux. A friendship developed. Tourgée was more radical and more inclined toward public scrapes, but by the time Phillips left North Carolina for a job in the Grant administration, he had acquired a reputation as a Republican who could be counted on. The Citizens' Committee agreed to pay Phillips a $250 retainer to secure his services, with the promise of a larger fee later.

Martinet was pleased with the team's progress, and his confidence in Tourgée was unflagging. "Go right ahead and do what you think best," Martinet wrote after the committee had reviewed Tourgée's latest recommendations, including the hiring of Phillips. "We agree with you in toto." Reiterating what he had said months earlier, Martinet reminded Tourgée that "you have full control of the case."

BY LATE APRIL OF 1893, impatience had taken hold in New Orleans and Mayville. From where Martinet and Tourgée sat, it seemed as if the case might easily slip into 1894 without a hearing date. They were asking Phillips: Could anything be done to speed up the schedule? Every day without movement was one more day of the Separate Car Act's injustices. It wasn't the only prejudice, or even the most important, but it was the battleground they had chosen. Living with the consequences of routine discrimination and oppression, Martinet later wrote to Tourgée, was a constant indignity that no one should have to endure.

The May 1 reply from Phillips was discouraging. We should not press for an expedited hearing on our own, he said. Solo requests rarely succeed. "If we can secure the Cooperation of the State," he wrote to Tourgée, "it would be much better."

Cooperation of the State? At this point, it was far more likely that the state would say no, thanks, the law is working just fine, we're in no rush. But following Phillips's advice, they decided they had to try. The job would fall to Walker.

Martinet wasn't even in New Orleans right now. He was away for the entire spring, living temporarily in Chicago, pursuing a change of career in his early forties. During the past several years, he had been studying medicine at a New Orleans university, along with editing the *Crusader*, directing the Jim Crow car case, and operating his notary business. When a well-known Chicago institution, the Policlinic, offered him a spot in one of its courses, Martinet had seized it, eager for an extended stay in the North.

The experience had been a revelation. "I have lived here a new man, a free/man," he exulted to Tourgée at the end of May. No one knew his race. No one asked. He looked white enough to say nothing, if he chose. "I return South with a heavy heart," he wrote, as his three-month sojourn was ending.

While he often enjoyed the advantages of his light skin color in New Orleans, he never felt truly safe. He tried to explain this to Tourgée. "You don't know what that feeling is, Judge. You may imagine it, but you have never experienced it—knowing that you are a free man and yet not allowed to enjoy a free man's liberty, rights, and privileges unless you stake your life every time you try it. . . . My heart is constricted at the very thought of returning to those scenes—it suffocates me."

The North was no paradise of liberty. Martinet's visit to the massive Chicago World's Fair, recently opened to great fanfare, had reminded him of that. He had strolled the six hundred acres of exhibitions on a mid-May afternoon, his resentment rising as he went through the American pavilions. How could this celebration of the nation's progress give such little attention to the contributions of its colored citizens? The metaphor was too much for Martinet. The World Fair's "very grandeur has filled me with bitterness," he told Tourgée. "I felt that if the whole thing could sink in Lake Michigan and disappear in toto, I would rejoice. There have been congresses here every week, of one thing or another, but I have not visited nor taken an interest in any. We are not wanted in them—except to fill the specific role of representing the race."

Limits, always limits. Frederick Douglass's long-ago words, reverberating through the cavernous buildings: "When we come as scholars or statesmen, the color line is raised."

Firm, sharp, ever present.

MARTINET HAD DELAYED his return to New Orleans for a week or so. Tourgée was coming to Chicago in early June for a convention, and Martinet was jubilant at the prospect of spending some time together. "I feel that you are our one friend in this land of oppression and that I may never meet you again," he wrote on May 30.

He hadn't intended, when he sat down that afternoon in his second-floor flat on Wells Street, to write a long letter. He would be seeing Tourgée in a matter of days, after all. But like a runaway train, Martinet could not stop. He kept writing, fulminating, his handwriting shrinking as he crammed more lines on each oversized sheet, eight pages in all.

Once again, thoughts of abandoning his native New Orleans were pressing upon him. So, too, were his qualms about the battle they were waging. Lifting the lid on his Pandora's box of doubts, Martinet let them rush out. "The question forces itself upon me: Are we not fighting a hopeless battle—a battle made doubly hopeless by the tyranny and cruelty of the Southern white and the Negro's own lack of appreciation, his want of energy, and his submissiveness?" he asked. "Are the Negroes progressing, or are they not retrograding under the yoke of the Southern barbarians, and are not our efforts for their betterment put forth in a method and manner calculated to do little good, or perhaps harm?"

He refused to allow despair to have the final word. He was willing to explore other paths, other methods. "But if our fight is fruitless, or rather our manner of fighting it makes it so—what is to be done?" His question was rhetorical, but his answer was not: Education first, defiance generally, disobedience when necessary. "The colored people must be given a chance to develop, to rise, and the hands of oppression must be stayed from them, and they must be taught properly—they must be taught, not only to read, write and pray, but also that to combat wrong and injustice, to resist oppression and tyranny, is the highest virtue of the citizen."

Even if he opted to withdraw from the conflict, he felt better knowing that Tourgée would be soldiering on. "You are fighting a great battle, Judge. You are, if not the only one, the foremost militant apostle of liberty in the whole land. . . . You may not live to see the fruits of your labors and sacrifices, or to receive the gratitude of those benefited by them—it will be reserved to a future generation to properly and justly estimate them."

A week later, after learning that Emma's mother had died and Tourgée had called off his trip to Chicago, Martinet felt even more alone. He boarded the cars for the long, tense return to New Orleans, his Northern interlude at an end.

IN WASHINGTON, the justices were preparing to scatter for the summer of 1893, some to their circuits to handle duties there, others directly to vacations. Their just-completed term had been an unusual one. They hadn't operated at full strength since December. Missing from the conference table for five long months, encompassing more than two hundred rulings, was John Harlan. He had gone to Paris, appointed by President Harrison to an obscure but important international tribunal, one of two American representatives. Harlan's absence had left his colleagues without one of their most prolific and reliable opinion writers.

While honored to be chosen, Harlan had protested. He did not see how he could possibly accept. These complicated international quarrels—this one involved a longstanding U.S.-Canadian dispute over seal fishing in the Bering Sea near Alaska—took months to sort through. He could not be away from his family for that long, he told Harrison. And besides, how could he justify a lengthy stay in Paris, given the backlog that the justices had vowed to reduce? The new U.S. circuit courts of appeals, recently created by Congress to ease the court's caseload, were just getting organized. Harlan did not think of himself as indispensable, but he was writing forty or more majority opinions each term. "My full share," he had written recently to a friend. Two ailing justices were coping with health problems. Who would take up Harlan's slack?

Harrison was not accepting "no" for an answer. As Mallie later recounted, the president had told her husband, "I do not wish you to leave your family; you must take them with you." The offer was tempting. Here was a second chance to live in Europe, one they thought had passed them by. President

Hayes had tried to entice Harlan into a diplomatic post during the summer of 1877, but Harlan had turned it down. Wrong job, wrong time. But this temporary assignment, with the government covering a good portion of the family's expenses, "put a different light on the matter," Mallie wrote. It would give them, she said, "the opportunity of seeing something of the Old World—an opportunity we had always longed for."

For Henry Brown, Harlan's prolonged absence meant more work and less conviviality. He and Harlan had grown to be friends as well as colleagues. They did not see eye to eye on everything, of course. But they often took the same side. Dissents were rare—about 90 percent of the court's rulings were unanimous—but when Harlan would write one, Brown was among his likeliest partners. During Brown's first two years on the bench, he had dissented with Harlan in seven, as had Brewer and Stephen Field. None of the other five justices had joined the Kentuckian more than once. A lawyer in a discrimination case, assessing which justices might be sympathetic, might start with Harlan and his trio of occasional dissenters.

One certainty: The court was not in any danger of needing Harlan's vote to break a tie. Only twice during Brown's tenure had a case ended with a five-to-four split. Twice in two years. More than five hundred rulings. That was the nature of how the Supreme Court operated. The justices preferred unanimity. They did not rule by public opinion, but they kept their eyes on it.

Given a choice between status quo and a new path, most justices favored status quo.

A FAMILY SORROW had weighed heavily on Harlan as he prepared for the Paris assignment, but it was one that he mostly kept to himself. Years of alcoholism had left his brother James in devastated straits. No longer able to work as a judge or lawyer, James was living a hand-to-mouth existence in Louisville, supported by others. James's condition was no secret, but it had tormented John for a long time. He had been depositing small sums of money with their former law partner, Augustus Willson, with instructions on when to spend it. Harlan did not know what else to do. He vacillated between shame and compassion, between anger and guilt. "The matter distresses me more than I can say," he wrote to Willson in December 1891.

Harlan had always relied on Willson to alert him to any emergency, and one of those letters had arrived as he was preparing for Europe. He replied to Willson immediately, apologetic but resolute. "James's collapses give me great pain," he said. "His condition is the one and only cloud upon my life." But he could not "abandon my duties or plans," and he could not come to Louisville before leaving for Paris. "Let me say now that if James should die, while I am in Europe, I will thank you [to see] that he is decently buried in the family lot at Frankfort."

Before leaving, Harlan mailed six checks to Willson, thirty dollars each, dated the first of the month, January through June. He asked Willson to use his discretion in dispensing them. They were for James's "comfort," not for his whiskey. He was sorry to burden Willson with this responsibility, but he knew no one else he could ask.

Wire me if necessary, he instructed, care of "United States Minister."

ON JULY 7, 1893, while Harlan was still in Paris with another month's work ahead of him, Justice Samuel Blatchford of New York died. There was no doubt about this vacancy. It would go to a Democrat, reducing the court's Republican contingent to five, the lowest total since 1870. When Cleveland announced his choice in late September, the news sent Tourgée spiraling into self-doubt. Their odds of success, never good, suddenly seemed bleak. What should they do?

Tourgée did not know. But if they were going to change their strategy, it would be best to do so quickly. In New Orleans, Walker had already arranged for a special emissary to intercede with the Louisiana attorney general, and ask his support for expediting the case. "My friend, Judge Ferguson, has kindly offered to see the Atty. Gen'l in person," Walker wrote to Tourgée excitedly in early October.

Having Ferguson make the approach had seemed like a brilliant idea. If both Plessy *and* Ferguson were keen to have *Plessy v. Ferguson* heard sooner than later, how could the attorney general say no? But that's what happened.

"The only answer obtained," Walker wrote dourly on October 23, "is that the case seems to be getting along well enough." There was nothing more Walker could do. He wasn't willing to beg. "Any further attempt on my part," he said, "would call for a condescension which I am not prepared to undergo."

Walker's defeat gave Tourgée the freedom to voice his misgivings in full. On the last day of October 1893, with a morning frost reminding Mayville of winter's specter, Tourgée sat with a fresh stack of paper, drafting an expansive letter to Martinet. It grew to thirty-four pages as he drifted from legal strategizing to the state of race relations in America. "I have been having some very serious thoughts in regard to Plessy's case," he began. "Shall we press for an early hearing or leave it to come up in its turn or even encourage delay?"

Encourage delay? After all their meticulous maneuvering to put the matter before the court as quickly as possible? "I know you will be surprised to hear this from me," Tourgée wrote, "and I will explain the reasons of it."

At the outset of the case, Tourgée had convinced himself that five justices were within reach—or, at least, not beyond reach. His optimism, hard to justify even then, had eroded. He went through his latest tally, sorting the justices by category, naming no one, but struggling to fashion a possible majority from wisps and wishful thinking.

Certainty: "There is but one who is known to favor the view we must stand upon."

Uncertainty: "One is inclined to be with us legally but his political bias is strong the other way. There are two who may be brought over by the argument."

Hopeless: "There are five who are against us." That included Cleveland's recent nominee, still unconfirmed. "Of these, one may be reached, I think, if he 'hears from the country' soon enough. The others will probably stay where they are until Gabriel blows his horn."

Gabriel blows his horn. A powerful allusion, well chosen. Four justices opposed until their dying days and beyond, until the angel Gabriel sounds his trumpet, announcing the Judgment Day.

Could anything be more unyielding, more definitive, more crushing than that?

PUTTING QUESTION MARKS next to four justices was a generous evaluation at best. Two probably did not belong in that category, not even as wishful thinking. But Tourgée wasn't willing to concede that. Instead, he offered a new strategy for achieving a majority: They should take their fight into the public arena, and make the justices feel the pressure of a mass movement. "The court has always been the foe of liberty until forced to move on by public opinion," he told Martinet, "but if we can get the ear of the Country, and argue the matter fully before the people first, we may incline the wavering to fall on our side when the matter comes up."

How would they create such a groundswell? Tourgée favored a new national newspaper, an extension of the NCRA. He had been nursing this idea for a while, and had made a preliminary start at soliciting backers. He wanted to call it the *National Citizen*, to come out monthly. He was aiming at ten thousand subscribers. Even a monthly publication would take time and money and energy, all commodities in short supply. But if successful, he said, the *Citizen* could become a beacon for the millions of white and colored citizens who believed in liberty and equality. The newspaper could rally public sentiment against the Supreme Court "as the ally of Slavery, Secession, and Caste." Such a crusade might not work, Tourgée acknowledged to Martinet, but "it could do no harm in comparison with an adverse decision."

Long ago, defeat had not made Tourgée's list of worries. He had once told Walker that a "square out adjudication" was vitally important to the Citizens' Committee, win or lose. Now, however, he was issuing a potent warning about losing. "It is of the utmost consequence that we should not have a decision against us, as it is a matter of boast with the court that it has never reversed itself on a constitutional question," he told Martinet. That wasn't entirely accurate, but the thrust of his statement was true: A precedent, once embedded, would be exceedingly hard to remove. Equal but separate, the law of the land.

Tourgée felt this burden, acutely. "I do not wish the responsibility of deciding this matter without the knowledge of the Committee," he wrote. He asked Martinet to "lay this letter before them," with the advice to let the case "come up when it will and not attempt to advance it." That would give them a chance to shape public opinion.

Biding their time now seemed acceptable, even wise. Without the Louisiana attorney general's support, they had no hope of expediting the case anyway. The committee endorsed Tourgée's recommendation. He was, after all, in "full control."

EMMA GREETED HER husband's plan for a national newspaper with gloom. He had been talking for months about this preposterous venture. Had he learned nothing from the failure of *Our Continent*? She had protested, but he had persisted, drafting a prospectus, stoking interest among colored editors, looking for partners. Frustrated, she had taken to her diary to record her fear and anger. "Began copying circulars for Albion . . . seeing nothing but disaster in the scheme if he attempts it alone," she had written on the last day of August 1893. "He will listen to no reason or persuasion on my part."

Hadn't the NCRA caused them enough problems? If Tourgée hadn't started the organization, he might still be writing for the *Inter Ocean*. The editors had suspended publication of the Bystander in early August, after a dispute over Tourgée's pay. What began as a misunderstanding had quickly mushroomed into acrimony. Nixon, the *Inter Ocean* editor, had felt for a long time that Tourgée had been using the Bystander column as a soap box for promoting the NCRA. Other tensions emerged as both Tourgées tried, in separate letters to Nixon, to repair the damages. Emma pleaded poverty, telling Nixon that they relied on their Bystander income to pay their mortgage. Albion's tone varied from conciliatory to feisty, from earnest to sarcastic, sometimes all in the same letter.

His threat to take his work elsewhere had brought a wounded but firm reaction from Nixon. "Of course you have a perfect right to sell your work wherever you think it will be of most personal benefit to you," Nixon had written in July. "We have given you the greatest and most congenial constituency that you could have found anywhere in the United States. . . . You have been allowed the broadest kind of latitude, in fact, have had the least possible restraint." Nixon rejected the idea that the *Inter Ocean* treated him with anything other than respect, saying that "the *Inter Ocean* has certainly been of as much benefit to you as you to the *Inter Ocean*."

No denying the truth of that, as Emma well knew. The Bystander had rescued her husband at a moment when he seemed to be fading. The lost income would hurt the most, in the short term. But it could be replaced. The lost identity and lost platform would be harder to replicate. To lose all three simultaneously, while watching Albion pour weeks of precious energy into a foolish new venture, well, the juxtaposition was too much for Emma.

"I have no faith in what he is doing—merely wasting time which should be given to other work, whereby we could have something to live on," she wrote in her diary on November 7. "My heart is very heavy."

LETTING THE CASE "come up when it will" did not mean going into hibernation. Tourgée and his legal team needed some inkling of the timetable, so they could write their briefs and prepare for the oral arguments. Walker sought to find out. "Kindly inform me," he asked the Supreme Court clerk in January 1894, "when you think it likely that the case of Homer Plessy etc. will come up for a hearing."

The clerk, accustomed to such queries, had answered promptly. His reply was brief and matter-of-fact. *Plessy* was far back in the docket. It would not be reached until spring of 1895 at the earliest, and perhaps not until the fall.

More than a year to wait! Possibly two. If time was what they needed, they now had plenty. But engineering a shift in public opinion was a monumental task, especially from the tiny village of Mayville, New York. Tourgée had promised Emma that he would not risk the family's meager assets. He might be stubborn, as she had said, but he did not want to duplicate the *Continent* fiasco. He had been soliciting stockholders, negotiating a printing deal with a Buffalo publisher, forcing himself to look hard at the economics—all while working on writing projects that, as Emma had put it, "could give us something to live on."

By April 1894, his nerves and his health had gotten the better of him. He decided to put the *Citizen* on hold. Emma was thrilled. "Returned all subscriptions to stock," she wrote happily in her diary. She had prayed for this outcome. She pronounced it "much to my gratification."

Many factors had played into the decision. Reconciliation with the *Inter Ocean* was one of them. At Emma's instigation, Tourgée had gradually worked his way back into Nixon's good graces. In January, the *Inter Ocean* had agreed to publish a new series of "Siva" columns, a sequel to Tourgée's anonymous series of open letters to Cleveland. The first round had spurred a national guessing game in 1885 about Siva's identity, and the *Inter Ocean* was hoping for a repeat success. As for the Bystander, a resurrection was about to occur. Loyal readers had howled at his suspension. That had certainly helped, but probably not as much as Tourgée's agreement to keep the NCRA out of the column and be more judicious in his criticism of the Republican Party. On May 12, 1894, after a nine-month absence, the Bystander returned to his perch. Soon, he was again writing about race in his distinctive way.

Tourgée had more irons in the fire than a blacksmith, so he wasn't at all disappointed at Walker's news that *Plessy* wouldn't be heard for a year or more. The court's composition had changed with Blatchford's replacement, as expected. But the outcome was even worse than Tourgée had feared. Cleveland's first two nominees, both New Yorkers, had failed to win confirmation, blocked by a New York Democratic senator flexing his political muscles in a showdown with Cleveland. But the Senate had speedily approved the third. The victor was a sitting U.S. senator. A Southern Democrat. A former Confederate. From Louisiana.

Of Tourgée's three categories, Justice Edward White could be easily assigned to the third.

Hopeless.

CARRY BROWN FELT well enough in the early months of 1894 to accompany her husband to a flurry of social events, well chronicled in the society columns of the *Evening Star* and the *Post*. A dinner party for twenty at a senator's residence. A state dinner at the White House. An afternoon tea at home—Carry's first in their splendid mansion on Sixteenth Street, ready for visitors after more than two years of construction headaches and noise.

For Justice Brown, seeing his wife on her feet was a great relief. As he would write years later, her recurring ailments had become a constant worry, unpredictable and debilitating enough that "I never dared to calculate upon her living from one month to another." Whenever she was feeling better, they tried to seize the moment. With her doctor's blessing, they arranged another European jaunt. By the time summer came, she was well enough to go.

They returned a few weeks earlier than usual, but the trip itself was a success. On September 11, 1894, they stepped off the SS *Trave* in New York, one month before the start of the fall term.

FREDERICK DOUGLASS'S SUDDEN death on February 20, 1895, brought forth a national outpouring of emotion that said as much about the country's continuing racial divide as it did about Douglass. He had been a lightning rod during his remarkable life. Death was no different. Those who disliked him found a way to indicate their disdain. Those who loved him, whether they knew him personally or not, grieved as if they had lost a dear family member.

On the Monday following his death, thousands streamed to the Metropolitan AME Church in Northwest Washington to pause at his heavy oaken casket, catch a last glimpse of his bearded face, and perhaps say a prayer, if they were quick enough. The crush of mourners made lingering impossible. Blue-coated police officers kept the line moving. "Some would have stood and shed their tears upon the casket," the *Evening Star* reported, but "no time was given for the demonstration of grief."

The sunny winter morning gave way to afternoon, and still the grievers came, a seemingly endless parade. Men, women, and children, mostly people of color, but whites, too. Not just a smattering of whites, but hundreds, the *Evening Star* said. Shortly after two o'clock, Mrs. Douglass and her family were ushered into their roped-off pews. Outside, carriages lined M Street in both directions. An immense throng still jammed the block, spilling around the corners, into Fifteenth and Sixteenth Streets, hoping in vain to gain admission for the service. Some ticketholders, holding passes for the block of five hundred reserved seats, couldn't get in. Every seat, every nook was filled, "to the last inch of standing room."

Near Mrs. Douglass, in rows set aside for guests of "special honor," sat two Republican senators and John Harlan. The justice had no role in the service. But Harlan had known Douglass for more than twenty years, going back to their campaign tour in Maine, stumping for Grant in 1872. Their paths had crossed occasionally in Washington. Douglass's 1883 letter, praising Harlan's dissent in the *Civil Rights Cases*, had called it a triumph of reasoning that should be "read and pondered by every citizen in the country." Harlan, alone in dissenting, was now the lone justice at the funeral.

It felt like the end of an era, not just the end of a life. As eulogy after eulogy often noted, not just in Washington but in dozens of memorial services around the country, Douglass's seventy-eight years stood as witness to a nation's evolution. That evolution was far from complete, as Douglass had often said in a lifetime of orations. Slavery, then liberation. The Emancipation Proclamation, then the color line. Legal subjugation, then legal separation. The Fourteenth Amendment's promise of equal protection, then whites holding conferences on "the negro problem."

On the day of Douglass's death, in Alabama, one of his successors to national leadership was presiding over the fourth annual meeting of the Tuskegee Negro Conference. More than five hundred farmers and teachers in the South, including some whites, had gathered at Booker T. Washington's Normal and Industrial Institute in Tuskegee. The agenda: to talk about how negroes could "cure the evils that lie in our power to remedy."

Militancy was not Washington's style. He favored improving the colored "condition" through education, land and home ownership, moral and religious training. Whites and the color line did not make many appearances in his speeches. Neither did confrontation. As the conference's final declaration said, "More can be accomplished by going forward than by complaining." The delegates endorsed a set of principles for negroes in the South to follow. Buy land and "cultivate it thoroughly." Give more attention to "the character of our leaders, especially ministers and teachers." Keep out of debt. Avoid lawsuits.

Martinet never much cared for Washington's philosophy. The Tuskegee educator liked to preach about the "dignity" of every job, skilled or unskilled, and surely that was true. But wasn't there also a risk of creating a docile generation of colored youth, doomed to menial labor in a white-dominated world, reluctant to stand up for their rights? That's what worried Martinet.

The *Crusader* editor could not shake the feeling that Washington's credo of hard work and self-reliance was missing a crucial element. "The Booker Washingtons . . . and others have their uses and are doing a useful work," Martinet told Tourgée in his brooding 1893 letter, written at the end of his Chicago stay. But what "colored youths most need," he wrote, is to be taught "manly courage and resistance to wrong and oppression," alongside "the 'dignity of labor' and the elevating influences of religion."

Martinet had chosen resistance and lawsuit, a difficult path. In September 1895, seven months after Douglass's death, a Booker T. Washington speech in Atlanta would garner national attention and praise for advocating very much the opposite.

JUSTICE HENRY BROWN labored on his June 1895 commencement address with a surgeon's care and a composer's ear. He had something important to tell the graduates of Yale Law School, as well as the rest of the country, and he wanted to express his fears with precision and verve. Speeches by Supreme Court justices were rare enough. A speech that warned about "municipal corruption, corporate greed, and the tyranny of labor" was certain to produce headlines. Brown wanted to appear thoughtful, not reckless. He wanted to play the role of philosopher, not politician. He was sounding an alarm about "the evils that threaten our future tranquility," not taking a side.

That wasn't exactly true. He was taking the side of moderation, stability, and the fair administration of law. As he made clear to the graduates, he did not oppose wealth or power. He opposed wealth in the hands of a few, and power in the hands of the corrupt. He did not oppose corporations, which provided incentives, jobs, prosperity. But he feared the growth of powerful "trusts," those combinations of corporations that "stifle competition and monopolize the necessaries of life." The country needed to corral the corporations, restraining their worst tendencies without hindering their ability to contribute to the public good. "The whole fabric of civilization is built upon the sanctity of private property," he said. "Were this foundation to be taken away, the structure would crumble into ruins."

The graduates were inheriting the consequences of thirty years of dramatic change and "social unrest," Brown told them. He did not mention, specifically, racial strife. "It has been given to the Nineteenth Century to teach the world how a great republic can be founded upon principles of justice and equality," he said. "It will be the duty of the Twentieth to show how it can be preserved against the insidious encroachments of wealth, as well as the assaults of the mob."

If moderation was the way forward, what was the path? The judicial system, Brown said. "At the basis of every free government is the ability of the citizen to apply to the courts for a redress of his grievances and the assurance that he will there receive what justice demands."

In bringing the *Plessy* case, Martinet and the Citizens' Committee were seeking "what justice demands." A few months after Brown's speech, as summer was ending, the Supreme Court clerk completed the docket for the October 1895 term. *Plessy's* new number in the queue: 210. At the court's usual pace, that meant a hearing sometime in the spring of 1896.

By then, the case would be nearly four years old.

THE SETTING WAS GLORIOUS for Booker T. Washington's Atlanta speech, yet another of the country's grand fairs, this one called the Cotton States and Industrial Exposition. On a September day so cruelly hot that the fair's organizers mercifully cut short the opening program, tens of thousands stood for hours in their sweat-drenched finery to watch a massive parade. The procession, including U.S. Army troops accompanied by a thirty-five-member military band, strode along the same streets that Sherman's army had left in ruins as they marched away in late 1864. In the headlines for September 19, 1895, Atlanta's rise from the ashes often played a featured role. "In Its New Pride," said the *Chicago Tribune*. "South Displays the Glories of a Prosperous Peace."

In the spirit of this new beginning, the exposition's organizers had established a Negro Board, asking it to create an exhibition, a move that avoided some of the criticisms leveled at the Chicago World's Fair. Washington had served as one of the board's commissioners, and now had the honor of addressing the immense crowd at the welcoming ceremony. The *Tribune* correspondent called his speech eloquent, "perhaps the best" of the day. Three times, Washington had to stop, and wait for the cheers to fade so that he could be heard again. What had brought the crowd of overwhelmingly white businessmen and politicians to its feet? In the words of the *Tribune* correspondent, "his ideas were not radical, and he did not stoop to the worn-out arguments of inequality but frankly acknowledged the deficiencies of his race."

Running through the speech were the familiar Washington themes—hard work, thrift, self-sufficiency, and the importance of moral character. But that wasn't what caught the crowd's attention or the public's imagination. Washington had tailored his message to his predominantly white audience. His tone was mollifying. His words were soothing. He evoked history in a way that Douglass and Martinet and Tourgée never had, never would. If whites wanted to know about the future of race relations, Washington kept saying, they should look to the past.

In the future, "as in the past," he said, "you and your families will be surrounded by the most patient, faithful, law-abiding and unresentful people that the world has seen. As we have proved our loyalty to you in the past, in nursing your children, watching by the sick bed of your mothers and fathers, and often following them with tear-dimmed eyes to their graves, so in the future in our humble way, we shall stand by you with a devotion no foreigner can approach, ready to lay down our lives, if need be, in defense of yours, interlacing our industrial, commercial, civil, and religious life with yours in a way that shall make the interests of both races one."

"Interlacing" did not include social equality, he said reassuringly. That was not necessary, or even desirable. "In all things that are purely social, we can be as separate as the fingers, yet one as the hand in all things essential to mutual progress," he said. "The wisest among my race understand that the agitation of questions of social equality is the extremest folly, and that progress in the enjoyment of all the privileges that will come to us must be the result of severe and constant struggle rather than of artificial forcing. . . . It is important and right that all privileges of the law be ours, but it is vastly more important that we be prepared for the exercise of these privileges."

Without mentioning the separate car laws sprouting in the South, Washington signaled his lack of interest in a protracted fight for equal accommodations. He had other priorities. "The opportunity to earn a dollar in a factory just now is worth infinitely more than the opportunity to spend a dollar in an opera house," he said. And: "No race can prosper until it learns that there is as much dignity in tilling a field as in writing a poem. It is at the bottom of life we must begin, and not at the top."

The speech was a sensation. White newspapers around the country reprinted substantial portions. In the South, where Tourgée still drew denunciations for his Bystander columns, accolades rained down. "Words of Wisdom From a Colored Man" was the *Asheville Daily Citizen*'s headline. The *Birmingham News* saluted the speech as "wise in counsel and sensible throughout," and declared: "The negroes need more men like Booker T. Washington." The *Times-Democrat*'s correspondent sent a dispatch to New Orleans that said: "I cannot recall an orator of more magnetism, more earnestness, more sincerity. . . . All in all, it was the most impressive speech I have ever heard, and doubtless the most remarkable that has ever fallen from the lips of a negro."

Martinet and Tourgée were hoping for a shift in public opinion, but not this kind. Here, many whites were saying with vigorous approval, was a colored man who wanted his people to work hard and raise themselves up, but not at the expense of whites. Here was a man who understood the negro's place in the world, who wasn't pressing those "worn-out arguments of inequality," as the *Tribune* correspondent had put it.

That was not the message that Tourgée and his team planned to deliver in their arguments to the Supreme Court.

The audience: The nine justices of the Supreme Court, 1896

(Library of Congress)

22

"In the Nature of Things"

March, April, May 1896

JUST A FEW MONTHS MORE. That's all Martinet and Tourgée wanted. Just a few months more—March, April, May—and the *Plessy* case would be pushed to the fall of 1896, along with all other leftovers on the court's endless docket. By then, the country's mood might be different. Republicans would be priming themselves for a national victory, and Grover Cleveland would be on his way out of the White House. "Don't you think it better to have the Plessy case fixed for November, after the election?" Martinet asked Tourgée in early March.

The two men had convinced themselves: Time was the remedy. Time would bring that much-needed shift in public sentiment. Already, the election excitement was building. The newspapers were giving Tourgée's old friend, Maine's Tom Reed, a slim shot at pulling an upset at the Republican convention. Swept up in the hoopla, Martinet told Tourgée: "If Reed were the Rep. nominee, and elected by a large majority, men's minds on questions of rights might be changed."

Their grand plans for pressuring the justices through public opinion hadn't amounted to much. The *Crusader* had gone to daily publication in 1894, but its modest circulation was dwarfed by its mounting losses. "*Crusader* is on its last legs," Martinet told Tourgée. In Mayville, Tourgée had founded a modest monthly magazine called *Basis: A Journal of Civilization*, featuring the Bystander, removed from the *Inter Ocean*. That meant the column was appearing less often, in a barely visible publication. Not the most effective way to influence public sentiment.

Initially, their strategy had been to seek the fastest possible route to Supreme Court review. Then, it had changed to "let the case come up in turn." Now delay was their desire. Tourgée had checked with Phillips in Washington. At the court's current pace, he said, oral arguments might be reached by "the very edge of the term." That meant late April or early May. To avoid that possibility, they needed to apply for a postponement until fall. Could the Louisiana attorney general be persuaded to support their request? Walker was asked to find out.

Meanwhile, they needed to be prepared if their luck ran out, and the case was called. They were nearly ready. Tourgée and Walker had written their portions of the brief. Phillips had promised to "block out" his section soon. He was finding the task daunting, he freely admitted. "There is a great deal in the case to think about," he told Tourgée. "I do not know how you ready writers" do it. As an "unready writer," he said, he would be drafting and redrafting "up to the last moment."

During their many months of correspondence, Phillips hadn't speculated about their chances. Now, though, he offered his understated view. It matched Tourgée's.

"It is hardly doubtful," he said, that "we have a Court somewhat adverse to our views."

TOURGÉE NEEDED NO reminder of the court's unfriendly inclinations. The justices loomed large in his mind as he wrote his brief. The court's composition had changed once again. Howell Jackson, Brown's good friend, had died the previous August after serving fewer than three years. His replacement: Rufus W. Peckham Jr., a New York Democrat and judge on the state's elected court of appeals. The newspapers described Peckham as "a warm personal friend of President Cleveland," a relationship forged in New York's political trenches. Peckham's friends and former law clients included several of the nation's most powerful tycoons, and his previous judicial rulings had shown a decided aversion to government intrusion into corporate affairs. Might Peckham be persuaded to feel the same about a legislative act that forced a Louisiana railway corporation to run separate cars?

Peckham's confirmation had boosted the court's Northern contingent to seven. But these were the sorts of Northerners that Tourgée had often railed against in his Bystander column. Not just white, but living above the fray. Their backgrounds did not suggest any notable interest in racial injustice or equal rights. Several had spent their legal careers working for large corporations or defending their interests. Chief Justice Melville Fuller fit that profile. A native of Maine, he had gone west to Chicago as a young man, and had made his name as a lawyer for the city's burgeoning railroad industry.

To sway four of the Northern-born justices to join Harlan for a five-vote majority, Tourgée was asking them to look beyond the confines of their lives, to see a world that did not align with the one that they knew. Three justices—Brown, George Shiras Jr. of Pennsylvania, and Peckham—were new to the court since the 1890 Mississippi separate car case. Tourgée would need them all, plus one more. Not impossible, but nearly so. Five-four splits on the court were still rare. In several recent terms, there hadn't been any. The last two terms, though, had brought three each. Hardly a pattern, but if the Citizens' Committee had a prayer of prevailing, five-four was its best hope, possibly its only hope.

Their final brief reflected Tourgée's belief, as he had told Walker long ago, that "it is better to have too many points than not enough." The nearly eighty pages teemed with arguments, a surfeit rather than a selection. They had worked on their portions separately, in Mayville, Washington, and New Orleans. The result was overlap and some duplication, even though they had divided up the many questions they needed to cover.

But it had one advantage. Instead of listening to a soloist's lonely voice, the justices were hearing a chorus. Three lawyers, from three different perspectives, amplifying each other, sounding the alarm, seeking converts to their cause.

IN WRITING THE BRIEF, the trio couldn't start over. They had to confine themselves to the established record and the five categories of errors they had cited in asking for the court's review. But like decorating a house with many rooms, the brief offered an abundance of opportunities for personal touches and embellishment. For Tourgée, the master of elaboration, the temptation proved irresistible. They might lose the case, but not because he had failed to argue, fully and forcefully, why the Separate Car Act was an insult to both the Thirteenth and Fourteenth amendments. He would show the justices the path to the correct ruling, morally as well as legally. Beyond that, what more could he do?

The brief needed to shine. Many Supreme Court cases were decided on briefs alone, with no oral arguments. Tourgée's portion came first, and within a few pages, it was abundantly clear that he was not following the familiar formula. He couldn't anchor his argument primarily in precedents, because he was asking the justices to apply the amendments differently than the majority had ever applied them before. To guide and school the justices, he had synthesized the issues into twenty-three "points of contention," gracing each with a roman numeral.

Point II unveiled an unorthodox argument, intended to resonate with those justices who saw themselves as staunch defenders of property rights. Race, Tourgée asserted, was a kind of property. It had economic value. If you were white—or could claim to be white—it enhanced your reputation. If you were black, it was a burden. "How much would it be *worth* to a young man entering upon the practice of law," he asked, slyly choosing the justices' chosen profession as his example, "to be regarded as a *white* man rather than a colored one?"

Look at the statistics, he urged. Whites owned 90 percent of the country's land. They controlled 99 percent of the business prospects. Who in the United States today, he asked, would choose to be black? "Probably most white persons, if given a choice, would prefer death to life" as a colored person, he wrote. Given that sensibility, "is it possible to conclude that the *reputation of being white* is not property? Indeed, is it not the most valuable sort of property, being the master-key that unlocks the golden door of opportunity?"

Think of a passenger, sitting in the white car, he told the justices. Under Louisiana's Separate Car Act, the conductor has the authority, with a snap judgment, to exile that passenger to the colored car, depriving him or her of "the reputation of being white." That amounted to a "forcible confiscation" of valuable property, "without evidence or investigation"—a clear violation, Tourgée said, of the Fourteenth Amendment's provision that no state shall "deprive any person of life, liberty, or *property*, without due process."

An inventive argument, but a risky one. What if the justices ruled that people of mixed race were exempt from the law, allowed to choose either the white or colored car? Separation would remain. Nothing would change. A winning point in a losing cause.

THE FOURTEENTH AMENDMENT was Tourgée's touchstone in his brief. If he strayed from it, he never strayed for long. Tourgée wanted the justices to think hard about the four provisions of the amendment's first section, harder than ever before. The clause granting citizenship. The prohibition against states making any law abridging the rights of U.S. citizens. The twinned guarantees of due process and equal protection. The Separate Car Act ignored or violated each, he argued, in multiple and nefarious ways.

He had combed the court's previous rulings on the Fourteenth. The questions surrounding race and the color line, Tourgée was saying, had too many permutations to have been settled with finality. The *Plessy* case, with its mixed-race plaintiff and a law making it a crime to sit in the wrong car, had triggered new issues that deserved their own careful analysis. The Fourteenth had created a "*new* citizenship," he asserted, "embracing *new* rights . . . controlled by *new* authority, having a *new* scope and extent," requiring the court to examine *Plessy* in a *new* context.

Similarly, he wanted the court to revisit the Thirteenth. The amendment's stated purpose was to abolish "slavery and involuntary servitude." But outlawing slavery, he said, did not banish the beliefs that sustained it. Those attitudes of superiority and dominance were embedded in the new Jim Crow laws. The Thirteenth was also meant, he argued, to rid the nation of the caste system that had nourished slavery. If the court allowed the Separate Car Act to stand, it would be allowing the States to reimpose that caste system.

Nor would it end there, he predicted. If a state had a right to separate the races on trains, what else might it do? The variations were endless, he said. "Why not require all colored people to walk on one side of the street and the whites on the other?" he wrote. "Why may it not require every white man's house to be painted white and every colored man's black?" To justify these new discriminations, the states would make ever more bizarre claims of "equality." One side of the street "may be just as good as the other," Tourgée said drily.

Instead of the naked prejudice of the earlier Black Codes, Tourgée told the justices, the State of Louisiana was now hiding its intentions, calling the Separate Car Act a "police regulation," necessary to protect the public's health. Tourgée was scornful. What was the danger? What was the disease?

And this: "Is it the white who spreads the contagion," he asked, "or the black?"

TOURGÉE HAD STACKED the deck with the cards that he wanted. Now he was ready to play them. From the earliest days of the case, he had thought that a nearly white plaintiff would make it easier to expose the law's unfairness and unenforceability. The justices in Washington, reading the case record, might well have wondered why a passenger who looked white, sitting in the whites-only car, had drawn a conductor's attention at all. Tourgée made no effort to enlighten them. He did not mention the arranged arrest. Instead, he deployed Plessy's mixed ancestry as a wedge, seeking to widen the justices' understanding of racial conditions in America.

He asked them to "take notice" of the "great numbers of citizens" of mixed race in "all parts of the country." Were they white? Colored? How was a conductor to make such a judgment? It was impossible to determine someone's ancestry, he argued, without "the most careful and deliberate weighing of evidence, much less by the casual scrutiny of a busy conductor." Even if a percentage could be determined, what then? "Will the court hold," Tourgée cried, "that a single drop of African blood is sufficient to color a whole ocean of Caucasian whiteness?"

No law could anticipate the various scenarios a conductor might face, he suggested. His passengers might include a "white" mother traveling with her "colored" child. "Has a State the right to order the mother to ride in one car, and her young daughter, because her cheek may have a darker tinge, to ride alone in another?" he asked. The mother's or daughter's discomfort would not alter the conductor's decision. This proved that the act was "intended to promote the happiness of one class" at the expense of the other. Invoking the iconic image of the blindfolded Lady Justice, arm extended, holding a scale as she weighs the evidence, Tourgée declared: "Justice is pictured blind and her daughter, the Law, ought at least to be color-blind."

Another lawyer might have stopped there. Not Tourgée. He opted for a novelist's memorable climax. "Suppose a member of this court, nay, suppose every member of it," he wrote, "should wake to-morrow with a black skin and curly hair—the two obvious and controlling indications of race—and in traveling through that portion of the country where the 'Jim Crow Car' abounds, should be ordered into it by the conductor. . . . What humiliation, what rage would then fill the judicial mind!"

If the justices could stand in those colored shoes, he said, they would "feel and know" the truth of his arguments. They would see that the act was not meant, as its preamble claimed, "to promote the comfort of passengers on railway trains." It was intended to "humiliate and degrade" people of color, and to "perpetuate the caste distinctions on which slavery rested."

SPURRED BY TOURGÉE'S long-ago question about whether Louisiana had ever defined "colored race" or "person of color," Walker had plumbed the legal and historical record for his brief. In a tone verging on astonishment, he revealed his findings. Unlike many states, "Louisiana law and precedents are silent on the subject." By failing to provide a definition, he argued, "successive legislatures" had made it impossible to enforce the Separate Car Act.

For Walker, his research had clarified the absurdity of designating train conductors as the "supreme judge" of a passenger's race or color. Nearly every state had a different standard, if it had any standard at all. There were "almost as many definitions," he wrote, "as there are lexicographers and courts." In Mississippi, he wrote, "a person of color means a person of African descent." In Alabama's courts, "negro means a black man, one descended from the African race, and does not commonly include a mulatto." In Michigan, anyone with "less than one-fourth of African blood" would be considered white, while in North Carolina, the percentage had to be "less than one-sixteenth." In South Carolina and Georgia, disputes over someone's color were matters for a jury to decide, governed by rules of evidence. Not a train conductor, acting alone, "without recourse to any of the courts in the State."

Fascinated by this "most unaccountable variance," Walker challenged the justices to consider the plight of a mixed-race traveler, bound for a distant destination. "How would it affect a citizen's constitutional rights to be classed by law as a white man in one state and as a negro or person of color in another state?" he wrote. "One would think that his reputation and social status as a white man ought to be worth something. . . . The rights and privileges of a white man, as such, are not to be taken from him by State legislation."

The rights and privileges of a white man. Another novel argument, echoing Tourgée's view that reputation was a form of property. But not a claim that would give much comfort to someone who had no intention or hope of passing for white.

EMMA COULD HARDLY believe it. She thought winter had said its farewell to Mayville. Then, on the morning of April 3, she woke to "a regular blizzard all day, almost equal to any the winter has produced." The nasty weather matched Albion's foul mood. From Washington had come an April 1 letter from Phillips, with the astonishing news that the court was about to hear *Plessy*. Phillips had been blasé about this dramatic turn of events. "I will represent the matter orally," he had written, anticipating that the oral arguments might take place the very next day. "Until now, I had thought that Mr. Walker and you—or you alone—could be here."

That was it. No expression of regret. No urgent telegram, seeking instructions. No explanation of why the case was called so suddenly. Nothing to show that Phillips understood how maddening it would feel for Tourgée to be stuck in Mayville, frozen out of the opportunity to address the justices in person. After all this time, all this work, all this worry.

Tourgée was already unhappy with his co-counsel. They had disagreed about a part of the brief in a recent exchange of letters. Phillips felt the tension. In his April 1 letter, he told Tourgée, "as you were annoyed . . . and did not come back at me about it—indeed having abandoned all communication with me since then—I will not aggravate matters." Now it looked as if Tourgée would be forced to rely on Phillips and his passion-free promise to "represent the matter orally." As if this were just another case on the court's crowded docket. Next up, *Plessy v. Ferguson*, number 210. All rise.

No, this would not do. Even if the hearing had already taken place without him, Tourgée could not stand by silently. He sent off a blistering protest to the Supreme Court clerk about the sudden call of the case. Later in the day, through the blizzard, came an unexpected reprieve. "Albion relieved by telegram from Mr. Phillips," Emma wrote in her diary that night. "Sep. Car case is put for the 13th."

April 13. Plenty of time for Tourgée to hurry to the capital, courtesy of a bit of luck at the previous day's session. The justices had stopped just short of the *Plessy* case, making it first in line for the court's next meeting. Fortunately, the justices also had announced a ten-day recess. April 13 would be their first day back.

A few days later, Court Clerk James McKenney replied to Tourgée's fiery letter, confirming the April 13 date and explaining that his office customarily relies on the local counsel, if there is one, to notify any out-of-town lawyers who "desire to argue the case." That's why the clerk had not contacted Tourgée directly. Reading between McKenney's diplomatic lines, it was clear that Phillips had known for several days that the case had reached the "call" list. But he had waited until nearly too late to inform Tourgée.

April 13. Tourgée would have his chance to speak after all, no thanks to his co-counsel.

EVEN AS TOURGÉE packed his bags for Washington, he was still hoping to hear from Walker that the Louisiana attorney general had agreed to postpone the case until fall. Unfortunately, Walker was getting nowhere. On April 9, with the oral argument four days away, Walker conceded defeat. "I have not the faintest hope" of obtaining the attorney general's support, he wrote Tourgée.

That wasn't his only disappointment, Walker wrote. He also wouldn't be making the trip to Washington for the oral argument. A lingering series of coughs and colds had weakened his health. The long journey seemed too much of a risk. He sent Tourgée into battle with a warm salute. "I hope your success will be commensurate with the energy, skill and earnestness which has marked everything you have said and done in the case," he wrote.

By the time Walker's letter reached Mayville, though, Tourgée was already gone.

EIGHT JUSTICES FILED into their customary meeting place, the Old Senate Chamber, at noon on April 13, 1896. Adjusting their dark robes to make themselves comfortable, they folded themselves into their chairs. Forty years before, at a desk in this same room, Charles Sumner had suffered the beating that nearly cost him his life. Now, in a few hours, Tourgée would rise to argue for the principles that had defined Sumner's career and legacy. Sumner was not Tourgée's hero. But in many ways, Tourgée was Sumner's heir and beneficiary.

Fuller presided from the center seat, while seniority dictated the rest of the tableau. At Fuller's right rested the longest-serving justice, Stephen Field, full-bearded in his fourth decade on the bench, but in declining health as he neared his eightieth birthday. On Fuller's immediate left perched John Harlan, still vigorous at sixty-two, wisps of gray at his temples, his stout neck barely visible above his judicial collar. Three seats to Fuller's right was Henry Brown, sixty and in his sixth year on the court, his bushy dark eyebrows a bold contrast to his thinning gray hair.

David Brewer's chair remained empty. No announcement was made to explain his absence, but anyone reading the newspapers would excuse him. On top of serving as chairman of an international tribunal charged with settling a territorial dispute between Venezuela and Great Britain, Brewer was coping with a family crisis. His oldest daughter Fannie was critically ill with consumption. Her doctors had sent her to Texas in November, hoping the milder weather would bring a miracle. Brewer had just returned from his latest visit, summoned because she seemed to be slipping away.

Brewer could still participate in *Plessy*. No court rule required the justices to hear the oral argument. Since January, when the territorial commission's work began, Brewer had joined in most rulings. Tourgée had no way of knowing whether Brewer could be turned into an ally. It seemed unlikely, given Brewer's majority ruling in favor of Mississippi's separate car law. But without him, assembling a majority would mean capturing someone from the "hopeless" group.

Tourgée's presence in the chamber caught the attention of the *Washington Post* reporter. Fashioning a short item for the newspaper's "Capitol Chat" column, he wrote: "Judge Albion W. Tourgee, the famous author of 'A Fool's Errand,' which created such a sensation a score of years ago, was in the Supreme Court yesterday arguing the case of H. A. Plessy vs. J. H. Ferguson."

And what did "the famous author" tell the justices? The *Post* reporter did not say. He did not quote a single word of Tourgée's oral argument. Relying solely on the briefs, the reporter offered instead a spare hundred-word summary of the facts, unaware that it was an arranged arrest. Plessy "claims to be one-eighth African and seven-eighths Caucasian," he told his readers, "and resented being ejected from the white coach on the East Louisiana Railroad."

Then, the reporter's verdict on Tourgée's chance of success, delivered like a punch line. "One of the visitors to the court expressed the opinion that it was another fool's errand," he wrote, "as the practical questions at issue in the case have already been decided in favor of the validity of the law involved."

TOURGÉE POSSESSED the oratorical skills that Brown had always envied. Apart from their eye afflictions and public stature, the two men shared little else. Tourgée had unpaid debts; Brown had financial security. Tourgée prized his unconventional view of life, his refusal to accept the rules of white society. Brown, on the other hand, was among the most conventional of men. He wanted to help steer the boat, not rock it.

For the oral argument, Tourgée had armored himself with a thick sheaf of notes, nearly fifty typewritten pages on half sheets of paper, which he had titled simply, "Plessy Vs. Ferguson. Argument of A. W. Tourgee." He would not have time to make more than a few of his many points. But he had a few good lines at the ready.

He hoped to jar the justices into rethinking their racial views by asking "how shall a man who may have one-eighth or one-sixteenth colored blood know to which race he belongs? . . . It is a question the law of Louisiana has not decided, and which science is totally unable to solve." He intended to spotlight his "reputation is property" argument, saying that "The most precious of all inheritances is the reputation of being white." Then, after laying bare the Separate Car Act's constitutional defects, he would declare that the entire law must fall, because "No man can be hanged with a rotten rope."

Oral arguments generally drew little attention from the Washington press corps, and *Plessy* was no exception. Other than the "Capitol Chat" item, Tourgée's presentation drew almost no coverage from white newspapers, even in New Orleans. The *Picayune* reduced the event to thirty-one words, saying only that "the court heard argument" and that the case "arose from enforcement of the Jim Crow car law." No mention of the Citizens' Committee and its work to challenge the law. No hint that it was a test case. The *Times-Democrat*'s account, limited to two paragraphs, said the Plessy team had run into skeptical questioning from Justices Stephen Field and Edward White. The duo had quizzed Tourgée and Phillips about the state's "inherent" police powers, the newspaper wrote, leading lawyers "who heard the argument" to surmise that the Separate Car Act was safe from being declared unconstitutional.

The Louisiana attorney general's brief had listed the state's police powers as its primary defense of the Separate Car Act. Did Field's and White's questions mean they were leaning toward the State's view? Until the court ruled, there was no way to know. Tourgée did not have a good feeling, though, when he left for Mayville the next day. He trudged home late on Wednesday night, April 15. "Albion pretty tired from the trip," Emma wrote in her diary.

Following their usual routine, the justices would debate the case in their weekly Saturday conference after the oral argument. Any wrangling, though, would likely stay behind those closed doors. Scuttlebutt was not among the court's traditions. "We have not yet heard anything about the case," Phillips told an impatient Tourgée on April 28. "Indeed, as you might guess, we never do, until some Judge has read for a minute or two upon his opinion!"

DONNING THEIR ROBES on Monday, May 18, the justices had a mountain of rulings to release, nearly three dozen in all, part of their rush to complete as many cases as possible before the term's end. The busy calendar drew no bigger crowd than usual, though. The press did not see the rulings as including any landmark pronouncements.

When the justices took their seats, Brewer's chair was vacant again. He was in Kansas, grieving with his family over his daughter Fannie's death. Before the devastating telegram from San Antonio, the justice had recorded his vote for most of the May 18 decisions. But not in *Plessy*. Later, there was talk that he had avoided the case. If true, he kept his reasons to himself. Following the court's custom, he did not explain his choice.

After the first dozen rulings came *Plessy*. The tally: Seven justices for the majority. One dissenter. Harlan stood alone. After four years of legal maneuvering, briefs, and oral argument, Tourgée's team had failed to swing a single vote. Writing for the majority? Not Fuller, or White, or Horace Gray, or anyone from the "hopeless" category. No, the author was Henry Billings Brown.

It made no difference, of course, that Fuller's assignment had gone to Brown. But it made the decision that much harder to take. Brown had been in Tourgée's "uncertain" category.

His ruling, though, had no such ambiguity.

BROWN'S HANDIWORK HAD circulated among the other justices in the weeks after the oral arguments. As the author, though, Brown was the one to read it aloud. If his eyes were causing him any problems that Monday, no reporter took any notice. He began with a brief review of the facts, captured from the Tourgée-Walker petition to the Louisiana Supreme Court in 1892: The passenger had been "ordered" to leave the whites-only car, had "refused to comply," and was "forcibly ejected." Unsuspecting readers of the ruling—now and in the future—would have no clue that the railroad had been a knowing participant. It seemed evident that Brown himself did not realize it.

At every turn, Brown opted for a narrow reading of the Thirteenth and Fourteenth amendments, hewing closely to the court's previous interpretations. Tourgée had wanted the court to accept a less literal view of "involuntary servitude." Tourgée had laid out his reasoning, arguing that separate car laws had one overriding purpose: to make whites into the dominant race. That essentially made separation into a form of servitude, he said—servitude to whites in their drive to establish their superiority.

Absurd, in Brown's view. Separate cars had nothing to do with servitude. For support, he quoted from Bradley's majority opinion in the *Civil Rights Cases*: "It would be running the slavery argument into the ground to make it apply to every act of discrimination."

In unsettling contrast to Tourgée's dark view, Brown offered a benign interpretation of the Separate Car Act. "A statute which implies merely a legal distinction between the white and colored races," he wrote, "has no tendency to destroy the legal equality of the two races, or reestablish a state of involuntary servitude." He saw nothing alarming in this "implied" distinction, saying it "must always exist so long as white men are distinguished from the other race by color." Then, underscoring the majority's incredulity at this part of Tourgée's argument, he added: "Indeed, we do not understand" why the Plessy team has so "strenuously relied" on the Thirteenth Amendment.

Brown's disbelief did not end there. Calling it a "fallacy" to assume that "the enforced separation of the two races stamps the colored race with a badge of inferiority," he wrote: "If this be so, it is not by reason of anything found in the act, but solely because the colored race chooses to put that construction upon it." Brown wasn't just dismissing the Thirteenth Amendment argument. He was scolding people of color for thinking the law's show of equality was a sham.

There were white people all over the country, North as well as South, who believed that the colored race was inferior. These whites had said so repeatedly—in speeches, in newspaper articles, in legislatures. Now Brown and the majority were declaring, essentially, that people of color could not believe their own ears, their own eyes, or their own experience.

WHAT ABOUT THE FOURTEENTH AMENDMENT, and its prohibition against the states making any law that "shall abridge the privileges or immunities of citizens of the United States?" That was the core of the *Plessy* argument. Couldn't the justices see that the Separate Car Act, passed by the state legislature, undermined the very notion of equal citizenship?

No, Brown and the majority could not. They saw no conflict at all between Louisiana's exercise of its "police power" and the Fourteenth Amendment. Thirty years after the amendment's creation—a contentious process that had involved many hands and compromises—Brown gave his view of what its drafters must have been thinking in 1866: "The object of the amendment was undoubtedly to enforce the absolute equality of the two races before the law, but, in the nature of things, it could not have been intended to abolish distinctions based upon color, or to enforce social, as distinguished from political, equality, or a commingling of the two races upon terms unsatisfactory to either."

In the nature of things. Not a legal phrase, certainly. Instead, Brown was endorsing custom and preference, from the white point of view, as it existed at the time—and, seemingly, as Brown thought it would exist for all time. An immutable condition, not open to question. Or, as Brown had said of his interpretation of the Thirteenth Amendment, "too clear for argument."

Courts had long recognized legislation based on separation, Brown pointed out. "Similar statutes for the separation of the races upon public conveyances," he wrote, have been "held to be constitutional." To support this conclusion, he listed a dozen rulings—including two that predated the Civil War. One was William Day's lawsuit against the Michigan steamboat, *Day v. Owen*, the 1858 case that Brown's first law firm had brought and lost. The other was a famous Boston schools case from 1849, with Sumner on the losing side, arguing unsuccessfully against separation before the Massachusetts Supreme Judicial Court.

By reaching back to a time before emancipation and the Fourteenth Amendment to supply two of his precedents, Brown had left himself open to an obvious criticism: He wasn't just relying on the past. He was living in it. How could rulings from 1849 and 1858, before the guarantees of equal protection and due process, have much bearing on *Plessy*?

His conclusion was shaky for another reason. He had said those dozen cases had upheld "similar statutes." But most of the twelve rulings didn't involve a statute at all. Homer Plessy's predecessors—William Day in Michigan, Mary Miles in Pennsylvania, William Heard before the Interstate Commerce Commission—were challenging company policies, not state laws.

It was a mystifying statement from a justice who prided himself on his careful research and respect for precedent.

THE RULING CONFIRMED Tourgée's and Martinet's worst fears. By bringing the case, he and the Citizens' Committee had opened the door to making matters worse, to hardening lines that had once been ambiguous, to the spread of separation. Brown could have let them down lightly. He chose not to. Instead, he and the majority delivered a stinging message: Laws and lawsuits were not the best way to achieve their goals. "The argument also assumes that social prejudices may be overcome by legislation, and that equal rights cannot be secured to the negro except by an enforced commingling of the two races," Brown wrote. "We cannot accept this proposition. If the two races are to meet upon terms of social equality, it must be the result of natural affinities, a mutual appreciation of each other's merits, and a voluntary consent of individuals."

Social equality. Not only had Brown and the majority cast aside the

Tourgée team's arguments, they had adopted that detested phrase, the same phrase that had prompted Frederick Douglass to write in response to the 1883 *Civil Rights Cases*: "What has riding in the same railroad car, being sheltered in the same inn, attending the same show, looking at the same animals, sitting in the same theater, to do with social equality?"

Martinet, Desdunes, and the Citizens' Committee didn't see themselves as seekers of "social equality." They weren't inviting themselves to private homes, or bursting into family gatherings. Like William Day on his steamboat trip, like Mary Miles in her train travels, like David Ruggles and Frederick Douglass at the birth of passenger railroads, they were seeking access to the same public spaces, the same rights and privileges, the same opportunities that whites enjoyed. If riding in a car or sitting in a restaurant was a "social" right, what else qualified for that distinction? They shuddered to think.

As for Tourgée's prophesy of proliferating separation, Brown was not worried. "The reply to all this," he wrote, "is that every exercise of the police power must be reasonable, and extend only to such laws as are enacted in good faith for the promotion for the public good, and not for the annoyance or oppression of a particular class." The case "reduces itself" to one question, Brown said: Is the Louisiana law "a reasonable regulation?" His answer was a meandering yes. It was reasonable to promote passenger "comfort." It was reasonable to preserve "the public peace and good order."

If Brown had any doubts that these goals were the act's purpose, he did not say so. Instead, he wrote: "We cannot say that a law which authorizes or even requires the separation of the two races in public conveyances is unreasonable, or more obnoxious to the Fourteenth Amendment than the acts of Congress requiring separate schools for colored children in the District of Columbia, the constitutionality of which does not seem to have been questioned."

That was the essence of Brown's overall approach. He saw his opinion as successor to all that had come before, the logical result of the court's previous pronouncements. He agreed with the Louisiana Supreme Court that the legislature could not exempt the conductor from a lawsuit for damages. That made sense, too, based on past rulings. But Brown shook his head at Tourgée's novel argument about property rights.

"It is claimed," he wrote, "that, in any mixed community, the reputation of belonging to the dominant race, in this instance the white race, is property. . . . Conceding this to be so for the purposes of this case, we are unable to see how this statute deprives him of, or in any way affects his right to, such property." A white man, if wrongly assigned, could sue the company. But a colored man had no cause for action, Brown said, because "he is not lawfully entitled to the reputation of being a white man."

But wait: Was Plessy white or colored? Tourgée had emphasized in his brief that Louisiana law had no definition, asking if the court would allow "a single drop of African blood . . . to color a whole ocean of Caucasian whiteness." Brown avoided the issue. While "it may undoubtedly become a question of importance whether . . . the petitioner belongs to the white or colored race," he wrote, "these are questions to be determined" by the states.

BROWN WAS NO NAÏF. He had encountered separation in his travels. So had all the justices. But they had convinced themselves that separate did not mean unequal—indeed, they told themselves that separating the races might make equality *easier* to achieve, by eliminating any friction that might arise from forcing them together. In the majority's ruling, Brown had put that thought into these words: "Legislation is powerless to eradicate racial instincts or to abolish distinctions based upon physical differences, and the attempt to do so can only result in accentuating the difficulties of the present situation."

The difficulties of the present situation. But how much did Brown and his Northern brethren know of the "present situation?" None had served in the war, a seminal point in the "difficulties" the country now faced. None had gone South, as Tourgée had, during Reconstruction. None had a firsthand view of what it meant to be a person of color in nineteenth-century America. All were Northern-born and bred, and by 1896, many white Northerners were exhausted by the race issue and what the *Chicago Tribune* correspondent had called the "worn-out arguments of inequality" in writing about Booker T. Washington's speech the previous year.

If the two races couldn't get along, if whites could not tolerate the company of any other color, Brown and the majority were saying, why wasn't "equal but separate" a legitimate answer, if equality could be maintained?

In the nature of things, the court had so ruled.

It was a resounding repudiation, one that Martinet and the Citizens' Committee found crushing. The majority opinion had rejected nearly every contention made by Tourgée and his legal team, while fully accepting the "police powers" argument from the Louisiana attorney general's counsel. "The majority of the judges of the highest tribunal of this American government have cast their voice against our just appeal," the committee later wrote. "Notwithstanding this decision, which was rendered contrary to our expectations, we, as freemen, still believe we were right. . . . In defending the cause of liberty, we met with defeat, but not with ignominy."

HARLAN DISSENTED, FORCEFULLY and with a clear-eyed vision of a sinister future. The Southerner, the son of a Kentucky slaveholder, saw the case in a practical and historical context that none of his Northern colleagues seemed to grasp. "In my opinion," he wrote, "the judgment this day rendered will, in time, prove to be quite as pernicious as the decision made by this tribunal in the *Dred Scott Case*."

Harlan not only accepted Tourgée's forewarning of separation spreading, he drew a more ominous picture. Why not laws requiring separate sections in courtrooms? In legislative halls? In any public assembly "convened for the consideration of the political questions of the day?" He took no comfort in Brown's reassurance that "reasonableness" would prevent abuses. Reasonable was too much in the eye of the beholder. Separation laws already allowed a "partition" within a railroad car as one method of keeping the races apart, he pointed out. Wasn't it "reasonable" to assume that partitions would migrate into other public spaces? He envisioned "astute men of the dominant race" demanding the partitioning of jury boxes so that "their integrity" wouldn't be "corrupted" by contact with colored jurors during trials and deliberations.

While striving to keep his dissent polite, Harlan left no doubt about his profound dismay with his colleagues' reasoning. Several times, he used language to suggest that "this day" would be remembered as a shameful one in the court's history. He and Brown were friends, and would remain so, but their friendship did not prevent Harlan from expressing his outrage that "this high tribunal, the final expositor of the fundamental law of the land, has reached the conclusion" that it was legitimate for States to use color and race as a dividing line in regulating civil rights.

The majority ruling, he was convinced, was an affront to the Constitution. It would "stimulate aggressions, more or less brutal and irritating, upon the admitted rights of colored citizens." It would "encourage the belief" that state law could be deployed to stymie the intentions of the three Reconstruction amendments. "We boast of the freedom enjoyed by our people above all other peoples," he wrote. "But it is difficult to reconcile that boast with a state of the law which, practically, puts the brand of servitude and degradation upon a large class of our fellow citizens, our equals before the law. The thin disguise of 'equal' accommodations for passengers in railroad coaches will not mislead anyone, nor atone for the wrong this day done."

Thin disguise. Brand of servitude. Unlike the majority, who had come within a hair of ridiculing Tourgée's Thirteenth Amendment argument, Harlan embraced it. This was nothing new for him. His dissent in the *Civil Rights Cases*, more than twelve years earlier, had strongly supported the premise. Now he reiterated that belief. The Thirteenth "prevents the imposition of any burdens or disabilities that constitute badges of slavery or servitude," he said. Banishing colored passengers to a separate car, on a "public highway," imposed just such a disability.

"It cannot be justified upon any legal grounds," he wrote.

THE "PUBLIC HIGHWAY" figured prominently in Harlan's thinking. The phrase appeared ten times in his dissent. Confronting the question of corporate ownership, Harlan had none of the trepidations that had handcuffed Charles Francis Adams in the Massachusetts legislature during the early 1840s. Railroad corporations might be private, Harlan said, but their roads were a public benefit, often built with public money and land. Their cars were not exempt from constitutional guarantees of equal access and protection.

Nor did he endorse the constant cries of "social equality" emanating from some white quarters. "Social equality no more exists between two races when traveling in a passenger coach," he wrote, "than when members of the same races sit by each other in a street car or in the jury box, or stand or sit with each other in a political assembly, or . . . when they approach the ballot box."

For Harlan, Louisiana's Separate Car Act was more indefensible than the Mississippi version, which had drawn his vigorous dissent in 1890. The Mississippi legislature had not made it a crime for a passenger to sit in the "wrong" coach. *A crime.* He could scarcely contain his disbelief at what the Louisiana lawmakers had done. As he understood the Separate Car Act, a "Chinaman" could ride legally in the whites-only coach. A Chinaman! A member of a race "so different from our own that we do not permit those belonging to it to become citizens of the United States." But "citizens of the black race in Louisiana," some of whom had "risked their lives for the preservation of the Union," must wear the label of "criminal" for claiming their constitutional rights? This incongruity was Harlan's version of absurd.

Harlan's view of equality did not extend to Chinese immigrants. In past years, he had joined with the majority in declaring the 1882 Chinese Exclusion Act to be constitutional. As a young man, he had taken up the cause of the anti-immigrant Know Nothings, and now he worried about the new waves of immigrants coming to America. He had his blind spots, his prejudices, his preconceptions. But unlike others, he had confronted his past, examined his fears, and had emerged with the belief that, for the white and black races, equality and opportunity could not survive if they came in different colors. He not only endorsed the Plessy protest, he encouraged new ones. Colored passengers, he said, "ought never to cease objecting, to the proposition that citizens of the white and black race can be adjudged criminals because they sit, or claim the right to sit, in the same public coach on a public highway."

Ignoring Tourgée's more radical arguments, Harlan tore away at the Louisiana law's "guise" of equality, just as Tourgée had in his brief. "Everyone knows that the statute in question [was intended] to exclude colored people from coaches occupied by or assigned to white persons," Harlan wrote. "No one would be so wanting in candor as to assert the contrary." These "state enactments," he said, had been "cunningly devised" to defeat the "legitimate results" of the Civil War. He offered a dire prediction: Such laws "can have no other result than to render permanent peace impossible and to keep alive a conflict of races."

Render permanent peace impossible. Now this was something extraordinary—a Supreme Court justice, openly worrying about racial warfare. His rhetoric, already blunt, turned sharper and starker as he outlined his fears. He talked about "race hate," and what must be done to prevent its proliferation. "Sixty millions of whites are in no danger from the presence here of eight millions of blacks," he wrote. "The destinies of the two races in this country are indissolubly linked together, and the interests of both require that the common government of all shall not permit the seeds of race hate to be planted under the sanction of law."

Harlan had started his political career as a proslavery candidate. After the war, he saw the rise of the Ku-Klux in Kentucky and elsewhere. Now, he made a direct plea to the people who shared his skin color and heritage. "The white race deems itself to be the dominant race in this country," he wrote. "And so it is in prestige, in achievements, in education, in wealth and in power. So, I doubt not, it will continue to be for all time if it remains true to its great heritage and holds fast to the principles of constitutional liberty. But in view of the Constitution, in the eye of the law, there is in this country no superior, dominant, ruling class of citizens. . . . Our Constitution is color-blind, and neither knows nor tolerates classes among citizens."

Color-blind. The same word Tourgée had used in his brief.

IF SOMETHING MOMENTOUS had just happened, it wasn't apparent to the nation's newspapers. Most paid scant attention to the *Plessy* ruling or to Harlan's objections. In 1883, his dissent in the *Civil Rights Cases* had been widely excerpted. But now, his warnings—"as pernicious as Dred Scott," and "the seeds of race hate," and "make permanent peace impossible"—stirred little commentary or alarm. In the North, there was an air of resignation and fatigue in the few editorials that appeared. In the South, there was satisfaction that the majority had recognized both states' rights and the wisdom of separation.

The common thread? A feeling that the matter was now settled, that the Supreme Court had spoken, for better or worse. As one editorial reprinted in several Northern papers put it, "Race questions, so far as the laws may regulate them, may now be considered to be fully determined in the South. The two races will have separate hotels, railroad cars, churches, and schools. . . . We have probably seen the end of the agitation for the indiscriminate mixing of the white and the black people in this country." In Rochester, New York, Tourgée's old stomping ground, the *Union* and *Advertiser* treated the decision as a narrow one, "purely a case of police power." *The New York Journal* also minimized its scope, saying the court "simply" said that a "local road can regulate local traffic . . . according to the custom which prevails in the South."

A sprinkling of newspapers, however, anticipated that the ruling would reach beyond "local traffic." The *New York Mail and Express* called the decision "a serious blow to the advancement of the South," and suggested that it should be fought, and even challenged. "The venerable and learned justices are human," the newspaper said, "and, therefore, not exempt . . . from error."

The *Richmond Planet* joined other black newspapers in denouncing the majority's cramped view of equality, equal protection, and due process. "We can be discriminated against, we can be robbed of our political rights, we can be persecuted and murdered, and yet we cannot secure a legal redress in the courts of the United States," the *Planet* said. "Truly has evil days come upon us."

EPILOGUE

ON JUNE 18, 1900, census enumerator John E. Duffs walked the streets of New Orleans's Seventh Ward, knocking on the doors of more than thirty households, collecting the bits of information he needed for the twenty-eight boxes on his questionnaire sheets. He had instructions for each entry, including Box 5, "Color or Race." The directions were simple enough: "Write 'W' for White. 'B' for Black (negro or negro ancestry). 'Ch' for Chinese. 'Jp' for Japanese. 'In' for Indian, as the case may be."

No need for any of those last three designations on today's visits. As for the first two, well, they posed a challenge for Duffs. He no longer had the option of "Mu" for "mulatto," a category in previous censuses, well used in New Orleans's French-speaking neighborhoods. Like a train conductor surveying the cars on the East Louisiana Railroad, the enumerator had only two choices for the multihued families on his route. White. Black. Not "FC" for French Creole, or "Mi" for mixed, or "O" for other. White. Black.

Duffs was nearing the end of his day when he reached the little rented house at 1438 North Roman Street where Homer and Louise Plessy lived, along with Louise's mother. When Duffs left, he had the 1900 census's answer to the question that Albion Tourgée and James Walker had posed in their brief to the Supreme Court: What color was Homer Plessy? He was "B." He would be "B" again in 1910, even though "Mu" had been restored as an option, and that's what Plessy had been in the 1880 census. Then, in 1920, at the age of fifty-seven, Plessy would be "W," completing his journey across the color spectrum and leaving a paper trail of racial confusion that would have delighted Tourgée.

The *Plessy* case had already slipped into the shadows of the city's history. It had come to a quiet end on January 11, 1897, when Plessy and Walker returned to Criminal Court A for a proceeding that merited no coverage at all in either the *Picayune* or the *Times-Democrat*. Judge Ferguson, his term up, was no longer sitting. His replacement, Joshua Baker, would handle the case from here.

The case had been docketed as an arraignment, the first step toward a trial. But the Citizens' Committee had no interest in a lingering battle that couldn't be won. Plessy changed his plea to guilty. Baker imposed the minimum twenty-five-dollar fine, the committee paid it, and the test case went into the records as one more conviction, indistinguishable from the dozens of others that Baker would preside over in the coming weeks.

A few months later, the committee issued a formal report laying out its reasons for challenging the Separate Car Act. Louis Martinet, Rodolphe Desdunes, and the committee's other members had heard the criticisms—lost cause, misguided strategy—and declared their belief that they had taken the right course, that pursuing justice cannot be done without risk. They praised Harlan's dissent as a "courageous" stand for "justice and equal rights," and then the committee dissolved. The *Crusader*, already in financial distress before the Supreme Court's ruling, went silent. "Seeing that the friends of justice were either dead or indifferent, [the editors] believed that the continuation of the *Crusader* would not only be fruitless but decidedly dangerous," Desdunes wrote later in his history of Creole leaders, published in French.

Like Martinet, who grew so discouraged that he eventually withdrew from the public arena, Tourgée had found the loss in *Plessy* hard to take. He was exhausted, personally and by the race issue. His devotion to civil rights activism had come at the expense of his writing career. A fall trip to New York, seeking a magazine job, left him feeling sorry for himself. "I have nothing to say that the world cares to hear," he wrote to Emma, a reprise of his pre-Bystander blues. "I don't want to come home, or try anything else. I merely want to die."

He had campaigned hard for Ohio's William McKinley in the 1896 presidential election, and when McKinley won, Tourgée sought a foreign post. For some months, it looked as if he might not get one. He was too controversial, some said, for a prominent posting. Friends from both races lobbied on his behalf. Emma made a special trip to Washington to make a plea. In May 1897, the appointment came through. Tourgée would go to Bordeaux, France, as the U.S. consul there. Martinet telegraphed his "sincere congratulations." Left unsaid: The country's best-known white advocate for civil rights was absenting himself from the field, at least for now.

A year later, in July 1898, James Walker died in New Orleans. His lengthy obituary in the *Times-Democrat* contained a remarkable error, never corrected. "He had charge of some very important cases in the city," the *Times-Democrat* wrote, "and some time ago went to Washington, where he gained a decided victory in the Jim Crow car case."

PRESIDENT THEODORE ROOSEVELT almost didn't make it to the special tribute for John Harlan on the night of December 9, 1902. He was sorry, very sorry, he had told his attorney general a few weeks earlier, but he had other commitments. The country's legal elite, aided by congressional and cabinet officers, would have to celebrate Harlan's twenty-fifth anniversary on the Supreme Court without a presidential speech.

But by the time the 280 guests had gathered that evening at the New Willard Hotel in Washington, word had spread. Roosevelt would be there. The printed program had him arriving at nine o'clock, somewhere between the "mignons de filet de boeuf a la Cheron" and the "glaces assorties." The president would speak first, naturally, then Harlan, then seven others. It would be a night of accolades and humility, of high-minded oratory and humorous barbs, of honoring a man and an institution. Dissent would have the evening off. Or so it seemed.

The master of ceremonies was Harlan's old friend, Wayne MacVeagh. The Pennsylvanian had toiled with Harlan on the Louisiana election commission in 1877, and impressed with the Kentuckian's temperament, had urged President Hayes to pick Harlan for the Supreme Court. On either side of Roosevelt and Harlan, at the long head table, sat Chief Justice Fuller and the rest of his colleagues, along with Harlan's three sons. James had traveled from Puerto Rico, where he was serving as the territory's attorney general. John, a lawyer, and Richard, a minister, had journeyed from their homes in Chicago.

The invitation list, drawn up by the bar, was exclusively male, but special provisions had been made for Mallie, to her delight. From her seat in the balcony, she and the rest of the Harlan entourage—daughters, daughters-in-law, close friends—had an aerial view of the entire floor. John rambled the room, bursting with good cheer, beaming with pride. He could retire with full pay next year, when he reached seventy, if he so desired.

He did not so desire. He desired to stay on the bench, to keep making his mark. Six years earlier, in a bantering letter to Fuller, he had given his boss some advice for the October 1896 term. Assign yourself fewer cases. We're in our sixties now. We don't want to wear out. "I have often heard men say that they were quite willing to die when the time comes, but I never believed any one said it in good faith," Harlan joked. "The fact is, I am afraid to die; for it might be my sentence that I should spend the balance of my days at 'Democratic headquarters.'"

Harlan, a Republican, and Fuller, a Democrat, enjoyed their good-natured jabs. Harlan told Fuller that he intended to stay on the bench until "December 10, 1927," the date of his fiftieth anniversary. Of course, he would be ninety-six then. Only a handful of justices had made it to their eighties. The court was a lifetime appointment, but it was not a job for a worn-out man. Harlan had seen colleagues in the throes of decline, the anguish of it. His friend Henry Brown was coping with his failed right eye. For now, Harlan had no such worries. He was still strong at sixty-nine, a few steps slower and a score of pounds heavier, but still engaged, still energetic.

At half past ten, Roosevelt lifted his burly frame, and the room quieted. Harlan's Civil War bravery was on his mind. "In the states of the farther North, it was easy for the man to make up his mind on which side he would unsheath his sword," Roosevelt said somberly. "In the states of the farther South, it was equally easy. In Kentucky, the task was a difficult one." Harlan chose the Union, the president said, but his service did not end there. He "continued to do his duty as a citizen all the better because he had done it as a soldier." He used his experience as "an incentive, as a spur, to make him feel ashamed that his present or his future should fall short of his past."

When the applause from Northerners and Southerners alike had died down, Roosevelt turned to Harlan. "I wish to express my personal debt to you, for your influence, for your example," the president said. "But I wish far more, speaking as the representative of all our people, to express the infinite sense of obligation we have to you for having shown by your life what the type of fearless American citizenship should be."

Roosevelt had not mentioned any of Harlan's dissents, nor any of the six hundred majority decisions he had written during his twenty-five years. It was not necessary. *Fearless American citizenship.* The crowd rose as one, its cheers washing over Mallie and the Harlan family in the balcony.

It was hard for any speaker to follow Roosevelt to a podium, but Harlan's rhetorical gifts had earned him a reputation as one of Kentucky's best orators. He took Roosevelt's lead, speaking reverently of those who had fought in the terrible war, on both sides, extolling "the memory of their splendid courage, their marvelous military skill and their high character." Now, though, he rejoiced at the thought that the "severed sections, weary of debate, are again one people, loving the one flag, acknowledging the one Constitution, and abiding loyally by the decisions of the one supreme tribunal."

One people, loving one flag. A rosy vision, and certainly not one that would draw universal agreement. But the court's most notable dissenter was not done. "Permit me to say," he told the rapt crowd, "that there has been no moment during my term of service when I have not been deeply sensible of the awful responsibility resting upon every member of that court." He paused. "The power of the Supreme Court for good, as well as for evil, can scarcely be exaggerated. . . . It can by its judgments strengthen our institutions in the confidence and affections of the people, or, more easily than any other department of the government, it can undermine the foundations of our governmental system."

He ended with an unusual twist on the usual political closing. "God bless our dear country," he said to the vast sea of white faces. "God bless every effort to sustain and strengthen it in the hearts of the people of every race subject to its jurisdiction or authority."

The hearts of the people of every race. The power of the court for good, as well as for evil. On this night of celebration, sober reminders of a nation's obligations, meant to linger long after the applause had faded.

A YEAR LATER, in early December 1903, Henry Brown's doctors told him to prepare for a final descent into blindness.

The justice had lived with this terror nearly all his life. His right eye had mostly quit on him two years ago, and now, after the latest episode of inflammation brought on by strain and overwork, his left eye had gone dark, too. For the moment, he could do nothing more than rest and pray for one more miracle.

Relying on the hands of others, he dictated several letters to send immediately. One went to his old friend Charles Kent in Detroit. Kent had seen the alarming headlines in the local papers—"The Specialists Hold Out No Hope of Recovery" was among those on the *Free Press*'s somber account—and had written a kind note. Brown wanted Kent to know that he had not given up hope. "I am taking encouragement from the fact that good work has been done by blind men," Brown wrote, "and that some distinguished justices have been forced to rely upon the sight of others to prepare their opinions."

If his eyes could be coaxed back to some sort of working order, Brown had every intention of remaining on the bench for now. He still liked the job, but more than that, he wanted to stave off retirement until he could leave with his full pension. He would reach the magic age of seventy in March 1906. "I would resign if I could do so and draw my pay," he told Kent, "but after nearly thirty years' service" in the federal judiciary, "I do not feel called upon to do so when I am within a little over two years of completing my term."

He was suffering in other ways. His wife had died in 1901, in Italy during one of their overseas trips, a cruel irony not lost on him—his two great loves, Carry and Europe, forever fixed in memories of joy and sorrow. He consoled himself with her doctors' assurances that the journey had done nothing to shorten her life. But nothing they could say would ease his grief at losing her company. He came back from Italy, and went to Stockbridge, his boyhood haunt in western Massachusetts, seeking solace in familiar surroundings and lifelong friends. "I am here at my old birthplace trying to get away from myself," he wrote to Fuller in late August, with the court's fall term just six weeks away. "I shall have a hard time going back to Washington where every object will suggest her presence, but I hope I shall be able to work to divert my thoughts. But it has been a horrible summer and I am simply broken hearted."

The day after writing Kent, he set to work on a more difficult and delicate letter. He needed to give Fuller a full account of his condition. The chief justice would want to know: Could he cast his votes? Could he take on any opinions? Brown chose honesty over vagueness. "My doctors held a consultation last evening and decided to put me to bed in a darkened room for some weeks," he told Fuller. "While confinement to a darkened room is a great affliction, my inability to keep my seat on the bench is heart-rending to one of my temperament. I have sacrificed myself to a determination to do my full share of the work, and the consequences are such that I hardly dare contemplate them."

After nearly two months in his darkened cocoon, with heavy bandages keeping all light away from his paralyzed optic nerves, he emerged to find the treatment had helped. His left eye was markedly better. His right eye, thought to be hopeless, had flickered tentatively back to life. "Regains His Sight," said the Washington *Evening Star*'s headline on January 30, 1904. "Justice Brown Will Not Be Blind."

He was not cured. He had to be careful, like a man rescued from a desert isle, to ease himself back into civilization. But he made plans to retake his seat in late February. Meanwhile, he sent a typewritten note to Fuller about an immigration case involving several Chinese merchants, explaining his qualms about their treatment. "I confess my sympathies are much awakened by the fact that these men have been in the country for twenty years, doing legitimate business and conducting themselves in a reputable manner, and this sudden awakening of activity of the authorities in their cases seems quite suspicious," he told Fuller. He had studied the matter as much "as my eyes will permit, but it seems to me so hard a case . . . that I am quite willing to construe all my doubts" in favor of the immigrants.

Gradually, he crafted a new routine. He even took on a few majority opinions, producing them for the end of the term. He still was not allowed to read, but he could surprise his friends. In late June, he remarried. He kept the small ceremony, in the New Jersey countryside, a secret until the wedding day. A "runaway match," Brown quipped to reporters.

His new wife, Josephine Tyler, was his cousin's widow. She and Carry had been close friends, and since Carry's death, Josephine's presence had helped ease his loneliness. "Mrs. Tyler," said one newspaper account of the ceremony, "is said to possess in no small degree the same qualities which distinguished the justice's first wife."

Celebrating his revived eyes and new companionship, they honeymooned in Europe.

ALBION TOURGÉE'S ASHES did not make it from France in time for his memorial service in Mayville on November 14, 1905.

Emma was heartbroken at the shipping delay, and still woozy from her rough Atlantic crossing four days earlier. Lodie wasn't feeling well, either. But they gathered themselves to greet the hundreds of guests, converging on western New York from every point of the compass. They had come, some at great distance and expense, to pay their respects to a man who had touched their lives—through his friendship or his Civil War comradeship, through his books or his Bystander column, through his speeches or his inspiration. As the visitors streamed toward the Methodist Episcopal Church, a light snow fell, dusting the green Chautauqua Hills in a curtain of white. For the next few hours, they sat and stood and sang together, white and black, equal and not separate, at least for that moment.

Tourgée had died the previous spring, in Bordeaux, during his eighth year as the U.S. consul. Acute uremia, the obituaries had said. But months before his kidneys had finally failed, his old war wounds and new ailments had wracked his body, a painful decline rather than a peaceful death. He was sixty-seven when the end came on May 21. Emma had arranged for cremation at the famous Père Lachaise cemetery in Paris, and had resisted the temptation to rush home. She had an entire household to pack up and ship, accounts to settle, a new consul to greet, a future to plan.

She and Lodie would spend the summer in Europe, visit ancestral grounds in England, and return in the fall. Albion's ashes would make their own way, bound for the Mayville cemetery. Emma had plans for a handsome memorial, an obelisk, to mark the spot. The inscription would be Albion's last message to his public: "Write me then as one who loved his fellow man."

From his distant outpost in Bordeaux, he had tried to keep his voice alive. But as his health deteriorated, he wrote less and less. By his death in 1905, he was so far offstage that many newspaper obituaries made no specific reference to his later civil rights activism or the NCRA. "Death Claims Noted Writer," was a favored headline.

The Northern papers used a combination of labels to describe him. Soldier, jurist, diplomat, man of letters. Southern papers were not as kind. The *New Orleans States* called him a "narrow and vicious partisan of ordinary talents" whose books had "fanned the flames of sectionalism," gaining him "temporary" fame by "traducing the people of the South and keeping alive the bitterness engendered by the Civil War."

Emma hired a clipping service to collect the obituaries. They filled more than one hundred scrapbook pages. Not one, not even from New Orleans, mentioned the *Plessy* case.

TWO WEEKS AFTER the memorial service in Mayville, on Thanksgiving Day 1905, a small band of "Negro-Americans" from sixteen states and the District of Columbia, calling itself the "Niagara Movement," made its debut with a "Friends of Freedom Day" in several dozen cities. The celebrations varied, but in the main, they exalted the lives and legacies of a trio of "Friends": abolitionist William Lloyd Garrison, Frederick Douglass, and Albion W. Tourgée.

The Niagara Movement had sprung from a July gathering in Buffalo, led by scholar and activist W. E. B. Du Bois, a professor at Atlanta University in

Georgia. He and his fellow organizers had circulated a "Private and Confidential" memorandum, inviting men of color to a conference that would "inaugurate a permanent national forward movement." Twenty-nine had come. A Declaration of Principles, issued later, vowed vigorous protest—"loudly and insistently"—of the color line in all its forms. Jim Crow laws had spread from Mississippi and Louisiana to nearly every Southern state, as Tourgée and Harlan had predicted in *Plessy*, and the Declaration specifically cited separate cars as an insult to "our manhood, womanhood, and self-respect." Any discrimination based on race, the Declaration said, was "barbarous," no matter "how hallowed it may be by custom, expediency or prejudice."

For the Niagara Movement, Tourgée was a trailblazer. Booker T. Washington was an adversary. The declaration, without mentioning Washington, endorsed militancy over accommodation. "We refuse to allow the impression to remain that the Negro-American assents to inferiority, is submissive under oppression and apologetic before insults," it said. "Through helplessness we may submit, but the voice of protest of ten million Americans must never cease to assail the ears of their fellows, so long as America is unjust."

Members of the Niagara Movement had been a major presence at the Mayville service. Crusading journalist Ida Wells, on behalf of the Illinois chapter, read a stirring tribute to Tourgée—"that strong and uncompromising friend of our race"—and asked the nation to "give heed to his words of patriotic pleading." Wells's sustained campaign against lynching, carried out in the 1890s through published articles and lectures, had been inspired in part by the Bystander's early and frequent alarms about lynching. He had written her an admiring note about her work, and she had responded in kind. "It is my earnest wish, and I know I voice the sentiments of thousands of my race, that the Bystander may live long to speak with clarion voice against wrong and injustice," she had told him in 1893.

Harry C. Smith, editor of Ohio's leading black newspaper, the *Cleveland Gazette*, was there with a delegation of "prominent African-American leaders," as he described them to Emma. Smith, as a member of the Ohio House of Representatives, had collaborated with Tourgée in writing an anti-lynching law. Its enactment in 1896 was a first for the state, and a first for the North. Booker T. Washington was not there. He sent a telegram, saying other engagements prevented him from coming. “My race owes much to the courage and helpful work of Judge Tourgee, which we shall not forget,” Washington wrote.

Now, with their “Friends of Freedom” events, the Niagara Movement was combining forces with Tourgée once again. Du Bois’s directives to each chapter called for a reading of the Declaration of Principles, followed by speeches on one or more of their “Friends.” Tell the audience, Du Bois suggested, that December 10 is the one-hundredth anniversary of Garrison’s birth. Du Bois had crafted a “Garrison Pledge” that ended: “I am in earnest. I will not equivocate. I will not retreat a single inch and I will be heard.”

In Washington, the “Friends of Freedom” celebration took place in the Metropolitan AME Church on M Street NW. Ten years earlier, thousands of both races had filled the church and the surrounding streets for Douglass’s funeral. On this night, November 30, a small but enthusiastic crowd pledged to support the movement’s goals. The *Washington Post* said the gathering of “several hundred negroes” heard speeches on Garrison and Tourgée, described in the headline as “Emancipators of Their Race.”

Tourgée would have hotly protested that description. In an 1891 Bystander column, he wrote of himself: “He was neither known as an abolitionist, nor did he devote himself to teaching those whose eyeballs slavery had seared. . . . He has advocated justice for the colored man, but has sacrificed nothing of consequence for his opinions.”

Emma would not have said that they had sacrificed nothing. In the spring of 1906, while living temporarily in Washington, she sought a special bill from Congress for an increase in Albion’s Civil War pension. The Pension Office had rejected her request, saying it lacked proof that his death had resulted from his war disabilities. She refused to give up. She had the house in Mayville, but with no reliable income, she felt she had no choice but to press for every penny. She managed to convince the House Committee on Invalid Pensions of her need. “Evidence shows she is left with little property,” the committee’s report said. “Finds herself in comparative poverty and makes her appeal to Congress.”

In June 1906, the bill was approved, boosting her widow’s pension from eight to twelve dollars a month.

AS FALL MADE ITS TURN toward winter in the waning months of 1910, bringing shorter days and dwindling daylight to the twenty-three rooms inside his stately mansion a mile north of the White House, Henry Brown coped with his own enveloping darkness.

His eyesight nearly gone, his days at the Supreme Court now in the past, he resisted the temptation to feel sorry for himself. After all, as he later wrote to his friend Charles Kent, he had achieved more than he had ever expected. "Death, which seems so horrible at twenty-five, loses all its terrors at seventy-five, and ought to be welcomed rather than feared. And these last years can be made so interesting picking up and disposing of the tangled threads of a lifetime."

His wife, Josephine, did most of his reading for him now. Perhaps this deprivation troubled him more than any other. For a man who kept a log of the books he read, in a leather-bound volume inscribed "H. B. Brown" on the front, losing the freedom to cast his own eyes over the pages . . . well, could there be a clearer reminder of how much his world was shrinking?

He could still see just enough to deliver a speech, as he did once or twice a year, most recently in April to the Ladies' Congressional Club of Washington, where he had outlined his opposition to women's suffrage. He could still draft a personal letter, which he sometimes preferred to dictation, but slowly and in a shaky hand. He could still turn out the occasional article, but at a fraction of the pace that gave him a reputation as one of the court's workhorses. But he was holding fast to his love of travel, spending some of his winter months in the Carolinas or Florida, and parts of his summer in Europe or New England. "It is upon these little outings I depend for much of the health and happiness I now enjoy," he told Kent.

To his great relief, blindness had not forced him into early retirement. He had been spared that humiliation. He had left on his own terms, two months after his seventieth birthday. At his retirement dinner on May 31, 1906, he did not have to rely on the sight of others to tell him whose hand he was shaking. As he gazed out through his damaged eyes at his fellow justices, at cabinet officers, at President Roosevelt and Vice President Charles

Fairbanks, he took no small pleasure in having a gaze at all. He believed with an almost religious fervor that he was handing over his judicial robes at just the right time. The country was entitled to "the services of judges in the full possession of their faculties," he later wrote, "and as my sight had already begun to fail, I took it as a gentle intimation that I ought to give place to another."

While other justices equated retirement with boredom, and even fretted they would lose their minds if they quit the court, Brown scoffed at this notion. "I think the stories that are often heard about men collapsing when they leave the Bench is all nonsense," he told Kent in 1908, after almost two years in retirement. "Of the four men of our Court who lost their minds, all of them lost them while they were still upon the Bench, while the four who left the Bench in sound condition, not one of them showed symptoms of mental weakness until their deaths."

He confronted his hampered circumstances with something approaching equanimity. "I am busier, perhaps, than you think, writing something every day, though to little purpose," he wrote in October 1910. "I know that my work is done, that I have lost all ambition and am living only in the present and the past. . . . I might easily rust out, but I will not permit myself to do so, if I can avoid it."

Spurred by Kent, he had been laboring on an autobiographical sketch, which Kent envisioned as the basis for a book that might come out after Brown's death. At first, Brown had resisted Kent's cajoling. The justice had a hard time believing that anyone would want to read such a thing. But he had eventually warmed to the idea. He pronounced himself pleased with his forty-page effort. "It is written in the first person, but may be readily turned into the third person," he told Kent. "It is a simple affair, but will be of assistance to anyone who may feel sufficient interest to write a brief memorial. I am not ambitious for a regular biography."

In the style of other such sketches, he chose his heritage as his starting point. "I was born of a New England Puritan family in which there has been no admixture of alien blood for two hundred and fifty years," he wrote. "Though Puritans, my ancestors were neither bigoted nor intolerant—upon the contrary, some were unusually liberal."

No admixture of alien blood. Neither bigoted nor intolerant. In the nature of things, an unusual juxtaposition of pride and prejudice, purity and protestation.

ON OCTOBER 14, 1911, as the day's first rays of sunlight were bathing the nation's capital that Saturday morning, Justice John Marshall Harlan died at his home, at the age of seventy-eight. Acute bronchitis had felled the court's oldest member. He had been ill only a few days. "Mourn for Harlan," the *Washington Post* headline declared the next day. "Supreme Court Justice's Death Shocks President Taft. Roosevelt Wires Sorrow."

All day long, telegrams flooded into the Harlan homestead on Euclid Street. "The country loses a great judge and jurist and a most patriotic and valuable servant," the president, William Howard Taft, wrote to Mallie. "He was a brave and effective soldier for the Union in the Civil War." Theodore Roosevelt's telegram employed the vigorous language that was his trademark: "He was a gallant soldier, a most useful citizen, an upright and fearless judge, deeply devoted to the interests of the people. All American citizens are his debtors, and we are better men because he lived."

In Louisville, where he had first made his name, a *Courier-Journal* headline took an early stab at his legacy: "Renowned as a Dissenter—Some Notable Opinions." The *Courier-Journal* picked out a half dozen of his more than three hundred dissents, including his opposition to striking down the nation's first income tax in 1894 and his stirring defense of Sumner's public accommodations law in the 1883 *Civil Rights Cases*.

The *Courier-Journal* did not mention his *Plessy* dissent, nor did any of the other papers in their lengthy accounts of Harlan's long and illustrious career.

BROWN TOOK HARLAN'S death as a personal blow. In the past year alone, he had lost two of his Supreme Court colleagues. Brewer, his Yale classmate. Then Fuller, a few months later. Now Harlan was gone, too.

Determined to pay tribute to Harlan, working as well as his fading eyesight permitted, Brown put together an article for the *American Law*

Review. He had never been inspired enough to write about any of his other colleagues, and by submitting his tribute to such a prominent journal, he was ensuring a wide audience for his words. Published as "The Dissenting Opinions of Mr. Justice Harlan" in the May–June 1912 issue, Brown's essay devoted just two paragraphs to the *Plessy* case. But by the time he was done with those paragraphs, he had come close to disavowing one of the central findings that had allowed the majority to endorse Louisiana's law requiring railroads to separate the races.

Obscuring his own role in the ruling, Brown resorted to the passive voice. "It was said," he wrote, "that separation of the two races did not involve any question of superiority or inferiority, and that the object of the Fourteenth Amendment was not to abolish the distinction based upon color or to enforce social as distinguished from political equality. The law was sustained as a reasonable exercise of the police power."

His next paragraph summarized Harlan's view: "He thought that the arbitrary separation of citizens on the basis of race, while they are on a public highway, was a badge of servitude wholly inconsistent with the civil freedom and equality before law established by the Constitution, and could not be justified upon any legal grounds. He assumed what is probably the fact, that the statute had its origin in the purpose, not so much to exclude white persons from railroad cars occupied by blacks, as to exclude colored people from coaches occupied or assigned to white persons."

What is probably the fact. Just five words, but if Brown and the majority had accepted them as true in 1896, if they had acknowledged that the law was *aimed* at keeping blacks away from whites, at discriminating against one race in favor of the other, they might have written a different, narrower decision. They might have stripped away the veneer of equality that allowed Louisiana and other Southern states to hurtle headlong into legal separation. They might have forestalled the nation's descent into nearly six decades when separate never meant equal.

Whatever Brown came to believe about Louisiana's true intent in passing the Separate Car Act, however, there's no evidence that he had changed his mind about relations between the races. He believed, as he wrote, that the Constitution could ensure political rights, but not "social rights."

Perhaps, in saying "what is probably the fact," Brown was merely being kind to his departed colleague. Whatever his intent, he spoke only for himself, and in such elliptical language that no one paid much attention. The damage predicted by Harlan in his dissent—the spread of separation to other states and other public spaces—had already come to pass. When Brown went to the South in 1912, he would have traveled on a train with separate cars. At the resort where he stayed, the only people of color he saw were the ones who served him.

Anyone scouring the justice's papers after his death in 1913 would find no other evidence to shed light on whether Brown had misgivings about his decision. He had not mentioned the *Plessy* case in his autobiographical sketch—or any other case, for that matter. He had purposely shied away from his years as a federal judge and Supreme Court justice, telling Kent that "it is more befitting" for others to tell the story of his "doings" on the nation's courts.

No one would undertake to write that story in depth. Within a few decades, Brown's name would be largely forgotten. After the Supreme Court issued its 1954 decision in *Brown v. Board of Education,* declaring separation to be inherently unequal, a new generation of scholars turned their attention to the *Plessy* ruling, and to Harlan's dissent. Full-length biographies were written on Harlan and Tourgée, while Brown's life went largely unplumbed. If historians paused to consider him at all, most dismissed him with harsh judgments. A lightweight. An undistinguished jurist. An unthinking racist. A liar. They call *Plessy* his legacy, and "separate but equal" his shame.

For Brown, the proud New Englander who had written as a young man of his ambitions to leave his mark upon this world, it was not the outcome that he had envisioned.

AFTER A FITFUL FIVE YEARS, plagued by financial woes and internal squabbles, the Niagara Movement frayed. Some of its leaders migrated to a new organization, the National Association for the Advancement of Colored People. In the late 1940s, the NAACP's legal department initiated the lawsuits that led to *Brown v. Board of Education* and the court's embrace of the Fourteenth Amendment as a bar against segregation in public schools. Six days after the unanimous *Brown* ruling in 1954, the *New York Times* chose an arcane headline for an editorial about the landmark decision, harkening back sixty years to a dissent that few of its readers knew or remembered: "Justice Harlan Concurring." The editorial said: "This is an instance in which the voice crying in the wilderness finally becomes an expression of a people's will." The editorial did not mention Tourgée or the Citizens' Committee.

In New Orleans, a historical plaque marks the place where Homer Plessy boarded the East Louisiana Railroad in June 1892. Descendants of Plessy and Ferguson led the group that unveiled the marker in 2009. "Plessy's act of civil disobedience was a test case," the plaque says. "The philosophy and strategies of the Comité des Citoyens foreshadowed Civil Rights movements of the 20th century."

Anyone curious enough to look online for a photograph of Homer Plessy will be disappointed, and even confused. A search on his name will turn up a striking image of a bearded man in a dark suit. It is not Homer Plessy but P. B. S. Pinchback, a misidentification made once and multiplied many times over.

There's another historical plaque, on Erie Street in Mayville, outside the house once known as Thorheim. The State of New York placed it there in 1936, three decades after Tourgée's death, in honor of its once-famous resident. The gold-lettered sign reads: "Here from 1881 to 1900 lived Judge Albion W. Tourgee—soldier, author, ambassador to France." A single sentence, embellishing his diplomatic service, awarding him a position he never had, and saying nothing of the civil rights work that inspired his life, that gave meaning to his Civil War ambition of creating a Union "better than it was."

Myth and missing pieces, etched in public memory, obscuring our vision of the racial hostilities and legal battles that defined one century, and profoundly, disturbingly, cruelly, and violently helped to shape the next.

ACKNOWLEDGMENTS

Books begin as ideas, but take flight with encouragement. In the spring of 2011, as I was making my first forays, I emailed Jim Campbell, a professor at Stanford University who has done notable research in the field of African-American history. Am I wrong, I asked, to think that historians have plumbed the *Plessy* case mostly for its legal and constitutional consequences? That no book has fully explored the story of separation in the nineteenth century?

The professor and I knew each other only slightly. In my role as editor of the *Washington Post*'s Sunday Outlook section, I had published a commentary that Campbell had written, and then several years later, we spent a pleasant hour having coffee when I happened to be visiting the Stanford campus. A few weeks went by, and then Campbell's reply landed. He had passed around my email to several colleagues, he said, and a consensus had formed. You're on to something, he told me. It's a good idea. Go for it.

Thanks, Professor Campbell. That shot of momentum at the right moment helped me believe that I could apply my researching and storytelling skills to this seminal period in American history.

One other professor deserves a shout. Unfortunately, he's not alive to hear it. Steve Botein served as my thesis adviser during my senior year in college. He had an expansive view of history—how to research it, how to tell it—and he regarded his neophyte students as flowers to be watered rather than clay to be sculpted. With a gentle hand, he allowed me to follow my instincts and make my own mistakes. My love of history grew stronger under his stewardship.

Grateful is a barely adequate word to describe my appreciation for the people who endowed the J. Anthony Lukas prizes for nonfiction writing, jointly administered by Columbia University and Harvard University. Receiving the 2016 Lukas Work-In-Progress Award gave me more than financial support. I admired Lukas as a journalist and author while he was living. His masterful 1985 book, *Common Ground*, inspired me as I thought about how to write *Separate.* I can only hope that my finished work honors Lukas's legacy.

John Glusman, my editor at Norton, urged me to apply for the Lukas award. I thought my chances were somewhere near zero. John firmly disagreed. On this and so many other matters, I have benefited from his counsel. His wisdom is exceeded only by his patience. He was the captain of this boat, a steady hand steering through the narrows. His assistant, Helen Thomaides, eased the journey with her adept and cheerful handling of seemingly endless questions. My warm thanks, too, to Rebecca Homiski, Steve Attardo, Anna Oler, Sarahmay Wilkinson, Ellen Cipriano, and others on Norton's art and production teams for embracing the book, and putting a high premium on its design and readability. Every author needs a publicist with Kyle Radler's passion and perceptiveness. He helps give a book its best shot in the crowded marketplace of readers and ideas. Likewise, I'm lucky to have Meredith McGinnis and her social media team looking for ways to put the book before interested readers. Copy editor Avery Hudson earned my admiration for his meticulous scrutiny and good-natured queries. Whatever flaws remain, I hid them too well for him to catch.

For a dozen years now, Gail Ross has acted as my agent. I couldn't ask for a better companion in the trenches. I know she will give me her best and honest judgment, which is the most valuable form of support. I treasure her friendship. Before my book proposal went to publishers, it profited from the penetrating comments of Gail's partner, Howard Yoon, and her associate, Anna Sproul-Latimer.

The *Washington Post* has been my professional home since 1985. Changing over to contract status and working full-time on *Separate* during the past few years has left me a distant observer of the newsroom's continuing transformation in the digital age. I am thankful to editor Marty Baron for allowing me to remain as an associate editor, if in name only, during my extended book leave. Many current and former *Post* colleagues have sustained me with their interest and questions about the book, perhaps without knowing how much those chats meant to me. They include David Brown, E. J. Dionne, Will Englund, Mike Fletcher, Glenn Frankel, Amy Goldstein, Don Graham, Kelly Johnson, Robert Kaiser, Kathy Lally, Charles Lane, Lori Montgomery, Robert O'Harrow, Dale Russakoff, Frances Stead Sellers, and Bob Woodward.

Writing a book can be a solitary enterprise. Several friends kept me tethered to the wider world. A heartfelt thanks to Scott Shane, my longtime pal and journalistic soulmate, for regular and lengthy conversations. His piercing questions and devil's advocacy led me to dig harder for answers, and his suggestions for the manuscript proved once again that he's as fine an editor as he is a writer. Likewise, I reaped the benefits of Bill Casey's insightful comments on the final draft. His reaction bolstered my confidence that this story needed to be told, fully and frankly.

My old friend Walter Isaacson, biographer extraordinaire and New Orleans native, met with me at the dawn of this effort, and offered sound advice on extracting a new story from the bits and pieces of an old one. He later described the *Plessy* case as "a knife that cleaved America," a phrase that I immediately envied for its clarity and brevity.

Thanks, also, to Robert Ruby, David Simon, Elaine Weiss, and Laura Wexler, good listeners as well as fine writers. Likewise, Francie Weeks, Jane Murphy, Coni Douglas, and Andrew Douglas helped spur me on, turning requests for progress reports into reflective discussions about history's enduring consequences. Dan Meyers, my artful neighbor, reprised his role as master of photo reproduction, fine-tuning my collection of nineteenth-century images to help them look their best in the twenty-first.

I could also fill several pages with the names of archivists and librarians who assisted my pursuit of facts, whether large or small. In my six years of work on *Separate*, I gained an ever-greater appreciation for the people who preserve the nation's past. If their generosity could be measured in dollars, their budgets would swell to a size that would ease their justifiable concerns about surviving in this belt-tightened age.

More than a baker's dozen qualify for above-and-beyond awards: Paul Espinosa at the incomparable Peabody Library, part of the Johns Hopkins University in Baltimore; Bonni Wittstadt at the Hopkins Eisenhower Library; Joanne Colvin at the University of Baltimore's Law Library; Jane Fitzgerald at the National Archives in Washington; Scott Forsythe at the National Archives regional branch in Chicago; John Paul Wolfe at the Chautauqua County Historical Society in Westfield, New York, home of the Tourgée papers; Emily Walhout at Harvard University's Houghton Library; Scott Campbell at the University of Louisville Law Library, home for one collection of John Marshall Harlan's papers; Tom Knoles at the American Antiquarian Society in Worcester, Massachusetts; David Kirkpatrick at the Kentucky Archives; Melissa Mead at the University of Rochester Library; Claudia Fitch at the Louisville Free Library; Emilie Leumas at the Archdiocesan Archives in New Orleans; Connie Phelps and James Hodges at the Louisiana and Special Collections department of the University of New Orleans; and Erin Sidwell at the Library of Congress.

Greg Osborn of the New Orleans Public Library, who happens to be a Plessy descendant, spent many hours educating me about his adopted city and offering advice on how to search the many collections at his library and elsewhere in New Orleans. In Washington, I spent a valuable afternoon in the company of Don Ritchie, the Senate historian, as he took me on a guided tour of the Old Senate Chamber, the Supreme Court's home at the time of the *Plessy* case. Michael Vorenberg, a professor of history at Brown University, shared his insights on Lincoln and reconstruction in Louisiana. Todd Mealy, who has spent years researching the life of William Howard Day, invited me to his Pennsylvania home to look through the many documents he had accumulated. In Connecticut, Ellington resident Lynn Fahy found illuminating snippets about Henry Brown's ties to that little village. Ken Aslakson, Claire Bettag, Mary Gehman, and Emily Landau shared thoughts and insights while answering some of my questions about New Orleans. My thanks to Tom (Artie) Martinet and Michael Henderson, a

Plessy relative on the Mathieu/Debergue side, for comparing notes from their research into their family roots.

I would have traveled great distances to scour collections at the Library of Congress and the National Archives, but I am fortunate that these two national treasures are an hour's train ride from my home. Baltimore, where I live, boasts many fine libraries, and I made use of nearly all of them in chasing down information. Thanks to Goucher College, Johns Hopkins University, University of Baltimore Law School, Enoch Pratt Free Library, Morgan State University, Loyola University of Maryland, and the University of Maryland Baltimore County for aiding my hunt.

Further afield, I owe special debts of gratitude to the Detroit Public Library's Burton Historical Collection and the University of Michigan's Bentley Historical Library. For explorers of Michigan's history, both are essential stops. Thanks, also, to Jennifer Fauxsmith and the staff at the Massachusetts State Archives for helping me locate the many abolitionist petitions to the state legislature in the early 1840s, including one that measured more than thirteen feet in length when unfurled. I was glad I did not have to refold it on my own.

In Michigan and Kentucky, both places that required multiple visits, I was fortunate to have friendly faces to greet me at the end of long days. Sally and Jimmy Rubiner, my wife's cousins, once again let me occupy their spare bedroom for extended stretches, just as they did when I was researching my first book in Detroit. Helen Cohen welcomed me to her Louisville home twice, and bore the intrusion with the gracious good cheer that is plentiful in the Bluegrass State. My cousin, Cindy Block, and her husband, Ian, made my trips to North Carolina and Raleigh so easy that I lamented when my research came to its natural end.

A trio of researchers pulled on specific strands of the story. Malissa Ruffner used her genealogy skills to ferret out leads from Albion Tourgée's family history. Michael Romary unearthed sources that illuminated the Ohio River's important role as a dividing line between North and South. Melissa Mason sifted through Detroit newspapers for articles that shed light on Henry Brown's experience with the Civil War draft in 1863 and 1864. Their missions were limited; their contributions were not.

The book's intersections with the French and Spanish threads of the New Orleans story sometimes required the reading of documents in those languages. When I exhausted my limited abilities to understand the words in front of me, several angels rescued me. *Muchas gracias* and *merci beaucoup* to Mariella Neyra-Brown; my Paris friend Joelle Tavano; Emilie Leumas at the New Orleans Archdiocesan Archives, and Sally Reeves at the New Orleans Notarial Archives.

Many hands helped in assembling the photographs in the book, but I need to single out the Chautauqua County Historical Society, custodians of the Tourgée collection. John Paul Wolfe and his small staff cheerfully sent reproductions of the many images that I requested. Warm thanks, too, to John Marshall Harlan's great-granddaughter, Edith de Montebello, for allowing me to use the Harlan wedding portrait at the beginning of Chapter Two. The University of North Carolina Press made available its copy of the photo, previously published in Professor Linda Przybyszewski's 1999 book, *The Republic According to John Marshall Harlan*. My appreciation to both publisher and author for their generous cooperation.

Behind most authors, and certainly behind this one, stands a family. Mary Jo Kirschman, my best friend as well as my spouse, embraced her role as first reader. Her critiques made every chapter better. Without her support, forbearance, enthusiasm, and love, there would be no book. Our grown children, Josh and Jill—along with Jill's husband, Mike, and my siblings—kept my spirits from flagging when the journey seemed too long or too difficult. Their interest served as energy boosters; their questions as guiding lights. I would need another lifetime to repay them.

NOTES

PROLOGUE

xiv **McKenney's courteous reply:** The correspondence between Tourgée and the Supreme Court clerk, James H. McKenney, can be found at the National Archives, Record Group 267, U.S. Supreme Court appellate case files, case 15248, folder 2. There are two rounds of letters between April 3 and April 7, 1896.

xv **the committee's invitation:** Louis A. Martinet to Tourgée, Oct. 5, 1891, document 5760, the Albion W. Tourgée papers, Chautauqua County Historical Society, Westfield, NY.

xv **prepare for a race war:** In 1893, with the *Plessy* case pending, Tourgée wrote several *Chicago Inter Ocean* columns warning of racial warfare. It was not his first ringing of this alarm, which began in earnest with his 1884 book, *An Appeal to Caesar.*

xvii **"the utmost consequence":** Tourgée to Martinet, Oct. 31, 1893, document 7438, Tourgée papers.

xvii **"prison bars":** Martinet to Tourgée, May 30, 1893, document 6998, Tourgée papers. Subsequent endnotes about the Tourgée papers will cite only the document number and date.

ONE: TAKING THEIR SEATS

3 **"receptacle of forgotten barbarisms":** From the 1844 annual report of the Massachusetts Anti-Slavery Society, pp. 6–8.

5 **shouts, groans, and hisses:** The best account of this first trip appeared in the *Salem Gazette,* Aug. 28, 1838. Other details from the *Boston Courier,* Aug. 28, 29, and 30; *Newburyport Herald,* Aug. 31, 1838, reprinting reports from the *Salem Gazette* and the *Boston Gazette*; and the *Gloucester Telegraph,* Sept. 1, 1838, reprinting a *Boston Transcript* article. Francis Crowninshield Bradlee's 1922 book, *The Eastern Railroad: A Historical Account of Early Railroading in Eastern New England,* also described the event, based on company records and newspaper accounts, pp. 12–15.

6 **A sumptuous London home:** Within a few years, Peabody would quit the Eastern Railroad presidency, sinking his time and energy into financing the westward expansion of the nation's railways. With no family waiting in the wings to inherit his massive fortune, he felt free to give

most of it away. He provided millions for museums and libraries, as well as housing for London's poor and aid for destitute Southern schoolchildren after the Civil War.

6 **overwhelmingly men:** Women, with the notable exception of those active in the Massachusetts abolitionist movement, rarely ventured to places where politics and business were transacted in 1838. They had no voting rights, could not serve on juries or bring lawsuits.

7 **A chagrined Peabody:** The *Boston Courier*, in a dispatch dated Aug. 29, 1838. The *Salem Gazette* printed the full text of Peabody's speech in its Sept. 7, 1838, issue.

8 **"afraid to speak":** Quoted from *Narrative of the Life of Frederick Douglass, an American Slave*, p. 108.

8 **life of a professional resister:** For a fuller understanding of Ruggles's life and his role in the abolitionist movement, see Graham R. Hodges's 2010 biography, *David Ruggles: A Radical Black Abolitionist and the Underground Railroad in New York City*.

9 **"more than a match":** From *Narrative of the Life of Frederick Douglass*, p. 109.

9 **"'Jim Crow' car":** The *Salem Gazette* account of the two drunken white sailors, on Oct. 12, 1838, is the earliest reference to a "Jim Crow car" that I could find in an American newspaper, using keyword searching of digitized newspaper collections. For another exploration of the origins of Jim Crow, see Elizabeth Anne Pryor's 2008 doctoral dissertation, "'Jim Crow' Cars, Passport Denials and Atlantic Crossings: African-American Travel, Protest and Citizenship at Home and Abroad, 1827–1865."

10 **Figurines:** *Newburyport Herald*, May 7, 1833.

11 **Ruggles told the judge:** From Ruggles's account in *The Liberator*, Aug. 6, 1841.

12 **Crapo declared:** Crapo's words quoted in the *Boston Weekly Messenger*, July 29, 1841, and cited in Kyle Volk's 2008 doctoral dissertation, "Majority Rule, Minority Rights: The Christian Sabbath, Liquor, Racial Amalgamation, and Democracy in Antebellum America."

12 **"dastardly assault":** Garrison's denunciation of Crapo's ruling in *The Liberator*, Aug. 6, 1841, under the heading "Lynching in New Bedford."

12 **"the greatest farce":** Ruggles in *The Liberator*, Aug. 6, 1841.

12 **"Action is everything":** From *The Liberator's* account of the Aug. 2 dinner, Aug. 20, 1841.

14 **Buffum confronted Chase:** Recounted in Bradlee's *The Eastern Railroad*, p. 28.

15 **Chase's fear of "mob violence":** The *Lynn Record*, reprinted in *The Liberator*, Oct. 8, 1841.

15 **"I am convinced":** Buffum's letter, Nov. 12, 1841, in *The Liberator*, headlined "Eastern Rail-Road Violence."

15 **Dozens of petitions:** I read these various petitions at the Massachusetts State Archives, where they are part of the legislative collection.

15 **counterpetitions:** Also at the Massachusetts State Archives. The one quoted is dated Feb. 17, 1842.

15 **"Who is to decide":** Douglass speech quoted in the *Hingham Patriot*, Nov. 20, 1841, and *The Liberator*, Dec. 10, 1841. Also in *Frederick Douglass Papers*, vol. 1, p. 9.

16 **"the stifling smoke":** The *National Anti-Slavery Standard*, reprinted in *The Liberator*, Jan. 14, 1842.

17 **could stay bundled:** My description of the House chamber is based on George Bothwell's 1902 memoir, *Reminiscences of Sixty Years in Public Affairs*, pp. 71–72.

17 **if only ten other "patricians":** From *National Anti-Slavery Standard*, Sept. 9, 1841, cited in Carlton Mabee's *Black Freedom: The Nonviolent Abolitionists from 1830 Through the Civil War* (1970).

18 **"the ablest man":** *Emancipator and American*, Feb. 17, 1842.

19 **"an entire abolitionist":** Charles Francis Adams, in his diary, Dec. 23, 1837. I have called it "CFA diary" in subsequent endnotes.

20 **a place of "little consequence":** CFA diary, Oct. 30, 1839.

20 **"political gamblers":** CFA diary, Mar. 7, 1842.

20 **"willing to advance their principles":** CFA diary, Jan. 11, 1843.

20 **much-anticipated report:** Massachusetts Senate report 63, Feb. 22, 1842.

20 **"this foolish mixing":** The newspaper accounts captured the tenor of the debate. See, for example, the *Boston Atlas*, Feb. 16, 1842, reporting on the marriage bill.

20 **"keep myself cool":** CFA diary, Feb. 16, 1842.

21 **"traveller's directory":** Garrison's list first appeared on Apr. 8, 1842. It ran in every issue until the practice of separate cars ended in late 1843.

21 **sixty-four thousand signatures:** *Boston Courier*, Mar. 17, 1843.

21 **"the most memorable event":** CFA diary, Feb. 1, 1843.

22 **"strong undercurrent of prejudice":** CFA diary, Feb. 6, 1843.

22 **With a dramatic air:** *Daily Atlas*, Feb. 7, 1843, and the *Courier*, Feb. 9, 1843. The *Courier* account specifically noted the Adams instruction to record his words.

22 **praised Adams:** Douglass, *My Bondage and My Freedom* (1855), p. 310.

22 **"I thought it dangerous":** CFA diary, Feb. 6, 1843.

23 **scribbled down:** From Brown's year-ending summary at the back of his 1859 pocket diary, part of the collection of his personal papers at the Detroit Public Library.

TWO: HARLAN OF KENTUCKY

25 **saw a strapping shape:** In recounting this first sighting years later, Malvina gave her age as fifteen. Inexplicably, this appears to be an error. She was born March 27, 1839, making her fourteen in the summer of 1853.

26 **that first night:** Malvina's recollections of her courtship come from her memoir, *Some Memories of a Long Life, 1854-1911,* mainly pp. 3–11. She completed the memoir in 1915, four years after her husband's death. It remained in the Harlan family papers for many years, consulted by scholars but unpublished until 2001.

27 **latest local novelty:** The Frankfort-to-Louisville railway portion opened for operation in May 1851.

28 **"special patrol companies":** The law went into effect July 1, 1852.

28 **icy dash to freedom:** For more on the river and runaway slaves, see Ann Hagedorn's *Beyond the River: The Untold Story of the Heroes of the Underground Railway.*

28 **On the Ohio:** Details on steamship operations from, among other sources, S. L. Kotar and J. E. Gessler's *The Steamboat Era: A History of Fulton's Folly on America's River, 1807–1860.* Also helpful: a traveler's account in the *New York Evangelist*, "A Sail Up the Mississippi and Ohio," May 5, 1853.

29 **"moved to tears":** My account of the Douglass-Remond scene comes from "Down the Ohio to the Underworld," *Fraser's Magazine,* Dec. 1866 (vol. 74, pp. 753–770). Reprinted in *Littell's Living Age*, Jan. 5, 1867. The author is not identified.

30 **At last count:** "Last count" refers to the 1850 census. In the 1860 census—the final one to include a "Slave Schedule"—the Harlans were recorded as having twelve slaves. The slave schedule did not provide names of enslaved people, only ages and gender. It appears that the Harlans replaced some slaves between 1850 and 1860, but it's hard to know for certain. Without names and dates of birth, it is impossible to compare the 1850 and 1860 lists with confidence.

30 **"Uncle Lewis":** The name comes from Mallie Harlan's memoir, *Some Memories.*

30 **settle the mystery:** The question of Robert Harlan's parentage has fascinated Harlan scholars

for years. See James W. Gordon's 1993 article, "Did the First Justice Harlan Have a Black Brother?" in *The Western New England Law Review* 15, no. 2. The 2002 edition of *Some Memories* included a family tree. Robert was shown in a box leading to James Harlan, with a question mark. About the same time, advances in DNA testing appeared to rule out James Harlan as Robert's father, showing no link between a descendant of Robert and two descendants of John Harlan. The editor of Mallie's memoir wrote in a footnote, p. 244, that Robert Harlan was "seven-eighths white in ancestry."

31 **his occasional letters:** Robert Harlan and John Harlan kept in touch throughout their lifetimes. Several of their letters can be found in the Harlan collections at the University of Louisville Law Library and at the Library of Congress. There is a good deal of overlap between the two collections. Both have been microfilmed, and some libraries have purchased copies. For the sake of simplicity, I will cite either one or the other, guided by where I first saw the document.

31 **recreating the scene for a reporter:** The journalist was James B. Morrow of the *Washington Post*, who interviewed Harlan for a lengthy profile piece, published Feb. 25, 1906. Mallie offered a slightly different account in *Some Memories*, pp. 20–21.

31 **"the highest cash prices for Negroes":** *Louisville Daily Journal*, Aug. 20, 1853.

33 **"seen me in my grave":** *Some Memories*, p. 10.

34 **copied several into a notebook:** Historians have cited these two selections as Harlan's own writing, and as evidence of Harlan's precocious intelligence. Writing before the Internet, they did not have the benefit of its search engines. Using phrases from both works, I found the original sources. The essay on liberty was a review of a published oration; it appeared in *The United States Literary Gazette*, July 15, 1825. The poem was the work of Irish writer Gerald Griffin, published in 1808. From what I could tell by looking at Harlan's papers, he did not claim these works as his own, but only copied them. That was a common way, then, to capture a favored piece of writing. The essay on liberty, as it appears in the Harlan notebook, opens with a quotation mark, which would be an odd beginning if it were Harlan's own work. The notebook is part of the Harlan collection at the Library of Congress, box 25, manuscript reel 15. My thanks to Ryan Reft, a historian at the library's manuscripts division, for granting me permission to view the original notebook.

35 **"You can fill the place":** Harlan's account from "My Appointment as Adjutant General of Kentucky," Harlan papers, Library of Congress, box 11, microfilm reel 8.

36 **loose network of 143 companies:** Harlan's report on the Kentucky militia, from the National Archives, Record Group 168, Records of the National Guard Bureau, which includes Annual Returns of Militia, 1822–1902.

36 **solemn face:** *Some Memories*, p. 45.

37 **the lecture so compelling:** The text of Robertson's Nov. 4, 1852, lecture appears in his 1855 collection of speeches and essays, *Scrap Book on Law and Politics, Men and Times*, pp. 246–256. That same book includes Robertson's correspondence with John Harlan's committee, p. 245.

37 **a speech hailing Robertson:** *Louisville Courier-Journal*, Nov. 24, 1908, also cited in David G. Farrelly's "Harlan's Formative Period: The Years Before the War," *Kentucky Law Journal* 46, no. 3 (1958).

37 **two hundred thousand people in slavery:** The Kentucky state auditor's annual reports to the legislature on taxable property included statistics on slavery by county. Those reports are at the Kentucky State Archives.

38 **"its appropriate grave":** Robertson's *Scrap Book*, p. 330.

38 **farewell oration:** Robertson's *Scrap Book*, p. 335.

38 **"lies in his throat":** James Harlan to D. Howard Smith, Aug. 5, 1851, Harlan papers, Library of Congress, box 2, microfilm reel 2.

39 **a new political movement:** John Harlan wrote about joining the Know Nothings in an autobiographical memo on his political years. The memo has a long title, beginning "The Know-Nothing Organization . . ." Peter Scott Campbell, manager of Harlan's papers at the University of Louisville Law School, dubbed this memo "John Marshall Harlan's Political Memoir," in annotating it for the *Journal of Supreme Court History*, Nov. 2008. For simplicity's sake, I'm adopting Campbell's label. From the Library of Congress collection, box 11, microfilm reel 8.

40 **mysterious rituals:** My research into the Know Nothing movement included original sources from the 1850s, primarily pamphlets and newspapers. Two scholarly works were particularly helpful: Agnes McGann's 1944 work, *Nativism in Kentucky to 1860*, and Carl Brand's 1916 thesis, "History of the Know Nothing Party in Indiana."

41 **ensuring slavery's expansion:** The Kansas-Nebraska Act of 1854 granted white male settlers in those two new territories the power to decide for themselves whether to embrace slavery. Before the law, slavery was restricted to states south of the 36°30' parallel. Kansas, north of the line, was known to favor slavery. Passage of the act led to the final rupture of the Whig Party.

42 **no plans to speak:** Harlan's "Political Memoir."

42 **"Grueling" could not begin:** My description of Harlan's 1855 speaking tour comes from historical Kentucky newspapers at the University of Kentucky library in Lexington, primarily those published in Frankfort, Lexington, Louisville, and Danville.

43 **"eloquent advocate":** *Kentucky Tribune*, reprinted in the *Frankfort Tri-Weekly Commonwealth*, July 16, 1855.

43 **"I had become conscious":** From Harlan's "Political Memoir."

43 **reappointed him:** Harlan served as adjutant general from 1851 to 1859, appointed by three different governors. His annual salary increased to $250 for the 1855 fiscal year.

44 **compiled a scrapbook:** Part of the Harlan collection at the University of Louisville.

44 **1848 Fillmore letter:** In Harlan's 1856 scrapbook, he labeled the letter, "Fillmore on Slave Trade—Letter to Gayle." He did not note the source. I found the reprint in the *Frankfort Commonwealth*, June 27, 1856.

44 **"the young giant":** *Louisville Daily Journal*, July 29, 1856.

44 **quoted him approvingly:** *Evansville Daily Journal*, Apr. 3, 1856.

44 **"unsurpassed eloquence":** *Cynthiana News*, June 26, 1856.

45 **a lasting image:** The Harlans' wedding scrapbook is part of the University of Louisville collection. The Willard Library in Evansville has a folder of articles on the Harlan wedding, including remembrances from guests who were interviewed after Harlan's death in 1911.

45 **"mounds of macaroons":** Eliza McCutcheon, Mallie's friend and later her sister-in-law, wrote about the Harlan wedding in a 1917 reminiscence. It appears in Kenneth P. McCutchan's compilation of Civil War letters written by her husband (Mallie's brother), titled *"Dearest Lizzie:" The Civil War Letters of James Maynard Shanklin*.

45 **her mother's parting words:** *Some Memories*, p. 11.

THREE: BROWN OF NEW ENGLAND

47 **doubts about his doubts:** The words and thoughts attributed to Henry Brown in this chapter come, largely, from two sources: a thirty-three-page autobiographical "Memoranda" that Brown wrote late in his life, and the yearly pocket daybooks that he kept from 1855 to 1875. Except for two missing volumes, those daybooks are part of the Brown collection at the Detroit Public Library.

48 **"which I veto":** Brown's daybooks for 1856 and 1857 are the missing ones. Fortunately, Brown's

close friend, Charles Kent of Detroit, quoted several entries from those two years in writing an "Addenda" to Brown's "Memoranda." After Brown's death in 1913, Kent arranged for the publication of Brown's "Memoranda" and his "Addenda" under the title of *Memoir of Henry Billings Brown.* Kent also arranged, with the permission of Brown's widow, to donate Brown's pocket calendars and other papers to the Burton Historical Collection, now part of the Detroit Public Library. A few months after Kent sent the collection to the Burton, Mrs. Brown requested the return of the 1856 and 1857 daybooks. They never made their way back to the Burton. For Brown's thoughts in the months after his graduation from Yale, I have relied on Kent's quotations. See "Addenda," *Memoir,* pp. 36–40.

48 **"Preceding Autobiography":** Brown's summary of his life to that point was written on the pages for Mar. 6–Mar. 25 in his 1855 daybook.

48 **written in her diary:** All quotes from Brown's mother's diary from "Memoranda," *Memoir,* pp. 3–4.

48 **"never so happy":** Brown's "Memoranda," *Memoir,* p. 4.

49 **the hands of Dr. Ebenezer Leach:** The Utica account is based on Brown's "Preceding Autobiography" in his 1855 pocket calendar. The information on Dr. Leach's background from *History of Oneida County, New York*, published 1878, pp. 353–354.

49 **"I want you to become a lawyer":** Brown's "Memoranda," *Memoir,* p. 5.

50 **"grim satisfaction":** Brown's "Memoranda," *Memoir,* p. 5.

50 **firmly mediocre average:** Brown's grades from the Yale College Book of Averages, on microfilm, HM69, at Yale's Sterling Memorial Library, Manuscripts and Archives Division.

50 **"we rose before dawn":** Brown's "Memoranda," *Memoir,* pp. 11–12.

51 **a miller and farmer:** Ten years before Henry was born, Billings Brown served a single term in the Connecticut House of Representatives, in 1826. He was thirty-two years old, had been married one year and had no children. He represented the town of Preston, where he was born in 1794. Whether this foray into public office was more dabbling or duty, it was certainly brief. Politics did not prove to be his calling or destiny.

51 **"highly respectable":** Brown's "Memoranda," *Memoir,* p. 11. Brewer had come to Yale in his junior year, transferring from Wesleyan College in Middletown, CT.

52 **"Half a mind not to speak":** From Brown's year-end summary for 1856, reprinted in Kent's "Addenda," *Memoir,* pp. 38–39.

53 **"All gross flattery, H.B.":** Brown's 1856 class album is part of his collection at Yale's Manuscripts and Archives, Sterling Library. A transcription of the mocking note he wrote to himself is among his papers at the Detroit Public Library.

54 **small armada:** The partnership of Silas K. Everett and Elias Brown had offices at 159 Front Street, within hailing distance of the Manhattan piers that served the company's fleet.

54 **well-to-do and well connected:** The list of Elias Brown's business and political offices come from several sources, including *Green's Annual Connecticut Register,* published regularly in the 1840s and 1850s, and Richard Anson Wheeler's *History of the Town of Stonington* (1900).

54 **a strong impression on Henry:** Brown's "Memoranda," *Memoir,* pp. 5–6.

54 **"I eagerly seized upon this opportunity":** Brown's "Memoranda," *Memoir,* p. 13.

55 **sailing for Liverpool:** Advertisements in the *New York Herald*, Oct. 23–24, 1856.

55 **unseasonably warm Saturday:** All mentions of New York's weather in this chapter are based on meteorological data collected daily at the Apothecary of New York Hospital from 1848 to 1870. These ledgers are now part of the Medical Center Archives at New York–Presbyterian Hospital/Weill Medical College of Cornell University.

55 **a city of half a million:** The 1850 census listed New York City's population as 515,547; Baltimore's as 169,054; and Boston's as 136,881.

55 **no factories:** Brown's "Memoranda," *Memoir,* p. 8. The town of Ellington's population was recorded as 1,255 in the 1850 census.

55 **so many horses:** From a July 26, 2013 article in the *New York Times*, headlined "Heat-Struck, July 1852," by Benjamin Weiser. Weiser quotes Joel A. Tarr, coauthor of *The Horse in the City* (2007), and Jon A. Peterson, an emeritus professor of history at Queens College, in describing the volume of manure and its smell.

55 **ten identifying details:** Brown's passport record, the National Archives, *Passport Applications,* 1795–1925, M1372, roll 58.

56 **"no law authorising me":** Secretary of State John Clayton's letters to the newspaper editors were published in the *Morning Chronicle and New-York Enquirer,* Aug. 18, 1849, along with official statements from two passport clerks explaining the department's longstanding policy regarding applications from people of color. That policy had never been as formal and clear as Clayton's letters suggested. For a fuller discussion of the controversy, and whether the passport was intended to be a document of citizenship or one of identification, see chapter eight of Craig Robertson's 2010 book, *The Passport in America: The History of a Document.*

56 **"Clayton's Law of Passports":** *North Star,* Aug. 24, 1849.

57 **paying three hundred dollars:** From the Academy of Music's advertisement in the *New-York Daily Times,* Oct. 23, 1856: "To let, on the off-nights of the opera, for concerts, lectures, &c. Accommodation for 4,000 persons. Price per night $300, including light."

58 **"ANOTHER GREAT MEETING":** The *Tribune,* run by Horace Greeley, was the most partisan of New York's three leading daily newspapers.

59 **"What will come before the country":** The three daily papers each carried some text of Robinson's speech. There are slight differences, but for the most part, none of consequence. The *Times* and *Tribune* accounts are somewhat longer than the *Herald's.*

59 **"SAILS THIS DAY":** As best as I could tell from newspaper shipping reports, the *Rathbone*'s departure was delayed a day. No ships on the New York–Liverpool route left Thursday. Four, including the *Rathbone,* left Friday.

60 **"beaten without mercy":** Brown's "Memoranda," *Memoir,* p. 14.

61 **"O climax of ecstasy":** Kent's "Addenda," *Memoir,* p. 39, quoting Brown's 1856 daybook.

62 ***Dred Scott v. Sandford*:** The correct spelling is Sanford; the error was made by the court, and became a permanent part of the official record. Also, "Dred" does not appear in the official case title, but I added it here because that's how most Americans know the ruling. The case is *Scott v. Sandford*, 60 U.S. 393. In reading Taney's decision, I paid close attention to his references to separation. For my brief narrative of the timing and circumstances surrounding the ruling, I consulted a variety of sources. *The Illustrated Biographies of the Supreme Court Justices, 1789–2012,* edited by Clare Cushman, was helpful. I also made use of the online collections of documents compiled by Supreme Court Historical Society, the Library of Congress, the Legal Information Institute at Cornell Law School, and the Oyez Project at the IIT Chicago–Kent College of Law.

63 **inherited his family's slaves:** Taney described his history of slave ownership in an Aug. 19, 1857 letter to Eliphalet Nott, president of Union College in Schenectady, NY, quoted in Bernard C. Steiner's 1922 biography, *Life of Roger Brooke Taney: Chief Justice of the United States Supreme Court*, p. 376. "I am not a slaveholder," Taney claimed, "More than thirty years ago, I manumitted every slave I ever owned, except two, who were too old when they became my property. These two, I supported in comfort, as long as they lived."

63 **"Our aged justice":** From Curtis's letter to his uncle, George Ticknor, Feb. 27, 1857. Cited in Steiner's *Life of Roger Brooke Taney*, p. 333.

64 **They stood separate, apart:** Taney described at some length what the "civilized portion of the

white race" believed about the "unfortunate" African race at the time of the Declaration of Independence. One sentence in this section included a phrase that quickly became the most quoted of any from his decision. Here is the full sentence, with the famous phrase italicized: "They had for more than a century before been regarded as beings of an inferior order, and altogether unfit to associate with the white race either in social or political relations, and so far inferior that *they had no rights which the white man was bound to respect*, and that the negro might justly and lawfully be reduced to slavery for his benefit." The italicized phrase is often quoted out of that historical context, and sometimes misquoted as "they had no rights which the white man *is* bound to respect." While I have no doubt that Taney believed that, and was perhaps cleverly working the statement into his decision, he did not use the present tense.

65 **plenty of company:** Passenger manifest for *City of Washington*, the National Archives, *Passenger Lists of Vessels Arriving New York, 1820–1897,* M237, microfilm reel 180.

66 **"mild epidemic insanity":** Emerson to his friend, Caroline Wilson, who was about to sail to Europe. Emerson had just said goodbye to another friend on his way to Europe, prompting him to say: "We all talk against it, but we all go. We preach America, but practise Europe. It is a mild epidemic insanity, & nothing but indulgence & a cloying operates a cure." The full letter appears in vol. IV of Ralph Rusk's *Letters of Ralph Waldo Emerson*, p. 441. The "insanity" phrase is quoted in Daniel Koch's *Ralph Waldo Emerson in Europe* (2012), p. 166.

66 **"wonderful expansion to one's ideas":** Brown's year-end summary to his 1857 daybook.

66 **"much to learn":** Brown's "Memoranda," *Memoir,* p. 13.

FOUR: TOURGEE OF OHIO

69 **could not sleep:** Letter from Emma Kilborn to Albion Tourgee, Oct. 29, 1858, document 31. The correspondence between Emma and Albion, which began in 1858 and continued throughout their lives, offers a remarkably intimate portrait of their courtship and marriage. In this chapter, I have drawn on more than fifty of their letters from 1858 and 1859. I also relied on two excellent books, Mark Elliott's *Color-Blind Justice: Albion Tourgee and the Quest for Racial Equality* (2006) and Otto Olsen's 1965 political biography, *Carpetbagger's Crusade: The Life of Albion Winegar Tourgee.* But I did not rely on their readings of the letters I have chosen to quote or characterize.

70 **his viewing perch:** From Ronald C. White Jr.'s *A. Lincoln: A Biography,* pp. 273–274. For more on the comet, and why it was regarded as "one of the most impressive astronomical events of the nineteenth century," see "The Worldwide Impact of Donati's comet on art and society in the mid-19th century," in *The Role of Astronomy in Society and Culture* (2011).

70 **the "sparkling tail":** *Ashtabula Weekly Telegraph*, Oct. 2, 1858.

70 **"earthly idol":** Emma to Albion, Oct. 29, 1858, document 51.

70 **"dreadful malady":** Emma to Albion, Mar. 1, 1858, document 45. I have chosen to use underlines, as Emma and Albion did in their letters. I think it captures their voice better than italics, the more conventional style for showing emphasis in print.

71 **he "had no home":** Albion to Emma, Mar. 8, 1859, document 57; **"orphan in spirit,"** May 29, 1860, document 126.

72 **"if I am successful":** Albion to Emma, June 9, 1859, document 74.

72 **"for my sake":** Emma to Albion, March 20, 1859, document 58.

73 **described her final hours:** From Valentine Tourgee's letter to Sophronia Winegar, May 14, 1843, document 26. Valentine's letters to his wife's family, while not frequent, were quite detailed about Louisa's failing health and his helpless despair in watching her decline. It is likely that Albion came across these letters while staying with the Winegar family in 1859.

He wrote to Emma, "I found a lot of my Father's letters in my rummaging and learned ever so much about my mother." Sept. 4, 1859, document 90.

73 ***"Memory has no magic power"*:** A handwritten version of this poem, with the date "November 1857" scrawled at the bottom, is document 60. In 1859, Tourgee collected his poems into a volume called "Sense and Nonsense," and contemplated having it published. He gave a copy to Emma.

74 **"a sink of corruption":** Valentine Tourgee to Sophronia Winegar, May 19, 1856, document 35.

74 **"out of debt":** Valentine's letter to "Respected Friends," one of several salutations he used in writing to Louisa's family, Oct. 30, 1836, document 8.

75 **"almost heart-broken":** Clarenia Ann Tourgee to the Winegar family, Feb. 14, 1843, document 22.

75 **"taught us how to die":** Valentine to Sophronia Winegar, May 14, 1843, document 26.

75 **a love for books:** Valentine's fond comments about Albion come from several letters to Sophronia Winegar—May 14, 1843, document 26; Oct 5, 1845, document 28; Sept. 19, 1847, document 31. Valentine rarely used punctuation in his writing style, so for easier reading in quoting these letters and others, I have taken the liberty of putting periods and commas where they appear obvious.

75 **"very near getting killed":** Valentine to Sophronia, June 4, 1848, document 32.

76 **his Kingsville kingdom:** Valentine's Sept. 19, 1847, letter to Sophronia, document 31, went into great detail as he tried to impress his in-laws with his newfound prosperity. By 1860, according to the census, Valentine had added 47 more acres and a herd of 96 sheep that produced 396 pounds of wool. Other totals: 600 pounds of butter, 350 pounds of maple syrup, and 150 pounds of cheese. The 1850 and 1860 censuses included Agricultural Schedules, offering a bounty of information on farm size and farm production.

76 **those he felt were immoral:** For Valentine's tight rein on Albion's reading material, I am relying on Roy Dibble's account in his 1921 book, *Albion W. Tourgee.* Dibble, who grew up near Tourgee's longtime home in Mayfield, NY, wrote the first version of his biography as a dissertation while a graduate student at Columbia University. Dibble's book lacks depth, and has few footnotes, but Dibble's proximity to Tourgee's family and his access to fresh memories made me comfortable enough to use his account.

76 **"a vast untrodden field":** Albion to Emma, July 25, 1859, document 80.

77 **Ohio had enacted "black laws":** I have condensed fifty years of history into a single paragraph, which cannot begin to do justice to this important subject. Others have delved more deeply. See Richard Sewall's *Ballots for Freedom: Antislavery Politics in the United States, 1837–1860.* Also, a wealth of information can be found in an 1845 report to the Ohio legislature, "Report of a Majority of a Select Committee Proposing to Repeal All Laws Creating Distinctions on Account of Color, Commonly Called the Black Laws, January 18, 1845."

78 **"Dear Father":** Albion to Valentine Tourgee, May 9, 1852, part of a letter begun by Jacob Winegar to Valentine on April 24, 1852. This letter is not part of the Tourgee papers. I'm grateful to Mark Elliott, author of *Color-Blind Justice,* for providing me with a copy. Elliott obtained it from Dean Keller, former librarian of Kent State University. Keller's index to the Tourgee papers, created in the mid-1960s, remains a useful if limited guide to the collection.

78 **"throwing stones":** Jacob Winegar to Valentine Tourgee, Apr. 24, 1852.

78 **determined not to show weakness:** This is Otto Olsen's observation in *Carpetbagger's Crusade,* p. 4. It seems apt, based on some of Emma's comments about Albion's feistiness.

79 **a clench-fisted letter:** Sophronia had asked Valentine to pay something for Albion's room and board. He reacted with incredulity and sarcasm: "We have a law in this State, and I presume in yours, providing for the maintenance of transient persons or persons who have no legal resi-

dence. If you occupy the position of overseer to such [a person], no doubt a draft on the county treasury will be duly honored." Valentine to Sophronia, May 15, 1856, document 35.

79 **Determined to repair the damage:** Emma to Albion, Mar. 2, 1859, document 56.

80 **"sail under false colors":** Albion to Emma, Mar. 8, 1859, document 57.

80 **"Have no hesitations":** Emma to Albion, Mar. 20, 1859, document 58.

81 **"universally pitied":** Emma to Albion, Apr. 3, 1859, document 61.

81 **his ode:** Albion copied the poem into a letter to Emma, May 3, 1859, document 60.

82 **"I feel stronger and happier now":** Albion to Emma, June 9, 1859, document 74.

83 **their plan of marrying:** The question of when they would marry was a frequent theme in their correspondence from 1859 through 1861. In January 1860, document 133, Albion wrote, "It requires not a little self-denial for two persons . . . to put off the state of their union for four, five or six years. It requires more power to quell the strong swelling passions of the human heart than to govern a nation."

83 **"Father and I had quite a talk":** Albion to Emma, Aug. 7, 1859, document 81.

84 **quizzed his aunt Ann:** Albion's letters during his month in Lee, beginning Aug. 7, 1859, provide a remarkable but still incomplete chronicle of his efforts to understand and collect his inheritances. To bolster my account, I obtained copies of his grandfather's and uncle's wills, filed in the Berkshire County Probate Court, along with all subsequent documents related to those two estates.

84 **"Ministre du Finance":** Albion to Emma, also Aug. 7, 1859.

85 **such low-life behavior:** Emma to Albion, Aug. 24, 1859, document 86.

85 **"slave in all":** Albion to Emma, in a letter begun Aug. 25, 1859, document 87.

85 **"She's a pretty doll":** Albion's account of his flirtation with his cousin from his Aug. 7 letter to Emma; **"I have some grit . . ."** from Emma's reply, Aug. 11, 1859, document 82.

85 **"he esteemed you":** Emma to Albion, Aug. 24, 1859, document 86.

86 **"I would have true greatness":** Albion to Emma, Aug. 25–28, 1859, document 87.

86 **"uproar in the courts":** Albion to Emma, Sept. 4 and 5, 1859, document 90.

87 **"waited long enough":** From the same letter, Sept. 4 and 5.

87 **enough cash to enroll:** Unfortunately, I could find no record of the payments to Albion, either by his aunt or the two estates. The court files show that the executors failed to file the required spending reports. The available facts, however, make clear that Albion did receive at least a portion of the five hundred dollars due to him under the terms of the two wills. Otherwise, he could not have enrolled at the University of Rochester in the fall of 1859, and he could not have returned for the start of the second year in the fall of 1860. It seems highly unlikely, though, that he received the full five hundred dollars while enrolled at Rochester. He ran out of money in the middle of his second year, withdrawing in January 1861.

87 **his quarters at 3 Kent Street:** Albion told Emma that he was rooming with a friend from Kingsville, Seneca Coon (who later changed the spelling to Kuhn). Letter to Emma, Sept. 18, 1859, document 95.

87 **"quite a lawyer":** Albion to Emma, Sept. 7, 1859, document 91.

87 **"a triangulated monomaniac":** Albion to Emma, Jan. 29, 1860, document 138.

88 **"life to your eyes":** Emma to Albion, Oct. 16, 1859, document 104.

88 **"none of the haggard":** Albion to Emma, Jan. 15, 1860, document 133.

FIVE: THE FREE PEOPLE OF COLOR

91 **that most memorable day in New Orleans history:** My description of the Eighth of January celebration for 1860 is drawn from New Orleans's seven daily newspapers at the time: the *Bee*

and its French edition, *L'Abeille de la Nouvelle-Orléans*; *Commercial Bulletin*; *Daily Crescent*; *Daily Delta*; *Daily True Delta*; and *Picayune*.

92 **nearly eleven thousand:** More free people of color lived in New Orleans than in all other parishes combined. The 1860 census shows 10,948 in Orleans parish, and 7,699 elsewhere in the state. New Orleans had a total population of 174,491, including 14,484 slaves. Louisiana's population in 1860 was recorded as 708,002, with 331,726 slaves, about 47 percent.

92 **Quadroon Boxes:** The theaters, in their daily advertisements, listed their ticket categories and prices. At the St. Charles, a "quadroon box" cost the same as the white dress circle seats. While the quadroon boxes did not appear to be off-limits to those who were more than one-quarter black, the name suggested that it was intended for the mixed-race elite.

93 **"the various grades of the coloured people":** The visiting New York journalist's list, displayed at the beginning of this chapter, comes from Frederick Law Olmsted's *Journeys and Explorations in the Cotton Kingdom*, p. 294. Olmsted, before becoming one of the nation's foremost landscape architects, had established himself as a writer. In 1852, the *New York Times*, then in its second year, hired him to travel through the South and record his impressions. He wrote under a pen name, "Yeoman." His dispatches formed the basis for several books.

93 **could trace their origins:** The past few decades have produced a wealth of well-researched books exploring the history of free people of color in New Orleans. My bibliography lists the books I consulted, but a half dozen deserve a special mention for this chapter: Kimberly Hanger's *Bounded Lives, Bounded Places* (1997); Kenneth Aslakson's *Making Race in the Courtroom* (2014); Emily Clark's *The Strange History of the American Quadroon* (2013); Mary Gehman and Lloyd Dennis's *The Free People of Color* (1994); Caryn Cossé Bell's *Revolution, Romanticism, and the Afro-Creole Protest Tradition in Louisiana* (1997); and Roland McConnell's *Negro Troops of Antebellum Louisiana* (1968). Except where noted, I looked at all primary source documents to draw my own conclusions about the events.

93 **"noble-hearted, generous":** For the full text of Jackson's appeal, see vol. 2 of *The Correspondence of Andrew Jackson*, edited by John Bassett, published 1929, pp. 58–59.

94 **the procession pushed off:** The *Daily Crescent* published the full "Order of Procession," Jan. 8, 1860.

94 **newly paved:** In 1859, New Orleans Mayor Gerard Stith undertook an extensive and expensive paving campaign to bring New Orleans out of the mud. The first phase included more streets in the American district than others, prompting complaints of favoritism from some property owners in the French-speaking neighborhoods.

94 **quite the stir:** The *Daily Crescent* wrote, approvingly, that the parade's "most interesting feature was the appearance of the colored veterans, who, with the whites, braved the dangers and assisted in achieving the victory. . . . They were placed in rear of the whites, and their appearance, many of them bowed with age, excited universal remark." *Crescent*, Jan. 9, 1851.

94 **"These faithful men":** The *Picayune's* effusive tribute to the colored veterans, also Jan. 9, 1851, caught the eye of abolitionists in the North. William C. Nell, a black antislavery activist, reprinted it in his 1852 book, *Services of Colored Americans, in the Wars of 1776 and 1812.*

96 **about two hundred:** Clark, *Strange History of the American Quadroon*, p. 98.

97 **Harang would not allow:** Clark offers a well-documented account of Agnes Mathieu's route to freedom in *Strange History*, pp. 97–101. I have relied on her reading of the primary documents, which she cites as Manumission of Agnes, December 16, 1779, Record Group 2, Spanish Judicial Records, the Louisiana State Historical Center in New Orleans. She and several New Orleans archivists were interviewed about Agnes Mathieu's story for a segment of the PBS show *History Detectives*, episode 810, which aired in 2011. The segment did not mention Agnes Mathieu's connection to the Plessy family.

97 ***un padre no conocido*:** See, for example, the baptism record for Agnes's son Louis Mathieu, *mulato libre*, St. Louis Cathedral, Baptisms for Slaves and Free People of Color, 1792–1798, baptism number 1032, p. 260.

98 **He signed the alteration:** The sacramental records of the New Orleans Archdiocese don't yield their secrets easily, and I benefited from the expertise of others in researching the Plessy and Mathieu families. Emilie Leumas, the archdiocese's chief archivist, explained some puzzling mysteries and translated several documents that were beyond my abilities. I also received invaluable assistance from Greg Osborn at the New Orleans Public Library, who also happens to be a Plessy descendant.

99 **he told the delegates:** *Journal of the Proceedings of the Convention of State of Louisiana*, p. 761 and p. 831.

99 **Hostility was nowhere in evidence:** My description of the St. Louis Hotel dinner from accounts in the *Daily True Delta*, Jan. 9, 1860; *Bee*, Jan. 9, 1860; *Picayune*, Jan. 10, 1860.

99 **after years without an association:** In 1853, thirty-one colored veterans announced that they were forming an Association of Colored Veterans. They sought the legislature's imprimatur, prompting a spirited debate about whether such official recognition would create a "dangerous" precedent. A New Orleans senator, John L. Lewis, said he knew most of the thirty-one petitioners, and praised them as "objects of veneration rather than suspicion." The Senate eventually went along, but the House never voted on the bill.

101 **did not require such an emphatic ruling:** The court majority chose to make its point in a murder case, *State v. Harrison*, that did not involve a free person of color. Harrison, identified only by that name, was a slave convicted of killing another enslaved man in East Feliciana Parish. The majority did not overturn Harrison's conviction; it only criticized the 1855 law's defects. *State v. Harrison* (11 La. Ann. 722).

101 **scornful dissent:** The two dissenting justices were aghast at the majority's logic. They wrote: "The argument that slaves are one object, and free colored people another, overlooks the fact, that both compose a single, homogenous class of beings, distinguished from all others by nature, custom and law, and never confounded with citizens of the State. No white person can be a slave, no colored person can be a citizen."

101 **One law offered "voluntary" slavery:** The 1859 laws were Act 275 (voluntary slavery), Act 16 (the ban on certain licenses for free people of color), and Act 87 (the ban on newly arriving people of color).

102 **"the kind of population we want":** *Opelousas Patriot*, July 23, 1859.

SIX: "THE HARLAN NAME"

107 **Mallie's memory remained scorched:** I have relied, for the most part, on Mallie Harlan's recollection of the fire, *Some Memories*, pp. 25–30. She wrote about it with detail and care, choosing to include small touches that didn't necessarily portray her in a favorable light. That said, it's important to note that *Some Memories* was written with her husband's reputation in mind, and should be evaluated in that light.

108 **cup of hot tea:** It's not clear from Mallie's memoir how often John experienced this. She describes one incident, in the early 1900s, when her husband poured hot tea on his hand, and lapsed into what a doctor called a "psychic stroke." *Some Memories*, p. 30.

108 **hurled himself into the race:** In his "Political Memoir," Harlan wrote of his campaign for county judge that he "visited every house and shook hands (as was the fashion) with nearly every man, woman and child in the county." A bit of mild overstatement seems a characteristic element of his storytelling.

109 **his son John prepared to help:** Loren Beth's 1992 book *John Marshall Harlan: The Last Whig Justice*, has a good chapter on Harlan's political activities before the Civil War. Louis Hartz's "John M. Harlan in Kentucky, 1855–1877," *Filson Club History Quarterly*, Jan. 1940, offered a good guide to relevant newspaper citations.

109 **"I started to jump up":** Harlan's account of his 1859 congressional race, in his "Political Memoir," must be read with the usual discerning eye. As he often did in recounting his personal history, he portrayed himself as an accidental beneficiary of events. If he truly did not want the nomination, or felt unprepared to take it on, he could have done as others did during the balloting: Withdrawn his name, bringing a swift end to his candidacy.

109 **narrowest of margins:** On the final ballot, Harlan defeated Roger W. Hanson, 36⅔ to 35½ in a complicated tabulation that involved fractional votes. See "Letter from Lexington," *Louisville Daily Courier*, May 20, 1859.

110 **"surprised, if not annoyed":** From Harlan's "Political Memoir."

111 **Stephen Douglas had amplified:** After Douglas held forth at length on nonintervention at the second Lincoln-Douglas debate in Freeport, IL, the policy acquired a label among Democrats: "the Freeport Doctrine."

111 **I ask you now, Captain Simms:** My account of the Georgetown debate is based on the *Louisville Daily Journal*, May 25, 1859, later references in the *Frankfort Daily Commonwealth*, and Harlan's "Political Memoir."

112 **"The Captain was stumped":** The *Journal*'s partisan correspondent, identified only as "IO," indulged freely in the mix of opinion and fact that was common in newspapers during the mid-nineteenth century.

112 **"high bred and aristocratic":** *Daily Courier*, June 7, 1859.

112 **evidence from newspaper clippings:** Harlan's "Political Scrapbook, 1859–1860," University of Louisville collection, box 17.

112 **"hang a negro-stealer as high as Haman":** The Simms quote was rendered slightly differently in three newspaper accounts. All agreed that he said "as high as Haman," but one quotes him as saying "nigger-stealer" rather than "negro-stealer." I chose the milder version because it appeared in two of the three papers, and absent other evidence, it seems best to go with the majority, particularly as most newspapers in those days had no hesitation in using the more offensive word.

113 **deal with the consequences:** The quotes in this paragraph from the *Courier*, June 7, 1859; *Lexington Observer and Reporter*, reprinted in the *Courier*, June 16, 1859; *Cynthiana News*, quoted in the *Frankfort Tri-Weekly Commonwealth*, May 30, 1859.

113 **"had my opponent on the run":** From Harlan's "Political Memoir."

113 **A truce emerged:** The duel negotiators included a former Kentucky governor (Charles Morehead) on Davis's side and a former U.S. vice president (Breckinridge) on Simms's. The *Courier* published a nearly complete record of the documents exchanged by the parties, on June 23, 1859. Harlan wrote his own account in 1908, "Debate with Simms," University of Louisville collection, box 25, folder 3.

114 **the final tally:** The official returns showed Simms the winner, 6,932 to 6,865. The *Courier* published a county-by-county breakdown, Aug. 11, 1859.

114 **"persons whom no one knew":** Harlan's account, in his "Political Memoir."

116 **Campaigning as an elector:** Electors acted, essentially, as surrogate speakers for the candidates. Harlan's appearances ran from late July into October. The schedule published in the *Courier*, Sept. 22, 1860, listed eight debates in twelve days in five counties.

116 **red, white, and blue landscape:** *Louisville Journal*, "Immense Mass Meeting in Richmond," July 25, 1860.

117 **never made it home:** *Some Memories*, pp. 47–48.

117 **a "chief amusement":** *Some Memories*, p. 30.

117 **Politicians from every part of the state:** *Courier*, Jan. 18 and 19, 1861.

117 **even more startling news:** The *Courier*, Jan. 18, 1861, reprinted a dispatch from the *New Orleans Daily Delta* about the raids on federal installations. Additional details from documents in the *Official Records of The War of the Rebellion*, ser. 1, vol. 1, chap. 6, pp. 489–492.

118 **slide toward secession:** The *Cincinnati Press* wrote that Kentucky was "drifting into disunion." The *Frankfort Commonwealth*, in reprinting the item on Jan. 24, 1861, said the *Press* was misreading the legislature's mood.

118 **"the wicked purpose of subduing":** The telegram is reprinted in *Official Records of the War of the Rebellion*, ser. 3, vol. 1, p. 70. Magoffin's reply provoked Kentucky's John L. Crittenden, then serving in Congress, to send an apologetic note to a Union general. Crittenden called Magoffin's telegram "hasty & unbecoming—and does not correspond with usual + gentlemanly courtesy." Still, Crittenden told the general, Magoffin was right not to offer troops, because it would have provoked the secessionists and severed Kentucky from the Union. Crittenden to General Winfield Scott, May 17, 1861, copy in the Abraham Lincoln Papers, Library of Congress.

118 **"a standing army of gigantic proportions":** "Governor's Message," *Frankfort Commonwealth*, May 8, 1861. Magoffin insisted that he was equipping the state militias only to ensure order, and not as a prelude to secession.

119 **Traitor:** In a 1911 "autobiographical letter" to his son Richard, Harlan wrote: "I was regarded by rebel leaders as a 'traitor to the Union,' because of my opposition to secession, and because I had announced that the Government was under a solemn duty to save the Union, if need be, by armed force." The 1911 letter runs thirty-two pages. It was intended, Harlan wrote, to "commit to paper" some of his Civil War experiences. Copies can be found in both Harlan collections. The text appears in Peter Scott Campbell's article, "The Civil War Reminiscences of John Marshall Harlan," *Journal of Supreme Court History* 32, no. 3 (Nov. 2007).

119 **his newspaper nights:** From Harlan's 1911 letter to son Richard, and from *Some Memories*, pp. 53–58.

119 **his father's clandestine footsteps:** John Harlan wrote an account of his role in the gun-running operation, and sent it to Thomas Speed for his 1907 book, *The Union Cause in Kentucky.* Speed published it, with Harlan's permission, pp. 117–121.

120 **The men all understood:** For an 1883 article in the *Magazine of American History*, Daniel Stevenson interviewed three men who attended the secret meeting in James Harlan's Frankfort office. "General Nelson, Kentucky, and Lincoln Guns," August 1883, pp. 115–139.

120 **sent a report privately to Lincoln:** Eleven men signed the letter, including James Harlan, May 28, 1861, Lincoln papers, Library of Congress, ser. 1, general correspondence.

121 **John had inside knowledge:** From Harlan's account in Speed's book, *The Union Cause in Kentucky.*

122 **get "ahead of the enemy":** For Polk's message to Magoffin and other documents on Kentucky's neutrality, see *Official Records of the War of the Rebellion*, ser. 1, vol. 4, chap. 12. The Confederate documents begin on p. 179, and the Union documents on p. 196.

122 **"I think to lose Kentucky":** Lincoln to U.S. senator Orville H. Browning, Sept. 22, 1861, in *The Collected Works of Abraham Lincoln,* vol. 4, pp. 531–533. This letter includes Lincoln's concern that "the very arms we had furnished Kentucky would be turned against us."

123 **"a most horrible one for me":** *Some Memories*, pp. 59–61.

123 **makeshift barge:** Harlan tells the story in "Some Experiences as a Captain of the Home Guards," the Harlan papers, Library of Congress.

123 **Summoning "all the courage":** *Some Memories,* p. 60. In his 1911 letter to son Richard, Harlan mentioned his agonizing choice and said Mallie "came to my rescue and urged me 'to go to the front,' saying she would care for our little ones. This relieved my anxiety somewhat."

123 **"To the People of Kentucky":** This recruiting announcement appeared in the *Louisville Democrat* and the *Louisville Journal* on multiple days between Sept. 27 and Oct. 10, 1861.

124 **placed announcements:** The ads ran in the *Journal* and the *Democrat,* Oct. 16–20, 1861.

124 **filled eight companies:** Recruitment totals from the *Democrat*, Nov. 10, 1861. For a full description of the Tenth's makeup, see Dennis W. Belcher's 2009 book, *The 10th Kentucky Volunteer Infantry in the Civil War.*

125 **"A most exciting trip":** *Some Memories*, pp. 61–62.

126 **"our gallant Col. Harlan":** A member of the regiment, undoubtedly with permission, described the miserable conditions in a letter dated Jan. 10, 1862, sent to the *Louisville Journal.* It appeared five days later under the headline, "Advance of Colonel Harlan's Tenth Kentucky Regiment," signed "W." Also, Belcher's book, p. 26, quotes a letter from Columbus Harshfield, a private in Company F: "I do not believe our clothing was thoroughly dry the whole way."

127 **a spot called Logan's Crossroads:** My account of the battle at Logan's Crossroads (more popularly known now as the Battle of Mill Springs) is based largely on *Official Records of the War of the Rebellion*, ser. 1, vol. 7, chap. 17. Harlan's regimental report, dated January 27, 1862, appears on pp. 88–90.

127 **"sore and grievously disappointed":** Harlan's 1911 letter to his son Richard.

SEVEN: "A WAR OF WHICH NO MAN CAN SEE THE END"

131 **homesick and frightened:** For this chapter, I have made liberal use of Brown's daybooks to illuminate his thoughts and feelings, as well as his 1908 autobiographical "Memoranda," keeping in mind that it was written many years after the events.

133 **a modest "governor's house":** The residence, at 612 S. Marshall Avenue, is now owned by the Marshall chapter of the Daughters of the American Revolution.

133 **"Went out with Gorham":** Brown's daybook entries for Dec. 6–10, 1859, describe his visits to Detroit law offices.

133 **such an eminent escort:** Details on Gorham's life from *Portrait and Biographical Album of Calhoun County, Michigan* (1891), pp. 190–192.

134 **the Crosswhites trapped inside:** The Marshall Public Library has an extensive collection on the Crosswhite case. Washington Gardner's *History of Calhoun County* (1913) devotes twenty-six pages to the episode, pp. 55–81, including transcriptions of several original court documents.

134 **"Resolved, That these Kentucky gentlemen":** Dispatch from "M.R.D." [Martin R. Delany] to the *North Star*, Frederick Douglass's newspaper, July 28, 1848, and cited in Martin R. Delany, *A Documentary Reader* (North Carolina Press, 2003).

134 **"write it in capital letters":** From Francis Troutman's affidavit, recounting the events, quoted in Gardner's *History of Calhoun County*, pp. 56–57. As far as I could find from the records, Gorham did not dispute the quote, but he did not mention it in his account, also quoted in Gardner's *History*, p. 58.

135 **walk to Firemen's Hall:** Brown's daybook, Feb. 22, 1860.

136 **"Phillips is a dangerous man":** Brown's daybook, May 25, 1859.

136 **"capital stump speech":** Brown's daybook, Mar. 28, 1859.

136 **"little better than absolute blindness":** Brown's daybook, Mar. 10, 1860.

137 **Spaciousness was its virtue:** Gary Ecelbarger's 2008 book *The Great Comeback: How Abraham Lincoln Beat the Odds to Win the 1860 Republican Nomination,* p. 203, called the Wigwam "a most impressive convention hall, not so much for the carpentry but for the spectacular décor."

137 **"Took nap in PM":** Details of Brown's trip to the Republican convention from his daybook, May 17–20, 1860.

138 **noisy approval:** Lincoln's backers did a masterful job of creating the impression of a groundswell for their candidate. "Tremendous applause" greeted the announcement of Lincoln's 181 votes on the second ballot, just shy of Seward's 184½. The convention chairman's call for quiet was even noted in the official *Proceedings of the Republican National Convention,* p. 115.

138 **declaring it "incomprehensible":** Brown heard two Emerson lectures in Detroit, on Feb. 18 and 19, 1860. He had no comment on the first, titled "Manners and Morals." Presumably it had some merit, because Brown chose to go to the second one the next day.

138 **Hubbard was an Easterner:** Biographical details from Hubbard's papers at the University of Michigan's Bentley Historical Library.

139 **qualifying him to appear:** Admission to the bar put Brown's name into the Detroit newspapers for the first time. *Free Press,* July 24, 1860.

139 **"my destiny":** Brown's daybook, Aug. 30, 1860.

139 **"not in my nature":** Brown's year-end summary for his 1860 daybook.

139 **"hard up for cash":** Brown's daybook, Oct. 22, 1860.

139 **more reading time than clients:** "Memoranda," *Memoir,* p. 19. Brown wrote that during the fall of 1860, he "devoted himself less to the practice of law, which was meagre enough, than to familiarising myself with the Michigan Reports." The Michigan Supreme Court's rulings were published as the Michigan Reports.

140 **"to establish a correct principle":** Day to abolitionist Gerrit Smith, Mar. 27, 1856, the Gerrit Smith papers, box 8, Syracuse University Libraries, Special Collections Research Center.

140 **fascinating reading:** Brown does not mention, in his daybooks or his "Memoranda," reading any specific Michigan Supreme Court case in the fall of 1860. But based on other information from later in his life, there's no doubt he read *Day v. Owen.* The case citation is *Day v. Owen,* 5 Mich. 520 (1858).

140 **The facts, as laid out:** The Michigan Supreme Court's file on the *Day* case, at the Archives of Michigan, includes documents from the lower courts and the original lawsuit. I have used information from that file to provide some of the context that the final ruling itself lacked. Record Group 96-169, box 48, F21, Michigan Supreme Court, 1858.

140 **sued the steamboat's captain:** The case file does not make clear whether Owen, the captain and owner, was directly involved in refusing Day's request for a cabin.

141 **"if sober, well-behaved and free of disease":** *New York Tribune,* "A Wholesome Verdict," Feb. 23, 1855.

141 **Day and his background:** I examined original records when possible, but two books made my research easier. One was Todd Mealy's 2010 biography, *Aliened American,* the first of two volumes on Day's life. Mealy unearthed a wealth of material, and he generously allowed me to review several documents relevant to this narrative. R. J. M. Blackett's 1986 book, *Beating Against the Barriers,* offers a briefer but illuminating glimpse of Day's world.

141 **only two identities:** In focusing on the legal principles at issue, appellate rulings often omitted such context.

141 **"adoptive father":** Day used this phrase in an Aug. 3, 1898 speech. Todd Mealy provided me with a copy.

141 **offsetting expenses:** Day's letter to R. E. Gillett, publisher of the *Oberlin Evangelist,* June 29,

1843, Oberlin College Archives, Record Group 7/1/5, box 7. Also, letters from Day's "guardian," John P. Williston, to Oberlin college officials, box 8, Feb. 14, 1845, July 17, 1845, and Dec. 17, 1846.

142 **"Address to the Colored People":** The full text appears in *Minutes of the Proceedings of the National Negro Conventions, 1830–1864.*

142 **"hardly inferior to Douglass":** *New York Tribune*, July 15, 1853.

142 **denied him a seat:** Day triumphed initially, triggering a backlash that led to a second vote and his expulsion. *Journal of the Senate of the State of Ohio*, 1854, p. 51 (Jan. 5), p. 102 (Jan. 20), and pp. 107–108 (Jan. 21).

142 **hinted at his reason:** Day to Gerrit Smith, March 27, 1856, and June 21, 1858, the Gerrit Smith Papers, box 8, Syracuse University Libraries, Special Collections Research Center.

143 **three of the four judges:** The court's fourth judge, James V. Campbell, opted to sit out. He had several conflicts with parties in the case, not uncommon in Michigan's small and tight-knit legal world.

143 **"eminently right":** The *Free Press* devoted a week's worth of articles to the *Day* ruling. This quote appeared in "The Supreme Court of the State of Michigan on the Social Status of Negroes," Oct. 20, 1858.

144 **unsure when he would return:** Day did not return to the United States for four years, after the Emancipation Proclamation. He and his wife Lucie later divorced, and both remarried. He had a long and distinguished career as a lecturer, editor, activist, and educator. He died in Harrisburg, PA, in 1900.

145 **They arranged for Henry's interview:** In his "Memoranda," *Memoir*, p. 19, Brown made a point of saying that Dickey was "a friend of the family."

147 **Drilling with the company:** Brown's daybook, Sept. 3, 1861.

147 **"obliged to advocate it":** Brown's daybook, Jan. 13, 1862.

147 **"little certainty in the law":** Brown's daybook, May 30–31, 1862.

148 **"Shall I go into the army?":** Brown's daybook, Sept. 1, 1862. Earlier, on July 14, 1862, he wrote, "Must I go into the army?" That earlier entry appears to be in response to public discussion of the first draft call.

148 **"Chairman Ward committee!!!":** Brown's daybook, Sept. 18, 1862.

148 **a leisurely trip:** Brown described his travel to Memphis in his daybook, May 11–21, 1863.

148 **souvenirs of the war:** Five of these official passes are among Brown's papers at the Detroit Public Library.

148 **approved a general draft:** The Enrollment Act of 1863, passed by Congress on Mar. 3, created a system of provost marshals to compile lists of all eligible men by April 1, a massive undertaking.

149 **failed to meet their quota:** Local newspapers often carried brief announcements of districts that had met their quotas. If a draft was held, the newspapers frequently published the names of those selected.

149 **amend the law:** Congress passed a revision of the Enrollment Act on Feb. 24, 1864.

149 **"desire in a wife":** From Brown's year-end summary in his 1863 daybook. He called Carry a "lovely damsel" in his entry for Nov. 24, 1862, the day they met. Their courtship began in earnest a few months later.

150 **three hundred or so:** The eligibility lists, compiled two years earlier, were out of date. After a reexamination, the Second Ward eligibility total dropped to two hundred fifty-six men, slightly increasing Brown's odds of being picked if a draft was needed.

150 **a draft looked unavoidable:** *Free Press*, Aug. 20, 1864, "The Draft."

150 **"Concluded to get a substitute":** It appears that Brown could have waited. On Aug. 29, the *Free Press* reported that the Second Ward had achieved its quota, and had a surplus of twenty-six men. No draft was necessary.

150 **driving substitute prices ever higher:** From the *Free Press*, Aug. 19, 1864: "The highest price that we have yet heard of was paid for two substitutes on Tuesday, at $1,850 each. The lowest price yesterday was $850. Nobody dares make an estimate what the price will be after the draft takes place."

150 **"John Peterson by name":** Hiring a substitute produced a paper trail, but one that proved challenging to reconstruct. John Peterson's agreement with Brown can be found among Peterson's enlistment papers, Record Group 94, entry 91, Adjutant General's office, ser. 1, box 617, at the National Archives in Washington. Peterson survived the war, serving in Tennessee and Georgia. He was discharged on July 17, 1866. See Register of Enlistments in the U.S. Army, 1798–1914, microfilm M233, National Archives, roll 30.

150 **Certificate of Discharge:** A record of Brown's certificate can be found at the National Archives in Chicago, Record Group 110, Provost Marshal General's Bureau, entry 5971, on "List of Furloughs Granted to Enlisted Men."

EIGHT: "FOR THIS I AM WILLING TO DIE"

153 **The city felt transformed:** My account of the scene in Rochester after the Fort Sumter attack is drawn from Tourgee's letters, Apr.–May 1861, and from Rochester newspapers.

153 **"One telegram falsifies another":** Tourgee to Emma, Apr. 14, 1861, document 268.

154 **"I don't read the Political news":** Tourgee to Emma, Feb. 4, 1860, document 139.

154 **"what the world calls Society":** Tourgee to Emma, Feb. 28, 1860, document 150.

154 **Those were the words:** Portions of Anderson's speech at City Hall appeared in the *Union and Advertiser*, Apr. 19, 1861. Anderson's Sunday sermon received a brief mention in the *Union and Advertiser*, Apr. 22, 1861.

155 **"no one knows why":** Tourgee to Emma, Dec. 15, 1860, document 231.

156 **"the world shall hear me":** Tourgee to Emma, Feb. 24, 1861, document 257.

156 **"erected on the ruins":** Tourgee to Emma, Mar. 3, 1861, document 260. For letters with an abundance of underlining, such as this one, I have chosen for readability's sake to describe rather than replicate all the underlines.

157 **"go—with great fortitude":** Emma to Tourgee, Mar. 10, 1861, document 264.

157 **"Tell me now":** Tourgee to Emma, Apr. 22, 1861, document 272. This six-page letter is the one that begins with Tourgee's account of Anderson's speech and Rochester's war fever.

158 **putting on a little weight:** Emma to Tourgee, Jan. 20, 1861, document 244.

158 **She did not even mind his flirtations:** Tourgee's friend Joe Webster found it hard to believe that Emma did not mind his friendships with other women. "So much frankness of expression was quite horrifying to him," Tourgee told her, July 1, 1861, document 291. "He really does not know us very well."

158 **"Oh, Albion, Albion":** Emma to Tourgee, Oct. 16, 1859, document 104.

159 **"wrong, vile, inhuman":** Tourgee to Emma, Nov. 12, 1859, document 114.

159 **ever went to trial:** Simeon Bushnell and Charles Langston, both black abolitionists, were the only ones tried and convicted. Langston was an Oberlin College graduate and friend of William Howard Day. The prosecutions were of questionable fairness. An example: The U.S. marshal in Cleveland, an appointee of the Buchanan administration, oversaw the assembling of the jury pool. In a region with a decided Republican majority, the pool of forty had only ten Republicans. The jury that heard the case did not have a single Republican.

159 **the legal battle:** For a deeper look at this seminal case, see Jacob Shipherd's *History of the Oberlin-Wellington Rescue*, published in 1859. Shipherd, a supporter of the rescuers, compiled a thorough record, featuring transcripts from court and newspaper accounts.

160 **One banner:** Reported May 29, 1859, in *The Anti-Slavery Bugle*, a weekly in Salem, OH.

160 **"rank little Republican":** Emma to Tourgee, Jan. 18, 1860, document 134.

161 **"go to Smash":** Tourgee to Emma, Feb. 4, 1860, document 139.

161 **"I bid this messenger":** Emma to Tourgee, Apr. 24, 1861, document 162. Unraveling the timeline of their letters during this period was an arduous process, complicated by the volume of letters, the lack of information about when they were delivered, and questionable legibility of some dates. I'm grateful for the extra eyes of Tom Knoles, an expert on historical letters at the American Antiquarian Society in Worcester, MA.

162 **hurriedly scrawled:** Tourgee to Emma, Apr. 23, 1861, document 275.

162 **Horace's words:** Translations abound for this line from Horace's *Odes* (III.2.13). Many choose "fitting" or "right" for *decorum*, rather than Tourgee's "noble."

163 **"keep him safe":** Emma to Tourgee, Apr. 25, 1861, document 274.

163 **Nine thousand:** *New York Herald*, May 28, 1861.

164 **"it had been promised me":** Tourgee to Emma, June 26, 1861, document 286. Was Tourgee exaggerating his chances for an officer's job? It's hard to know, but he wasn't the only one frustrated by politics in the selection process. The man who became the Twenty-Seventh's first commander, Colonel Henry W. Slocum, said years later at a regimental reunion that there was so much "wire-pulling" for the leadership posts that he became disgusted. He went home to Syracuse, and had to be persuaded to take over the Twenty-Seventh, according to Charles B. Fairchild's *History of the 27th Regiment N.Y. Vols* (1888), p. 3. Fairchild was a corporal and later a sergeant in Company D.

164 **his blind eye:** Twice in the days before his health inspection, Tourgee expressed concern to Emma that he would be rejected because of his blind eye. Apr. 27, 1861, document 276, and May 8, 1861, document 278.

164 **"go & see & feel":** Tourgee to Emma, June 20, 1861, document 287.

164 **Albion had arranged:** Tourgee to Emma, July 1, 1861, document 291.

164 **"We had a good laugh":** Tourgee to Emma, July 1, 1861, document 291.

165 **refused to take the oath:** Fairchild, *History of the 27th Regiment N.Y. Vols*, p. 6.

165 **"sacrifice of a whole generation":** The text of Anderson's speech appeared the following day in the *Union and Advertiser*, and is reprinted in *Papers and Addresses of Martin B. Anderson*, "The Issues of the Civil War—Address to the Class of 1861," vol. 1, pp. 130–138.

165 **mountain of headlines:** *Union and Advertiser*, July 22, 1861.

166 **sometimes plain wrong:** For Emma's frustration with the newspapers, and the confusion over Colonel Slocum's condition, see her letter to Tourgee, document 299, July 28/29, 1861. Her reactions to the news from Bull Run come from this letter and July 25, 1861, document 297.

166 **the company's second lieutenant:** Lieutenant Edward Gould's account comes from his affidavit, Feb. 11, 1862, part of Tourgee's military records and pension file at the National Archives.

166 **the many ifs:** I have based this series of "ifs" on several documents from July and August that reveal Tourgee's thinking. Among them: a July 23, 1861, letter to Emma, document 295, and a Tourgee dispatch in the *Union and Advertiser*, dated Aug. 5 and published Aug. 10, 1861. His dispatch offered a series of veiled criticisms of the war's conduct. In an editor's note, the newspaper said it had decided not to publish a separate Tourgee account on the Bull Run defeat because it had arrived too long after the battle "to retain its freshness."

167 **"I am safe":** Tourgee to Emma, July 23, 1861, document 295. Tourgee wrote the letter on pages 163–164 of a notebook, and then tore out the pages for mailing to Emma. The notebook, docu-

ment 980, also contains the beginning of an article for the *Union and Advertiser*, perhaps the one deemed too late to merit publication.

167 **alarming rumors from town:** These rumors appeared in Emma's Aug. 4, 1861, letter to Tourgee, document 300, and Angie's subsequent letter to him, Aug. 17, 1861, document 303.

167 **"Don't believe any rumors":** Tourgee to Emma, Aug. 15, 1861, document 301.

167 **He must tell Emma everything:** Angie warned him that they would "swarm" to his bedside if he did not reveal the truth.

167 **Even before Angie's reprimand:** Tourgee's letter, document 304, was dated Aug. 18, and postmarked the same day as Angie's reprimanding letter, Aug. 19, so he could not have seen it.

168 **"wholly unfit for military service":** Quoted from Tourgee's Certificate of Disability for Discharge, Aug. 12, 1861, part of his military and pension records at the National Archives.

168 **miraculously, his legs:** Tourgee to Emma, Sept. 19, 1861, document 315.

168 **"I am completely discouraged":** Tourgee to Emma, Oct. 17, 1861, document 328.

169 **"a sin of no slight magnitude":** Tourgee to Emma, May 14, 1862, document 399.

169 **a month of speeches:** In 1895, Tourgee completed the 105th Infantry's official history, *The Story of a Thousand.* He said, p. 22: "The writer recruited the larger part of Company G, traveling from town to town, holding personal interviews by day and public meetings usually at night. In the month that he was engaged in this service, he held more than forty public meetings."

169 **the "Hell-March":** Chapter VIII in *The Story of a Thousand,* pp. 64–95, is titled, "The Hell-March."

170 **commanding general had shouted:** Recounted in *The Story of a Thousand*, pp. 88–92, also cited in Mark Elliott's *Color-Blind Justice*, p. 87.

170 **"my blood boils!":** Tourgee to Emma, Nov. 23/24, 1862, document 446. For other letters from his convalescence at the Danville farm, see documents 440–445, Oct. 22 to Nov. 17, 1862.

171 **"I am willing to die":** Document 454, Jan. 1863. The day of the month is obscured by cross-writing along the top, but "Sunday" is visible. The document appears to be a completed draft of the letter, with parts written on the diagonal and in the margins. Even if Tourgee never sent this "Brothers of the Upsilon" letter, it still provides an extraordinary glimpse of his evolution from sideline observer to radical thinker.

172 **notoriously foul Libby Prison:** One of the other captives during Tourgee's time at Libby was John Maynard Shanklin, Mallie's brother and John Harlan's brother-in-law. Shanklin was freed in the same prisoner exchange as Tourgee, on May 6, 1863. They probably traveled on the same Union ship to Annapolis.

172 **"Freedom!":** Tourgee to Emma, May 6, 1863, document 467.

172 **"American citizen of African descent":** From Tourgee's Civil War diary, Oct. 24, 1863, document 577.

173 **"serve the country best":** Tourgee's Civil War diary, June 22/23, 1863.

NINE: "CLAIM YOUR RIGHTS"

176 **the hall echoed:** My description of the June 29, 1863, rally draws on the June 30, 1863, account in *L'Union*, written in French. The newspaper added an English edition the following month, but the French and English versions were intended for different readerships and were rarely the same in content. For the articles in French, I relied on the help of French-speaking friends, my own limited skills, and the translations of several *L'Union* articles in James McPherson's 1965 book, *The Negro's Civil War.* Those published translations were done by Roger Des Forges.

176 **The committee's minutes:** *Minutes of the Union Association of Orleans and Jefferson Parishes, May–October 1863,* a single ledger book that is part of the New-York Historical Society's

Thomas J. Durant collection. Durant was chairman of the General Committee, and attorney general under Shepley's military government.

177 **Two Northerners:** In writing this chapter, I benefited from the Shepley collection at the Maine Historical Society and the Banks papers in various archives. I also consulted a privately published biography of Banks, *King of Louisiana,* written by Raymond H. Banks (no known relation). The biography, available online, is an excellent guide to archival documents on the general's Civil War years.

178 **"noble-hearted old patriot":** *New York Times,* Feb. 11, 1863.

178 **had acquired a seat:** On June 26, 1863, Fernandez and four other delegates from his Union Republican Club, Second District, presented their credentials to the Union Association's General Committee. They were immediately accepted, and Fernandez was appointed chairman of a subcommittee. *Minutes of the Union Association of Orleans and Jefferson Parishes, May–October 1863.*

178 **Fernandez, an auctioneer:** Biographical details on Fernandez from newspaper accounts and census records. Caryn Cossé Bell's *Revolution, Romanticism, and the Afro-Creole Protest Tradition in Louisiana, 1718–1868*, describes Fernandez's relationship to *L'Union*, pp. 247–248.

179 **besieging City Hall:** From a Mar. 21 dispatch for the *New York Tribune*, published Apr. 3, 1863, under the pen name "Umbra." The dispatch was written by Union loyalist William Baker, who later became an active member of the Union Association while continuing his correspondence for the *Tribune*.

179 **"vagrancy and crime":** On Jan. 29, 1863, General Banks issued a directive (General Orders, No. 12) that provided the legal underpinning for the arrests and essentially established a system of enforced labor to replace slavery. The order promised "just compensation," but once arranged, the plantation owners could expect "continuous and faithful service, respectful deportment, correct discipline, and perfect subordination." For the full order, see *Official Records of the War of the Rebellion*, ser. 1, vol. 15, pp. 666–667.

180 **His January 29 dispatch:** With no working telegraph lines between New Orleans and Washington, steamboat was the carrier of choice for newspaper dispatches and government messages. Typically, newspaper correspondence from New Orleans was published somewhere between ten and fourteen days after they were written.

180 **"respectably dressed females":** A few weeks later, Hamilton ("Nemo") turned his words into an illustration for *Frank Leslie's Illustrated Newspaper*, which ran in the Mar. 7, 1863 issue. His scene, which appears at the beginning of this chapter, featured several people of color in police custody. The most prominent was a light-skinned woman, respectably dressed.

180 **four hundred and eighty signatures:** The full petition can be found in the Shepley papers, Maine Historical Society, collection 117, box 7.

181 **He hadn't come to Economy Hall:** My account of the Nov. 5 rally at Economy Hall draws on a lengthy report in the *New Orleans Times*, Nov. 6, 1863.

183 **Homere Patris Plessy:** New Orleans Birth Records Index, 1790–1899, vol. 30, p. 17.

184 **"it would not be objectionable":** Lincoln to Banks, Aug. 5, 1863, Lincoln Papers, Library of Congress.

184 **"This disappoints me bitterly":** Lincoln to Banks, Nov. 5, 1863, Lincoln Papers.

185 **The official proceedings:** Published as *Proceedings of the Convention of the Friends of Freedom: Held in Lyceum Hall, New Orleans, Dec. 15 and Dec. 22, 1863.*

185 **Banks blamed:** Banks to Lincoln, Dec. 6, 1863, Lincoln Papers, the Library of Congress.

187 **"faction is treason":** Banks, aware of the autocratic nature of his order, sought to explain his reasons for the shift. Operating under martial law, he wrote, requires "some sacrifice of individual prejudices and interests. . . . In great civil convulsions the agony of strife enters the

souls of the innocent as well as the guilty." *Official Records of the War of the Rebellion*, ser. 3, vol. 4, pp. 21–23.

188 **nearly every newspaper story:** Many historical accounts have given Mar. 12, 1864, as the date for Lincoln's meeting with Bertonneau and Roudanez. I'm not certain why; it clearly took place March 4. Newspaper editions of Mar. 5 reported in detail on the meeting.

188 **three sheets of ordinary lined paper:** Bertonneau and Roudanez both signed the addendum, which is undated. That document, and the petition, can be found at the National Archives, Senate Records, 38th Congress, Committee on Territories, SEN38A-H19. My thanks to archivist Adam Berenbak for his help in locating the documents.

189 **submitted them to the Senate:** *Congressional Globe*, Mar. 15, 1864, Senate Proceedings, p. 1107.

189 **"only a suggestion":** Lincoln to Hahn, Mar. 13, 1864, Lincoln Papers.

189 **"I am anxious":** Lincoln made plain that he wanted the new constitution ratified. He told Banks "to let the civil officers in Louisiana . . . know that this is my wish, and to let me know at once, who of them openly declare for the Constitution, and who of them, if any, decline to so declare." Aug. 9, 1864, Lincoln Papers.

TEN: CHOOSING SIDES

194 **Principle and duty:** My portrayal of John Harlan's mindset in 1865 is based on a variety of sources, including speeches, letters, comments in his autobiographical sketches, and positions he took as attorney general. I have used the term "negroes" here to reflect Harlan's language in these speeches and letters. While I examined many original documents, I also benefited from reading the work of Harlan scholars, particularly Alan F. Westin, Loren Beth, Louis Hartz, Thomas Owen, Linda Przybyszewski, and Peter Scott Campbell, as well as Mallie Harlan's *Some Memories.*

194 **appreciative crowds:** *New Albany Daily Ledger*, Oct. 4, 1864, and *Louisville Daily Journal*, Oct. 6, 1864.

194 **it was Lincoln who had changed:** For Harlan's critique of Lincoln during the 1864 campaign, see the *Louisville Daily Journal*, Sept. 12, 1864 (speech in New Castle, KY) and *New Albany Daily Ledger*, Oct. 4, 1864 (speech in New Albany, IN).

195 **taking his shots:** This account of Harlan's speech in New Castle from the *Louisville Journal*, Sept. 8 and 12, 1864.

196 **sudden death in February 1863:** James Harlan died February 18. That's the date recorded in his estate papers and in newspapers at the time. But the headstone on his grave says Feb. 23, for unknown reasons, and that date appears in several historical accounts, an understandable error.

196 **promotion to brigadier general:** Lincoln included Harlan on a list of nominees sent to the Senate on Jan. 19. *Senate Executive Journal*, Jan. 22, 1863. Harlan asked for his name to be withdrawn when he decided to resign.

196 **his resignation letter:** The *Louisville Daily Journal*, Mar. 11, 1863. The handwritten original can be found in Harlan's microfilmed Compiled Military Service Record, National Archives, M397, roll 238.

196 **"I deeply regret":** Harlan's regret was tempered by an understandable war weariness. He had spent much of the first half of 1862 leading troops decimated by disease and illness. More than one hundred had died, and on a march from Mississippi to Tennessee during that summer, "at least seventy-five were sick or so weak from sickness they could not carry a gun," Harlan wrote in his 1911 letter to son Richard, pp. 21–22.

196 **financial problems:** Harlan was worried about his personal finances even before his father's

death. In late Jan. 1863, he formally requested a leave of absence for "15 or 20 days" to take care of business matters at home: "I have bank obligations of a (to me) large amount, hanging over my head, and involving others, which my honor compels me to arrange." Harlan's Compiled Military Service Record, National Archives.

197 **His father's money:** My account of the estate is based primarily on two sets of documents at the Kentucky state archives: the estate inventory records (from the Franklin County Inventory, Appraisement and Bill Sale Book G) and a civil lawsuit filed in Franklin County Court (*Harlan's administrators v. James Harlan's heirs*).

197 **He had guaranteed loans:** From an Oct. 31, 1877, letter that Harlan wrote to U.S. senator James Beck. The National Archives, Record Group 46, Records of the United States Senate, 45th Congress, Judiciary Committee, 45B-A5, Harlan, John M.: Nomination of as a Justice of the Supreme Court.

197 **an intricate puzzle:** I'm indebted to Yvonne Pitts, a professor of history at Purdue University, for her help in understanding Kentucky inheritance laws at the time of James Harlan's death. She plumbed the subject for her 2013 book, *Family, Law, and Inheritance in America: A Social and Legal History of Nineteenth Century Kentucky.*

198 **"barter and sale of human beings":** *Some Memories,* pp. 66–67.

198 **on sale at public auction:** In *Some Memories,* Mallie does not mention the auction. The information comes from the Harlan estate file.

199 **"a most fortunate purchase":** *Some Memories,* pp. 68–70, in a section Mallie titled "A Tale of Two Cooks."

200 **"I feel confident":** My account of Palmer's tenure in Kentucky is drawn from newspapers and his memoir, *Personal Recollections of John M. Palmer: The Story of an Earnest Life*, published after his death in 1900.

201 **Five thousand crossed:** That was the figure Palmer reported to President Andrew Johnson in a July 27, 1865, letter, published in newspapers at the time.

202 **"Interesting Letter":** The *Lexington Observer & Recorder* published Harlan's letter twice, June 10 and 14, 1865. The newspaper was supporting the Conservative Unionists, and would have agreed with Harlan's position.

203 **"The negroes in Kentucky believed":** Palmer's account, *Personal Recollections*, pp. 240–243.

203 **"every nook and hiding-place":** *Personal Recollections,* p. 254.

204 **jammed with refugees:** As reported by the Paris (KY) *Western Citizen*, reprinted in the *Chicago Tribune*, July 31, 1865.

204 **the first of several indictments:** It appears that Palmer was indicted three times by grand juries in Louisville during the fall of 1865. See "Annals of Kentucky," a year-to-year digest of news events, published in *History of Kentucky* by Lewis and Richard Collins, 1874 edition, vol. 1, pp. 163–165. The original indictment papers are missing; the Kentucky state archives reports a two-year gap in the county's criminal records, covering 1864 and 1865. For specifics, I relied on the Court of Appeals case file at the Kentucky state archives. The case was known as *Commonwealth v. John M. Palmer.*

205 **stand and fight:** In his "Political Memoir," cited earlier, Harlan wrote of himself during this period, "I was an intense Nationalist, as well as an intense believer in State Rights, as they were left or defined by the Constitution."

205 **John's argument was short:** Harlan's brief is part of the Court of Appeals file at the Kentucky state archives. *Commonwealth v. Palmer*, case number 13, summer term 1866.

205 **The court's opinion:** *Commonwealth v. Palmer*, 65 Ky. 570 (1866).

206 **dominated by ex-rebels:** In a July 13, 1866, speech, Harlan said: If the Democrats kept winning elections in the state, "it will not be long before Kentucky will become an uncomfortable

place for anyone except a rebel soldier, a rebel sympathizer, or a Union man who will apologize for his love of the Union and sympathy for the Union army." The *Cincinnati Daily Commercial*, July 20, 1866.

207 **new outbreaks of legal conflict:** See Victor B. Howard, "The Black Testimony Controversy in Kentucky," the *Journal of Negro History* 58 (Apr. 1973): 140–165.

207 **appealed his conviction:** William Bowlin was convicted by a jury of stealing twenty-two dollars in cash and six dollars in postal currency from George Gardner while spending the night at Gardner's house. In Mar. 1867, Bowlin was sentenced to five years in prison.

207 **an unusual one-paragraph "Suggestion":** Harlan's brief note can be found in the Court of Appeals case file for *Bowlin v. Commonwealth*, case 3, summer term 1867.

208 **overturning Bowlin's conviction:** The ruling is *Bowlin v. Commonwealth*, 65 Ky. 5 (1867).

208 **not much of a choice:** Harlan wrote, in his "Political Memoir," of his switch to the Republicans: "I was then of the opinion that the general tendencies and purposes of the Democratic Party were mischievous, while those of the Republicans were the better calculated to preserve the results of the War and to maintain the just rights of the National Government."

208 **the new "Ku-Klux":** Newspapers adopted a variety of spellings for the marauding bands sprouting throughout the South. Kukluk, Ku Klux, and KuKluk were all used frequently, along with Ku-Klux.

208 **kindled a friendship:** Harlan wrote, in 1877, that he and Bristow first met in 1865. Bristow was a state senator and Harlan was attorney general. "We became very intimate, and 'took to each other' at once," Harlan recalled. See Harlan's "one-day diary," Aug. 21, 1877, Library of Congress collection, box 25, microfilm reel 15.

209 **warm friends:** Ross A. Webb's 1969 biography, *Benjamin Helm Bristow: Border State Politician*, has a good account of the Harlan-Bristow relationship.

209 **announced their law partnership:** *Louisville Courier-Journal*, Feb. 15, 1870. The *Courier* and the *Journal* had merged in 1868.

210 **"leave this rebel state":** Ever since the war began, Harlan had proudly pointed out that Kentucky had remained part of the Union. For him to call it a "rebel state" in 1870, even in banter, clearly showed the extent of his unhappiness. His Nov. 16, 1870, letter is part of the Benjamin Bristow collection at the Library of Congress, box 1, folder of correspondence, 1839–1870. A substantial excerpt appears in Alan F. Westin's article, "The First Justice Harlan: A Self-Portrait From His Private Papers," *Kentucky Law Journal* 46 (Spring 1958): 340.

210 **Downplaying his ambition:** Harlan's account evolved and subtly changed over his lifetime. During the campaign, he said frequently: "I did not seek the nomination," but said nothing about being surprised by it. Forty years later, in his "Political Memoir," he added that the nomination had caught him unaware.

211 **"It is quite certain":** *Cincinnati Daily Gazette*, May 15, 1871.

211 **"a call to duty":** Harlan's "Political Memoir."

211 **"calm, thoughtful and argumentative":** *Cincinnati Daily Enquirer*, June 28, 1871.

211 **"a sprinkling of ladies":** *Cincinnati Daily Gazette*, June 3, 1871. Both the *Gazette* and the *Louisville Courier-Journal*, also June 3, published full texts of the Vanceburg debate.

212 **John would retort:** See, for example, the transcript of their debate in Flemingsburg, *Cincinnati Daily Enquirer*, June 28, 1871.

213 **"Social equality can never exist":** *Louisville Daily Commercial*, July 29, 1871, also cited in Louis Hartz's article, "John M. Harlan in Kentucky, 1855–1877," *Filson Club History Quarterly*, January 1940, pp. 34–35.

213 **Republican Party's Radical wing:** The Radical wing was a complicated group that did not speak with one voice. Charles Sumner was often at odds with his Senate colleagues on how best

to achieve their goals. The primary author of the Civil Rights Act of 1866 was Senator Lyman Trumbull of Illinois.

213 **"the most perfect despotism":** From a Harlan speech in Livermore, KY, July 26, 1871, quoted in the *Louisville Daily Commercial*, "General Harlan's Republicanism," Nov. 1, 1877.

213 **might be in his future:** *Louisville Courier-Journal*, Aug. 11, 1871, in a piece headlined "Harlan Looming," mentioned the *Cincinnati Gazette* and the *New York Tribune* suggestions.

ELEVEN: "A TASTE FOR JUDICIAL LIFE"

215 **share their stories:** Brown's personal scrapbook, which includes a copy of the Tenth Reunion program, is part of Yale's Manuscripts and Archives collections. His family donated the scrapbook after his death. Other reunion details from the Class of 1856 records at the Yale University Library.

216 **Edwin Pollard's:** Brown's daybook, Feb. 17, 1866. I have not cited daybook entries if the specific dates already appear in the narrative.

216 **worked hard on it:** Brown's daybook, Feb. 23 to Mar. 6, 1866.

216 **paid the price:** Brown's daybook, Mar. 10, 1866.

217 **"with an axe":** Brown's daybook, Jan. 8, 1866.

217 **he judged himself:** Brown chronicled his up-and-down feelings about the murder trial, daybook, May 3–10, 1866.

217 **"not enough of a lawyer":** Brown often chastised himself for losing cases. A few years later, on Feb. 1, 1868, he wrote: "I desire to put in my diary this humiliating confession that the case tried yesterday was lost mainly thro[ugh] my mismanagement."

217 **recording his barbs:** Brown's comment about Watch Hill from his daybook, Aug. 5, 1866. The other barbs from entries on Feb. 13, 1866; July 4, 1865; and July 4, 1866.

217 **"Beautiful quadroons":** Brown's daybook, Aug. 14, 1866.

217 **more than a million people:** Summary of Michigan's population, including racial breakdown, from the 1860 and 1870 censuses.

218 **his commercial empire:** My Crapo synopsis is based in part on a 1933 biography, *The Story of Henry Howland Crapo, 1804–1869*, written by his grandson, and in part on the Crapo papers at the University of Michigan's Bentley Historical Library.

219 **"Malignant Official Insult":** *Free Press*, Apr. 6, 1866.

220 **"let them howl":** Crapo's letter to his son, William, Apr. 6, 1866, Crapo papers. Also quoted in *The Story of Henry Howland Crapo*, pp. 233–234.

220 **visible prejudice in the North:** Northern hypocrisy was an argument that the *Detroit Advertiser and Tribune* often used during the early years of Reconstruction. In 1867, after Ohio voters refused to eliminate the whites-only voting clause in the state's constitution, the newspaper editorialized: "Every Republican vote against equal suffrage at the North is a blow against Congressional Reconstruction at the South." *Tribune*, Oct. 11, 1867.

220 **"so strong is the popular current":** *Tribune* (Detroit), June 3, 1867.

221 **marked the date:** Brown made a special effort to hear Sumner, writing in his daybook, Oct. 10, 1867: "Concluded not to go to Marshall this morning and was glad I did not, in consideration of the eloquent lecture from Chas. Sumner." An advertisement in the *Free Press*, Oct. 7, 1867, included the lecture title and admission fee.

221 **spend a few minutes:** Brown's daybook, Oct. 6, 1867: "Charles Sumner called on Sam [Pitts] after tea. I seized the opportunity to see him."

221 **"masterly piece of strategy":** Brown's daybook, Feb. 8, 1866.

222 **keep it in his pocket:** Brown's daybook, May 25, 1868.

222 **"charmed" the audience:** Coverage of Sumner's lecture in the *Free Press* and *Tribune*, both Oct. 11, 1867.

223 **"the plea of inferiority":** *Tribune*, "Fred. Douglass's Lecture," Feb. 3, 1868.

223 **Female suffrage lost:** *Free Press*, Aug. 14, 1867.

223 **swarming into Michigan:** *Free Press*, Feb. 17, 1868.

224 **The rhetorical battle escalated:** The quotations are from the *Free Press*, Mar. 30, 1868 ("Nineteen Reasons . . .") and the *Tribune*, Apr. 6, 1868 ("The great bugbear . . .").

224 **failed miserably:** The revision lost by more than 38,000 votes, out of 182,315. From *Michigan Manual 2013–2014*, "Constitutions," p. 28.

224 **the Republican soul:** *Tribune*, Apr. 8, 1868.

225 **"White Man's Government":** Headlines in the *Free Press*, Apr. 7, 1868, reproduced in the image at the beginning of this chapter.

225 **receive her share:** Sam Pitts estate, Wayne County Probate Court records, packet #5665, Archives of Michigan.

226 **"Carry unable to sit up":** Brown's daybook, May 7, 1868. Brown never wrote anything specific about Carry's illness. Charles Kent, Brown's lifelong friend, probably knew something of Carry's condition, but in his "Addenda" for the *Memoir of Henry Billings Brown*, p. 53, he wrote only: "She suffered much from ill health."

226 **loved to entertain:** Based on a ten-page reminiscence that Carry Brown's sister, Isabelle (Pitts) Goodwin, wrote in 1915. "From the first," Isabelle wrote, "their home was a social centre. . . . Henry and Caroline's delight was to entertain, and make welcome, all their friends, particularly people in whom they were interested, who were, perhaps, passing through the city." "Notes by Mrs. Goodwin," Brown papers.

226 **"not to become paterfamilias":** Brown's daybook, Apr. 22, 1865. He did not say anything more illuminating in this entry, or elsewhere.

226 **"got tickets":** Brown's daybook, May 21, 1868.

227 **"completely taken aback":** Brown's daybook, May 28, 1868.

227 **entire matter would end:** Brown's daybook, June 1, 1868.

227 **News of his appointment:** While it seems unlikely that Brown learned of his selection from the *Tribune*, that's what his daybook entry for June 25, 1868, says. "Saw a notice of my appt. as Circuit Judge this morning," he wrote.

228 **"I am painfully conscious":** Brown's remarks from the *Tribune*, "Judge Brown Takes His Seat," July 2, 1868, and *Free Press*, "The Courts," July 3, 1868.

228 **"How I sweat!":** Brown's daybook, July 2, 1868.

229 **plenty else coming at him:** Statistical breakdown of Brown's fall docket from the *Free Press*, Sept. 8, 1868.

229 **missed his own renomination:** The *Free Press*, Sept. 15, 1868.

229 **"Beaten without a doubt":** Brown's daybook, Nov. 3, 1868.

229 **"Glorious Results":** *Free Press*, Nov. 5, 1868.

230 **"taste for judicial life":** Brown's "Memoranda," *Memoir*, p. 20.

230 **one prominent member:** Brown's daybook, Apr. 3, 1869.

230 **Federal judges in Michigan:** Until 1891, when salaries became uniform, there were quirks in the federal system that allowed each state to set different pay scales. Michigan federal judges were paid $3,500 a year in 1870, the standard sum, while neighboring Ohio paid $4,000 in the Southern District and $3,500 in the Northern District.

231 **a formidable figure:** Details of Russell's career from a variety of sources—newspaper accounts, *Cyclopedia of Michigan* (1890), *Bench and Bar of Michigan* (1897), and a 1904 commemorative

book, *Under the Oaks*, issued in conjunction with the Fiftieth Anniversary celebration of the Republican Party's first-ever state convention, held in Jackson, Michigan, July 1854.

231 **"Russell is a scamp":** Brown's daybook, Nov. 13, 1867.

231 **resent Russell's extended travels:** Brown's daybook, Dec. 8, 1865, and Mar. 7, 1866.

231 **"Nothing to distinguish":** Brown's daybook, Apr. 3, 1869.

232 **he felt strapped:** Brown's daybook, July 24, July 28, and Aug. 11, 1869.

232 **"Lots of bills":** Brown's daybook, Jan. 28, 1870.

232 **"busy, busy, busy":** Brown's daybook, Jan. 8, 1872.

233 **"Terrific headache":** Brown's daybook, Feb. 2, 1872.

233 **"short unsatisfactory speech":** Brown's daybook, July 10, 1872.

233 **wondering if he should withdraw:** Brown's daybook, July 18, 1872.

234 **Stay with Grant:** The *Tribune* published most of Brown's oration, July 26, 1872. As far as I could find, the *Free Press* did not cover the event.

235 **"care not a fig":** Brown's daybook, Aug. 6, 1872.

235 **he withdrew:** For the convention balloting, see the *Free Press* and *Tribune*, both Aug. 8, 1872.

235 **"but not a sadder man":** Brown's daybook, Aug. 7, 1872.

TWELVE: TOURGEE GOES SOUTH

237 **"Dear Wifey":** Tourgee to Emma, July 25, 1865, document 617. For this chapter, I again relied on original documents whenever possible, but I reaped the benefit of Elliott's *Color-Blind Justice* and Olsen's *Carpetbagger's Crusade*. Both provide richly detailed explorations of the Tourgees' years in North Carolina, including aspects of their lives outside the scope of my narrative.

238 **Holden himself had replied:** Holden to Tourgee, June 16, 1865, document 614. If Tourgee's letter to Holden survives, it is well hidden. A thorough hunt through Holden's collected papers at three archives in North Carolina turned up no evidence of it.

238 **yet he had found time:** Holden's activities for June 16, 1865, included "Letter of A.W. Tourgee, Erie, Pa., answered." North Carolina State Archives, Governor's Papers 186, correspondence, folder June 16–18, 1865.

238 **Abandoned farms:** After the war, a fierce debate raged within the U.S. government about whether to continue to confiscate land belonging to rebel leaders. While wholesale confiscation did not occur, the Freedmen's Bureau moved to take control of abandoned property owned by rebels who had fled to other parts of the Confederacy. National Archives, Freedmen's Bureau, North Carolina, Assistant Commissioner's Records, 1862–1870, letters sent, July 1865, microfilm M843, roll 1.

238 **"acts of unlawful violence":** Brevet Major General Thomas H. Ruger to Governor William Holden, Aug. 1, 1865, *The Papers of W. W. Holden*, pp. 222–224. In June 1866, the Freedmen's Bureau began preparing a "Semi-Monthly Report of Outrages by Whites Against Blacks in the State of North Carolina." For these reports, see Freedmen's Bureau, North Carolina, Assistant Commissioner's Records, 1862–1870, microfilm M843, roll 33.

239 **pledging their allegiance:** New appointees had to be willing to take the Union's "iron-clad test oath" for office holders, swearing they had never "voluntarily" aided the rebellion.

239 **stark message:** "Proclamation by William W. Holden, provisional governor, to the people of North Carolina," June 12, 1865.

240 **Unionists like Holden:** For a deeper exploration of Holden's life, see Horace W. Raper's 1985 biography, *William W. Holden: North Carolina's Political Enigma*. I also consulted Holden's autobiography, *Memoirs of W. W. Holden*, published in 1911.

240 **better for his precarious health:** Tourgee wrote years later that his "first object" in going to North Carolina was to restore his health. *Appeal to Caesar*, pp. 59–61. But in April 1866, while drafting an article about his reasons for the move, he did not mention his health as a factor.

240 **borrowed revolver:** In his first letter to Emma after leaving Erie, he asked her to thank a friend "for the loan of his revolver." July 20, 1865, document 414.

240 **"my Southern scheme":** Tourgee to Emma, July 20, 1865, document 414.

241 **a pair of North Carolinians:** The pair was Kemp Battle and J. M. Heck. Battle would later serve as North Carolina's state treasurer from 1866 to 1868, during Governor Jonathan Worth's administration.

241 **"nothing shall discourage me":** Tourgee to Emma, July 22, 1865, document 616.

241 **The streets hummed:** My depiction of New Berne from newspaper accounts, including the *New Berne Times*, "Increasing Commerce," July 31, 1865. I have chosen to call it New Berne, because that spelling seemed the most common at the time, but it was also known as Newbern and New Bern, as it is spelled today.

242 **swarming with supplicants:** Description of Raleigh during June–July 1865 based on newspaper accounts and Holden's letters.

242 **Three thousand five hundred appointments:** Holden to President Andrew Johnson, July 24, 1865, in *The Papers of W. W. Holden*, pp. 220–221.

242 **was turned away:** *Memoirs of W. W. Holden*, p. 58.

242 **"I see men hourly":** Tourgee to Emma, July 27, 1865, document 618.

242 **"two very satisfactory interviews":** After reviewing the available evidence, I came away strongly doubting Tourgee's claim of two interviews with Holden. This appears to be an example of Tourgee's fondness for embellishment, possibly because he did not want to admit to Emma that he hadn't seen the governor.

243 **Captain was not his rank:** In subsequent years, "Captain Tourgee" frequently cropped up in print, and Tourgee even referred to himself as "Captain Tourgee" on occasion.

243 **a tough fight:** Details on the Clingman court-martial from the case file at the National Archives in Washington, Record Group 153, Records of the Office of the Judge Advocate General, Court Martial Files, 1809–1894, box 1201, case MM2619.

244 **left a scar:** Tourgee took extensive notes during his court-martial in 1863, recorded in a notebook, document 980, pp. 49–62.

245 **a ten-point proposal:** Eliphalet Whittlesey, assistant commissioner for North Carolina, sent Tourgee's plan to Oliver O. Howard, head of the Freedmen's Bureau, July 21, 1865. Record Group 105, Records of the Commissioner, 1865–1872, letters received, T–Y, Mar.–Oct. 1865.

245 **"From personal interviews with him":** Whittlesey letter to Washington, July 31, 1865, Record Group 105, Records of the Assistant Commissioner for North Carolina, 1862–1870, endorsements sent, July 11, 1865–Sept. 20, 1866.

246 **their weekly ads:** The first appeared on Feb. 2, 1866, in the *Greensboro Patriot*, under the heading "West Green Nurseries, Tourgee & Kuhn."

247 **"as slaves again":** Whittlesey to Howard, Aug. 21, 1865, quoted in Olsen, *Carpetbagger's Crusade*, p. 32.

247 **an act "concerning negroes":** The *Charlotte Democrat* published the new law in its entirety on Mar. 20, 1866, headlined "The Freedmen's Code."

248 **Servitude:** Fears of reenslavement were a much-discussed concern at the Freedmen's Bureau. Tourgee and others called attention to it in their speeches. For a deep exploration, see Douglas Blackmon's *Slavery by Another Name*, his exhaustively researched 2008 book on forced labor in the South, covering many decades after the war.

248 **drafting an essay:** The draft can be found in document 980, a notebook, pp. 80–84 and 100–102.

249 **"misrule of traitors":** This phrase appeared at the end of thirteen resolutions adopted at a Unionist gathering near Greensboro on Aug. 16, 1866, quoted in the Raleigh *Daily Standard*, Sept. 4, 1866.

249 **"true Southern men":** *Greensboro Patriot,* "A Radical Meeting in Guilford," Aug. 24, 1866.

249 **lengthy and indignant response:** Tourgee's letter, dated Aug. 24, 1866, ran in the *Greensboro Patriot* on Sept. 14. The *Patriot* was a weekly, so his letter had missed two editions.

250 **"What right has he":** *Greensboro Patriot,* editorial on the "Mulatto Convention," Sept. 14, 1866.

250 **"I have written this lying down":** Emma to Tourgee, Sept. 3, 1866, document 646.

250 **Emma's health on his mind:** Tourgee's letters to Emma from Philadelphia, Aug. 31–Sept. 5, 1866, documents 644, 647, and 648.

250 **tens of thousands:** Tourgee estimated the crowd at the astounding figure of "100,000" in his Sept. 5 letter to Emma, document 648.

251 **a marked man:** The *New York Herald* carried a lengthy report on Tourgee's Philadelphia speech. Tourgee kept a clipping of the *Herald's* account, pasted into a scrapbook, with the annotation "The Phila. Speech—so notorious—the Herald report." Document 2428.

252 **"this vile wretch Tourgee":** Governor Worth's campaign against Tourgee was a sustained one. See Worth to Nereus Mendenhall, Sept. 10, 1866; Worth to the *Greensboro Patriot*, Sept. 10, 1866; Worth to John A. Gilmer, Sept. 11, 1866; Worth to A. M. Tomlinson, Sept. 13, 1866. All in *The Correspondence of Jonathan Worth*, vol. II, published by the North Carolina Historical Commission, pp. 780–782.

252 **"the vital air":** Document 657, anonymous letter to Tourgee, Sept. 24, 1866. The other threatening letter is document 659. A third unsigned letter, document 669, came in mid-October.

252 **their emissary wrote:** The young man was James Sampson. For Sampson's letters, see documents 661, 663, 664, and 670, all written between Oct. 1 and Oct. 21, 1866.

254 **"cold, hungry and alone":** Emma to Tourgee, Dec. 18, 1875, document 1877. She was pregnant in 1867. The pregnancy apparently ended with a miscarriage, according to Elliott, *Color-Blind Justice*, p. 139.

254 **"our battle cry":** A copy of Tourgee's handbill is at the end of a scrapbook, document 2428.

254 **forty-three votes:** *Greensboro Patriot,* Nov. 29, 1867.

254 **"a long one":** Tourgee to Emma, Jan. 17, 1868, document 761.

255 **a prime seat:** Tourgee to Emma, also Jan. 17, 1868.

255 **"Gorilla Convention":** As the convention opened, the *Wilmington Morning Star* explained its standing headline: "The real Gorilla being a native of *Africa,* and Barnum's Gorilla being a *white man wearing a monkey skin,* we think we have discovered the name that expresses the true character of the great Unconstitutional Convention." *Morning Star,* Jan. 11, 1868.

255 **Albion rose to reply:** Draft of Tourgee's speech, document 801, "Speech on Elective Franchise, delivered in Convention of 1868." The full text can be found in *Undaunted Radical*, a selection of Tourgee's speeches and writing, edited by Mark Elliott and John David Smith.

256 **unpunished perpetrator:** Tourgee, in his speech, referred to the Confederate commanding officer as the "fiend who walks today unhung, and clamors for a white man's government." The officer was Lieutenant General Nathan Bedford Forrest. After the war, Forrest played a prominent role in the founding of the Ku-Klux.

256 **"mingled blood":** Tourgee used the word "mingled" three times in his speech, document 801.

256 **"The Tourgee brayed":** *North Carolinian,* Feb. 22, 1868.

256 **a clarifying message:** "Address to the People of North Carolina," *Journal of the Constitutional Convention of the State of North Carolina*, 1868, p. 485.

257 **petitions of support:** Tourgee to Emma, Feb. 19, 1868, document 774, and Mar. 4, 1868, document 781.

257 **"every possible vilification":** Tourgee to A. G. Wilcox, Apr. 2, 1868, document 1239, a notebook with drafts and copies of letters, pp. 62–63. Wilcox, an Army friend in Fremont, OH, was considering a move to the South.

258 **"a carpet bagger!":** The quotation comes from an unidentified, undated newspaper clipping in the Tourgee scrapbook, document 2428. Based on clues in the clipping, it appears to have been published by the *Dansville Advertiser*, a weekly in Livingston County, NY. Tourgee spoke at a Dansville rally for President Grant's reelection campaign in the summer of 1872.

THIRTEEN: EQUAL BUT SEPARATE

261 **"Gay parties":** From the *Picayune*, "The City," Apr. 29, 1867, a daily column featuring observations about the people and places of New Orleans. This chapter is based largely on original sources, primarily newspaper accounts, legal rulings, and public records. But I also benefited from Roger A. Fischer's 1974 study, *The Segregation Struggle in Louisiana, 1862–77*; John Blassingame's 1973 work, *Black New Orleans, 1860–1880*; and Ted Tunnell's 1984 book, *Crucible of Reconstruction: War, Radicalism, and Race in Louisiana, 1862–1877.* For context on travel in the South after the Civil War, Blair L. M. Kelley's *The Right to Ride* (2010), was helpful for this chapter and others.

261 **the iron track:** In advertising for construction bids, the New Orleans city government offered a wealth of detail on the street railway system's operation in 1865. Those advertisements were published in the *Picayune*, *Philadelphia Inquirer*, and *New York Herald*, among others.

261 **as good a right:** My account of the William Nichols case is drawn from testimony as reported in the newspapers, primarily the New Orleans *Republican*, "The Star Car Question," May 1, 1867; the New Orleans *Times*, "The Street Cars and the Reserved Rights," May 1, 1867; and the *New Orleans Tribune*, Apr. 30 and May 1, 1867.

261 **too few of them:** One rider of color, in a letter to the *Tribune*, claimed he often had to wait about forty-five minutes for a star car because there were so few, about one in seven. When a star car did come, he complained, "it may be full of whites, for star cars are generally filled with whites." R. I. Cromwell to the *Tribune*, June 25, 1865.

261 **more white riders than colored:** In 1865, the railway said one-third of its fleet was devoted to star cars, but passengers of color made up only 6 percent of its ridership. By 1867, the railway had adjusted the ratio, converting several star cars to whites-only. The New Orleans *Times*, in a May 25 editorial, called this "an economic necessity," saying it was unprofitable to run near-empty star cars. But even half-full cars in an overcrowded system made sense only because separation was a given.

262 **"a brand put upon us":** *New Orleans Tribune*, Feb. 28, 1865.

262 **his last speech:** On Apr. 11, 1865, Lincoln appeared at an upstairs window to give his first substantial speech since the surrender at Appomattox two days earlier. Congress had just rejected Louisiana's bid for readmission to the Union, prompting his comments.

263 **"These two populations":** *New Orleans Tribune*, Dec. 29, 1864.

264 **"ambitious mulattoes":** *Picayune*, May 5, 1867, from an editorial headlined "Black Against White." Not only were they "ambitious mulattoes," the newspaper claimed, but in times of slavery, they were "the most exacting and frequently most cruel masters."

264 **a case "of vast importance":** *Tribune*, Apr. 30, 1867.

264 **Sheridan had replaced:** The general also used his power to oust the governor, attorney general, and a judge.

265 **"claim the right":** New Orleans *Republican*, May 1, 1867.

265 **stinging dust clouds:** *Picayune*, May 5, 1867.

265 **"dusky son of Africa":** New Orleans *Times*, May 5, 1867. My account of Guillaume's arrest and court hearing is drawn from the *Times* and the *Tribune*, also May 5.

266 **Nichols's affidavit:** After that week of protests, Nichols dropped his complaint. According to Fischer, *The Segregation Struggle*, p. 33, Nichols explained that his "sole objective" was to test the company policy.

266 **a long evening of protest:** In piecing together my narrative of the May 4–5 uprising, I found that some secondary sources tended to be more vivid in their reconstructions than the newspaper accounts on which they were based.

266 **the wife of a Hungarian dignitary:** Theresa Pulzsky's journal of her visit to the American South was published in 1853 as part of a two-volume book, coauthored with her husband. The portions on New Orleans appear in volume II of *White, Red, Black: Sketches of Society in the United States*, pp. 93–108.

267 **The death toll:** Casualty figures from *Report of the Select Committee on the New Orleans Riots*, Thirty-Ninth Congress, Second Session, Report No. 16, p. 12.

267 **"a concert of action":** New Orleans *Times*, "The Negroes and the City Railroads," May 7, 1867.

268 **one hundred and fifty cars:** Details on the railway system's operations from a report on its fifth anniversary, New Orleans *Times*, Oct. 7, 1865.

269 **"I entertain no doubt":** Ogden's letter to Mayor Heath, in the *Tribune*, May 16, 1867.

269 **centerpiece of subsequent commentaries:** See the *Picayune*, Aug. 18, Oct. 27, and Oct. 29, 1867. The Oct. 27 commentary, looking back at the five months since the end of the star cars, said: "We thought then, and think now, that the better course would have been to forbid any whites getting into the star cars, and any colored people, under any pretence, into the white cars."

270 **Catto and his allies:** For more on Octavius Catto, see Harry C. Silcox's "Nineteenth Century Philadelphia Black Militant: Octavius Catto," in *Pennsylvania History* 44 (Jan. 1977): 53–76. Also, *Tasting Freedom: Octavius Catto and the Battle for Equality in Civil War America*, by Daniel R. Biddle and Murray Dubin (2010).

270 **left stranded:** Mary Miles's ejection received no newspaper coverage when it happened, or at least none that I could find. My narrative of her case is based on her lawyers' statement of facts in their brief to the Pennsylvania Supreme Court, and the appeals court's eventual ruling.

270 **1861 precedent:** The case was *Goines v. McCandless*, in Philadelphia Reports, 1861, vol. 4, pp. 255–258.

270 **"public mark of degradation":** The Earle and White brief was printed in pamphlet form, and can be found online and in libraries under the title *In the Supreme Court, for the Eastern District of Pennsylvania: The Philadelphia and Westchester Railroad Company, Plaintiffs in Error, vs. Mary E. Miles, Defendant in Error.*

270 **sweeping new law:** *Annual Digest of the Laws of Pennsylvania*, 1867, "Railroads," pp. 1476–1477.

271 **announced a public effort:** From "Report of the committee appointed for the purpose of securing to colored people in Philadelphia the right to the use of the street-cars," May 1867.

271 **"passenger railway insanity":** The quote appeared in Frederic W. Speirs's 1897 monograph, *The Street Railway System of Philadelphia, Its History and Present Condition*, pp. 23–27. Other facts from "The Street Railways of Philadelphia," *The Quarterly Journal of Economics* 22 (Feb. 1908): 233–260.

271 **a sliver of the white population:** Between the 1860 census and 1870 census, the city's population zoomed from 565,529 to 674,022. The black portion remained about the same at just under 23,000.

272 **For or Against:** The railways published a sample ballot as part of an advertisement in the Philadelphia *Daily Age*, Jan. 28, 1865.

272 **"with great violence":** *Derry v. Lowry*, Philadelphia Reports, 1865, vol. 6, pp. 30–31.

273 **extraordinary in its fervor:** The ruling is *West Chester and Philadelphia Railway Co. v. Miles*, 55 Pennsylvania 209 (1867).

274 **"all who read it":** *Ohio Statesman*, Nov. 16, 1867.

274 **"We are satisfied":** *Harrisburg Telegraph*, Nov. 11, 1867.

275 **all but two delegates calling themselves Republican:** The *Picayune*, Oct. 19, 1867, wrote that all but two were "Radicals." That was far from accurate, reflecting the newspaper's antipathy toward the Sheridan-directed process.

275 **the same insult:** For example, see the *Louisiana Democrat,* published in Alexandria, Dec. 4, 1867.

275 **glaringly apparent:** For my narrative of the convention's work, I relied on newspaper accounts and the official record, *Journal of the Proceedings of the Convention, for Framing a Constitution for the State of Louisiana.* The *Journal* is an excellent record of the process—amendments, motions, roll call votes—but a poor source for the debates. The newspapers provided fuller accounts of the more dramatic moments.

275 **eager to engage:** Philip Dray's 2008 book, *Capitol Men*, has a fine chapter on Pinchback's early life, titled "Pinch." Pinchback's wild career included a one-month stint as Louisiana's governor, beginning in Dec. 1872.

275 **not a "colored convention":** Quoted in the *Picayune*, Dec. 6, 1867.

276 **the delegates dueled:** *Journal of the Proceedings*, Dec. 31, 1867, Jan. 2–3, 1868, pp. 121–125.

276 **"a war of races":** Ludeling quoted in the *Picayune* and the *Crescent*, both Jan. 3, 1868.

276 **Mandating "social equality":** *Journal of the Proceedings*, p. 121.

277 **I don't want to force:** Bertonneau, quoted in the *Picayune*, Jan. 3, 1868.

278 **"If left to time":** From a draft of a Pinchback speech, Jan. 4, 1868, in his papers at Howard University's Moorland-Spingarn Research Center, quoted in Dray's *Capitol Men*, p. 109.

278 **use the protections:** *Tribune*, Feb. 4, 1869.

278 **a thousand-dollar damage award:** Sauvinet's lawsuit covered in the *Picayune*, Jan. 28 and Apr. 28, 1871.

278 **colored-only viewing stand:** The race track's newest addition wasn't mentioned in the *Picayune's* lengthy report on the meet's opening day, Apr. 4, 1871. But it brought fury from the editors of the *New Orleans Weekly Louisianian*, founded by Pinchback after the *Tribune* closed. "The demoniac spirit of caste, had been aroused again," the *Louisianian* wrote on Apr. 9, 1871. "The managers of the course have pandered to the ignoble passions and prejudices of those who possess no other claim to superiority than the external shading of a skin."

FOURTEEN: "IS NOT HARLAN THE MAN?"

281 **wasn't being coy:** During May 1875, Harlan wrote to several friends, saying that he could not possibly campaign for governor until after the courts had adjourned in late June. See his letter book, May 1875 to Oct. 1876, University of Louisville collection, microfilm reel 6.

281 **"it would have been ungracious":** From Harlan's "Political Memoir." Four days after the convention, Bristow wrote to him that "it must be quite a sacrifice for you to accept the nomination,

and yet I do not see how it was possible for you to avoid it under the circumstances." Bristow to Harlan, May 17, 1875, Library of Congress collection, box 3, microfilm reel 3.

281 **"the brains of his entire party":** *Hartford Herald*, June 23, 1875. The *Herald's* comment came in an editorial criticizing Harlan for his "blunders" in talking about the state's financial condition, and wondering why a "seasoned politician like Harlan" hadn't prepared better.

282 **"sense of duty":** From J. H. Wilson's letter to Harlan, May 15, 1875, Library of Congress collection, box 3, microfilm reel 3. Reflecting that sense of duty, Harlan wrote to Bristow that day: "I was so completely cornered that I could not escape—for it was demonstrated that my acceptance was necessary to prevent the Convention from being a failure . . . it did not suit me to get into politics now. But I am in it and will do the best I can." Harlan to Bristow, Bristow papers, box 5, correspondence folder, Apr.–Aug. 1875.

282 **dozens of appeals:** The quoted examples come from Harlan's Letter Book, May 1875 to Oct. 1876, University of Louisville collection.

282 **improve on those numbers:** In a July 21, 1875, letter to a supporter, Harlan said, "I am confident that I will poll at least 105,000 votes and by hard work between this and the election it can be raised to 110, or 112,000, which will either elect me or make it very close." University of Louisville collection, box 2, folder 7, microfilm reel 8.

283 **know "the facts":** Harlan's retelling of the Douglass story from his "Political Memoir." Alan Westin accepted Harlan's version without caveat in "John Marshall Harlan and the Constitutional Rights of Negroes: The Transformation of a Southerner," *Yale Law Journal*, Apr. 1957, p. 665.

283 **this vital mission in the North:** Blaine's touring troupe of speakers appeared at rallies throughout Maine in the late summer of 1872, well chronicled in New York and New England newspapers.

284 **In John's memory:** I could not find a contemporaneous account in a Kentucky newspaper of Harlan's "ugly question" moment during the 1875 campaign.

285 **"balance between State and Federal power":** The quote appears near the end of the majority opinion in the *Slaughter-House* cases, 83 U.S. 36. This 1873 ruling was the court's first major interpretation of the Fourteenth Amendment, and it was a complicated one, decided by a five-to-four vote, unusual in that era.

286 **"rampant rule of ignorance":** *Hartford Herald*, June 9, 1875.

286 **"root out the evil":** Harlan to Bristow, Sept. 16, 1871, Bristow papers, box 1, correspondence folder, Jan.–Sept. 1871.

286 **hired him to assist:** Telegram from U.S. attorney general George H. Williams, Feb. 11, 1873, University of Louisville collection, box 2, folder 7, microfilm reel 8.

287 **"An Important Decision":** *Detroit Free Press*, Mar. 23, 1875.

287 **3,000-word explanation:** Instructions to a grand jury were rarely considered noteworthy enough for publication, but this one can be found at 30 Federal Cases 1005. Several law journals also printed the full text. The *Central Law Journal*, in St. Louis, wrote in its Apr. 2, 1875 issue: "We are not in the habit of publishing charges to grand juries . . . but our readers will, no doubt, justify us in making an exception this week in case of the charge of Mr. Circuit Judge Emmons to a grand jury in Memphis."

287 **Enforcement Act of 1870:** The act was one of several enacted by Congress in response to Ku-Klux violence.

288 **"I concur":** From Harlan's July 2, 1875, speech in Elizabethtown, KY, published in full by the *Louisville Courier-Journal*, July 5, along with his opponent's address.

289 **"absurd" interpretation:** From Harlan's Elizabethtown speech.

290 **"goodly mixture of the colored element":** *Courier-Journal*, May 19, 1876.

290 **not to seek it:** For example, see Bristow to E. A. Starling, Jan. 27, 1876, Bristow papers. Cited in Ross Webb's *Benjamin Helm Bristow*, p. 217.

291 **Ninety seats!:** The 1874 elections for the House represented the party's worst defeat in its short history. The Republicans would probably have lost its Senate majority, too, if the Senate seats had all been contested at once.

291 **"My candid conviction":** Harlan to John H. Reno, Dec. 17, 1875, Harlan Letter Book, May 1875–Oct. 1876, cited earlier.

291 **path to second choice:** Talk of a "second choice" was a common topic in the weeks leading up to the national convention. The *Cincinnati Daily Star*, for example, wrote on May 19 that the New Jersey delegation was supporting Blaine, with Ohio governor Rutherford B. Hayes as its "second choice." The *Star* claimed this development was a boost for Hayes because "the second choice usually gets the nomination."

291 **eleven-point plan:** The *Courier-Journal*, May 19, 1876.

292 **"hand-shaking and hat-throwing":** *Cincinnati Enquirer*, May 19, 1876.

292 **Impromptu speeches:** *Chicago Tribune*, June 15, 1876.

292 **the prevailing wisdom:** The newspapers of the time, fueled by their Democratic or Republican sympathies, offered a wealth of information and speculation. I relied on the Louisville, Cincinnati, New York, Chicago, Pittsburgh, Boston, and Washington papers to sketch the scene at the convention.

293 **"wrath of our infuriated masters":** For the text of Douglass's speech, see *Proceedings of the Republican National Convention Held at Cincinnati, Ohio,* June 14–16, 1876, pp. 26–27.

293 **powerful quotes:** Harlan's nominating speech, *Proceedings of the Republican National Convention*, pp. 68–70.

294 **"our case was hopeless":** Harlan to Bristow, June 19, 1876, Bristow papers.

294 **"The effect was electrical":** *New York Times*, June 17, 1876.

295 **"those gallant men":** *Proceedings of the Republican National Convention*, p. 107.

295 **found the moment so memorable:** The reporter's description of Harlan was tinged with the euphoria of the moment, calling him "that splendid specimen of American manhood, that true, lion-hearted Republican, John M. Harlan." See the *New York Times*, June 17, 1876, "Closing Day of the Convention."

295 **withdraw Bristow's name:** Three days after the convention, Harlan wrote a long letter to his dejected friend. Characteristically, he wanted to explain what he had done. Once it became clear that Bristow could not win, Harlan said, "My determination was to seize the first opportunity to retire in a becoming manner, and so throw our votes . . . to secure a good nominee." Bristow said he understood. He praised Harlan's decision to support Hayes as "exactly in the right time, and done in the right way." Harlan to Bristow, June 19, 1876; Bristow's reply, June 20, 1876, both in the Bristow papers, box 7.

295 **jotting the names:** From the *Diary and Letters of Rutherford Birchard Hayes,* Jan. 17, 1877, vol. 3, p. 402. This five-volume compilation is a robust selection of Hayes's papers.

295 **nothing for Blaine or Bristow:** Hayes's aversion to appointing either of his two rivals was political, it appears, not personal. Writing in his diary before the convention, with no other eyes to please, Hayes expressed his respect for Bristow. "His war on the whiskey thieves gives him prestige as the representative of reform. I am not sure but he would be the best candidate we could nominate. I am sure I prefer him to any man. It will be a small disappointment for me to give up my chances." *Diary and Letters*, Mar. 21, 1876, vol. 3, p. 309.

296 **dueling accusations:** The 1876 election has attracted the attention of many historians. Roy Morris Jr.'s 2003 book, *Fraud of the Century*, offers a lively and in-depth account.

296 **"abide the result":** Hayes to Carl A. Schurz, Jan. 19, 1877, *Diary and Letters*, vol. 3, p. 403.

296 **"We want a united country":** For Hayes's thoughts on his inaugural address, see his Feb. 25, 1877, entry, *Diary and Letters*, vol. 3, pp. 420–421.

297 **"could appoint a Southern Democrat":** Hayes diary, Feb. 17, 1877, *Diary and Letters*, vol. 3, pp. 416–417.

297 **"not the duty of the President":** Hayes diary, Mar. 23, 1877, *Diary and Letters*, vol. 3, p. 429.

298 **Mallie made plans:** *Some Memories*, p. 83.

298 **"an utter confusion":** Harlan to Bristow, Apr. 13, 1877, Bristow papers, box 7, correspondence folder, 1877.

298 **several possible nominees:** The *Chicago Inter Ocean* summarized Hayes's rumored choices in a Washington dispatch, "Speculations as to Judge Davis' Successor," Sept. 25, 1877. In reading the Bristow and Hayes papers, I came to believe that Hayes never developed a solid interest in appointing Bristow to the court. Miscommunication seemed rife in their relationship. Hayes couldn't seem to fathom what Bristow wanted, in part because Bristow didn't seem to know himself.

298 **if Bristow wasn't in the running:** As with the Republican presidential nomination, Bristow wasn't willing to make his intentions entirely clear, frustrating supporters such as H. V. Boynton, the *Cincinnati Gazette's* Washington correspondent. Bristow told Harlan that the Supreme Court job didn't pay enough, and he told his friends that he might take the job if offered, but he would not seek it. Bristow's mixed signals led to a series of misunderstandings with Harlan about each other's intentions.

299 **"take the Circuit Judgeship":** MacVeagh to Harlan, May 12, 1877.

299 **resisted the idea:** On his return to Louisville in mid-August, Harlan wrote a private account of his meetings with Hayes, and more generally, of his quest for a federal appointment. Harlan intended the account to be the start of a diary, but he soon abandoned the effort. In a preface to the lone entry, Aug. 21, 1877, he wrote, "What is found here is written in the belief that no human eye except my own shall see it." Library of Congress collection, box 25, microfilm reel 14. Mallie, in *Some Memories*, p. 87, wrote that Harlan rejected the diplomatic post because "he could not bear the thought of being out of his native land for four years."

299 **"meets all the requirements":** MacVeagh to Hayes, Aug. 21, 1877, Library of Congress collection. MacVeagh sent Harlan a copy of his letter.

299 **"is not Harlan the man?":** Hayes to William Henry Smith, Sept. 29, 1877, and Smith's reply, Oct. 3, 1877, the Hayes papers. Quoted in Beth's *John Marshall Harlan*, pp. 123–124.

300 **they were fuming:** An accusation was afoot that Harlan had made a deal with the Hayes forces at the 1876 convention, and that he was reaping his reward. Decades later, the quid quo pro story gained new momentum when Walter Gresham, a well-known Indiana judge and politician, claimed in his memoir that Harlan had been promised a Supreme Court seat in return for backing Hayes at the convention. I don't find the story credible. The facts and Hayes's actions suggest otherwise. He did not appoint Harlan to his cabinet, and he took seven long months before choosing Harlan for the court. There's ample evidence, in Hayes's diary, that he seriously considered other candidates, and no hint of a deal with Harlan.

300 **how dare he?:** In the months after Bristow's failed bid for the presidential nomination, several of his most ardent supporters began to blame Harlan for the loss. Some thought Harlan had given up too soon at the convention; others thought he made a deal to benefit himself. It appears that Harlan's detractors created enough doubt in Bristow's mind about Harlan's motives to cause Bristow to become disenchanted with his old friend.

300 **"snapped the cords of a friendship":** From Harlan's "one-day diary," Aug. 21, 1877. For more on the rift, see Beth, *Harlan*, pp. 113–118, and David G. Farrelly, "John Marshall Harlan's

One-Day Diary, Aug. 21, 1877: An Interpretation of the Harlan-Bristow Controversy," in the *Filson Club History Quarterly*, April 1950.

300 **upset with Hayes's Southern policy:** Hayes was acutely aware of his party's discontent. On Oct. 24, 1877, he wrote in his diary: "It is now obvious that there is a very decided opposition to the Administration, in both houses of Congress, among the Republican members." But he was undeterred. "How to meet and overcome this opposition is the question. I am clear that I am right. I believe a large majority of the best people are in full accord with me. Now my purpose is to keep cool." *Diary and Letters*, vol. 3, p. 449.

301 **seventeen-page reply:** Handwritten letter at the National Archives, Record Group 46, Records of the U.S. Senate, 45th Congress, Judiciary Committee, NA No. 45B-A5, Harlan, John M.: Nomination of as a Justice of the Supreme Court.

301 **"you can't be beaten":** Beck to Harlan, Nov. 30, 1877, University of Louisville collection, box 2, folder 9, microfilm reel 8.

301 **Lucy Hayes's carriage:** *Some Memories*, p. 91.

301 **Given "the importance":** Harlan to Waite, Dec. 15, 1877, Morrison Waite papers, Library of Congress. Cited in Beth, *Harlan*, p. 139.

301 **he let those go:** The court reporter at the time, William T. Otto, wrote a preface to vol. 95 of U.S. Reports that provides a road map to Harlan's participation and nonparticipation in the cases decided during his early weeks on the bench.

302 **a dissent of any kind:** I compiled these figures by going through the decisions, and cross-checking them with the Supreme Court Database, a remarkable online resource created and maintained by Harold Spaeth, Lee Epstein, and a host of others, in affiliation with Washington University at St. Louis. I used SCDB Legacy 03, covering cases from 1791 to 1945.

302 ***Benson v. Decuir*:** The case came to the court under this name. By the time it was decided, though, Benson had died. The administrator of his estate was substituted as the lead name, so the case became *Hall v. DeCuir*, 95 U.S. 485 (1878). The Supreme Court clerk capitalized the "c" in Decuir for unknown reasons. At the lower court level, and in official records filed by her lawyer, the spelling is Decuir. I have stuck with that.

302 **"She was never a slave":** From Judge E. North Cullom's ruling in the Fifth District Court of New Orleans, June 14, 1873, in the Transcript of Record, *Benson v. Decuir*, U.S. Supreme Court, pp. 74–80.

303 **dreary, dark places:** Transcript of Record, *Benson v. Decuir*, p. 65.

303 **gone to Louisville:** Harlan missed all oral arguments during the first two weeks of Jan. 1878, but still participated in deciding most of those cases.

FIFTEEN: "UNCONGENIAL STRIFES"

305 **The fear—the dread:** My narrative about Brown's disabling headaches is drawn from his daybooks from 1872 to 1875. The earliest sign of trouble is his entry for Feb. 2, 1872: "Terrific headache—worst of the season. Too sick to argue [a] motion in U.S. Court." After twenty years of writing in these daybooks, Brown stopped the practice in Sept. 1875.

306 **"head over ears":** Brown noted his European acquisitions in his daybook, July 22 and Aug. 7, 1873.

306 **"Swell court, big dignity":** Brown's comments on his trip to Washington from his daybook, Oct. 20–27, 1873.

306 **"will never they cease":** Brown's daybook, Mar. 3, 1874.

306 **"uncongenial strifes":** Brown's "Memoranda," *Memoir*, p. 21.

306 **"Judge Longyear dead!":** Brown's daybook, Mar. 12, 1875.

307 **"The salary of a district judge":** In *Memoir,* Kent noted several times that Carry's inheritance freed Brown to pursue his judicial ambitions. See, for example, pp. 72–73.

307 **nerve-wracking crawl:** Brown's daybook, Mar. 16–23, 1875.

308 **"incalculable relief":** Brown's "Memoranda," *Memoir,* p. 21.

308 **his Southern sojourn:** Brown wrote of his 1876 visit to Memphis in *Memoir,* pp. 22–24.

310 **The company's ads:** *Philadelphia Times,* Nov. 22, 1875; *Chicago Tribune,* Jan. 6, 1876; *Memphis Daily Appeal,* Jan. 23, 1876.

310 **"genuine negroes and mulattoes":** *Memphis Daily Appeal,* Jan. 23, 1876.

310 **charmed the *Tribune*'s reviewer:** *Chicago Tribune,* Jan. 15, 1876.

310 **applauded his stand:** *Memphis Daily Appeal,* Mar. 4, 1875.

311 **colorful, gregarious impresario:** Davey's funeral in 1879, held in Detroit, drew hundreds of people and long accounts in the Detroit newspapers. *Detroit Free Press,* Dec. 5 and 7, 1879.

311 **"or I will close it":** From a *Memphis Daily Appeal* interview with Davey, Mar. 4, 1875, under the headline, "Civil Rights: The First Test of the Great Infamy at the Memphis Theater."

311 **"keen black eyes":** Brown's "Memoranda," *Memoir,* p. 26.

311 **proprietor named Tom Maguire:** In early 1876, the U.S. district attorney in San Francisco brought separate cases against Maguire and his doorkeeper, Michael Ryan, alleging that they had excluded ticketholders of color from the dress circle and parquette seats. Ryan's case went to the Supreme Court, joining four others that the justices combined in a single 1883 decision on the act's constitutionality, now known as the *Civil Rights Cases.*

313 **"Yours respectfully":** Tourgee to Edward J. Taylor, May 3, 1875, Tourgee papers, document 1807.

313 **darling daughter Lodie:** Her parents used the nickname Lodie exclusively in their letters. Lodie's full name was Aimée Lodoilska Tourgee. Lodoilska was Emma's middle name.

314 **"clothed like a queen":** Tourgee to Emma, Jan. 5, 1873, document 1649.

315 **"pure folly":** Tourgee to Martin B. Anderson, president of Rochester University, May 11, 1874, document 1739. The letter is also the source for the "Canaan of my aspirations" quote about Tourgee's hopes of winning a seat in Congress.

315 **"take care of my civil rights bill":** Among others, poet Henry Wadsworth Longfellow reported on Sumner's last words in a letter, Apr. 5, 1874, to Lady Elizabeth Georgina Campbell, Duchess of Argyll. See *The Letters of Henry Wadsworth Longfellow,* letter 3435, p. 734.

316 **"forget the negro for a bit":** Tourgee to Anderson, May 11, 1874, cited earlier. Quoted in Olsen, *Carpetbagger's Crusade,* p. 193.

316 **adopted a young girl:** Addie Patillo's letters to the Tourgees hint at her complicated relationship with her benefactors. In 1875, while living in Brattleboro, VT, she wrote at length of her insecurities and aspirations, and even commented on the strains in the Tourgees' marriage, saying "I am so glad you are feeling good natured toward each other for it be so much for the best." July 18, 1875, document 1822. For more on Patillo, see Elliott, *Color-Blind Justice,* pp. 135–139, and pp. 149–152. For a present-day newspaper account based on an interview with a Patillo descendant, see "A Magical Mystery Tour Into Family, History, Heritage and Color," *Greensboro News and Record,* Feb. 20, 2000.

317 **wake from their slumber:** *Raleigh News,* Feb. 13, 1875.

317 **"repellant to my instincts":** Tourgee to E. S. Parker, editor of the *Alamance Gleaner,* a weekly in Graham, NC. The letter is dated May 25, 1875. The *Gleaner* published it on June 1.

317 **series of essays:** In early 1875, under the same pen name ("Henry Churton") that he used in publishing his first novel, Tourgee wrote a four-part essay titled "Why Reconstruction Was a

Failure." He sent it to the *Northampton Journal*, a weekly in western Massachusetts. The *Journal* published the four parts over a month-long period. The clippings can be found in document 2428, a scrapbook that includes two other lengthy Tourgee critiques of Reconstruction.

319 **"No reconciliation, no peace":** *Alamance Gleaner*, June 29, 1875.

319 **"One of the amusements":** Tourgee letter to the *Wilmington Post*, May 28, 1875.

319 **"I am now fully armed":** For the Tourgee-Emma correspondence on the Ransom threat, see documents 1856–1858, Sept. 23–24, 1875.

320 **thirty-one days of wrangling:** My narrative of Tourgee's activities at the convention is drawn from his letters to Emma, newspaper accounts, and the official record, *Journal of the Constitutional Convention of the State of North Carolina, Held in 1875.*

320 **"did not like the language":** Raleigh *Daily Constitution*, Sept. 25, 1875. The debate on separate schools took place primarily on Sept. 25 and Sept. 30, 1875.

321 **"no one who deserves more":** Letter from Thomas B. Keogh to President Grant, in the Senate's files for 1876. National Archives, Record Group 46, Sen 44B-A4, box 7, nominations.

321 **the capital in a tizzy:** Tourgee to Emma, Nov. 24, 1875, document 1875.

322 **"horrors of the last week":** Emma's extraordinary letter to Tourgee is document 1877, Dec. 18, 1875.

322 **drafting and redrafting:** Tourgee saved the early draft of his letter to the Committee on Pensions. I compared that draft, document 1878, to the final version in his nomination file at the National Archives.

322 **prisoner of war:** Tourgee's final draft inflated his length of time as a prisoner of war from four months to "nearly six months." Also, he added his childhood eyesight injury to the list of insults he had suffered during the war. He wrote: "As the result of one wound received at the first Battle of Bull Run, I lost an eye."

324 **ratcheted up the pressure:** Tourgee's letters to O'Hara can be found at p. 330 and p. 336 of "Letter Book 3, April 13, 1876 to May 8, 1877," document 2200. O'Hara's response to Tourgee's Aug. 4 letter is not part of the collection, but Tourgee quotes from it in his second letter on Aug. 12.

324 **replace him with a white candidate:** Several newspapers reported that O'Hara had been "compelled" to withdraw. The *Raleigh News*, on Oct. 20, 1876, wrote that "O'Hara, the negro, is taken off the ticket by the Republicans in the vain hope of appeasing white folks."

324 **attacked him with a cane:** The newspapers reported on the assault and trial with some relish. *Charlotte Observer*, Apr. 7, 1878, and *Raleigh Observer*, June 5, 1878.

325 **he felt bereft:** My narrative on his congressional race is drawn largely from twenty-five letters he wrote to Emma from late August to mid-November, documents 2224 to 2250. Emma's letters for this period are not part of the collection, suggesting that she saved his, but that he lost track of hers during this hectic time.

325 **"my mistaken life":** Tourgee to Emma, Oct. 1, 1878, document 2236.

325 **"I shall lose 500 votes":** Tourgee made this estimate early in the campaign, Aug. 29, 1878, document 2227. It's hard to know for sure, but there's no evidence that Emma's absence hurt his campaign in any measurable way.

325 **"Whether it was true or not":** Tourgee's letter to the Wilmington *Morning Post*, May 28, 1875. Tourgee, in saying he did not know or care if the man's story was right, was unapologetic. "Such fish," he wrote, employing an insensitive metaphor, "have been found in mill ponds in this district since. I say *that* now."

326 **"down on his all-fours":** *Raleigh Observer*, Oct. 12, 1878.

326 **allowed himself to think:** After telling Emma on Oct. 28, 1878, document 2244, that it looked as if he would lose by six hundred, he wrote on Nov. 3, document 2246, that his sup-

porters were predicting victory by five hundred votes. He was estimating a narrower win, he told her—perhaps two hundred.

326 **"Pity me darling":** Tourgee to Emma, Nov. 6, 1878, document 2248. He also wrote: "Oh my punishment is greater than I can bear. Why did I not die in this campaign? Why did I not die years ago?"

326 **"This is very bitter":** Tourgee to Emma, Nov. 11, 1878, document 2250.

326 **"nothing for me here":** Tourgee to Emma, Apr. 13, 1879, document 2315.

SIXTEEN: FOOL'S ERRAND

329 **newspaper advertisements:** For example, see *New York Times*, Nov. 22, 1879.

329 **"the fame of it":** *New York Tribune*, Dec. 3, 1879.

330 **opposing sendoffs:** Contrasting farewells from the *Greensboro North State*, Aug. 28, 1879 ("Reconstruction Hero Gone"), and *Charlotte Observer*, Sept. 10, 1879 ("vindictive, malicious man").

330 **four full columns:** *New York Tribune*, Nov. 18, 1879.

331 **"dreadfully lonely":** Emma to Tourgee, Jan. 7, 1880, document 2365.

331 **"black silk dress":** Emma to Tourgee, Jan. 20, 1880, document 2369.

331 **Fifty thousand:** The *Rochester Democrat and Chronicle*, Mar. 28, 1880, reported forty thousand sold since December 1, 1879, without citing a specific source. The *Washington Post*, Mar. 29, 1880, reported that Tourgee "is said to have the pleasure of seeing his book" sell at the rate of ten thousand a month.

331 **Enthusiasm waned:** Quotes in this paragraph from the *Louisville Courier-Journal*, Nov. 17, 1879 ("bigoted and malignant"); *Raleigh Observer*, Nov. 11, 1879 ("destined, we fear"); and *Memphis Daily Ledger*, Jan. 22, 1880 ("Radical campaign volume").

332 **Albion renewed the arguments:** For his critique of Reconstruction in *A Fool's Errand*, see chap. 20 and 21, pp. 112–129 in the 1879 edition.

332 **"No better campaign document":** The correspondent's "Washington letter," quoting Garfield and others, was written for the *Indianapolis Journal*. It was widely reprinted.

332 **serious financial trouble:** In September 1875, George Hurlburt informed Tourgee that the publishing company was working on a plan that would pay its creditors "thirty-five cents on the dollar." Document 1837. Tourgee had a major stake in the publisher's financial health; his first novel, *Toinette*, had just come out. Hurlburt assured Tourgee that the company would stay in business under a new ownership arrangement, and that it was planning to promote *Toinette* in another round of advertising.

333 **Ford was resolute:** My account of Tourgee's dealings with Edward Ford in the spring of 1880 is drawn from a long newspaper essay that Emma wrote in October 1908, headlined "Memories of the Campaign of 1880." The clipping is document 10532. The newspaper is not identified, and my efforts to trace it were unsuccessful.

333 **items were popping up:** *Chicago Tribune* and *New York Tribune*, both Apr. 25, 1880, and *New Orleans Picayune*, Apr. 29, 1880.

334 **Certainly not Garfield:** Some historical accounts raise the possibility that a brokered convention was Garfield's plan all along, but I do not subscribe to that theory. Certainly, there were Garfield supporters who hoped the convention would turn to him, but unlike Hayes in 1876 or Lincoln in 1860, Garfield was not a declared candidate. Also, Garfield's letters and diary entries do not read like someone committed to a candidacy or strategy.

334 **"Presidential fever":** Cited in Allan Peskin's *Garfield: A Biography*, p. 454, and Ira Rutkow's *James Garfield*, p. 48.

334 **nothing to thwart:** See Garfield's diary, Feb. 11 and 18, 1880, in *The Diary of James A. Garfield, Vol. IV, 1878–1881*, pp. 365 and 369, for his commitment to helping Sherman.

334 **Garfield protested:** *Proceedings of the Republican National Convention* (1880), p. 269.

334 **"Rally 'Round the Flag":** Most newspapers, in reporting on the celebration triggered by Garfield's nomination, used this alternate title for the famous Civil War song. A few used "The Battle Cry of Freedom," the composer's original and now better-known title.

334 **cannon thundered:** *Chicago Tribune*, "The Victory. How the Battle Was Won," June 9, 1880.

335 **"my friend, Judge Tourgee":** From *Proceedings of the Republican National Convention*, p. 284. The speaker was William W. Hicks, nominating Thomas Settle for vice president. Settle did not win the nomination, which went to Chester A. Arthur.

335 **brotherly pals:** There isn't a great deal of information about Tourgee's boyhood relationship with Garfield. Roy Dibble, in his 1921 biography of Tourgee, has several details that came from family members, p. 76. Tourgee said, in a speech later in his life, that he met Garfield when he was ten years old, suggesting it was the summer of 1848. As best as I could determine, they probably met the following summer, which was Garfield's first at Geauga Academy, a school near Tourgee's relatives in Chester Township, OH.

336 **"I can face these hisses":** Details of the Cooper Union event from the *New York Tribune* and *New York Times,* both June 13, 1880.

337 **"the Nation can justly afford":** Garfield's letter of acceptance, July 10, 1880, in *Proceedings of the Republican National Convention*, pp. 298–301.

337 **"good 'popular' talker":** Asa Lamb to Garfield, Sept. 18, 1880, the Garfield papers, Library of Congress, series 4, microfilm reel 65. Cited in Elliott's *Color-Blind Justice*, p. 186.

337 **Garfield wants to confer:** Tourgee met with Garfield twice in September 1880. See Tourgee to Garfield, Sept. 5, 1880, Garfield papers, series 4, reel 64, and Tourgee's telegram to Garfield, series 4, reel 57.

338 **"death to intolerance":** Quoted in the *Chicago Tribune*, Oct. 1, 1880.

338 **somewhat startled:** After the election, Tourgee wrote an unsolicited note to Garfield, document 2389, expressing some ideas about the South. He wasn't expecting a response, much less an immediate and encouraging one. The Tourgee-Garfield relationship, as seen through their letters, is also chronicled in Elliott, *Color-Blind Justice,* pp. 186–191, and Olsen, *Carpetbagger's Crusade*, pp. 245–247.

338 **"dangerous as ever":** Tourgee's papers contain two drafts that appear to be the basis for a fourteen-page letter to Garfield on Dec. 14, 1880. Documents 2386 and 2389, both undated. The final Dec. 14 letter can be found in the Garfield papers, series 4, reel 81.

338 **"a mere negation":** Tourgee to Garfield, also from the Dec. 14, 1880, letter.

339 **forthcoming essay:** Published in the *North American Review* as "Aaron's Rod in Politics," Feb. 1881.

339 **"quarter of a million copies":** Tourgee to Garfield, Dec. 23, 1880, document 2388. Three months later, the publisher sent Emma a report on sales of all Tourgee titles for the first two months of 1881. Tourgee's share—10 percent of revenues—was $1,979. Document 2399. Translating that amount into today's dollars is an imprecise art, with many factors at work, but a rough estimate would be $45,000 for just that ten-week period.

339 **delivered his verdict:** Hinsdale to Garfield, Jan. 4, 1881, in the *Garfield-Hinsdale Letters: Correspondence between James Abram Garfield and Burke Aaron Hinsdale* (1949), p. 473. For other letters about Tourgee and his education plan, see pp. 469–470, and p. 478. Also, Hinsdale to Garfield, Dec. 21, 1880, Garfield papers, series 4, reel 82.

340 **"heartily pleased":** Tourgee to Garfield, Mar. 4, 1881, Garfield papers, series 4, reel 93.

340 **"new and brighter era":** Tourgee to Garfield, also Mar. 4, 1881.

340 **he petitioned Garfield:** Tourgee to Garfield, Mar. 6, 1881, Garfield papers, series 4, reel 93.

340 **"The Judge was greatly moved":** *Diary of James A. Garfield, Volume IV, 1878–1881*, Apr. 7, 1881, p. 571.

340 **Their irritation showed up:** *Washington Post*, May 11, 1881.

340 **a provocative speech:** Quoted in the *Cincinnati Enquirer*, June 20, 1881.

341 **Fourth of July poem:** Tourgee titled it simply: "One Hundred and Fifth Birthday." Document 2411.

341 **another long voyage:** On July 2, 1881, the *New York Times* listed "The Hon. H.B. Brown" and "Mrs. Brown" among the *Main*'s 125 cabin passengers. By 1881, Europe had become a favored summer destination for wealthier Americans, reflected in the *Times* headline: "Still Flocking to Europe."

341 **"easily dispose":** Brown's "Memoranda," *Memoir*, p. 24.

342 **his "natural vitality":** Brown's "Memoranda," *Memoir*, p. 21.

342 **"unusually good night":** *The Times of London*, Sept. 13, 1881.

343 **not for five hundred dollars:** The Fisk Jubilee Singers' Washington visit received wide newspaper coverage. I relied on accounts from the *Wilmington* (DE) *Morning Journal*, *New York Times*, *Nashville Daily American*, *Decatur* (IL) *Herald*, all Feb. 18, 1882; the *Cincinnati Enquirer*, Feb. 20, 1882; the *Baltimore American* and the *Cincinnati Gazette*, as reprinted in the *Chicago Tribune*, Feb. 21, 1882.

344 **time-consuming and expensive:** Robert J. Kaczorowski's 1995 article, "Federal Enforcement of Civil Rights During the First Reconstruction," *Fordham Urban Law Journal* 23, focuses on the period before the 1875 Civil Rights Act, but it provides a well-researched understanding of the limitations faced by the U.S. attorney's offices in enforcing the broad federal laws passed by Congress after the Civil War.

344 **a brutal attack on Republican freedmen:** For an excellent account of this extraordinary case, see Charles Lane's *The Day Freedom Died: The Colfax Massacre, the Supreme Court, and the Betrayal of Reconstruction* (2008). While writing this book, I benefited from several conversations with Lane, who is a *Washington Post* colleague. The Supreme Court's ruling in the Colfax Massacre is *U.S. v. Cruikshank*, 92 U.S. 542. Seven justices joined Waite in his majority opinion; the ninth justice, Nathan Clifford, wrote a concurring opinion that said he did not need to assess the constitutional issues in the case because, in his view, the indictment against the massacre's alleged perpetrators was fatally flawed.

345 **"useless and played-out":** *Memphis Daily Appeal*, Jan. 28, 1880.

345 **"an epidemic of 'civil rights'":** *Memphis Daily Appeal*, Oct. 5, 1881.

345 **"Our Colored Friends":** *Nashville Daily American*, Oct. 18, 1881.

346 **seriously ill:** Several newspapers, in explaining Harlan's absence at the court, mentioned his daughter's dire condition and his rushed trip to Chicago. See the *National Republican*, Nov. 11, 1882.

346 **a hasty note:** Harlan to Chief Justice Waite, Nov. 9 and 10, 1882, cited in Beth, *John Marshall Harlan*, p. 147 and p. 291.

346 **vivid memories of Edith:** See "My Eldest Daughter's Marriage and Death," in *Some Memories*, pp. 114–116.

347 **"I refrain from":** Senator George F. Edmunds to Harlan, Dec. 1, 1882, in the "Family Scrapbook Civil Rights Case 1883," University of Louisville collection, microfilm reel 7.

347 **given them a nudge:** Jury deliberation records, *Robinson v. Memphis and Charleston Railroad*, Record Group 21, U.S. Circuit Court, Western District of Tennessee, Memphis Division, law case files, box 49, case no. 2611, National Archives in Atlanta.

348 **rising in the darkness:** *Some Memories*, pp. 108–114.

348 **"legislative extravaganza":** *Baltimore Sun*, Oct. 16, 1883.

349 **"You, sir, have won a place":** Walter S. Thomas to Harlan, Oct. 16, 1883, in the "Civil Rights Case" scrapbook. Thomas was a prominent figure in the Ohio Republican Party, serving as a regular delegate to state conventions. Later, he was president of the Ohio Afro-American League.

349 **"test of time":** George M. Thomas to Harlan, Nov. 8, 1883, "Civil Rights Case" scrapbook.

349 **no such aspiration:** *New York Times*, Oct. 26, 1883.

SEVENTEEN: THE COLOR LINE SHARPENS

351 **"quagmire of logic":** In *Some Memories*, pp. 108–114, Mallie offers a lengthy description of Harlan's difficulties in drafting his dissent. While her account may lean slightly toward the dramatic (like her husband, she was a good storyteller), there's no doubt that the dissent took him longer than others. Using other documents from the Harlan collections, I was able to improve on the vague chronological references in her account.

352 **nearly fourteen thousand words:** The Supreme Court's ruling is commonly referred to as the *Civil Rights Cases*, even in legal journals, rather than by its formal name, *U.S. v. Stanley et al.* The citation is 109 U.S. 3.

355 **he collected the clippings:** The newspaper articles quoted are from the *New York Tribune*, Nov. 22, 1883; *New York Times*, Nov. 21, 1883; *Chicago Inter Ocean*, Nov. 20, 1883.

356 **a second note:** Hayes to Harlan, Nov. 28, 1883, and Jan. 19, 1884. The MacVeagh letter was Nov. 20, 1883. All from Harlan's "Civil Rights Case" scrapbook.

356 **"not a single weak point":** Douglass wrote Harlan twice, once after the justice announced he was dissenting, and again after the dissent was released. Oct. 16 and Nov. 27, 1883, "Civil Rights Case" scrapbook.

356 **heartfelt letter:** William Howard Day to Harlan, Nov. 17, 1883, "Civil Rights Case" scrapbook.

356 **"Dear Mallie":** Harlan's undated note to his wife, recounting his conversation with former Justice William Strong, is the second item in the "Civil Rights Case" scrapbook.

358 **best political hope:** In an Oct. 3, 1883, letter, Douglass told a friend, "I am thought to be an Independent, and so I am, but I am an Independent inside of the Republican party. . . . My advice to colored men everywhere is to stick to the Republican party. Tell your wants, hold the party up to its profession, but do your utmost to keep it in power in State and Nation." Douglass to James M. Dalzell, Douglass papers, Library of Congress.

358 **made Douglass cringe:** Douglass referred to the *New York Evening Post* editorial as "a great mistake" in speaking to the National Convention of Colored Men. See the *Chicago Tribune*, Sept. 26, 1883. The comment does not appear in the "official" published text of his convention speech.

358 **"bettering our condition":** From a Douglass interview with a *Washington Evening Star* reporter, reprinted in the *Washington Bee,* May 12, 1883. The *Bee* was one of the leading black newspapers at the time.

359 **now was it?:** I synthesized these questions about Douglass's call for a convention from a variety of white and black newspapers, too numerous to cite, and from Douglass's comments on the criticisms that he was hearing.

359 **"safety valves of the republic":** Also from the *Star* interview, as quoted in the *Bee.*

360 **"a fine body of men":** *Louisville Courier-Journal*, Sept. 25, 1883.

360 **"a French colored man":** See, for example, the *Courier-Journal*, Sept. 27, 1883.

360 **The Martinet family's story:** My narrative of Louis Martinet's family background is based, in part, on records from the St. Martin Parish courthouse and from the Diocese of Lafayette. My

appreciation to Candy Brunet, associate archivist at the diocese, for tracking down the Dec. 7, 1869, marriage record for Louis Martinet's parents, which lists their eight children. Thanks, also, to the staff of the St. Martin Parish library for unearthing other genealogical material on the Martinet family.

360 **bought her freedom:** The 1848 record of Hippolyte Martinet's purchase of Mary Louise Benoit, leading to her subsequent freedom, can be found at the St. Martin Parish courthouse, book 17, p. 112. The document, written in French, identified her as "*une mulatresse*." As part of that same sale, Hippolyte Martinet also bought Mary Louise's mother, Hortense, and Mary Louise's infant son, Pierre, who was the couple's first child.

361 **"raised the uproar":** *Louisville Courier-Journal*, Sept. 27, 1883.

361 **scanning the crowd:** The reporter's dispatch appeared in many papers, including the *Chicago Inter Ocean* and the *Nashville Daily American*, both Sept. 26, 1883.

361 **he inserted new ideas:** The prepared text of Douglass's speech, delivered Sept. 25, 1883, was published by the *Louisville Courier-Journal* the next day, and later as a pamphlet. That version has appeared in anthologies of Douglass's writings. It does not include, however, the portions he added as he was speaking, as reported by various newspapers. I have quoted from both.

363 **The unkind ones:** "Roaring farce," from the *Memphis Daily Appeal*. "Buncombe," from the *Nashville Daily American*. "A ceaseless stream of valueless talk" showed up in a dispatch that many papers used, including the *Chicago Tribune*. All from papers of Sept. 27, 1883.

363 **"I am not ashamed":** Douglass to an unidentified recipient, Oct. 4, 1883, the Douglass papers, Library of Congress.

363 **"objectionable and abhorrent":** The *Picayune* quotes in this section are from Oct. 16 and Oct. 30, 1883.

364 **"if not a disgrace":** The quotes from the weekly *Louisiana Standard* come from an article headlined "Civil Rights," mostly likely published on Saturday, Oct. 20 or 27, 1883. The undated clip is among many in Harlan's "Civil Rights Case" scrapbook.

365 **all-too-believable encounter:** My narrative of the William H. Councill case is drawn largely from the extensive ICC files at the National Archives II in College Park, Maryland. The bulk of the documents can be found in Record Group 134, Operating Division, Formal Dockets, 1887–1924, dockets 19–24, container 4. The folders for docket 21 include Councill's original complaint, the Western & Atlantic's responses, testimony transcripts, witness depositions, and briefs. The documents leave no doubt about the correct spelling of Councill's last name, often misspelled by newspapers at the time. He sent letters to the commission on his personal stationery, with the double l.

365 **twelve hundred railroad lines:** From the ICC's first annual report, Dec. 1, 1887.

366 **"please notify us":** Letter from Councill's lawyers, John D. Brandon and Oscar R. Hundley, to ICC chairman Thomas Cooley, May 27, 1887. ICC files, docket 21, correspondence, folder 2.

366 **his distinguished career:** Among other accomplishments, Cooley was the author of several widely used textbooks on constitutional and civil law, and a professor at the University of Michigan's law school.

366 **make a success of it:** Cooley's papers at the Bentley Historical Library, University of Michigan contain a wealth of material on his work as the ICC's first chairman. His diaries begin Aug. 31, 1887, six months after the ICC was created.

366 **"good deal of feeling":** Cooley to his wife Mary, July 23, 1887. Cooley papers, box 3, correspondence.

367 **an impressive witness:** The ICC hearing was featured prominently in two major New York newspapers on July 24, 1887, with headlines sympathetic to Councill and disparaging of the South. From the *Tribune*: "Civil Rights In Trains. Some Light on Southern Brutality. A Rail-

road Company That Took all the Money It Could Get and Then Allowed a Colored Passenger to be Maltreated." From the *Times*: "Ejected From His Seat/The Color Line South—A Case Before the Inter-State Commerce Commission."

367 **"I knocked him out of his seat":** Whitsett deposition, July 9, 1887, taken in Ringgold, GA. ICC files, docket 21.

368 **defying the color line:** Western & Atlantic's superintendent, in his written reply to Councill's complaint, said the railroad "insists that it has a right to classify its passengers by the line either of color or sex . . . provided the two cars are in every respect equal and equally comfortable." Superintendent R. A. Anderson, June 16, 1887, ICC files, docket 21.

369 **Morrison's ruling:** For the full text of the *Councill* ruling, see *Interstate Commerce Commission Reports, Reports and Decisions of the Commission*, vol. 1, pp. 339–347. The citation is 1 I.C.C. 339 (1887).

369 **Separate is legal:** The day after Councill's July 23 hearing, Cooley again mentioned the case while writing to his wife. "We heard the case of the darkey yesterday," he wrote. His casual use of that belittling term—the same word that Charles Whitsett had used in recounting his attack on Councill—reflected Cooley's blindness to bigotry's pervasive nature. His prejudices did not prevent him from finding in Councill's favor, within the confines of the color line. For the letter to his wife, see box 3, correspondence, July 24, 1887, Cooley papers.

370 **The trouble began:** My synopsis of the William H. Heard case is drawn largely from the ICC files, Record Group 134, Operating Division, formal dockets, 1887–1924, docket 46.

371 **"not open for discussion":** For the full text of the *Heard* ruling, see *Interstate Commerce Commission Reports, Reports and Decisions of the Commission*, vol. 1, pp. 428–436. The citation is 1 I.C.C. 428 (1888).

371 **both men of color:** A few hours after the hearing, Cooley wrote to his wife about his favorable impression of Heard's lawyers, J. W. Cromwell and W. C. Martin. "Two colored lawyers were in charge of the case for the complainant, and one them made a really good sound sensible speech," he wrote. "It showed want of education and training, but in point of substance and appropriate logic, would have done credit to any one." Dec. 15, 1887, box 3, correspondence, Cooley papers.

EIGHTEEN: "THE NEGRO QUESTION"

373 **"such an outburst":** Tourgee to Nixon, editor of the *Inter Ocean*, July 11, 1889, document 3916.

373 **mountain of mail:** "A Bystander's Notes," *Inter Ocean*, Aug. 31, 1889, and Tourgee to Nixon, Aug. 31, 1889, document 3986.

373 **"earnest-hearted lovers of liberty":** "A Bystander's Notes," *Inter Ocean*, June 29, 1889.

373 **Unable to write:** "Bystander," *Inter Ocean*, Aug. 31, 1889. Tourgee quoted the "colored Mississippian's" letter in his column; if the original survives, I could not find it in the Tourgee papers. That didn't seem surprising, given the volume of mail he received from "Bystander" readers. (There is an extensive cache from 1892, collected as document 7614.)

374 **"most powerful champion":** William T. Green to Tourgee, Nov. 7, 1889, document 4124. Otto Olsen, a pioneering Tourgee scholar, wrote a notable essay in 1964 about the Bystander's influence, "Albion W. Tourgee and Negro Militants of the 1890's," in *Science and Society* 28, no. 2 (Spring 1964). Olsen expanded on that essay for his 1966 biography, *Carpetbagger's Crusade*.

374 **tried out different voices:** The examples cited in this paragraph were culled from the first two years of "Bystander" columns: "campaign song," June 23, 1888; "miasma of intolerance," May 10, 1890; brag about himself, Mar. 8, 1890; lament his graying hair, May 10, 1890.

374 **embellish for effect:** Carolyn L. Karcher's 2016 book, *Refugee From His Race: Albion Tour-*

gée and His Fight Against White Supremacy, describes one instance in which Tourgee embellished a reader's letter, adding phrases to sharpen points he wanted to make in his column. She concludes that Tourgee remained "faithful overall" to the letter writer's "language and style," pp. 107–109. She is more forgiving than I would be. Her book offers a probing examination of Tourgee's rise as a civil rights advocate, as well as his evolution as a writer.

374 **soliciting his thoughts:** *Frank Leslie's Illustrated Weekly* editor John Sleicher to Tourgee, July 17, 1889, document 3929; *Tribune* editor Donald Nicholson to Tourgee, July 29, 1889, document 3939.

375 **"I will offer it to the newspapers":** S. S. McClure to Tourgee, Mar. 20, 1888, document 3419.

375 **"get along without the Bystander":** Nixon to Tourgee, June 14, 1889, document 3868.

376 **"I take the 'cussing!'":** Tourgee to Nixon, July 11, 1889, document 3916.

376 **preferred pronunciation:** In his preface to *Color-Blind Justice*, p. ix, Elliott wrote: "In 1882, after he became a nationally recognized novelist, Albion Tourgée added an accent mark over the first *e* in his last name to assist the public in its correct pronunciation." Elliott chose to use the accent throughout *Color-Blind Justice*, except in quoted material. I have opted for chronological integrity. In my narrative, he is Tourgee in earlier chapters, and Tourgée once he makes the addition permanent. In quotes, I preserved whatever spelling appeared in the original.

376 **amiably reversed:** Nixon to Tourgée, Aug. 23, 1889, document 3980.

376 **"I will continue the Bystander":** Tourgée to Nixon, Aug. 31, 1889, document 3986.

377 **"My poor husband":** Emma to her lawyer, Adelbert Moot, June 17, 1905, document 9771.

377 **"unfortunate, penniless novelist":** *Boston Globe*, Jan. 13, 1885.

377 **"get out of the way":** *Watchman and Southron*, Dec. 9, 1884.

377 **"whip this debt":** Tourgée to Emma's sister, Millie Kilborn, Mar. 1, 1886, document 2496.

378 **"a certain sense of shame":** *Detroit Free Press*, Feb. 9, 1886.

378 **"their money's worth":** Tourgée to Emma, Feb. 9, 1886, document 2482.

378 **"outlived my time":** Tourgée to Emma, Feb. 18, 1886, document 2487.

378 **"a man that was":** Tourgée to Emma, Feb. 27, 1886, document 2493.

378 **"guard me from myself":** Tourgée to Millie Kilborn, also from his Mar. 1, 1886, letter.

379 **"be perfectly happy":** Tourgée to Emma, Mar. 8, 1886, document 2502.

379 **hard feelings on both sides:** Tourgée to Adelbert Moot, Sept. 20, 1887, attached to an unrelated letter, part of document 2900. Tourgée's letter begins, "I am very sorry that Mr. Mathews is dissatisfied with my work . . ." Tourgée had chosen fiction and an elliptical route to write about monopoly power, and his benefactor wanted something more straightforward.

379 **various pseudonyms:** Tourgée wrote for the *Inter Ocean* as "Siva" from Dec. 1884–Mar. 1885, as "The Veteran and His Pipe" from Apr.–Sept. 1885, as "Trueman Joyce" from Sept.–Dec. 1885, and again as Siva from Mar.–Dec. 1886.

379 **stoked the speculation:** *Inter Ocean*, Dec. 20 and 27, 1884. The Dec. 27 item said, "The letters of 'Siva' addressed to the President-elect have attracted more attention and caused more excitement than any other political letters published within the last thirty years."

379 **"My name has become a trademark":** Tourgée to J. N. Mathews, editor of the *Buffalo Express*, Mar. 4, 1886, document 2498.

380 **"pay his respects":** From the *Chicago Tribune's* lengthy July 27, 1889, account of Harrison's search for a nominee, headlined "They Want the Ermine; Candidates for the Vacant Place on the Supreme Bench." Among other accounts consulted: the *Baltimore Sun*, *Pittsburgh Commercial Gazette*, *Chicago Inter Ocean*, *Detroit Free Press*, *New York Times*, and *Pittsburgh Dispatch*, all from July 27 and 28, 1889.

381 **"Write me what you know":** Harrison to Robert S. Taylor, July 23, 1889, Harrison papers, Library of Congress, series 1, microfilm reel 21.

382 **"anxious to have him":** *Chicago Tribune*, July 27, 1889. Was this true, or a bit of propaganda from Brown's champions? I lean toward propaganda. It's entirely possible that several justices told Harrison that they thought well of Brown's work as a federal judge. But it seems a stretch to say that "three or four" were "anxious" to have him, essentially endorsing him over other qualified candidates.

382 **once and forever rival:** Kent mentions the Brown-Russell rivalry in his "Addenda," *Memoir*, p. 76.

382 **Yale classmate:** In his "Memoranda," *Memoir*, p. 29, Brown praised Brewer and their relationship.

382 **"unable to tell what impression":** *Free Press*, Nov. 15, 1889. A month earlier, Stockbridge had received a rather formal letter from Harrison, thanking him for "letter of October 14, in which you set forth very forcibly and earnestly the qualifications of Judge Brown," and promising to give "careful attention" to Stockbridge's "suggestions." I can imagine that the president's neutral tone was discouraging to Stockbridge. Harrison to Stockbridge, Oct. 17, 1889, Harrison papers, series 1, reel 23.

382 **Russell's supporters claimed:** *Chicago Tribune*, Sept. 26, 1889.

382 **Stockbridge's spirits lifted:** *Free Press*, Nov. 27, 1889.

382 **private letter from Brewer:** *Detroit News*, Dec. 4, 1889, "D. J. Brewer the Man."

383 **"Bystander Day":** Emma coined this phrase in her diary, Sept. 20, 1889, document 9906.

383 **"Southernism":** "Bystander," *Inter Ocean*, Jan. 4, 1890.

384 **special delivery stamp:** Emma's diary, Jan. 2, 1890.

384 **Rulings in fifty cases:** From the entry for Mar. 3, 1890, Minutes of the Supreme Court, National Archives, M215 (microfilm), reel 18, vol. 54–57, May 1889–Mar. 1892.

385 **Did it run afoul:** My account of *Louisville, New Orleans and Texas Railway Company v. State of Mississippi* is drawn from three sources: The Supreme Court of Mississippi's ruling, cited as 66 Miss. 662 (1889); the Transcript of Record at the U.S. Supreme Court, filed Aug. 13, 1889; and the Supreme Court's ruling, 133 U.S. 587 (1890).

387 **reflecting a weariness:** In reviewing the newspapers for Mar. 3–6, 1890, I found it striking how many treated the Supreme Court's decision in the Mississippi case as routine. The *Washington Post* was a notable exception, calling attention to the ruling's significance in its headline: "Separation of Races. The Supreme Court Decides an Important Railway Question."

387 **The "negro apologists":** *New Orleans Times-Democrat*, Mar. 6, 1890.

388 **"take lunch with him":** Presidential secretary E. W. Halford to Tourgée, Mar. 5, 1890, document 4548.

388 **"dangerous and unjust method":** "Bystander," *Inter Ocean*, Mar. 8, 1890.

389 **"Pardon my plainness":** Tourgée to J. C. Price, document 11043, undated but almost certainly drafted on Jan. 25, 1890. Emma mentioned the letter in her diary entry for that day: "Albion wrote letter to Pres. of Afro-American League, of which I did not approve."

389 **"I cannot see":** Price to Tourgée, Mar. 18, 1890, document 4568.

389 **"If the Nation is not willing":** "Bystander," *Inter Ocean*, Nov. 28, 1889. The draft of his education bill was published in his next column on Dec. 7.

390 **his disability claim:** Tourgée's war wounds were a significant problem for him, but his decision to press the disability claim also reflected their continuing financial woes.

390 **"poor health":** Washington *Evening Star*, Mar. 15, 1890. Emma expressed her concerns in diary entries on Mar. 8, Mar. 14, and Mar. 20, 1890.

390 **"an educator of white old men":** Quoted in the *Evening Star*, Mar. 25, 1890.

390 **"first Mohonk Conference":** Invitation to Tourgée, Mar. 13, 1890, document 4563.

391 **the colored press reacted with scorn:** The quotations in this paragraph are from the *Detroit*

Plaindealer, June 20, 1890, and *New York Age*, June 14 and 21, 1890. Also see the *Cleveland Gazette*, June 14, 1890, "Negroes Not Wanted."

391 **boycotting:** George Washington Cable of New Orleans, a white Southerner famous for his writing about racial injustice, refused to attend. Cable, Tourgée, and others urged the conference's organizers to expand the guest list to include people of color, without success.

391 **decided to go:** In an undated letter to Anderson, document 5147, Tourgée outlined his reasons for attending the conference, saying he was mostly going for "the fun." He said he had no expectations of the conference producing any sort of meaningful result.

391 **"Don't be silent at Podunk":** Anderson to Tourgée, May 19, 1890, document 4738.

392 **his main speech:** The proceedings were published as *The First Mohonk Conference on the Negro Question, Held at Lake Mohonk, Ulster County, New York, June 4, 5, 6, 1890.* For Tourgeé's spontaneous remarks, see pp. 24, 54, and 103. His lengthy prepared speech can be found on pp. 104–117.

392 **he could never repair:** Choosing Hayes as the conference chairman did not sit well with Fortune, the editor of the *New York Age*. He called Hayes "a traitor to black Republicans of the South" for ending Reconstruction.

392 **"pungent, dramatic, original":** *The Diary and Letters of Rutherford Birchard Hayes,* entry for June 6, 1890, vol. 4, p. 579.

392 **"the sensation of the Conference":** Emma's diary, June 6, 1890.

392 **House Bill No. 42:** The bill passed the House on June 3, 1890, fifty-six to twenty-three, with fifteen absent. *Official Journal of the Proceedings of the House of Representatives of Louisiana*, session beginning May 12, 1890, pp. 200–204.

393 **armed with a petition:** *Baton Rouge Advocate*, May 28, 1890, "Official Journal of the House." Also cited in Keith Medley's well-researched book, *We as Freeman: Plessy v. Ferguson*, pp. 96–97. Medley's work is the best look at the New Orleans committee that brought the *Plessy* case, with the richest detail from Louisiana sources.

393 **rose to speak:** The *Crusader* published the text of Senator Henry Demas's speech in its July 19, 1890, edition. No full set of the *Crusader* survives, but the July 19, 1890, issue is part of a microfilm collection, "Miscellaneous Negro Newspapers," filmed by the Library of Congress in 1947 for the Committee on Negro Studies of the American Council of Learned Societies. In addition, there are *Crusader* clippings in several collections of papers at the Amistad Research Center, located at Tulane University, and at Xavier University, both in New Orleans.

393 **"We cannot afford to surrender":** *Times-Democrat*, "Separate Car Bill," July 9, 1890.

394 **reprinted the telegram:** *Crusader*, July 19, 1890.

NINETEEN: "IN BEHALF OF 7,999,999 OF MY RACE"

398 **another Straight University attendee:** The Straight University catalogues in the 1890s listed previous graduates by year. Eli Freeman's name appeared under "College Department," along with his occupation of "teacher." Martinet's name was included among the 1876 graduates of the "Law Department," but as Carolyn Karcher documented in *A Refugee From His Race,* p. 346, Martinet wrote in an 1885 letter to a newspaper that he did not receive a degree. He helped found the Law Department, he said, but later withdrew to study the law independently, as many still did at that time.

398 **"intelligent and thoughtful":** *Manhattan* (Kansas) *Daily Republic*, Mar. 17, 1890.

398 **"7,999,999 of my race":** Eli Freeman to Tourgée, Aug. 4, 1890, document 4872.

398 **offer his suggestions:** Tourgée's reply to Freeman is not among the many documents in the Tourgée collection, and other historians have said it does not survive. I believe, however,

that Freeman brought it to a Dec. 1890 rally in Manhattan, KS, held to support the New Orleans Citizens' Committee in its fight against the Separate Car Act. From the *Manhattan Daily Republic* for Dec. 2: "A long letter was read from Judge Albion W. Tourgee, editor of Bystander's Notes in the Chicago Inter Ocean, and a great friend of the colored people. . . . He says the separate car law is a great insult to the colored citizens of the United States, and advises that . . ."

398 **take up that dime collection:** Freeman's efforts in Kansas helped raise $7.15. The amount is listed in the Citizens' Committee's official account of its activities, the 1897 *Report of Proceedings for the Annulment of Act 111 of 1890 by the Citizens' Committee of New Orleans.* A copy is in the Charles Rousseve papers, Amistad Research Center, box 1, folder 13.

399 **drenched Mayville:** Emma's diary, entries for Aug. 21–25, 1890.

399 **"The Celebrated Novelist":** *Pittsburgh Press*, Apr. 27, 1890.

399 **late-afternoon breaks:** Emma's diary for Aug.–Sept. 1890 has multiple entries that mention Tourgée's fishing. It seems that she was bothered at times by these excursions, and that's why she kept noting them.

399 **stiffly worded letter:** Tourgée to Robert Bonner's Sons, Sept. 11, 1890, document 4930.

399 **repayment of $2,500:** Ezekiel Fleming, after obtaining a judgment against the Tourgées for that amount, had been trying for months to recover it. The debt stemmed from the failure of the *Continent* magazine in 1884.

400 **upheld the order:** Special Judge George R. Butts of Chautauqua County issued the contempt order. Emma's appeal was heard by Judge Loran Lewis, of the Supreme Court in Buffalo. Emma's lawyer, Adelbert Moot, kept her informed of the proceedings by letters, Sept. 1 and 6, 1890, documents 4911 and 4921.

400 **got it wrong:** Headlines from the *Evening Star*, Sept. 6, 1890, and *Inter Ocean*, Sept. 7, 1890.

400 **"such newspaper thrusts":** Adelbert Moot to Emma, Oct. 20, 1890, document 5006.

400 **"the day was lost":** Emma's diary, Sept. 19, 1890.

401 **"cut itself loose":** Tourgée was reacting to a speech by Indiana's Republican representative, Joseph Cheadle, who said: "If the Republican party is ever to gain a foothold" in the South, "it must appeal to the respectable white voters, the ex-Confederates, and the white men of the South who are tired of Bourbon rule." Cheadle later switched parties to run as a Democrat.

402 **"Although of Southern blood":** *Detroit Free Press*, "National Capital Topics," Oct. 15, 1890.

403 **"well disposed toward Judge Brown":** *Chicago Tribune*, "National Capital Notes," Nov. 30, 1890.

404 **"tugging at his coat":** *Washington Post*, "A Surprise to Judge Brown," Dec. 24, 1890.

404 **provoked no opposition:** The Senate Judiciary Committee's nomination file for Brown, at the National Archives, is skimpy. The committee wrote to both Michigan senators, asking their opinion of Brown. They each sent back brief statements, vouching for Brown's upright character and legal acumen. Neither reply exceeded thirty-five words. Record Group 46, Records of the United States Senate, 51st Congress, Judiciary Committee, Senate 51B-A4, number 224, Henry B. Brown nomination, Dec. 23, 1890.

404 **Unanimous approval:** The *Congressional Record, Proceedings and Debates*, Dec. 29, 1890, shows no discussion of Brown's nomination. Vol. 22, Fifty-First Congress, Session II, part 1, pp. 843–863.

405 **"more gratifying to one's ambition":** Brown's "Memoranda," *Memoir*, p. 29.

405 **her sister Isabelle emphasized:** From Isabelle Goodwin's biographical sketch of Brown, "Notes by Mrs. Goodwin," cited earlier.

405 **Alger's specifications:** The description of Alger's private car is based on the original contract,

dated Apr. 9, 1886, in the Pullman Palace Car Company collection at Chicago's Newberry Library, Record Group 02/01/06, box 56.

405 **several friends:** The *Free Press*, Jan. 3, 1891, listed a traveling party of twelve. Alger's private car could not accommodate that many for sleeping, so presumably several had accommodations in the train's regular sleeper.

406 **escorted Bush:** The *Free Press* conducted a lengthy interview with bailiff Richard Bush, published Jan. 8, 1891. That article is the source for Bush's account of Brown's reaction to his nomination. The *Free Press* reporter did not ask Bush about his travel to Washington, or where he sat on the train. The *Free Press* article of Jan. 3, listing the dozen members of Brown's entourage, did not mention Bush.

406 **ears seemed to disappear:** The borrowed robe came from Justice Stephen Field. My account of Brown's swearing-in from the *Free Press*, Jan. 6 and 8, 1891, and *Detroit News*, Jan. 5, 1891.

406 **"a slap in the face":** Desdunes column, "To Be or Not to Be," the *Crusader*, July 4, 1891. Rousseve papers, Amistad Research Center, box 1, folder 8.

407 **the entire "black race":** In his effort to build a movement that spanned the color spectrum, Desdunes named three men as prime candidates for raising the money needed for the test case. One was a prominent black minister, Reverend Alexander S. Jackson, who was clearly not a member of *les gens*. The olive branch to Jackson did not work. He did not like the men who ran the *Crusader*, and he criticized them publicly. See Martinet's letters to Tourgée, Dec. 7 and Dec. 28, 1891, documents 5737 and 5377.

407 ***"guerre à mort"*:** From Desdunes's essay, "Forlorn Hope and Noble Despair," *Crusader*, Aug. 15, 1891, Rousseve papers, box 2, folder 6. The column that brought out Desdunes's ire had run the previous week. It is not part of either the Amistad or Xavier collection, but fortunately, Desdunes quoted from it and provided the headline, "The Cause of the People's Apathy on the Jim Crow Car."

408 **wanted him to know:** Tourgée's letter to John Mitchell Jr., editor of the *Richmond Planet*, Aug. 30, 1891, document 5742, mentions Mitchell's unhappiness with the Bystander column's broad criticism of the colored press.

408 **Martinet took a different tack:** Tourgée, in his Sept. 12, 1891, "Bystander" column, quoted Martinet's comments. If Martinet made those comments in a personal letter to Tourgée, as seems likely, that letter is not among those in the Tourgée papers. The first Martinet letter in the collection, dated Oct. 5, 1891, makes clear that the two men had exchanged previous letters.

410 **From that meeting had emerged:** Keith Medley's book, *We As Freemen*, offers a wealth of information about the eighteen men who met at the *Crusader*, pp. 118–127. Most lived, he wrote, "within walking distance of each other in Faubourg Tremé, Faubourg Marigny, New Marigny, and the French Quarter." They included teachers, businessmen, lawyers, government employees, and writers.

410 **the committee's manifesto:** The text can be found in the committee's 1897 *Report of Proceedings for the Annulment of Act 111*. Tourgée ran excerpts in his Oct. 3, 1891, column.

410 **without taking a fee:** In its 1897 report, the committee thanked Tourgée for services "cheerfully rendered, without compensation." *Report of Proceedings*, p. 9.

411 **"you shall have control":** Martinet to Tourgée, Oct. 5, 1891, document 5760.

411 **needed some tutoring:** Martinet's guidance for Tourgée also from the Oct. 5, 1891, letter.

413 **"the most refined society":** Brown's "Memoranda," *Memoir*, p. 30.

413 **two years to complete:** Details on the Browns' house and its construction from *District of Columbia Building Permits, 1877–1949* at the National Archives, microfilm M1116, reel 168.

Also cited, along with the land deed records, in Sue Kohler and Jeffrey R. Carson's *Sixteenth Street Architecture*, vol. 1, pp. 275–276.

413 **six servants:** From the 1900 census record for Henry and Carry Brown.

414 **His evaluations were generous:** Brown's "Memoranda," *Memoir*, pp. 30–32.

414 **another lengthy tour:** The Browns left for Europe in early July. Passenger records show they returned to New York on Sept. 29, 1891, aboard the SS *Ems*.

414 **"Big Day in Yale's History":** *New York Times*, June 25, 1891.

414 **satire and song:** Details on the Class of '56's Thirty-Fifth Reunion from the class collection, Yale University Library, Manuscripts and Archives.

415 **"A million names":** Bystander, *Inter Ocean*, Nov. 7, 1891.

415 **The workload was staggering:** On Nov. 24, Emma wrote in her diary: "Filled out the last of first series of certificates and added about 40 new names" to the roll. On Dec. 11, "Busy with Association matters all day."

415 **coming exposition:** Tourgée mentioned Lodie's California assignment in an unrelated letter to a company interested in buying some of her work. Document 5901, undated.

416 **this part of the puzzle:** Martinet described his dealings with the railroads in two letters to Tourgée, Dec. 7 and Dec. 28, 1891, documents 5837 and 5877.

417 **served three years:** Details on Walker's life from his Confederate pension records, Louisiana State Archives; from obituaries, *Picayune* and *Times-Democrat*, July 9, 1898; and from the 1880 census.

417 **"a good, upright, conscientious man":** Martinet to Tourgée, also Dec. 7, 1891.

TWENTY: ARREST

419 **memorable winter storm:** Emma's diary, Jan. 3–10, 1892.

419 **His telegram to Emma:** From her diary, Dec. 22, 1891: "Telegram from Albion that he feared he must come home, as he was so ill."

419 **Lodie would go on:** Tourgée, undated letter, document 5901.

420 **Walker had flagged:** My account of the initial exchange between Walker and Tourgée is drawn from these letters: Walker to Tourgée, Jan. 2 and Jan. 9, 1892, documents 5915 and 5938; Tourgée to Walker, undated but almost certainly Jan. 14, 1892, document 6502. (Walker mentioned Tourgée's reply "of the 14th" in his next letter, Jan. 21, document 5969.)

422 **saw this case in its own light:** Historians of the *Plessy* case, particularly constitutional scholars, have written at length about how Tourgée and his team chose to construct their case. Several have said it was a mistake not to raise questions more sharply about the supposed equality of the separate cars. Previous lawsuits had done that, without much success.

423 **five hundred Republican delegates:** Details of the state convention from the *Picayune* and the *Times-Democrat*, Jan. 20, 1892, and several Martinet letters to Tourgée, particularly Feb. 3, 1892, document 6007, and July–Aug. 1892, document 6377.

423 **registered colored voters:** The *Times-Democrat*'s Jan. 18, 1892, editorial, quoting a Louisiana secretary of state report, said there were "126,884 whites and 127,923 colored voters at the last election, a colored majority of 1039." That did not mean registered colored voters had gone to the polls in greater numbers. Republicans alleged that intimidation, or the threat of it, had deterred some from voting.

426 **their own interpretations:** For the newspaper accounts of Daniel Desdunes's arrest, see the *States*, Feb. 24, 1892, and the *Picayune* and *Times-Democrat*, both Feb. 25, 1892.

426 **"make no clamor":** Tourgée to Walker, Mar. 1, 1892, document 6073; **"avoid sensational discussions,"** Walker to Tourgée, Feb. 25, 1892, document 6058.

427 **"in the traces":** Tourgée to Walker, Jan. 14, document 6502, cited earlier.

427 **"virtual defeat":** Tourgée to Walker, also from the Mar. 1, 1892, letter.

427 **"sacrifice every conviction":** Walker to Tourgée, Mar. 6, 1892, document 6086.

427 **"a presumption of common sense":** Tourgée to Walker, Mar. 11, 1892, one of two letters catalogued as document 6101.

428 **dry sense of humor:** Walker to Tourgée, Mar. 14, 1892, document 6109.

428 **"I like it":** Tourgée to Walker, Mar. 12, 1892, document 6104.

428 **Let's deny that Desdunes:** Tourgée to Walker, undated, document 6101, but from its contents, clearly written between Mar. 16 and 21, 1892.

429 **"submit gracefully":** Walker to Tourgée, Mar. 18, 1892, document 6125.

429 **last sighting:** "Judge Marr Missing," the *Picayune*; "Still Missing," the *Times-Democrat*, both Apr. 21, 1892.

430 **The Pullman ruling's effect:** The case is *State ex. rel. Abbott v. Hicks*, 44 La. Ann. 770 (1892).

430 **a second dispatch:** Martinet's telegrams to Tourgée, May 26 and June 1, 1892, documents 6271 and 6302.

430 **He had speeches:** *Inter Ocean*, June 4, 1892, and *St. Paul Daily Globe*, June 6, 1892.

430 **"better and grander things":** From a Bystander dispatch at the convention, *Inter Ocean*, June 11, 1892.

430 **twenty-five thousand copies:** "Is Liberty Worth Preserving?" is reprinted in *Undaunted Radical: The Selected Writings and Speeches of Albion W. Tourgée*. Details on the pamphlet's printing and distribution at the convention from *Undaunted Radical*, p. 14 and p. 252.

431 **proud to say:** Tourgée mentioned the 100,000 figure in his Bystander column, June 4, 1892, on the eve of the convention. Keeping pace with the NCRA's growth, he wrote, required "the attention of one, two, three members of his family. Even the servants were utilized, and finally he was compelled to employ a young lady as clerk." For a thorough discussion of the NCRA's rise and subsequent decline, see Karcher's *Refugee from His Race*, pp. 159–195. Elliott offers a less detailed but still insightful look in *Color-Blind Justice*, pp. 253–259, 273–277.

431 **"Agree with Walker":** Tourgée telegram to Martinet, undated, but likely June 1 or 2, 1892, document 6363.

431 **stepped to the ticket window:** I have based my account of Plessy's arrest on the Citizens' Committee's *Report of Proceedings*, as well as court records and newspaper accounts.

432 **two different committees:** *Times-Democrat*, Jan. 7, 1887, and the *Weekly Pelican*, Sept. 3, 1887.

432 **hired a private detective:** The Citizens' Committee's *Report of Proceedings*, issued nearly five years after Plessy's arrest, was the group's first public mention of the arranged nature of the *Desdunes* and *Plessy* cases. The report's account was vague enough to be overlooked. It said the committee "had officers on hand to effect the arrests, and thus have the proper charges made," which prevented "any friction with unauthorized parties; this will explain the item '*Private detectives and incidental expenses*' in the column of expenditures."

432 **all the newspaper accounts:** *Picayune* and *Times-Democrat*, both June 9, 1892. The *Crusader* account, likely June 11, 1892, is part of the Desdunes collection at Xavier University, folder 1/12, marked "June-July 1892." Excerpts from all three appear in Medley's *We As Freeman*, pp. 145–146.

433 **first week on the bench:** Appointed for the four years remaining in Marr's term, Ferguson was sworn in on July 6, 1892. *Picayune* and *Times-Democrat*, July 1 and 7, 1892.

433 ***State v. Desdunes*:** The original case file, No. 18685, is part of the Criminal Court's historical records at the New Orleans Public Library. The University of New Orleans Library has a photocopied set. I'm indebted to Greg Osborn at the Public Library, and Connie Phelps at the UNO Library, for their help in making it possible for me to locate and see the complete record.

434 **"Jim Crow Is Dead":** The *Crusader,* almost certainly July 16, 1892, Desdunes collection, folder 1/9. The folder is marked "May 28, 1892," clearly an error.

435 **twenty-eight pages:** Martinet to Tourgée, July–August 1892, document 6377. This section, and the next, is based largely on this extraordinary letter.

435 **"the Hon. Fred Douglass":** Newspapers frequently used the shorthand "Fred. Douglass," and his collection of papers at the Library of Congress shows that letter writers often adopted that form, perhaps not realizing that its informality irritated Douglass.

437 **"the silly negroes":** *Times-Democrat,* Nov. 19, 1892.

437 **"the colored people are not alone":** The date of Rodolphe Desdunes's blistering reply to the *Times-Democrat's* Nov. 19 editorial isn't known for certain. It probably ran Nov. 26, 1892, a Saturday, which was the *Crusader's* publication day. The Xavier University Library has the clipping incorrectly filed in folder 1/15, marked "vol. 4, 42, ca Oct 1894." When the library acquired the collection years ago, many clippings were loose, and the archivists sometimes had to make their best guess. I am grateful to the Archives and Special Collection staff, particularly Irwin Lachoff and Eric Joseph, for helping me as I read through the many clippings.

438 **The Citizens' Committee liked:** In its 1897 report, the committee emphasized that it had not wanted "to impose any hardship" on Desdunes or Plessy for their services, arranging to post bond for each, limiting their time in jail.

438 **a quickly prepared writ:** The initial *Plessy* case, no. 19317 in the Criminal Court for the Parish of Orleans, went to the Louisiana Supreme Court as *Ex parte Homer A. Plessy,* case no. 11134, when Walker applied for the writ of prohibition. The *Ex parte* file can be found in Supreme Court of Louisiana's Historical Archives, at the University of New Orleans, collection 106. Much of the record has been digitized, and can be accessed online through the Louisiana Digital Library website, louisianadigitallibrary.org.

438 **"my friend":** Walker to Tourgée, Oct. 4, 1893, document 7379, and Oct. 23, 1893, document 7428.

438 **a Massachusetts native:** Ferguson was born on Martha's Vineyard in 1838, and studied law in Boston before leaving for New Orleans in 1865. For more on his background, see *We As Freeman,* pp. 37–52.

439 **His only question:** It's important to remember, in reading Ferguson's ruling, that he was not doing a full constitutional review. He was deciding whether the prosecution had the legal authority to bring the charges to trial. He did make one observation about the Fourteenth Amendment, saying that the Separate Car Act did not violate the equal protection clause because the act's provisions applied equally to both races.

439 **unanimous approval:** The Louisiana Supreme Court's ruling is *Ex parte Homer A. Plessy,* 45 La. Ann 80 (1892).

440 **Other states had legal definitions:** Before the Civil War, in the 1856 case *State v. Harrison,* the Louisiana Supreme Court had drawn a sharp distinction between *les gens de couleur* (free) and "negroes" (those in slavery). But neither that ruling, nor earlier ones, defined "the colored race." For more on Louisiana's racial classifications, see Kenneth Aslakson's fascinating 2014 book, *Making Race in the Courtroom: The Legal Construction of Three Races in Early New Orleans.*

TWENTY-ONE: "YOU ARE FIGHTING A GREAT BATTLE"

443 **deep in Brown's bones:** Brown described his close friendship with Jackson in "Memoranda," *Memoir,* pp. 27–29.

443 **vocal in their opposition:** Washington *Evening Star,* Feb. 1, 1893, "The Judge Jackson Petition."

444 **"not a Bourbon Democrat":** *Inter Ocean*, Jan. 30, 1893.

444 **ten or so official visitors:** *Evening Star*, Feb. 1, 1893.

445 **"cold, calculating economist":** "Bystander," *Inter Ocean*, Feb. 11, 1893.

446 **number 15248:** Later, when the case reached the hearing stage, it would be given a another number, representing its place on that term's schedule. But the clerk's office kept track of the case's progress under the original number, and that is how the file is catalogued at the National Archives: Record Group 267, U.S. Supreme Court, appellate case files, box 2555, number 15248.

447 **fought on the same side:** Tourgée and Phillips had a longstanding correspondence, dating back to 1869. Two dozen of those letters are part of the Tourgée collection.

447 **"do what you think best":** Martinet to Tourgée, Feb. 2, 1893, document 6547.

447 **"If we can secure":** Phillips to Tourgée, May 1, 1893, the second of two items identified as document 6921.

448 **"it suffocates me":** This section, and the next, is based on Martinet's letter to Tourgée, May 30, 1893, document 6998. Like his lengthy letter from the previous summer, it is a remarkably personal exploration of Martinet's feelings about racial matters at that time.

448 **such little attention:** Ida Wells, the crusading black journalist, felt so strongly about this issue that she and others produced a pamphlet, "The Reason Why the Colored American Is Not at the World's Columbian Exposition." Frederick Douglass wrote the introduction. Wells sent a copy to Tourgée with the inscription, "To Judge A. W. Tourgee, whose suggestion it was that originated the preparation of this volume, 20,000 of which were distributed at the World's Fair." Document 7608.

449 **"his want of energy":** In his May 30, 1893, letter, Martinet made several unflattering generalizations about "the Negro race." As an advocate, he identified with all people of color. But like many mixed-race Creoles in New Orleans, he seemed to think of himself as neither "Negro" nor white, but as part of a third group.

450 **"My full share":** Harlan to his former law partner in Louisville, Augustus Willson, Dec. 24, 1891, University of Louisville collection, box 5, folder 23, 1890-1891 correspondence, microfilm reel 11.

451 **"something of the Old World":** *Some Memories*, pp. 126–150.

451 **Dissents were rare:** My analysis of Supreme Court outcomes and workload during the first two years of Brown's tenure, including the number of dissents and which justices participated, was aided by the invaluable online resource, the Supreme Court Database, mentioned in a chap. 14 endnote.

452 **"the one and only cloud":** Harlan to Willson, July 2, 1892. The Harlan-Willson correspondence, from 1877 to 1894, contains multiple references to Harlan's brother and his alcoholism. University of Louisville collection, microfilm reels 8, 10, and 11. Toward the end of James Harlan's life, the local newspapers reported on his failing condition. From the *Courier-Journal*, Dec. 1, 1894: "He Will Go to the Almshouse; Judge James Harlan Does This As a Last Effort to Break Himself of Drinking."

452 **"My friend, Judge Ferguson":** Walker to Tourgée, Oct. 4, 1893, document 7379.

453 **"not prepared to undergo":** Walker to Tourgée, Oct. 23, 1893, document 7428.

453 **"some very serious thoughts":** Tourgée to Martinet, Oct. 31, 1893, document 7438. In addition to laying out reservations about the case, Tourgée's letter dealt with his reasons for wanting to start a national newspaper devoted to civil rights, and how he planned to get it off the ground. The letter is reprinted on p. 78 of Otto Olsen's 1967 compilation of important documents in the *Plessy* case, titled *A Thin Disguise*.

454 **"the foe of liberty":** Also from Tourgée's letter to Martinet, Oct. 31, 1893.

455 **"nothing but disaster":** Emma's diary, Aug. 31, 1893.

455 **"the broadest kind of latitude":** Nixon to Tourgée, July 12, 1893, document 7120.

456 **"Kindly inform me":** Walker to James McKenney, Supreme Court chief clerk, Jan. 18, 1894, and McKenney's reply, Jan. 20, 1894, both in the *Plessy* file at the National Archives.

457 **"much to my gratification":** Emma's diary, Apr. 5 and 7, 1894.

457 **the society columns:** *Evening Star,* Jan. 6 and 25, and Feb. 2, 1894, and *Post,* Jan. 13, 1894.

458 **"never dared to calculate":** Brown to Charles Kent, Aug. 2, 1901, reprinted in *Memoir,* pp. 90–91. In this same letter, Brown referred to his wife's "long invalidism," without giving any specifics on the nature of her illness.

458 **the SS *Trave*:** Passenger manifest, National Archives, microfilm M237, frame 631.

458 **last glimpse:** Details on Douglass's funeral from the *Evening Star, Washington Post, Chicago Tribune, Inter Ocean, New York Times,* and *New York Tribune,* Feb. 25–26, 1895.

459 **memorial services:** Held primarily in churches and political venues, the services took place in a variety of towns and cities, many with a significant population of African Americans. A partial list from newspaper reports: Chicago, Atlanta, Boston, Kansas City, Brooklyn, Detroit, Nashville, Pittsburgh, St. Louis, San Francisco, Springfield, MO, Wichita, KS, Jackson, MS, Rochester, NY, Butte, MT, Newport, RI, and Montgomery, AL.

459 **the conference's final declaration:** From the monthly magazine *Lend a Hand,* Apr. 1895, vol. 14, pp. 247–248.

460 **"manly courage and resistance":** Martinet to Tourgée, May 30, 1893, document 6998.

460 **certain to produce headlines:** The *Chicago Tribune* published excerpts of Brown's speech under the headline "Perils in Our Path," while the *New York Tribune* opted for "Perils of the Republic," both June 25, 1895. A more complete text appeared in the *Albany Law Journal,* July 13, 1895, pp. 18–21.

462 **He evoked history:** Quotations from Washington's speech as published in *The Booker T. Washington Papers,* vol. 3, 1889–1895, pp. 578–587.

463 **saluted the speech:** Quotes in this paragraph from the Ashville *Daily Citizen,* Sept. 20, 1895; *Birmingham News,* reprinted in the *Nashville Daily American,* Sept. 22, 1895; and *New Orleans Times-Democrat,* Sept. 23, 1895.

TWENTY-TWO: "IN THE NATURE OF THINGS"

465 **"Don't you think":** Martinet to Tourgée, Mar. 4, 1896, document 9014.

465 **"on its last legs":** Martinet to Tourgée, also Mar. 4, 1896.

466 **delay was their desire:** Martinet telegram to Tourgée, Jan. 29, 1896: "Think best let Plessy case go next session." Document 8953.

466 **"the very edge of the term":** Phillips to Tourgée, Jan. 20, 1896, document 8936.

466 **"unready writer":** Phillips to Tourgée, Feb. 4, 1896, document 8969.

466 **"a Court somewhat adverse":** Phillips to Tourgée, also Jan. 20, 1896.

466 **"warm personal friend":** The day after Peckham's nomination, dozens of newspapers carried a dispatch with this phrase. The *Philadelphia Inquirer* and the *Baltimore Sun,* among many others, Dec. 4, 1895.

467 **most powerful tycoons:** Those included Cornelius Vanderbilt, J. Pierpont Morgan, Jay Gould, and William Rockefeller. See Melvin Urofsky's *The Supreme Court Justices: A Biographical Dictionary,* pp. 351–352.

467 **Might Peckham be persuaded:** While Tourgée's letters make clear that he was thinking about the justices and their background, he did not pose this specific question about Peckham. It

seems to me a logical one, though, based on Tourgée's awareness that some justices might find certain arguments more appealing than others.

467 **nearly eighty pages:** The full "Brief of Plaintiff in Error" is part of the *Plessy* case file at the National Archives. My narrative in this section, and the next two, is based on the brief.

472 **this dramatic turn of events:** Phillips to Tourgée, Apr. 1, 1896, document 9071.

473 **"you were annoyed":** Phillips to Tourgée, also Apr. 1, 1896.

473 **"Albion relieved":** Emma's diary, Apr. 3, 1896, document 9906.

473 **McKenney replied to Tourgée's fiery letter:** The Tourgée-McKenney exchange is part of the *Plessy* file at the National Archives, folder 2. The public file contains photocopies of their letters; the originals have been placed in the archives vault. The final two pages of Tourgée's April 3 letter, however, aren't visible on the photocopies. My thanks to archivist Jane Fitzgerald for allowing me to see the originals, which are faded but readable.

474 **"not the faintest hope":** Walker to Tourgée, Apr. 9, 1896, document 9091.

475 **critically ill with consumption:** Widely reported in newspapers. See the *St. Joseph* (MO) *Weekly Gazette,* Jan. 4, 1896, and *Kansas City Gazette*, Mar. 23, 1896. Also, Brewer's letter to Chief Justice Melville Fuller, Dec. 8, 1895, Fuller papers, box 3, Library of Congress.

475 **slipping away:** Brewer's letters to his daughter Etta in San Antonio, Feb. 3 and 8, 1896, Brewer papers, Yale University Library, Manuscripts and Archives Division, MS99, folder 51.

475 **Brewer had joined in:** My analysis is drawn from the *Minutes and Dockets of the Supreme Court*, National Archives, microfilm M215, roll 20.

475 **"Capitol Chat" column:** *Washington Post,* Apr. 14, 1896.

476 **nearly fifty typewritten pages:** Tourgée's notes for the oral argument, document 6472.

476 **Tourgée's presentation:** The Supreme Court's minutes for April 13, 1896, say that Tourgée and Phillips spoke for Plessy, and Alexander Porter Morse argued for the State of Louisiana. Like Phillips, Morse was a Washington lawyer, hired to serve as the Louisiana attorney general's local counsel.

476 **skeptical questioning:** New Orleans *Times-Democrat*, Apr. 14, 1896. The *Picayune's* one-paragraph account appeared the same day.

476 **its primary defense:** Defendant in Error's Brief, Transcript of Record, *Plessy v. Ferguson*, p. 3.

477 **"Indeed, as you might guess":** Phillips to Tourgée, Apr. 28, 1896, document 9130.

477 **grieving with his family:** *Austin Weekly Statesman*, May 14, 1896; *Leavenworth Times*, May 16, 1896; *Wichita Daily Eagle*, May 20, 1896; Washington *Evening Star*, May 21, 1896.

477 **talk that he had avoided:** See J. Gordon Hylton's Fall 1991 article in the *Mississippi Law Journal*, "The Justice Who Abstained in *Plessy v. Ferguson*." I saw no evidence to support or refute that thesis. (Hylton wrote that Brewer missed the oral arguments on Apr. 13, 1896, so he could attend his daughter's funeral. That's incorrect. She died nearly a month later, on May 11.)

477 **Fuller's assignment:** Historians have speculated about why Brown might have been assigned the *Plessy* case, without much concrete evidence. I reviewed Fuller's papers at the Library of Congress, which includes a smattering of correspondence with all the justices. There's no mention of *Plessy*, and nothing that sheds light on why Brown ended up with the assignment. One historian's account suggested that Fuller saw Brown as a malleable tool, but that seems unlikely. In various exchanges with Fuller over the years, Brown displayed a streak of independence and earnest diligence. See Fuller papers, box 3, folder marked "Brown, Henry B."

478 **Brown's handiwork:** The case citation is *Plessy v. Ferguson*, 163 U.S. 537 (1896).

479 **the amendment's creation:** For an evocative narrative history of the Fourteenth Amendment's origins and enactment, see Garrett Epps's 2006 book, *Democracy Reborn: The Fourteenth Amendment and the Fight for Equal Rights in Post–Civil War America.*

480 **famous Boston schools case:** *Roberts v. City of Boston,* 5 Cush. 19.

483 **"but not with ignominy":** From "Statement of the Citizens' Committee," in the 1897 *Report of Proceedings of the Citizens' Committee.*

485 **now he worried:** In the spring of 1889, during an exchange of letters with Dean Henry Rogers of the University of Michigan Law School about a possible commencement speech, Harlan suggested immigration as a topic. On Apr. 25, Harlan wrote: "What would you think of a subject that would enable me to speak of the damage to our institutions arising from excessive immigration to this country?" Harlan's schedule prevented him from speaking that year. He spoke at the next commencement on "National Rights and States' Rights." Henry Rogers papers, correspondence files, Bentley Historical Library, University of Michigan.

487 **"Race questions":** This editorial appeared in several newspapers, including the *Wilkes Barre Leader,* May 24, 1896, and the *Des Moines Register,* May 26, 1896. It did not identify the originating newspaper.

487 **minimized its scope:** The Rochester *Union and Advertiser,* "State Sovereignty," May 19, 1896, and the *New York Journal,* "According to the Custom," May 20, 1896, both cited in Olsen's *A Thin Disguise*, pp. 125–128.

487 **"justices are human":** From the *New York Mail and Express,* quoted in the New Orleans *Times-Democrat*, under the headline "The Jim Crow Car Law," May 23, 1896.

487 **"evil days":** *Richmond Planet,* May 23, 1896.

EPILOGUE

489 **little rented house:** From the 1900 census, New Orleans, Enumeration District 69, Sheet 20A, Seventh Ward.

490 **a paper trail:** Plessy family information from the 1910 Census, Enumeration District 98, Sheet 2A, Sixth Ward, and the 1920 Census, Enumeration District 103, sheet 8A, Sixth Ward.

490 **Plessy changed his plea:** From "Statement of the Citizens' Committee," *Report of Proceedings of the Citizens' Committee.*

490 **"dead or indifferent":** Quoted from *Our People and Our History,* a 1973 edition of Rodolphe Desdunes's 1911 book, translated from the French, p. 147. Originally titled *Nos Hommes et Notre Historie.*

490 **"I merely want to die":** Tourgée to Emma, Nov. 17, 1896, document 9172.

491 **lobbied on his behalf:** For Tourgée's efforts to secure a diplomatic post, see Karcher, *Refugee from His Race*, pp. 295–298.

491 **"sincere congratulations":** Martinet telegram, May 12, 1897, document 9383.

491 **"a decided victory":** New Orleans *Times-Democrat,* July 9, 1898.

491 **sorry, very sorry:** Theodore Roosevelt to Attorney General Philander C. Knox, Nov. 29, 1902, Theodore Roosevelt papers, Library of Congress.

491 **"boeuf a la Cheron":** From Washington and New York newspaper reports on the celebration, Dec. 10, 1902. Additional details from *Some Memories*, pp. 167–172.

492 **bantering letter:** Harlan to Melville Fuller, Aug. 24, 1896, Fuller papers, box 5, folder for John Harlan.

493 **"his duty as a citizen":** Roosevelt's speech, as quoted in the *Evening Star,* Dec. 10, 1902.

494 **linger long after:** Harlan's speech was selected for *Kentucky Eloquence: Past and* Present, a 1907 anthology of "orations, after-dinner speeches, popular and classic lectures."

494 **"No Hope of Recovery":** *Detroit Free Press,* Dec. 5, 1903.

494 **"I am taking encouragement":** Brown to Kent, Dec. 7, 1903, in *Memoir,* pp. 93–94.

495 **consoled himself:** In his Aug. 2, 1901, letter to Kent, Brown wrote that Carry's doctors had

advised him to take her abroad. "I can now see that was a great mistake, though I doubt whether it shortened her life materially, as her disease was such as must ultimately and inevitably result in her death; and her long invalidism rendered it less a surprise and a shock that it would have been had she been taken away in perfect health." *Memoir*, pp. 90–91. As in other instances, Brown gave no specifics on the nature of Carry's "disease."

495 **"simply broken hearted":** Brown to Fuller, Aug. 27, 1901, Fuller papers, box 3, folder for Henry B. Brown.

495 **"my full share of the work":** Brown to Fuller, Dec. 8, 1903, Fuller papers, Brown folder.

495 **the treatment had helped:** Brown's primary doctor was William H. Wilmer, a pioneering eye specialist at Johns Hopkins Hospital in Baltimore.

495 **"Regains His Sight":** Other details about Brown's treatment and recovery from the *Chicago Tribune*, Jan. 29, 1904, and *Detroit Free Press*, Jan. 31, 1904.

496 **"so hard a case":** Brown to Fuller, Feb. 6, 1904, Fuller papers, Brown folder.

496 **A "runaway match":** Brown's remarriage prompted widespread newspaper coverage for several days, including prominent accounts in the *New York Tribune*, *Chicago Tribune*, *Philadelphia Inquirer*, *New York Times*, and Washington *Evening Star*, June 26–27, 1904.

496 **"the same qualities":** *Pittsburg Post*, June 26, 1904, "Jurist, at 68, Weds."

496 **shipping delay:** *Altoona Tribune*, Nov. 17, 1905. Emma complained to the American Express Company, and the company's Paris manager politely suggested the arrangements had been too tightly scheduled, leaving no margin for error. W. S. Dalliba, American Express, to Emma, Nov. 27, 1905, document 9858.

496 **new ailments:** Documents in Tourgée's pension records at the National Archives state that he was being treated for diabetes mellitus in the months before his death.

497 **keep his voice alive:** In late 1896, Tourgée resumed his Bystander column. After a little more than a year in France, the column ceased, this time for good.

497 **one hundred scrapbook pages:** Document 9907, the Tourgée papers.

498 **"Private and Confidential":** The quoted Niagara Movement documents are part of the W. E. B. Du Bois papers at the Du Bois Library, the University of Massachusetts, Amherst. A digital set is available online on the library's website.

498 **"strong and uncompromising friend":** The Illinois division of the Niagara Movement had the tribute printed, and sent a copy to Emma, document 9838, "In Memoriam, Tribute of Respect by Colored Citizens of Chicago to the Memory of Judge Albion W. Tourgee."

498 **"with clarion voice":** Ida Wells to Tourgée, Feb. 22, 1893, document 6645.

498 **"African-American leaders":** Harry C. Smith to Emma, Nov. 8, 1905, document 9828.

498 **collaborated with Tourgée:** For Tourgée's role in drafting and lobbying for Ohio's anti-lynching law, see *Color-Blind Justice*, pp. 237–238, and *Refugee from His Race*, pp. 246–250.

498 **Washington was not there:** Several newspaper accounts said that Washington "was expected" at the service. See the *Altoona Tribune*, Nov. 17, 1905, and *New York Age*, Nov. 23, 1905. Washington's telegram quoted in *Carpetbagger's Crusade*, p. 350.

499 **"I will not equivocate":** Draft of the "Garrison Pledge of the Niagara Movement," in Du Bois's handwriting, Du Bois papers, University of Massachusetts, Amherst.

499 **"Emancipators of Their Race":** *Washington Post*, Dec. 1, 1905.

499 **"sacrificed nothing of consequence":** "Bystander," *Inter Ocean*, Sept. 12, 1891.

499 **"comparative poverty":** House Committee on Invalid Pensions, Fifty-Ninth Congress, First Session, report no. 5801.

500 **"loses all its terrors":** Brown to Kent, Mar. 22, 1912, in *Memoir*, pp. 114–117.

500 **leather-bound volume:** Part of the Brown papers, Detroit Public Library.

500 **his opposition to women's suffrage:** In January 1913, after Michigan voters rejected a state

constitutional amendment that would have given women the right to vote in state elections, Brown cheered the result in a Jan. 4 letter to Kent, reprinted in *Memoir*, pp. 124–125. For a powerful account of the women's suffrage movement, built around the last state's ratification of the Nineteenth Amendment in 1920, see Elaine Weiss's 2018 book, *The Woman's Hour: The Great Fight to Win the Vote.*

500 **"these little outings":** Brown to Kent, Oct. 30, 1910, *Memoir*, pp. 106–107.

501 **The country was entitled:** Brown's "Memoranda," *Memoir*, p. 32.

501 **"lost their minds":** Brown to Kent, Feb. 20, 1908, *Memoir*, pp. 94–95.

501 **"I might easily rust out":** Brown to Kent, also Oct. 30, 1910, *Memoir*, pp. 108–109.

501 **"I was born":** "Memoranda," *Memoir*, p. 1.

502 **telegrams flooded into:** Taft and Roosevelt telegrams quoted in the *Washington Post*, Oct. 15, 1911.

502 **"Renowned as a Dissenter":** *Louisville Courier-Journal*, Oct. 15, 1911.

504 **"more befitting" for others:** Brown to Kent, Aug. 10, 1908, *Memoir*, p. 99.

505 **"Justice Harlan Concurring":** *New York Times*, May 23, 1954.

505 **a misidentification:** At some online sites, warnings have been posted about the mix-up with Pinchback, but it hasn't stopped the proliferation of the misidentification. No photograph or other likeness of Homer Plessy appears to have survived, or at least none has been found.

SOURCES

Writers of narrative history need a puzzle solver's patience and a detective's doggedness. We also need luck. In my six years of work on *Separate*, I was constantly amazed by the richness of the records that have been preserved, even as I mourned the inevitable gaps. Mirroring the narrative structure, I have grouped many of the sources by geography and the principal figures.

ARCHIVAL AND MANUSCRIPT COLLECTIONS

Adams family papers: Charles Francis Adams's diary and letter books, 1839–1843, from *Microfilms of the Adams Papers*, viewed at the Eisenhower Library, the Johns Hopkins University.

Amistad Research Center (based at Tulane University in New Orleans): Papers of Charles Rousseve, including clippings from the *New Orleans Crusader* and documents related to the Citizens' Committee that challenged the constitutionality of the Separate Car Act.

Archives of Michigan: Michigan Supreme Court case files for *Day v. Owen* (1858); Wayne County probate records.

Bentley Historical Library at the University of Michigan: Papers of Thomas Cooley; Henry H. Crapo; Bela Hubbard; Henry Wade Rogers.

Chautauqua County Historical Society (Westfield, New York): Papers of Albion W. Tourgée.

Detroit Public Library, Burton Historical Collection: Papers of Henry Billings Brown; James McMillan.

Diocese of Lafayette, Louisiana: Martinet family records.

Kentucky State Archives: Franklin County civil lawsuits and estate records; governor's records; legislative records; militia records; Court of Appeals case files.

Library of Congress: Papers of Benjamin Bristow; Frederick Douglass; Melville Fuller; James A. Garfield; John Marshall Harlan; Benjamin Harrison; Abraham Lincoln; Morrison Waite.

Maine Historical Society: Papers of George F. Shepley.

Marshall (Michigan) Public Library: Probate records; collection on the Crosswhite case.

Massachusetts State Archives: Legislative collection, including petitions from abolitionists in the 1840s.

National Archives, Washington, DC: Supreme Court appellate case files, *Plessy v. Ferguson*, number 15248; *Minutes and Dockets of the Supreme Court*; Senate Judiciary Committee records for the Supreme Court nominations of John Marshall Harlan and Henry Billings Brown; *Passport*

Applications, 1795–1925; *Passenger Lists of Vessels Arriving New York, 1820–1897*; records of the Civil War era, including those from the Adjutant General's Office, the Freedmen's Bureau, the Provost Marshal General, Office of the Judge Advocate General, as well as the Compiled Military Service Records for individual soldiers.

National Archives II, College Park, Maryland: Files of the Interstate Commerce Commission, 1887–1889.

National Archives, Atlanta: Case files for the U.S. Circuit Court, Western District of Tennessee, records for *Robinson v. Memphis and Charleston Railroad.*

National Archives, Chicago: Records of the Civil War era for the Michigan regiments, including those from the Adjutant General's office and the Provost Marshal General.

New Orleans Archdiocese: Baptism, marriage and death records, Plessy family.

New Orleans Public Library: Property records; criminal case files; mayoral records; maps.

New-York Historical Society: Papers of Thomas J. Durant, including records of the Union Association of New Orleans.

Newberry Library, Chicago: Pullman Palace Car Company records.

St. Martin Parish (Louisiana) Courthouse: Martinet family records.

University of Louisville Law Library: Papers of John Marshall Harlan.

University of New Orleans Library: Files on the *Plessy* and *Desdunes* court cases.

Willard Library (Evansville, Indiana): Collection on the Shanklin and Harlan families.

Xavier University of Louisiana, New Orleans: Desdunes family papers.

Yale University, Sterling Memorial Library: Records of Henry Billings Brown, David Brewer, and the class of 1856.

NEWSPAPERS

Illinois: *Chicago Inter Ocean; Chicago Tribune*

Kentucky: *Covington Journal*; *Cynthiana News*; *Frankfort Commonwealth*; *Georgetown Herald*; *Kentucky Tribune* (Danville); *Kentucky Yeoman* (Frankfort); *Lexington Observer and Recorder*; *Louisville Commercial*; *Louisville Courier*; *Louisville Courier-Journal*; *Louisville Democrat*; *Louisville Journal*

Louisiana: *Baton Rouge Daily Gazette*; *Black Republican* (New Orleans); *Daily Delta* (New Orleans); *Daily Louisianian*; *L'Abeille de la Nouvelle-Orléans*; *Louisanne Courier* (New Orleans); *L'Union* (New Orleans); *New Orleans Bee*; *New Orleans Crescent*; *New Orleans Crusader*; *New Orleans Picayune*; *New Orleans Republican*; *New Orleans Times*; *New Orleans Tribune*; *Sunday Delta* (New Orleans); *True Delta* (New Orleans)

Massachusetts: *Boston Courier*; *Boston Daily Atlas*; *Boston Evening Transcript*; *Lynn Record*; *Hampshire Gazette*; *Newburyport Herald*; *Salem Gazette*

Michigan: *Detroit Free Press*; *Detroit News*; *Detroit Plaindealer; Detroit Advertiser and Tribune*; *Marshall Daily Chronicle; Marshall Statesman*

New York: *Albany Journal*; *Frank Leslie's Illustrated Weekly*; *Harper's Weekly*; *New York Age*; *New York Herald*; *New York Times*; *New York Tribune*; *North Star; Rochester Union and Advertiser*

Ohio: *Anti-Slavery Bugle* (New Lisbon); *Ashtabula Sentinel*; *Ashtabula Telegraph*; *Cincinnati Commercial*; *Cincinnati Daily Enquirer*; *Cincinnati Daily Gazette*; *Cleveland Evening Leader*; *Cleveland Gazette*; *Western Reserve Chronicle*

Washington: *Congressional Globe* (record of congressional debates, 1833–1873); *Washington Post; Evening Star*

SELECTED BOOKS AND ARTICLES

General

American Annual Cyclopedia and Register of Important Events. New York: D. Appleton, 1863, 1864.

Barnes, Catherine A. *Journey from Jim Crow: The Desegregation of Southern Transit*. New York: Columbia University Press, 1983.

Blackett, R. J. M. *Beating against the Barriers: Biographical Essays in Nineteenth-Century Afro-American History*. Baton Rouge: Louisiana State University Press, 1986.

Blaine, James Gillespie. *Twenty years of Congress, from Lincoln to Garfield: with a review of the events which led to the political revolution of 1860*. Norwich, CT: 1884–1886. Vol. 2.

Catterall, Helen T. *Judicial Cases Concerning American Slavery and the Negro*. Washington: Carnegie Institution of Washington, 1932. Vol. 3.

Cox, LaWanda C. F. *Lincoln and Black Freedom: A Study in Presidential Leadership*. Columbia: University of South Carolina Press, 1981.

Cox, Samuel Sullivan. *Union—disunion—reunion: three decades of federal legislation, 1855 to 1885. Personal and historical memories of events preceding, during and since the American Civil War*. Providence: J. A. and R. A. Reid, 1888.

Crapo, Henry H. *The Story of Henry Howland Crapo, 1804–1869*. Boston: Thomas Todd Company, 1933.

Cutler, Carl C. *Queens of the Western Ocean: The Story of America's Mail and Passenger Sailing Lines*. Annapolis, MD: U.S. Naval Institute, 1961.

Douglass, Frederick. *Life and Times of Frederick Douglass: His Early Life As a Slave, His Escape From Bondage, and His Complete History* (1892). New York: Collier Books, 1962.

Douglass, Frederick. *Narrative of the Life of Frederick Douglass: an American Slave* (1845). Cambridge, MA: Belknap Press, 1960.

Douglass, Frederick, John W. Blassingame, and John R. McKivigan. *The Frederick Douglass Papers: Series One: Speeches, Debates, and Interviews*. New Haven, CT: Yale University Press, 1979.

Douglass, Frederick, James McCune Smith, and Gerrit Smith. *My Bondage and My Freedom* (1855). New York: Dover Publications, 1969.

Dray, Philip. *Capitol Men: The Epic Story of Reconstruction Through the Lives of the First Black Congressmen*. Boston: Houghton Mifflin, 2008.

Ely, James W. *The Chief Justiceship of Melville W. Fuller, 1888–1910*. Columbia: University of South Carolina Press, 1995.

Epps, Garrett. *Democracy Reborn: The Fourteenth Amendment and the Fight for Equal Rights in Post-Civil War America*. New York: Henry Holt, 2006.

Foner, Eric. *Reconstruction: America's Unfinished Revolution, 1863–1877*. New York: Harper & Row, 1988.

Goldstone, Lawrence. *Inherently Unequal: The Betrayal of Equal Rights by the Supreme Court, 1865–1903*. New York: Walker & Company, 2011.

Hagedorn, Ann. *Beyond the River: The Untold Story of the Heroes of the Underground Railroad*. New York: Simon & Schuster, 2002.

Harris, William C. *With Charity for All: Lincoln and the Restoration of the Union*. Lexington: University Press of Kentucky, 1997.

Helper, Hinton R. *The Impending Crisis of the South: How to Meet It*. New York: Burdick Brothers, 1859.

Hunter, Louis C. *Steamboats on the Western Rivers: An Economic and Technological History*. Cambridge, MA: Harvard University Press, 1949.

Kelley, Blair L. M. *Right to Ride: Streetcar Boycotts and African American Citizenship in the Era of Plessy v. Ferguson*. Chapel Hill: The University of North Carolina Press, 2010.

King, Willard L. *Melville Weston Fuller, Chief Justice of the United States, 1888–1910*. New York: Macmillan, 1950.

Kluger, Richard. *Simple Justice: The History of Brown v. Board of Education and Black America's Struggle for Equality*. New York: Knopf/Random House, 2004. Revised and expanded edition.

Kotar, S. L., and J. E. Gessler. *The Steamboat Era: A History of Fulton's Folly on American Rivers, 1807–1860*. Jefferson, NC: McFarland & Co., 2009.

Lincoln, Abraham, and Roy P. Basler. *The Collected Works of Abraham Lincoln*. New Brunswick, NJ: Rutgers University Press, 1953.

Lincoln, Abraham, John G. Nicolay, and John Hay. *Abraham Lincoln: Complete Works, Comprising His Speeches, Letters, State Papers, and Miscellaneous Writings*. New York: Century Co., 1894.

Mealy, Todd. *Aliened American: A Biography of William Howard Day, 1825 to 1865*. Vol. 1. Baltimore, MD: PublishAmerica, 2010.

Minutes of the Proceedings of the National Negro Conventions, 1830–1864. Edited by Howard H. Bell. New York: Arno Press, 1969.

National Park Service. "Civil Rights in America: Racial Desegregation in Public Accommodations." Monograph, 2004.

Oates, Stephen B. *With Malice Toward None: The Life of Abraham Lincoln*. New York: Harper & Row, 1977.

Proceedings of the Republican National Convention Held at Cincinnati, Ohio, June 14, 15, and 16, 1876. Concord, NH: Republican Press Association, 1876.

Quarles, Benjamin. *Lincoln and the Negro*. New York: Oxford University Press, 1962.

Quarles, Benjamin. *The Negro in the Civil War*. Boston: Little, Brown, 1953.

Rapport, Leonard. "The Interstate Commerce Commission Formal Case Files: A Source for Local History." *Prologue*, vol. 15, no. 4 (Winter 1983).

Sievers, Harry Joseph. *Benjamin Harrison*. Chicago: H. Regnery Co., 1952.

Socolofsky, Homer E., and Allan B. Spetter. *The Presidency of Benjamin Harrison*. Lawrence: University Press of Kansas, 1987.

Southwick, Sarah H. *Reminiscences of Early Anti-Slavery Days*. Cambridge, MA: Riverside Press, 1893.

Sproat, John G. "Blueprint for Radical Reconstruction." *The Journal of Southern History* 23, no. 1 (1957): 25–44.

Steiner, Bernard C. *Life of Roger Brooke Taney: Chief Justice of the United States Supreme Court*. Baltimore, MD: Williams & Wilkins, 1922.

Toll, Robert C. *Blacking Up: The Minstrel Show in Nineteenth Century America*. New York: Oxford University Press, 1974.

U.S. War Department. *The War of the Rebellion: a Compilation of the Official Records of the Union and Confederate Armies*. Government Printing Office, 1880–1901.

Volk, Kyle G. "Majority Rule, Minority Rights: The Christian Sabbath, Liquor, Racial Amalgamation, and Democracy in Antebellum America." PhD diss., University of Chicago, Department of History, 2008.

Way, Frederick Jr., *Way's Packet Directory, 1848–1983*. Athens: Ohio University Press, 1983.

Welke, Barbara Y. *Recasting American Liberty: Gender, Race, Law, and the Railroad Revolution, 1865–1920*. New York: Cambridge University Press, 2001.

Woodward, C. Vann, *The Strange Career of Jim Crow*. 3rd revised ed. New York: Oxford University Press, 2002.

Massachusetts Railroads and the Abolition Movement

Annual Report of the Board of Managers of the Massachusetts Anti-Slavery Society, with Some Account of the Annual Meeting. Boston: The Society, 1840–1845.

Boutwell, George S. *Reminiscences of Sixty Years in Public Affairs: Governor of Massachusetts, 1851–1852.* New York: McClure, Phillips and Co., 1902.

Bradlee, Francis B. C. *The Eastern Railroad: A Historical Account of Early Railroading in Eastern New England.* Salem, MA: The Essex Institute, 1922.

Duberman, Martin B. *Charles Francis Adams, 1807–1886.* Boston: Houghton Mifflin, 1961.

Garrison, William L. *Letters of William Lloyd Garrison.* Edited by Walter M. I. Merrill and Louis Ruchames. Cambridge, MA: Belknap Press of Harvard University Press, 1971.

Hallowell, Richard P. *Why the Negro was enfranchised: Negro suffrage justified: published at the request of the colored citizens of Boston.* 2nd ed. Boston, 1903.

Hodges, Graham R. *David Ruggles: A Radical Black Abolitionist and the Underground Railroad in New York City.* Chapel Hill: University of North Carolina Press, 2010.

Johnson, David N. *Sketches of Lynn, Or, the Changes of Fifty Years.* Lynn, MA: T. P. Nichols, 1880.

Johnson, Oliver, and John G. Whittier. *William Lloyd Garrison and His Times: Or, Sketches of the Anti-Slavery Movement in America, and of the Man Who Was Its Founder and Moral Leader.* Boston: B. B. Russell & Co., 1880.

Mabee, Carelton. *Black Freedom: The Nonviolent Abolitionists from 1830 Through the Civil War.* New York: The Macmillan Company, 1970.

Mayer, Henry. *All on Fire: William Lloyd Garrison and the Abolition of Slavery.* New York: St. Martin's Press, 1998.

Morris, J. B. *Oberlin, Hotbed of Abolitionism: College, Community, and the Fight for Freedom and Equality in Antebellum America.* Chapel Hill: University of North Carolina Press, 2014.

Pillsbury, Parker. *Acts of the Anti-Slavery Apostles.* Concord, NH: Clague, Wegman, Schlicht & Co., Printers, 1883.

Quincy, Josiah. *Figures of the Past: From the Leaves of Old Journals.* Boston: Roberts Brothers, 1883.

Ripley, C. P. *The Black Abolitionist Papers:* Vol. 3. Chapel Hill: University of North Carolina Press, 1991.

Ruchames, Louis. "Jim Crow Railroads in Massachusetts." *American Quarterly* 8, no. 1 (1956): 61–75.

Ruchames, Louis. "Race, Marriage, and Abolition in Massachusetts." *The Journal of Negro History* 40, no. 3 (1955): 250–273.

John Marshall Harlan

Alsetter, Mabel, and Gladys Watson, "Western Military Institute, 1847–1861." *Filson Club History Quarterly*, April 1936.

Belcher, Dennis W. *The 10th Kentucky Volunteer Infantry in the Civil War: A History and Roster.* Jefferson, NC: McFarland & Co., 2009.

Beth, Loren P. *John Marshall Harlan: The Last Whig Justice.* Lexington: University Press of Kentucky, 1992.

Brand, Carl Fremont. "History of the Know Nothing Party in Indiana." Thesis, Indiana University, 1916.

Campbell, Peter Scott. "John Marshall Harlan's Political Memoir." *Journal of Supreme Court History* 33, no. 3 (November 2008).

Campbell, Peter Scott, editor. "The Civil War Reminiscences of John Marshall Harlan." *Journal of Supreme Court History* 32, no. 3 (November 2007).

Collins, Lewis, and Richard H. Collins. *Collins' Historical Sketches of Kentucky: History of Kentucky.* Frankfort: Kentucky Historical Society, 1966.

Daniel, Larry J. *Days of Glory: The Army of the Cumberland, 1861–1865.* Baton Rouge: LSU Press, 2006.

Farrelly, David G. "Harlan's Formative Period: The Years Before the War." *Kentucky Law Journal* 46, no. 3 (1958).

Farrelly, David G. "John Marshall Harlan and the Union Cause in Kentucky, 1861." *Filson Club History Quarterly* (January 1963).

Farrelly, David G. "A Sketch of John Marshall Harlan's Pre-Court Career." *Vanderbilt Law Review* 10, no. 2 (1957).

Greenberg, Amy S. *A Wicked War: Polk, Clay, Lincoln, and the 1846 U.S. Invasion of Mexico.* New York: Alfred A. Knopf, 2012.

Harlan, Malvina S. *Some Memories of a Long Life, 1854–1911.* New York: Modern Library, 2002.

Harrison, Lowell H. *The Civil War in Kentucky.* Lexington: University Press of Kentucky, 2009.

Hartz, Louis. "John M. Harlan in Kentucky, 1855–1877: The Story of his Pre-Court Political Career." *Filson Club History Quarterly* (January 1940).

McCutchan, Kenneth P. *At the Bend in the River: The Story of Evansville.* Woodland Hills, CA: Windsor Publications, 1982.

McGann, Agnes. *Nativism in Kentucky to 1860.* Washington, DC: The Catholic University of America, 1944.

Military History of Kentucky: Chronologically Arranged. Frankfort, KY: The State Journal, 1939.

Miller, Milford M. "Evansville Steamboat Clippings, 1848–1875." Willard Library, Evansville, IN.

Owen, Thomas L. "The Pre-Court Career of John Marshall Harlan." Master's thesis, University of Louisville, 1970.

Palmer, John M. *Personal Recollections of John M. Palmer: The Story of an Earnest Life.* Cincinnati: R. Clarke, 1901.

Przybyszewski, Linda. *The Republic According to John Marshall Harlan.* Chapel Hill: University of North Carolina Press, 1999.

Robertson, George. *Scrap Book on Law and Politics, Men and Times.* Lexington, KY: A. W. Elder, 1855.

Shanklin, James M, and Kenneth P. McCutchan. *"Dearest Lizzie": The Civil War As Seen Through the Eyes of Lieutenant Colonel James Maynard Shanklin of Southwest Indiana's Own 42nd Regiment, Indiana Volunteer Infantry.* Evansville, IN: Friends of Willard Library Press, 1988.

Speed, Thomas. *The Union Cause in Kentucky, 1860–1865.* New York: G. P. Putnam's Sons, 1907.

Stevenson, Daniel, "General Nelson, Kentucky, and Lincoln Guns." *Magazine of American History* 10, no. 2 (August 1883).

Webb, Ross A. *Benjamin Helm Bristow: Border State Politician.* Lexington: The University Press of Kentucky, 1969.

Westin, Alan F. "The First Justice Harlan. A Self Portrait From His Private Papers." *Kentucky Law Journal* 46, no. 3 (Spring 1958).

Westin, Alan F. "John Marshall Harlan and the Constitutional Rights of Negroes: The Transformation of a Southerner." *The Yale Law Journal* 66, no. 5 (Apr. 1957).

Whitney, Thomas R. *A Defence of the American Policy, As Opposed to the Encroachments of Foreign Influence: And Especially to the Interference of the Papacy in the Political Interests and Affairs of the United States.* New York: De Witt & Davenport, 1856.

Yarbrough, Tinsley E. *Judicial Enigma: The First Justice Harlan*. New York: Oxford University Press, 1995.

Henry Billings Brown

Broad, Trevor. "Forgotten Man in a Tumultuous Time: The Gilded Age as Seen by United States Supreme Court Justice Henry Billings Brown." Senior's honor thesis, University of Michigan, 2005.

Brown, Henry Billings. "Dissenting Opinions of Mr. Justice Harlan." American *Law Review* 46 (1912): 321.

Brown, Henry Billings. "The Twentieth Century: An address delivered before the graduating classes at the seventy-first anniversary of Yale Law School, on June 24th, 1895." New Haven, CT: Hoggson & Robinson.

Brown, Henry Billings, and Charles A. Kent. *Memoir of Henry Billings Brown: Late Justice of the Supreme Court of the United States: Consisting of an Autobiographical Sketch*. New York: Duffield, 1915.

Kohler, Sue A., and Jeffrey R. Carson. *Sixteenth Street Architecture*. Vol. 1. Washington, DC: Commission of Fine Arts, 1978.

Albion Winegar Tourgée

Current, Richard N. *Those Terrible Carpetbaggers*. New York: Oxford University Press, 1988.

Elliott, Mark. *Color-Blind Justice: Albion Tourgée and the Quest for Racial Equality from the Civil War to Plessy v. Ferguson*. Oxford: Oxford University Press, 2006.

First Mohonk Conference on the Negro Question: Held at Lake Mohonk, Ulster County, New York, June 4, 5, 6, 1890. Reported and edited by Isabel C. Barrow. Boston: G. H. Ellis, 1890.

Garfield, James A., Burke A. Hinsdale, and Mary L. Hinsdale. *Letters: Correspondence between James Abram Garfield and Burke Aaron Hinsdale*. New York: Kraus, 1969.

Garfield, James A., Harry J. Brown, and Frederick D. Williams. *The Diary of James A. Garfield, Volume IV, 1878–1881*. East Lansing: Michigan State University Press, 1967.

Garfield, Lucretia, James Garfield, and John Shaw. *Crete and James: Personal Letters of Lucretia and James Garfield*. East Lansing: Michigan State University Press, 1994.

Holden, W. W., and William K. Boyd. *Memoirs of W. W. Holden*. Durham, NC: Seeman Printery, 1911.

Journal of the Constitutional Convention of the State of North-Carolina, at Its Session of 1865. Raleigh, NC: Cannon & Holden, convention printer, 1865.

Journal of the Constitutional Convention of the State of North-Carolina, at Its Session, 1868. Raleigh, NC: J. W. Holden, convention printer, 1868.

Karcher, Carolyn L. *A Refugee from His Race: Albion W. Tourgée and His Fight against White Supremacy*. Chapel Hill: The University of North Carolina Press, 2016.

Keller, Dean H. *An Index to the Albion W. Tourgée Papers in the Chautauqua County Historical Society, Westfield, N.Y.* Kent, OH: Kent State University, 1964.

Olsen, Otto H. *Carpetbagger's Crusade: The Life of Albion Winegar Tourgée*. Baltimore, MD: Johns Hopkins Press, 1965.

Olsen, Otto H. *The Thin Disguise: Turning Point in Negro History: Plessy v. Ferguson: A Documentary Presentation, 1864–1896*. New York: Humanities Press, 1967.

Proceedings of the Southern Loyalists' Convention Held in Philadelphia, Pennsylvania, September 1866. Washington, DC: McGill & Witherow, 1866.

Raper, Horace W. *William W. Holden: North Carolina's Political Enigma*. Chapel Hill: University of North Carolina Press, 1985.

Tourgée, Albion W. *An Appeal to Caesar*. New York: Fords, Howard, & Hulbert, 1884.

Tourgée, Albion W. *Toinette: A Tale of the South*. New York: Fords, Howard, & Hulbert, 1879.

Tourgée, Albion W. *A Fool's Errand, by One of the Fools: The Famous Romance of American History*. New York: Fords, Howard, & Hulbert, 1879.

Tourgée, Albion W. *Bricks Without Straw: A Novel*. New York: Fords, Howard, & Hulbert, 1880.

Tourgée, Albion W., Mark Elliott, and John D. Smith. *Undaunted Radical: The Selected Writings and Speeches of Albion W. Tourgée*. Baton Rouge: Louisiana State University Press, 2010.

Wilson, Edmund. *Patriotic Gore: Studies in the Literature of the American Civil War*. New York: Oxford University Press, 1962.

New Orleans, Louisiana, and the *Plessy* Case

"Address of Colonel James B. Walton." Delivered at the May 27, 1882, reunion of the Washington Artillery. Reprinted in *Southern Historical Society Papers* 11 (Jan.–Dec. 1883): 210–217.

Aslakson, Kenneth R. *Making Race in the Courtroom: The Legal Construction of Three Races in New Orleans*. New York: New York University Press, 2014.

Banks, Raymond H. *King of Louisiana, 1862–1865, and Other Government Work: A Biography of Major General Nathaniel Prentice Banks, Speaker of the U.S. House of Representatives*. Las Vegas, NV: R. H. Banks, 2005.

Bearss, Edwin C. "The Seizure of the Forts and Public Property in Louisiana." *Louisiana History: The Journal of the Louisiana Historical Association* 2, no. 4 (1961).

Bell, Caryn Cossé. *Revolution, Romanticism, and the Afro-Creole Protest Tradition in Louisiana, 1718–1868*. Baton Rouge: Louisiana State University Press, 1997.

Belz, Herman. *A New Birth of Freedom: The Republican Party and Freedmen's Rights, 1861 to 1866*. Westport, CT: Greenwood Press, 1976.

Brasseaux, Carl A. *French, Cajun, Creole, Houma: A Primer on Francophone Louisiana*. Baton Rouge: Louisiana State University Press, 2005.

Broyard, Bliss. *One Drop: My Father's Hidden Life: A Story of Race and Family Secrets*. New York: Little, Brown and Co., 2007.

Chase, Salmon P., and John Niven. *The Salmon P. Chase Papers*. Kent, OH: Kent State University Press, 1993.

Clark, Emily. *Strange History of the American Quadroon: Free Women of Color in the Revolutionary Atlantic World*. Chapel Hill: University of North Carolina Press, 2015.

Desdunes, Rodolphe L. *Our People and Our History: A Tribute to the Creole People of Color in Memory of the Great Men They Have Given Us and of the Good Works They Have Accomplished*. Baton Rouge: Louisiana State University Press, 1973. Translated from the French by Dolores McCants.

Fortier, Alcée. *A History of Louisiana*. New York: Goupil & Co. of Paris, 1904.

Fischer, Roger A. "A Pioneer Protest: The New Orleans Street-Car Controversy of 1867." *The Journal of Negro History* 53 (July 1968).

Fischer, Roger A. *The Segregation Struggle in Louisiana, 1862–77*. Urbana: University of Illinois Press, 1974.

Gehman, Mary, and Lloyd Dennis. *The Free People of Color of New Orleans: An Introduction*. New Orleans, LA: Margaret Media, 1994.

Hanger, Kimberly S. *Bounded Lives, Bounded Places: Free Black Society in Colonial New Orleans, 1769–1803*. Durham, NC: Duke University Press, 1997.

Hollandsworth, James G. *The Louisiana Native Guards: The Black Military Experience During the Civil War*. Baton Rouge: Louisiana State University Press, 1995.

Houzeau, Jean-Charles, and David C. Rankin. *My Passage at the New Orleans Tribune: A Memoir of the Civil War Era*. Baton Rouge: Louisiana State University Press, 1984.

Kein, Sybil. *Creole: The History and Legacy of Louisiana's Free People of Color.* Baton Rouge: Louisiana State University Press, 2000.

Kinzer, Charles E. "The Tio Family: Four Generations of New Orleans Musicians, 1814–1933." PhD diss., Louisiana State University, 1993.

Lofgren, Charles A. *The Plessy Case: A Legal-Historical Interpretation*. New York: Oxford University Press, 1987.

McConnell, Roland C. *Negro Troops of Antebellum Louisiana: A History of the Battalion of Free Men of Color.* Baton Rouge: Louisiana State University Press, 1969.

McCrary, Peyton. *Abraham Lincoln and Reconstruction: The Louisiana Experiment*. Princeton, NJ: Princeton University Press, 1978.

Medley, Keith W. *We As Freemen: Plessy v. Ferguson*. Gretna, LA: Pelican Publishing Co., 2003.

Official Journal of the Proceedings of the Convention: For Framing a Constitution for the State of Louisiana, 1867–1868. New Orleans: J. B. Roudanez, 1868.

Olmsted, Frederick L. *Journeys and Explorations in the Cotton Kingdom: A Traveller's Observations on Cotton and Slavery in the American Slave States*. London, 1861.

Owen, William M. *In Camp and Battle with the Washington Artillery of New Orleans: A Narrative of Events During the Late Civil War from Bull Run to Appomattox and Spanish Fort*. Boston: Ticknor & Co., 1885.

Parton, James. *General Butler in New Orleans: History of the Administration of the Department of the Gulf in the Year 1862: with an Account of the Capture of New Orleans and a Sketch of the Previous Career of the General, Civil and Military*. New York: Mason Brothers, 1864.

Proceedings of the Convention of the Friends of Freedom: Held in Lyceum Hall, New Orleans, December 15th, 1863.

Rankin, David C. "The Origins of Black Leadership in New Orleans During Reconstruction." *The Journal of Southern History* 40, no. 3 (1974).

Reinders, Robert C. *End of an Era: New Orleans, 1850–1860*. New Orleans: Pelican Publishing Co., 1964.

Report of Proceedings for the Annulment of Act 111 of 1890 by the Citizens' Committee of New Orleans. Crusader, 1897.

Roland, Charles P. "Louisiana and Secession." *Louisiana History: The Journal of the Louisiana Historical Association* 19, no. 4 (Fall 1978).

Roumillat, Shelene C. "The Glorious Eighth of January." *Louisiana Cultural Vistas*, Winter 2014.

Scott, Rebecca J., and Jean M. Hébrard. *Freedom Papers: An Atlantic Odyssey in the Age of Emancipation*. Cambridge, MA: Harvard University Press, 2012.

Sterkx, H. E. *The Free Negro in Ante-Bellum Louisiana*. Rutherford, NJ: Fairleigh Dickinson University Press, 1972.

Thomas, Brook. *Plessy v. Ferguson: A Brief History with Documents*. Boston: Bedford Books, 1997.

Thompson, Shirley E. *Exiles at Home: The Struggle to Become American in Creole New Orleans*. Cambridge, MA: Harvard University Press, 2009.

Tunnell, Ted. *Crucible of Reconstruction: War, Radicalism, and Race in Louisiana, 1862–1877*. Baton Rouge: Louisiana State University Press, 1984.

Vincent, Charles, ed. *The African American Experience in Louisiana: Part B: From the Civil War to Jim Crow*. Carbondale: Southern Illinois University Press, 2011.

INDEX

Page numbers in *italics* refer to illustrations.
Page numbers marked with an "n," refer to endnotes.